PARADIGMS OF THE PAST

PARADIGMS OF THE PAST

The Story of Missouri Archaeology

Michael J. O'Brien

University of Missouri Press / Columbia and London

Copyright © 1996 by
The Curators of the University of Missouri
University of Missouri Press, Columbia, Missouri 65201
Printed and bound in the United States of America
All rights reserved
5 4 3 2 1   00 99 98 97 96

Library of Congress Cataloging-in-Publication Data

O'Brien, Michael J. (Michael John), 1950–
    Paradigms of the past : the story of Missouri archaeology /
  Michael J. O'Brien.
      p.   cm.
    Includes bibliographical references and index.
    ISBN 0-8262-1019-8 (pbk. : alk. paper)
    1. Indians of North America—Missouri—Antiquities. 2. Excavations
(Archaeology)—Missouri—History. 3. Missouri—Antiquities. I. Title.
E78.M8037 1996   95-36754
977.8′01—dc20   CIP

∞This paper meets the requirements of the
American National Standard for Permanence of Paper
for Printed Library Materials, Z39.48, 1984.

Designer: Kristie Lee
Typesetter: BOOKCOMP
Printer and binder: Thomson-Shore, Inc.
Typefaces: Minion and Frutiger

*Jacket illustrations courtesy of the American Museum of Natural History,
the Missouri Historical Society, and the St. Louis Post-Dispatch.*

Frontispiece: *Carl H. Chapman and Jesse E. Wrench at Graham
Cave, Montgomery County, Missouri, 1955.*

To Beverly, Nathan, Kimberly, and Aaron

CONTENTS

FIGURES

3.17. Gerard Fowke, archaeologist with the Missouri Historical Society, showing some of the vessels in the society's collection, ca. 1931

3.18. Map of the Forest Park mound group, St. Louis, made by David Bushnell Jr., ca. 1903

3.19. Map showing locations of rock cairns in Missouri excavated by Gerard Fowke in 1906–1907

3.20. Map of the Old Fort, Saline County, Missouri, made by Gerard Fowke in 1907

3.21. Photograph of the internal structure of Brenner mound number 2, Platte County, Missouri, excavated by Gerard Fowke in 1906 or 1907

3.22. Drawings of a burial vault in Pike County, Missouri, made by Solomon Giddings ca. 1820

3.23. Photograph of a burial vault in Pike County, Missouri, excavated by Gerard Fowke in 1906 or 1907

3.24. Drawings of two burial vaults in Pike County, Missouri, made by Garland Carr Broadhead, probably in the 1860s or 1870s

4.1. Franz Boas demonstrating the use of an Eskimo harpoon, ca. 1900

4.2. Maxey Cave, Pulaski County, Missouri

4.3. Map showing locations of rock shelters and other sites in Missouri visited by Gerard Fowke ca. 1920

4.4. Plans of Miller Cave, Pulaski County, Missouri, by Gerard Fowke and Charles Markman

4.5. Photograph of the main chamber of Miller Cave showing remnants of the large trenches excavated by Gerard Fowke

4.6. Nels Nelson and associates at Castillo Cave, Spain, 1913

4.7. Stratigraphic cut made by Nels Nelson through midden deposit at San Cristobal, New Mexico

4.8. Plan of 1903 excavation grid at Jacobs Cavern, McDonald County, Missouri, devised by Charles Peabody and Warren Moorehead

4.9. Photograph showing arrangement of the excavation grid at Jacobs Cavern, McDonald County, Missouri, 1903

4.10. Drawings of artifacts recovered from Jacobs Cavern, McDonald County, Missouri, by Vance Randolph and Jay Taylor

4.11. Revision of Charles Peabody and Warren Moorehead's original grid plan of Jacobs Cavern, McDonald County, Missouri, showing locations of excavations undertaken in 1921, 1923, and 1924

4.12. Photograph showing stalagmitic material from Jacobs Cavern, McDonald County, Missouri, with flint and bone embedded

4.13. Cross section showing Vernon Allison's depiction of strata in Jacobs Cavern, McDonald County, Missouri

4.14. James Ford in front of Harold Fisk's Mississippi Valley map

PREFACE

The prehistory of Missouri is a fascinating subject that has attracted an odd assortment of students over the years—not odd in the sense that they necessarily were unusual (though some certainly were) but in the sense that they came from diverse quarters. If the voluminous literature on the subject that has grown up over the last century and a half is any gauge, then those students of Missouri prehistory have undertaken a considerable amount of work. Their accomplishments have indeed demonstrated that the record of Missouri's prehistoric past is exceedingly rich and complex, a phenomenon, we are told (Chapman 1980: 225), that is attributable in part to the state's geographical position astride two major biomes—the tall-grass prairies to the north and west and the oak-hickory forests to the south and east—and in part to the lack of natural boundaries that otherwise might have inhibited human movement from one locale to another. The oldest firmly dated archaeological remains in the state are about 11,200 years old and anchor one end of a long cultural sequence that in some respects parallels sequences in adjacent parts of the midcontinent and in other respects differs radically from them.

These similarities and differences have been of interest to antiquarians and archaeologists since at least the first half of the nineteenth century, but it was not until 1975 that the long and varied nature of Missouri's archaeological record was chronicled in any depth. In that year Carl H. Chapman published the first volume of a projected three-volume series entitled *The Archaeology of Missouri*. The second volume followed in 1980, and Chapman planned to have the third volume ready for publication before the end of the decade. Tragically, Chapman and his wife, Eleanor, were killed in an automobile accident in February 1987, and volume 3 never appeared. The two volumes that Chapman completed, however, cover an enormous amount of material that only he was capable of reporting. He began his career in archaeology a full half century before his death and built a reputation that led to his being widely regarded as the dean of Missouri archaeology.

Throughout Chapman's career, his interest in Missouri prehistory never wavered. He received his undergraduate degree in sociology from the University of Missouri, and after brief stints in graduate school at the universities of New Mexico (for his master's in anthropology) and Michigan (for his doctorate in anthropology), which were sandwiched around a hitch in the Air Force during World War II, Chapman returned to the University of Missouri to begin a distinguished career as professor and researcher. All his fieldwork was performed in Missouri, conducted in large part with volunteers from the Missouri

Archaeological Society (MAS), an organization comprising mainly avocational archaeologists from around the state. His friendship with the hundreds of people in that group—most of whom were artifact collectors and knew the locations of literally thousands of sites—made him privy to details of the archaeological record that were unavailable to other professionals. For decades the name Carl Chapman was synonymous with Missouri archaeology. Between 1946 and 1970, of all the fieldwork done in Missouri archaeology, Chapman either conducted the work himself or oversaw the work of others. Some of those "others" were research associates he hired through the American Archaeology Division at the University of Missouri, many were his students, and even more were members of the MAS. Chapman decided where people would work, he designed the work, and he negotiated with the contracting agencies. A look at Chapman's list of publications boggles the mind: it includes several books and literally hundreds of articles and unpublished reports—all of them on Missouri prehistory.

It is difficult to imagine doing archaeological work in Missouri without using Chapman's two volumes, the first of which covers the preceramic period of the state's prehistory, ca. 9200–1000 B.C., and the second, the ceramic period, ca. 1000 B.C.–A.D. 1200. Volume 3 would have covered the remainder of the late prehistoric period and the ethnohistoric period, up through Euro-American contact with indigenous groups in the eighteenth century. The completed volumes cover a considerable body of archaeological data by time period and geographic region and provide detailed descriptions and drawings of projectile-point types and ceramic types—the main objects used by archaeologists to mark time. Charts at the back of each volume summarize various cultural sequences by drainage region, and there are comprehensive lists of radiocarbon dates for various sites. Especially helpful are roughly 1,500 references to works that Chapman consulted in his research.

However, Chapman's volumes have little or nothing to do with how Missouri's past has been studied. Rather, what they have to do with is the *archaeological record* of various locales and how one person chose to interpret that record. Readers are not given the opportunity to learn how archaeology has changed over the years or how the study of Missouri's past fits into a broader perspective of contemporary Americanist archaeology. In essence, what was omitted, as Wood (1984: 1) noted, was a history of *how* archaeological work has been conducted in Missouri and *why* it was conducted the way it was. By using the references in Chapman's volumes, one can construct a rough chronological ordering of the work that took place throughout the state, but Chapman does not give readers insight into why certain sites were excavated or what guided archaeologists' reasoning (including his own) as they reached the interpretations given in the literature.

With a subject as complex as the archaeological record of Missouri, which chronicles over 11 millennia of human occupation of a 69,000-square-mile area, it would be helpful for students of archaeology to have not only the details of that record but also the details of how we have come to know what we think we know about that record. In some respects, this topic is as interesting as, or perhaps even more interesting than, a detailing of the prehistoric past. It is one thing to know what happened between 1000 B.C. and A.D. 1000, but it is another thing to know *how* we know—or at least how we *think* we know— what happened during that 2,000-year span of time. And that, in essence, is the goal of this book: to develop an understanding of how archaeologists and their antiquarian predecessors have structured their fieldwork, their analyses, and perhaps even their thought processes to arrive at the various pictures of Missouri's past. Those pictures have changed considerably over the years, in part a result of continuing fieldwork conducted within Missouri's borders and in part a result of changes in Americanist archaeology as a discipline.

Archaeological investigation in Missouri did not begin with Chapman's work. In fact, the archaeological record of the state figured prominently in several important debates that took place in the nineteenth century, in particular (a) the mound-builder debate—whether the earthworks evident across much of the eastern United States were built by American Indians or by a vanished race of people—and (b) the debate over whether humans were in North America during the last great ice age. Chapman mentions these controversies and lists several references on the subjects, but it is difficult if not impossible to determine from his brief summaries how important the issues were in professional and popular circles of the time. In point of fact, the origin of the mounds and the antiquity of humans in North America were *the* two hottest topics in mid- to late-nineteenth-century archaeology. Without knowing the importance of the former issue, for example, one would not understand why so much fieldwork was undertaken in eastern Missouri by the Bureau of Ethnology (which changed its name to Bureau of American Ethnology in 1894) in the 1880s and 1890s. Likewise, without understanding the nature of the debates that were going on over the antiquity of humans in the New World, work undertaken in a tiny rock shelter in southwestern Missouri by the American Museum of Natural History in the 1920s would lose much of its significance. At one level it is interesting to know that the work was carried out, but it is even more interesting to know the full story behind *why* it was carried out. To obtain a broader perspective, one has to step back from the archaeological work that was done in Missouri and place it in the intellectual context of the time.

It is reasonable to believe that the archaeology of Missouri, or of any other state, for that matter, was and is a microcosm of events, ideas, and movements in the profession at large—that studying how the past has been pursued by archaeologists in one state will tell us a great deal about how the past was pursued by the majority of archaeologists elsewhere. We probably would not expect to find a one-to-one correlation because of the variable nature of the archaeological record from one locale to another and personal predilections about how best to study that record, but we might expect to find common theoretical and methodological approaches. After all, archaeologists communicate with each other, they read common journals, and they attend meetings to find out what is going on in other parts of the country. I became interested in the archaeological history of Missouri in the late 1970s, but it took almost a decade to familiarize myself with the literature. Like all graduate students from the 1970s on, I was exposed to Gordon Willey and Jeremy Sabloff's *History of American Archaeology* (1974), now in its third edition. Their book traces the intellectual growth of Americanist archaeology, beginning with the early explorers and coming up to the present, and summarizes theoretical and methodological conceptions and misconceptions that advanced or retarded our understanding of the past. An important thread woven through their account is how archaeological theory, method, and strategy have changed over time and how innovative methods and concepts developed by archaeologists working in one geographic area were adopted by archaeologists working elsewhere.

Encouraged by Willey and Sabloff's success in assembling a large and disparate body of information and placing it in a reasonable format, I decided to undertake this volume. Because of my more limited focus, I am able to discuss case examples in more depth than Willey and Sabloff could. I also am able to spend more time examining the question of *why* certain things happened as they did, both in Americanist archaeology generally and in Missouri archaeology specifically. In case you are wondering, I use the term *Americanist* archaeology (as opposed to *American* archaeology) to emphasize archaeology undertaken by American-trained archaeologists, regardless of where in the world their research area is. This usage has become fairly standard, and I follow the tradition here even though I focus almost exclusively on fieldwork undertaken in North America.

The treatment presented here is not intended to be encyclopedic, and to the reader I can only offer the same words used by James B. Griffin in his review article "The Pursuit of Archaeology in the United States" (Griffin 1959: 379): "If I have omitted your favorite area, archaeologist, or attitude, adopt a divine view and forgive my human errors." I could never hope to include every article and report that has been written about the archaeological record of Missouri, nor is there any reason to think that someone would want to read a book that included the thousands of references that would result from such an effort. Besides, Chapman's two volumes already contain much of the material written before about 1980; of course, if he were writing the books today he would have to add the 500–1,000 additional references that have appeared since 1980 to the 1,500 or so that he included. My rationale for what to include was based on my perception either of how important the work is in Americanist archaeology or of how representative the work was of Missouri archaeology at a particular time.

Archaeologists knowledgeable about the intellectual history of the discipline may well find little new here and may rightfully grumble that the discussions are too brief and synoptic. On the other hand, a perspective that is broader than simply the events that occurred in Missouri archaeology should be of interest to most readers and at the very least will serve as general background. For example, most readers will have some familiarity with archaeological types, which are units designed to partition materials in the archaeological record into manageable groups. Similarly, many readers will be familiar with temporal-spatial units such as phases, which have been created to emphasize similarities between or among various components and sites. But most readers probably do not know the history behind the various systems that have been proposed for keeping track of time, space, and form. If one were to glance through volumes of the *Missouri Archaeologist* spanning 1940 to 1948, it would be immediately obvious that some means had been devised to group the artifacts and archaeological "cultures" of Missouri. Articles written in the 1950s and those written in the 1960s discuss entirely different systems. Where did these systems come from? Who developed them? How long were they in use? And, most importantly, did the systems allow us to develop a better understanding of the archaeological record, or did they cloud our perceptions?

I must confess that in several instances my decisions about what to include were guided by personal interest. For example, I have long been fascinated with one of the lesser-known frauds in American archaeology—a deer bone containing an engraving of a mastodon, supposedly found in a small cave located in the extreme southwestern corner of Missouri. The public is aware of some of the more well known archaeological and paleontological frauds of the twentieth century, such as Piltdown Man, but the story of the carved mastodon from Jacobs Cavern is more or less forgotten lore. In addition to being an interesting story, the case is a textbook example of how logic and the rules of empirical examination can be applied to rebut a dubious claim. The Jacobs Cavern incident can also be used to showcase advances in stratigraphic analysis that took place in Americanist archaeology after 1916.

My decisions about what to include were guided by another consideration— the age of the research. Even if you are not a careful reader, you will undoubtedly notice some inequalities among the chapters. Some are longer than others, and the longer ones often contain considerable detail. This is especially true of chapters 6 through 8, in which I examine some of the more recent work undertaken in Missouri, much of which has significantly changed our perceptions of the prehistory of the state. I also tended to go into considerable detail in discussing some of the work done in the nineteenth century, for the reason that it is interesting in its own right and has never been treated adequately. Anyone doing research on nineteenth-century archaeology should find the primary references cited here an excellent starting point for more intensive examination of specific aspects.

With the exception of a few personal communications, the references I make throughout the volume are to published works or to manuscripts (primarily survey and excavation reports) on file at the Archaeological Survey of Missouri, located on the University of Missouri–Columbia campus. I did not make much use of archival documents, other than those held by the Missouri Historical Society (St. Louis), though without question there are numerous state, federal, and private archives that hold information useful in understanding particular aspects of Missouri archaeology. The Western Historical Manuscript Collection at UMC, for example, houses all of Carl Chapman's papers and is a gold mine of information on Chapman's long career, especially his legislative efforts in the 1970s in conjunction with federally sponsored archaeology. Undoubtedly, an entire volume could, and eventually should, be written about the dominant figure in Missouri archaeology, but I will leave that to someone with expertise in biography.

Several methods of organization occurred to me while preparing the book, none of which I particularly liked. One method would have been to treat the material topically, with chapters arranged around subjects such as method and theory, environmental analysis, and the like, but I quickly abandoned that notion because of the large number of topics that I wanted to include and the impossibility of linking the individual discussions into a coherent story. After toying with several other ideas, I decided to organize the discussion into a chronological framework, which made it easier to parallel developments in Missouri archaeology with those in Americanist archaeology. However, I was still forced in some instances either to go back and pick up a story line from a previous point or to jump ahead to finish a story. I also tried to select chapter titles that encapsulate major topics of the periods under consideration, though in many instances they include only one or a few issues of the many that were involved.

The chronological ordering will definitely appeal to those with little interest in Americanist archaeology but who want to know who did what in Missouri, where they did it, and when they did it. Quite frankly, I wish I had had such a guide in 1977, when I arrived in Missouri to begin my professional employment. I picked up Chapman's first volume to read as background, but there was more information than I could remember easily, and I quickly became lost in terms of time and space. I remember wishing for an easy-to-read guide to what had been done in Missouri and by whom. As I made my way through the chapters on the different Archaic-tradition periods, which were cross-cut by Chapman's spatial units (see Chapter 1), I kept running across the same site names and the same reservoir names, but I remember it took considerable research to ferret out the fact that Rodgers Shelter was in Kaysinger Bluff Reservoir, which in turn was located in portions of Benton, Hickory, Henry, and St. Clair counties. However, the only impoundment in those counties listed on a modern state map was Harry S. Truman Reservoir. It took more research to figure out (I think someone actually had to tell me) that Congress had changed the name of the reservoir from Kaysinger Bluff to Truman.

Using a chronological ordering for the chapters meant that I had to decide on beginning and ending dates for them. My choice of dates represents my attempt to juggle information concerning overall trends in Americanist archaeology with occurrences in Missouri archaeology. The lengths of the time periods involved vary considerably and in some cases represent compromises made in ordering various topics. Chapter 1 is an introduction to several important issues discussed in more detail in subsequent chapters. My thought in writing the chapter was to call attention to some of the problems with which archaeologists wrestle as they attempt to understand the past. What I hope becomes obvious is that several underlying issues in Americanist archaeology have been there from the beginning and undoubtedly always will be there. One concern with which archaeologists have long wrestled is how to keep track of what happened prehistorically, where it happened, and when it happened. Probably no other issue has been of such key concern throughout the history of Americanist archaeology; hence, time-and-space systematics is one of the common threads that unites all the chapters in this book.

In that regard, I also include in Chapter 1 an abbreviated overview of the archaeological record of Missouri, primarily for those readers who have little or no previous experience with the subject. I hasten to underscore the word *abbreviated,* because the discussion is nothing more than a thumbnail introduction to a very complex subject. I subdivide the archaeological record in terms of time periods, from the earliest evidence for human occupation in the state, ca. 9250 B.C., up to A.D. 1860. I should point out that because of space limitations, I focus little attention on archaeological work that has dealt primarily with remains from the historical period—that time period beginning in 1541, when it is believed contact occurred between Native American groups in extreme southeastern Missouri and a party attached to the de Soto expedition—unless the work was part of a larger project that also focused on the prehistoric archaeological record. I admit that this is an unfortunate omission in light of the importance of some of the archaeological study of historical-period sites in Missouri, but I had to draw the line somewhere.

Chapter 2, "Mound Builders and Amateur Scientists," treats the period before 1880, which was the heyday of speculation about human prehistory but was also a period that after midcentury saw the rapid growth of scientific societies across the United States and a flurry of antiquarian research in Missouri and other states. Several archaeological sites in the state became as well known as any in the country because of the intense curiosity and press coverage they generated. Until now, that flamboyant era of Missouri archaeology has been underreported. Some of the most interesting characters ever to study the prehistory of Missouri worked during the period, and one in particular made several discoveries that grabbed national as well as international attention and held it for some time.

Chapter 3, "Mounds and the American Paleolithic," spans the period 1881–1910, during which numerous field projects in Missouri were carried out by crews from the Bureau of (American) Ethnology (BAE), by researchers funded by private museums and scientific societies, and by self-funded individuals. Two topics were of particular archaeological interest during that period—the antiquity of humans in North America and the groups responsible for mound construction—and work in Missouri figured in discussions of both topics. Some previous reviews of that important period in Americanist archaeology have painted an all-too-brief and rosy picture of the legacy of the BAE, usually pointing out how the bureau crushed the view that historically known Indian groups couldn't possibly have been responsible for constructing the elegant earthworks so evident across the eastern United States. In one respect, it *is* difficult to overemphasize the positive effect bureau prehistorians had on how the archaeological record came to be viewed, but there also is no denying that some of the positions they took, as well as their strident opposition to anyone who questioned their positions, slowed the growth of Americanist archaeology.

Chapter 4, "The Birth of a Discipline," examines the period 1911–1940, a long time span during which significant strides were made in archaeological methods and techniques. It was during the early stages of that period that some of the methods archaeologists now routinely take for granted—such as stratigraphic excavation and seriation—were developed in the American Southwest and soon had diffused across the country. By the end of the period, archaeologists had begun to shift their interest away from the examination of single sites to analysis on the regional scale, and several in-depth treatments of the archaeological record, along with the first widely used classificatory system for archaeological units, had begun to appear. State and national archaeological societies began to spring up in the 1930s, which was also the decade in which federally sponsored research by nongovernment archaeologists made its appearance.

Chapter 5, "Understanding Time, Space, and Form," covers the period 1941–1960, which witnessed a heightened involvement in archaeology by the federal government. Much of the archaeological work carried out in Missouri during the latter half of the period was a result of federally sponsored excavations in proposed reservoir areas. The refinement of temporal-spatial units continued unabated from the previous period, as did the focus on analysis at the regional level. The ending date of the period, 1960, is in my mind the most significant of all the dates I use to segment the periods. In many respects, what came after that date, although not independent from what preceded it, caused a major reorientation in the aims and goals of Americanist archaeology.

Chapter 6, "Salvage Archaeology and the Emergence of Environmental Studies," examines one of the critical periods in the development of archaeology,

1961–1976, during which an emerging perspective, the study of culture process—the study of what culture is and how it functions—rose to challenge "traditional" archaeology—the study of artifacts, with little or no regard for what culture is—as the dominant paradigm in the discipline. It was also during that period that traditional archaeology, with continued funding from the federal government, reached its peak in Missouri. As we will see, the debate that was raging in Americanist archaeology over the proper goals of the discipline had little effect on how archaeology was carried out in Missouri. That period also witnessed the birth of one of the most important projects ever undertaken in the Midwest—an interdisciplinary program aimed at understanding changing patterns of human adaptation in the lower Pomme de Terre River valley of the western Ozarks. Many archaeological projects conducted during and after the 1960s had human-environment interaction as a research focus, but few if any could match the Pomme de Terre project in terms of research results.

Chapter 7, "Archaeology as Big Business," discusses a topic that is integral to understanding the archaeology of Missouri or of any other state from 1970 on—the phenomenon that became known as cultural-resource management (CRM). I focus considerable attention on two large-scale CRM programs undertaken in Missouri—the Truman Reservoir Archaeological Project and the Cannon Reservoir Human Ecology Project. The latter was the largest archaeological study, in terms of funding, ever undertaken in the state. The projects were in some ways novel experiments in meshing the goals of traditional archaeological research with the dictates of contract archaeology.

Chapter 8, "Archaeology as the Science of Artifacts," is a discussion of several trends that have characterized Americanist archaeology from about 1980 to the present. As the chapter title suggests, there has been an increasing emphasis in Americanist archaeology on the creation of a study of the past that has as its base an empirical context. In several key respects this emphasis differs significantly from previous attempts to make archaeology a science and represents a decided departure from the heavily interpretive approach that has characterized much of the archaeology conducted during the twentieth century. The 1980s also ushered in several ethical and legal issues that radically affected archaeology in the United States—the curation of archaeological materials and the repatriation of human remains and associated grave goods. I discuss these at some length because both have had and will continue to have important implications for how archaeological research is conducted not only in Missouri but across the United States.

Chapter 9, "Interpretation versus Explanation: A Reflection on Missouri Archaeology," is a retrospective look at how the archaeological record of Missouri has been viewed over the last century and a half and how those views have changed. The chapter also focuses directly on an issue that has been with archaeology almost from its inception—the difference between interpretation and explanation—and examines how each approach has manifested itself in Missouri archaeology. I suspect this chapter will be the most interesting to read, as it was for me to write.

As almost a postscript, I have to say that I am a firm believer in knowing the history of one's discipline. In writing this book I learned more about Americanist archaeology in general, and certainly more about Missouri archaeology specifically, than I ever thought possible. There is a lot of originality in what I read, and when placed in proper perspective it makes for a fascinating story of how archaeologists have come to view the past. Most importantly, the characters in the story—the archaeologists themselves—are as important as any of the action that takes place around them. In a very real sense, the central characters wrote their own lines for the story. I have merely chronicled their efforts. Yes, I know that what I have written *is* a story (at least the title of the book says so), which is ironic because I come down so hard on storytelling in archaeology. My only answer is that the book is about people and what *they* thought about the archaeological record; it's not about the record itself. And, with maybe a few exceptions, I was not about to try to explain (or interpret) why people thought the things they did. I'll leave that to you.

ACKNOWLEDGMENTS

Several people contributed to this project in important ways. As in the past, the staff of the University of Missouri Press was extremely encouraging throughout the writing and production phases, which made the entire process a pleasant experience. I thank Beverly Jarrett for her interest in the project from the beginning and Clair Willcox and Jane Lago for their advice on what parts of the manuscript were and were not essential to the final product. I also thank Gloria Thomas, my editor at the University of Missouri Press and the person responsible not only for keeping my writing style consistent but also for correcting glaring mistakes. This is the second project on which we have worked, and, as in the past, Gloria's attention to detail and genuine enthusiasm for the project greatly simplified my life.

Four of my research assistants spent countless hours on technical aspects of production: Mike Lindsey and Dan Glover drew all the maps and redrafted various line drawings from earlier publications, and Lynden Steele and Colin Spitler photographed various plates from earlier publications and processed numerous negatives found in public and private archives. My library assistant, Nan Jones, tracked down several references for me and photocopied a seemingly endless stream of articles. Neil Trubowitz, Duane Sneddeker, and Kirsten Hammerstrom of the Missouri Historical Society helped me secure photographs in the society archives; in addition, Trubowitz graciously provided me with an unpublished manuscript pertaining to archaeological activities of the society in the late nineteenth and early twentieth centuries. Sara W. Germain of the Robert S. Peabody Museum of Archaeology, Phillips Academy, Catherine Burek of the American Museum of Natural History, Martha Labell of the Peabody Museum of Archaeology and Ethnology (Harvard), and Paula Fleming of the National Anthropological Archives (Smithsonian Institution) assisted me in locating a number of important photographs. Numerous other people were generous in providing me with photographs of various individuals who figure prominently in the book or of important sites. These include Bruce McMillan, Dale Henning, Raymond Wood, Jeffrey Saunders, Russell Graham, Patrice Teltser, Mary Dunnell, Donald Grayson, David Meltzer, Bruce Smith, Michael Schiffer, Dennis Lewarch, LuAnn Wandsnider, and Lewis Binford.

I benefited from the advice of numerous persons who read either the entire manuscript or key portions of it. David Meltzer, who knows more about nineteenth- and early-twentieth-century Americanist archaeology than most of us know about what happened last year, read chapters 2 and 3 and caught several serious errors in citations and offered critical insight into the inner workings of the Bureau of American Ethnology. Robert Dunnell read Chapter 9 and forced me to rethink several subtle but important differences between inferential and noninferential explanation. I also am indebted to him for over a decade's worth of fairly intense conversations on various aspects of method and theory in Americanist archaeology, especially the methodological debates of the 1940s and 1950s. Bruce Smith and Bruce McMillan, both of whose fieldwork and analysis figure prominently in the book, read the entire manuscript, caught numerous errors, and offered constructive advice on how to present clearer arguments. Lee Lyman, a scholar in the field of the history of Americanist archaeology, read the entire manuscript in detail, suggested the addition of numerous citations, and, through literally dozens of conversations, helped me better understand many of the foundations of modern archaeology, especially those that developed in the 1930s and 1940s. John Marshall provided me with newspaper articles and various pieces of information relating to the mapping and destruction of the St. Louis mound group and offered numerous additions and corrections to Chapter 2.

Since my goal was to produce a book that would be of interest not only to professional archaeologists but also to interested nonprofessionals—and, importantly, a book readable by people in both groups—I sought the advice of two individuals who, though they know quite a bit about archaeology, are not at a level where they have succumbed to using archaeological jargon. Also, both of them know me well enough to give me their opinion, no matter how critical it might be. My wife, Beverly, read the entire manuscript and pointed out numerous places where even the most knowledgeable reader would have a difficult time understanding the discussion. She also, with great patience, pointed out several places where the prose sounded self-serving, which I ended up deleting. I thank her not only for reading and commenting on the manuscript but also for her understanding of the long hours involved in writing the manuscript. I thank my son Aaron for understanding as well.

The other person whose opinion I sought was my dad, E. J. O'Brien, who spent two months poring over the manuscript and offering literally hundreds of editorial comments. He not only proofread the manuscript but did such things as check every reference mentioned in the text against the list of references; make dozens of suggestions about what to cut, expand, or move; and devise better figure captions. He also suffered through the long peer-review period with me, probably by that point feeling that the manuscript was as much his as it was mine. For any archaeologist who complains that his or her parents don't really understand what their son or daughter does for a living, I suggest giving them a 1,200-page manuscript to edit. It was a great, if somewhat humbling, experience for me to work with my dad, probably in no small part because it brought to mind the old days, when even then I thought I knew more than I actually did.

PARADIGMS OF THE PAST

1

Introduction

Archaeology is a subject of broad interest to a wide audience—a point that receives support from several lines of evidence. Witness the number of archaeology-related articles in popular magazines such as *National Geographic* or the long lines that form in museums for new displays of archaeological materials from various parts of the world. If you are still unconvinced, keep track of the number of articles on archaeological finds that appear in your daily newspaper over the course of a year or the number of television shows that address various aspects of archaeology. The fascination that many of us have with the past (Figure 1.1) stems in large part from artifacts—those things of beauty and exquisite workmanship that have lain buried in the ground for millennia. To be sure, artifacts hold a lure in and of themselves—otherwise they wouldn't command the prices they do on the antiquities market—but I suspect the fascination that most people have with the past transcends the beauty and value of the artifacts. That is, we believe the objects can somehow tell us something about a people who no longer are around—a people who, although they had lifestyles radically different from ours, were faced with the same problems we have, such as how to obtain enough food to feed a family, how to raise children, how to get along with the neighbors, and how to appease the Supreme Being. These are not trivial pursuits today, and they weren't in the past.

It is often said that the real reason the past should be studied is because it holds the key to the future. In other words, as Carl Chapman (1980: 264) put it, "A better knowledge of the past could be a guide to coping with the future." But I don't hold to that tenet. The mistakes of the past were as context specific as the ones of the future will be, and unless someone has a cure for human nature being what it is, we'll continue to muddle along, making mistakes here and there, many of them of the same kind made by our forebears. No, I think the right reason to study the past is simply because it is there. Sir Edmund Hillary didn't need any more reason to scale Mount Everest, and we don't need any more justification to do archaeology or to be interested in what it can tell us about people who came before us.

Figure 1.1. Open house at Jakie Shelter, Barry County, 1956. It was common in the 1950s and 1960s for the Missouri Archaeological Society and the University of Missouri to sponsor open houses to showcase fieldwork that was being done. By all accounts, the events were extraordinarily successful. The open house at Jakie Shelter, held on Sunday, May 6, 1956, drew over 5,000 people, despite the fact that the site could only be reached after a 12-mile drive over gravel roads (from Chapman 1957).

My experience has been that people with an interest in the past tend to be more interested in what happened in their own backyards than in what happened in someone else's. Nebraskans tend to be interested in the prehistory of Nebraska, Missourians in the prehistory of Missouri, and so forth. This statement is not meant to imply that Missourians are uninterested in the prehistory of Mexico and the Aegean, but rather that people are naturally intrigued with learning more about their home range. Unfortunately, archaeologists working in Missouri, like those working elsewhere, for the most part have not done too good a job of educating the general public about the prehistory of the state. Most people are astounded when they learn of the breadth and depth of Missouri's archaeological record and what it can tell us about the past.

This lack of knowledge on the part of the public makes it appear that archaeologists have only recently discovered that Missouri's archaeological record is both rich and complex. Such a belief, however, is incorrect, as even brief perusal of the references in Chapman's two volumes on the prehistory of Missouri (1975, 1980) makes clear. Interest in the prehistory of Missouri dates to the first half of the nineteenth century, though much of the work that was carried out prior to roughly 1880 was antiquarian as opposed to archaeological in nature, meaning that it was carried out by curiosity seekers who had no real research agenda other than to excavate new and wonderful items with which to line either personal shelves or those of museums. (Antiquarianism is still very much around.) Interest in Missouri's archaeological sites and artifacts accelerated throughout the latter half of the century, and by the early decades of the twentieth century hundreds of sites across the state—in regions as diverse as the Mississippi River floodplain and the steep, forested valleys of the central and eastern Ozark Highland—had been examined.

The antiquity of interest in Missouri's prehistoric past, however, in no way implies that *specific* interests have remained constant or that the ways in which the past is examined have not changed. Quite to the contrary, many topics that concerned nineteenth-century prehistorians working in the United States, regardless of where they were working, were of little or no interest to later archaeologists. Certainly many of the contentious issues that concern archaeologists today—such as the proper criteria to use for determining whether a site should be placed on the National Register of Historic Places or the most appropriate technique to use in surface collecting a site—were never discussed even as recently as 25 years ago. The disparity in goals and issues in Americanist archaeology is not simply a product of time. At *any* given point there will be differences in perspective on the past, with no two people necessarily agreeing even on how the archaeological record should be approached. Most archaeologists view what they do as scientific; others see the study of the past as more of a humanistic endeavor. Some opt for investigative procedures that allow them to rigorously examine the validity of the propositions they put forth about the past; others take a less rigorous approach to interpretation. A few archaeologists would even argue that there is no objective means of assessing the validity of individual interpretations and that we should scrap the exercise entirely and concentrate instead on explaining "the hard phenomena of the archaeological record" (Dunnell 1978a: 195). Needless to say, if disagreement exists over *how* the record should be examined, there is little chance of wide consensus on *what* the archaeological record is telling us about the past.

Why Study the History of Archaeology?

There are several possible answers to the question of why one should study the history of archaeology. The one I like best is because it's there and it's interesting. Americanist archaeology is a fascinating subject, complete with boiling controversies and colorful characters. Likewise, Missouri archaeology has had its share of both. In several respects, a novelist could not have picked better topics and characters. Given these ingredients, what further rationale does one really need to study the subject?

On the other hand, I believe there are several additional reasons that *professional* archaeologists should be well grounded in the history of the discipline. In archaeology, how we approach the past is, to a large degree, conditioned by such things as where we received our training, who trained us, where we received our first exposure to fieldwork, who our colleagues are, and what we read. It stands to reason that the broader one's background, the better perspective one brings to problem-solving. In the mid to late 1960s and early 1970s, Americanist archaeology went through a reorientation in terms of its goals, one early result of which was a decided aversion to the older literature—anything written before 1962. On the other hand, there were at least a few archaeologists who believed differently. Writing toward the end of that period of reorientation, Gordon Willey and Jeremy Sabloff, in their preface to *A History of American Archaeology*, noted that

> American archaeology—as all archaeology—is now in a phase of critical self-appraisal. Recent innovations in method and theory have aroused interest and argument in a way that has never occurred before within the discipline. This is the occasion, we believe, for a review of the full course of its development. In this way we can appreciate new developments in relation to those that have gone before; and from this historical perspective we may also see more clearly the significance of the new directions in which the field is moving. (Willey and Sabloff 1974: 9)

I agree with Willey and Sabloff that a knowledge of history helps us appreciate new directions, but I believe the reasons for the importance of such knowledge go deeper than this. For example, Bohannan and Glazer (1988: xv) state that we should study the history of a discipline to "save [ourselves] a good deal of unnecessary originality." Despite the humorous tone of their statement, their point is excellent. It would be difficult to count the times that archaeologists (myself included) truly believed they had devised a new concept or method and published a paper on it, only to have someone point out that so-and-so said the same thing 30 years ago. Worse yet is when you completely misrepresent a fact or argument because you cited a secondary source in which the author scrambled the original information. These rather embarrassing predicaments are simply a result of being ignorant of a discipline's history.

On a different note, it is often said that by understanding the history of a discipline, one can avoid the mistakes of one's predecessors (Mayr 1982: 20; see Daniel 1981 for an example from archaeology). I agree with the general point of this statement, but I do not particularly like the word *mistakes*. Errors have been made in archaeology, but many of the things that we might count as mistakes were simply the results of honest attempts at a particular time to use the best available information to solve an intellectual problem. For example, the advent of radiocarbon dating in the early 1950s demonstrated that some previous estimates of the ages of archaeological materials were wrong. To call the earlier estimates mistakes implies ignorance on the part of whoever made the estimates, which clearly is unwarranted. Similarly, only intellectual arrogance would lead us to label someone's approach to solving a problem a "mistake." This does *not* mean that we can't take exception to the approach or point out its problems, but we do have to be clear about our motives.

Later in this chapter I discuss the differences between two approaches— *interpretation,* concocting a story that accommodates the data, and *explanation,* deriving an answer based on theoretical expectations—that have been used in archaeology. I do so because the issue of interpretation versus explanation, the roots of which are buried in 150 years of Americanist archaeology, is fundamental to everything archaeologists do. As David Meltzer (1989: 12) notes, "The best way to understand why we do what we do is to unfold the beliefs that have structured, and continue to structure, our work." The belief that has structured much of Americanist archaeology and the overwhelming percentage of Missouri archaeology is that we can "interpret" the past. In the following chapters, I want to unfold that belief and determine where it has led us in our search for the past. As you will see, I am critical of interpretation as an approach in archaeology, but my opposition does not stem from any feeling that explanation is the "right" approach and interpretation is the "wrong" one. Rather, the question really boils down to which one is more useful.

A Reflection of Americanist Archaeology

Archaeology came through that phase of critical self-appraisal to which Willey and Sabloff referred, but there is still a great need to review its development,

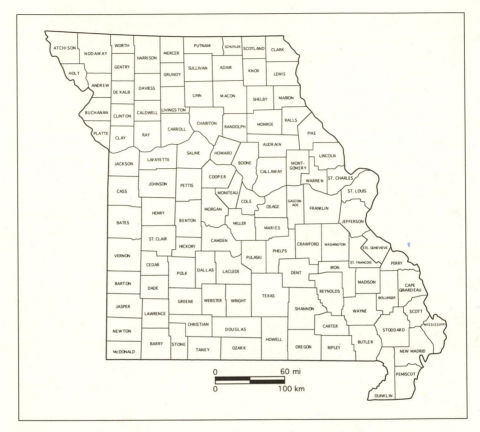

Figure 1.2. Outline of Missouri showing locations of 114 counties.

especially at a scale that was impossible for Willey and Sabloff to even contemplate.[1] One logical place to begin such a review is by choosing a geographically defined region that has witnessed extensive research and thus has a fairly well known archaeological record. Since I do the majority of my work in Missouri and its 114 counties (Figure 1.2) and am somewhat familiar with the literature that pertains to its archaeological record, I selected it as my sampling universe.

A sample of one is really no sample at all, especially given that there are 49 other states that could have been selected, and I don't pretend that the

1. Surprisingly, Willey and Sabloff's volume, which is now in its third edition, remains one of the few scholarly overviews of the discipline and certainly the one with which most archaeologists are familiar. I take the fact that so few overviews have been written to mean either that archaeologists believe Willey and Sabloff have covered everything that is important (which the authors themselves don't believe [see Sabloff 1989: 34]) or that archaeologists still aren't too concerned with the historical development of the field.

archaeological work that has been carried out in Missouri mirrors that conducted in other states. For example, Missouri obviously did not participate in the federally funded projects carried out in Tennessee Valley Authority basins during the 1930s—projects that produced not only important substantive results in terms of understanding local cultural sequences but also improvements in excavation techniques and advances in analytical methods. Regardless, the more important question is, did the innovative field methods and analytical methods produced by those projects have any effect on the manner in which archaeology was conducted in Missouri? Conversely, did work conducted in Missouri have important implications for archaeologists working elsewhere? Have archaeologists working in Missouri been leaders in the field from a theoretical and/or methodological standpoint? If not leaders, have they at least quickly recognized theoretical and methodological advances made elsewhere and incorporated those advances into archaeological work in Missouri? In short, were archaeologists working in Missouri innovators or at least borrowers of innovative techniques, or did they operate in a vacuum, seldom if ever bringing in theoretical and/or methodological innovations from outside the state? If they *did* import innovative concepts and methods, did they truly understand them or did they simply use them as window dressing?

Making these determinations requires a knowledge not only of what was occurring in Missouri at various times but also of what was going on in the profession at large. Willey and Sabloff (1974: 16) argued that "American archaeology is as good as its concepts" and that "the history of its development is related very directly to the addition of new and better concepts as these apply to the dimensions of form, space, and time and to the circumstances of context, function, and process." What Willey and Sabloff did *not* say, but which in my mind needs clarification, is that while the concepts themselves have been important to Americanist archaeology, it is how those concepts have been *applied* that is the really important issue. What has been the end product of those applications? Has it been an interpretation or an explanation? Any discussion of Americanist archaeology, and by extension the archaeology undertaken in any state, must have as its basis a clear understanding of the difference between explanation and interpretation.

Interpretation and Explanation: A Fundamental Dichotomy

The distinction between interpretation and explanation has much more to do with the discussions in the following chapters than I can convince you of at this point, perhaps, but I hope at least to provide you with some of the critical differences between the two and to show you that failure on the part of archaeologists to make the distinction has weakened the discipline considerably. Instead of offering solid *explanations* of why the archaeological record is structured the way it is—what I consider to be the ultimate goal of archaeology—archaeologists all too often offer only personal *interpretations* of its structure. The difference between these two products is anything but subtle.

Archaeologists, if they have a penchant for anything, love to interpret the record they study. Satisfactory interpretations of the archaeological record are pleasing not only to us and to our peers but also to a public fascinated with the past. Part of this fascination has to do with objects, but an even larger part has to do with the people who made, used, and abandoned the objects. Archaeologists are constantly bombarded with questions such as "Who lived at this site?" "What language did they speak?" "What kinds of houses did they live in?" "What foods did they eat?" The public, for the most part, does not take too kindly to the answer "We don't know." Most people have an appreciation for the fact that the dead don't speak, but they still feel that archaeologists should be able to answer what appear to be simple questions. If you can't get the dead to speak, so the reasoning goes, then at least get the objects they left behind to do the talking for them. And, as history has borne repeated witness, archaeologists *have* succeeded in getting objects to speak, though only after the right questions have been asked—questions based on years of experience in getting to know the artifacts.

What a wonderful freedom this silence of the dead imparts to the archaeologist, who can pursue interpretation without fear of criticism. You might, as Robert Dunnell (1988b: 6) once noted, be unpopular or even be labeled anachronistic because of your interpretations, but you can't be wrong. On the other hand, "One cannot help but be impressed by the parallel with *A Connecticut Yankee in King Arthur's Court*. So long as we are content to make statements, the truth of which cannot be ascertained, we are great magicians. But we might do well to keep an eye peeled for Yankees" (Dunnell 1988b: 6). There haven't been many Yankees who have cast an eye on the way archaeology has been undertaken in Missouri, but if they had, they would have been overwhelmed with information.

There is no way of ever knowing the number of sites in the state that have been subjected to some type of archaeological work, but it would easily reach into the thousands. Perhaps this is not surprising given that the Archaeological Survey of Missouri, the official repository for site locations in the state, now lists over 30,000 entries. The number of publications and unpublished manuscripts that pertain to archaeological work in Missouri probably exceeds 5,000. Further, the number of newspaper articles that have described archaeological finds in Missouri is anyone's guess. All of this adds up to a tremendous amount of information on the prehistory of the state. No one could ever hope to know all the information, though the person who undoubtedly came the closest was Carl Chapman (Figure 1.3).

Chapman had a penchant for detail, as even a casual reader of his two volumes will quickly notice. He might not have given the reader much, if any, information about why a particular site was excavated or why it was excavated in the manner that it was, but he left nothing out in discussing the number of projectile points by type from a certain level of a rock shelter or the number of shell-tempered sherds from the floor of a Mississippian-period house. Also highly visible is Chapman's proclivity for interpretation, which he liberally inserted throughout the volumes. He not only interpreted how the artifacts from a particular locality fit into the local archaeological sequence for the region but also expanded his interpretation to include such things as interrelationships between the people who made and used the artifacts in a particular locale and their contemporary groups in other regions. He relied on the old archaeological standbys—trade, diffusion, and migration—to explain the movement of artifact styles and people from one locale to another. When an item found in region A resembled in shape, form, or design an item found in region B, the only possible interpretive recourse was to infer (a) that the group in area A traded it to the group in area B (or vice versa), (b) that one group learned from the other how to make the item, or (c) that the group in one of the areas migrated from the other locality and brought the item (or knowledge of how to make it) with them.

Figure 1.3. Carl Chapman in Vernon County, Missouri, 1984 (courtesy *St. Louis Post-Dispatch*).

A classic example of Chapman's interpretive reasoning is his formulation of a model for the collapse of the "Hopewell interaction sphere," a now-outdated term used to refer to a short-lived network that supposedly distributed nonlocal materials such as mica, obsidian, copper, and grizzly-bear canines from the West to groups throughout the East and Midwest shortly after the birth of Christ. Chapman (1980: 71–72) noted, "None of the suggested causes for the decline and fall of the Hopewellian Interaction Sphere networks is satisfactory or wholly supportable. A new look needs to be taken at the evidence now available, new questions need to be asked of the data, and new hypotheses need to be proposed and tested. Perhaps we already have most of the data necessary to *explain* the change" (emphasis added). Chapman (1980: 72) cited as evidence of the collapse the absence or deterioration of certain Hopewellian traits in slightly later sites. These included the loss of elaborate decorations on pots, the absence of nonlocal materials, deterioration of the flaked-stone industry, the absence of log-tomb burials and geometric earthworks, and the absence of maize as a cultigen. Based on his review of these data, he arrived at the following conclusion:

> The overall impression gained from the evidence is that the change that took place was in the sociopolitical or politico-religious organization, concomitant with a breakdown of interregional interaction transactions that involved exchange of exotic status-ceremony-related materials. Within the local societies it was as if those with the knowledge and skill or the right to produce the distinctive, finely modeled and painted figurines, sculptured pipes, copper ornaments, and tools . . . were prevented from passing their knowledge and skill to the succeeding generations, or perhaps had no reason to do so. (Chapman 1980: 72)

Chapman (1980: 72) added, "The preceding is not an explanation of the breakdown of the interaction sphere but only a speculation. The basic question remains: Why did the regional interaction center break down?" Chapman's answer lay in perceived disruptions to what he termed "the corn-tobacco ceremony." He proposed that Hopewellian society operated in the following way: (1) Hopewellian organizational leaders held special ceremonies at special centers, during which time they would exchange nonlocal materials and items; (2) a necessary item of these ceremonies was a food or drink made from corn; (3) the food or drink was served in special ceramic or conch-shell vessels; (4) the ceremonies "were held at regularly scheduled times, perhaps when the corn was first harvested, with a green-corn ceremony coming near or soon after the summer solstice. An alternative might be a 'feast of the dead,' held yearly in different interaction centers . . . similar to the Algonkin Feast of the Dead in the seventeenth century"; (5) "the smoking of tobacco in a special pipe was a part of the ceremony, and the pipe was used as a passport for safe travel between regional centers"; and (6) unscheduled ceremonies were held upon the death of an important individual.

In Chapman's scheme, the explanation for the "collapse" of Hopewell was a change in the growing season of corn, which was brought about by climatic cooling ca. A.D. 400 (Bryson and Wendland 1967). Chapman was not the first archaeologist to propose that a link existed between climate change and Hopewellian culture change (see Griffin 1960; Struever and Vickery 1973; Vickery 1970), but he concluded that one had caused the other. Simply because two things *appear* to be correlated (and even here, there were problems [see below]) does not mean that one caused the other. Climatic change *could* have affected the Hopewellian food base, which in turn *could* have affected Hopewellian sociopolitical organization, but how do we know? *Could have affected* is the key phrase here.

Is Chapman's answer satisfactory as an explanation? A more fundamental question is, is it even an explanation? At first glance it might appear that it comes close to being an explanation because it addresses why the system collapsed, but it most assuredly is not. It actually fails on several counts, though the one that concerns us here is the lack of congruence between evidence and conclusion. *Explanation* is a system that works through a series of approximations until it can go no further given the data at hand. And, importantly, explanations are derived from a body of theory, not from any experiential realm. The ultimate arbiters of "an" explanation, as Dunnell (1988b) notes, are *performance criteria,* that is, how well a proposition works in an empirical context. Chapman's proposition does not work in an empirical context.

We now know that many of the changes Chapman cited as evidence of the Hopewell collapse did not occur simultaneously, though, in fairness to him, this was unclear when he originally formulated his model. But one fact that *was* well known when Chapman published his volume in 1980 was that there were few unquestionable occurrences of corn growth in the Midwest before ca. A.D. 900. Even if corn *had* been used in the ceremonies—and again, there is little evidence that corn was being grown (and none that it was being grown in abundance), let alone being used in ceremonies—why did the entire system of dispute resolution and prestige collapse? If, as Chapman suggests, Hopewellian peoples were having a difficult time growing corn, why didn't they switch to something else? At an even more basic level, what led to the development of such an elaborate system in the first place? We might *guess* that it was a form of dispute resolution, but this is only a guess.

Chapman used ethnographic data from the seventeenth century (the "Algonkin Feast of the Dead") as an analog to what happened in the first and second centuries A.D. He also used ethnographic information for the basis of his assumption that pipe-smoking assured safe passage from one territory to another. He interpreted rituals as being necessary confirmations of relationships between exchange groups and as assurances that certain individuals or social units had the right to continue the exchange, though he did not tell the reader what led him to those conclusions. Chapman admitted that his model was hypothetical but offered his rationale for using it:

> The preceding hypothetical model and the discussion of it and the analogs used are necessarily derived from a period separated by nearly two thousand years from the time of the Hopewellian Interaction Sphere. However, we need only look at the philosophies and ceremonies of the Christian religion today to see that philosophy, concepts, practices, and even artifacts (especially religious) can survive through several millennia and major cultural changes. (Chapman 1980: 75)

The key word in the above quote is *can*. It is possible for things such as religious practices to survive for several millennia (but even then, probably not in an unaltered form), but how does one document that they *did* survive? And why would we use a ceremony from the seventeenth century to "explain" something that happened 1,500 years beforehand (not to mention hundreds of miles away)? What we have here is an *interpretation* of why the Hopewellian system collapsed, not an *explanation* of it.

Explanations derive from well-grounded theories about the way things work, and Chapman had no theory from which to derive an explanation. And, I would argue, the interpretation itself is not even well grounded. An explanation of the collapse of the Hopewell interaction sphere, as I implied earlier, would have to begin with why the sphere (or whatever it was) began in the first place. What kind of theory can we draw on to explain why Middle Woodland people would begin importing various objects from faraway places and would start decorating their pots similarly? It is evident to me (O'Brien 1987), as it was to Braun and Plog (1982) before me, though they were more implicit, that Hopewell—both its "rise" and its "collapse"—is explainable in terms of Darwinian fitness. As I point out in Chapter 8 and in detail in Chapter 9, Darwinian evolutionary theory has considerable explanatory power relative to the archaeological record. At this point we don't need to concern ourselves with what that theory entails. What is important is that it *is* a theory and it is capable not only of providing explanations of the way things are but also of guiding the methods used to generate data. We don't have to rely on guesswork and interpretation, that is, on storytelling. This is the way science operates—the way it *has* to operate. To quote biologist Richard Lewontin (1974: 8), in science "We cannot go out and describe the world in any old way we please and then sit back and demand that an explanatory and predictive theory be built on that description."

Regardless of the differences between them, both interpretation and explanation *must* be based not only on evidence but also on *rules* of evidence. If a person is going to interpret the archaeological record, it is incumbent upon that person to follow the rules of evidence, which at the very least entails stating specifically the grounds upon which an interpretation is made (as Chapman did, at least in part). The rules of evidence are not a new invention but rather have been around in one guise or another for a long time. Neither are they limited to science, which renders irrelevant the argument over whether archaeology is a science or a humanistic discipline. Classics scholars, for example, might argue over interpretations of Greek political life in the third century B.C., but we assume that they have solid lines of evidence with which to support their claims. And we would likewise assume that their conclusions not only are based on a logical thought process but also are framed in such a way that if one piece of evidence used to support the claim were shown to be false, the argument would also be shown to be suspect. Such is not necessarily the case in archaeology.

One result of archaeologists' lack of adherence to rules of evidence has been the inability of the general public to separate archaeological "fact" from archaeological interpretation, the latter of which, when you strip the veneer off, is really nothing more than storytelling. And who among us can't tell stories? Even nonprofessionals can excavate a site and then create a story, and who is to say that their stories aren't as valid as the ones told by professionals? The question we should be asking, then, is not, who produces the more believable story? but rather, is the conclusion warranted? Even more importantly, has the conclusion been reached only after all other reasonable conclusions have been shown to be false? The issue of falsification in archaeological analysis became a focus of attention in the 1960s (see Chapter 6), but as I attempt to point out in Chapter 3, the issue really isn't new. Interestingly enough, several excellent examples grew out of archaeological work in Missouri.

We will leave the issue of interpretation versus explanation for the time being, but it will crop up repeatedly in various guises throughout the following chapters. It will become a central focus in Chapter 9. My reason for bringing it up here is to place firmly in your mind that there are major differences between the two approaches to the archaeological record and that they have conditioned our views of prehistory. Perhaps at this point a more important matter for you to consider is that if interpretations are being made—and I would guess that 99% of archaeology has centered around interpretation—on what basis are they being made? Much of what I discuss in chapters 2 through 8 hinges on this issue.

Keeping Track of Time, Space, and Form

Although it will be important to examine the basis on which interpretations are being made as you make your way through the book, perhaps an equally important issue will be keeping track of what is meant by certain terms that crop up during the course of discussion. Although I have intentionally tried to downplay the use of esoteric archaeological terminology, there is, on occasion, a need to use specific terms. Some of these are defined in the context of usage, but I introduce below a few that will appear with regularity, especially those related to chronological, spatial, and formal ordering of archaeological materials.

Archaeologists have long wrestled with the problems of space and time—where and when various cultural traits arose, how long they lasted, and when they died out—and a significant portion of the literature has been dedicated to how best to record this kind of information. My intention here is not to preempt later discussion but to provide a basic introduction to the issue. This brief presentation will also provide a convenient segue into a similarly brief overview of the archaeological record of Missouri in terms of time, space, and form. Knowing at this point what the record contains and the dates that have been assigned to it will in no way detract from the later story line and actually should make it easier to follow.

The chronological ordering of prehistoric materials is not a recent endeavor, with most Western chronicles assigning the Greeks the honor of being the first to develop a formal system subdividing artifacts not only by time but also by material class—stone, bronze, and iron, in that chronological order. In some circles there is sympathy for other groups' having established priority in this regard (the Chinese, for example [Olsen 1987]), though archaeological credit usually is given to Christian J. Thomsen (1848), curator of antiquities at the Museum of Northern Antiquities in Copenhagen. It was his student J. J. A. Worsaae, however, who actually provided the stratigraphic evidence (see below).

Thomsen's problem of deriving a basic cultural sequence is similar to the problem facing archaeologists today. At the most general level, we now know which artifact forms appeared before or after others on the North American continent. For example, we know that lanceolate-shaped blades containing flutes on each face appear to be among the oldest artifacts yet discovered in the United States. In the Southwest, tools of this form, commonly referred to as Clovis projectile points, named for the town in New Mexico near where they were first identified, have been recovered in association with mammoths. In Missouri, several have been found associated with mastodons. The relative positions of the Clovis points—deeper stratigraphically, compared to specimens of other projectile-point types—as well as the absolute dating of organic materials in association with the points lead us to pinpoint the dates of the objects at ca. 9250–8950 B.C. Wherever we find a Clovis point, whether it be in a buried context or on the ground surface, we suspect the point was made during that period.

Likewise, the beginnings of pottery production in the large midwestern river valleys can be traced to ca. 500–600 B.C. On a finer scale, we have documented that sometime after A.D. 800 potters in many localities in the Midwest and East shifted from using various minerals as tempers to using burned, crushed mussel shell—a shift that eventually had profound effects on vessel-production technology (see Chapter 8). However, shell-tempered pottery by no means occurs in all ceramic assemblages in those regions. The appearance of flat-topped, pyramidal-substructure mounds coincided in many areas with the beginnings of shell-tempered pottery, but not all groups who made shell-tempered pottery constructed mounds. Thus, even among archaeological sites in the Mississippi River valley that postdate ca. A.D. 1000, there is tremendous variation in site plan and artifact content. If this is true for sites in one region that are more or less contemporary, how much more spatial and temporal variation is there when sites from the preceding 10 millennia are added? The answer is that the variation expands exponentially. How do archaeologists sort this variation in order to create meaningful categories? The various approaches that have been proposed to keep track of space, time, and form are not difficult to understand; the difficult part is applying one approach consistently. We are going to look closely at some of those systems in chapters 4 and 5, but as background I will discuss two generic methods that are routinely used to partition the archaeological record, each of which emphasizes time but only one of which emphasizes form. I hasten to point out that archaeology has endured the creation of literally dozens of partitioning systems, some of which emphasized form over time and/or space, but I defer discussion of them until later.

The Cultural-Tradition System

What I will call the "cultural-tradition" system comprises unit names that connote, at least to those who use the system, a considerable amount of information about time and artifact form and less information about space. For example, the term *Mississippian* is used in the sense of a *tradition* (literally, a way of doing things) to refer to sites that contain shell-tempered pottery, perhaps mounds, and usually corn. The sites occur in a wide variety of contexts in the midwestern and southeastern United States and were occupied anytime between roughly A.D. 800 and 1600. Some archaeologists would argue that the Mississippian tradition began slightly later; others would argue that the terminal date should be moved in one direction or the other. Regardless, most archaeologists would agree that the Mississippian tradition (or, as is commonly written, Mississippian *culture*—a term used in archaeology but which was borrowed uncritically from ethnology [for our purposes defined as the study of indigenous peoples]) fits somewhere in that age range.

Archaeologists have even developed subunits within larger units to account for the waxing and waning of various cultures. For example, the term *emergent Mississippian* is now commonly used to refer to the first hundred years or so of what is viewed as Mississippian development in the Midwest and Southeast—that period when some prehistoric groups residing in those regions began growing corn, shifting from various mineral tempers to shell temper in their pottery, and rearranging themselves socially and politically into larger and more complex sociopolitical groups—what have commonly been referred to as chiefdoms.

Archaeologists have long recognized, however, that not all prehistoric peoples in the Midwest and Southeast grew corn, shifted to shell tempering, or reorganized into chiefdoms. In other words, some groups were not "Mississippianized." In some instances, they lived alongside their Mississippian neighbors, but their sites are usually found on the periphery of the major river valleys or in what archaeologists refer to as "the hinterland." It would appear for all practical purposes that these groups continued living as they had for the preceding several centuries, whereas their neighbors developed or acquired new ways of doing things. Ignoring for now the question of why those groups didn't adopt the traits of their Mississippian neighbors, what are we to do with the non-Mississippian artifacts in terms of placing them in a time-space-form category? The usual answer is to extend the chronologically earlier tradition—Late Woodland—up in time to accommodate the non-Mississippian artifacts, thereby creating parallel, contemporary traditions. Whereas in the central Mississippi River valley we might terminate the Late Woodland tradition at ca. A.D. 900 and replace it with the emergent-Mississippian tradition, in the eastern Ozarks we might run the Late Woodland tradition up to the sixteenth century.

Even the occurrence of shell-tempered pottery and corn is no assurance that the term *Mississippian* will be used to group contemporary artifact assemblages. Archaeologists have developed a host of terms to signify major differences among shell-tempered-pottery assemblages from portions of the midwestern and eastern United States. For example, the term *Oneota* has been used for materials from the upper Midwest, including portions of Missouri; *Fort Ancient* applies to materials from the Ohio River valley; and *Plaquemine* is often used for materials from the lower Mississippi River valley. Thus, under this system, the Oneota tradition of the upper Midwest was contemporary with the Mississippian tradition of the central Mississippi River valley and with a portion of the long-lived Late Woodland tradition of the Ozark Highland.

Another example that bears brief discussion is the aforementioned Hopewellian tradition—a cultural manifestation that has been identified in all states of the Midwest as well as portions of the South and Southeast. Hopewell derives its name from a site in southern Ohio that produced a wealth of items made of nonlocal materials. Artifact assemblages from Hopewell and related sites in the Scioto River valley and neighboring drainages in southern Ohio contain such things as grizzly-bear canines from the western United States, copper from the Great Lakes, shark teeth from the Gulf Coast, obsidian from Wyoming, and mica from various regions. More often than not, these materials were worked into exquisite objects that found their way into burials. The vast majority of these items occur in Ohio, but west-central Illinois also contains a fair amount, as do a few other localities across the eastern half of the United States.

In addition to objects manufactured from nonlocal materials, many Hope-wellian sites contain elaborately carved and stamped ceramic vessels—decorative techniques that appeared in west-central Illinois sometime around 200 B.C. and disappeared around A.D. 300 (Figure 1.4). For many years any site in the eastern United States that produced a pottery sherd exhibiting fancy carved or stamped designs was labeled Hopewell. By the late 1930s it was obvious to archaeologists that southern Ohio and west-central Illinois were the two major "hearth" areas for Hopewell and that other regions were only minor players. It also became obvious that while many sites in the eastern United States contained one or a few fancy sherds, these numbers were dwarfed by thousands of nondecorated sherds from the same time period. In other words, the absence of decorated sherds at a site was not necessarily an indication that the site was not occupied during the time of the Hopewellian tradition. Hopewell thus was (and still is) viewed as a tradition that at most sites was represented, if at all, by a thin veneer of material that itself represented only a tiny fraction of the total kinds of materials being produced (or procured) by the inhabitants. In other words, the Hopewell tradition crosscut the longer-lived Middle Woodland tradition.

The Chronological System

In opposition to the tradition-based system is the strictly chronological system, wherein many of the same units used in the tradition-based approach are employed, but they are used strictly as time markers. In other words, the term *Mississippi(an)* is used as a period, as opposed to a tradition, without regard for artifact content and with little regard for spatial distribution. Thus any prehistoric site in Missouri dating after A.D. 900 would be assigned to the Mississippi(an) *period*—instead of the Mississippian *tradition*—regardless of whether it produced shell-tempered pottery or not, just as any site dating 5000–3000 B.C. would be assigned to the Middle Archaic period.

Compound Systems

Perhaps not surprisingly, few archaeologists use the units in a strictly chrono-logical sense. More commonly, some units are used in a chronological sense and others are used to mark time *and* tradition. In the Midwest and Southeast, for example, one typical procedure is to use the preceramic units—Paleo-Indian through Late Archaic (see below)—in a strictly chronological sense (e.g., the Paleo-Indian period, the Late Archaic period) and then to switch gears and use the ceramic units in the traditional sense (e.g., the Mississippian tradition). And it certainly is not uncommon to find references to the *Mississippian tradition* in the same paragraph with references to the *Mississippi(an) period*. As I noted earlier, these systems for keeping track of time, space, and form are not difficult

Figure 1.4. Middle Woodland–period, Havana-tradition sherds from the Burkemper site, Lincoln County, Missouri. Vessels carrying stamped and/or incised designs similar to those shown here were once lumped under the term *Hopewell,* which is now a more restrictive label (from O'Brien and Hoard 1996).

to understand, but to judge from the literature, they are difficult to apply consistently.

Notice that in the preceding paragraphs I bracketed the *-an* on the end of *Mississippi* in some cases. I did so because over time there has been a move toward using *Mississippi* to refer to the *period* and *Mississippian* to refer to the *tradition.* The term *Mississippian,* which as Chapman (1980: 6) noted "has a prominent place in the description of archaeological materials and cultures in Missouri and throughout the Mississippi River valley," probably dates from the late nineteenth century. Bureau of Ethnology prehistorian William Henry Holmes (1886b) used the designation *Middle Mississippi Valley* group to segregate ceramic vessels from the central Mississippi River valley from those found farther north, which he labeled the *Upper Mississippi Valley group.* As Chapman pointed out, Illinois archaeologists Fay-Cooper Cole and Thorne Deuel (1937) later employed those same designations to refer to two separate culture types that they identified. Midwestern archaeologist W. C. McKern coined the term *Mississippi pattern,* which had two manifestations—*the Middle Mississippi phase* and the *Upper Mississippi phase* (McKern 1939). James Griffin, whose command of prehistoric pottery from the eastern United States is unparalleled, used the term *Mississippi* to refer to a period as well as a culture type (Griffin 1952b). He subdivided the culture types into *Middle* and *Upper Mississippian* and the period into two parts, *early* and *middle Mississippian.* Gordon Willey, in his summary volume on the archaeology of North America and Mesoamerica (Willey 1966), used the designation *Mississippian tradition,* the term commonly used today. It should be apparent—and will become more so later—that the situation has become confusing.

The problem is by no means limited to the Mississippian tradition/period, as Chapman (1980: 2) again points out:

> *Woodland* is the term that seems to have been used the most to describe the cultural developments that took place in the relatively short period from 1000 B.C. to A.D. 900 in the central Missouri-Mississippi valley, which encompasses the present state of Missouri. Similar to terminology for other periods, it was found that the term *Woodland* has been used to describe pattern, stage, culture, tradition, and period (Anonymous 1943; Cole and Deuel 1937; Deuel 1935; Griffin 1952b; Jennings 1968; McKern 1939; Willey and Phillips 1958).

There have been efforts to rectify problems caused by terminological confusion, usually by substituting new terms for the old ones (e.g., Stoltman 1978), but few archaeologists have used the new terms.[2] There also have been numerous

---

2. In many respects, these newer formulations contain the same problems as the older ones (Dunnell 1978a).

attempts to cross correlate the tradition-based and purely chronological systems. Usually in such cases an author will use the units to refer to traditions and then present a table that contains periods and dates. Chapman (1975, 1980) modified this approach by developing an entirely new series of tradition units and then correlating those with time periods, noting, "Cultural periods roughly equate with time periods" (Chapman 1980: 1). His scheme is presented below:

Tradition	Period
Village Farmer	Late Mississippi (A.D. 1450–1700)
	Middle Mississippi (A.D. 1200–1450)
	Early Mississippi (A.D. 900–1200)
Prairie-Forest Potter	Late Woodland (A.D. 400–900)
	Middle Woodland (500 B.C.–A.D. 400)
	Early Woodland (1000–500 B.C.)
Forager	Late Archaic (3000–1000 B.C.)
	Middle Archaic (5000–3000 B.C.)
	Early Archaic (7000–5000 B.C.)
Hunter-Forager	Dalton (8000–7000 B.C.)
Early Hunter	Paleo-Indian (12,000–8000 B.C.)
Unspecialized Hunter-Gatherer	Early Man (?–12,000 B.C.)

Chapman's "traditions" are more in line with what Fitzhugh (1972, 1975) referred to as *adaptation types,* defined as general constructs that integrate physical-environmental variables with human responses to the environment. Chapman coined his traditions "with the view that the names of traditions should include an identifying cultural criterion" (Chapman 1980: 1). Thus, regarding the Prairie-Forest Potter tradition, Chapman (1980: 4) stated that "in line with the use of the term *tradition* to describe the general way of life or the primary economic base of a culture's participation in a tradition, the term *Prairie-Forest Potter Tradition* has been used for the culture that occurred most consistently in the time approximately from 1000 B.C. to A.D. 900, and *Woodland period* has been used to designate the time period." The period names and dates Chapman employed are those in common use in the eastern United States, summarized in Griffin's (1967) overview of the archaeology of the region.

What are we to make of all these schemes? Are the terms and accompanying dates useful for segmenting the archaeological record in terms that are meaningful, or, conversely, do they attempt to lump too much variation under a single heading? Actually, they do both. Regardless of whether one uses the units in the sense of traditions or in a strictly chronological sense, the terms impart a certain amount of information. If I told you I found a piece of Mississippian pottery, you immediately would know something about the temper in the sherd—that it probably is shell—as well as its date of manufacture—after ca. A.D. 800. You also would have some *general* indication as to where I found the sherd (probably the eastern half of the United States). My telling you that a sherd came from a Mississippian site also might lead you to ask whether the site had mounds or wall-trench houses—which Mississippian peoples often built—or whether any evidence of corn had been found. On the other hand, if I told you I found a piece of pottery that dates ca. A.D. 800, it could have any number of materials as a temper and could have come from just about anywhere. Thus a certain amount of information is imparted by using either a tradition-related unit or a purely chronological unit, with more information imparted by the former.

However, I have glossed over a significant amount of information in my shorthand approach, which is not necessarily problematic as long as I (and you) realize I have done so. If all I am trying to do is quickly impart some information to you, the units are adequate. But when I start using the designators as data-reporting units, such as stating that such-and-such region has 60 Mississippian sites, then I am using the units for purposes that they are ill prepared to handle. This does not mean that they have *not* been used as end-all categories in and of themselves; in fact, the units have become a mainstay of Americanist archaeology. Standard archaeological practice since the 1950s has been to subdivide the archaeological record into finer and finer temporal-spatial units for the purpose of combining things that appear to be similar and segregating things that appear to be dissimilar. Such normative categories—normative in the sense that the units are defined in terms of "normal" characteristics (which themselves are ill defined)—have assumed an importance that far exceeds their limited utility as bookkeeping devices. In the central Mississippi River valley, where I do the majority of my research, the number of such units, usually referred to as phases, has proliferated to the point where one now needs a user's guide to read an archaeological report. The same could be said relative to pottery types and projectile-point types, which are also used to partition the archaeological record.

Time-and-Space Systematics and the Archaeological Record of Missouri

I began this section by mentioning that I wanted not only to present a brief overview of some of the terms that will be encountered in the following chapters but also to introduce in abbreviated form several aspects of the archaeological record of Missouri. Keep in mind that the brief overview presented below is a *modern* summary of the archaeological record, not one that could have been written even a few years ago. The unit designations I use for the prehistoric period are, for the most part, those used by Griffin (1967) in his overview of the prehistory of the eastern United States, though I have modified the dates to reflect modern chronological assessments. Although I generally omit from later discussion the period postdating A.D. 1541, there is an incredibly rich archaeological record in Missouri that dates to the last four hundred years, that is, the period after contact between Native American groups and Euro-Americans. To give you at least some idea of what that record contains, I briefly touch on a few aspects of the historical period.

This overview takes into account several topics that will be covered in later chapters—topics that at one time or another became important areas of research in Missouri archaeology. One such area of investigation has to do with human responses to physical-environmental changes that have occurred over the last 12,000 years. Missouri is a complex amalgam of many different kinds of physiographic settings. The Ozark Highland presents the greatest amount of relief, the southeastern corner of the state exhibits the least amount, and the northern and western prairies are intermediate between the two. Although these elevational differences were the same 12,000 years ago as they are today, the landscape of Missouri underwent dramatic alterations during the intervening millennia. For example, the vegetation cover evident when it was mapped in the nineteenth century (Figure 1.5)—both in terms of composition and position—is nothing like it was at the end of the last glaciation (roughly 11,000–12,000 years ago), when spruce and larch extended their range deep into the Ozarks. The modern positions of the two major biomes in Missouri—the tall-grass prairies and the oak-hickory forests—stand in contrast to their positions at the height of the prolonged warm, dry climatic episode that gripped much of the Midwest between ca. 7000 and 3000 B.C., when prairie grasses claimed many of the areas previously covered by oak-hickory forests. Trying to understand human responses to environmental change is not a new area of archaeological research, but it has only been in the last few decades that the data needed to examine the evolution of paleolandscapes in Missouri have been available.

The Paleo-Indian Period (9250–8950 B.C.)[3]

Missouri contains ample evidence that prehistoric peoples hunted and lived within the state's boundaries by ca. 9250 B.C.—evidence consisting of a variety of bifacially flaked stone implements that have been found in parts of the western United States in association with mammoths and other now-extinct animals, including several forms of bison. As mentioned earlier, some of these stone tools have been found in Missouri in direct association with mastodon remains. Many of the implements undoubtedly served as projectile points—probably on spears,

---

3. Small portions of the following synopsis are from Warren and O'Brien 1982a.

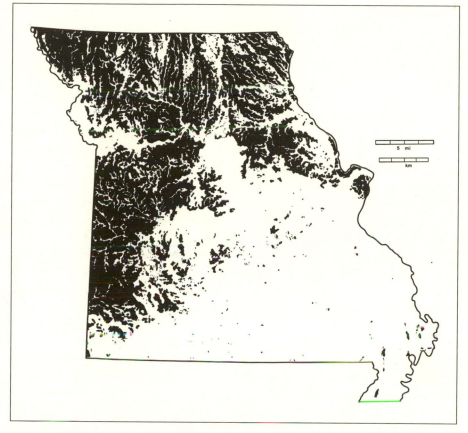

Figure 1.5. Nineteenth-century distribution of prairie (dark area) and timber (light area) across Missouri as determined from General Land Office survey records (after Schroeder 1981).

some perhaps on darts—but some apparently also doubled as knives. The earliest form appears to be the aforementioned Clovis point, which in various parts of the western United States was replaced sometime around 8950 B.C. by the smaller Folsom point, which in turn was replaced by several different point forms.

The exact timing of the arrival of humans into the New World is a subject of debate. Some archaeologists, including Chapman (e.g., 1975), place the event late in the Pleistocene epoch, a two-million-year-long geological unit that for very good reasons has been termed the "ice age." Others place the arrival within the last thousand years of the Pleistocene, ca. 12,000–11,000 years ago. Throughout the Pleistocene, temperatures in the Northern Hemisphere fluctuated dramatically, with prolonged periods of cold followed by periods of higher temperatures. This is not to say that temperatures dropped precipitously and remained consistently lower for tens of thousands of years, or, conversely, that temperatures rose and remained at a consistently higher level for long periods. In reality, annual mean temperatures might have risen or declined relative to those of the previous year; what we see in the environmental record—the advance and retreat of glacial ice—are long-term trends.

Late Pleistocene climatic conditions in the Midwest led to the development of mixed hardwood-and-coniferous forests that stretched from the Plains eastward and at least as far south as the Ozark Highland. In Missouri these forests were composed primarily of spruce in the north, grading into mixed spruce-birch-maple forests in the south. In the one locality where an extensive pollen record has been found in association with a likewise extensive mammalian record—the lower Pomme de Terre River valley of southwest Missouri—evidence indicates that at least some of the forests were interrupted by patches of grassland. Several bogs in that locality produced the remains of mastodons—browsers that lived on leaves and branches of conifers—but one bog also produced bones of mammoths—grazers that ate primarily grasses and shoots (see Chapter 6). Thus the presence of mammoths alongside mastodons, with their contrasting diets, suggests that the forests were more open than they were in more northerly latitudes.

The beginning of the Holocene epoch ca. 11,000 years ago[4] coincided with the introduction of dry Pacific air masses that dominated the midcontinent, leading to the final great retreat of glacial ice in Canada, the disappearance of intermontane glaciers in the continental United States, and the replacement of coniferous forests with deciduous forests in areas such as Missouri and steppe-tundra with grasslands in the Great Plains. Certainly by 8500 B.C. mastodons and mammoths had disappeared from the Midwest and the Plains and had been replaced by more-modern-looking forms of bison as the largest animals roaming the landscape.

The Dalton Period (8950–7900 B.C.)

By ca. 8950 B.C. the midcontinent was inhabited by an essentially modern suite of plants and animals, and it was on these resources that early Holocene hunter-gatherers focused their attention. In contrast to the paucity of radiocarbon dates from the Midwest falling in the Paleo-Indian period, several dates from midwestern contexts exist for the time span 8950–7900 B.C., what has become known as the Dalton period. Precise dating of the Dalton period is problematic—Chapman (1975) dated it from 8000 to 7000 B.C.—though the span assigned

---

4. Specialists on the subject might argue with the date used here, with some preferring to move it a thousand years forward. However, with new dates for the Younger Dryas stadial, a 1,300-year-long cold period between ca. 11,600 and 12,900 years ago (Edwards et al. 1993), I believe the beginning date of 11,000 B.P. for the Holocene is acceptable.

here probably brackets it fairly (Goodyear 1982). Dalton points—thin, concave-base, unnotched forms—have been found across Missouri in all physiographic settings, from the prairies of northern and western Missouri to the Ozark Highland to the older, braided-stream surfaces in the Mississippi alluvial valley. Social groups probably were small and mobile; most encampments appear to represent temporary occupations. Sites appear in upland contexts, often near small ephemeral streams in areas dominated historically by grassland flora (O'Brien and Warren 1983).

Incidentally, the Dalton point, and by extension the Dalton period, were named for the owner of the land in Cole County, Missouri, containing the type site (the site after which the artifact type was named), Judge Samuel P. Dalton (Figure 1.6), who served on the Missouri Supreme Court from 1950 until his death in 1965. Dalton was an avid collector of artifacts, a member of the Missouri Archaeological Society, and, according to his son Andy Dalton, "very proud of his association with the University and particularly with . . . Dr. Chapman" (W. A. R. Dalton, pers. comm., 1994).

The Early Archaic Period (7900–5000 B.C.)

Around 7900 B.C., perhaps later in some areas, the Dalton point disappeared and was replaced by corner-notched and basal-notched projectile points. All areas of Missouri, except the meander-belt portion of the Mississippi Valley, have produced numerous examples of these points, suggesting that use of the prairies and forests by human groups was fairly intensive. The Early Archaic period corresponds to the onset of the Hypsithermal, or Atlantic, climatic episode (Deevey and Flint 1957). Environmental conditions during the Hypsithermal (7000–3000 B.C.) were radically different from those of the earlier Holocene and also may have been quite different from those of subsequent times. Because of the increasing persistence of dry westerly winds across the midwestern United States (Webb and Bryson 1972), prairies expanded eastward beyond their modern limits (H. E. Wright 1976) and probably captured many localities that previously were forested. These conditions also affected streams and verte-brate resources, and we might expect that human settlement patterns changed as well.

The Middle Archaic Period (5000–3000 B.C.)

Temporally diagnostic artifacts of the Middle Archaic period include numerous side-notched projectile points/knives that replaced the Early Archaic–period forms. Grinding stones appear in significant quantities, apparently signifying a greater reliance on plant foods than seen previously. By 5000 B.C. moisture stress became severe in some parts of the Midwest, as evidenced by the continued eastward expansion of prairies, which reached their maximum extent around

Figure 1.6. Judge Samuel P. Dalton and his wife, Edna Rusk Dalton, with two of their grandchildren, Kimball S. Anderson (left) and Renner S. Anderson, at an open house at Van Meter State Park, Saline County, Missouri, 1960. By the mid-1950s, the name Dalton had become as common in Missouri archaeology as it was in Missouri politics and jurisprudence. Carl Chapman and Judge Dalton were close friends, and Dalton showed Chapman several lanceolate points that had come from his property near the mouth of the Osage River. Chapman called them Dalton points and the name stuck.

that time (H. E. Wright 1968). In some areas prairie intrusion into previously forested areas was preceded by accelerated rates of erosion and deposition of wind-blown sediments (Ahler 1973a; Butzer 1977). Faunal assemblages from Middle Archaic sites provide further evidence of dramatic changes in vegetation. For example, remains of several prairie species such as bison and pronghorn have been found in the Ozark Highland (McMillan 1976c; Purdue 1982), and higher-than-expected incidences of prairie-timber-edge species such as white-tail deer and cottontails have been found in historically forested regions of central Missouri (McMillan and Klippel 1981).

Evidence of the ways in which animals were affected by the Hypsithermal include decreases in body size of deer, cottontails, and gray squirrels toward sizes that today are found in animals located much farther west (Purdue 1980).

Decreases in stream discharge (Hill 1975; Klippel et al. 1978) and the lowering of water tables in swamps in the central Mississippi River valley (King and Allen 1977) suggest that aquatic species were also affected. All of these data suggest that the middle Holocene was a period of severe and recurrent droughts across much if not all of the Midwest. Some "protected" localities, such as major river valleys, could have offered refuge from some of the more profound effects, but even there resources attractive to Middle Archaic groups might have changed in terms of quantity and proportion from those present previously.

The Late Archaic Period (3000–600 B.C.)

By about 3000 B.C. the climatic trends of the Hypsithermal were reversed as a result of the diminishing strength of westerly winds and concomitant increases in rainfall. Prairies began a slow westward retreat, and forests began to reclaim terrain. Despite this general amelioration of conditions, not all regions rebounded at the same rate, and probably no area rebounded to match pre-Hypsithermal conditions. Prairies still maintained their positions in the flat upland areas of northern and western Missouri, and forests thrived best in wetter environments, such as along stream courses and on valley sides.

Extensive evidence of human use of Missouri's landscape between 3000 and 600 B.C. exists in the archaeological record. It probably is fair to say that every county in the state has provided large numbers of projectile points and other artifacts that can be securely dated to the Late Archaic period. Burial mounds appear in fairly sizable numbers for the first time during this period (Bacon and Miller 1957; Klepinger and Henning 1976), and there is substantial evidence of permanent or semipermanent houses, storage pits, and deep trash middens. Evidence from several areas in Missouri indicates that at least some groups were engaged in two-part seasonal migrations composed of large, upland warm-season villages and small, bottomland winter encampments (Bozell and Warren 1982; Reeder 1980; Reid 1980). Deer and other mammals were still important staples for humans, but fish, wild seeds, and nuts increased in importance. Additional supplements to the diet included two cultigens—squash and gourds—that appeared in the lower Pomme de Terre River valley ca. 2200 B.C. (Chomko and Crawford 1978; Kay et al. 1980).

The Early Woodland Period (600–250 B.C.)

The Early Woodland period is poorly documented in Missouri, primarily because of a paucity of recognizable chronological markers diagnostic of that time span. In other regions of the Midwest, such as western and west-central Illinois, mineral-tempered pottery appeared ca. 600 B.C. and within a few hundred years became ubiquitous in the larger drainages, such as the Illinois River valley and portions of the Mississippi River valley. In Missouri, the earliest pottery, known as Marion thick, occurs in only a few isolated localities on the west bank of the Mississippi River north of St. Louis. Specimens of a later type, known as Black Sand, occur in northeastern Missouri and in a few localities along the Missouri River. Pascola pottery, contemporary with Black Sand, occurs sporadically on sites in southeastern Missouri. Several straight- and contracting-stem Early Woodland point types occur over most of Missouri, but it is unclear how late in time some of the types extended. The paucity of Early Woodland ceramic material on Missouri sites has, from time to time, been cited as evidence of a decline in population size, though such speculation is unwarranted.

In parts of the Midwest a warming trend, termed the Sub-Atlantic, began ca. 800 B.C. and lasted for about 1,100 years. Pollen records indicate that the Great Plains witnessed lower levels of effective moisture (Wendland 1978), but any climatic changes probably had little or no effect on regional fauna and flora. Faunal remains from archaeological sites exhibit high diversity, and mast (nut) resources, especially hickory-nut shell, dominate floral assemblages. The role of pottery in the processing and preparation of some of these foods is poorly understood—a subject that has recently become a focus of concerted study (D. T. Morgan 1992; O'Brien et al. 1994).

The Middle Woodland Period (250 B.C.–A.D. 450)

In contrast to the poorly understood role pottery assumed in the processing of foodstuffs during the Early Woodland period, a wealth of information exists concerning the role it played during the few centuries prior to and just after the beginning of the Christian era. By that time pottery was widespread across the Midwest, including most if not all parts of Missouri. Regional ceramic traditions—one of which, the Havana (earlier termed Hopewell) tradition, occurs in western and west-central Illinois—are evident fairly frequently in the Mississippi River valley and sporadically across other portions of the Midwest. Havana-tradition pottery is distinctive in its decorative treatment, often comprising zoned, stamped, and/or incised designs (Figure 1.4), and thus has become a widely used temporal marker. As mentioned previously, the absence of Havana pottery in a region has often been used as evidence that the region was depopulated—a line of reasoning that overlooks the tremendous regional ceramic variation that existed during the Middle Woodland period.

One area of the Middle Woodland archaeological record that has received considerable analysis is pottery technology and use. In fact, the ceramic portion of the midwestern Middle Woodland archaeological record has become a virtual laboratory for understanding how changes in the design and performance of ceramic vessels were integrated with other dimensions of human adaptation (O'Brien and Holland 1990, 1992; O'Brien et al. 1994). David Braun (1985a, 1987) first documented the complex changes in cooking-vessel shapes and sizes that occurred in western Illinois between ca. 200 B.C. and A.D. 700—an analysis that has been duplicated for materials from other regions, including eastern Missouri (Hoard 1992; O'Brien 1987; O'Brien and Hoard 1996; O'Brien et al. 1994). These various analyses have documented a trend toward production of thinner-walled cooking vessels, which has been linked to changes in methods of cooking and in diet—for example, the use of starchy and oily seeded plants such as goosefoot and sunflower increased dramatically during the Middle Woodland period.

It has been proposed (O'Brien 1987; Styles 1981) that local population growth in the resource-rich midwestern river valleys could have caused resource zones to shrink in size, and that increased reliance on the seeds of native annuals such as goosefoot, maygrass, little barley, sumpweed, knotweed, and sunflower (Asch and Asch 1985a, 1985b; Asch et al. 1979; Pulliam 1987) was part of the human response to this condition. Population-growth rates are difficult to estimate (Asch 1976), but the large number of Middle Woodland sites in the Illinois Valley and other localities suggests that conditions could have become crowded as the population expanded, perhaps in large part due to the attraction provided by the resource-rich locales (O'Brien 1987).

Some areas, especially the lower Illinois River valley, have produced convincing evidence of status differences within groups. Burials within mounds often contain a wide variety of grave goods—objects made of obsidian, mica, copper, and marine shell; grizzly-bear teeth; and shark teeth—and the differential distribution of these materials among the burials indicates that some form of personal status differentiation was practiced. Although some archaeologists (e.g., Tainter 1975, 1977, 1978, 1981, 1983) have concluded that the distribution suggests that at least some Middle Woodland groups had a rigid hierarchy of hereditary ranking, Braun's (1979, 1981) demonstration that supposed status symbols fail to crosscut all age and sex categories argues strongly that status positions were not ascribed.

The Late Woodland Period (A.D. 450–900)

Archaeological remains dating to the Late Woodland period have been documented across Missouri in all physiographic contexts. Literally hundreds of Late Woodland–period sites have been at least partially excavated, resulting in large quantities of materials and numerous radiocarbon dates for them. Myriad pottery types and projectile-point types have been formulated to encompass the tremendous variation that exists in the material record, and many of these are excellent chronological markers. Clearly absent in the early half of the Late Woodland–period record is the decorated Havana-tradition pottery that dominated some ceramic assemblages during the Middle Woodland period. By A.D. 450 most cooking vessels either were left plain-surfaced or were marked by stamping the exteriors with cord-wrapped paddles. The abandonment of highly decorated vessel exteriors has led some archaeologists to suggest that Late Woodland groups became more localized in terms of their social interactions and as a consequence intergroup interactions ceased. Braun (1977, 1985b; see also Braun and Plog 1982), on the other hand, argues that intergroup interaction actually increased during the early half of the Late Woodland period, to the point where it was no longer necessary to exchange elaborate goods or to create elaborate vessel decorations.

Faunal and floral remains recovered from early Late Woodland–period sites indicate a continued intensification of food procurement efforts (O'Brien 1987, 1996; Styles 1981), and toward the end of the period, people began growing maize. Agricultural intensification had several important biological consequences. Although maize is an important source of carbohydrates, it is a poor source of protein and other nutrients. And if there is a drought, not even that source of carbohydrates is available. Not surprisingly, comparisons of Middle Woodland and terminal Late Woodland skeletal samples (Buikstra 1979; Cook 1976) show, among the later samples, decreasing signs of acute stress (e.g., Harris lines [a sign of interrupted growth]) but more frequent signs of chronic stress (e.g., growth rate and cortical thickening of juvenile long bones); a higher incidence of weanling-age death; a 5–7-year drop in life expectancy of young adults; and an earlier onset of dental caries.

The Mississippian Period (A.D. 900–1541)

In some parts of the Midwest a radical change in how people distributed themselves across the landscape occurred ca. A.D. 900–1000, the date normally used to signal the beginning of the Mississippi(an) period/tradition. I mentioned some of the hallmarks of the new pattern earlier—mound construction, shell-tempered pottery, and a heavy reliance on maize agriculture. Underlying this veneer of homogeneity, however, is a tremendous amount of variation, one aspect of which is site size. At one end of the spectrum is Cahokia, a mound center the core of which is spread over more than 6 square miles of rich alluvium east of St. Louis. Smaller in size are numerous mound centers located up and down the west bank of the Mississippi River, many of which were fortified (J. R. Williams 1964). None of these centers, whose functions are poorly understood, existed throughout the entirety of the Mississippian period. Rather, each center reached its zenith at some point between ca. A.D. 900 and 1541 and then was abandoned. Hundreds of smaller sites are located in the meander-belt floodplain of the Mississippi River as well as on portions of the Pleistocene braided-stream surfaces associated with the ancestral Mississippi and Ohio rivers.

Excellent chronological markers, especially ceramic vessels, allow us to date many of the Mississippian-period sites in the Mississippi River valley, but most of those types are specific to their localities. It is in regions such as the Ozark Highland where we have a difficult time assessing the ages of archaeological sites that date post–A.D. 900, since the material record in many sites resembles that from the Late Woodland period. Also, several regions of Missouri contain sites with materials assigned to well-documented traditions that were contemporary with the Mississippian tradition. For example, sites in central Missouri have produced shell-tempered Oneota-tradition pottery, sites in the northwestern corner of the state exhibit Central Plains–tradition materials, and several sites in extreme southwestern Missouri contain examples of classic Caddoan pottery.

The European Period (A.D. *1541–1800*)

I chose to arbitrarily end the Mississippian period at A.D. 1541 because that date coincides with the arrival of the Spaniard Hernán de Soto and his expedition into northeastern Arkansas and perhaps into southeastern Missouri. This early entrance of Europeans into the United States did not necessarily signal an immediate end to then-existent lifeways, but it was a portent of things to come. Articles left behind by de Soto's expeditionary force have been found throughout the Southeast. In Missouri, such objects—iron fragments, brass bells, and glass beads—have been recovered from Mississippian-period burials at several sites in Pemiscot County (O'Brien 1994).

The next contact Europeans had with Native American groups in Missouri resulted from the 1673 exploration by Jacques Marquette and Louis Jolliet of the Mississippi River valley, a voyage followed by the expedition of Robert Cavelier, Sieur de la Salle later that decade. Until around 1718, French occupants of the central Mississippi Valley—the region that has commonly become known as the Illinois, or Illini, Country—were predominantly traders involved in exchanging European goods for native furs collected by various Native American groups. A few priests, primarily Jesuits, also came to the Illini Country, and missions began to dot the landscape by the early eighteenth century. As late as 1711 the total French population in the Mississippi Valley was less than 200 (Walthall and Emerson 1991: 7), most of whom were located along the Gulf Coast.

Unfortunately, the archaeological record in Missouri for the period of French contact in the late seventeenth century is virtually unknown. We know little archaeologically of groups residing on the west bank of the Mississippi River that might have been visited by Marquette and Jolliet, though at least one site in northeastern Missouri appears to be an excellent candidate for such a village. Our knowledge improves for the early eighteenth century, though it is limited to a few communities constructed by the Missouri and Osage. It is difficult to reconcile historical accounts of the Missouri and Osage—written in the nineteenth and twentieth centuries—with the archaeological record of the eighteenth century. Chapman (1946, 1959), Bray (1961, 1991), and others tied the Missouri group to the 120-acre-plus Utz site in Saline County, recognizing the Missouri as having developed out of an Oneota-tradition base. Trade goods are present in considerable quantities at Utz, which is not surprising given its location near de Bourgmond's Fort Orleans.

At least one village of Osage was located in Saline County in the early eighteenth century, with the majority of villages located to the southwest, in Vernon County, Missouri. Known Osage sites produce inordinate amounts of European trade goods, including brass kettles and beads; iron hoes, axes, and knives; gun flints; and glass beads. By the nineteenth century, the Osage were living in permanent villages only during part of the year, with the majority of the population involved in hunting-and-gathering activities during the warmer months. By 1808 the Osage had given up much of their land to the United States and were living in only three villages—two in Vernon County and one near Claremore, Oklahoma. In 1823 they moved west to Oklahoma and Kansas and in 1825 ceded all Missouri land to the federal government.

Back in Time

As we will soon see, it was not the archaeological record of the historical period that first attracted the attention of antiquarians to Missouri. Rather, it was the remains from much earlier periods. Early investigators had no way of accurately estimating the ages of most of the archaeological remains they encountered, and they often concocted what now appear to be bizarre interpretations of what they found. It is important to keep in mind that in many respects the basic interests of early prehistorians were the same as those of most archaeologists today—variation in time, space, and form. As today, some of them were better than others at making sense out of that variation.

2

Mound Builders and Amateur Scientists

The Pre-1880 Era

Modern students of archaeology have a rather difficult time believing that a scant hundred years ago many prehistorians, as well as the general populace, were convinced that the thousands of earthworks evident over the eastern United States, especially in valleys associated with larger rivers such as the Ohio and Mississippi, were erected by a race of people who had suddenly and mysteriously vanished—either of their own accord or driven out by Native Americans—leaving behind only their earthen structures, their dead, and the materials they placed in with the deceased. Various groups at one time or another were tabbed as the mound builders, including the Toltecs, the Vikings, the Danes, the Ten Lost Tribes of Israel, and even the Spanish party headed by Hernán de Soto that traversed the South in 1540–1541. Some of the scenarios concocted by eighteenth- and nineteenth-century writers were fairly involved and included several stages; in Caleb Atwater's 1820 sketch, the "Hindoos" constructed the mounds and then were driven out by Asian immigrants, who later evolved into the American Indian.

These runaway scenarios seem silly today, but when they are viewed within the broader American social and political realm of the nineteenth century, we can begin to appreciate the self-fulfilling nature of the stories. Given the manner in which the American Indian was viewed at the time, is it really that difficult to understand how the mound-builder myth was perpetuated? The question at the time was, how could a race of "ignoble savages" have constructed enormous earthworks—many involving complex geometric proportions and alignments—or manufactured such elaborate pottery? The answer was simple: they didn't. What they *had* done was run off the mound builders, just as they had tried to rout Euro-American colonists and settlers who were bringing with them the trappings of civilization.

These scenarios were fueled in part by information supplied by what we might loosely term "prehistorians." Most of these individuals had received no formal archaeological training (what little there was available at the time), and although we might criticize their interpretations, some of their fieldwork leaves little to criticize when viewed in the proper historical context. For example, Atwater's article "Description of the Antiquities Discovered in the State of Ohio and Other Western States," which appeared in the first volume of the *Transactions and Collections of the American Antiquarian Society* (Atwater 1820) and was reprinted by Atwater in 1833 as "Description of the Antiquities Discovered in the Western Country," provided fairly detailed plan maps of prehistoric earthworks, especially those centered around the junction of the Scioto and Ohio rivers in southern Ohio. In 1848 Ephraim G. Squier and Edwin H. Davis published a lengthy treatise in the *Smithsonian Contributions to Knowledge* series entitled "Ancient Monuments of the Mississippi Valley," in which they, like Atwater, provided detailed plan maps of numerous mounds (Figure 2.1).[1] And, as Atwater had, Squier and Davis included speculative statements about the origins of the earthworks, attributing them to a group of mound builders separate from the American Indian.

Any volume on the history of American archaeology will dedicate at least a few pages to the work of Squier and Davis, a newspaperman and a physician, respectively, and usually a paragraph or two to the work of Atwater, a postmaster, because the publications they produced document an archaeological resource base that has all but disappeared as a result of land clearing and urban expansion. Their work is justifiably recognized as some of the most extensive archaeological research conducted in the United States prior to the federal government's entry into the field in the final decades of the nineteenth century. Histories of American archaeology either gloss over or ignore completely the myriad field programs and investigations that were carried out at the local level throughout the nineteenth century—programs directed not by professional prehistorians but again by interested laypersons. Because those projects were less encompassing than the large regional programs conducted by Squier and Davis and by Atwater, they received much less attention in print and for the most part have slipped into obscurity. These less-publicized efforts produced results that deserve our consideration. In many instances the short reports that resulted from such work represent all that is known of sites, and though the information is biased, it can sometimes be used to complement the results of more modern work.

From a historical perspective, the smaller projects are even more interesting in that they represent microcosms of the larger ones. As we will soon see, the mound-builder myth was alive and well in regional societies such as the Academy of Science of St. Louis, whose members stood ready and able to

---

1. The title of the work by Squier and Davis is misleading, since they spent most of their time in the Ohio River valley and its tributary valleys and very little time in the Mississippi Valley.

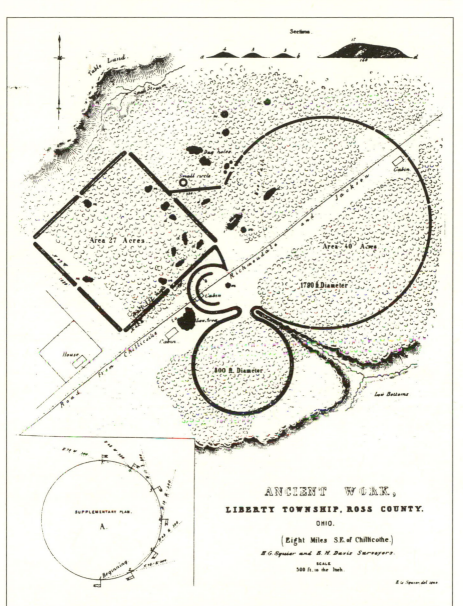

Figure 2.1. The Liberty Earthworks, Ross County, Ohio, as mapped by Ephraim G. Squier and Edwin H. Davis in the 1840s (from Squier and Davis 1848).

contribute supporting information. Such groups may have been small, but they were active and made their voices heard in the leading debates of the day. Some easterners in the mid–nineteenth century undoubtedly thought Missouri to be little more than a provincial outpost, but it certainly generated its fair share of national archaeological attention. Ironically, the attention focused on the archaeological record of Missouri during the 70 years between 1850 and 1920 probably exceeds that of the 70 years after 1920. A significant portion of the attention was focused on the thousands of mounds that existed across Missouri and on what was in them.

The Mound Builders—A Majority Opinion

Despite the best efforts of Joseph Henry, the first secretary (director) of the Smithsonian Institution, to excise from Squier and Davis's memoir any speculative statements regarding the mounds (as he did with other archaeological monographs published through the *Smithsonian Contributions to Knowledge* series [e.g., Haven 1856; Lapham 1855; Whittlesey 1852]), and despite the fact that Henry at one point threatened to withdraw support for its publication (Hinsley 1981: 36–37), the final product was replete with overt as well as thinly veiled speculation regarding the function of the mounds and the ties between the mound builders and groups in Mexico and Central America (see Schwartz 1967). Similarly, Atwater (1833: 150) noted with authority, "That this people were not ancestors of our present Indian race in the United States, seems to me a well established fact. Our common Indian has not a single idea necessarily derived from Asia; whereas, the men who raised the tumuli in the valley of the Mississippi, in all their emigrations, showed their Asiatic origin every step they took, and in all they did." Atwater, especially, was given to flights of fancy regarding the functions of the earthworks: "Though they were used as places of sepulture and of worship, yet, were they not sometimes, in the last resort, used also as places of defense?" (Atwater 1833: 96). He also was not above borrowing hyberbolic statements such as those made by Henry M. Brackenridge, an early traveler in the Midwest who, as Atwater (1833: 94) put it, had "discriminating powers of mind [with which] the public are acquainted":

> The tumuli, as well as the fortifications, are to be found at the junction of all the rivers, along the Mississippi, in the most eligible positions for towns, and in the most extensive bodies of fertile land. . . . Their great number, and the astonishing size of some of them, may be regarded as furnishing, with other circumstances, evidence of their antiquity. I have been sometimes induced to think, that, at the period when these were constructed, there was a population as numerous as that which once animated the borders of the Nile, or of the Euphrates, or of Mexico. The most numerous, as well as the most considerable of these remains, are found precisely in those parts of the country where the traces of a numerous population might be looked for, viz. from the mouth of the Ohio, on the east side of the river, to the Illinois river, and on the west side from the St. Francis to the Missouri. I am perfectly satisfied that cities similar to those of ancient Mexico, of several

hundred thousand souls, have existed in this country. (Atwater 1833: 94, quoting Brackenridge)[2]

Brackenridge, through the use of his "discriminating powers," might have been "perfectly satisfied" with his population estimates, but they were too large by at least one order of magnitude, and this for the largest site he is known to have visited (Cahokia, located in western Illinois across from St. Louis). As opposed to many of the writings of others who opined on the subject, however, the work of Brackenridge, Atwater, and Squier and Davis was at least wrapped in a mantle of what then passed for scientific examination. After all, Atwater's work was published by an organization—the American Antiquarian Society—that had been formed by men such as Henry Clay, Thomas Hart Benton, and DeWitt Clinton. Squier and Davis's work appeared in the first publication of the Smithsonian Institution, which had been established by Congress in 1846 as a private scientific organization and which exhibited a scientific aura even at that early date. It is no wonder that when antiquarians who kept such good company spoke authoritatively on the origin of the mounds, people listened.

It wasn't only authoritative-sounding antiquarians who captured the minds and ears of a general public fascinated with the subject of Indians, mounds, and buried antiquities. Perhaps the most widely read tale spinner of the mid–nineteenth century was William Pidgeon, a man who, while not exactly a modern household name, had a nation of people sitting on the edges of their seats soon after his best-seller, *Traditions of De-coo-dah*,[3] was published in 1858. Pidgeon claimed to be a wandering trader who had spent two winters with an old Indian named De-coo-dah, "a man of undoubted veracity, revered and respected by those that knew him" (p. 7). For whatever reason, De-coo-dah trusted Pidgeon and told him the history of the American Indians, including the history of their forebears, the mound builders. Soon after relating his story, De-coo-dah died, and Pidgeon decided to pass the old man's teachings on to the American public. Further "research" by Pidgeon, to provide a proper time depth for De-coo-dah's account, demonstrated that Adam had built the first mounds in America and that his efforts were followed by those of the Egyptians, the Phoenicians, and other Africans. Even Alexander the Great, in his efforts to conquer the

2. This quotation, which Atwater took from Brackenridge, must have appeared in one of the numerous newspaper articles Brackenridge wrote, since it does not appear in his compilation of accounts entitled *Views of Louisiana* (H. M. Brackenridge 1814).

3. The shortened title used here does little justice to the precise title Pidgeon picked for his treatise: *Traditions of De-coo-dah and Antiquarian Researches: Comprising Extensive Explorations, Surveys, and Excavations of Earthen Remains of the Mound-builders in America; The Traditions of the Last Prophet of the Elk Nation Relative to Their Origin and Use; and the Evidences of an Ancient Population More Numerous than the Present Aborigines.*

world, had gotten into the act and built a few mounds in the New World. Alexander apparently was followed by the Romans, an occurrence for which Pidgeon furnished evidence (pp. 16–17):

> On the bank of the river Desperes [Des Peres, in south St. Louis], in Missouri, was found by an Indian and presented to Governor [William] Clark, a genuine Roman coin. . . . Many enclosures, similar to the Roman camps described by Josephus, may yet be seen in the valley of the Mississippi . . . and various other earth-works, similar in construction, may be seen north to the [Great] lakes, and west to the Mississippi, west of which, we doubt whether the Romans ever held empire.

Pidgeon's doubts appear to have been justified: to date, except for the reported coin from the River Des Peres, no evidence of a Roman occupation of Missouri has been identified.

Pidgeon offered the Smithsonian Institution the rights to the manuscript, but the story was just too outlandish, and the board of regents refused to publish it. Apparently the book made a fortune for its author during its long run in print. Not only did the general public fall prey to the outlandish story, but "gullible historians who should have known better" (Fagan 1977: 226) also quoted from it. Finally, in 1884, a surveyor named Theodore H. Lewis, as a result of carefully checking Pidgeon's supposed findings and interviewing people who knew him, debunked the myth and showed Pidgeon to have been a fraud. Not mincing words, Lewis (1886: 69) stated that "the Elk nation and its last prophet De-coo-dah are modern myths." By that time, the tide was beginning to turn against the myth of the mound builders, and within another decade or so, the number of prehistorians still looking for pre-Indian mound builders had declined dramatically. But that's getting ahead of the story. Despite the overwhelming popularity of the mound-builder myth, there was, by midcentury, an opposition that, though small, was quite vocal.

The Mound Builders—A Minority Opinion

Perhaps the two most outspoken opponents of the notion that the mounds were constructed by a vanished race were Samuel F. Haven and Henry Rowe Schoolcraft. In 1856 Haven, librarian of the American Antiquarian Society, published "Archaeology of the United States" in Joseph Henry's *Smithsonian Contributions to Knowledge* series. In his review he examined not only the archaeological data available at the time but also linguistic and human-physiological data, concluding that the Indians and the mound builders were one and the same. Willey and Sabloff (1974: 47) refer to Haven's treatise as "a model of reasoned description and discussion in comparison with the speculative works which had dominated the literature until then." This is a fair assessment, though

Willey and Sabloff do not mention what I consider to be the centerpiece of Haven's argument, namely, that early explorers, especially those who traversed the southern United States, actually saw Indian groups building and using earthen mounds:

> In the letters of Charlevoix and Father le Petit, and in the "History of Louisiana," by Du Pratz, we have very minute accounts of the Natchez Indians, who, with the Arkansas, were the most civilized of the North American aborigines. We learn that they worshipped the sun, had temples in which was kept the "eternal fire," and a despotic government; that their chiefs were the high priests, and were called suns, or children of the sun; and that the temples and the dwellings of the chiefs were raised upon mounds, and for every new chief a new mound and dwelling were constructed. Thus, a civil and religious system, with customs and ceremonials pertaining to it, is described, which explains the use of some of the artificial elevations, and may indicate the purpose of others. (Haven 1856: 18)

The accounts of early Spanish and French explorers were easy to come by in the nineteenth century, and one can only wonder why more writers did not reach the same conclusion that Haven did: "the absence of archaeological discoveries and speculations, on the part of the intelligent and well-informed men who first visited the interior parts of the present United States, is somewhat singular, in view of the fact that so much has since been brought to light in the very paths on which they trod" (pp. 18–19). In other words, Haven was suggesting that the lack of comment, or of speculation, by early explorers relative to the origins of the earthworks indicated that the mounds were considered to be nothing out of the ordinary, that is, they were made by the same groups of people who were using them in the sixteenth and seventeenth centuries.

Schoolcraft, in a manner similar to that of Haven, noted commonalities between the material cultures of the mound builders and those of ethnohistorically known Indian groups, but his six-volume work published in the early 1850s, entitled *Historical and Statistical Information Respecting the History, Condition, and Prospects of the Indian Tribes of the United States,* was so rambling and disjointed that it was examined only by the most diehard readers. He clearly recognized the link between the American Indian and the mounds, and he saw little reason to think of the mounds as the result of anything *other* than the work of "barbarians," or Indians (Schoolcraft 1854).

The Mound Builders in Missouri

References to earthworks in Missouri, as well as speculation about their origins, were common in narratives and gazetteers from the first half of the nineteenth century, such as Lewis C. Beck's *Gazetteer of the States of Illinois and Missouri* (1823) and Alphonso Wetmore's *Gazetteer of the State of Missouri* (1837). By 1850 several sites in Missouri had been discussed in the literature, especially those in the eastern half of the state. Why wouldn't that area of Missouri receive the lion's share of attention, if we are to believe Alban Jasper Conant, who, writing in the *Transactions of the Academy of Science of St. Louis* in 1878, prosaically characterized the region as an antiquarian's paradise:

> There is, doubtless, now no richer field for archaeological research in this great basin of the Mississippi Valley than is to be found in the State of Missouri. The wonderful extent and variety of the ancient works and monuments therein, the relics they disclose, the huge burial mounds filled with the bones of the dead, disposed in orderly array, as though by loving hands, along with vessels of pottery of graceful forms and varied patterns, often, too, skillfully ornamented,—all bear witness to a settled and permanent condition of society and government and obedience to law, and to certain convictions of a future life. (Conant 1878: 353)

Conant doesn't tell us exactly how he was able to reconstruct those aspects of prehistoric life, but we can be certain that his insights were not the products of methods that would bear much resemblance to those in use today. In fact, they would not bear much resemblance to those of the early twentieth century. One reason for this difference is simply the factor of time and the natural improvements that an emerging discipline makes in method and technique—improvements that steadily build on previous advances. But to treat all method-ological changes as the natural result of time's arrow belies the exponential growth in methodological improvements that occurred in the opening decades of the twentieth century. Such an exponential change in method was impossible in the mid to late nineteenth century—impossible, in fact, until the mind-sets of prehistorians and ethnologists changed relative to the questions of who constructed the earthworks in the midwestern and eastern United States and when they constructed them. In essence, all other queries were outgrowths of those two overarching concerns.

With several exceptions, such as the work of Samuel Haven, the overwhelming consensus prior to roughly 1890 was that the American Indians, regardless of where they originated, were in no way related to their predecessors the mound builders and in fact probably had led to the latter group's removal. Once that scenario was in place, one could get on with the business of describing the material remains of the two separate groups. Any concern with method was directed entirely toward fleshing out the particulars of mound-builder life, using the rich archaeological record contained in the mounds to provide the answers. For the most part, the battery of methods employed was straightforward: Go to the field, excavate a mound or two, and report what you find. In fact, the methods were so straightforward that one did not need formal training to be a prehistorian. There were plenty of people such as Conant who were trained in other professions (Conant was an artist) but who were eager to be prehistorians. These people found the perfect vehicle through which to carry out their passion for the past—the amateur scientific society.

The Golden Age of Scientific Societies

Conant was one of a growing number of individuals who came to archaeology from other disciplines, such as law, medicine, and art—individuals who had a love for all phases of natural history but who had no extensive training in any of them. American universities and colleges, with few exceptions, did not offer courses in archaeology and ethnology,[4] but then men such as Squier and Davis had shown that one did not need formal training to make a name for oneself in the study of prehistory. Still, not every would-be archaeologist had the backing, monetary and otherwise, of groups such as the American Ethnological Society (which sponsored Squier and Davis), nor were most people in a position to give up their regular employment to spend months mapping and excavating mounds. Most people had to be content to join a group of like-minded individuals and pursue their interest as an avocation. Across the United States literally hundreds of interest groups that were organized loosely around the pursuit of scientific knowledge, with a heavy emphasis on archaeology and paleontology, sprang up in the nineteenth century. The scientific and literary societies in eastern cities such as Boston, New York, and Philadelphia had long and established traditions by the time midwestern cities such as St. Louis, Kansas City, and Chicago began to witness the growth of such organizations. In turn, the eastern societies were supplements to larger, national organizations, such as the American Antiquarian Society (founded in 1812), the American Ethnological Society (1842), and the American Association for the Advancement of Science (1847). Given the prestige associated with the eastern societies, it is no surprise that the newer societies mimicked the older ones in terms of charter and purpose. At least for a few hours every other week, "gentlemen in the various professions and departments of trade who manage to find time for some scientific and literary recreation" (*Kansas City Review of Science* III: 61) could join together to create an atmosphere in which to catch up on the latest news carried in the journals, exchange papers they had read or written, examine specimens brought in by other members, and expound on whatever topic had been chosen for that evening's discussion. Conant joined a group that called itself the Academy of Science of St. Louis (ASSL).

It is impossible to comprehend the nature and background of archaeological work undertaken in Missouri after the midcentury mark without examining the

---

4. Ethnology is the study of nonindustrialized peoples and includes such topics as language, religion, kinship, marriage, tool manufacture and use, trade, and diet.

role played by regional academies of science and historical societies. In fact, the vast majority of archaeological investigations undertaken in Missouri between 1860 and 1880 were conducted by members of the Academy of Science of St. Louis and slightly later by members of two other St. Louis organizations—the Missouri Historical Society and an offshoot of the local chapter of the Archaeological Institute of America. In terms of its impact on archaeology in the latter half of the nineteenth century, the ASSL had primacy, though by the early twentieth century its important role was eclipsed by the MHS. The first meeting of the ASSL was held on March 10, 1856, and was attended by 15 members—7 medical doctors, 3 lawyers, and 5 professors. The constitution, which along with the bylaws was adopted at the first meeting, spelled out the objectives of the fledgling society:

> Section 1. It shall have for its object the promotion of Science: it shall embrace Zoology, Botany, Geology, Mineralogy, Palaeontology, Ethnology (especially that of the Aboriginal Tribes of North America), Chemistry, Physics, Mathematics, Meteorology, and Comparative Anatomy and Physiology.
>
> Sec. 2. It shall furthermore be the object of this Academy to collect and treasure Specimens illustrative of the various departments of Science above enumerated; to procure a Library of works relating to the same, with the Instruments necessary to facilitate their study, and to procure original Papers on them.
>
> Sec. 3. It shall also be the object of this Academy to establish correspondence with scientific men, both in America and other parts of the world.

The academy might have been small in 1856, but it was anything but dormant. In terms of the topics pursued by its members, there appears to have been little in the vast realm of science that did not fall under their purview, but topics that fell under the general rubric of natural history, including ethnology, archaeology, and paleontology, enjoyed greater interest than some of the others. One of the board's first official acts was to pay the expenses of one of its members, Albert C. Koch (we will see a lot more of Koch shortly), to travel to Mississippi to investigate new and interesting fossil discoveries and to report back to the membership through letters. The academy was also reaching out to the eastern societies and institutions, perhaps as a means of gaining recognition but probably also because of an insatiable thirst for knowledge on the part of its highly educated members.

The ASSL had established two types of membership in its constitution, associate and corresponding, the former for members living in St. Louis County, and thus able to attend meetings, and the latter for persons living elsewhere. Corresponding memberships were offered free of charge, whereas associate members paid an up-front charge plus annual dues. If one reads between the lines of various entries in the *Journal of Proceedings*,[5] it appears that corresponding

---

5. The *Proceedings* were published as part of the *Transactions of the Academy of Science of St. Louis*.

members didn't even have to apply for membership. Instead, they simply were nominated by a member and then elected. It is obvious from examining the *Journal* for the first month and a half of the organization's existence that members were interested in adding to the corresponding membership some of the most well known names in science—men such as Joseph Henry of the Smithsonian Institution; Ferdinand V. Hayden, geologist with the U.S. Geological Survey; and Joseph Leidy of Philadelphia, arguably the top vertebrate paleontologist of the time.

On August 25, 1856, members of the ASSL formed 14 standing committees, one of which dealt with ethnology. Over the next 20 years, numerous reports, comments, and pieces of correspondence relating to the prehistory not only of Missouri but of North America found their way into the *Transactions* and *Proceedings*. It is obvious that the members were not content only to hear about subjects of archaeological and ethnological interest but also were interested in leaving their marks in the fields. As it turned out, their own backyard provided plenty of interesting information.

St. Louis and the Big Mound

St. Louis early on had been dubbed the Mound City because of the large number of earthworks contained within its corporate limits, the most impressive of which, called the Big Mound, lay on the second terrace of the Mississippi River in what by the 1850s was the north-central part of the city. The Big Mound might have been the most impressive earthwork, but it was only one of at least 25 Mississippian-period mounds that existed in downtown St. Louis in the first half of the nineteenth century (Figure 2.2). Perhaps the earliest mention of the mound group was by the aforementioned Brackenridge, who described in 1814 what he had seen in 1811:

> I have frequently examined the mounds at St. Louis: they are situated on the second bank [terrace?] just above the town, and disposed in a singular manner; there are nine in all, and form three sides of a parallelogram, the open side towards the country, being protected, however, by three smaller mounds, placed in a circular manner. The space enclosed is about four hundred yards in length, and two hundred in breadth. About six hundred yards above there is a single mound, with a broad stage on the river side; it is thirty feet in height, and one hundred and fifty in length; the top is a mere ridge of five or six feet wide. Below the first mounds there is a curious work, called the Falling Garden. Advantage is taken of the second bank, nearly fifty feet in height at this place, and three regular stages or steps, are formed by earth brought from a distance. (H. M. Brackenridge 1814: 189)

Brackenridge's description might have been fairly accurate, but his map, re-drafted in Figure 2.3, was crude. Note that he states that there are 9 mounds in the

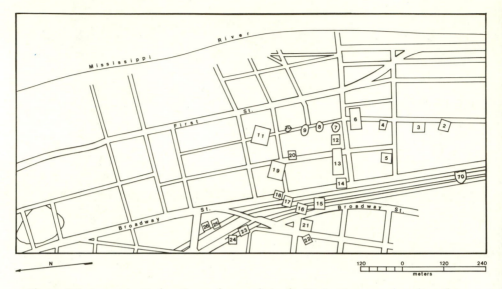

Figure 2.2. Approximate locations of mounds in the St. Louis group, based on data derived from various nineteenth-century maps and other documentary sources (from Rogers and Pulcher 1987).

circular arrangement, but his diagram shows 10. In fact, Brackenridge underestimated the true number of mounds that dotted the terrace. Thomas R. Peale, who along with Thomas Say mapped the St. Louis mound group in 1819 (see below) but didn't publish the sketch (Figure 2.4) until more than 40 years later in an *Annual Report of the Board of Regents of the Smithsonian Institution* (Peale 1862), shows the locations of no less than 27 mounds.[6] Apparently what Brackenridge mapped was only the circular arrangement of mounds shown in the center of Peale's map. Peale's mound 27—the Big Mound—corresponds to Brackenridge's mound B, and Peale's tri-level mound 6 corresponds to Brackenridge's "falling garden" (Peale 1862: 389). It is difficult to believe that Brackenridge, given that he "frequently examined the mounds," could have so severely underreported the number of mounds present.

On the other hand, there is little reason to suspect the veracity of Peale's map. He was a junior member of the engineering expedition headed by Major S. H. Long (who later became chief examiner in the U.S. Patent Office) that set out from Pittsburgh in the spring of 1819 to explore the upper reaches of the Missouri River. Together with Say, another member of the expedition, Peale used a tape and compass to map the positions of the mounds and to measure

---

6. Two mounds identified by Peale and Say, numbers 1 and 2, may have been natural knolls (J. Marshall, pers. comm. 1994).

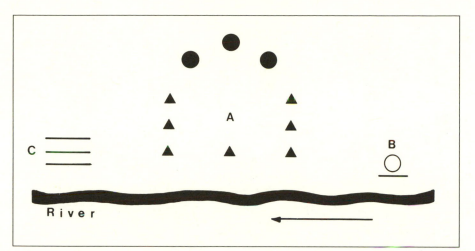

Figure 2.3. Sketch map of mounds in the St. Louis group, as depicted by Henry M. Brackenridge in 1811 (after Brackenridge 1814).

their dimensions. The measurements were published as part of the account of the Long expedition (James 1823: 59–60 [reprinted in Thwaites 1905: 117–18]), but the map "was omitted to give place to what was considered more important matter" (Peale 1862: 388). In addition to constructing a base map and taking measurements, Peale and Say also opened five graves on the summit of the Big Mound (James 1823: 60; Peale 1862: 391), but they recovered nothing other than a rat tooth and some snake bones. In his later published recollections, Peale (1862) noted that the grave pits were lined with vertical stone slabs, though as Stephen Williams and John Goggin (1956: 12) pointed out, Peale was confusing the graves on the Big Mound with some he and Say excavated along the Meramec River south of St. Louis.

The fate of the St. Louis mound group was sealed by its location. Urban expansion throughout the first half of the nineteenth century led to the destruction of almost all the mounds, including the Big Mound, portions of which were removed as early as the 1850s by grading operations connected with street and sidewalk construction.[7] The majority of the mound fill was hauled off in the 1860s for brick-making[8] and, especially in 1869, by the North Missouri Railroad Company (later the Northern Pacific) for use as roadbed fill. These operations were watched carefully by St. Louisans, who provided reports of what they observed in the way of internal features of the mound. Thanks to Thomas

7. *Missouri Republican* (St. Louis), February 13, 1854; *St. Louis Dispatch*, May 31, 1865.
8. *Missouri Republican* (St. Louis), February 13, 1854, and April 9, 1868.

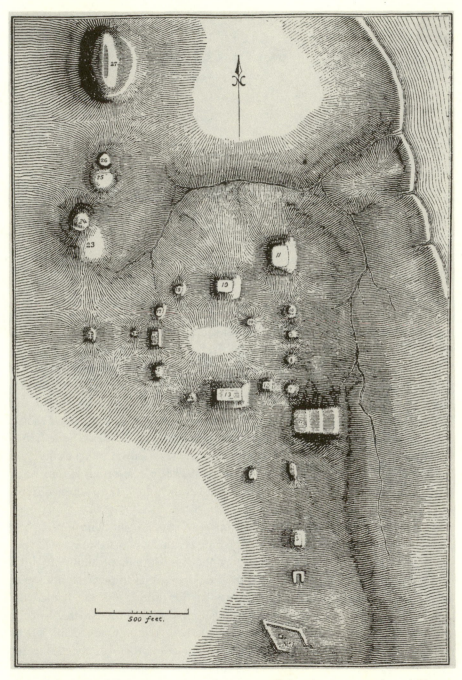

Figure 2.4. Map of the St. Louis mound group made by Thomas R. Peale and Thomas Say in 1819 (from Peale 1862).

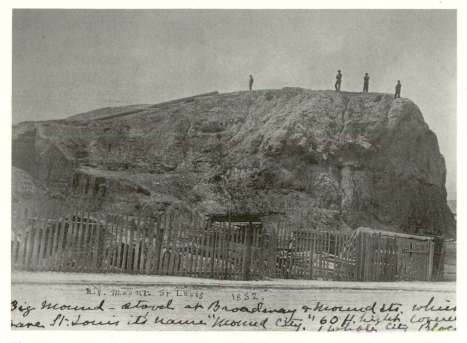

Big. Mount. St. Louis   1852.

Big Mound - stovel at Broadway & Mound sts. which gave St. Louis its name "Mound City." 60 ft. high. Covers whole city Bloc...

Figure 2.5. Copy of a daguerreotype made by Thomas Easterly in 1852 of the Big Mound in St. Louis, looking east (courtesy Missouri Historical Society).

Easterly, a professional photographer, we have excellent daguerreotypes of the mound during its final days (Figures 2.5 and 2.6).

One of those who reportedly kept a watchful eye on the destruction of the Big Mound was Conant, who several years later provided written commentary not only on the events surrounding the removal of mound fill but also on internal features of the mound. If Conant's reports (1877, 1879a, 1879b)[9] are to be believed, the Big Mound contained a number of interesting features, including skeletons interred with shell beads and copper ornaments (discussed in more detail later). The most impressive feature, however, was a central burial chamber located toward the bottom of the mound:

> The original length of the chamber could only be conjectured, as portions of the mound had been removed when the street was cut through upon the southern

9. Conant's three published versions are essentially identical. The easiest reference to find is the one included in *Switzler's Illustrated History of Missouri* (Conant 1879a).

Figure 2.6. Copy of a daguerreotype made by Thomas Easterly in 1869 (?) of the Big Mound in St. Louis, looking northeast. Compare the size of the mound with the size evident in the 1852 photograph (Figure 2.5) (courtesy Missouri Historical Society).

end, as seen in the engraving [Figure 2.7]. It could be traced, however, for seventy-two feet. For this distance the sides were perfectly smooth and straight, and sloped outwardly a few degrees from the perpendicular, and the marks of the tool by which the walls were plastered could be plainly seen. . . .

The manner of its construction seems to have been thus: The surface of the ground was first made perfectly level and hard; then the walls were raised with an outward inclination, which were also made perfectly compact and solid, and plastered over with moist clay. Over these, a roof was formed of heavy timbers, and above all the mound was raised of the desired dimensions. The bodies had all been placed in a direct line, upon the floor of the vault, a few feet apart, and equidistant from each other, with their feet towards the west. (Conant 1879a: 42–44)

Despite Conant's supposedly firsthand account of the "vault,"[10] there is every reason to question whether what he was viewing was a covered tomb as such—

10. There are good reasons to suspect that Conant was not the firsthand witness he said he was (see his note 10).

since, as he reported in a footnote, no timbers were recovered—or simply an extremely large burial pit (Williams and Goggin 1956: 21). A later visit to the mound yielded further information on the "vault":

> The night before, the workmen had made a vertical cut directly across the northern end of the small portion of the work which yet remained. What was there revealed is well represented in the engraving [Figure 2.7]. The sloping walls were of compact yellow clay, the intermediate space filled with blue clay in a much looser condition, in perfect agreement with the idea of its having fallen in from above by the decay of its support. Here too, at the northern end, I conjectured, was the entrance to the sepulcher, for the reason that here the walls were about eight feet in height, from six feet to eight feet apart, whereas the first measurements at the top, when the walls were discovered, showed a diameter of eighteen feet. (Conant 1879a: 44–45)

Conant's interpretation of events surrounding the construction and use of the mound throughout its history are fairly typical of the speculative statements that were made by antiquarians during the middle decades of the nineteenth century. More importantly, they underscore both the overwhelming sentiment that the mound builders and the American Indians were two separate groups and the

Figure 2.7. Engraving of the Big Mound in St. Louis, looking east-southeast, used by Alban J. Conant in his article in Switzler's *Illustrated History of Missouri, from 1541 to 1877.* Conant's rendering probably was either taken directly from Thomas Easterly's daguerreotype of 1852 (Figure 2.5) or was made at about the same time (from Conant 1879a).

manner in which supporting information for this belief was marshaled. With regard to who built and used the Big Mound, Conant's major piece of evidence was, interestingly enough, stratigraphic in nature. According to his reasoning, skeletons found in the large burial pit were the remains of the mound builders; those found outside the pit at higher positions stratigraphically were the remains of the later Indians, who had had no part in the mound construction:

> This mound, as is well known, was used by the Indians as a burial place, and only about sixty years since, it was visited by a small band, who disinterred and carried away the bones of their chief who had been buried there. But their interments here, as was their unvarying custom, were near the surface. I have observed the same in other localities, sometimes not more than eighteen inches from the top of the mound, —as was the case with some I examined in Washington County, on the banks of the Missouri. On account of this it is not difficult to distinguish the Indian burials from those of the Mound-builders. Had this fact been better understood, we would have been spared many erroneous statements, as well as hasty generalizations upon articles taken from the mounds, which were attributed to their builders, but which, in fact, were deposited by the Indians; and many of them even, subsequent to their first acquaintance with our own race. A striking example of this occurred during the removal of the "Big Mound." Near the northern end, and about three feet from the surface, two skeletons were discovered very near each other, one evidently that of a male, the other a female. With the larger of the two were found the spiral spines of two conch shells, much decayed, nine ivory beads of an average size, as near as I can recollect, one inch in length and nearly one-half in diameter, an ivory spool with short shaft but very wide flanges, which were much broken around the edges, and two curious articles of copper [Figure 2.8], about three inches in length and about half as wide, resembling somewhat in shape the common smoothing iron of the laundry. . . .
>
> Embedded in the verdigris with which they were encrusted were plainly visible the marks of a twisted string just like ordinary wrapping twine, which had been clumsily tied about them, and upon which the beads had been strung. . . . I have been thus particular in the account of this "big Indian" and treasures . . . because these articles of copper, and the ivory spool . . . have been taken as the exponents of the state of the arts among the Mound-builders, and have been made the subject of the most extravagant statements. (Conant 1879a: 41–42)[11]

11. Conant's description of the copper pieces pales in comparison to that carried in an article in the *Missouri Republican* (April 17, 1869), apparently written by someone who actually saw the pieces: "The nose is greatly prolonged, and more nearly resembles the beak of a bird than the proboscis of a man or animal. The eyes and mouth are distinctly observable, but with the extraordinary beak the effigy has the appearance of a caricature. . . . The length of the masque from the top of the forehead to the chin is about two inches, while the breadth across the region of the eyes is one inch and a half. The copper plates are about the thickness of a table spoon. . . . They may have been used as ear jewels, which supposition is confirmed from the fact that they were found lying on both sides of the skull." The account also indicates that the "graves in which the copper ornaments were found were about twenty-five feet below the original surface of the mound," which contradicts Conant's account.

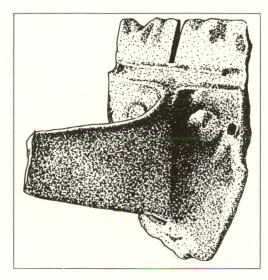

Figure 2.8. Drawing of the copper long-nosed-god mask found in the Big Mound in St. Louis in 1869 (from Williams and Goggin 1956, courtesy Missouri Archaeological Society).

In other words, Conant, using stratigraphic superpositioning to separate the pit burials from the nonpit burials, not only drew the distinction between the mound builders and the Indians but also demonstrated that artifacts commonly thought of as belonging in the realm of the mound builders (e.g., copper ornaments) were actually manufactured by the Indians or received in trade from Europeans. In short, Conant was right, but he was right for the wrong reasons. He simply could not escape the notion that the American Indians were incapable of erecting large earthworks and burying their dead in deep pits. To Conant (1879a: 78), archaeological fieldwork was demonstrating that a "broad chasm" existed between the abilities of the mound builders and those of the Indians—a chasm that was rapidly turning into an "impassable gulf."[12] Conant would have been surprised to learn that within a decade a nineteenth-century scientist, Cyrus Thomas, would come along and cross that gulf.

The Mounds—Natural or Artificial?

The Big Mound is interesting not only in terms of its content but also as an example of the controversy that often surrounded the origins of the earthworks—controversy of a different kind than that surrounding the question of who had constructed the mounds. The controversy was over whether the mounds were of natural or human origin. Given what we know today of geological and

---

12. Conant borrowed this metaphor from J. W. Foster (1873b: 347).

soil-formation processes, it might seem odd that as recently as the second half of the nineteenth century learned persons had varied opinions concerning the origin of a structure as large as the Big Mound—especially one sitting in the middle of a fairly flat alluvial terrace. After all, Sir Charles Lyell's *Principles of Geology* had been through nine editions in the short span between 1830 and 1853, and anyone who claimed even a modicum of competence in natural history was familiar with his discussions of sedimentary superpositioning and landforms. But competence or no, the scientific literature of the nineteenth century is dotted with skeptical statements about the role of humans in creating the mounds (or at least many of the mounds), including those in St. Louis and those across the river in the American Bottom. No more vociferous denouncement of such heresy exists than that uttered by Wills de Hass[13] at the 1868 annual meeting of the American Association for the Advancement of Science in Chicago:

> A fluviatile origin [of the mounds] has been a ready and plausible theory with many persons. Another respectable authority regards them as outliers of loess brought to their present form by denudation. . . .
>
> It is not surprising that novices should commit egregious blunders in attempting to discuss subjects they do not understand; but it is surprising that those whose position and investigations should have induced them to examine carefully the character of those works before expressing positive opinions, have failed to do so. The only charitable conclusion is they never examined the mounds. No man whose opinions are worth quoting could have examined even one of these interesting monuments, and not declared, unequivocally, in favor of artificial origin. The proofs are clear, abundant and conclusive. Externally and internally, character, structure, position and contents, all incontestably prove them the work of man's labor, industry and spirit of combined action. All, from the largest to the smallest, are the result of human agency. On this point there need be no farther cavil or doubt. (de Hass 1869a: 291)

By 1868 there may have been no need in de Hass's mind for "farther cavil or doubt," but the matter was far from completely clear in the scientific community as late as 1860. The *Proceedings of the Academy of Science of St. Louis* for April 2, 1860, record that "Mr. N. Holmes[14] presented a fragment of Indian pottery, made of sun-dried clay, which he had obtained from the big mound at St. Louis." Today, the presence of a piece of pottery in mound fill is not taken as anything out of the ordinary, since it is clear that village debris often was scooped up

---

13. The spelling of *de Hass* is inconsistent in the literature; sometimes it is spelled with a small "d" and sometimes with a capital "D."

14. Chapman (1980) erroneously assigns this statement to William Henry Holmes, a prehistorian with the Bureau of (American) Ethnology and someone who will figure prominently in Chapter 3. He would have been only 14 years old in 1860. Nathaniel Holmes was a St. Louis lawyer (later a judge) and member of the Academy of Science of St. Louis.

to use in forming a mound. But to Holmes, the idea of its being evidence that the mound was not a natural feature was a new one. The *Proceedings* state that Holmes went on to address the membership:

> He remarked that the streets in the vicinity of the mound had been cut down . . . [and that] In this section, the line of level of the natural surface, as he had frequently observed, was distinctly marked through the entire base of the mound and of the terrace on the eastern side. Below the surface level, the lines of stratification as of deposits out of water were very evident; above it, the section presented a nearly uniform appearance and almost homogeneous structure, with only here and there some patches of lighter or darker shades of color. The color in general of the upper portion was grayish, indicating vegetable or surface soil; that below the original surface was yellowish like the clay of our hills. He had found this fragment of pottery imbedded in the upper and artificial portion of this section, about two feet above the natural surface line, on the western side.
>
> It was highly improbable that this pottery could have been drifted to that position, on the supposition that the mound was a natural formation. The conclusion was inevitable, that it must have been carried thither by the Indians mixed with the materials of which they were constructing the mound; and it may be safely taken as an additional proof of the artificial character of the structure; if, indeed, any other evidence of that fact were required than what is afforded by the appearance of the section alone.
>
> Mr. Schoolcraft, some years ago, and Dr. Koch, more lately, had supposed this mound to be a natural formation. Messrs. Squier and Davis, before the section was made, judging from its situation and form . . . had entertained no doubt of its artificial character. . . . That the views of Messrs. Squier and Davis were correct, there could be no reasonable doubt. (*Transactions of the Academy of Science of St. Louis* I: 700–701)

But there *was* doubt, whether reasonable or not, over the origin of the Big Mound, and it lasted through the 1860s.[15] The source of that doubt lay in published pronouncements by geologists, professional and otherwise, who had personally inspected the mound profiles as the structure was slowly being razed. Modern archaeologists would examine the profiles and easily reach the same conclusion Holmes had, that is, that the mound was artificial, but perhaps we

15. Spencer Smith also presented a paper before the academy in 1869, in which he argued against the theory that the Big Mound was artificial. References to the paper in published form exist (e.g., Brinton 1881; F. W. Putnam 1870: 63; Scharf 1883: 96; Williams and Goggin 1956: 71), though it was not published in the *Transactions of the Academy of Science of St. Louis*. A copy of the original text exists in the Missouri Historical Society in St. Louis; the text was printed in the *Missouri Democrat* (September 7, 1869). Frederic W. Putnam (1870: 63), second curator of anthropology at the Peabody Museum (Harvard), references Smith's presentation in urging caution in assuming the Big Mound was artificial. Daniel Brinton, who eventually founded the anthropology program at the University of Pennsylvania, accepted as fact that the mound was of natural origin.

should not be too hard on those who examined the same sections and reached the opposite conclusion. To understand the reasoning of those whose opinions differed from that of Holmes, one needs a bit of background not only on the stratigraphic section of the Big Mound itself but also on how geologists of the time viewed the sedimentary history of the Mississippi River valley.

In the mid–nineteenth century, two volumes on midwestern geological history and process were published that soon became standard reference books on the subject—George C. Swallow's *First and Second Annual Reports of the Geological Survey of Missouri* (1855) and Amos H. Worthen's *Geological Survey of Illinois* (1866). Considerable space in each report was dedicated to a discussion of sedimentary processes and the types of deposits produced by each. In the mid– nineteenth century continental subsidence and rebound were well-known phe- nomena, and it was an accepted fact that the midcontinent had been covered at various times by ocean waters. It was also known that much of the midcontinent had been subjected to cycles of glacial advance and retreat. What was not well understood, however, was the timing of the various events that had shaped the landscape. More pertinent to our discussion here, it is clear that geologists of that period often misidentified depositional processes.

One of the errors made by both Swallow and Worthen was the assumption that the thick mantles of loess soil found in Missouri and Illinois were riverine, or fluvial, as opposed to eolian in nature, that is, that they were deposited by river water instead of by wind. In fact, it is obvious that what they termed *loess* was in many cases different kinds of clay, defined in most areas by their colors and by their positions above a composite unit termed *drift*, which was viewed (in most cases) as a marine unit containing several subunits of rounded pebbles, gravel, organic debris, and series of different-colored clays. In light of the time period in which they were reached, Swallow's and Worthen's conclusions were reasonable. They knew that marine deposits predated fluvial deposits, and they observed the unconformity between the underlying mixed beds of the drift and the overlying loess/clays. Thus, they reached the conclusion that the unconformity represented the switchover from marine to fluvial regime. They also realized that, depending on locale, the composition of the drift (and sometimes the loess) varied significantly, and they relied heavily on the color of the different clays to make their assignments as to whether a particular bed belonged in the loess or drift categories.

Worthen (1866: 34) actually examined the mounds in the American Bottom area across the Mississippi River from St. Louis and concluded that they were natural deposits of drift clay overlain by loess. He then examined the exposed sections of the Big Mound in St. Louis and found the mound to consist of "about fifteen feet of *common chocolate brown drift clay* at the base, which was overlaid by thirty feet or more of the ash-colored marly sands of the Loess, the line of separation between the two deposits remaining as distinct and well-defined as they usually are in good artificial sections in the railroad cuts through these deposits" (Worthen 1866: 34).

But Holmes, a lawyer, knew that Worthen, the state geologist of Illinois, was wrong, and he again addressed the Academy of Science:

> I know, as many others do . . . that what Mr. Worthen has taken to be a line of separation between the upper and basal portions of his mound [see Figures 2.6 and 2.7], is only the line that marks the bottom of the original mound where it stood upon the natural surface of the ground; and the idea that the basal portion was composed of the drift clay, and the top part of loess, is so far a mere illusion. . . . It is very possible that it may be a knoll of loess left standing there on a ground of the marine drift brown clay or loam; and if the characteristic fossils of the Loess were found in it, it might certainly be declared to be a remnant of the loess. No such fossils have been found in it; but I have found embedded in it a fragment of pottery, which is now in the Museum of the Academy.
>
> This pottery may furnish some evidence that the mound is artificial, though not conclusive. If the mound be natural loess, then the pottery would furnish another proof that man existed here in the age of the Mastodon and the Loess deposit; but if it be artificial, the pottery may have been carried into the mound with the materials of which it was constructed, at a much later date. . . .
>
> The observations of Messrs. Squier and Davis upon this mound, and that called Monk's Mound in the American Bottom, comparing them with other similar mounds of the Mississippi valley, which were ascertained to be artificial, satisfied them that these two, at least, were artificial, and belonged to the class of Temple Mounds; but it may still be possible, however, that these, like the smaller mounds of the Illinois bottom, were naturally formed, and they were only used, as found by the Indians, for superstitious purposes. The facts known are all against such an hypothesis. (*Transactions of the Academy of Science of St. Louis* II: 568–69)

The Honorable Nathaniel Holmes's elegantly reasoned address, only part of which is reprinted above, apparently closed the book forever on the question of the origin of the mound—at least the question of whether it was artificial or not. As we will see, it did nothing to answer the question of who erected it. Holmes's address rightfully deserves a place in the annals of Missouri archaeology, but we must add an asterisk to his name, for he did not quite have the last word on the question of origin at that January 7, 1867, meeting of the St. Louis academy. That honor belonged to Wills de Hass, who, the secretary noted in the *Proceedings*, "being present,[16] upon invitation, stated, in confirmation of

16. Williams and Goggin (1956: 23) are apparently incorrect in their statement that de Hass was a member of the Academy of Science of St. Louis. His name does not appear in any published membership lists, nor could I find any mention in the *Proceedings* of his membership being proposed. The fact that the *Proceedings* noted that he was "invited" to make a statement, whereas in other cases the *Proceedings* simply noted that a particular member stated such-and-such, suggests he was in

the artificial character of the Big Mound at St. Louis, that his investigations had left no doubt on his mind as to its artificial origin" (*Transactions of the Academy of Science of St. Louis* II: 569). And what of de Hass and his investigations—the investigations that caused him to deliver at the 1868 AAAS meeting in Chicago such a vocal attack on those who would believe the mounds to be the result of natural forces?

Interestingly, in the paper in which de Hass (1869a) excoriated those who thought that the mounds so evident across the eastern United States were of natural origin, he mentioned only the mound groups located in the American Bottom, which today are known collectively as the Cahokia mound group. Although he claimed to have "examined, located, measured and mapped over one hundred and fifty mounds, excavating many, and collecting several hundred specimens of ancient art" (de Hass 1869a: 292), he described none of his findings. Instead, he droned on about "a vast city of mounds in ruin . . . a community, little less populous, perhaps, than that now centering within an area of twenty miles of this great modern metropolis of the West [St. Louis]" (de Hass 1869a: 293).[17]

De Hass made no mention of the Big Mound at St. Louis in any of his publications. In fact, there is no incontrovertible evidence that de Hass ever conducted any work at the mound. Williams and Goggin (1956: 16) cited de Hass's statement at that January 7, 1867, meeting of the St. Louis academy as evidence that "certain excavations were made in graves at the north end [of the Big Mound] by De Hass" (Williams and Goggin 1956: 16), but the only statement recorded in the *Proceedings* is that de Hass noted that "his investigations had left no doubt on his mind as to its artificial origin." De Hass never said what his "investigations" included. Williams and Goggin (1956: 16) also cited as evidence of de Hass's work a letter written by Nathaniel Holmes to Jeffries Wyman, the first curator of the Peabody Museum (Harvard),[18] in which he offered the museum a number of artifacts from the burial pit, including a lock of what was thought to be human hair. In the letter, Holmes stated, "A few years ago, Dr. De Hass obtained some articles of stone and similar shell-beads from graves opened at the northern end by the excavations then made, of which he has given some account." Holmes did not state that de Hass conducted the investigations, only that he obtained some of the materials.

De Hass was, of course, familiar with what had transpired during the final days of the mound's existence, and, as Williams and Goggin (1956: 23) pointed out,

---

attendance at the meeting but not actually a member. The *Proceedings* of meetings after the January 7, 1867, meeting are silent on de Hass.

17. De Hass's paper is also quoted at length in Scharf 1883 (101–2).

18. Because of the existence of more than one Peabody Museum, I always assign an institutional affiliation in parentheses.

it was de Hass who provided the only known photograph of an artifact from the Big Mound. Sometime near the final days of the Big Mound, T. T. Richards of St. Louis had acquired the two small copper long-nosed-god masks (probably ear ornaments) that came from one of the two burials that Conant (1879a) described as being near the surface of the mound. In 1870 Richards submitted a letter on the find to the *American Naturalist* (Richards 1870), one of the editors of which was Frederic Ward Putnam of the Peabody Museum (Salem), later curator of the Peabody Museum at Harvard and for over two decades permanent secretary of the American Association for the Advancement of Science. Putnam added a footnote commenting on Richards's letter and asking for "carefully made figures of the ear ornaments" (F. W. Putnam 1870: 63) for inclusion in a future issue of the journal. Wills de Hass must have been allowed to see the copper masks, for he, instead of Richards, sent Putnam a photograph of one of them (see Figure 2.8 for a drawing of the object).

Cranial Observations and Measurements

Putnam concluded the brief note on the copper masks with the following question:

> Can any one inform us whether the skulls found in this grave on the "Great Mound" have been compared with those of undoubted mound skulls? For there seems to be much uncertainty relating to this mound. Was it really formed by the mound builders, or even used by them, or were the skeletons found there of the present Indian race? It will be remembered that Professor Smith, of St. Louis, who watched the leveling of the mound [see footnote 7], was satisfied that it was a river deposit, and not an artificial mound. (F. W. Putnam 1870: 63)

Thus, there were still some doubts about whether the Big Mound was natural or artificial in 1870. More important here is Putnam's question on the similarity of skulls from the Big Mound and those from earthworks known to have been produced by the mound builders. This was a common theme in much of the nineteenth-century antiquarian literature, with elaborate schemes being devised to track the movement of peoples throughout prehistory—schemes based on cranial indices that supposedly could be used to distinguish among different races and subgroups. One of the most elaborate treatises, and certainly the one most often cited in the antiquarian literature of the mid to late nineteenth century, was Samuel G. Morton's *Crania Americana* (1839). Morton, a Philadelphia physician and anatomist, developed two major, closely related objectives for his research: (1) to examine the skulls of over 40 ethnic groups from North and South America to determine what the similarities and differences were and (2) to determine whether one race or more than one race of people had lived in North America in the prehistoric past.

Conant cited Morton's craniometric work in his April 5, 1876, address to the St. Louis academy (Conant 1878) on the archaeology of southeastern Missouri. Conant excavated several sites in New Madrid County, including the multi-mound site later known as Sikeston, from which he obtained ceramic vessels and several skulls. His comments regarding the skulls and their chronological placement were reminiscent of his statements regarding the skeletons in the Big Mound at St. Louis, but they also reflected the inflexibility that existed in the thinking of most antiquarians regarding the place of the American Indians relative to that of the mound builders. Cranial measurements were viewed as a rational basis for making the separation, despite what other evidence might have suggested. At least two of the skulls from Sikeston were "normal," according to Conant, and both exhibited evidence of occipital flattening (Figure 2.9, top and middle)—a not uncommon occurrence on Mississippian-period skulls from southeastern Missouri (Holland 1991, 1994) and northeastern Arkansas (M. L. Powell 1989). On one poorly preserved specimen (Figure 2.9, bottom), however,

> The forehead is lower and more retreating than any I have seen from the mounds or caves, while the superciliary ridges are largely developed, altogether suggesting a mental organization but little above the ape. It bears a closer resemblance to the pictures of the Neanderthal skull [from near Düsseldorf, Germany] than any which have come under my observation. When my eyes first rested upon this remarkable skull, I had no doubt that it was an intrusive burial by the Indians, such as I had frequently seen near the surface of other mounds which were unmistakably such, and my suspicion was strengthened by the fact that it was located upon the very outer edge of the mound; but, upon careful examination of its position, I found that it was deposited in the usual manner with the head towards the centre, with the drinking vessels in the usual position, also, beside the head, and corresponding in all particulars of its interment with the rest. From all these circumstances it was impossible to escape the conviction, that, to whatever distinctive race or tribe the individual may have belonged, he was buried by those who erected the mound, and in the same faith. (Conant 1878: 364).

Thus, Conant's inescapable "conviction" was that some poor savage, whose intelligence was little more than that of an ape, had died and been interred by the mound builders, who buried him in the same manner and with the same funeral offerings afforded one of their own. Conant simply could not believe that someone with an "abnormal" skull and who had been buried on the "very outer edge" of a mound could have been a mound builder. The fact that the individual had been interred with the same type of vessels that "known" mound builders had been interred with meant, obviously, that the mound builders had interred him.

Conant was only one of many antiquarians who believed that craniometric measurements could be used to distinguish between mound builders and Indians

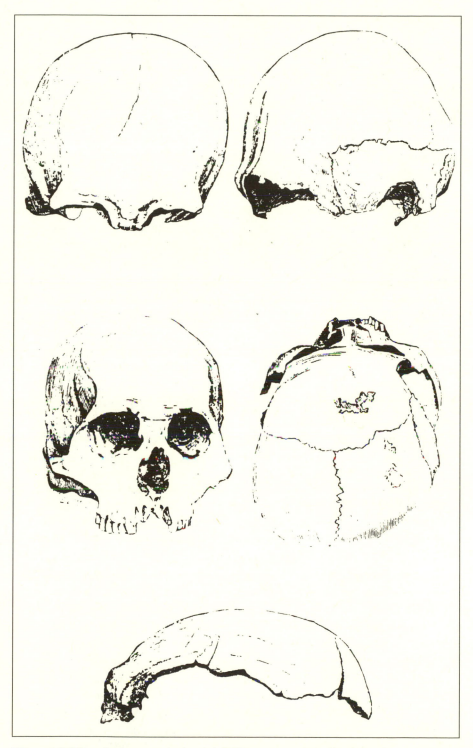

Figure 2.9. Three human crania from the Sikeston site, New Madrid County, Missouri, discussed by Alban J. Conant (from Conant 1879a).

(e.g., Daniel Wilson's treatise "Physical Anthropology," published in the *Smithsonian Institution Annual Report for 1862* [D. Wilson 1863]). The Smithsonian went so far as to enlist the help of laypersons in securing cranial information, especially from travelers to "the Indian country," by publishing in the 1861 annual report "Instructions for Archaeological Investigations in the United States" (Gibbs 1862). Even Wills de Hass brought craniometrics into his rambling address before the AAAS membership (de Hass 1869a). In concluding his paper, de Hass noted, "We have not reached that advance in science attained by the anthropologists of Great Britain, who pronounce the character of crania from the form of the tumuli in which they appear. These researches [in the United States] have not yet determined the interesting anthropological fact, if a fact it is, that *long* mounds contain *long* or dolichocephalic skulls; and *round* or conical mounds, cover a round-headed, or *brachycephalic* race" (de Hass 1869a: 302). Although no attempt to use such a scheme was made in Missouri, cranial shape would continue to play a role during the nineteenth century as one basis for distinguishing between the remains of mound builders and those of Indians. By the end of the nineteenth century and well into the first quarter of the twentieth century, after it had been fairly well concluded that the mound builders and the Indians were one and the same, cranial analysis would play an even larger role in disputes over exactly how long humans had been in the New World (see Chapter 4). This time, physical anthropology would be held in the hands of one powerful and outspoken person, Aleš Hrdlička, who had the requisite experience in ethnology and archaeology as well as in anatomy to provide an authoritative opinion.

Mound Exploration across Missouri

Though I have to this point focused on the reports of Alban Conant, he was not the only recorder, nor even the most important recorder, of archaeological sites in the state in the nineteenth century. For example, E. P. West was an untiring, if somewhat speculative, recorder of archaeological remains in the western part of the state and adjacent regions. His articles (West 1877a, 1877b, 1880, 1882a, 1882b, 1883), which appeared in numerous issues of the *Kansas City Review of Science and Industry* (renamed in 1878 from the *Western Review of Science and Industry*), suggest that his driving ambition was to demonstrate the antiquity of the mound builders and to link the mounds with a vanished race. Other antiquarians working in western Missouri included W. H. R. Lykins (1878), S. V. Proudfit (1881a, 1881b), Garland C. Broadhead (1880a, 1880b), and C. W. Stevenson (1878). In the northeastern quadrant of the state, G. L. Hardy and F. B. Scheetz (1883) excavated a series of mounds in Ralls County, and J. C. Watkins (1883) reported on mounds in Pike County. In central Missouri, W. H. Ficklin (1894) excavated a few mounds, but the bulk of excavation there would not occur for another decade after his work. The results of some of this work were published in various proceedings and transactions of state organizations (e.g., the *Missouri Historical Society Collections* and the *Transactions of the Academy of Science of St. Louis*), but some of it made its way into national publications such as the *Annual Report of the Smithsonian Institution* (e.g., Broadhead 1880a; Hardy and Scheetz 1883; Lykins 1878; Watkins 1883). Quite often, published reports were abstracted in other journals for the benefit of their readers (e.g., reports by Broadhead and Stevenson in *The American Antiquarian and Oriental Journal* I: 103).

By far the most-intensive investigations took place in southeastern Missouri, some of them through the efforts of the St. Louis academy. The Mississippian-period mounds in southeastern Missouri figured only sporadically in early accounts—for example, Henry M. Brackenridge (1814) mentioned the Lilbourn site in New Madrid County (Figure 2.10)—but it was not until the 1870s that fairly large scale investigations began to be centered in the region. By that time several Mississippian-period palisaded mound sites in southeastern Missouri were well known for the large numbers of burials and ceramic vessels they produced—in short, an antiquarian's dream. Horatio N. Rust (1877) excavated several mounds at Sandy Woods in Scott County (Figure 2.10), as well as mounds at sites the locations of which are unknown, and it appears his work was done for commercial purposes (a portion of his pottery was purchased by the Peabody Museum [Yale]). Colonel Caleb Croswell (1878) excavated at Matthews, in New Madrid County (Figure 2.10), and at Sandy Woods, and Conant (1878) apparently excavated the above-referred-to skeletons at Sikeston, also in New Madrid County (Figure 2.10). Slightly earlier, the well-published antiquarian J. W. Foster (1864) worked at Beckwith's Fort, in Mississippi County (Figure 2.10), as did the owner, Thomas Beckwith, who between 1884 and 1887 assembled a collection of "about sixteen hundred pieces in all, consisting of pottery, tools, ornaments etc." (Beckwith 1887: 239).[19] The largest of the palisaded centers, Lilbourn, had been investigated by George Clinton Swallow, a professor at the University of Missouri (the same Swallow who had been the director of the Geological Survey of Missouri), who made brief reports on what he recovered (*Transactions of the Academy of Science of St. Louis* I: 36) and described his excavations in a manuscript that accompanied his artifact collection when it was donated to the Peabody Museum at Harvard twenty years later (F. W. Putnam 1875a, 1875b).[20]

19. A sizable portion of Beckwith's collection is housed at Southeast Missouri State University in Cape Girardeau.

20. Putnam 1875a is usually listed as Swallow 1875. However, the entry in the *Eighth Annual Report of the Peabody Museum* was written by Putnam, who abstracted portions of Swallow's manuscript

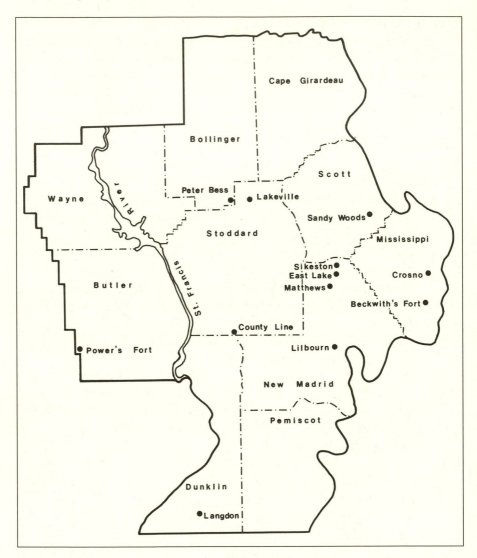

Figure 2.10. Locations of 12 fortified Mississippian-period sites in southeastern Missouri, many of which were excavated in the late nineteenth century.

Swallow's excavation of the "Big Mound" at Lilbourn probably is the largest single excavation of a mound ever undertaken in Missouri. He claimed that he and 10 associates used their "servants and teams" to "cut a passage six feet wide

that accompanied the collection. Putnam 1875b is identical to Putnam 1875a except for the addition of a short introductory remark and the addition of woodcuts from Foster 1873b.

entirely through the 'Big Mound' from side to side [east to west] and from top to bottom, laying open its entire structure" (F. W. Putnam 1875b: 322). Swallow and several of his friends accomplished the work in December 1856 and January 1857, using their servants to excavate and horse-drawn wagons to remove the mound fill. The trench was still five feet deep in 1916 (Moore 1916: 503), and its outline can be seen today.

As Conant (1878) was to do in his description of the internal structure of the Big Mound at St. Louis, Swallow noted that the Lilbourn mound contained a central vault:

> A room seems to have been built by putting up poles (like rafters in the roof of a house); on these rafters were placed split cane *(Arundinaria macrosperma)*; plaster, made of the marls of the bluff formation, was then applied above and below so as to form a solid mass, inclosing the rafters and lathing of cane, and this held all in place; over this room was built the earth work of the mound, so that when it was completed the room was at its centre. The earth work was then coated with the plaster, and over all nature formed a soil. (F. W. Putnam 1875b: 322, quoting Swallow).

This central "room" actually may have been no more than the remains of a well-preserved house that at one time had been erected on a smaller substructure mound within the larger mound (S. Williams 1954: 162–63). The "plaster" probably was fired clay that had lined the walls of the house. Swallow excavated at least one other mound at Lilbourn and found "ashes, shells, charcoal, fragments of bones and pots. Nothing of any great value" (F. W. Putnam 1875b: 333). He also excavated a mound about six miles east-northeast of New Madrid (site unknown), which produced numerous Mississippian-period vessels (F. W. Putnam 1875b).

The work of Rust, Croswell, Conant, Beckwith, and others might have been conducted on a fairly large scale, but it produced little in the way of useful information concerning the archaeological record of the sites. Artifact descriptions were almost always vague, and almost no intrasite locational information was reported. There also was apparently little in the way of planning or structured research guiding the excavations, other than what Beckwith (1887: 228) stated as his aims: "I have been exploring the mounds in this section more or less, the last three years searching for Mound Builders' relics, not to sell, but to collect for my own satisfaction." There was, however, one major exception to those personalized collecting expeditions, and what was produced as a result of it stands in direct contrast to the other results. That noteworthy project was the mound survey headed by W. B. Potter of the Academy of Science of St. Louis, listed in the *Transactions* as a professor.

It was not uncommon for scientific societies of the time to have a large number of standing committees that were supposed to further the various specific scientific interests of the organization. So it was that the ASSL formed a committee on mound exploration and appointed Potter as chairman. On April 3, 1876, Potter informed the general membership, "The committee have examined and made a survey of five groups of mounds" and collected 200 vessels and 20 skulls (*Transactions of the Academy of Science of St. Louis* 3: ccvii). The committee spent a grand total of $88 on labor, transportation, and other items—which, even adjusting for inflation, was a bargain. This was not the first time the academy had paid the costs associated with fieldwork, but the work that finally resulted from the 1876 investment was far superior to anything produced previously by academy members. In December 1876 the academy reorganized the committee on mound exploration into a formal archaeology section, and in June 1877 Potter reported on the section's recent work and promised publication of a four-part series. One of the four parts—the only one ever published—appeared in 1880 as *Contributions to the Archaeology of Missouri by the Archaeological Section of the St. Louis Academy of Science*.[21] The first section, "Archaeological Remains in Southeastern Missouri," was written by Potter (1880), and the second section, "The Ancient Pottery of Southeastern Missouri," was written by physician Edward Evers (1880).

Potter's maps and descriptions of the five mound sites included in the report are unduplicated in terms of what they tell us about the configuration of large middle-Mississippian-period fortified communities in the region. All five sites—Sikeston (Potter's "settlement C" [Figure 2.11]), East Lake ("settlement D"), Matthews ("settlement A" [Figure 2.12]), Lilbourn ("settlement B" [Figure 2.13]), and Sandy Woods (Figure 2.10)—as I noted above, had been examined by other antiquarians, and all five have figured prominently in subsequent archaeological reconstructions of the period A.D. 1000–1300. Two sites—Lilbourn and Matthews—have received considerable excavation in the twentieth century (Chapman et al. 1977 [Lilbourn]; Walker and Adams 1946 [Matthews]).

Potter's maps in some cases provide the only evidence that the communities were fortified, since erosion and agricultural activities have subsequently destroyed embankments and ditches. Potter also plotted the locations of mounds, house depressions, and large depressions that resulted from the removal of soil for use in mound construction. In most cases the dimensions he listed for the mounds, walls, and ditches are at odds with those given by other investigators, such as Rust, Croswell, and Conant, but their estimates were, as we now know, erroneous. Potter's descriptions, on the other hand, correlate well with what is shown on his maps, and subsequent investigations have supported most of his measurements (e.g., Chapman et al. 1977; Walker and Adams 1946).

21. For some reason, this publication lists the name of the organization as the St. Louis Academy of Science instead of the Academy of Science of St. Louis.

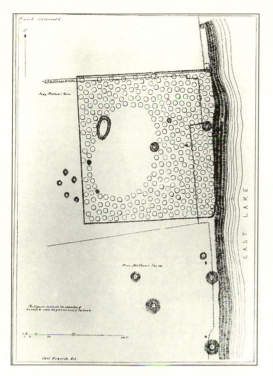

Figure 2.11. Map of the Sikeston site, New Madrid County, Missouri, prepared by W. B. Potter (from Potter 1880).

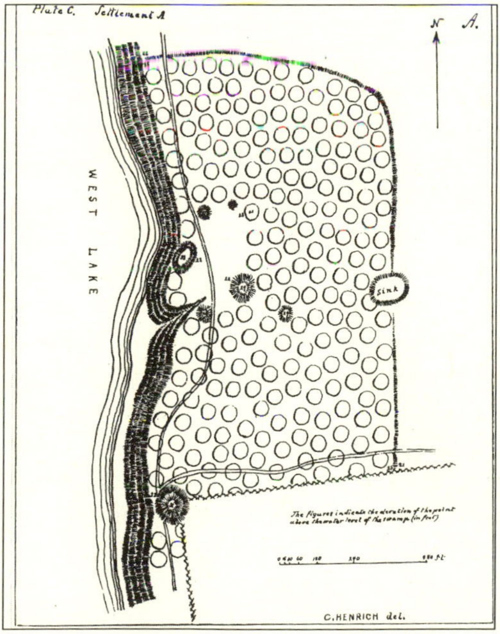

Figure 2.12. Map of the Matthews site, New Madrid County, Missouri, prepared by W. B. Potter (from Potter 1880).

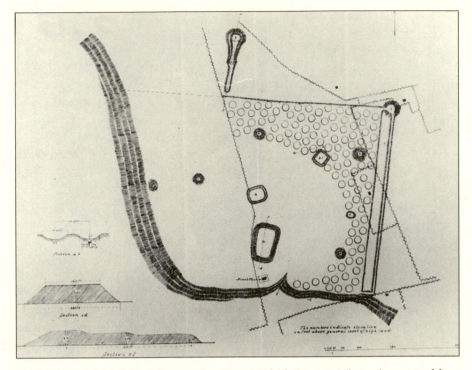

Figure 2.13. Map of the Lilbourn site, New Madrid County, Missouri, prepared by W. B. Potter (from Potter 1880).

If one reads Potter's descriptions of his excavations carefully (e.g., Chapman 1980; J. R. Williams 1964), it is not difficult to relate them to individual mounds and sectors of the sites. Potter numbered the most visible topographic features at the site and referred to them in the text when he discussed what was found in each. Unfortunately, he provided no excavation plans, which was typical of most works of the nineteenth century. What is apparent in Potter's descriptions is that the mounds he excavated served different purposes—some were burial mounds and others were substructure mounds for buildings. For example, several of the larger mounds at Sandy Woods were said to contain nothing, while Potter (1880: 9–10) estimated that two of the mounds—both of which had been looted over a period of years—produced 800–1000 ceramic vessels and 100–200 skeletons.

Potter's report contrasts with others of the period, not only in terms of what is contained in his short monograph but also in terms of what it does not contain. The purpose of these reports by the academy's archaeology section, which is stated in the preface (unattributed, but probably authored by Potter, the section head), is clear: "These papers [Potter's and Evers's] are intended not so much to express the theories and opinions of individual members of the Section, as to be the means of furnishing to those interested in the archaeology of the country, a reliable statement of facts connected with the occurrence of prehistoric remains in this important region." In other words, Potter did not view the reports as a place in which to engage in speculation over who built the mounds, and in fact he uses the term *mound builders* only three times, the first time even placing it in quotation marks.

Potter concluded his report with eight summary points, some of which required considerable insight and an eye for detail. For example, he recognized the numerous bayous in the region as former channels of the Mississippi River and noted that the mounds were made primarily of clay that had been hauled from the clay plugs that choked the former channels. Although his work was limited to five sites, he detected patterns in the numbers and locations of mounds and in their functions. He also noticed that fortification ditches were always located outside the palisades and that house depressions were "thickly scattered over the surface within the walls of the settlements, with the exception of an elliptical area generally 600′ to 800′ by 300′ to 400′" (Potter 1880: 18).

Potter's concern with fact as opposed to speculation is nowhere more apparent than in his quotation of a statement made earlier by another member of the archaeology section, Caleb Croswell (1878: 535), who excavated a number of burials at Matthews: "Col. Croswell, who devoted some time in excavating this mound, states that 'there appeared to have been no observance of order in depositing the dead in this mound'" (Potter 1880: 11). Potter truncated Croswell's quote, which continued "but this seeming carelessness may have been methodical and attributable to some peculiarity in their customs; of course, I make an exception of the systematic care practised in gradually drawing in the circle [of the mound] and increasing the height to the centre" (Croswell 1878: 535). Potter clearly wanted no part of speculation. Despite the precision with which the map of Matthews was prepared, clearly showing the locations of house depressions (though drawn grossly oversize on the plan), Potter did not attempt to duplicate Croswell's scheme of deriving a population estimate:

> I have computed the . . . number of excavations [depressions] at thirty-five to the acre, making the number of dwellings one thousand seven hundred and fifty. If we base our estimate on [five persons per family], we shall have as the result eight thousand seven hundred and fifty, a population more than sufficient to entitle any of our modern settlements to the denomination of *city*. I consider, however, that the estimate falls short of the reality, if we take into consideration the prevalence of polygamy among all barbarous and semi-civilized nations. (Croswell 1878: 533)

Potter's ability to withstand such seductive analyses probably made for boring reading in the highly speculative period of the late nineteenth century, but on the other hand it was a model of objectivity. It would not be long, however, until his report became simply one of many nonspeculative statements on the earthworks that stretched across the midwestern and eastern United States. Its importance in Americanist archaeology is that it was one of the first.

To this point we have spent considerable time talking about the mounds themselves, but what of the artifacts that came from the mounds? In Chapter 3 I examine the collecting habits of scientific groups in Missouri; my purpose here is to discuss the role played by artifacts in formulating various scenarios that ostensibly "explained" the past. As we will see, material remains from the mounds played important roles in the creation of various evolutionary schemes that exerted a stranglehold on the broad field of anthropology—a stranglehold that would not be broken until the mound-builder myth was laid to rest. Note carefully that I am *not* implying that evolutionary schemes died with the mound-builder myth, for they most assuredly did not. But what *did* happen was that analysis of the material record began to shift away from identifying artifacts as being products of mound builders versus Indians and toward documenting such things as functional and technological variation on a regional scale.

Material Remains and Evolutionary Schemes

After we peruse archaeological reports from the mid to late nineteenth century, we see clearly that the vast majority of these excavations were little more than indiscriminate treasure hunts. Rarely is there mention of anything more than human-skeletal elements and large, intact artifacts, especially ceramic vessels. Certainly no excavators mentioned thus far separated materials by anything more than the grossest of proveniences (e.g., material from mound 1 was kept separate from that from mound 2), and given the manner in which most mounds were excavated—using picks and shovels or, in some cases, mule teams—it is a wonder that anything was recovered intact. Excavators were for the most part uninterested in reporting the nature of what they had dug through, and even in cases where artifact descriptions were included, they were done in the most cursory manner. Some artifact descriptions were provided either by the individuals who had excavated the material (e.g., Croswell 1878) or by interested laypersons (e.g., Evers 1880 [Figures 2.14 and 2.15]), but the most useful information was that written by museum personnel, who not only cataloged archaeological items on a daily basis but also had seen enough items from other areas to make useful comparisons. For example, Putnam (1875a, 1875b) described pottery and a few stone artifacts in the collection from New Madrid County that Swallow donated to the Peabody Museum (Harvard). Putnam's descriptions were straightforward and concise—what one would expect from a museum curator.

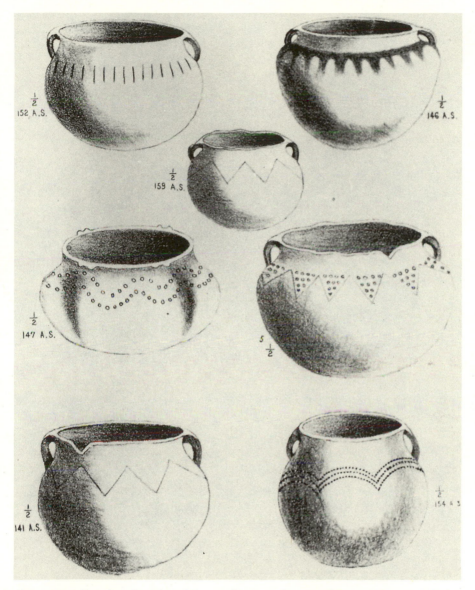

Figure 2.14. Drawings by Edward Evers of pottery from southeastern Missouri (from Evers 1880).

He provided exact dimensions (sometimes weights as well) of each piece, as well as the Peabody Museum accession number and an engraving (Figure 2.16).[22]

22. The engravings deserve more than passing mention, since several of them appear in numerous publications of the period. Individual pieces in Swallow's collection formed the basis for numerous

Figure 2.15. Drawings by Edward Evers of pottery from the central Mississippi River valley (probably northeastern Arkansas) (from Evers 1880).

articles, such as Conant's (1878) summary in the St. Louis academy's *Transactions* and his longer works (Conant 1879a, 1879b). Conant (1878: 358) states in a footnote, "For the plates here given I am indebted to the kindness of Dr. G. C. Swallow, Dean of the Agricultural College of the State University of Missouri." The woodcuts used to produce the plates apparently were made by one G. A. Bauer, whose name or initials appear under many of the pieces.

For comparison with material found elsewhere, he included several engravings from J. W. Foster's (1873a) *American Naturalist* article on the pottery of the mound builders (Figure 2.17), referencing the pieces to pages in Foster's (1873b) *Pre-historic Races of the United States.*

The descriptions of Missouri pottery by Foster (1864, 1873a, 1873b), an attorney by training, were more in line with the spirit of the times—fanciful, to be sure, and certainly not very informative. For example, in his short article on pottery from unspecified mound sites in Perry and Mississippi counties, he opined on the artistic ability of the mound builders relative to the American Indian and various European groups:

> In the specimens of pottery which have been recovered from the mounds, there is displayed a skill in the selection of the materials, and in the moulding of them into artistic forms, which far surpass the specimens which are characteristic of the Bronze Age of Europe. . . .
>
> When we examine this [effigy] head critically we are convinced that the unknown artist had the skill to impress upon the plastic clay the features of his race. Those features are not characteristic of the Red man. The facial angle is not as obtuse as in the European; the eyes have not the obliquity of the Indian; the jaws are not extraordinarily prognathous, and altogether, the contour of the face is indicative of intelligence. The head is covered with a fillet, the material of which was probably cloth. Have we in this model the characteristic features of the Mound-builder? (Foster 1873a: 94–95)

In one brief article, Foster not only identified the makers of the pottery but proved that they were far superior in their ability as potters to the Bronze Age peoples of Europe. This was quite a feat, especially in light of the fact that he accomplished it in about nine pages. What evidence for superiority did he produce?

> While the inhabitants of the European Bronze Age were content, in their artistic delineations, with simply curved lines and chevron-like markings, the Mound-builders adopted not only the bold swell of the scroll-like ornamentation, but grappled with the delineation of the human figure and human face,—the highest perfection of art; and in this range of modelling, it will be admitted, from the examples submitted, that they soared far above mere caricature,—that they imprinted upon the plastic clay the characteristic features of their race. (Foster 1873a: 95)

Equating perceived artistic ability with such things as intelligence and social complexity was common practice in the nineteenth century. Samuel Haven, in his efforts to prove the antiquity of American "races," concluded, "Their religious doctrines, their superstitions . . . and their arts, accord with those of the most primitive age of mankind" (Haven 1856: 159). Efforts to understand the

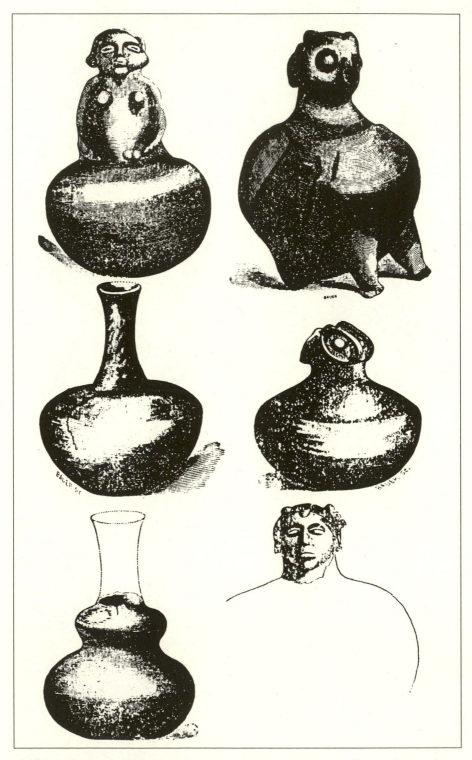

Figure 2.16. Drawings by G. A. Bauer of pottery in the G. C. Swallow collection from New Madrid County, Missouri (from F. W. Putnam 1875b).

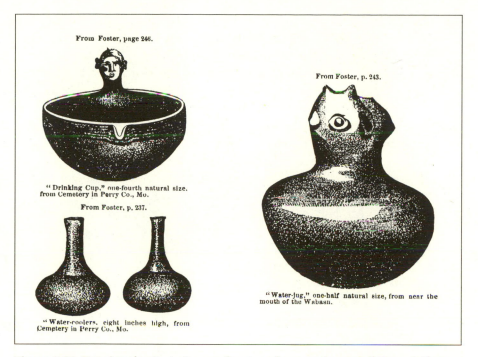

From Foster, page 246.

" Drinking Cup," one-fourth natural size, from Cemetery in Perry Co., Mo.

From Foster, p. 237.

From Foster, p. 243.

" Water-jug," one-half natural size, from near the mouth of the Wabash.

" Water-coolers, eight inches high, from Cemetery in Perry Co., Mo.

Figure 2.17. Drawings by G. A. Bauer of pottery from southeastern Missouri (from Foster 1873a).

developmental stages that humankind appeared to have gone through reached a pinnacle in the work of ethnologists such as Herbert Spencer, Lewis Henry Morgan, and Edward Tylor. Morgan, in particular, in his book *Ancient Society* (1877), broke new ground in attempting to classify world cultures into a ladderlike progression of stages (his "ethnical periods"), from savagery, through barbarism, to civilization, on the basis of whether or not the cultures had developed certain technological innovations. Development, to Morgan, meant independent invention or adoption through diffusion: "Some of these inventions were borrowed, not unlikely, from tribes in the Middle Status [barbarism]; for it was by this process constantly repeated that the more advanced tribes lifted up those below them, as fast as the latter were able to appreciate it and to appropriate the means of progress" (L. H. Morgan 1877: 540). Once a group was able to "appreciate," for example, pottery, that group had automatically jumped to "lower barbarism." Under Morgan's scheme, that group rested in that category until its members invented or adopted maize cultivation, irrigation, and stone or adobe architecture, at which point they automatically moved up a square, to "middle barbarism."

Despite being grounded in an intractable evolutionary scheme, many of the artifact studies written in the last three decades of the nineteenth century carried snippets of information that are useful for modern archaeological studies, especially those concerned with the geographic distribution of various artifact classes. By 1880 most books and journal articles were accompanied by engravings of artifacts, especially ceramic vessels carrying effigy heads on the rims or molded into effigy shapes. Not surprisingly, the vast majority of studies focused on vessel decoration and form, though many mentioned at least in passing various nondecorative characteristics, such as those pertaining to function and technology. Few if any studies attacked the problem of vessel function head on, employing instead a variety of formal-functional names derived from everyday use. For example, globular vessels with tall, thin necks were invariably labeled as water jugs, and large, everted-rim vessels were referred to as urns.

With regard to technological aspects of pottery production, some reports noted how the vessels were made (e.g., that they were the products of adding coils of wet clay to a flat or rounded base). Less frequently, mention was made of such things as temper and firing regime. Despite other inadequacies in his report, Conant's (1878) description of the pottery from southeastern Missouri actually was exceptional in terms of the information it carried. He described the pottery as being "so similar, that it would seem as though it might all have been the product of one manufactory. The clay seems first to have been mixed with pounded shells, and the articles then subjected to various degrees of heat. Some of the largest pots were burned till they became red; the medium sizes are usually dark gray; while some of the animal forms are of a yellow-drab, and seem to have been made of clay of much finer quality, and with a very smooth surface" (Conant 1878: 362).

Frederic Ward Putnam, a curator of ethnological and archaeological materials, would be expected to pay attention to such details. In describing materials in the Swallow collection, he noted:

> The clay in some of the vessels had been mixed with more or less finely pounded shells, probably of fresh water mussels. . . . In a few of the specimens sand was mixed with the clay, and in several, the clay was apparently without any mixture. These last are generally thick and rude in their finish, while those in which charcoal is now seen are generally the thinnest and among the more finely finished vessels. (F. W. Putnam 1875b: 323)

Putnam was accurate in some of his assessments of temper and firing, as work conducted many decades later has borne out. On the other hand, Conant's observation that different clays were used to create different vessel forms was probably inaccurate. As opposed to different clays, what he probably was observing were the effects of different-sized shell particles and different firing regimes.

Mounds and ceramic vessels were not the only things on the minds of American prehistorians during the nineteenth century, though they certainly received the lion's share of attention in print. There was another issue on the table that, while not totally separate from the mound builders, was distinct enough that it deserves separate consideration. That issue concerned the antiquity of the human presence in North America, specifically, whether humans were present during the tail end of the Pleistocene. In Europe, the question of human antiquity assumed the forefront in research after the middle of the nineteenth century, receiving its impetus from the discovery of obvious flaked tools from river deposits that appeared to have considerable time depth. As a further spark to the rapidly rising interest in the distant past, excavators began to recover bones of extinct animals from gravel beds and caves, where they were found in association with tools. These discoveries, assuming the contexts were undisturbed, could be explained in one of two ways: either there was considerable antiquity to the human presence in Europe, or the animals whose remains were found associated with tools had become extinct at a much later date than assumed previously. By the middle of the nineteenth century it was quite obvious to most (but certainly not all) European prehistorians that the first answer was correct. American prehistorians took note of this fact and began wondering just how long humans had been in North America.

Humans and Mastodons in the Same Bed?

As I noted in Chapter 1, the answer to the question of how long humans have been on this continent is about 11,200 years, give or take a few hundred years. Not every archaeologist would agree with this answer, but those who take a conservative approach—basing their assessment on completely unambiguous, well-dated contexts—would not argue too much with that date. I hasten to add that there is nothing that says humans *couldn't* have arrived here at an earlier time, but there is no unambiguous evidence that shows they did.[23] Radiometric dating was not around in the nineteenth century (it was developed in 1949), and prehistorians had to rely on other means for assigning ages to artifacts. One method of assigning age was through assessing the antiquity of the context in which artifacts occurred. The American literature of the nineteenth century is replete with references to discoveries of tools in what were presumed to be glacial gravels. Prehistorians reasoned that if the gravel beds dated to the glacial period, and the beds contained tools, then the obvious conclusion was that humans had inhabited North America during the so-called "ice age."

A second method of assigning age was by comparing stone tools found in North America with those found in European gravel beds. If the forms were similar, then perhaps North America had experienced its own Paleolithic period.

23. Missouri has had its share of purportedly "early sites," the most well known being Shriver, in Daviess County (Reagan et al. 1978). A Clovis point was found at the site, but few archaeologists believe claims of a pre-Clovis occupation below the level containing the point.

I delay discussion of this very important issue until Chapter 3, since it was during the last two decades of the nineteenth century that acrimonious debate arose over the existence of a North American Paleolithic.

A third method of assigning age was by basing it on the association of the remains of extinct animals and stone tools. There are numerous references in the literature of the nineteenth century to artifacts and even human bones in place alongside the remains of ice-age mammals such as the mastodon. For example, human bones were found associated with the remains of extinct animals at Natchez, Mississippi, in the 1840s (Dickeson 1846; Leidy 1889)—a find that received its scientific imprimatur when, decades later, Thomas Wilson (1892, 1895a) ran chemical tests on the human bone and on mylodon bones and declared them (erroneously, it turns out) to be of the same age. As David Meltzer (1983: 6) points out, even Charles Lyell (1863: 203) was not wholly convinced that the association was meaningful. Attacks on the reliability of the Natchez find occasionally were made (e.g., Hrdlička 1907), but it was not until well into the twentieth century that the putative association was conclusively shown to be false in that case.

Relative to all other claims of associations between the remains of humans and of extinct mammals in North America that were made during the nineteenth century, those made on the basis of materials from Missouri rank first in terms of the controversy they created and the length of time during which the evidence was debated. Even then, I would probably dedicate only a couple of paragraphs to the story, since these particular claims, as it turns out, were unfounded. My reasons for devoting more space to the story have as much to do with the personalities behind those claims as they do with demonstrating how archaeological evidence can be misinterpreted. The fact that the claims persisted for as long as they did tells us something about the prejudice of the antiquarian mind of the mid–nineteenth century to a human presence in North America during the last glacial period.

Neither the discovery in Missouri of bones of extinct mammals nor the discovery of such bones in association with human tools was a unique phenomenon in the nineteenth century. The remains of large, extinct mammals, including mastodons, were reported throughout the century and from all parts of North America. The *Proceedings of the Academy of Science of St. Louis,* for example, are replete with notations of members discovering fossils in Missouri and other states. Recall that in 1856 the academy had even paid the way for one of its members—Albert C. Koch—to travel to Mississippi to view fossil discoveries firsthand. As we will see shortly, Koch already had some firsthand experience at this sort of thing. Geologist Garland C. Broadhead, another member of the St. Louis academy (Figure 2.18), was constantly making reference throughout the second half of the nineteenth century to fossil mammals as well as Indian sites that he happened upon in his travels. He finally found what he was looking for,

Figure 2.18. Geologist Garland Carr Broadhead (1827–1912) in 1897 (courtesy Missouri Historical Society).

reporting in 1881, at the height of the mastodon craze, that he had discovered a mastodon associated with stone artifacts in a spring in Pettis County (Broadhead 1881). The artifacts were described as a few flint implements and a stone club, and they occurred with the mastodon bones in a 15-foot-diameter funnel-shaped area.[24] Broadhead's report is too sketchy to be of much use, and the whereabouts of the artifacts are unknown. But regardless, he was decades too late with his discovery to make it big news in Missouri, for Albert Koch had already brought the attention of the paleontological and archaeological world to Missouri.

Albert Koch and His Traveling Road Show

Numerous articles and compilations have appeared that chronicle Albert Koch's exploits (e.g., McDermott 1948; McMillan 1976a), but it is probably impossible to capture the true spirit of one of the strangest characters who ever graced the study of Missouri's prehistory. Koch was born in Germany in 1804 and immigrated to the United States when he was 22 years old (McDermott 1948: 233), changing his name from the German Albrecht Karl to Albert Carl. He

---

24. Chapman (1975: 53) notes that the spring is still in use and that later materials probably washed down into the funnel, where they became mixed with the bones.

took up residence in St. Louis in the early 1830s and between 1836 and 1841 was able to fulfill his lifelong penchant for collecting things by operating a museum that, by most accounts, was for a while highly successful (Stadler 1972). Koch had an eye for the bizarre as well as for the bazaar, combining wax figures of famous and infamous persons (including Don Antonio López de Santa Anna, president of Mexico and commander-in-chief of the Mexican army), exotic animals (including live alligators), and carnival acts in his multisalon museum (McDermott 1948). For example, a six-legged lamb was displayed alongside the ever-popular "Miss Zelina-Kha-Nourhina, the Peri of the Caspian," who, accompanied by her father, performed the "Feast of Miracles" during her well-publicized engagement.

Koch may have earned at least a portion of his living through his "museum," but his passion was collecting fossil vertebrates. The majority of Koch's fossils came from three Missouri localities (Figure 2.19), two of which—Sulphur Springs, located south of St. Louis, and a bog in the Pomme de Terre River valley of central Missouri—would, in the second half of the twentieth century, figure prominently in the archaeology of the state. The third site (actually the first investigated by Koch), located on the Bourbeuse River in Gasconade County, is historically important because it was there, in October 1838, that Koch first found what he believed to be indisputable proof that prehistoric people had slain giant animals that had since become extinct. He based his belief on two points: (1) many of the animal bones were blackened, thus appearing to have been burned, and (2) among the bones there were a number of rocks that apparently had been brought in by humans to kill and/or butcher the animals. Koch's discovery was first reported in the October 13, 1838, edition of the *Missouri Saturday News* and subsequently appeared (anonymously) in the January 12, 1839, edition of the *Philadelphia Presbyterian* newspaper: "It is with the greatest pleasure, the writer of this article can state, from personal knowledge, that one of the largest of these animals has actually been stoned and buried by Indians, as appears from implements found among the ashes, cinders, and half burned wood and bones of the animal." The article (I cite it as Koch 1839a) must have been written by Koch himself, as he almost admits in a later publication (Koch 1857: 62). In the article Koch never tells the reader what kind of animal he found, though the headline must have referred to the animal as a mammoth, because when the article was reprinted in *The American Journal of Science and Arts* (vol. 36 [1839]), the editor placed *Mastodon?* in parentheses after the title, *The Mammoth*. The editor also asked that the unknown author communicate with the journal directly. Koch (1839b) did so, but he had no more to say on the Gasconade County discovery, preferring instead to concentrate on a description of an animal he had recovered from a newly found locality 22 miles south of St. Louis, a site he termed Sulphur Springs (Figure 2.20).

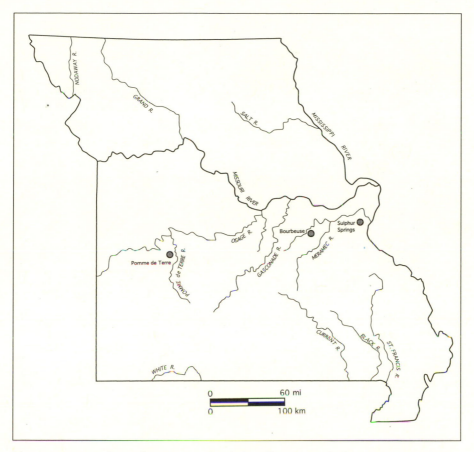

Figure 2.19. Locations of excavations made by Albert C. Koch (location on Bourbeuse River is approximate).

Chief among Koch's finds at Sulphur Springs was a large cranium of a mastodon, though, not recognizing it for what it was, he labeled it as a new animal, *Missourium Kochii*.[25] In a privately printed circular (Koch 1840), he described it in the following manner (as quoted by Buckingham 1842: 134–36):

> I will now endeavour to point out the principal parts in which the formerly found large Mastodon (Mastodon giganticum)[26] differs from the large animal found by me. The first and most remarkable difference between the two animals is the formation of the extremity of the forehead as the one discovered by me has

25. Koch usually capitalized species names, which by convention are lowercased.
26. Here Koch is referring to the remains he had found in Gasconade County, which he evidently realized were of a mastodon by the time he wrote this.

Figure 2.20. Vignette from *Panorama of the Monumental Grandeur of the Mississippi Valley*, by John J. Egan, showing Albert C. Koch's excavations at Sulphur Springs, Jefferson County, Missouri (courtesy St. Louis Art Museum).

a nose projecting 15 inches over the lower jaw, formed of a bony substance, interwoven with cells, and which is flat, so that it bears much resemblance to the upper jaw of an alligator; it ends in two nostrils, which are somewhat raised on the face; the lower part of the said projection is connected with the upper lip, which is somewhat arched on both sides, forming a ridge in the centre. There is no indication of any canine, or front teeth, whereas the skull of the previously found Mastodon shows a hole, in place of the beforementioned projection, which evidently was occupied by its proboscis, or trunk, with its powerful muscles. . . .

In the head of this huge monster we observed particularly, that while the tusks of the elephant go downward, and those of the mastodon upward, these of the new animal go out *horizontally* in curves, bending backward towards the ear, like the horns of some kinds of oxen, or of the buffalo; and that they are solid ivory tusks, proceeding from the upper parts of the mouth, instead of hollow horns proceeding from the temples or sides of the head.

Unfortunately, Koch did not have a complete *Missourium* skeleton to mount for his museum, and in the spring of 1840 he moved his project west to a boggy spring along the Pomme de Terre River in present-day Hickory County[27] that over the years had produced mastodon remains. There he was able to recover enough bones to complete his mount of the *Missourium,* an animal that he was convinced had been

27. Hickory County was formed from a portion of Benton County in 1845; thus Koch's references are to what was then Benton County.

an inhabitant of water courses, such as large rivers and lakes, which is proven by the formation of the bones; 1st, his feet were webbed; 2d, all his bones were solid and without marrow, as the aquatic animals of the present day; 3d, his ribs were too small and slender to resist the many pressures and bruises they would be subject to on land; 4th, his legs are short and thick; 5th, his tail is flat and broad; 6th and last, his tusks are so situated in the head that it would be utterly impossible for him to exist in a timbered country. His food consisted of as much vegetables as flesh, although he undoubtedly consumed a great abundance of the latter, and was capable of feeding himself with his fore foot, after the manner of the beaver or otter, and possessed, also like the hypopotamus, the faculty of walking on the bottom of waters, and rose occasionally to take air. (Koch 1841b: 7)

As McDermott (1948: 244) notes, "Such an animal was well worth going to see!" Koch obviously was a neophyte at best in comparative zoology and had even less knowledge of functional anatomy. He was wrong on almost every count, from the notion that the *Missourium* had webbed feet to his conclusions that the creature could feed itself with its forelimbs. Mastodons never ate meat, did not have broad, flat tails, and certainly lived in timbered country. But, of course, Koch was convinced he was dealing with something other than a mastodon; he just wasn't too sure of its taxonomic position. He had started out calling it *Missourium Kochii* (Koch 1840), but after his Pomme de Terre discoveries added information on its anatomical features (and after he had compared the remains to the creature described in the 41st chapter of the Book of Job), he revised his taxonomic nomenclature first to *Leviathan Missouriensis* (Koch 1841a, 1841b) and then to *Missourium Theristocaulodon* Koch (Koch 1842a, 1845) (Figure 2.21).

For whatever reason, it was several years after the discoveries on the Bourbeuse and Pomme de Terre rivers that Koch made more than casual mention of the precise circumstances surrounding the occurrence of artifacts and the remains of extinct animals. He had briefly noted in the *Philadelphia Presbyterian* article that humans had killed the proboscidean that he recovered on the Bourbeuse River, but he had provided few details. It was not until 1857, in a paper read before the Academy of Science of St. Louis and published shortly thereafter (Koch 1857), that Koch laid out the evidence, "inasmuch as this work has never appeared in the English language, and is, perhaps, little known in America"[28] (Koch 1857: 61–62). Incredibly, in the same paper he claimed to have found *similar* evidence of humans and mastodons in the Pomme de Terre bog from which he had recovered his *Missourium* (which by 1857 he had conceded was a mastodon [see below]).

Regarding the Bourbeuse River discovery, he stated that he had recovered "several arrow-heads, a stone spear-head, and some stone axes, which were taken out in the presence of a number of witnesses, consisting of the people of the

---

28. Koch had summarized a bit of the evidence in a book printed in Germany (Koch 1845).

neighborhood, attracted by the novelty of the excavation" (Koch 1857: 63).[29] More importantly, he had found, he believed, proof that the people who left the tools had actually killed the mastodon:

> The greater portion of these [mastodon] bones had been more or less burned by fire. The fire had extended but a few feet beyond the space occupied by the animal before its destruction. . . . The fire appeared to have been most destructive around the head of the animal. Some small remains of the head were left unconsumed, but enough to show that they belonged to the Mastodon. There were, also, found mingled with these ashes and bones, and partly protruding out of them, a large number of broken pieces of rock, which had evidently been carried thither from the shore of the Bourbeuse river, to be hurled at the animal by his destroyers. (Koch 1857: 63)

Regarding the Pomme de Terre discovery, Koch (1857: 63) noted, "This discovery is already so well known, that I will merely mention the circumstance, in this connection, that the two arrow-heads found with the bones were in such a position as to furnish evidence still more conclusive, perhaps, than in the other case [the Bourbeuse River find], of their being of equal, if not older date, than

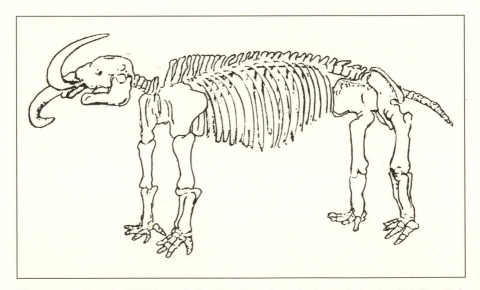

Figure 2.21. Drawing of Albert C. Koch's *Missourium theristocaulodon* Koch (after Koch 1845).

---

29. Gross (1951: 107) illustrated four of the artifacts, now in the Berlin Museum of Natural History, that are cataloged as having come from the Bourbeuse River, presumably from Koch's site.

the bones themselves" (Koch 1857: 63). He also noted that "one of the arrow-heads lay underneath the thigh-bone of the skeleton, the bone actually resting in contact upon it; so that it could not have been brought thither after the deposit of the bone; a fact which I was careful thoroughly to investigate" (Koch 1857: 63). The stone point, illustrated by Wood (1976b: 105 [originally in Rau 1873]) and Chapman (1975: 50), is actually a Late Woodland artifact, with a date of manufacture of ca. A.D. 400–900.

As McMillan (1976a: 92) points out, despite Koch's flair for the theatrical, there is no evidence that he faked any associations of stone tools and mastodons. In fact, at both the Bourbeuse and Pomme de Terre localities it seems clear that Koch found what he reported, that is, mastodon bones and evidence of human use of the areas. It is equally clear that Koch had no concept of artifact movement in a peat bog or of natural processes that could alter the positioning of animal remains. In fact, the purported association at the Bourbeuse River locality can be explained in exactly the manner noted by Adolphus Wislizenus in a presentation before the ASSL in 1857, in which he stated, "I take this opportunity of expressing my belief, and of trying to convince the members, that all the facts, stated by D[r]. Koch, can be accounted for in a far more simple and natural way, than by the hasty and thus far unwarranted supposition, that man has existed contemporaneously with the mastodon" (Wislizenus 1860: 169). The objectivity and clarity of Wislizenus's argument, tied as they were to natural processes and time lag, were extraordinary for the time and deserve careful consideration. To understand his argument one needs to know that Koch, according to his own report (1857: 62), recovered the mastodon in an upright position and that the *head, spine, and ribs* were charred—not the upper portions of the leg bones. Wislizenus (1860: 170) asked the obvious question: "Now, if men, as Dr. Koch supposes, had found the mastodon there while being mired and alive, and, unable to kill it in that helpless condition by weapons and stones, had resorted to fire, is it likely that they would have made a fire above the animal instead of around it[?]" He continued:

The following combination of circumstances appears to my mind the most natural and likely to solve the question:

An Indian family, attracted perhaps by the springs, selected centuries ago that place for a residence . . . where, unknown to them, the bones of the mastodon rested below. . . . [Indians] make their fires . . . on the bare ground, in a hollow circle. . . . Such underground kitchen work would, of course, exert a still more powerful and speedy effect in partially burning underlying bones, and would account, at the same time, for the presence of stones in the ashes. . . .

That in the course of centuries, after the spot was left undisturbed, alluvial ground could have accumulated over it to the depth of eight or nine feet, burying both the mastodon with its partially burned bones and the traces of the Indians, will scarcely need a word of comment.

> This combination of simple and throughout natural circumstances, though it will by no means give us certainty, seems to me to deserve after all more credit than the forced explanation by assuming the coexistence of man and the mastodon, for which no incontrovertible proof has yet been given, or the still more fanciful suggestion of intelligent apes. (Wislizenus 1860: 170–71)

This was not the only time Koch was skewered in public or in print. None other than the most well known prehistorian of the mid–nineteenth century, the great comparativist Sir John Lubbock, fired a broadside across Koch's bow. In an extended book review that focused on, among other works, the monographs by Haven and by Squier and Davis, Lubbock took note of Koch's Bourbeuse River find. His reference to Koch's work was intended as a shot at Haven, who himself dedicated a long paragraph to the find (Haven 1856: 142–43) "without a word of caution" (Lubbock 1863: 335). Lubbock was amazed that anyone would quote from the Koch communiqué reprinted in *The American Journal of Sciences and Art* "as if they were quoting from an article communicated to that respectable journal. Now, the fact is that the only authority for the statement is an anonymous correspondent of the Philadelphia Presbyterian" (p. 335). Lubbock also caught the editorial query that had appeared in the title of that reprinted communiqué: "The original communication to the Philadelphia Presbyterian *never alludes to the mastodon at all,* but refers the skeleton to the mammoth; and the mastodon was first suggested by the editor of the American Journal. Under these circumstances it certainly seems to us that some better evidence will be required before we can be expected to believe that any mastodon was ever stoned to death by North American Indians" (pp. 335–36).

Another shot was fired at Koch by Charles Whittlesey, the well-known and widely published Ohio prehistorian who in 1868 was vice president of the American Association for the Advancement of Science. At that year's annual meeting of the AAAS, Whittlesey took a swipe not only at Koch but at unnamed British scientists:

> Mr. Koch, who furnished a skeleton of the *Mastodon Ohioensis,* from the recent alluvium of the Pomme de terre River, Mo., to the British Museum at London, convinced the English geologists, that he found a flint arrowhead at the depth of fifteen feet beneath the skeleton. . . . He also stated that near the skeleton, and full as deep, were three other flint arrowheads. . . . This statement of Mr. Koch, is, however, contradicted by one of the men who assisted him in exhuming the skeleton. (Whittlesey 1869: 278)

Whittlesey apparently was wrong, for there is no evidence that Koch ever fooled any British scientist. Koch had, however, taken his traveling road show—complete with full mounts of his fossils—to England, where "their scientific value [was] . . . more fully acknowledged" (Koch 1857: 61), in the 1840s. Even with the addition of the *Missourium* fossils from the Pomme de Terre locality, attendance at his museum in St. Louis had sagged, and he had decided to sell the museum—but not before he staged one final extravaganza built around his completed mount. Apparently the complete Leviathan was a hit with the crowds, no doubt lured by the three-piece band who played in the rib cage of the giant creature. Koch had sold his museum in 1841 and taken the Leviathan on a whirlwind tour of the South and East before heading off to Europe, where he hoped to attract giant crowds.

McMillan (1976a: 89–90) is of the opinion that Koch's exhibition in Philadelphia probably was the first occasion for most scientists to view the remains firsthand, and unfortunately for Koch, his *Missourium* mount did not pass muster. In fact, he was blistered. For example, naturalist Paul B. Goddard announced at an October 1841 meeting of the Academy of Natural Sciences of Philadelphia[30] that he had examined Koch's *Missourium* skeleton and found several errors: The spine had 11 too many vertebrae; the first pair of ribs was misplaced on the bones of the shoulder to resemble clavicles (which mastodons did not possess); an ethmoid bone had been glued on the skull to resemble a snout; the tusks were distorted laterally; and the feet contained four phalanges per toe. Another naturalist, Richard Harlan (1843), after examining the mount, identified the remains of at least six different genera, including those of a new species that eventually became known as *Mylodon harlani* (Harlan's ground sloth) (Owen 1843).

In 1841 Koch took his collection to London, where he exhibited the Leviathan (incorrectly mounted [Figure 2.22]) to massive crowds at the Piccadilly. But again, reception of the Leviathan by the scientific circle was cool. In an address to the Geological Society of London, later published in the society's *Proceedings,* the noted anatomist Sir Richard Owen (1842) pointed out many of the anatomical mistakes Koch had made and stated his opinion that the beast was nothing more than a mastodon—albeit composed of the bones of several individuals. Koch (1842b) answered Owen somewhat halfheartedly; he later conceded the argument altogether (Koch 1857). Interestingly, in what could have been Koch's finest hour—a rebuttal of Owen—he (1842b) did little more than show his naïveté in anatomy and his almost childlike belief in any reconstruction that he created. Isaac Hays, a medical doctor with expertise in vertebrate anatomy, noted during an 1843 meeting of the American Philosophical Society that Koch's (1842b) paper read before the Geological Society of London, in which he compared the mastodon and *Tetracaulodon* (which by that time Koch assumed his *Missourium* to be), contained numerous errors:

> Mr K. asserts that the Mastodon in the Philadelphia Museum is a male, according to the construction and size of the pelvis, and the magnitude of the tusks in the upper jaw; yet there are no traces of tusks in the lower jaw: and

---

30. *Proceedings of the Academy of Natural Sciences of Philadelphia* 1:115–16.

Figure 2.22. Lithograph by G. Tytler of Albert C. Koch's *Missourium*, produced in London in 1842 during the height of Koch's exhibit in the Piccadilly. Koch completely misidentified (and misassembled) the mastodons he unearthed. Mastodons were never as large as the creature in the photograph. Visible in the lower-left corner of the lithograph is a live *Missourium* lurking in shallow water near the riverbank (courtesy Missouri Historical Society).

the specimen at Baltimore, which is considered to be indisputably a male, is also destitute of inferior tusks.

Now, Dr. H[ays] remarked, if even we were sufficiently well acquainted with the osteology of the Mastodon to distinguish the male from the female pelvis, which he thought we were not, still Mr. Koch's inferences would be unfounded, because, 1st. the pelvis and the lower jaw in the Baltimore skeleton belonged to different individuals: and 2d. the lower jaw in the Philadelphia one was of *wood,* modelled after the former, whilst the pelvis belonged to a third individual. (*Proceedings of the American Philosophical Society* 2: 265–66)

Despite the chilly reception Koch received from British scientists relative to his new genus, he was able to sell the *Missourium* mount, along with other pieces of his collection, to the British Museum for £1,300 in 1843. Owen then reassembled the skeleton into its proper anatomical position (though the skeleton still comprised parts of more than one individual), where it remained with its new label, *Mammut americanum.* Koch eventually returned to St. Louis and in the late 1850s was an active member of the Academy of Science of St. Louis. Ironically, in 1857, the same year he made his presentation on the association of human and mastodon remains, he was listed as chairman of the academy's standing committee on comparative anatomy (*Journal of Proceedings* January 26, 1857).

At this point we leave the fascinating Mr. Koch, though we should note that well after his discoveries the mastodon-human debate still continued (e.g., Andrews 1875; Dana 1875).[31] Even William H. Holmes of the Bureau of American Ethnology eventually entered the fray, as evidenced by a photograph of him taken at the Sulphur Springs site in 1901. We will pick up the story of the Sulphur Springs mastodon again in Chapter 8. When Koch left the site in 1840, he could not have known that 139 years later Sulphur Springs—ironically the one locality at which he found no evidence of human activity—would produce one of the most significant finds in North American archaeology—indisputable proof of mastodons having been killed by humans. On the other hand, if he *had* known, he probably would have shrugged off such news. After all, he had already proved such an association in Missouri, at least to *his* satisfaction.

The Bureau of Ethnology

If one were forced to pick a particular year that highlighted the pre-1880 period in American archaeology, it would have to be 1879—a year that was to leave a lasting impact not only on the manner in which archaeology was conducted but, perhaps more importantly, on the manner in which it was reported. In that year Congress created the Bureau of Ethnology (which changed its name to the Bureau of American Ethnology in 1894) within the Smithsonian Institution. It would be 90 years or so before another congressional action would have such a widespread effect on how archaeology was carried out in the United States. Personnel connected with the bureau would come to dominate Americanist archaeology in the final decades of the nineteenth century and the early decades of the twentieth century, holding sway in a manner that would never be seen again. To be sure, archaeologists connected with private museums and eastern universities, especially Harvard, would leave their mark on the profession in the closing decades of the nineteenth century, but it was the bureau's staff that set the tone for how archaeology was conducted and reported.

For a variety of reasons, archaeologists equate the Bureau of Ethnology with archaeological investigations, though it was formed for anything but that purpose. In fact, its first director—John Wesley Powell (Figure 2.23), the director

---

31. Although James D. Dana's review was published well after the fact, it was particularly damaging to Koch's claim of contemporaneity between humans and mastodons. The fact that Dana was a well-respected professor of geology at Yale University and editor of *The American Journal of Science and Arts* gave his review of the evidence all the more credibility.

Figure 2.23. John Wesley Powell (1834–1902), first director of the Bureau of Ethnology, in his office in the Adams Building on F Street, Washington, D.C., date unknown (photograph by De Lancey Gill, courtesy National Anthropological Archives, Smithsonian Institution).

of the U.S. Geological Survey—was not even interested in archaeology, viewing it initially as a drain on resources. Powell is more remembered in American science for his geological work, especially the mapping of the Grand Canyon, but he had long shown an interest in ethnology (especially linguistics), particularly the study of groups in the western United States (see Darrah 1951 and Stegner 1954 for excellent biographies), and his new bureau's goal was to formalize the scientific study of various indigenous peoples. Over the years, the ethnological side of the bureau established an excellent name for itself, made all the more impressive by the credentials of its staff. Many of the leading ethnologists of the time were either employed directly by the bureau or collaborated with bureau investigators. It is difficult, however, *not* to associate the Bureau of Ethnology with archaeology, if for no other reason than that the members of its prehistory staff were embroiled in two of the most contentious issues facing the emerging discipline of anthropology (which attempted to unite ethnology and archaeology): the identity of the mound builders and the antiquity of human occupation of North America. Those two issues came to dominate a sizable portion of the bureau's attention in the last two decades of the nineteenth century—attention that carried with it a set of enormous egos and powerful voices for the bureau's "official" positions. Archaeological remains from Missouri would, from time to time, figure rather prominently in the formation of those national positions.

3

Mounds and the American Paleolithic

1881–1910

The winds of change were in the air by 1880, and within a surprisingly short time—about a decade and a half—the once widely held belief that the mound builders and the Indians were separate groups was all but dead. Given its longevity in American anthropological thought, it is somewhat surprising how short a time was needed to demonstrate to most prehistorians' satisfaction that the belief was no longer tenable. There undoubtedly was a certain amount of preadaptation that went on during the last quarter of the nineteenth century, by which I mean that a significant number of ethnologists and archaeologists must have been independently coming to the conclusion, if slowly, that the mound builders and the American Indians were one and the same. The contortions that prehistorians were going through in attempting to force the available information into constantly shrinking pigeonholes points out the predicament they faced.

On the one hand, their preconceived, and deeply held, notion was that there were separate groups—a preconception bolstered in part by the disparity between the types of artifacts found in the mounds and those known to have been made by Indians. As long as the two groups could be separated by a large gulf of time, no threat to the proposition existed. In a time when chronological control was simply a matter of the distant past versus the period from 1541 on, the writings of persons such as Samuel Haven were no competition for the wild and speculative stories that made the newspapers, periodicals, and popular books of the United States and Europe. Certainly the evolutionary schemes of Lewis Henry Morgan and others, rather than jeopardizing the notion of two separate groups, reinforced it.

On the other hand, that gulf of time was beginning to shrink little by little. It was becoming obvious that at least some of the materials found in mounds were contemporary with materials recovered from sites with no mounds. Also, despite protestations, it was becoming increasingly obvious that some artifacts from the sixteenth century and later were as elaborately made as any of those derived from mound contexts. In short, it was becoming a strain intellectually to continue to create such scenarios, and I suspect that even some of the more dyed-in-the-wool "separatists" were beginning to concede that the "impassable gulf" to which Conant (1879a: 78) had referred was shrinking to more of a crack.

The nails that were eventually to seal the mound-builder coffin were forged in 1881, when, at the behest of Congress, the Division of Mound Exploration was formed within the Bureau of Ethnology. Received wisdom has long held that John Wesley Powell was the driving force behind the formation of the division, but this is incorrect, as Smith (1990a), Meltzer (1983, 1985), and others have pointed out. Recall that Powell was interested in ethnology, not archaeology. In fact, the amendment to the 1881 bureau appropriations bill that mandated establishment of the mound division apparently came as a surprise to Powell (1894), and he was not an amateur in political matters. He appointed none other than Wills de Hass to head the newly created division, though de Hass's long-searched-for fame was exceedingly short-lived.

De Hass, you may remember, had delivered a vociferous attack at the 1868 annual meeting of the American Association for the Advancement of Science against those who thought there was anything other than an artificial origin to the mounds in the eastern United States. The presentation in which he made his critical remarks was not the only one that he made at the meeting. The more important one was his report as chairman of the AAAS Special Committee on American Archaeology and Ethnology—a position to which he had been appointed at the 1858 meeting in Baltimore. According to de Hass, the work of his committee was spectacularly successful, a success made all the more impressive by a lack of funds:

> The Committee from the first labored under many disadvantages, and serious embarrassment, for want of funds. The anticipated aid from the Government and Societies having failed, the Committee alone relied upon private liberality for means to prosecute the work committed to their charge. A comparatively small fund having been realized from private sources, the system of research which had been adopted was prosecuted with industry and success. The work principally devolved upon the chairman; he laboring without remuneration, and most of the time at his own expense. Notwithstanding these discouragements much has been accomplished. Some of the most interesting localities in the United States have been visited; thousands of earthworks, mounds, circumvallations, etc., examined; specimens of ancient art and industry collected; numerous mounds excavated; extensive groups measured, mapped and described. The result of researches thus far prosecuted have been altogether satisfactory. (de Hass 1869b: 303)

De Hass carefully sowed in his self-aggrandizing remarks the seeds of what he hoped would be a national archaeological movement with himself at the helm:

The chairman would respectfully suggest that some decided action be taken by the Association for promoting inquiry and research. That the functions of the old Committee be either revived, or a new Committee appointed. He is ready and willing to cooperate in any way that may be desired.

He would specially recommend that measures be adopted for securing a National Museum for American Antiquities. To effect this he is willing to make large contributions. He is also willing to devote a portion of his time towards prosecuting scientific research. (de Hass 1869b: 304)

The national museum that de Hass envisioned would eventually be formed within the Smithsonian Institution, but he would not have a part in either its formation or its operation. Of course, he could not have anticipated this in 1868, when he was setting his sights on a position more prestigious even than chairman of a committee on archaeology sanctioned by the most influential scientific organization in America. De Hass's name does not appear in the AAAS membership list for 1869, though he does show up as one of the founding members of the Anthropological Society of Washington (the forerunner of the American Anthropological Association), which was founded in 1879. He was even appointed to a committee to help draft the constitution of the organization, which comprised the leading anthropological figures of the nation's capital. He was elected as one of the vice presidents in 1879 and again in 1880, and during his tenure he presented two papers at regular biweekly meetings (de Hass 1881a, 1881b).

Interestingly, another person who attended the organizational meeting of the ASW in February 1879 was Spencer Baird, who had recently succeeded Joseph Henry as secretary of the Smithsonian Institution. If Meltzer (1985: 251) is correct, it was Baird who lobbied Congress for the rider that established the Division of Mound Exploration within the Bureau of Ethnology. However, Powell (1894) later claimed that "certain [unnamed] archaeologists" had engineered the rider. Meltzer argues that Powell was too good a tactician and lobbyist to allow his opponents to outflank him and that the evidence points to Baird as the stimulus, especially in light of the latter's insistence that the bureau should serve as a source of museum collections (see Hinsley 1981)[1]—a view that Powell did not wholeheartedly share. Smith (1990a), on the other hand, fingers de Hass as the instigator of the congressional creation of the mound-exploration division, that is, as one of the "certain archaeologists" that Powell mentioned in 1894. Indeed, Powell himself noted that "in compliance with the terms of the statute the work of investigating the mounds of the eastern half of the United States was at once organized, and Mr. Wills de Hass was placed in charge, as he was one of the men who had interested himself to have the investigation enlarged" (Powell 1894: xli).

1. Republished as *The Smithsonian and the American Indian: Making of a Moral Anthropology in Victorian America* (Hinsley 1994).

Smith's argument has considerable merit, especially given what we can deduce about de Hass and his ambitions. In fact, there is every reason to suspect that both Meltzer and Smith are correct—that it was de Hass, working through Baird, who effected the creation of the mound-exploration division. But it was Powell, not Baird, who appointed de Hass to head the newly created division, perhaps realizing that by appointing one of his severest critics he could head off any further congressional meddling in the bureau's affairs (Smith 1990a: 28). Ian Brown (1990: 25) suggests that Powell may have found it difficult to immediately jettison de Hass, but the act must have been inevitable. As Smith (1990a: 28) notes, de Hass "just didn't seem to work out," and within a year he resigned his post. Cyrus Thomas (Figure 3.1) replaced de Hass in 1882, and it was he, not de Hass, who was to leave a deep and indelible mark on American archaeology. We can only speculate on the loss of face Wills de Hass suffered, but it is clear that by 1882 he was no longer a member even of the Anthropological Society of Washington.

The Division of Mound Exploration

It appears that from the start Thomas's directive from Powell was to solve the problem of who built the mounds. Writing several years later, in the *Twelfth Annual Report of the Bureau of Ethnology,* Thomas (1894: 21) stated, "The Director of the Bureau of Ethnology was desirous, therefore, that this important question, the origin of the mounds, should if possible be definitely settled, as it is the pivot on which all the other problems must turn." Powell himself early on was convinced that the mound builders and the American Indians were one and the same. In 1881 he noted, "With regard to the mounds so widely scattered between the two oceans, it may also be said that mound-building tribes were known in the early history of discovery of this continent, and that the vestiges of art discovered do not excel in any respect the arts of the Indian tribes known to history. There is, therefore, no reason for us to search for an extra-limital origin through lost tribes for the arts discovered in the mounds of North America" (Powell 1881: 74). The *Transactions of the Anthropological Society of Washington* for January 6, 1884, state that

> President Powell said that papers read before the Society during the past two years seemed to establish the fact that the mound-builders were Indians, and that many Indians built mounds. While small burial mounds were frequent and widely distributed, the larger mounds and earthworks with circumvallation— once probably crowned with palisades—were confined to narrower limits. The old theory that attributed these remains to an extinct high grade of civilization seemed to be well nigh abandoned.

Figure 3.1. Cyrus Thomas (1825–1910), second director of the Mound Exploration Division of the Bureau of Ethnology, ca. 1890 (courtesy National Anthropological Archives, Smithsonian Institution).

However, the fact that Powell was convinced did not mean that everyone else viewed the issue as settled. As Smith (1990a: 29) points out, the debate over who had constructed the earthworks created an obstacle to Powell's drive to obtain a detailed record of North American Indians. Too much time was being taken up by the project, and he told Thomas to get on with the job. Powell obviously wanted no more "blind groping by archaeologists for the thread to lead them out of the mysterious labyrinth" (Thomas 1894: 21).

From more or less the start of his work with the Division of Mound Exploration, Thomas apparently was convinced of the continuity of the mound builders and the American Indian. Writing in *The American Antiquarian and Oriental Journal*, Thomas asked and then answered the question, "'*Who were the mound-builders?*' We answer unhesitatingly, Indians—the ancestors of some, perhaps of several of the tribes of modern or historic times" (Thomas 1884: 90). Based on inspection of his published record, Thomas fulfilled his duties as director of the division admirably, with his crowning glory being the publication of the "Report on the Mound Explorations of the Bureau of Ethnology" in the *Twelfth Annual Report of the Bureau of Ethnology 1890–1891* (Thomas 1894). In it he discussed in great detail the mound explorations carried out by members of his crews as they worked their way over 24 states. Smith (1981, 1985, 1990a) plotted the distribution of the projects, which clearly demonstrates the grouping of activity along the major water courses of the eastern United States, especially the Mississippi River. The major part of the work undertaken by personnel connected with the division took place between July 1882 and June 1885 (Smith 1990a: 34–35), but the work continued into the 1890s. Work in Missouri was conducted mainly under the auspices of Col. P. W. Norris, with the assistance of L. H. Thing (F. S. Earle and James D. Middleton also conducted some work in Missouri). Most of the work in the state was concluded by June 1883 (Perttula and Price 1984; Smith 1990a). During the first year, Norris apparently worked in at least 9 or 10 other states, and Thing spent portions of his time in Arkansas and Illinois (Smith 1990a: 34). From Smith's assessment of the correspondence between Thomas and his field chiefs, one gets the feeling that Thomas was not an easy man to work for. He kept his crews moving around the country at a fevered pace, always tying the next month's paycheck to adequate performance. During the course of the project, the crews visited 140 counties and investigated over 2,000 mound sites.

Some of the information that Thomas demanded of his assistants included "topography of the immediate locality, the form, characters, and dimensions of the works and their relations to one another" (Thomas 1894: 21). Detailed diagrams of excavations and illustrations of artifacts (many prepared by William H. Holmes) accompanied the general descriptions. Smith (1990a: 29–30) points out that Thomas was determined to establish a series of mound types and to determine the geographical range of the various types: "Particular attention has been paid to the mode of construction and methods of burial in the ordinary conical tumuli, because these furnish valuable evidence in regard to the customs of the builders and aid in determining the different archaeological districts" (Thomas 1894: 23).

Historians of archaeology such as Jesse Jennings (1974: 39) have rightfully noted that "Thomas' huge report of a decade of mound exploration by the Bureau of American Ethnology can be thought of as marking the birth of modern

American archeology." In fact, it would be difficult to overemphasize the role played by Thomas and his crews in changing forever the way archaeology is conducted. Thomas had an agenda and demanded rigor in the methods used to gather materials and information. Much of the information generated both by Thomas and by his field parties on mounds in the eastern United States never made it into the 1894 volume. For example, the twelfth *Bulletin of the Bureau of Ethnology* (not to be confused with the *Annual Report* series), entitled "Catalogue of Prehistoric Works East of the Rocky Mountains" (Thomas 1891), contains a state-by-state listing of archaeological sites that were either found by or reported to the survey or that were gleaned from the literature. Of Missouri's 114 counties, 41 are reported to contain sites, the great majority of which are listed as "groups of mounds" (Thomas 1891: plate XI, reproduced here as Figure 3.2). The greatest concentration of sites shown occurred in the southeastern corner of the state, along the Mississippi River and its tributaries.

In preparing his 1891 catalog, Thomas relied for the most part on earlier accounts of the mounds. He gleaned published information from various Smithsonian annual reports, state gazetteers, and journals, as well as from letters sent in to the bureau as a result of a general call for information the Smithsonian sent out as Circular 316,[2] which was similar to the earlier call for assistance put out by the Smithsonian (Gibbs 1862). In the process of compiling the site inventory, Thomas actually added very little in the way of new information. In fact, until publication of his magnum opus in 1894, Thomas's published works were, for the most part, compendia of information on previously discovered sites or short treatises on subjects unrelated to the mounds.

Long delays occurred in producing the final volume on the mounds (Silverberg 1968), though one notes with amusement Powell's repetitive pronouncements in his annual reports that the work was just about completed. These delays undoubtedly caused some concern within the Smithsonian, especially within the Bureau of Ethnology, and probably led to Thomas's having to come up with all kinds of filler to include in the annual reports. Powell apparently wanted to publish the final report, possibly in more than one volume (Silverberg 1968: 215), in the occasional *Contributions to North American Archaeology* series, as

2. Some of the information used in the "Catalogue" can be found in the following sources, with the Missouri counties listed after the references (listed in parentheses after the O. T. Mason 1880 reference is the name of the actual informant listed for each county in Otis T. Mason's summary of correspondence the Smithsonian received as a result of the call for information in Circular 316): Broadhead 1880a—Boone, Callaway, Clay, Franklin, Johnson, Pike, Ralls, Saline; West 1877a—Clay, Platte; Watkins 1883—Pike; Hardy and Scheetz 1883—Ralls; H. L. Mason 1878—Holt; Lykins 1878—Clay; Snyder 1877—Chariton; O. T. Mason 1880—Boone (J. L. Stephens), Buchanan (J. W. Beach), Jasper (W. S. Newlon), Lawrence (J. W. Black, I. S. Drake), Mississippi (W. H. Ballou), Pike (J. C. Watkins), Saline (J. N. Dunlap), Stoddard (Q. C. Smith).

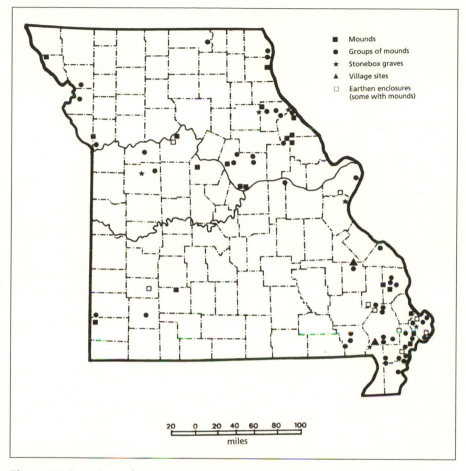

Figure 3.2. Locations of sites in Missouri mentioned in Cyrus Thomas's "Catalogue of Prehistoric Works East of the Rocky Mountains" (after C. Thomas 1891).

Thomas (1891: 9) indicates in his "Catalogue of Prehistoric Works." It is evident that although final publication of the report was delayed until 1894, Thomas had, by the time he wrote the "Catalogue," decided exactly what would go into the report. In the "Catalogue" he used the term *In report* "to denote that the description of the work alluded to will be found in the General Report of the Explorations of the Mound Exploring Division" (Thomas 1891: 9).

Of all the sites listed in the 1891 "Catalogue," only 18 earthworks or sets of earthworks in 9 Missouri counties[3]—Clark, Lewis, St. Louis, Cape Girardeau,

---

3. Actually, because of a locational error, only eight counties were represented. The one site assigned to Scott County actually was in Mississippi County.

Bollinger, Stoddard, Scott, Mississippi, and Butler (Figure 3.3)—were discussed in the 742-page "Report on the Mound Explorations of the Bureau of Ethnology" (Thomas 1894). These ranged from brief excavations in single mounds to extended examinations at larger sites. Marvin Jeter (1986, 1990) points out, correctly I think, that Thomas directly influenced the amount of coverage that any region received, which resulted in overemphasis on regions that he personally considered interesting. The state containing the most counties mentioned in the report was Arkansas (21 counties), followed by Tennessee (13), Illinois (12), Alabama (11), and Ohio and Missouri (9 each). However, in terms of the number of pages in the report dedicated to each state, Tennessee easily ranks first. Perhaps this is not surprising in light of the fact that Thomas was born in Kingsport, Tennessee, and spent the first 24 years of his life there.

Excavations were carried out at 14 of the 18 Missouri sites mentioned in the 1894 report—an unnamed mound group (see also Thomas 1887b) and the Boulware mound group in Clarke County; an unnamed mound in Lewis County; a "salt kettle" pottery scatter in St. Louis County; Lakeville and Rich Woods in Stoddard County; Baker's Mound, Gum Tree Mound, Beckwith's Fort, Beckwith's Ranch, and Meyers mounds in Mississippi County (Meyers mounds were erroneously listed as being in Scott County); and two sets of unnamed mounds and Powers Fort in Butler County. Four sites—the Ben Proffer mound group and an unnamed mound group in Cape Girardeau County, Peter Bess in Bollinger County, and County Line in Stoddard County—were mapped but not excavated.

Excavations ranged from small test trenches placed through small mounds to more thorough examinations at the larger sites. For example, the unnamed mound in Lewis County was examined by means of a single trench, which yielded decayed human bones, ash, and a few pieces of pottery. Thomas (1894: 167) dedicated only two paragraphs to the work, noting that the character of the mound was similar to that of mounds in Clarke County, where the field party had excavated 18 mounds in 2 different groups (Figure 3.4). The longest and most detailed discussions revolved around the work done at the large Mississippian-period sites, namely, Beckwith's Fort (Figure 3.5), Powers Fort, and Rich Woods. Eleven of the 35 mounds Thomas's crew identified at Rich Woods (Figure 3.6) were excavated, as were all 5 mounds at Powers Fort (Figure 3.7). The descriptions of the excavations range from excellent to poor in terms of the amount of detail included, probably a result of the importance Thomas placed on a particular excavation and no doubt a result of the completeness of the field records. Thomas described fill sequences that were evident in some of the mound cuts, but only 2 profiles were illustrated—one from Baker's Mound (Figure 3.8, top), which shows little detail, and one made by Norris of mound 1 at Powers Fort (Figure 3.8, bottom), which is an excellent cross-sectional diagram. Thomas was able to use the field notes and diagram to interpret the successional stages

Figure 3.3. Locations of sites in Missouri mentioned in Cyrus Thomas's "Report on the Mound Explorations of the Bureau of Ethnology": 1, unnamed mound group; 2, Boulware mound group; 3, unnamed mound group; 4, unnamed "salt kettle" pottery locality; 5, Ben Proffer mounds; 6, Witting mounds; 7, Peter Bess settlement; 8, Lakeville settlement; 9, settlement at the county line; 10, Rich Woods mounds; 11, Pin Hook Ridge mounds (Baker's mound, Gum Tree mound, Beckwith's Fort, and Beckwith's Ranch); 12, Meyers mounds (listed in Scott County but actually in Mississippi County); 13, unnamed mound group; 14, unnamed mound group; 15, Powers Fort (after C. Thomas 1894).

of mound construction, in the process producing the first published sectional plan of a Missouri mound that was more than a simplistic sketch.

More important than the excavation descriptions are the site plans and descriptions of site layout. The scale at which they were reproduced makes them difficult to use, but, as with the site plans produced by Potter (1880), they illustrate features that were subsequently destroyed through agricultural

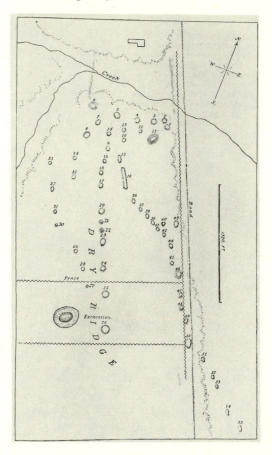

Figure 3.4. Map of mounds in the Boulware group, Clarke County, Missouri (from C. Thomas 1894).

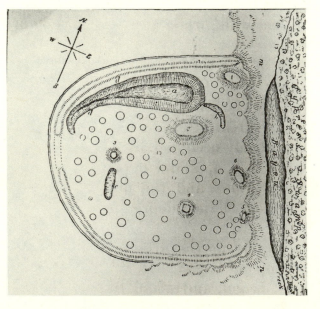

Figure 3.5. Map of Beckwith's Fort, Mississippi County, Missouri (from C. Thomas 1894).

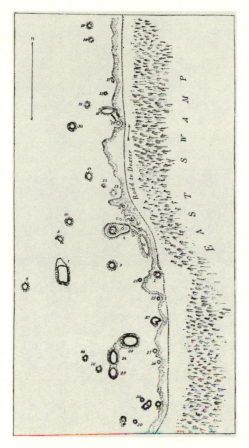

Figure 3.6. Map of the Rich Woods mound group, Stoddard County, Missouri (from C. Thomas 1894).

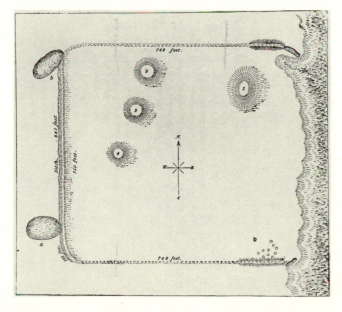

Figure 3.7. Map of Powers Fort, Butler County, Missouri (from C. Thomas 1894).

practices during the twentieth century. An example of the detail evident in the published maps is shown in Figures 3.9 and 3.6, which reproduce Thomas's map of Lakeville and Rich Woods, respectively. Despite the amount of detail shown, the maps are not without their problems. Thomas did not visit each site to check the information supplied by his assistants, though in some cases he did make field inspections and correct earlier information (Thomas 1894: 181). For example, Chapman (1980: 188), in referencing Thomas's (1894: 173–74) description of Lakeville, notes that Thomas's published north–south distance of "200 paces" (using 2.5–3 feet per pace) for the distance between the east–west earthworks severely distorts the map that Thomas produced. In other cases, such as at Rich Woods, Thomas published the actual distances and bearings used to create the maps.

Silverberg (1968: 216) wryly notes that "the [1894] report was not intended for laymen, and little of it makes for lively reading." This is an understatement. The vast majority of the report is given over to describing the mounds and excavations in a language that Silverberg rightly characterizes as methodical, grim, and ponderous. Thomas developed a final list of 11 "theses" that were set forth in the report, up from an earlier 8 that had appeared in the *Fifth Annual Report of the Bureau of Ethnology* (Thomas 1887a) and down from the 13 theses that had appeared in the fourth *Bureau of Ethnology Bulletin* (Thomas

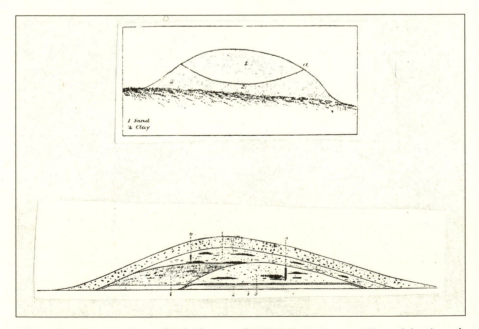

Figure 3.8. Cross sections of Baker's mound, Mississippi County, Missouri (top), and mound I at Powers Fort, Butler County, Missouri (bottom) (from C. Thomas 1894).

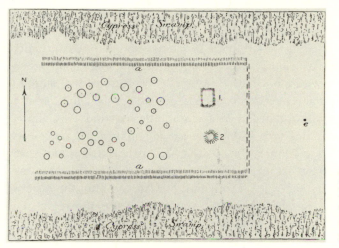

Figure 3.9. Map of the
Lakeville site, Stoddard
County, Missouri
(from C. Thomas
1894).

1887b). The first and the last two of his theses were the most important, and the majority of the nondescriptive portions of the report were dedicated to marshaling support for these three points:

(1) That the mound-builders of the area designated consisted of a number of tribes or peoples bearing about the same relations to one another and occupying about the same culture-status as did the Indian tribes inhabiting this country when first visited by Europeans. . . .

(10) The testimony of the mounds is very decidedly against the theory that the mound-builders were Mayas or Mexicans who were driven out of this region by the pressure of Indian hordes and migrated to the valley of Anahuac [the Valley of Mexico] or plains of Yucatan. It is also as decidedly against Morgan's theory that they were related to the Pueblo tribes of New Mexico. It likewise gives a decided negative to the suggestion that the builders of the Ohio works were pushed south into the Gulf states and incorporated into the Muskokee group.

(11) Although much the larger portion of the ancient monuments of our country belong to prehistoric times, and some of them, possibly, to the distant past, yet the evidence of contact with European civilization is found in so many mounds where it can not be attributed to intrusive burial and in such widely separated localities, that it must be conceded that many of them were built subsequent to the discovery of the continent by Europeans. (Thomas 1894: 17–18)

It took him 730 pages, but Thomas effectively laid to rest most of the major speculations regarding the nature of the earthworks and the groups responsible for erecting them. Thomas claimed the evidence was there if anyone but examined it halfway critically, especially the fact that late-period earthworks—the ones with European items in them—were similar to those from earlier periods. And, importantly, Thomas noted that there was no logical reason to suspect that the mound builders were of Mexican origin or that Indian groups had pushed the mound builders south. In other words, the archaeological record demonstrated to Thomas's satisfaction that a high degree of cultural continuity had existed in the eastern United States for an untold number of millennia and that that thread of continuity showed no major disruptions. It is clear to twentieth-century archaeologists that change had occurred; this is indicated in the myriad forms of earthworks recorded and the different kinds of artifacts found within them—but this type of change was an orderly progression as opposed to a punctuated, disruptive progression such as that that would have occurred had the Indians in fact pushed out the mound builders. In Thomas's mind, however, continuity had ruled throughout human tenure in the eastern United States, and it is clear that he favored tribal differences to explain the immense variation evident in the archaeological record.

An Increasingly Minority Opinion

Not all prehistorians necessarily shared Thomas's opinions on orderly continuity, and there certainly was still disagreement over the relationship between mound builders and Indians, though most opponents of the Indian-as-mound-builder view probably admitted privately that the weight of evidence was becoming difficult to bear. For some, Lewis Henry Morgan's (1877) notion of cultural "progress" among ancient peoples—a type of progress that was fueled by just the type of disruptive processes that were anathema to Thomas's scheme—was too ingrained to jettison simply because people such as Cyrus Thomas disdained it. As we will see in the next section, even William H. Holmes, Thomas's colleague at the Bureau of American Ethnology (BAE), had a difficult time expunging Morgan's terminology from his artifact studies. It was just too easy to fall back on the notion of a ladder of progress as an explanation for culture change.

Nowhere is this disruptive progression more evident than in numerous articles that appeared in *The American Antiquarian and Oriental Journal,* one of the major ethnological and archaeological journals of the late nineteenth century. The journal was edited by Stephen D. Peet, a minister, who never missed an opportunity, through both articles and editorials, to educate the large readership on the differences between the mound builders and the American Indians. Ironically, Peet had worked for a while as an assistant to Thomas, though it is abundantly clear that he was not a convert to the Indian-as-mound-builder way of thinking. To be more precise, he waffled on the subject, which was not unusual in the last decade of the nineteenth century. As more and more evidence piled up against the mound-builder myth, proponents found their position increasingly untenable. However, instead of abandoning the notion entirely, they often created various hybrid scenarios that seemingly bridged the gulf between the two viewpoints. These were last-ditch efforts that were doomed to failure because of the irreconcilable nature of the dichotomous positions. In 1893, when he was in a decidedly pro-mound-builder mood, Peet wrote an editorial entitled "The Archaeologists and the Geologists," which is a classic example of how Morgan's tripartite scheme was applied to the archaeological record:

> The system Mr. L. H. Morgan has given fits remarkably well into the geography [of North America]; and the prehistoric map of America [Figure 3.10] wonderfully illustrates the different stages of human growth. The social status is divided into first, second and third grade of savagery; first, second and third grade of barbarism; and two grades of civilization. The social grades seem to be dependent upon the means of subsistence, the material surroundings and other physical causes. (Peet 1893: 51–52)

Peet's point was that the map could be read by archaeologists in exactly the same manner as a geologist reads a column of rock, using the law of superposition, that is, older things will be on the bottom (to the south on the map) and younger things will be on the top (to the north on the map):

> The strata appear, as we pass over the continent from south to north, exactly in the order in which they would appear if we were going down beneath the surface in certain localities. We find the relics and remains, the symbols and ornaments, the tribal and religious customs, growing simpler and ruder as we traverse the continent, each one fairly representing the different ages and periods. These are as instructive in reference to the culture periods and many other subjects which we are investigating, as are those which come from deep explorations, and we conclude that the study of the map will be as profitable as the study of the uncertain horizon of the gravel beds. (Peet 1893: 47)

It was obvious, at least to Peet (and he was by no means alone), that the center of civilization in North America lay in the warmer latitudes, in Mexico and Guatemala. Groups such as the Mayas and Toltecs (who themselves, Peet suspected, were descendants of Asian peoples who migrated to the New World) were obviously capable of building cities containing impressive stone architecture and thousands of people. Note in Figure 3.10 that as one moves northward, civilization declines and one passes through successive levels of barbarism until finally, at a latitude roughly equal to the border between the United States and Canada, one passes into the highest level of savagery. By the time the Arctic Circle is reached, one enters the lowest level of savagery and encounters rude "Hyperboreans," who barely eke out an existence in an ice-covered land.

In an earlier article, Peet (1890) had noted the differences between mound-builder and Indian implements and had reached a startling conclusion: that

Figure 3.10. Stephen Peet's grades of culture in North America. Note the decrease in "grade" from south to north, corresponding to what Peet perceived as responses to the degrees of harshness of the physical environment. People living in the temperate climate of southern Mexico thus were able to reach civilization, but people at the Arctic Circle had the wherewithal to exist only as savages (from Peet 1893).

contact with Euro-Americans had led to the decline in the ability of Native Americans to manufacture high-quality articles. He raised an interesting question—one that must have been going through the minds of many prehistorians: Was the mound builder–Indian dichotomy real, or was it a matter of semantics? In other words, did the Indians displace the mound builders or had they evolved out of the mound builders? Regardless, according to Peet, there was a stark contrast between the elaborate items found in the earthworks—highly decorated ceramic vessels, ornate pipes, copper ornaments, and the like—and the rather drab items that early Europeans and Euro-Americans had seen the Indians make and use. To Peet, if one accepted that the mound builders *had* evolved into the Indians, then the decline in artistic ability could only have been a result of direct contact between early Indian groups and Europeans:

> The character of the art which was introduced at an early date and copied by the aborigines and embodied in their relics was, to be sure. very rude compared with that which had existed earlier; but the very advance of the white man's art had a tendency to overshadow and supplant the aboriginal art. Now we have only to apply the term Indian to this deteriorated art, as we do Mound-builder to the art before it had deteriorated, and we shall at once notice a marked distinction between them. The Mound-builder changed to Indian merely by contact with the white man. (Peet 1890: 253)

This tidy scenario ostensibly accounted for the difference between the chrono-logically older mound-builder items and the newer Indian material, but Peet must have realized that he had another problem to contend with. By the 1890s excavations were beginning to document that "crude" items often occurred alongside the more ornate items in burial contexts. If the Indians evolved out of the mound builders, then crude items should only be found in chronologically late contexts. How did one explain the contemporaneity? Peet's answer was that there were "Indianlike" groups along the Atlantic coast that were contemporaries of the mound builders and that at various times overran the mound builders and transplanted their cruder material culture. In essence, Peet *had* to develop some such proposition to explain the presence of "ornate" as well as "crude" objects in contemporary contexts in the earthworks.

What apparently had not occurred to Peet in 1890, though it certainly had by 1893, was that this scheme ran counter to those proposed by Morgan and others. The evolutionary progression, which Peet embraced in his later article, was supposed to run directionally from savagery, to barbarism, to civilization, not the other way around. Thus the mound builders should be the last step on the ladder, as opposed to the first, and their contact with Europeans should have bumped them up the ladder one step, not back down. But Peet had no conceptual problem in having the technologically superior Europeans adversely affect the artistic ability of the mound builders. Thus, it was easy for him to explain away crude but chronologically late artifacts as being tied to the collapse of the artistic ability of the mound builders.

But where did the mound builders come from? If we read between the lines of what Peet (1890) wrote, they had evolved from less-civilized groups, some of which were still around during the golden age of the mound builders. Where did these uncivilized groups come from, and how long were they on the North

American continent before some of them became mound builders? As we will see shortly, the questions of where and when had been brewing for decades and would reach the boiling point before the close of the century.

Artifact Analysis: Beyond Simple Description

One of the quirks of Cyrus Thomas's work is that he never expended much energy describing the artifacts recovered from the numerous excavations he directed. Thomas (1894: 22–23) noted, "The number of specimens collected by the division since its organization is not less than 40,000. . . . Perhaps the most important portion of the collection from an archaeological view is the pottery, of which some 1,500 specimens have been obtained, including most of the known varieties and several that are new in form and ornamentation." He did not elaborate on what he meant by "specimens," though I take it to mean complete or nearly complete vessels. We know, for example, that "some 45 or 50 whole vessels" were recovered from Beckwith's Ranch in Mississippi County, Missouri (Thomas 1894: 191), and that many of those were given to the landowner. In other cases, landowners and tenants donated pieces to the field parties. Thomas made it clear that his priority was not artifact descriptions: "It is proper to state here that only a partial study of the articles collected has as yet been made. Papers by specialists, describing and discussing them, are being prepared and will appear hereafter" (Thomas 1894: 25).

The most encompassing studies of aboriginal pottery conducted during the pre-1910 era were those by William Henry Holmes (Figure 3.11), an energetic scholar who at various stages of his career was a member of the U.S. Geological Survey under Powell, honorary curator of aboriginal pottery at the U.S. National Museum (Smithsonian Institution), illustrator of BAE reports, and, in 1889, the person responsible for carrying out the bureau's archaeological fieldwork. Holmes left the Smithsonian in 1894 to accept a curator's position at the newly founded Field Museum in Chicago but returned to the National Museum as head curator of anthropology in 1897. He subsequently, upon Powell's death in 1902, assumed the directorship of the BAE, a position he held until 1909, when he returned to the National Museum as head curator; he later served as director of the newly created National Gallery of Art.

As discussed in the next section, Holmes worked mightily to debunk the idea that humans had been present in North America during the Pleistocene—a mission that led him to investigate and report on the famous gravel beds and chert quarries of the time. He also had an interest in aboriginal mining, which led to an article in the *American Anthropologist* on prehistoric iron mining near Leslie, Missouri (Holmes 1903b). But it is his sustained interest in pottery that concerns us here. In 1884, while working for the U.S. Geological Survey and on

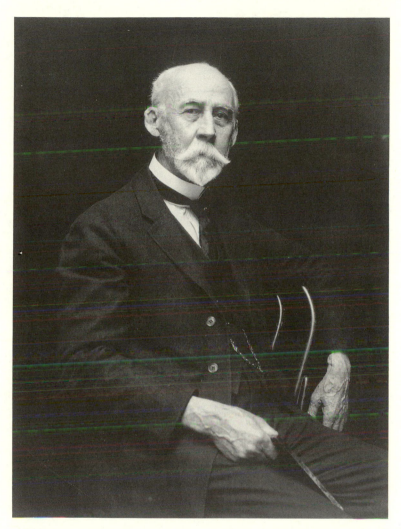

Figure 3.11. William Henry Holmes (1846–1933), second director (he changed the title to "chief" upon assuming office) of the Bureau of American Ethnology, 1925 (photograph by De Lancey Gill, courtesy National Anthropological Archives, Smithsonian Institution).

the side as illustrator for the Bureau of Ethnology, Holmes produced the first of three large overviews of pottery from the Mississippi Valley. That work, entitled "Illustrated Catalogue of a Portion of the Collections Made by the Bureau of Ethnology during the Field Season of 1881," was published in the *Third Annual Report of the Bureau of Ethnology* (Holmes 1884) and was exactly what its name implied: drawings and descriptions of some of the items recovered by Thomas's field parties.

That work was followed by "Ancient Pottery of the Mississippi Valley" (Holmes 1886b), which appeared in the *Fourth Annual Report of the Bureau of Ethnology* (the report also carried a more general work by Holmes entitled "Origin and Development of Form and Ornament in Ceramic Art" [Holmes 1886a]). The "Ancient Pottery" article was an intensive examination of ceramic vessels from what Holmes termed the Middle Mississippi Province, that portion of the Mississippi River valley centered on southeastern Missouri, northeastern Arkansas, and northwestern Tennessee. The third summary, entitled "Aboriginal Pottery of the Eastern United States," appeared in the *Twentieth Annual Report of the Bureau of American Ethnology* (Holmes 1903a). That study, widely recognized as Holmes's greatest work, had a tremendous effect on how the archaeological record was viewed throughout the first quarter of the twentieth century. In their introduction to the reprint of Holmes's magnum opus, Meltzer and Dunnell point out that Holmes

> spent considerable effort in providing a background and theoretical rationale for the study of pottery (1903a: 15–79), but this section is a series of warnings rather than directives. The investigation of pottery was conceived as having one of two ends, as a tool for the investigation of the "histories of peoples" and as the development of a particular technology (art). For the first purpose, though limited to the upper savages and barbarian grades, Holmes saw pottery as second only to readable written records because of the near universality of pottery (near universal availability of materials and a universal need for containers), its chemical stability, and its ability to reflect different cultural elements in its manufacture (1903a: 18). He warned against strictly homologous interpretations, pointing out the possibility for parallelisms as well as accidental resemblances (1903a: 19). Similarly, although he adopted geographic groupings as his main structure from his earlier work in the Mississippi Valley (Holmes 1886b), he cautioned against regarding such groupings as having ethnic or cultural significance (1903a: 21, 81), a caution he frequently forgot later in the work (e.g., 1903a: 130, 145, 159, 178). Holmes appreciated that ceramics had the potential for providing chronology: "We may reasonably anticipate that in time the ceramic evidence will materially assist in determining the succession of peoples and also in arriving at a somewhat definite chronology of events" (Holmes 1903a: 116). Yet Holmes did not explore such avenues himself. (Meltzer and Dunnell 1992: xxxvii)

Holmes's 1903 report contained numerous drawings by the author (Figure 3.12), some in color, of ceramic vessels from Missouri, many of which were recovered by Thomas's field parties. It also contained vessels in the collections of the Peabody Museum (Harvard), the Academy of Natural Sciences of Philadelphia, and the Academy of Natural Sciences at Davenport, Iowa. As important as the report was, especially in terms of its ability to draw together diverse information on pottery manufacture and design from different regions of the eastern United States, it perhaps was Holmes's second volume, "Ancient Pottery of the Mississippi Valley" (1886b), that was his most significant report. In it Holmes focused primarily on materials from northeastern Arkansas that were in the Davenport academy, supplementing the discussion with a few pieces from Tennessee and a couple of items from Arkansas that were in the National Museum. Holmes's description of the pottery was remarkably insightful and for the most part has passed the test of time. For example, with regard to technological variables he noted:

> The material employed was usually a moderately fine-grained clay, tempered, in a great majority of cases, with pulverized shells. The shells used were doubtless obtained from the neighboring rivers. In many of the vessels the particles are large, measuring as much as one-fourth or even one-half of an inch in width, but in the most elegant vases the shell has been reduced to a fine powder. Powdered potsherds were also used. The clay was, apparently, often impure or loamy. It was, probably, at times, obtained from recent alluvial deposits of the bayous—the sediment of overflows—as was the potter's clay of the Nile. There is no reason for believing that the finer processes of powdering and levigation were known. A slip or wash of very finely comminuted clay was sometimes applied to the surface of the vessel. The walls of the vessels are often thick and uneven, and are always quite porous, a feature of little or no importance in the storage of drinking-water, but one resulting from accident rather than from design. (Holmes 1886b: 372–73)

In that one short paragraph Holmes identified the key elements that, as we shall later see, formed the basis for the archaeological categorization of ceramic materials from the central Mississippi River valley. He recognized two distinct size grades of shell temper—coarse and fine—and noted the presence of clay temper in some vessels. The last line of the above-cited paragraph is important in several respects, the most significant being that Holmes denied that the porosity of shell-tempered pottery was purposeful. In other words, he was removing direct human intent as a cause of something. Such a view was rare in the late nineteenth century, even if the something being referred to was as mundane as vessel porosity. Compare Holmes's statement on porosity with that by J. W. Foster on "water jugs" from the central Mississippi River valley: "Being unglazed, they would permit water to permeate slowly through the pores, and thus, by evaporation, produce a temperature below that of the surrounding air,—a device resorted to, at this day, in tropical climates, to keep water cool" (Foster 1873a: 95). One does not have to read much into that statement to see that Foster saw the high porosity of the "water jugs" as an intentional result.

As interesting and informative as Holmes's analyses were, one variable was left out of the equation. At the time, this omission probably went unnoticed, but in retrospect it can be seen as symptomatic of not only Holmes's work but also that of other bureau prehistorians. That omission had to do with time. It is difficult to read Holmes's accounts of pottery from the Mississippi Valley and obtain

Figure 3.12. Drawings by William Henry Holmes of Mississippian-period vessels from southeastern Missouri and northeastern Arkansas that appeared in his "Aboriginal Pottery of the Eastern United States" (after Holmes 1903a).

any kind of feel for how he treated chronological development. In fact, time meant little to Holmes, as he himself noted (Holmes 1903a: 116), and he treated all of the material remains he analyzed as having been produced by various Indian groups—groups that were geographically separate (hence the variation in vessel manufacture and decoration) and essentially timeless. The manufacturers were Indians (albeit in different stages of orderly progress), and that was all that really mattered. From the bureau point of view, archaeological analysis should be geared toward sorting out geographically induced variation—without much regard to chronologically induced variation—and tying that geographic variation to specific Indian tribes. That perspective is evident in Holmes's work, and it certainly shows clearly in Thomas's (1894) final report on the mound exploration.

The role that this perspective played in shaping American archaeology during the last decade of the nineteenth century and the first two decades of the twentieth century is difficult to overestimate. Most treatments of American archaeology during that period reference the contentious issues of the time, but they tend to ignore a deep philosophical split that occurred in the discipline and, more importantly, the underlying reasons for that split. The split was not over the mounds and who built them—that issue was settled, for the most part— but rather over the antiquity of human occupation of North America. Holmes was at the center of the split, as were his contemporaries at the BAE and their intellectual adversaries at several universities, particularly those at the Peabody Museum at Harvard. Several sites in Missouri had figured prominently in earlier discussions of human antiquity in America, and another would soon be in the spotlight. To put all these stories in perspective, we have to examine more closely the debates over human antiquity that took place at the end of the nineteenth century and the beginning of the twentieth.

How Long Have Humans Been in North America?

In Chapter 2 I mentioned in passing several lines of reasoning that were employed in the mid–nineteenth century to judge the antiquity of humans in North America, but, because I chose to focus on Koch and the story of his mastodons, I ignored the others. However, those other lines—the positioning of stone tools in glacial gravels and the similarity of stone tools found in North America to those found in European gravel beds—were as important as the association of stone tools and mastodon bones in the great debate over human antiquity in North America. The two lines of reasoning were interrelated. As the reasoning went, if the forms of certain tools from North America were identical to those recovered from undisputed European Paleolithic (translated literally as "old stone" age) contexts, then perhaps North America had experienced its own Paleolithic period of human occupation. American prehistorians were, of course, familiar with the findings of their European colleagues[4]—findings that were given a tremendous boost through the publication in 1863 of Sir Charles Lyell's

4. Joseph Henry, for example, published a translation of A. von Morlot's article on Danish shell middens and Swiss lake dwellings in the Smithsonian *Annual Report* series (von Morlot 1861).

Geological Evidences of the Antiquity of Man, which added instant credibility to the claims of great antiquity that had earlier been made by antiquarians such as Jacques Boucher de Perthes (1847). The European claims of great antiquity were based on the same evidence used in part by American prehistorians: (1) the positioning of flaked-stone tools in glacial-gravel deposits and (2) the recovery of stone tools in association with extinct mammals. And, unlike in America, in Europe there were clear associations of tools and extinct mammals.

I want to examine the issues of stratigraphic position and association with extinct mammals separately, because it becomes too easy to miss several subtle yet important points when one considers them together. As I hope to show, the stratigraphic issue was by far the more important of the two during the late decades of the nineteenth century.

Stratigraphic Position and an American Paleolithic

One characteristic of many of the chipped-stone pieces recovered from supposedly glacial-period contexts across the midwestern and eastern United States (e.g., Babbitt 1884a, 1884b; Claypole 1896; Cresson 1890a, 1890b) was their crude appearance—cruder certainly than the well-made projectile points and other tools that were familiar to North American prehistorians. Given the then-current views on cultural evolution and the ladderlike nature of unilinear evolutionary schemes, it was difficult *not* to make the assumption that technologically "inferior" tools (or, more precisely, what were *assumed* to be tools) were left by earlier people.

Six vocal advocates of the presence of Paleolithic humans in North America were Charles Abbott (e.g., 1872, 1876, 1877, 1881, 1888), Frederic W. Putnam (1888, 1890), Thomas Wilson (1889, 1895b, 1899), W J McGee (1889) (who later switched positions), Henry W. Haynes (1893), and G. Frederick Wright (1888, 1890, 1892, 1893, 1895a–b).[5] Their arguments in favor of great antiquity for humans on the continent were based not only on the stratigraphic position of artifacts in glacial deposits but also on the similarities between Paleolithic tools in the Old World and the rather crude tools found in various North American gravel deposits, including the most publicized of all, the Trenton gravels in New Jersey. Proponents argued that since the two sets of tools looked the same, they must date to the same time period (e.g., T. Wilson 1889, 1895b).

The faulty logic behind this argument was not lost on Holmes, who began as early as 1892 a series of articles aimed at discrediting the great antiquity of humans in the New World (e.g., Holmes 1892, 1893a–f, 1894, 1897a–b). Part of

---

5. This is an extremely abbreviated list of citations. For example, in his article "On 'Paradigms' and 'Paradigm Bias,'" Meltzer (1991) cites 22 articles and books by Charles Abbott and 27 by G. F. Wright, and even his list is selective.

his strategy was to demonstrate the stages of manufacture that stone implements went through and thereby to show that items others had bandied about as ancient implements were instead preforms or quarry rejects of comparatively recent age. This led to his excavations in Piney Branch[6] and related quarries in the Washington, D.C., area and finally to his article "Stone Implements of the Potomac-Chesapeake Tidewater Province," published in the *Fifteenth Annual Report of the Bureau of Ethnology* (Holmes 1897b). In it Holmes conclusively demonstrated the universal reduction process that raw stone goes through on its way to being a finished piece and the similarity in form between rejects and blanks in American quarries and Paleolithic implements from Europe. The take-home message was clear: Don't confuse relatively recent, crude American quarry waste and "blanks" (the word archaeologists use for unfinished tools) with finished implements, even though the waste or blanks resemble true European Paleolithic tools.

The Trenton gravels quickly assumed center stage in the battle over a North American Paleolithic. Proponents and opponents alike visited and revisited the gravel beds, examining firsthand the thick stratigraphic sections and the tools that were purportedly being found there. One of the most widely read summaries of the work—written from a Paleolithic proponent's point of view—was G. Frederick Wright's *Man and the Glacial Period*, published in 1892 and revised in 1895 (Wright 1892, 1895a). In it Wright discussed evidence for the European Paleolithic, which by that time was overwhelmingly accepted as fact, and compared European materials with items from the Trenton gravels and other North American sites. He reached what was for him an inescapable conclusion: the chipped-stone pieces that had been recovered from deep within the gravel beds at Trenton during the 1880s were indeed tools. Their similarity in form to European paleoliths and the fact that they were in the glacial gravels was overwhelming evidence that humans were in the Delaware Valley during the glacial period.

Holmes, in a review of Wright's book, questioned not only the nature of the context in which the supposed paleoliths occurred—"The uprooting of forest trees intermingles the contents of the soil to the depth of three or four feet and the various excavations conducted upon a town site in 200 years of occupation makes 'recorded' depths to twice or thrice that depth of most uncertain value" (Holmes 1893f: 35)—but also the assumption that the so-called artifacts from the Trenton gravels were tools. He argued that

> these objects are referred to as *implements,* as if no question as to their exact nature had ever been raised. It is upon the assumption that they are bona fide

6. Holmes consistently spelled it "Piny."

implements, that the theory of a culture otherwise unobserved in America is set up and elaborated. Implements are objects adapted to a use, and the evidence of their status as implements is specialization of shape or indications of modification by use, neither of which features is observed in any single one of the sixty-four specimens upon which so much has been predicated of peoples and culture and age. That they resemble certain types of European paleolithic implements is sufficient for our author, who overlooks the important fact that they bear a much closer resemblance to the thousands of rude failures found upon Indian work shops in all parts of this country. (Holmes 1893f: 35–36)

Of course, it was only Holmes's opinion that the pieces from the Trenton gravels and other gravel beds bore more of a resemblance to quarry waste than to European paleoliths, a point raised forcefully by geologist and paleontologist Henry W. Haynes (1893) in a rejoinder to Holmes's review of Wright's book. What Holmes probably should have said was that *some* of the Trenton "tools" resembled quarry waste and some resembled tools, because there probably were some specimens from Trenton and elsewhere that did resemble European Paleolithic tools (Haynes 1892 [see Meltzer 1991]). But one or two implements did not imply that the European Paleolithic had been duplicated on the North American continent, as Holmes (1892: 297) had earlier pointed out: "Even if rude flaked stones are found in gravels ten times as old as the Trenton gravels, it must still be shown that they are not neolithic before it can be safely asserted that they are palaeolithic, for the exclusively rude period of flaked art observed in Europe is so extraordinary that its repetition in other countries would approach the marvellous." To Haynes (1893: 39), however, such a repetition was anything but extraordinary: "Is there anything marvelous in the fact that man everywhere should have passed through similar stages of progress, if he is everywhere the same being?"

Haynes (1893: 42) concluded his attack on Holmes with the Latin phrase *Magna est veritas et prae-vale-bit.* He was correct in this; truth *is* great and it *did* prevail. However, the truth that eventually emerged from the bitter and acrimonious debate over the American Paleolithic was not quite what Haynes had foreseen. In retrospect, Haynes was wrong and Holmes was right—the American Paleolithic was not "Paleolithic" at all—but it would be the height of arrogance to suggest that he was anything but a highly competent observer. He understood well the sequences of gravel terrace deposits in the Somme Valley region of France, where the European Paleolithic was first defined (he had viewed the deposits and implements from them firsthand, as had Wright) as well as sequences of deposits in North American localities, and he made explicit distinctions between the Paleolithic and Neolithic periods (e.g., Haynes 1888). His only error was in assuming that tools from North American and European gravels that were similar in form were also similar in age—a fatal error, but one not committed because of ignorance.

Most histories of archaeology, in treating the issue of an American Paleolithic, concentrate on what was said during the debate and ignore the underlying reasons for the rift that developed in American archaeology over the question of human antiquity. Meltzer (1983, 1985, 1991), in an excellent analysis of the period, points out that the fundamental issue was in the way the BAE archaeologists viewed the past, as opposed to the way archaeologists working outside the bureau viewed it. Bureau personnel saw the North American archaeological record as essentially one that had been left by the Indians and not by an unrelated group of mound builders that had preceded them. Powell's whole strategy had been to use archaeology to extend back in time the story of the American Indian, and that story certainly did not need "the idea of an earlier, unrelated Paleolithic 'race'" (Meltzer and Dunnell 1992: xxxiii). Non-BAE prehistorians, however, did not share this atemporal view, and it was they who argued vehemently that the gravel beds contained rich in-situ deposits of Paleolithic tools.

Meltzer considers the differences in outlook brought to bear on the question of human antiquity in North America to have been in large part natural outgrowths of differences in education:

> Most BAE archaeologists had earned their scientific credentials on geological and natural history expeditions to the deep canyons and vast Plains of the American West. This education was a wholly democratic American experience: anyone could be a scientist given a sufficient amount of energy and intellect. Formal training in a European university was not only unnecessary, it was viewed with a certain amount of disdain. The result was an innovative and highly nationalistic archaeology, with the American Indian as its centerpiece. . . .
>
> This was not the case among archaeologists outside the BAE, particularly those in the universities, which closely followed European lines. Contemporary European archaeologists viewed their discipline as an extension of history into prehistoric times (Trigger 1978). The strategy was historical rather than anthropological, with attention to sequence and detail. (Meltzer 1985: 251 [see also Meltzer 1991])

Meltzer is correct that scientific education for BAE personnel was a "wholly democratic American experience"; none of the leading figures in the bureau were trained ethnologists or archaeologists, yet all had the opportunity to join the field. For example, Powell was a geologist; Thomas had been, among other things, an entomologist; Holmes an artist; William J. (known almost exclusively as W J) McGee a geologist who did not even have an eighth-grade education; and Henry Henshaw an ornithologist. But all had received extensive on-the-job training in various aspects of anthropology, and most had carried out their new duties in admirable fashion. Meltzer further draws the distinction between BAE personnel and those prehistorians trained in European universities by examining how they lined up on the question of human antiquity in North America. On

Figure 3.13. Frederic Ward Putnam (1839–1915), second curator of the Peabody Museum of American Archaeology and Ethnology (Harvard), ca. 1909 (courtesy Peabody Museum, Harvard University).

the side arguing that there had not been a North American Paleolithic period were Powell and his BAE associates, notably Holmes, McGee, and to a lesser extent Thomas; on the other side, arguing that a North American Paleolithic had existed, were prehistorians Frederic Ward Putnam (Figure 3.13) of the Peabody Museum (Harvard), Warren K. Moorehead of the Phillips Academy in Andover, Massachusetts, Thomas Wilson of the National Museum, geologists G. Frederick Wright and Henry Lewis, and geologist and paleontologist Haynes.

One curious feature of the BAE team roster is the inclusion of McGee, who I earlier noted was a proponent of a Paleolithic occupation of North America. But that had been the early W J McGee (Figure 3.14), before Powell brought him into the bureau in 1893. Once there, he became a total convert to whatever line of thought Powell espoused. Other BAE archaeologists certainly were capable of lambasting their opponents in print, but it was Powell's bulldog, McGee, who specialized in character assassination. In reviewing Wright's *Man and the Glacial Period,* McGee labeled Wright's evidence of human occupation of the North American continent during the glacial period a "tissue of error and misinterpretation" and Wright himself a "betinseled charlatan whose potions are poison" (McGee 1893a: 94, 95).[7] McGee, as Meltzer (1985) and Hinsley (1981)

---

7. See Meltzer 1983 (17–20) for an overview of McGee's vitriolic reviews of Wright's book. McGee's various private and published reactions were at best nothing more than ad hominem attacks and

Figure 3.14. W J McGee (1853–1912) and friends on an outing to the soapstone quarry in west Washington, D.C.: W J McGee and Anita McGee at the left; Otis T. Mason, with staff; Rollin D. Salisbury at far right, ca. 1900 (from Hinsley 1994, courtesy National Museum of American Art, Smithsonian Institution).

at worst libelous accusations. Some of the things McGee had to say were so offensive (e.g., McGee 1893a, 1893b) that many individuals who disagreed with Wright over his interpretations offered him their personal support relative to his integrity.

point out, positioned himself in Washington academic circles to become the leading critic of "glacial man." And he positioned himself in many scientific groups: when the Washington Academy of Science was founded in 1898, McGee was the only person who belonged to all 12 constituent societies of the umbrella organization.

At the 1897 meeting of the American Association for the Advancement of Science, McGee, who was president of Section H (anthropology), chaired a symposium that featured expert opinions on the nature of the Trenton gravels, which were famous by then. Did they, as Putnam and Abbott had long claimed, contain conclusive evidence of human occupation of the Delaware Valley during the last glaciation, or did they contain objects that had been modified by nature to resemble stone tools and/or tools from a much later period that had made their way into the early deposit? The scholarly exchanges changed no one's mind (Holmes 1897a; F. W. Putnam 1897), which is not surprising in light of the fact that even firsthand inspections of the gravel beds had resulted in an impasse. McGee, as Meltzer (1985: 255) points out, had the last word on the matter: "Fifteen years ago there was hardly an archaeologist who did not regard the Trenton region as affording conclusive evidence of glacial man; today the manner in which the evidence has been torn to shreds is apparent to everyone" (W J McGee 1897a; see also W J McGee 1897b and A. N. McGee 1897[8]). McGee was correct; as Meltzer and Dunnell (1992: xvi) note, "The controversy over human antiquity in America would last another three decades (see Meltzer 1983, 1991), but . . . the American Paleolithic was lost. By the turn of the century, new 'discoveries' of American paleoliths had virtually ceased (Meltzer 1991)." The controversy that was to continue into the first couple of decades of the twentieth century would be over human skeletons, not stone tools. Interestingly, when it came to the mound-builder issue, BAE personnel were the clear winners. On the matter of a Paleolithic in North America, their game plan was executed superbly in that they effectively killed any analogy between North American stone tools and those from the Old World. But they overextended those efforts in an attempt to squelch any possibility of deep antiquity of humans in North America. It would be stone tools that eventually proved them wrong.

Humans and Mastodons

If the scientific world would, finally, abandon the notion of Paleolithic remnants buried deep in the glacial gravels of the northern third of the North American continent, what would they do with the occurrence of artifacts found

---

8. Anita Newcomb McGee, W J McGee's wife, was secretary of Section H and summarized the meeting for *Science* (Meltzer 1985: 255).

in association with the remains of extinct mammals, especially when those large mammals—mastodons, mammoths, and the like—were known to have lived during the Ice Age? It was one thing to find crudely flaked pieces of stone in glacial gravels—they could be explained away too easily—but it was another to find well-shaped dart and spear points in association with late-glacial-period animal remains. Those instances were difficult to dismiss out of hand. Certainly by the second half of the nineteenth century British and French geologists, paleontologists, and prehistorians were being won over to the notion that there was considerable antiquity to the human presence in Europe and, importantly, that humans had coexisted with mammals that since had become extinct.

Not everyone in Europe was satisfied with the evidence; in fact, there was a splinter opinion that perhaps the animals had survived longer than commonly assumed and therefore their association with humans was not of great antiquity. As Grayson (1983: 206) notes, an anonymous reviewer of Lyell's book in the *Westminster Review* had made just this point, stating that cave associations "might as well be explained by the prolongation of the period of the great extinct Pachyderms into the human period, as by carrying back the origins of Man to the epoch specially marked by their prevalence" (Anonymous 1863: 522). This point was long debated in North American circles, helped along by such spurious discoveries as Koch's purported associations at spots along the Bourbeuse and Pomme de Terre rivers as well as by, of all things, two pipes from Iowa cornfields that had been carved in the shape of elephants, or, if you wanted to believe it, in the shape of mastodons.[9] The discovery of the pipes, which we know now to have been part of a broader attempt at outright scientific fraud (McKusick 1970, 1991), clouded considerably the question of mastodons and humans and embroiled many of the leading prehistorians of the day in the controversy over their authenticity. In one respect, the pipe discovery was a continuation of the carnivalesque atmosphere that surrounded Koch and his mid-nineteenth-century exploits.

The pipes (Figure 3.15) were similar in design to the many Middle Woodland–period animal-effigy platform pipes that have come from midwestern sites and would have raised no more than the usual interest in such artifacts were it not for the fact that the pipes carried carvings of elephants instead of owls or squirrels. Both pipes came from Louisa County, Iowa. One reportedly was found in a mound by members of the Davenport Academy of Natural Sciences in 1880; the other was purchased for the academy in the late 1870s from the brother-in-law of the farmer who had found it. As McKusick (1970: 27) points out, from the start

9. Dave Meltzer pointed out to me another reason that some people in the United States believed in a recent extinction of mastodons: most of the mastodon bones that had been found in the eastern United States were so close to the surface that they *had* to be recent.

Figure 3.15. Fraudulent elephant pipes from Louisa County, Iowa, found by Rev. Jacob Gass ca. 1880 (from McKusick 1991, courtesy Iowa State University Press).

the professional journals—some of them at least—urged caution in accepting the discoveries as genuine. The most critical article was written by Henry Henshaw of the Bureau of Ethnology. He attacked the authenticity of the pipes in a wider study in which he examined the taxonomic identity of animals commonly found on platform pipes, his thesis being that if the animals were local species, then support would be provided for the proposition that the mound builders were not recent immigrants to the Midwest. In other words, they were Indians. But what about those pipes carved in the shape of elephants? Did they provide support for human migrations to the New World, perhaps from India or Africa, or did they suggest that humans and proboscideans were New World contemporaries? Or were they fakes? Henshaw came down hard on the side of fraud, scripting a cogent and insightful essay but at the same time impugning not only the authenticity of the pipes but the reputation of the man who had obtained the first pipe for the Davenport academy and who had found the second:

Bearing in mind the many attempts at archaeological frauds that recent years have brought to light, archaeologists have a right to demand that objects which afford a basis for such important deductions as the coeval life of the Mound-Builder and the mastodon, should be above the slightest suspicion not only in respect to their resemblances, but as regards the circumstances of discovery. If they are not above suspicion, the science of archaeology can better afford to wait for further and more certain evidence than to commit itself to theories which may prove stumbling-blocks to truth until that indefinite time when future investigations shall show their illusory nature. (Henshaw 1883: 158)

Henshaw's potentially libelous comments were directed at Jacob Gass, and it didn't exactly help Henshaw's case that the person whose character he was impugning was a man of the cloth—*Rev.* Jacob Gass. Several years later W J McGee, in attacking a clergyman from Ohio (G. F. Wright), would be viewed in some circles as simply doing John Wesley Powell's dirty work for him, and Henshaw was viewed in many quarters as doing the same thing—in his case promoting Powell's Indian-as-mound-builder proposal at anyone's expense, including that of a poor cleric from Iowa. Undoubtedly some of the outpouring of sentiment for Gass came from quarters who saw the Henshaw article as an attempt by the Washington elite to force its ideas down the throats of the supposedly less well informed masses in the provinces. The masses fought back, with one of the wealthiest Davenport businessmen, Charles E. Putnam, at the center of the attack. Putnam wrote in 1885 a vigorous defense of Gass and his finds that was circulated widely. He noted that Henshaw had never seen the pipes and instead had relied on a crude and inaccurate sketch. Neither had he questioned any of those involved in the discoveries—men of outstanding character and social position who were beyond reproach. When Putnam's defense was published in the academy's *Proceedings* (C. E. Putnam 1886 [cited in McKusick 1970]), there were also 30 pages of letters from individuals who had read the defense and had felt compelled to write and offer their opinions. Almost all were in agreement with Putnam's position. Anthropologist Daniel Brinton of Philadelphia considered Henshaw's attack "a paper not composed in the true spirit of science and out of place in the publications of the Bureau." J. P. MacLean, a noted antiquarian and minister from Ohio, wrote, "You certainly have literally annihilated Henshaw, and it is to be hoped that he will at once retire into the obscurity from which Major Powell has dragged him forth, and that his like may never again be seen in the land." Another "testimonial" came in to Putnam: "The elephant pipes, which have elicited so much criticism, I consider as genuine as the most undoubted specimens in the museum. Subjected to the sharpest tests, they pass successfully." "Sharpest tests," indeed. The comments were from Wills de Hass.

Despite these protestations, opinion soon began to turn against Gass and his finds, with even Stephen Peet, who earlier defended Gass in the pages of *The American Antiquarian and Oriental Journal* (Peet 1887) and who argued as late as 1903 that mastodons had become extinct only in the recent past (Peet 1903), finally throwing in the towel. Other claims of mound builder–mastodon contemporaneity would appear in the next two decades, but to most prehistorians the issue was dead. Almost everyone began to accept the fact that by the time the mounds were being built, the mastodon was nowhere to be found. Mastodons *had* been confined to the glacial period, with or without humans around to occasionally pick them off. But the big question, of course, was whether humans had been around then. The controversy stirred up by the Davenport pipes, at least in its original form, centered around mound builders and mastodons. Although the objects were found to be fraudulent, that conclusion said nothing about human antiquity or human-mastodon contemporaneity. The issue was still very much alive at the end of the century and would continue to simmer until the third decade of the twentieth century, when a most remarkable discovery was made, in a small cave in the extreme southwestern corner of Missouri, that once again drew considerable attention from the archaeological community and heated up the pages of respected journals. I will return to that discovery in Chapter 4.

Gerard Fowke and the Birth of Missouri Archaeology

Cyrus Thomas's massive report must have spurred archaeologists and antiquarians to follow in his footsteps, for in the waning years of the nineteenth century the investigation of archaeological sites across the Midwest and East accelerated rapidly. This was certainly true in Missouri. Pre-Thomas references to archaeological sites in Missouri are, as we have seen, not rare, but on the other hand earlier work was more sporadic and hit-or-miss than that conducted in some other states. By 1910, however, large portions of the state had been surveyed, at least in cursory fashion, and numerous sites had been excavated.

One of the most ambitious archaeological projects ever undertaken in Missouri was headed not by an archaeologist but by a historian, Louis Houck, of Cape Girardeau, Missouri, who in 1908 published a three-volume work entitled *A History of Missouri*, which covered the time period from the earliest prehistoric occupations up to the admission of the state into the Union in 1821. Although he was not an archaeologist, Houck was familiar with the major works that pertained to the prehistory of Missouri, and he provided an interesting if somewhat undiscriminating review of the literature. But Houck's main objective was not to review the literature but to provide the locations of virtually all known mounds in Missouri:

> This history of the state manifestly would be incomplete without, at least, an
> attempt to record where this pre-historic race, or it may be different races dwelling

in the land at different times or epochs, apparently had their habitat. . . . My main object . . . has been to accurately and definitely locate every mound and settlement of these pre-historic denizens of the state, and to that end every county has been visited during the last two years, at my insistence, by Mr. Lewis M. Bean and Mr. D. L. Hoffman. It is not asserted that they found every existing mound, or discovered every pre-historic settlement, but it is reasonably certain that all of the most conspicuous and remarkable mounds have been by them definitely located. (Houck 1908: 41)

Incredibly, Bean and Hoffman recorded the locations of some 28,000 mounds, the majority in the eastern half of the state (Houck 1908: 52). The variation in number of mounds per county was enormous. For example, the surveyors found 4 mounds in Daviess County, in northwestern Missouri, and 4,292 mounds in Scott County, in southeastern Missouri. However, the mound figures are greatly inflated because Bean and Hoffman could not discriminate between artificial mounds and natural topographic highs, especially "prairie mounds," which are ubiquitous sedimentary features (usually a meter or two high and up to 10 to 15 meters in diameter) on the Pleistocene-age braided-stream surfaces of southeastern Missouri counties such as Cape Girardeau, Scott, Bollinger, Ripley, and Butler. Note the dense concentration of mounds that Houck mapped in western Scott County (Figure 3.16), an area whose surface comprises Pleistocene deposits associated with the ancestral Mississippi River. The age of the prairie mounds appears to fall sometime during the middle Holocene (O'Brien, Lyman, and Holland 1989), though the process or processes that created them is still unknown. Many of the prairie mounds, because they were topographic highs in an otherwise low-lying, swampy region, were used prehistorically as campsites, as evidenced by the scatters of material found by Hoffman and Bean as they conducted their fieldwork.

Houck's survey of Missouri counties might have been the most ambitious project in Missouri from the period immediately following publication of Thomas's manuscript, but it was not the most significant, in my estimation. I would award that honor to the survey and excavation program carried out along the Missouri River by former Thomas field assistant Gerard Fowke (Figure 3.17). The title of his work, "Antiquities of Central and Southeastern Missouri" (Fowke 1910), is misleading since the bulk of the report, which was published in the *Bureau of American Ethnology Bulletin* series, dealt exclusively with sites along the Missouri River and near the junction of the Missouri and its major tributaries. Fowke dedicated less than 10 pages to southeastern Missouri, though in those pages he documented several copper plates that had recently been found in northern Dunklin County (see V. D. Watson 1950).

If ever there was an archaeologist whose life was ripe for a biographer, it is Gerard Fowke. Very little is known about him except for his archaeological work—primarily that undertaken in Missouri and in the James and Potomac

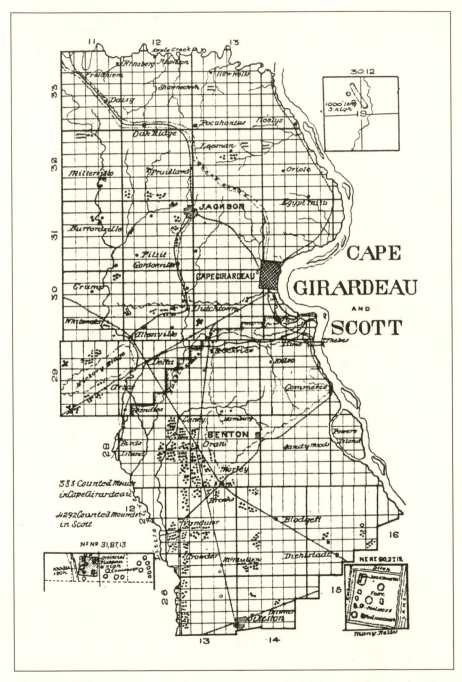

Figure 3.16. Map of Cape Girardeau and Scott counties, Missouri, showing locations of mounds plotted by Louis Houck (from Houck 1908). In the lower left-hand corner, Houck noted that 388 mounds had been recorded in Cape Girardeau County and 4,292 in Scott County. Most of those were natural "prairie mounds," not mounds constructed by humans. The small map at the lower right is of Sandy Woods (see Figure 2.10).

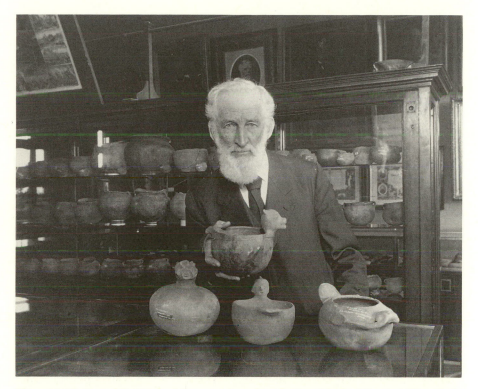

Figure 3.17. Gerard B. Fowke (1855–1933), archaeologist with the Missouri Historical Society, showing some of the vessels in the society's collection, ca. 1931 (courtesy Missouri Historical Society).

river valleys of northern Virginia (Fowke 1894). David Meltzer found a 4½-page typed manuscript in the National Anthropological Archives at the Smithsonian Institution (Record Group no. 3113) that provides a synopsis of Fowke's life. He was born Charles Mitchell Smith in 1855 (near Maysville, Kentucky), but changed his name legally to Gerard Fowke in 1887 (Smith [1990a: 33] notes that he also used the name Kentucky Q. Smith at some point in his life). The manuscript notes that throughout his adult life he was employed by numerous universities, museums, and scientific societies and that "In the course of these researches he has explored mounds, graves, village-sites, and other remains of prehistoric American Indians, as well as those of later tribes, in nearly every State from the Atlantic Coast to the tier of States west of the Mississippi" (p. 2). The manuscript also makes the points that "Fowke has not been a voluminous writer; he waits until he has something to say," and that he "is not connected with any church, club, fraternity, secret society, protective association, social organization, benevolent institution, or mutual admiration circle" (pp. 4–5). I leave it to the reader to speculate as to who wrote the short manuscript.

Fowke worked for Thomas in 1887, after the vast majority of mound surveys and excavations had been completed. His involvement in Missouri archaeology came a number of years later, during one of the most interesting and certainly one of the least-documented periods of work in the state. The story of Fowke's work in Missouri is important from several standpoints. First, his investigations represented an enormous step forward in terms of the quality of both fieldwork and reporting. Because he dealt with a much smaller inventory of sites than Thomas had, Fowke was able to spend more time discussing the excavations and the materials recovered. He had his intellectual biases, to be sure, but his reporting was unusually clear and concise. And, importantly, Fowke included numerous excavation photographs in his monograph—something that was lacking in Thomas's work. Second, Fowke's involvement in Missouri archaeology was tied directly to the efforts of national as well as local organizations, which, from a historical point of view, set a precedent in the state—a precedent that helped guide Missouri archaeology into the shape it would ultimately assume. Fowke provided the link between local learned societies and national organizations and institutions that up to the turn of the century had been missing.

Previously, members of local societies such as the Academy of Science of St. Louis and later the archaeological section of the Missouri Historical Society had carried out their own research, but such efforts rarely involved persons from eastern universities and institutions. When individuals with national prestige worked in Missouri, such as Thomas, albeit through his crews, that work was accomplished not necessarily in a vacuum but with little give and take with local antiquarians. Fowke, however, changed that. He had acquired a degree of prominence through his association with the BAE, and he aligned himself with the St. Louis Society of the Archaeological Institute of America, an organization of prominent St. Louisans who had an interest in Missouri's prehistory. It was the local organization that sponsored Fowke's work, but it was the national organization that transmitted the final report of the work to the BAE for publication in the *Bulletin* (Fowke 1910).

To note that Fowke aligned himself with the St. Louis chapter of the AIA does not do justice to an important episode in the history of Missouri archaeology, because the relationship that apparently developed between Fowke and the chapter was much more productive than what is evident on the surface. In many respects the relationship between the professional Fowke and the nonprofessional chapter members foreshadowed what was to come several decades later with the founding of the Missouri Archaeological Society. Understanding that relationship requires a brief discussion of a group with the bizarre name "the Knockers" that was formed by members of three local St. Louis organizations: the

AIA, the Academy of Science, and the Missouri Historical Society.[10] The spark of this group was a father-and-son combination—David I. Bushnell Sr. and Jr.—the younger of whom had begun to make a name for himself in archaeology. Bushnell Jr. worked in the 1890s as an assistant for the University of California, between 1901 and 1904 for the Peabody Museum (Harvard), and, beginning in 1907, as an employee of the BAE. His work in Missouri included excavating salt-processing areas and stone-box burials in Jefferson County (Bushnell 1907, 1908) and Ste. Genevieve County (Bushnell 1914) and mapping some of the mound groups in western and northern St. Louis County (Bushnell 1904a). The mound-group article is extremely short on detail (as is his synopsis of archaeological remains in the Ozarks [Bushnell 1904b]), though he produced what I believe to be the only map ever made of the mound group in Forest Park in St. Louis (Figure 3.18), which had received passing comment in various earlier reports.

Bushnell erroneously interpreted the Forest Park mounds as the ruins of earthlodges, as he did the thousands of natural prairie mounds that dot the state (Conant [1879a: 66] made a similar mistake, concluding that the prairie mounds were "garden mounds"). Bushnell excavated five of the mounds in the upper Forest Park group (labeled A–C, E, and F in Figure 3.18), though he presented little in the way of information on what was recovered. He must have realized later the inadequacy of his reports, because by the time he published the three papers on his work in Jefferson and Ste. Genevieve counties (Bushnell 1907, 1908, 1914), he had begun to describe his excavations in more detail, to present fairly detailed drawings of the excavations, and to include photographs in the reports. His interpretation of the salt-manufacturing area near Kimmswick (Bushnell 1907) in Jefferson County represents a considered opinion and is by far the best of his reports published before 1910 (discussed further in Chapter 4).

David Browman (1978: 2) suggests, and I think he is correct, that it was Bushnell's emerging prominence in the field and his ties to institutions such as the Peabody Museum that acted as a magnet in attracting other professional archaeologists such as Gerard Fowke to St. Louis. And it wasn't only Fowke who began keeping company with the Knockers. Browman notes that leading archaeologists of the day—men such as Earl Morris, who went on to have a distinguished career as a Southwestern archaeologist with the Carnegie Foundation, and Edgar Hewett, a Southwesternist and Mayanist who in 1906 became director of American Research with the AIA—regularly turned up at various meetings of the Knockers. Apparently by 1910 the ties between the Knockers and Morris were

10. A good portion of what I know of the Knockers comes from a short article by David Browman (1978), who pieced together bits of information as he attempted to catalog some archaeological collections that had been deposited at Washington University in St. Louis.

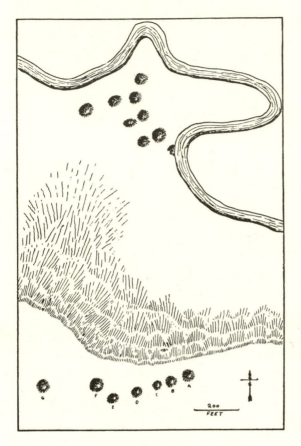

Figure 3.18. Map of the Forest Park mound group, St. Louis, made by David I. Bushnell Jr. (1875–1941), ca. 1903 (from Bushnell 1904a).

so close that members John M. Wulfing, George Mepham, Mepham's wife, and David I. Bushnell Sr. joined Morris's excavation team at Aztec Ruins in northern New Mexico (Morris 1919, 1921).

It is clear that one of the goals of the Knockers, and other groups like them, was to assemble collections of artifacts that could be studied and admired not only by members but also by the public. It is equally clear that the various organizations had two strategies for acquiring material: collect it themselves or buy it from other collectors. Browman (1978: 2) notes that it was not accidental that the travels of the Knockers coincided with where Bushnell Jr. and Fowke happened to be working: "It was a two-way street; at times the professionals found the sites, and the Knockers followed, and at other times the Knockers conducted the early excavations and those were followed up by the BAE personnel."

Some of the most important collections of Missouri artifacts ever assembled were made by members of the Knockers and later donated directly to that organization, to Washington University, or to the Missouri Historical Society. These include the famous eight copper repoussé plates that were found near

Malden, in Dunklin County, and purchased by Wulfing in 1907 (V. D. Watson 1950). Other groups were doing the same thing—sponsoring fieldwork and buying collections. Witness an advertisement placed by the Missouri Historical Society in the January 23, 1881, edition of the *Missouri Republican* (cited in Trubowitz 1993): "The Society particularly wishes to procure archaeological specimens, popularly known as Indian curiosities or stones, flint arrow and spear heads, chisels, discoidal stones, stone axes, pottery from mounds, etc., and will be thankful for every object of this class." The historical society was extremely successful in acquiring various collections, as Trubowitz documents. For example, George E. Leighton, who served as president of the society from 1882 until 1892, purchased and donated several large holdings, including the William J. Seever collection in 1889 and the John J. R. Patrick collection in 1891. An inventory of society holdings made by Bushnell Sr. in 1903 showed that the organization had at least 11,000 artifacts in storage and 13,828 on display in 42 cases (Trubowitz 1993: 3).[11]

It was the promise of artifacts hidden deep in the mounds of the Illinois River valley that in 1905 lured Wulfing and Bushnell Sr. to a set of earthworks near the town of Montezuma in Pike County, Illinois. There they began work on what was then termed the McEvers mound, the largest of 15 earthworks in what is now known as the Montezuma mound group. Within a short time they had unearthed about 1,200 "Hopewellian" flint disks and other artifacts. Whether they realized their inexperience in dealing with a complex archaeological context or hoped to bolster the significance of their work by getting advice from a professional archaeologist, they hired Gerard Fowke—who Trubowitz (1993: 4) notes had made use of the society's facilities as his winter quarters in 1904—to continue the excavations. For whatever reason—perhaps out of respect for the organization that hired him (or perhaps because of the low quality of the work that members had carried out)—Fowke published his brief report not in a journal with national visibility but in the *Missouri Historical Society Collections,* giving credit (or perhaps assigning blame) to the original investigators by including their names in the title (Fowke 1905).

The Missouri Historical Society hired Fowke again in May 1911 to pack its collections for storage (Trubowitz 1993). His employment lasted until April of the following year, and in August 1912 the society rehired him to compile a brief overview of Missouri prehistory (Fowke 1912). In December of that year the society hired him as full-time staff archaeologist, a position he held until December 1915. He returned to St. Louis briefly in 1926, 1928, and 1930 to relabel materials, accession new artifacts, and generally lend his advice to the society. He died in 1933.

---

11. The Missouri Historical Society began a thorough inventory of its archaeological holdings in 1990.

Fowke's Central-Missouri Mound Study

Gerard Fowke, like most of his contemporaries, was interested in mounds, but when he began his investigations in Missouri it was not the large earthworks of southeastern Missouri that attracted his attention but rather the ubiquitous low, earth-covered stone burial vaults of central and northeastern Missouri (Fowke 1910). In fact, his interest led to the excavation of 60 mounds, all except 1 (in Pike County) along the Missouri River—8 in Gasconade County, 12 in Osage County, 32 in Boone County, 1 in Howard County, and 6 along the Platte County–Clay County line (Figure 3.19). Numerous vaults in Missouri had been examined by previous investigators, especially G. C. Broadhead (see below), but the reports that had been produced were brief and speculative. Fowke also mapped and excavated a portion of the "Old Fort," a Mississippian-period earthen embankment in Saline County (Figure 3.20) that had long fascinated prehistorians and had received extensive commentary in print (e.g., Broadhead 1880a; T. H. Lewis 1892; West 1882a).

Fowke described the structures he mapped and excavated in varying degrees of detail and took excellent photographs of the stone vaults after they had been excavated. If we want to pinpoint the first extensive use of photographs in Missouri archaeology, then we have to assign primacy to the work of Gerard Fowke. David Bushnell Jr. made use of photographs in his reports of work in St. Louis and Jefferson counties, which were published slightly before Fowke's monograph, but it was Fowke who first published extensive photographic documentation of archaeological excavations undertaken in Missouri. The photographs are all the more important because Fowke's sampling area was large and the number of burial structures he excavated was sizable, thus allowing the reader to visually gauge the amount of variation among the structures.

In archaeology, descriptions of excavations are important not only for conveying information to the reader but also for acting as a permanent record of what was found. Archaeology is in the curious position of destroying what it studies, and up until the early twentieth century, the record of what had been destroyed through the act of excavating a mound or burial vault was severely lacking in detail. And, as we saw in Chapter 2 with the various eyewitness accounts of the interior configuration of the Big Mound at St. Louis, reports, though detailed, were not always more than fanciful summaries of what was found. A picture, the Chinese remind us, is worth a thousand words, but in archaeology pictures can be worth even more, especially in presenting complex stratigraphic sections and the like. But pictures can be drawn from many points of view and can be intended to show whatever it is that the artist wants us to see. Photographs, however, unless they are staged or retouched, do not lie. They faithfully record whatever is in front of the camera, be it a large earthen mound or a stone vault. And it was Fowke's extensive use of photography relative to the stone

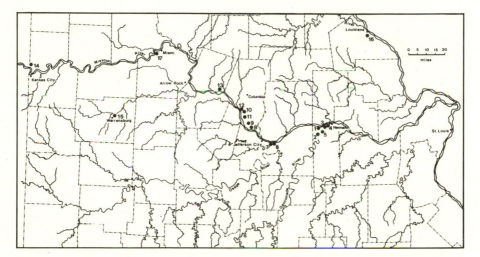

Figure 3.19. Map showing locations of rock cairns in Missouri excavated by Gerard B. Fowke in 1906–1907: 1, Granmann mounds; 2, Ruegge village; 3, Uffman mound; 4, Birkle mound; 5, Smith mounds; 6, Ewing mounds; 7, Dallmeyer mound; 8, Shaw mounds; 9, Dawson mounds; 10, Easley mounds; 11, Baumhoefer mounds; 12, Buescher mounds; 13, Kurtz mound; 14, mounds opposite Kansas City, Missouri; 15, mounds in vicinity of Warrensburg; 16, the "Indian house"; 17, Old Fort and village (now referred to as the Utz site) (after Fowke 1910).

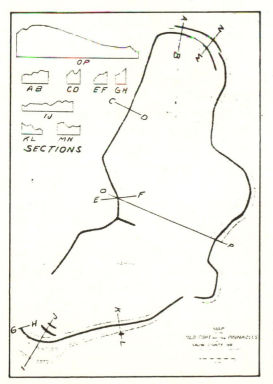

Figure 3.20. Map of the Old Fort, Saline County, Missouri, made by Gerard B. Fowke in 1907 (from Fowke 1910).

Figure 3.21. Photograph of the internal structure of Brenner mound number 2, Platte County, Missouri, excavated by Gerard B. Fowke in 1906 or 1907 (from Fowke 1910).

vaults he excavated that settled once and for all the nature of the structures (Figure 3.21). One vault, located in Pike County (number 16 on Figure 3.19), is of particular interest because of the status it attained in various nineteenth- and early-twentieth-century publications.

Of all the mounds in Missouri that had been examined in the nineteenth century, the one in Pike County probably ranks second only to the Big Mound in the number of references to it. Fowke (1910: 75) said of the mound, "Among the remains which have aroused great interest, but which have been instrumental in creating a false impression concerning the aborigines of the Mississippi valley, is a peculiar stonework in Pike county, near Louisiana." The mound was first described in Lewis C. Beck's (1823) gazetteer of Illinois and Missouri and was accompanied by a drawing of the internal structure. The illustration and description were done by Rev. Solomon Giddings of St. Louis, who gave them to Beck. The drawing (Figure 3.22) was widely copied in various forms (e.g., Broadhead 1880a; Conant 1879a; Houck 1908) and used as an example of the careful manner in which the mound builders constructed tombs. Fowke (1910: 75) stated that the drawing

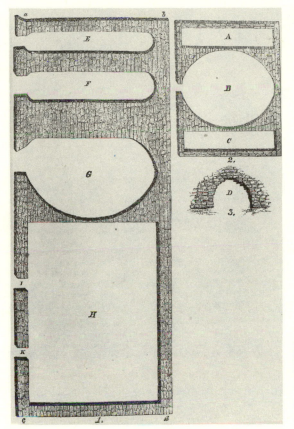

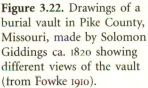

Figure 3.22. Drawings of a burial vault in Pike County, Missouri, made by Solomon Giddings ca. 1820 showing different views of the vault (from Fowke 1910).

[with its] complete lack of resemblance to anything ever constructed by a "Red Indian," or by his mythical predecessor, the "Mound Builder," has furnished a basis for all sorts of fanciful theories. The smoothness and regularity of the walls, the accurate alignment of the stones, as portrayed in his cut . . . might well excite the envy of a skilled stone mason of our own day. The statement in [Beck's] text that "all the walls consist of rough unhewn stone" proves the inaccuracy of the drawing, in which they are shown as smooth and even as they could be made with modern tools and machinery. Nevertheless, writers imbued with the idea of a "lost race" or a "high civilization" overlook this inconsistency and take only the drawing as a text.

Fowke's own work at the site, coupled with his discussions with the landowners, further convinced him that nothing of the sort described by Giddings had ever existed on the site and that it was "quite likely that the original sketch, made on the spot, was rather crude, its present finished appearance being

Figure 3.23. Photograph of a burial vault in Pike County, Missouri, excavated by Gerard B. Fowke in 1906 or 1907 (from Fowke 1910). Compare the photograph with Solomon Giddings's fanciful sketch shown in Figure 3.22.

such as would accord with the ideas of a draftsman who drew the stones after the conventional manner of text-books" (Fowke 1910: 78). Fowke's excavations produced the remains of the structure shown in Figure 3.23.

Many of the vaults excavated by Fowke—those that had withstood the ravages of time and vandalism—were quite remarkable in terms of the precise manner in which the rock walls had been constructed (Figure 3.21), but none approached the degree of precision evident in Giddings's drawing or even in those of Broadhead (Figure 3.24), who tended to illustrate vault walls in stairstep fashion. In most cases the limestone slabs were stacked a few feet high and enclosed the burial chamber on either three or four sides. Fowke also correctly noted that the vaults had been covered by mounded earth and that the occurrence of stone slabs inside the crypts was attributable to wall collapse as opposed to roofs that had collapsed (e.g., Broadhead 1880a).[12]

12. Broadhead was not the only investigator to believe, mistakenly, that the central chambers had once been roofed. For example, F. W. Putnam, addressing the October 15, 1879, meeting of the Boston

Into the Teens

Interestingly, the myth of the mound builders may have died in 1894 with the publication of Thomas's landmark work, but the demise of the myth did not signal an end to speculation about which groups of American Indians were responsible for the various earthen and stone mounds in the midwestern and eastern United States. Nor did it signal the end of loosely constructed evolutionary arguments in which phenotypic characteristics, especially cranial features and artistic ability, were used to place particular groups of prehistoric peoples. Fowke, who in his discussion of the Pike County crypt lampooned those who used the "mythical" denominator of mound builder, ironically stated early in his treatise on burial structures, "The mounds along the lower Missouri plainly owe their origin to a people whose grade of culture was much inferior to that of the mound builders east and south. The skulls are of the low type. . . . The methods of interment, as a rule, show but little reverence or respect for the dead" (Fowke 1910: 4). He was unsure of the dating of the mounds, though he accepted the absence of iron and glass objects in the crypts as evidence that the mounds predated the arrival of Europeans. He also suspected that the mounds

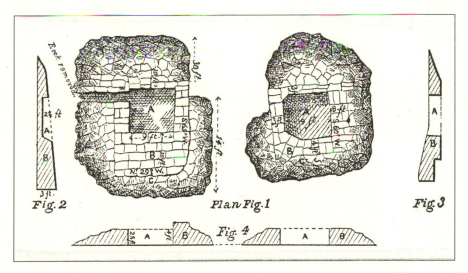

Figure 3.24. Drawings of two burial vaults in Pike County, Missouri, made by Garland Carr Broadhead, probably in the 1860s or 1870s (from Broadhead 1880a).

Society of Natural History, noted that Mr. E. Curtiss, who was making explorations in Clay County, Missouri, for the Peabody Museum (Harvard), stated that the stone chambers he was excavating "seem to have been closed over with wood" (*Proceedings of the Boston Society of Natural History* 20: 305).

predated the Siouan speakers noted by early Euro-American explorers, since no mention was made of Siouan burials in mounds in any of the early chronicles and diaries.

Fowke's speculations about which group or groups of "inferior" peoples had erected the thousands of burial mounds across Missouri were typical of the ruminations of prehistorians in the early twentieth century. By 1910 linguistic and ethnological information was pouring in to the BAE from across the country, and prehistorians, some of whom had little or no experience in ethnological studies, were quick to go through the compilations in search of clues that would help them put a name to the tribe responsible for leaving the archaeological materials they were collecting. After all, this had been the driving idea behind Powell's BAE—to flesh out all aspects of Indian life, especially language. His goals were reached in the BAE's publication of the two-volume *Handbook of American Indians North of Mexico*, edited by Frederick W. Hodge (1907–1910). Holmes had assumed the directorship of the BAE as those volumes were being prepared, and he and Hodge were able to draw on almost the entire anthropological community to produce a masterful work that, in the words of Hinsley (1981: 282), mixed "invaluable synonymy, bibliography, history, census statistics, and respectable ethnography with occasional judgmental generalization." The volumes were immensely popular, especially among archaeologists, who embraced them for the detail they provided. They were, to quote Hodge (1907–1910: viii), "designed to be a complete summary of existing knowledge respecting the aborigines of northern America." In retrospect, the volumes were "a model of nineteenth-century popular science—a generation late. . . . Quite aside from its clear merits as a resource book in anthropology, the *Handbook* was a fascinating historical product of clashing suppositions and grinding institutional change" (Hinsley 1981: 282–83).

The grip the BAE exerted on Americanist archaeology and ethnology, together with its rigid approach to the gathering of information and its abhorrence of speculation, was slowly being eclipsed by a new generation of students trained specifically in the integrative discipline of anthropology—an "inquiring community being nurtured, at great personal expense and exertion, in Cambridge, New York, and elsewhere" (Hinsley 1981: 283). It would be those students and not Powell's colleagues who would lead the archaeology of the 1920s. Compared to the feverish pace of the work of Thomas and his division crews and the massive output of Holmes on several fronts, the work conducted in the 1910–1940 era might appear to pale in comparison. But this appearance is deceiving, because it was during that 30-year period that Americanist archaeology came of age in terms of method and technique.

4

The Birth of a Discipline

1911–1940

The marriage between archaeology and ethnology that grew out of the Bureau of American Ethnology produced a strange hybrid that, at the time, no one knew was essentially sterile. Each parent on its own was quite capable of reproducing itself, at least for a while, but the union of the two eventually became an exercise in futility. Archaeology, as it turned out, was poised to embark on a long search for its true identity, and its decades-long association with ethnology was wearing thin. That fact, however, was lost on prehistorians and ethnologists connected with the BAE. They continued to view themselves as the ones who had defined the goals of ethnology and archaeology, and they were able to continue furthering their agenda through their control of or significant influence in scientific societies such as the American Anthropological Association, the Anthropological Society of Washington, and the American Association for the Advancement of Science.

The agenda for archaeology under the leadership first of Powell and then of Holmes called for ridding the scientific world of speculation about such things as extinct races of mound builders and glacial-period humans in North America and then setting about the business of describing the material culture of American Indian groups. Similarly, the goals of ethnology were to chronicle Indian life and to document differences among various groups. The BAE position was that archaeology and ethnology should complement each other, thus providing the link between the present and the fairly recent past. When the mold in which Holmes and others were casting the complementary disciplines began to wear out, they had nothing with which to replace it. Others did, however. One of those who did was Franz Boas (Figure 4.1), a young ethnologist who, ironically, held the title of honorary philologist on Powell's staff. The agenda that he soon established for the future directions of Americanist ethnology and, through his students, Americanist archaeology was more far-reaching than anything that had been proposed previously, and it quickly replaced the by-then stale agenda of the bureau.

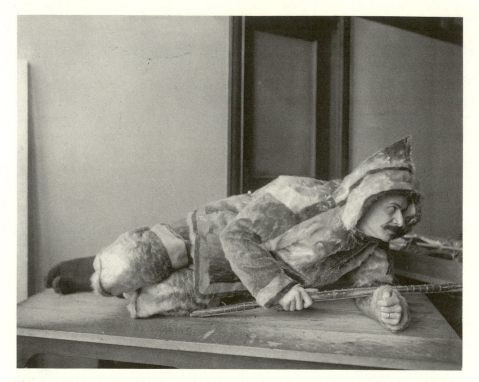

Figure 4.1. Franz Boas (1858–1942) demonstrating the use of an Eskimo harpoon, ca. 1900 (photograph by R. Weber; negative no. 3220, courtesy Department of Library Services, American Museum of Natural History).

Boas's training had been as a physicist and geographer, but a trip to Baffin Land in 1882 to study the Eskimo apparently convinced him that ethnology was his proper calling. After a brief stint teaching at Clark University, he served in several positions under Frederic W. Putnam, first as his assistant at the Field Columbian Museum (now the Field Museum of Natural History) in Chicago, then as his understudy at the American Museum of Natural History in New York. In 1899 Boas assumed a permanent professorship at Columbia University while maintaining his ties at the American Museum, and it was from this joint position that he set about to change the face of the emerging discipline of anthropology. Dexter (1966: 315) credits Putnam with introducing anthropology—a hybrid of ethnology and archaeology with a dose of skeletal biology thrown in—as a science, but it was Boas who made it a household word.

To those familiar with the history of anthropology, it might seem strange to include a discussion of Boas in a book on Missouri archaeology. To be honest, I doubt whether Franz Boas ever set foot in Missouri—in fact, I'm pretty sure he didn't—but whether he did or not is irrelevant. What is relevant is the effect he had on Americanist ethnology and, by extension, archaeology—an effect that can be measured not only in terms of *what* he produced but also in terms of *whom* he produced. It would be some of those he produced or at least influenced who would bring significant attention to Missouri archaeology. During the first three decades of the twentieth century, Americanist anthropology was in very large part a product of Boas's students and their students, and it is difficult to place the development of archaeology during that period in an intellectual framework without at least brief mention of this physicist-turned-anthropologist who once stated, "I have the conviction that in certain lines at least I know exactly what is needed for furthering our knowledge of American ethnology, and I believe that the method which I am pursuing is more systematic than that followed by many others. It is only for this reason that I have ventured to concentrate in my hands a considerable part of the ethnological work that is being done on our continent" (quoted in Parmenter 1966: 99).

Franz Boas and the Birth of Americanist Anthropology

It is often claimed that Boas was an anti-evolutionist, but he most decidedly was not. What he was, though, was a careful observer who advocated a wait-and-see attitude on such things as evolutionary explanations until all available data were in. If there *were* certain regularities that appeared in data sets from different geographic areas, then anthropologists certainly needed to understand the basis for the regularities, but this did not necessitate jumping on an evolutionary bandwagon. Boas, as opposed to most of his contemporaries, well understood the biological principle behind analogous features (convergence in terms of functional similarity), and he was able to make the application to human traits. Despite the evidence for this tempered view of Boas, there is no doubt that he was highly critical of loosely constructed evolutionary schemes that were based on absurd comparisons of human features such as skin color, number of words in a dialect, or cranial characteristics. He also tended to come down hard on diffusionist explanations, especially when they were interwoven in a mantle of evolutionary progress, but it was the comparativists who typically drew Boas's greatest wrath (e.g., Boas 1896).

Late-nineteenth-century anthropology was afloat with comparative studies, the vast majority of which were designed, implicitly or explicitly, to demonstrate Anglo-Saxon superiority over other groups. The classical evolutionists, such as Lewis Henry Morgan and Edward Tylor, were comparativists, and they were followed by scores of others who attempted to fine-tune the various evolutionary constructions that had been developed. It was difficult to dispel these schemes, coming as they did from leading figures in anthropology who held influential positions in the field—individuals such as W J McGee, first president of the

American Anthropological Association, and Daniel Brinton, president of the American Association for the Advancement of Science and an ardent supporter of the separateness of Indians and mound builders—but Boas made it his business to discredit them.

Boas was an empiricist, and the term *particularism*—the tendency to focus on particular details of a culture or cultures—has been applied to his work as well as to the work of his students. This appellation, however, only characterizes their work and does not signify a school or movement within anthropology. The only movement Boas acknowledged was toward making anthropology a science. And doing that meant uniting what to that point had been rather disparate endeavors. In describing his plans for an anthropology department at Columbia University, Boas explained in a letter to Zelia Nuttall:

> Since I took hold of the work in New York, I have tried to develop the same in such a way that it will ultimately result in the establishment of a well-organized school of anthropology, including all the different branches of the subject. I consider this one of the fundamental needs of our science, because without it we can never hope to thoroughly investigate and explore all the numerous problems of American anthropology. For this reason I am trying to develop the collections of this Museum in such a way that they will ultimately form the basis of university instruction in all lines of anthropological research. . . . I want to see represented anthropology as well in its physical side as its psychological, comparative side, and also specialists capable of carrying on work in archaeology. . . .
>
> I am confident that in this manner we shall be able inside of a few years to give a young man a thorough all-round schooling, which cannot be had at the present time anywhere. (quoted in Parmenter 1966: 98–99)

And train students Boas did. The list of students he produced—Margaret Mead, Ruth Benedict, Robert Lowie, Clark Wissler, Fay-Cooper Cole, Leslie Spier, Edward Sapir—is a who's who list of influential anthropologists of the first half of the twentieth century, many of whom left the Columbia nest to found graduate departments of anthropology elsewhere. Perhaps the greatest of Boas's students was Alfred L. Kroeber, who graduated from Columbia in 1901 and soon established the anthropology department at the University of California, Berkeley.

It is difficult to define Kroeber's particular niche in anthropology, because he really didn't have one. He was at once an ethnologist capable of unraveling complex kinship systems (e.g., Kroeber 1909a, 1917a), an archaeologist interested in California prehistory (e.g., Kroeber 1909b), and an anthropologist deeply interested in the meaning of culture (e.g., Kroeber 1917b). The notion of culture was certainly embodied in Boas's work, but the concept was carried to a new height by Kroeber. It is Kroeber's archaeological work that is of particular interest here, especially in terms of its influence on the field during the first three decades of the twentieth century. Some of the most well known archaeologists of the period trained under him at Berkeley, and it was to a certain extent Kroeber who set both the standards for archaeological fieldwork during the period and the tone of much of the research that was done, especially in his emphasis on defining cultural patterns through careful, particularistic analysis and tightly structured (*tortuous* might be a better word) description.

Alfred Kroeber and Historicism

Kroeber considered himself a historicist; in fact, he believed that he was more of a historicist than even Boas had been: "Boas may have seemed, possibly even to himself, to be following historical method. But it was merely historical method applied as a critical safeguard; the problems with which he concerned himself were not historical except in minor cases, but concerned with process as such" (Kroeber 1935: 542). There is no doubt that throughout his career Kroeber held to the belief that history and process were two different things and that one was attainable through anthropological research while the other was not:

> The causality that is involved in culture has normally accumulated so long and so intricately that on the whole very little of it can be specifically unraveled with authenticity. Boas was big enough to realize this. But the pioneers like Morgan, the men trained in laboratories like [W. H. R.] Rivers, the ruck of social scientists hoping somehow to imitate physics, kept and keep trying; and yet they achieve either only bits or constructs that are mainly unreal. It is the pattern rather than precise causation that is the meaningful result by and large achievable in the study of culture—as the history of linguistics should long ago have sufficed to teach us. (Kroeber 1952: 173)

To Kroeber, then, history was largely a matter of pattern; therefore, the task of an anthropologist was to recognize pattern and to describe it. But what about time? Where did it fit into the picture? How could one understand patterns without time? The answer was, patterns *couldn't* be understood without the element of time eventually thrown in—something that Kroeber never denied and indeed considered during his fieldwork in the Southwest. But early on he was not particularly enthused about trying to establish long cultural sequences based on stratigraphic columns, a point he made (Kroeber 1909b) relative to Max Uhle's (1907) cultural reconstructions based on California shell-midden excavations. Kroeber, still reflecting the position taken by his former professor, had seen enough of archaeologists' attempts to sort things temporally by means of rough-and-dirty methods, and he was not particularly impressed with the chronology-related debates that had seized archaeology for decades.

Powell's bureau had taken a similar stance and had effectively buried the notion of an American Paleolithic, and the bureau would continue to chip away at the notion of a long occupational history in North America. Here, at least for a while, bureau archaeologists and some university archaeologists were in agreement: instead of worrying about establishing hypothetical sequences, why not concentrate on using ethnological data for pattern recognition and then trying to extend those patterns back in time through archaeology? This had been Powell's dream from the beginning. History was, then, for Kroeber, as it was for Holmes, a description of the near past. The excesses that had recently ensnared ethnologists and archaeologists were replaced with moderation in the form of description.

What Kroeber had in mind for archaeology was in some ways not all that different from what a few people such as Cyrus Thomas had been doing all along. Unfortunately, Thomas usually gets cast in with his contemporaries in the bureau, most of whom were wedded to an evolutionary framework that viewed time in terms of progress. The evolutionary schemes that were proposed for prehistory were based on a comparative method that recognized individual cultures as simply points along a continuum. Some points were ahead or behind other points, and the points certainly were spread out spatially, but by using ethnological and archaeological data one was able to assign various human groups to their correct developmental stages. Thomas, and Holmes to a large degree, saw the proper role of archaeology and ethnology as being tools for precise description, *irrespective* of progressive evolutionary schemes (which, it must be admitted, even they themselves used on more than one occasion). To counteract the effects of those schemes, they in essence gave up on time. Kroeber, too, following Boas, attempted to counter the comparative-based evolutionary schemes, in his case by working out the developmental histories of individual cultures and carefully describing the materials left by the cultures. This led eventually to the formulation of culture areas and the age-area hypothesis, whereby analysis was directed toward assessments of when certain traits arose and when they spread to other areas.

These concepts are explored in a bit more detail later because of their direct bearing on Americanist archaeology; suffice it to say here that Kroeber and some of his contemporaries such as Wissler were in the forefront of such efforts. The point I am making is that it was not so much that Kroeber ignored time as it was that there were few if any concrete data on which to base temporal assignments of cultural traits. In the absence of those data, the age-area concept and its principal cultural process, diffusion, eventually arose as the theoretical underpinnings for interpretations of cultural variation.

A Kroeber contemporary, archaeologist Alfred Kidder, later commented that, as a reaction to all the hyperbole about the vast antiquity of human occupation in North America, "archaeology accordingly became preponderantly descriptive; effort was directed toward identification of ancient sites with modern tribes; research upon American prehistory, striking forward rather than back, upward rather than downward, was left without foundations. . . . many of us merely dodged the issue of origins and comforted ourselves by working in the satis-factorily clear atmosphere of the late periods" (Kidder 1936: 146). This was not necessarily a boring experience, given the richness of the late-period archae-ological record in many areas of the United States, but until the late 1920s the question of origins was indeed unattended to, save for a few instances. And when on occasion people would postulate that particular remains were old, especially human skeletons, Aleš Hrdlička would show them the error of their ways. It was this physical anthropologist who, even more than Holmes, kept the spirit of the traditional bureau approach to archaeology alive during the second decade of the twentieth century.

Aleš Hrdlička and the Fight against Glacial-Age Humans

In 1903, the year after Holmes took over as chief of the BAE, he hired Hrdlička away from the American Museum of Natural History and gave him the title of assistant curator in charge of the newly established Division of Physical Anthropology in the National Museum. By 1910, Hrdlička had worked his way up to the position of curator (Schultz 1945). Hrdlička came to share Holmes's intense opposition not only to a North American Paleolithic but also to great human antiquity on the continent. Hrdlička's reputation was such that anytime human remains were unearthed in the Americas, the chances were excellent that either Hrdlička or someone on his staff would see them. It would be almost impossible to count the acknowledgments from archaeologists that Hrdlička received in print during the early decades of the twentieth century or the brief reports that he produced based on his examination of skeletons recovered from archaeological sites. For example, he analyzed the poorly preserved skeletal material found by Fowke in the stone burial vaults of central Missouri (Hrdlička 1910). That report is typical of others he produced in that he immediately called attention to the fact that the remains were those of Indians and that they compared favorably in shape and measurement to remains from other regions of North America. Hrdlička had seen literally thousands of prehistoric skeletons from around the continent (as well as from South America), and there was no one more qualified to make comparisons among skeletal series. His detailed measurements far surpassed anything done previously, and the absence of speculation in his reports contrasted strongly with the likes of Morton's (1839) *Crania Americana,* which throughout much of the nineteenth century had been the standard reference work on North American skeletal material. Hrdlička's vaunted status in the field also meant that few questioned his identifications and opinions.

Hrdlička developed somewhat of a negative image over the years with regard to the power he wielded in knocking down one by one various claims of skeletal antiquity, but some of the negativity is unwarranted. There can be no doubt either of Hrdlička's skepticism of deep antiquity relative to the occupation of North America or of his adherence to the BAE official line. Holmes, in his preface to Hrdlička's summary of the major purported early remains from North America, made it perfectly clear what the party line was:

> The Bureau of American Ethnology from its foundation has taken a deep interest in all researches relating to the antiquity of man in America, and its attitude in considering the various questions that have arisen has been conservative. In the earlier years of the investigations there existed a rather marked tendency on the part of students, and especially on the part of amateurs and the general public, hastily to accept any testimony that seemed to favor antiquity, and the conservative attitude of the Bureau was emphasized by a desire to counteract and correct this testimony. (Holmes 1907: 3)

Hrdlička's numerous pronouncements of the lack of antiquity among skeletal series presumed to be ancient (e.g., Hrdlička 1907, 1912, 1918) may have contributed to the negative effect on the field that Kidder noted when he commented that reports had become "preponderantly descriptive," since probably few prehistorians were willing to go up against Hrdlička, but I think history has tended to overplay this notion. In reality, Hrdlička was open to the question of antiquity, but he was not open to speculative statements based on inconclusive evidence. In his 1907 summary of reportedly early skeletal material, he noted that although the material he had examined did not pass muster, this conclusion "must not be regarded as equivalent to a declaration that there was no early man in this country; it means only that if early man did exist in North America, convincing proof of the fact from the standpoint of physical anthropology still remains to be produced" (Hrdlička 1907: 98). He continued in a somewhat hopeful, forward-looking vein:

> There may be discouragement in these repeated failures to obtain satisfactory evidence of man's antiquity in America, but there is in this also a stimulus to renewed, patient, careful, scientifically conducted and checked exploration. . . . A satisfactory demonstration of the presence of a geologically ancient man on this continent would form an important link in the history of the American race, and of mankind in general. The Missouri and Mississippi drainage areas offer exceptional opportunities for the discovery of this link of humanity if such really exists. (Hrdlička 1907: 98)

Hrdlička was correct; the Mississippi drainage would eventually produce a "link of humanity," but that link was preceded by a discovery made in August 1927 in the Rio Grande drainage of New Mexico, a discovery that even Hrdlička and Holmes couldn't overlook. I take up the circumstances of that important discovery later in the chapter.

Clarence B. Moore and the Southeastern Waterways

The changing face of American anthropology in the opening decades of the twentieth century may have posed theoretical and methodological problems for professional archaeologists who were eager to stake out new claims, but those problems appear to have had little effect on the enthusiasm of members of various scientific societies across the country. One of those societies was the Academy of Natural Sciences of Philadelphia, whose membership had long been interested in archaeology—an interest constantly being whetted by illustrated reports of artifacts being excavated in the southeastern United States by a wealthy Harvard graduate, who by 1916 had plied the waters of virtually every navigable river from Florida to Louisiana in search of antiquities.

It is difficult to even briefly summarize archaeological work in the United States during the first two decades of the twentieth century and not discuss the work of Clarence B. Moore, an indefatigable researcher who carried with him on his 100-foot sternwheeler a complete excavation team and a physician-cum-skeletal analyst. For 25 years or so—a period stretching from the 1890s to the second decade of the twentieth century—Moore explored southern rivers and bayous in search of burial mounds, in the process excavating several thousand skeletons and recovering thousands of ceramic vessels and other artifacts. He sponsored his own fieldwork and underwrote the production costs of 20 reports dealing with the excavations, which appeared in the *Journal of the Academy of Natural Sciences of Philadelphia*. The reports were often rather sketchy, but the field photographs and artifact illustrations that accompanied the reports—especially the color drawings—were state-of-the-art. Moore gave artifacts from the collection to various museums in the East, but the bulk of his collections was donated to the Academy of Natural Sciences of Philadelphia, which, in what turned out to be a scandal, sold it to the Museum of the American Indian in New York City (Wardle 1929).

Moore actually did little fieldwork in Missouri, spending much of his time in the Midwest in the waterways of northeastern Arkansas. He did, however, spend a few weeks during 1916 exploring several mound groups in Pemiscot, New Madrid, and Mississippi counties in southeastern Missouri. He excavated three mounds in Pemiscot County, finding single burials placed in pits below clay mounds. He visited the Lilbourn mound group in New Madrid County, doing no excavations but noting the still-visible trench left by Swallow in 1856–1857 (Moore [1916: 503] erroneously listed the year as 1858). He also visited Beckwith's Fort in Mississippi County, placing a few "trial holes" in some of the mounds and in the area around the mounds.

Moore's major work was conducted at what he termed the Davis place (now known as Double Bridges), a mound group along the north bank of Portage Open Bay (Moore called it Open Bayou), a crevasse channel of the

Mississippi River that forms the dividing line between Pemiscot and New Madrid counties. Moore identified 23 mounds on the property and excavated 2, finding a submound burial in 1 of them. The site has figured fairly prominently in the archaeology of southeastern Missouri. Robert McCormick Adams and Winslow Walker (1942: 11) mentioned the location, as did James Ford et al. (1955: 47, 51) in their discussion of the geographic distribution of Poverty Point clay balls, which date to the Late Archaic period. James Hopgood (1967) referred extensively to the site, and J. R. Williams (1968) excavated 1,600 square feet of village area in 1967. In that year only 3 mounds were visible, though the original number probably was closer to Adams and Walker's count of 7 or 8 than to Moore's 23 (J. R. Williams 1968: 120). It is evident from his reports that Moore could usually discern the difference between artificial mounds and natural topographic highs, since the former were usually constructed of clay and the latter of coarser sediments. But in many cases such a distinction is not easily made unless a mound is excavated. In the case of Double Bridges, Moore probably counted as mounds the ubiquitous small sand ridges—actually relict-levee remnants—that dot the floodplain landscape of southeastern Missouri.

Much of what we know about prehistoric material culture in the central Mississippi Valley stems from Moore's investigations. His work, along with Holmes's (1903a) pottery treatise, called attention to the Mississippi Valley and formed the basis for many of the projects initiated several decades later. With regard specifically to Missouri, Moore's collections have allowed us to place material remains from the southeastern part of the state in a broader perspective than would otherwise have been possible. D. F. Morse and P. A. Morse (1983: 21) note, "It has become almost traditional to deplore the work of Moore, because of his emphasis on recovery of fine specimens from burials," but they also point out that he kept excavation records, cataloged his materials, and donated his collections to museums (primarily to the Academy of Natural Sciences of Philadelphia).

My primary reason for including a discussion of Moore and his work transcends what he found and goes more toward what was happening to the archaeological record in the central Mississippi River valley before and after the turn of the century. In late 1909 and early 1910, Moore turned his attention to northeastern Arkansas and its two major tributaries of the Mississippi—the St. Francis and White rivers. He offered the following rationale for the work:

> The St. Francis valley has yielded more examples of its ware than has any equal area in the United States, and while this pottery has shared in the full description which has been accorded the earthenware of the region to which it belongs, and while we can hope to shed but little new light upon the pottery itself, we shall try to describe in this report the conditions under which the vessels were placed with the dead and the burial customs of the aborigines who made the vessels, details

which former seekers of aboriginal remains along the St. Francis have failed to make public. (Moore 1910: 259)

It is apparent from Moore's following comments that the central Mississippi River valley was witnessing widespread destruction of its archaeological record through commercially motivated looting:

As the St. Francis (with the possible exception of the Mississippi, a river very many times the length of the St. Francis) long has had the reputation of being richer in aboriginal earthenware than is any other river in the United States, the territory through which the river passes has been for years the headquarters for collectors and for persons wishing to make a livelihood or to increase their means by the sale of Indian pottery, and these individuals have worked for long periods and with indefatigable zeal. Moreover, vast numbers of vessels have been destroyed along the St. Francis in the process of cultivation of cemeteries in which they lay, while others have been dug out or have been shattered in the digging by unskilled local endeavor. Consequently the limitations of the scientific worker along St. Francis river at the present time are apparent. (Moore 1910: 259)

At the Parkin site (P. A. Morse 1981), one of the large, late-Mississippian-period villages in Cross County, Arkansas, Moore (1910: 303) remarked, "The Lumber Company, which later had acquired the property on which the cemetery is, and erected a sawmill nearby, in dull times when the mill was closed, permitted its employees to eke out a livelihood by digging for pots, and this became the avocation of many. Men were actually seen by us at Parkin walking around with sounding-rods in their hands, as elsewhere they might carry canes."

Pothunting was not an occurrence limited either to the twentieth century or to Arkansas. In his 1894 report, for example, Cyrus Thomas noted the following occurrence:

In 1879 and 1880 the people in the neighborhood of Charleston, Mississippi county [Missouri], discovered that the pottery, in which the mounds of this region seem to have been unusually rich, had a considerable commercial value. A regular mining fever at once broke out and spread so rapidly that in some instances as many as twenty-five or thirty men, women, and children could be seen digging for pottery in one field at the same time.

The specimens obtained were taken to Charleston and sold to the merchants, who in turn sold them to various museums, scientific institutions, and relic hunters. It is said that this trade brought to town several thousand dollars. (C. Thomas 1894: 183)

Given the statements by Moore and Thomas regarding the wholesale looting of sites in the central Mississippi River valley, it is a wonder that anything exists today of the archaeological record in vast portions of the valley. This destruction actually accelerated throughout the twentieth century until enactment of legislation in Missouri and Arkansas in the 1980s led to a decrease in activity. However, the more than a century of indiscriminate digging, coupled with new farming technologies—especially those related to land leveling—has seriously depleted the archaeological record and has led to severe underrepresentation of certain material classes, especially intact ceramic vessels. No one will ever know the precise number of vessels removed from southeastern Missouri over the past century, but it surely is in the tens of thousands.

While Clarence Moore was searching the Mississippi River valley for undisturbed mound sites, Gerard Fowke was discovering that it was not only mound sites that were being destroyed. During the second decade of the twentieth century, Fowke turned his attention away from the burial vaults of central Missouri that he had examined in 1906 and 1907 (Fowke 1910) and toward another well-represented class of archaeological sites, the caves and shelters formed by rock overhangs (rock shelters) that are prevalent in the Ozarks.

Gerard Fowke and Cave Archaeology

"When a cavern is fairly lighted and has a dry floor," began Fowke (1922: 14) in his summary entitled "Cave Explorations in the Ozark Region of Central Missouri," "it forms an excellent abode for a small community unable or not disposed to construct shelters more comfortable or convenient; and there is abundant evidence that many caves in the Ozarks were utilized as habitations by the aborigines" (e.g., Figure 4.2). In his report Fowke described more than 75 caves and rock shelters in 11 Missouri counties, with those in Phelps and Pulaski heading the list (Figure 4.3). Many of the sites would later figure prominently in the development of an understanding of Missouri prehistory, but unfortunately Fowke's excavations, which were considerable, are of little analytical use. He presented numerous photographs of excavated items, especially complete skulls, but he listed no intrasite provenience information for the materials.

Fowke's work is interesting here not for what it tells us about the archaeological record of the north-central Ozarks, but for what it tells us about how some prehistorians continued to view the archaeological record late in the second decade of this century. For example, Fowke was still seized by the notion that the skeletal remains he was excavating from the rock shelters, as with the remains he had earlier excavated from the rock crypts (Fowke 1910), were of a different people than those responsible for building the large earthen mounds of the eastern United States. Not that he viewed the mound builders as a vanished race—recall that he had taken an active role in producing the evidence needed by Cyrus Thomas (1894) to dispel that myth. Rather, even as late as 1920 Fowke— and he wasn't alone—suspected that Indians of one group were responsible for the earthen mounds and that Indians of another group lived in the rock shelters and buried their dead in rock crypts:

Figure 4.2. Maxey Cave, Pulaski County, Missouri.

In view of the very primitive conditions under which cave dwellers lived, as denoted by the artificial objects which they left, and the low mentality indicated by the skulls, Mr. W. H. Holmes suggests that a careful and extended study of these abodes may disclose a culture lower than that prevailing among out-door dwellers in the same localities. As no effort would be required to secure warmth and shelter, and as food was abundant and easily procured, the people may never have advanced from savagery, or may have retrograded. (Fowke 1922: 15)

Fowke, who still accepted the Holmesian notion of lower and higher orders of prehistoric people, went to considerable lengths, however, to dispel any notion that he was referring to a long-extinct race of cave-dwellers:

If "Cave Man"—using this term to designate the predecessor of any race or tribe known to history—ever existed in the Mississippi Valley he would not find in any part of it natural features better adapted for his requirements than in the Ozark hills. But, so far, not the slightest trace of his presence has been revealed. Products

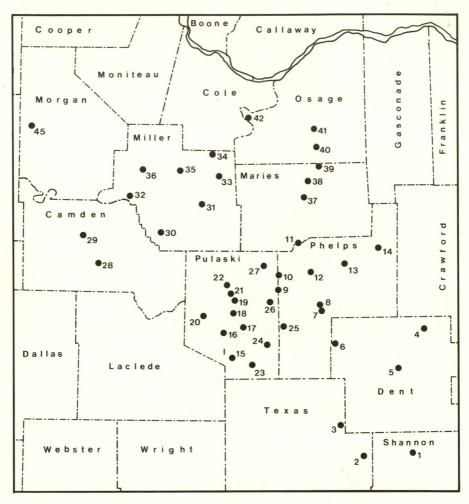

Figure 4.3. Map showing locations of rock shelters and other sites in Missouri visited by Gerard B. Fowke ca. 1920. Numbers were taken directly from Fowke's plate 3, though not all the numbers can be tied directly to the sites he discussed in the text. He conducted excavations at sites 8, which included cairns near the mouth of Gourd Creek, as well as Gourd Creed Cave; 10, Goat Bluff Cave; 18, Sell Cave; 24, Miller's Cave and Ramsey's Cave; and 26, walled graves at Devil's Elbow (after Fowke 1922).

of human industry have been reported as occurring at great depths under other conditions, even at the bottom of loess; though in all such cases there is some uncertainty as to the correctness of the observations. No similar reports have been made in regard to any cave yet explored. On the contrary, whatever may be the depth of the deposit containing them, the artificial objects exhumed are uniform in character from top to bottom; the specimens found on the clay or solid rock floor are of the same class as those barely covered by the surface earth. (Fowke 1922: 15)

In that single passage Fowke buries the notion of "cave men" and also establishes a criterion for distinguishing the remains of early humans from those of the Indians, that is, differences in morphological (shape related) characteristics, though he also states (Fowke 1922: 15) that "it may be necessary, also, to discover with [the remains of early humans] bones of extinct animals." The "uniformity in character" of the artifacts recovered from the myriad rock shelters led Fowke to believe that, at most, the artifacts covered a thousand years or so of occupation, even in the larger shelters such as Miller's Cave[1] in Pulaski County (Figures 4.4 and 4.5). His failure to recognize changes in artifact form was based in part on the way the shelter deposits were excavated but also in part on the fact that he was looking for changes of such magnitude that he failed to see the differences that were present.

The Development of Stratigraphic Excavation

Fowke's lack of understanding of stratigraphic-excavation techniques and subtle morphological changes in artifacts was not an isolated incident but was fairly endemic in Americanist archaeology as a whole. The excavation techniques that today's archaeologists take for granted—excavating through the use of a common grid, for example—were almost unheard of in the United States before 1910 and did not really become commonplace until the 1930s (Dunnell 1986: 28). It should not be surprising that at first researchers such as Kroeber (1909b) did not put much faith in the ability of stratigraphic excavation to provide the key to culture reconstruction and instead relied on geographic patterning. Only when it became obvious that there was considerable antiquity to the archaeological record of North America and that individual sites were capable of containing significant portions of that time depth did stratigraphic excavation become routine in some (but only some) archaeological circles.

Modern students of archaeology find it difficult to believe that stratigraphic excavation, so routinely is it used now, was not always standard practice. However, even a casual glance through almost any archaeological article from before 1910 will demonstrate that sites were rarely excavated by level then.[2] There were, of course, exceptions, such as Holmes's work in the Washington, D.C., quarries and in some cases the work of Thomas's crews, but by and large the standard practice was to open trenches and remove the fill until an object was reached, at which point it was drawn and then removed. Interestingly, profiles of trench

1. Now referred to as Miller Cave (e.g., Markman 1993).
2. Curiously, geologists had used stratigraphic analysis for decades, and certainly this had spilled over into archaeology with regard to the age and positioning of "Paleolithic" artifacts in the New Jersey and Ohio quarries.

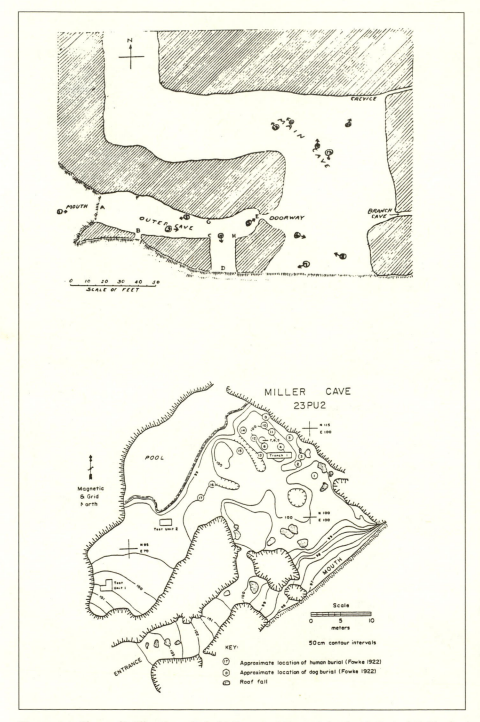

Figure 4.4. Plans of Miller Cave, Pulaski County, Missouri, by (top) Gerard B. Fowke (from Fowke 1922) and (bottom) Charles W. Markman (from Markman 1993). Note the similarities between the two maps (shown at approximately the same scalé) in terms of accuracy in distance (Fowke used only a compass and tape). Fowke, however, was not particularly interested in elevational differences within the cave.

Figure 4.5. Photograph of the main chamber of Miller Cave, Pulaski County, Missouri, showing remnants of the large trenches excavated by Gerard B. Fowke (from Markman 1993).

walls were drawn and the different fill sequences described, but most of the work could not even loosely be termed stratigraphic. Excavations with even less control were carried out by persons such as Moore, whose crews used probing rods to locate pots and burials.

One of the first uses of stratigraphic excavation was naturalist W. H. Dall's excavation of a series of Aleutian Island shell middens (Dall 1877), in which he was able to recognize three distinct strata, though as Willey and Sabloff (1974: 62–63) point out, "in typically unfortunate 19th century terminology he talks of 'lower' and 'higher' stages of culture." They also note that it probably was Dall's knowledge of geology and his background as a naturalist that allowed him to view the archaeological record differently than his contemporaries. Regardless, his work had little if any effect on other archaeologists.

Another archaeologist who made use of stratigraphic excavation was Max Uhle, whose work at the Emeryville shell midden in the San Francisco Bay area produced a lengthy sequence of change in the material record (Uhle 1907). As noted earlier, Kroeber would have no part of Uhle's conclusions, largely because Kroeber was looking for large and sweeping changes in the archaeological record, not small additions and subtractions.

Kroeber's views at the time may have slowed the growth of stratigraphic excavation, but they certainly did not kill the concept. In fact, shortly after

Figure 4.6. Nels Nelson (left), Abbe Henri Breuil, Hugo Obermeier, Paul Wernert, and Pierre Teilhard de Chardin at Castillo Cave, Spain, 1913 (photograph by M. C. Burkitt, negative no. 124770, courtesy Department of Library Services, American Museum of Natural History).

Kroeber published his conservative views (Kroeber 1909b), a former Boas student, Manuel Gamio, used the method to demonstrate the existence of a pottery horizon in the Valley of Mexico that underlay both Aztec and Teotihuacán levels (Gamio 1913). Shortly thereafter, Nels Nelson, a former Kroeber student who had excavated several California shell middens (Nelson 1909, 1910), was hired by the American Museum of Natural History to oversee a major project centered around pueblo occupation in the Galisteo Basin of New Mexico. His upbringing in the Kroeber tradition may have caused an early reluctance to use stratigraphic data to examine small-scale cultural change, but perhaps his trip in 1913 to St. Acheul, France (Nelson 1921: 541), and subsequent work in Paleolithic deposits in Spain (Willey and Sabloff 1974: 92) (Figure 4.6) boosted his confidence. Certainly by the time he had completed two seasons of work in the Galisteo Basin, Nelson had become convinced that careful stratigraphic work would allow him not only to date associated dwellings but also to develop a master ordering of pottery types—an ordering that was aimed at examining change over time in the region. Nelson's (1916) resulting publication of pottery-type counts from a 10-foot-deep trench at San Cristobal, New Mexico (Figure 4.7), was one of the first—if not *the* first—accounts of how types varied in frequency through

Figure 4.7. Stratigraphic cut made by Nels Nelson through midden deposit at San Cristobal, New Mexico (from Wissler 1921 [courtesy American Museum of Natural History]).

time, backed up by actual depth-dependent type frequencies. Willey and Sabloff (1974: 215) remind us that although Nelson was not the first prehistorian in the Southwest to excavate stratigraphically, he was the first to use the method to detect cultural change, since "in none of these [previous] instances was gradual cultural change plotted by means of stratigraphy." Clark Wissler (1917) hailed the stratigraphic excavations as "the new archaeology," a term that, interestingly enough, would be co-opted several times over the following five decades.

By 1920, stratigraphic excavation was certainly not a routine occurrence, though its use was growing, especially in the Southwest. At the center of these examinations of cultural change was pottery, a ubiquitous class of material on Southwestern sites. Wissler noted in one of his reports of the American Museum of Natural History's work on Pueblo sites that "the best indexes to time differences are the changing styles of pottery, so the large historical periods under which the ruins are grouped are named in terms of pottery. This does not mean that these styles of pottery are the only distinguishing characteristics between the periods; each of them can be checked with architectural features, for example, but pottery characters are the most accessible and lend themselves most readily to the method of superposition" (Wissler 1921: 23).

As I point out later, other methods for assigning chronological ordering were also coming into existence, and together they offered archaeologists the opportunity to expand the time line of human occupation in North America. The picture that I hope will emerge from the discussion is that things were perhaps not as bleak as Kidder indicated in his retrospective statement, quoted earlier, that many researchers dodged the issue of origins and comforted themselves by working in the clear air of the late periods. Archaeological materials were being put in some kind of temporal sequence, and archaeologists *were* beginning to identify subtle variations in the archaeological record that seemed to be related to both space and time.

Before we turn to some of those other methods, I want to discuss a case of stratigraphic excavation in Missouri that was conducted on and off between 1903 and 1924, though the controversy that arose from the work lasted much longer. By the time the story was over, it had involved two of the eminent anthropologists of the day, Nelson and Wissler, and had been reported in premier journals. It was not the opportunity to examine minute cultural change stratigraphically that brought Nelson and Wissler to Missouri; rather, it was a small carved bone from the floor of a cave. There is nothing particularly uncommon about a piece of bone that carries a carving of an animal—unless, of course, the animal is a mastodon.

Jacobs Cavern

In 1902 the Department of Archaeology at Phillips Academy, Andover, Massachusetts, sent a circular to newspapers around the country, the purpose of which "was to direct the attention of those especially who reside in the remoter districts to the importance of finding, preserving, and studying specimens of archaeological value" (Peabody and Moorehead 1904: iii). Undoubtedly, the purpose of the circular was also to identify potential sites for the academy to excavate. One of the academy's respondents was E. H. Jacobs of Bentonville, Arkansas, who alerted the staff to the presence of caves and rock shelters in northwestern Arkansas and southwestern Missouri that contained archaeological material. One of those caves, located in the extreme southwestern corner of Missouri, in McDonald County, came to be known as Jacobs Cavern.[3] The academy staff apparently was sufficiently impressed by the gift of specimens that Jacobs sent that they spent about five weeks in April and May 1903 excavating the site.

3. This name has been variously spelled Jacobs, Jacob's, and Jacobs'; the original publication (Peabody and Moorehead 1904) on the site spells it Jacobs, and I use that spelling throughout.

There was nothing out of the ordinary about Jacobs Cavern, at least nothing in its physical appearance that would set it off from the hundreds of other rock shelters and small caves in the region. When Peabody and Moorehead visited the site, the opening was about 21 m across, and the top of the deposit extended about 14 m back into the cave. The floor of the cave, that is, the top of the archaeological deposit, sloped back from the drip line, with the distance from floor to ceiling varying anywhere from a half meter to over 2.5 m. What was remarkable was how Peabody and Moorehead set about excavating the deposit. In what must have been the first use of an excavation grid in Missouri, they laid out the cave floor in a series of 1-m² units and then removed the deposits "in order, front to back, using the lines of stakes as coordinates to determine the position of any objects found. The linear distances of 1 m. were numbered from northwest to southeast in Arabic numerals from 1 to 21, and lettered from southwest to northeast from A to Q" (Peabody and Moorehead 1904: 13) (Figures 4.8 and 4.9). Their system for keeping track of provenience has seen few improvements in the nine intervening decades.

Peabody and Moorehead recognized three levels in the deposit. The upper level, which averaged about 70 cm in thickness, was apparently almost pure ash and contained numerous pieces of animal bone and lithic (stone) items. The middle level, which was about 65 cm thick, consisted of ash and limestone blocks and apparently very few artifacts and animal bone. The lower level was about 95 cm thick and was composed of clay and limestone fragments. Peabody and Moorehead developed a fairly sophisticated (for the time) typological scheme to categorize the lithic artifacts, using a mix of metric, morphological, and functional variables to create the categories. For example, they separated pieces that were over 5 cm long from those that were under 5 cm; then they placed the pieces into one of five categories—pieces without stems, pieces with stems, shouldered knives, perforators, and pieces of doubtful form—the first three of which contained subcategories.

Peabody and Moorehead concluded that the crudeness of the stone tools and the paucity of arrow points and pottery indicated that Jacobs Cavern was occupied by a group or groups of people who had preceded what they termed "the so-called 'mound builders'" (Peabody and Moorehead 1904: 27). Peabody and Moorehead attributed the six bundle burials that were found in the ash level to a group that had occupied the cave after the group responsible for the ash deposit but before the Osage had assumed control of the region.[4] They had no

---

4. Whether the Osage ever inhabited Jacobs Cavern is a moot point. David I. Bushnell Jr. (1915) described and illustrated five pieces of textile from "the valley of Little Sugar Creek," which he assumed was Jacobs Shelter. He identified E. H. Jacobs as having donated the pieces, some of which compare favorably with known Osage items.

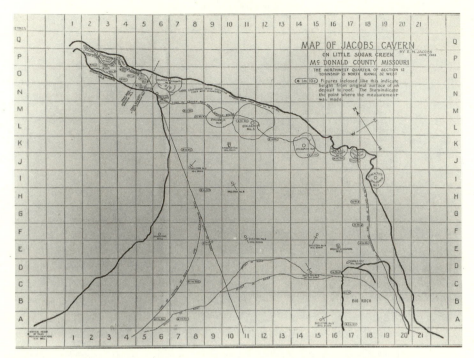

Figure 4.8. Plan of 1903 excavation grid at Jacobs Cavern, McDonald County, Missouri, devised by Charles Peabody and Warren K. Moorehead (map drafted by E. H. Jacobs) (from Peabody and Moorehead 1904 [courtesy Robert S. Peabody Museum of Archaeology, Phillips Academy, Andover, Mass.]).

Figure 4.9. Photograph showing arrangement of the excavation grid at Jacobs Cavern, McDonald County, Missouri, 1903 (from Peabody and Moorehead 1904 [courtesy Robert S. Peabody Museum of Archaeology, Phillips Academy, Andover, Mass.]).

way of estimating when occupation might have begun, except to note that no bones of extinct animals were found.

On the other hand, they laid the foundation for a later piece of what we might term unfortunate work that was used to provide evidence of the cave's occupation by Pleistocene groups. Peabody and Moorehead noticed that all of the stalagmites in the cavern had their points of origin on the surface of the clay-and-limestone deposit and that they had grown up through the ash deposit as a result of continued water seepage through the fissure-ridden overhang. In fact, part of the stalagmitic composition was bone, ash, and chert flakes. They noted that the rate of growth of stalagmites in general should be investigated, though they were unable to provide additional insight. They concluded their report by stating, "The evidence from the quantity of the ashes, the types of implements, the stalagmitic deposits, is toward the assumption of a very early and protracted occupancy of Jacobs Cavern by man" (Peabody and Moorehead 1904: 29). Nothing in their report would have led one to suspect that within two decades the cave would figure prominently in the continuing controversy over the antiquity of human occupation of the New World—that is, unless one could have presaged the "perfection" of techniques to date stalagmite growth and the finding in Jacobs Cavern of a broken white-tailed-deer bone that carried the engraving of a mastodon.

The October 14, 1921, issue of *Science* carried a surprising announcement by Jay L. B. Taylor[5] of Pineville, Missouri:

> To the Editor of Science: It may be of interest to you to learn of the recent reexamination of Jacobs' Cavern . . . [originally] examined by Dr. Charles Peabody and Mr. Warren K. Moorehead, of Phillips Academy. . . .
>
> Subsequent periodical and amateur investigations carried on by the writer, who now owns the land upon which this cavern is located, have resulted in the discovery of a number of very interesting artifacts. . . .
>
> The latest discovery was made on April 17, 1921, when the writer and Mr. Vance Randolph exhumed several engraved, perforated, and otherwise ornamented bones. . . . Immediate preservative treatment was resorted to but was so limited by local conditions that it was found impossible to save more than the most important specimen. . . .
>
> In many respects this bone is very interesting. One side bears an engraving which prominent archaeologists have agreed seems to resemble a mammoth or mastodon. . . .
>
> The writer felt that Phillips Academy was naturally entitled to priority rights of reexamination of the cavern. However, Mr. Moorehead found it impossible to visit the cavern and recommended that Dr. Clark Wissler, of the American Museum

---

5. Taylor worked with Mark R. Harrington during the New York–based Heye Foundation explorations of the Ozarks in the 1920s (see M. R. Harrington 1924a, 1924b).

of Natural History, make the examination. Dr. Wissler is now on the ground for that purpose.

Photographs of the most important specimens are in process of preparation and a detailed report of operations will be made public as soon as practicable. (J. L. B. Taylor 1921a: 357–58)

Taylor (1921b) quickly published a full description of the carved piece in *Natural History*[6] and included a photograph of the mastodon carving and a drawing of the other artifacts, which reportedly had decomposed shortly after they were found (Figure 4.10). The drilled bones and shell, Taylor reported, had come from around a stalagmite, the one he thought was labeled number 4 on Peabody and Moorehead's map (Figure 4.8). Luckily, the night of the discovery Randolph made life-size drawings of the pieces, after which Taylor locked them away. Taylor (1921b: 595) reported that "professional duties had prevented me from making frequent examination of my collection," though in the same article he mentioned that he had become worried about the possibility that the specimens were frauds and that he had "no desire to be severely ridiculed if the 'relics' proved to be fakes" (J. L. B. Taylor 1921b: 595). If he was so worried, one wonders why he didn't pull the specimens back out for another look from time to time.

In any event, when he did reinspect the specimens, he was horrified to discover that they had begun to disintegrate. Coating them with oil did nothing to stop the disintegration, and when, on professional advice, he switched to paraffin, the only specimen that had not disintegrated completely was the one with the mastodon carving! The bone remained in its paraffin casing until Clark Wissler's visit on August 17, 1921.

Wissler never reported on his examination except in a letter to Taylor, which the latter published at the end of his article in *Natural History* (J. L. B. Taylor 1921b). Wissler was guarded in his opinion of the find, though he was so tactful that Taylor never realized he was straddling the fence:

The question your find raises is whether the person who made the sketch on the bone that has been preserved saw a mastodon or mammoth. This cannot be answered positively, but the probabilities of the case can be estimated. . . .

At once the objection will be raised that the bone is recent. Though the mastodon and mammoth are characteristic of Pleistocene time, it is not known

6. In one of those strange twists of fate, Taylor's article on the mastodon bone appeared in the same issue of *Natural History* as, and in fact followed directly, Henry Fairfield Osborn's article arguing for the authenticity of Piltdown Man. This would not be the only time that Osborn, who was the director of the American Museum and a powerful figure in comparative anatomy, would later be embarrassed by his pronouncements of authenticity. He was quick to embrace a tooth from Nebraska as being from a fossil human, later having to admit that the tooth was indeed from a pig.

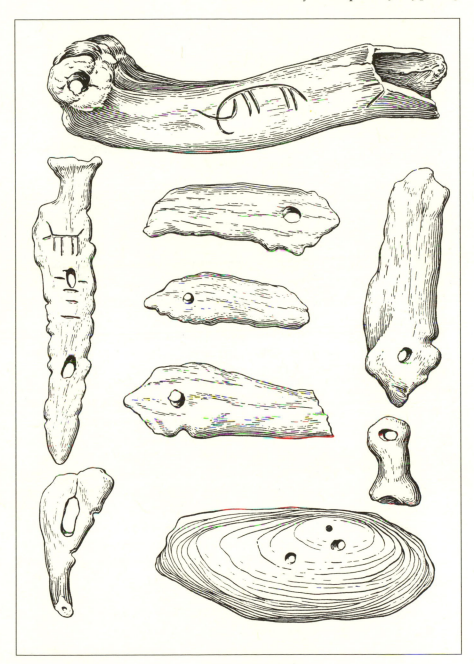

Figure 4.10. Drawings of artifacts recovered from Jacobs Cavern, McDonald County, Missouri, by Vance Randolph and Jay Taylor (from J. L. B. Taylor 1921b [courtesy American Museum of Natural History]).

when they became extinct; for all that is known to the contrary, these great mammals may have held out to within three thousand years ago. . . . there is nothing zoological that makes your interpretation improbable.

It appears that this bone was found in the present surface of the cave, but approximately five feet of deposit were taken out by Moorehead in 1903; hence this bone is older than anything found by him. . . . Also, there are still in the cavern almost five feet of deposit, in the main clay, through which you were so kind as to sink a shaft in my presence. This excavation indicated the presence of man's handiwork in all parts of this deposit. . . . One must conclude, therefore, that there are remains in the cavern that are of even greater age than the bone in question. . . .

The writer will do everything he can to further this investigation to the end that the complete story of Jacobs' Cavern may be revealed. It is to be hoped that at last we are on the trail of early man in America.

Perhaps it was Wissler who persuaded Nels Nelson, one of his colleagues at the American Museum of Natural History, to follow that trail of early man by renewing excavations at Jacobs Cavern in 1923. Nelson excavated a 16-meter-long trench, from the back of the cave to the front, reaching bedrock at the bottom of the excavation. He then extended the trench 30 meters down the talus slope to the valley floor and also connected the portion of the trench within the cave to Taylor's excavation made in 1921 (Figure 4.11). A thin cultural deposit—the same one found in 1903 by Peabody and Moorehead—occurred in the extreme upper level of the cave trench, thickening as it ran downslope. Below that, "we found nothing," Nelson (1928a: 330) stated five years later—not in a report on the excavations but in a book review of a volume produced by his own institution. That volume, which appeared in *The Anthropological Papers of the American Museum of Natural History,* was entitled "The Antiquity of the Deposits in Jacob's Cavern" and was written by geologist Vernon C. Allison (1926). In it, Allison claimed great antiquity for the deposits. In fact, he claimed that a tiny stratum containing bone fragments at the base of the clay deposit was evidence of continuous occupation by humans over the period from 16,080 to 11,730 B.C. How did he arrive at this remarkably precise estimate? He simply took Peabody and Moorehead's suggestion and dated the stalagmites.

As a first step, Allison, encouraged by A. E. Douglass's work on tree-ring dating, attempted to count the rings in one of the dirty stalagmites that Peabody and Moorehead found extruding through the ashy level (Figure 4.12). He discovered he couldn't actually count the rings, so he ingeniously rigged a contraption on the hill above the cavern and over a period of months trapped windblown sediments to calculate an average yearly buildup. He then divided that figure (0.8 mm of sediment per year) into the figure representing the total length of the stalagmite to calculate the number of years (1,213) represented in the ashy stalagmite. Then, to tie the floating estimate to a fixed date, he superimposed his growth rings on a growth curve for a California redwood, arriving at a date of 730 B.C. for the year during which the rising ash level reached the growing stalagmite. If you think Allison's reasoning is slightly bizarre, you might be interested to know that he earlier (Allison 1924) had reasoned that stalagmite growth was tied to the late Pleistocene glacial sequence in Europe. During the supposedly wet period between 16,080 and 11,730 B.C., the stalagmites started forming. Since the climate was cool and wet, humans had to live indoors. With the amelioration of conditions around 11,730 B.C., stalagmite growth slowed, and humans "abandoned the cavern and lived in the open" (Allison 1926: 324). That's quite a leap of faith. By the way, Allison never stated where he obtained such precise dates for the European glacial wet period.

As an addendum to his report, Allison tacked on a vigorous defense of the carved bone, noting that, as a result of Nelson's excavations in 1923, "there were formulated three tentative questions reflecting, in a purely negative manner, upon the genuineness of the 'mastodon' bone" (Allison 1926: 328). The questions, it turns out, were conveyed by Nelson to Allison at the time the latter was attempting to publish his monograph (Nelson 1928a: 332), though Allison does not reveal that fact. Nelson asked (1) why no other carved or drilled bone had been recovered by Peabody and Moorehead or by Wissler; (2) why he (Nelson) had found no similar items among the 6,000 animal bones excavated in 1923; and (3) why the other drilled objects had disintegrated but the mastodon bone remained intact. Allison answered simply that all other investigators had missed a tiny deposit that he (Allison) had discovered in 1924. The deposit (labeled "3" on Figure 4.13) thinned out toward the back of the shelter, but from it Allison recovered enough faunal material to suit himself that the tiny scraps were from large Pleistocene animals. It was from this deposit, Allison averred, that the mastodon carving had come.

Allison conducted several tests to determine whether the bone with the carving more closely resembled other bones from the deposit or a modern bone. Using a series of filters, he photographed the bone in question alongside one from the ash deposit and a piece of modern animal bone obtained from a butcher, on both of which he duplicated the mastodon carving. He found that in almost all cases the "mastodon" bone and the ash-deposit bones contrasted sharply with the recently butchered bone. Here, Allison said, was evidence of contemporaneity between the "mastodon" bone and the ash-deposit bones, making the "mastodon" bone at least 3,000 years old (based on his stalagmite date).

Readers, especially professional archaeologists, interested in how best to attack poor archaeological analyses should read Nelson's (1928a) review of Allison's report. It is a brilliant and at the same time withering, point-by-point analysis of Allison's conclusions, including that on the purported authenticity of the mastodon engraving. Nelson ridiculed the dating techniques and excoriated Allison for his absurd calculations; pointed out that the bone fragments in the

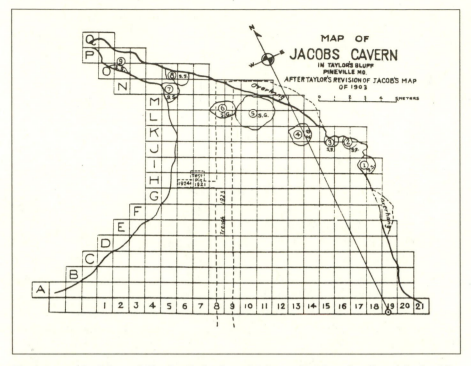

Figure 4.11. Revision of Charles Peabody and Warren K. Moorehead's original grid plan of Jacobs Cavern, McDonald County, Missouri, showing locations of excavations undertaken in 1921, 1923, and 1924 (from Allison 1926 [courtesy American Museum of Natural History]).

Figure 4.12. Photograph showing stalagmitic material from Jacobs Cavern, McDonald County, Missouri, with flint and bone embedded (from Allison 1926 [courtesy American Museum of Natural History]).

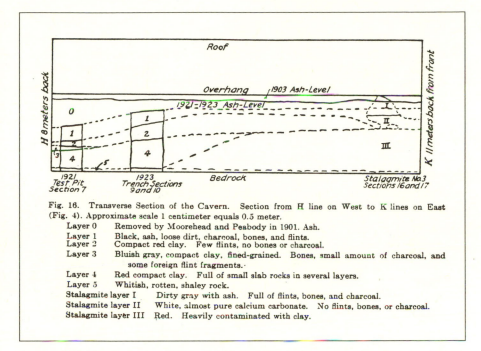

Fig. 16. Transverse Section of the Cavern. Section from H line on West to K lines on East (Fig. 4). Approximate scale 1 centimeter equals 0.5 meter.

Layer 0	Removed by Moorehead and Peabody in 1901. Ash.
Layer 1	Black, ash, loose dirt, charcoal, bones, and flints.
Layer 2	Compact red clay. Few flints, no bones or charcoal.
Layer 3	Bluish gray, compact clay, fined-grained. Bones, small amount of charcoal, and some foreign flint fragments.
Layer 4	Red compact clay. Full of small slab rocks in several layers.
Layer 5	Whitish, rotten, shaley rock.
Stalagmite layer I	Dirty gray with ash. Full of flints, bones, and charcoal.
Stalagmite layer II	White, almost pure calcium carbonate. No flints, bones, or charcoal.
Stalagmite layer III	Red. Heavily contaminated with clay.

Figure 4.13. Cross section showing Vernon Allison's depiction of strata in Jacobs Cavern, McDonald County, Missouri (from Allison 1926 [courtesy American Museum of Natural History]).

lowest level, even if they were in primary context as opposed to having somehow worked their way down into the lowest level, were of modern animals; and noted that the tests used to determine the antiquity of the mastodon carving had not been established properly. Nelson probably was greatly upset that the American Museum would publish such foolishness, and he came out swinging, stating in his opening paragraph, "This paper is primarily a geological study and as such should be reviewed by one or more competent geologists. Unfortunately I have not yet found anybody willing to undertake the task" (Nelson 1928a: 329).

Nelson's points of criticism are too numerous and involved to include in much detail here, but in brief, he reiterated the same points he had raised earlier, including the fact that Jay Taylor had found the only carved or drilled bone on the site, despite the presence of thousands of faunal specimens there. He also pointed out that the edges of the engraving were sharp, which should not have been the case if the bone were ancient, and that the surface of the bone inside the engraved lines was of a different color than the rest of the bone. Also, he asked, "how comes it that the cracks [that had developed as a result of post-recovery deterioration] should have steered so nearly clear of the incised figures, especially as the artificial incisions would naturally have tended to weaken the bone within the limits of their own particular range and not outside?" (p. 332). Nelson never came right out and said that Taylor was guilty of fraud; rather, he stated, "In this particular case, moreover, I have no grounds even for suspicion. I don't know the people around Pineville, having resided there only three weeks. Messrs. Taylor and Randolph, the discoverers of the engraved bone in question, are, on the other hand, in far better position to judge of the probabilities of the case" (p. 332).

Regardless of what Nelson thought on the matter of fraud, he was more than direct in his criticism of Allison's method of calculating dates of occupation: "Dr. Allison resorts to what seems to a mere archaeologist an exceedingly hazardous performance: he superposes his stalagmitic growth curve on a California redwood growth curve and tells us in effect that the inhabitants of Jacob's cavern became frisky enough to kick up the ashes in exactly the year [11,]730 B.C.! The scientifically minded are supposed to court accuracy, and I personally would welcome nothing so much as an absolute chronology for prehistoric times, but this is too much" (p. 333). Nelson implored at the end of his review, "let the Jacob's cavern mastodon rest in peace" (p. 335). Allison (1928) made a halfhearted rejoinder to Nelson's attack, which Nelson (1928b) answered briefly, but the issue was dead—that is, until 20 years later, when Taylor resurrected the mastodon once again.

That final piece was a rather sad attempt by a man to clear his reputation by reiterating that he had not faked the carving. A good portion of his defense consisted of attempting to demonstrate that Nelson was predisposed against great antiquity because of a bad experience he had once had. It had been almost 25 years since Nelson had been to Pineville, but Taylor remembered that in 1923 Nelson had confided to him that during a trip to Europe he had purchased a number of specimens that had later been shown to be fakes. Was Nelson, Taylor asked, so embittered by this experience that he was determined to view every purportedly old artifact as fraudulent? Or, he continued, did Nelson think that Taylor was in financial straits at the time of the discovery (which he admitted he was) and did Nelson conclude "that in my hill-billy simplicity I had faked this discovery in order to raise money?" (J. L. B. Taylor 1947: 693). In a fit of pique or maybe because the site had become a millstone, Taylor sold the site, noting that he had spent 40 years and several thousand dollars protecting it. He added only, "Much as I regretted the necessity for that action, I felt under no further obligations to science" (J. L. B. Taylor 1947: 695).

So ended the saga of the Jacobs Cavern mastodon. The carved bone was once on display in the capitol museum in Jefferson City, but its current whereabouts are unknown. As for Taylor and Randolph, the question remains: did they fake the carving to draw national attention, or did they simply fall prey to someone else's prank? Of course, we'll never know the answer to this question, but if we consider all the events, we are almost forced to conclude that they staged the whole affair. If they had found a single bone with a mastodon carved on its side, one conclusion would be that someone mucking about in the cave—Taylor (1921b: 591) stated that the deposit had been rummaged through by "hunters, tourists, and the like"—had sat down, picked up a piece of bone from the ash deposit, etched a mastodon in it, and then discarded it. Not a particularly reasonable conclusion, but at least a plausible one. But it wasn't just one bone that Taylor and Randolph found, but rather a cache of eight drilled bones and a drilled shell, which seems to negate that conclusion. It also tends to cast doubt on the possibility that someone else perpetrated a hoax. In fact, Taylor (1921b: 594) admitted that it was only by chance that he saw the first piece and that if he and Randolph hadn't started poking around they wouldn't have found the other pieces.

No, I believe that the evidence points to a hoax and that it was perpetrated by Taylor and Randolph. A good guess would be that they found the cache of bones and shell, which probably were burial goods, and that the bones bore the drill holes and perhaps the etching shown in Figure 4.10—all but the mastodon, that is. To increase the excitement of their find, one of them added the mastodon later. Also, it is inconceivable that the other specimens deteriorated to the extent that nothing was left. Rather, Taylor and Randolph probably discarded them to keep comparisons from being made. Nelson noted that the edges of the mastodon engraving were still sharp; it would have been interesting to compare those edges with the edges of the other engraved piece (Figure 4.10). The comparison probably would destroy their story, as would a comparison of the drill hole on the "mastodon" bone with those on the other bones.

Regardless of the accuracy of any suspicions regarding the discovery, the Jacobs Cavern mastodon carving assumes an important place in American archaeology alongside other curiosities such as the Davenport, Iowa, elephant pipes and the mastodon on the Holly Oak shell gorget from Delaware (e.g., Meltzer and Sturtevant 1983). Their value, if there is any, is in reminding us that things aren't always as they first appear. They also stand as testament to the vast amount of time and money that can be wasted in an attempt either to verify an item's authenticity or to demonstrate its fraudulence. Archaeologists are constantly barraged with either fraudulent materials or legitimate materials from highly questionable contexts, and they often become enmeshed in controversies that quiet down for a while, only to flare up again. The best advice was offered by Nelson: Give your best opinion and then let the matter rest in peace.

Folsom and Related Discoveries

Coincidentally, as Nelson was laying the Jacobs Cavern mastodon carving to rest, Americanist archaeologists were coming face to face with the prospect of having to accept that humans and now-extinct fauna had in fact lived side by side on the American continent. Prior to 1927, purported finds of early tools had been invalidated on various grounds, but the "breakthrough," as Willey and Sabloff (1974: 126) term it, came that year, when several small, fluted points were recovered in clear association with the remains of extinct bison *(Bison antiquus)* near Folsom, New Mexico (Figgins 1927). The stratigraphic association was in a geological context that beyond question lay on the temporal border between the late Pleistocene and the early Holocene; eventually, the remains of 23 bison and 19 Folsom points would be unearthed. The Folsom discovery, however, was only the first of many finds that would be made during the next decade and a half (e.g., Howard 1935; F. H. H. Roberts 1935, 1940) in which evidence of a temporal association between humans and extinct fauna would be equally clear.

One important feature of those associations was the nature of the projectile points themselves: they were easily recognizable because of the fine flaking and the presence of channel scars down both faces that resulted from the removal of long flakes. It was thus impossible to confuse the points with more recent examples, and the points became instant chronological markers. In those early days no distinction was made between Folsom points and what would later be known as Clovis points. Neither was it then recognized that Folsom points dated slightly later than Clovis points over most of the West and Midwest. It was clear, however, that also associated with extinct forms of bison were well-flaked, unfluted points that were unmistakable in terms of their morphological characteristics. These points, which were correctly assumed to postdate the use of Folsom points, were eventually given the name Yuma (see F. H. H. Roberts 1940)—a name that has given way to numerous point types. The vast majority of these early points were not found in stratigraphic context, but their relative ages were indisputable. Once archaeologists recognized the antiquity of the points, reports on the distribution of Yuma and Folsom points started flooding in (e.g., Fischel 1939; Renaud 1932).

Time-and-Space Systematics: Beyond Stratigraphic Excavation

The intermittent work that was undertaken in Jacobs Cavern during the early twentieth century is an example of the growth of stratigraphic excavation as an analytical method nationwide. Peabody and Moorehead noted only two levels in their 1903 work; Allison later recognized five (Figure 4.13), one of which was his purported Pleistocene stratum. In fact, a significant portion of Allison's support for the antiquity of the deer bone containing the mastodon carving was the fact that its original stratigraphic context was deep in level 3, or the lowest level, which he claimed he and Nelson had found in 1923.[7] Regardless of the validity

---

7. Nelson's (1928a: 334) comments lead one to believe that Nelson never saw the level during his work.

of Allison's claims, it is apparent that by the early 1920s stratigraphic context was being used routinely to provide support for chronological assessments: the deeper a deposit, perhaps the farther back in time it went.

Not all archaeological deposits are 10 feet deep like those in Jacobs Cavern, and even in those cases where they *are* deep, they do not always contain the full cultural sequence that archaeologists hope for. Wissler (1921: 15) summed up the problem nicely:

> If the people once living in what is now a ruin in southwestern United States had never moved away and had always rebuilt near the same spot, there would be little difficulty in reading their history. All we would then need to do would be to dig a trench through the accumulated ashes, sweepings, etc., and study the markings and contents of the exposed sections, where everything is laid down more or less successively in order of time. But nowhere is the problem so simple. Every now and then the population shifted. For aught we know, new peoples came as conquerors and evicted the rightful owners. Anyway, what we do find is that some ruins were occupied for a very long time, others for but a brief time, but none of them for all of the time. So, to get a time chart for the Southwest as a whole, the results obtained from many, many different ruins must be patiently pieced together and by precise methods.

What *were* some of these precise methods, and how did they affect both the growth of Americanist archaeology and the creation of various interpretations of the archaeological record? I use most of the remainder of this chapter to examine some of those methods, because together they laid the groundwork for what transpired in archaeology from 1940 on. Some of the methods remain essentially unchanged today; others have fallen out of common use over the years. Regardless, it is difficult to understand why certain interpretations grew out of archaeological work during the post-1940 period without understanding the historical background to the methods used, in a sense, to generate the interpretations. As I hope to show, Missouri archaeology was as much a product of those methods as was Americanist archaeology generally.

Cross-Dating

One means of assigning time to an archaeological deposit is by matching artifacts from the deposit with look-alike specimens from a deposit of known age. This method, as I noted above, was used to identify Paleo-Indian sites after the Folsom and related discoveries were made. The Folsom point type, for example, was so distinctive and apparently so short-lived that it made an excellent temporal marker. One did not need to recover the remains of extinct animals with every newly discovered Folsom point to determine its age. As more deep, stratified sites were excavated across the United States, various ceramic and lithic items were found to be excellent temporal markers that could be extended to assist in dating nonstratified sites. In those days before the advent of radiocarbon as a dating method it was not always clear what the absolute dates of the markers were, but they certainly could be used to tell time in a relative sense. For example, if projectile points of style A consistently occurred below points of style B, then it was assumed that points of style A were older than those of style B. Points of style A found at other sites were presumed to be similar in age to the one from the stratified site. Thus, as Wissler (1921: 15) had noted, chronological ordering on a regional scale was being "patiently pieced together." By the middle of the second decade of the twentieth century, ceramic types began to figure importantly in another method of dating that was quite distinct from cross-dating.

Seriation

As the stratigraphic method of telling time began to be fairly routine, archaeologists added another means of controlling for time in a relative sense, and the method, seriation, soon became widespread in Americanist archaeology. By 1917 the basis of the method had been established in print through the publication of two seriation studies, Kroeber (1916) and Spier (1917). Seriation, a term used by Spier but not by Kroeber (Willey and Sabloff 1974: 101), is based on the same basic premise as stratigraphically defined changes in artifact types: through time, people change the way they make and decorate things such as ceramic vessels. For example, at time A they paint vessel exteriors with red paint; at time B they paint vessels white; and at time C they paint them black. An important piece of the premise is that when they begin to paint vessels white, they are still painting some of them red. Likewise, when they shift to black paint, they are still painting some vessels white.

Nelson, Wissler, and others (e.g., Alfred V. Kidder) had amply demonstrated through stratigraphic excavation that this principle held and that changing percentages of pottery types could be a useful way to track time. What Kroeber and Spier did was to show that sites could be ordered by using surface-collected sherds to create the ordering. Surface collections from each site could be subdivided and the percentages of each type computed:

> The first subgroup (of pottery collections) contains thirty-five samples from as many ruins. The wares are corrugated, black-on-white, black-on-red, and black-on-white-on-red. These samples may be arbitrarily ranked according to their percentages of corrugated ware from highest to lowest. The test of such a seriation as an historical series will lie in the observed seriation of the accompanying wares; for when a group of three or more distinct, but mutually dependent, values are ranked according to some postulated sequence for one, and the other values are found to present serially concurrent variations, it may be concluded that the result is not fortuitous. (Spier 1917: 282)

Figure 4.14. James A. Ford standing in front of Harold Fisk's (1944) map of the Mississippi alluvial valley (ca. 1961) (courtesy Roger T. Saucier).

I agree with Willey and Sabloff's (1974: 101) comment, "This is one of the best and most concise definitions of archaeological seriation in the literature." So was Spier's defense of seriation as a method: "We have no reason to doubt that the samples of potsherds collected from successive levels of ash heaps present us with valid chronological indices. Why then cavil at the use of similar samples from the surfaces of ash heaps?" (Spier 1917: 326).

It wasn't ash heaps but rather the black gumbo of the Gulf Coast from which James A. Ford (Figure 4.14) removed pottery sherds for his 1936 publication, "Analysis of Indian Village Site Collections from Louisiana and Mississippi." Ford used stratigraphic evidence from the Peck site in Catahoula Parish, Louisiana, and surface collections of sherds from over a hundred sites in both Mississippi and Louisiana to define seven ceramic complexes, four identified with historic tribes that occupied the lower Mississippi River valley in the sixteenth and seventeenth centuries—the Tunica, the Caddo, the Choctaw, and the Natchez—and three that were prehistoric—Coles Creek, Deasonville, and Marksville. Ford's use of the word *complex* for the units implied that each unit comprised specimens of a number of ceramic types and other items, some of which overlapped from one complex to the next. Proportional seriation (often referred to as *frequency seriation*) was used to order sites chronologically; once the sites were ordered, certain breaks in the sequence were made, thus yielding the complexes.

Typological Classification

As important as Ford's contributions were to seriation as a developing method (culminating in his 1962 paper entitled "A Quantitative Method for Deriving Cultural Chronology"), it is his explicitly stated notions of what types are (and, as importantly, what they are not) that are of particular importance here. In fact, without an understanding of his notion of what types are and what they can be used for, it is impossible to place his seriational study in proper perspective. Prior to the late 1930s, few if any archaeologists were concerned either with how to construct artifact types or, more importantly, with the formulation of general principles for typing artifacts. As we have seen, earlier archaeologists certainly created types—for example, Peabody and Moorehead (1904) used a morphological scheme to discriminate among stone artifacts from Jacobs Cavern—but they never gave their reasons for choosing one particular typological system over another.

In the Southwest, pottery types were used to create chronological structure in archaeological deposits, but this approach was not universally accepted in Americanist archaeology. In the Midwest, pottery types were used more as descriptive units. For example, Holmes's (1903a) term *Mississippi* was in use in the 1930s as a pottery-classification unit, but there was no integration of the term into a coherent statement that addressed the nature of the pottery-bearing portion of the archaeological record. Ford's real contribution was, as Willey and Sabloff (1974: 108) note,

> to present pottery typology as a part of the "package" of stratigraphy-seriation-typology which made possible regional chronologies first in the Southeast and then in the Ohio Valley–Upper Mississippi area. In his seriational and survey monograph of 1936 Ford made the case for the pottery type as the measuring device of cultural variation in space and time; but it was in a conference report on Southeastern pottery classification and nomenclature [Ford 1938a] that he set down his most unequivocal statements on this theme.

That conference report, carrying no author but written by Ford, contained the descriptive standards of southeastern ceramics (Dunnell 1986: 172) that became widely used (see Guthe 1934 for a precursor). In it, Ford was, as Willey and Sabloff (1974: 108–9) note, unequivocal over both the way types had been used up to that point and the way types *should* be used: "The inadequacy of the procedure of dividing pottery into 'types' merely for the purposes of describing the material is recognized. This is merely a means of presenting raw data. Types should be classes of material which promise to be useful tools *in interpreting culture history*" (Ford 1938a as cited in Willey and Sabloff 1974: 109; emphasis added). Here Ford established a position that would remain essentially unchanged in his mind: artifact types are tools created and used by the archaeologist to order archaeological deposits, that is, to interpret culture history. Later, Americanist archaeology would become embroiled in a debate over the meaning of types— we'll examine this debate shortly—but Ford's views on types for a time carried the day in midwestern and southeastern United States archaeology.

The standardization of terminology relative to pottery categorization may, as Dunnell (1986: 165) points out, have eased communication between and among archaeologists, but it had another, lasting consequence. For Ford and the host of midwestern and southeastern archaeologists who followed him and/or were his contemporaries, types were formulated on the principle "use whatever works." Unfortunately, although Ford and his colleagues had worked diligently to set up a series of terms that could be used consistently, the results were inconsistent from region to region and from investigator to investigator. It is important to point out why this was (and continues to be) so, because the classificatory system has contributed directly to how the archaeological record of Missouri has come to be viewed. I quote Dunnell at some length, because he has produced the best exposition of these problems. He notes the strongly dimensional nature of twentieth-century Americanist artifact classifications (see Dunnell 1971), particularly pottery classifications.

> Although the list of dimensions varied somewhat from area to area based on tradition and the variable character of archaeological materials, this approach provided that a type hold some value in each of a standard set of dimensions of observation and measurement. Just as importantly, beyond setting limits on the dimensions that could be used, this approach did not provide any guidance in the *selection* of definitive attributes. They were literally *descriptions of pottery assigned to a particular type*, not definitions of the type. While a value or set of values was required for each dimension (e.g., a particular paste texture, a particular temper, or a particular exterior and surface treatment), which dimensions were definitive varied from type to type and were unmarked in the descriptions themselves. Thus, type descriptions embodied a very substantial amount of operational ambiguity. One had to know, case by case and a priori, which attributes were cause for the assignment of type and which were simply attributes associated

typically with the definitive elements. Because the type descriptions were in fact descriptions of particular pottery assemblages (how else could one obtain a "thickness" range, for example), a further and even more far-reaching structural ambiguity was introduced. Were types the creations of archaeologists and, thus, definitionally associated sets of attributes (i.e., analytic tools for the dissection of the archaeological record), or were they empirically associated sets of attributes that "discovered" existential entities? Either interpretation was possible, and both would be pursued. (Dunnell 1986: 165–66)

One of the problems inherent in Ford's work—and one that continues to plague Americanist archaeology—was his failure to distinguish between the type as a class and the objects that were assigned to the types (Dunnell 1986: 173). Types were established through reference to certain criteria, whatever those criteria might be (they differed from type to type, as Dunnell stated). Any object that had those essential characteristics was placed in that type. If it exhibited other characteristics, it was placed in another type. And if an object came along that did not meet the specifics of an established type, a new type was created to accommodate it. But artifacts and the types constructed to accommodate them are not the same thing; unfortunately, "Ford never clearly distinguishes between the type as a class and objects that are assigned to it" (Dunnell 1986: 173).

Symptomatic of the internal inconsistency of the classificatory schemes of the period was the pervasive notion, usually implied, that there was an "evolution" of ceramic types as pottery makers added more attributes[8] to their repertoire— attributes that might be related to design (style), function, or technology. One has only to look at many of the articles and monographs of the period to see the way in which the archaeological record was being characterized, that is, as a steady stream of pottery types, one following on the heels of another. But types can't evolve. Types can't even change. What *can* change is how people make or decorate pots. Rim angles can change, lip form can change, temper can change. It is important to keep in mind that these dimensions change through *replacement* of one feature by another and not through some kind of transformation. We can use observed changes in the frequency of various attribute states of the dimensions to measure change; we cannot use types for the same purpose. The study that came closest to making this position explicit was by a contemporary of Ford's, Irving Rouse, whose *Prehistory in Haiti* (1939) is an often overlooked classic of the period. In it, Rouse made a telling statement: "Each type . . . is . . . by definition . . . an immutable pattern. Hence it cannot grow or evolve" (p. 14). In other words, Rouse eschewed the notion of transformation.

---

8. Attributes are alternate states of dimensions. For example, one analytical dimension could be "kind of temper"; the attribute states would be "shell," "limestone," "sand," and so on.

Direct Historical Approach

Recall that four of Ford's (1936) ceramic complexes assumed the names of Indian groups that had resided in the southeastern United States and that had been in contact with Euro-Americans. Archaeologists came more and more to recognize the value of historical-period documents both in unraveling the question of which groups were where during which time periods and in documenting various aspects of Indian life. If one could begin with the known and work backward in time, tracing cultural continuities and noting points of divergence, then one was, in effect, creating culture histories in reverse. No one can argue with the approach, which came to be known as the *direct historical approach* (Wedel 1938), but it still carried with it the baggage of the ill-defined type concept. The approach was not new in the 1930s but rather had been the strategy adopted by Powell and Thomas for the Division of Mound Exploration: First, document the similarities in cultural patterns between those evident from ethnographic and ethnohistorical research and those evident archaeologically (see Meltzer 1985: 254). Second, connect the patterns and you have a continuous thread from the past to the present. In "An Introduction to Nebraska Archeology," William Duncan Strong (1935; see also Strong 1936) noted the same thing:

> It is the firm belief of the author that the possibilities of historic archeology in North America are not fully realized by the majority of anthropologists at the present time. Wherever the approach has been from the known historic into the unknown prehistoric, the results have more than justified the method, as the present superior status of archeology in the Iroquoian and Pueblo areas amply demonstrates. It seems surprising, therefore, that even today there are archeologists more interested in segregating obscure early cultures of unknown periods and affiliations than they are in determining the historic cultures and sequences represented in the regions to be worked. Obviously, in such work the historic cultures need not be an end in themselves, but they do seem to represent *the threads that give most promise of untangling the complex skein of prehistory.* (Strong 1935: 296; emphasis added)

Writing a few years later, Strong (1940: 377) tempered his zeal somewhat:

> With the protohistoric period the need for a general methodology to supplement and extend the direct historic approach becomes acute. Once beyond the historic period specific tribal organization merges into the complex streams of culture history. The known tribal terminations of these streams are essential to link history and prehistory. They convert archeological sequence into historic reality and anchor archeology to social science. Yet, from the protohistoric to the earlier periods, all tribal and linguistic appellations become increasingly fallacious. The anthropologist can legitimately trace the history of a specific tribe or even linguistic stock down into the successive prehistoric archeological constellations of

which it becomes a part, but the archeologist as a technician must eschew ethnic terminology for prehistoric horizons.

What Strong was arguing for was the use of the direct historical approach but without the terms used to categorize the material culture of ethnohistorically known groups. Strong was never precise about how far one could push ethno-historic analysis backward in time. As we will see, pattern-similarity studies of the time were loaded with functional assignments of artifacts based solely on analogs in the ethnohistorical record. This is what Strong (1940) was arguing against, though for the most part his call went unheeded.

Regional Synthesis

Despite the enormous amount of fieldwork that was being undertaken in the eastern United States during the 1930s, few efforts were made to integrate the information that was coming in. This information was in the form of a dizzying array of artifact variation, though if one was familiar enough with materials from different regions, one could see numerous threads of continuity running through various artifact assemblages. Archaeologists began wondering how best to categorize the remains in terms of time and space. Never far removed from archaeological thought during the 1930s was the notion that diffusion of peoples or ideas had led to some of the broad patterns seen in the archaeological record, but how could one isolate this process to the exclusion of others? It appeared that as a first step some system was needed that would categorize the patterns evident in the record.

One system that appeared was the midwestern taxonomic method. The system was developed initially in 1932 and appeared in its final form seven years later (W. C. McKern 1939). Although the system was more or less abandoned in the 1950s, it enjoyed wide usage in the Midwest during the 1940s, especially in Illinois and Missouri. The system was simple in its organizing principles, but it has come to be misunderstood in terms of the purpose for which its proponents intended it. It was not, at base level, a method for ordering things in terms of time, which to today's archaeologist might appear curious as well as counterproductive. Why would any system abandon time as an important dimension?

In reality, the developers of the method never intended that time would be ignored; they simply focused attention initially on pattern recognition. They did, however, make it clear that the taxonomic method was *independent* of time. As McKern explained, the "archaeologist requires a classification based upon the cultural factor alone; temporal and distributional treatments will follow as accumulating data shall warrant. Moreover, the archaeological classification *necessarily must be based upon criteria available to the archaeologist*" (McKern

1939: 303; emphasis added). What were those criteria that were available to the archaeologist? They were the artifacts that had been gathering dust in so many museums over the years—artifacts that had, from time to time, figured in museum displays but that had rarely been used to recognize cultural patterns.

Consider the sources of many of the midwestern artifacts that were available to archaeologists in the 1930s. The Midwest had not enjoyed the large, well-funded archaeological expeditions that areas such as the Southwest had witnessed, and thus the majority of collections in midwestern museums came from private collectors who either had picked up the material from the surfaces of sites or had excavated sites but often had kept no field notes. Archaeologists working in the Southwest had deep midden and room deposits in which to work, and deep middens produced lots of artifacts. Sites with similar depth were rare in the Midwest (but see Chapter 6). Hence, it is not surprising that southwestern archaeologists were more concerned with artifact types as time markers than were midwestern archaeologists. Willey and Sabloff (1974: 112) are entirely correct when they note that the midwestern taxonomic method "was a response to these circumstances and needs."

The frustration that midwestern archaeologists were feeling as a result of having boxes of artifacts but no organizing scheme was evident in W. C. McKern's words:

> Any statement that the archaeologist has no need for a culture taxonomic method is in conflict with the facts which all students of the subject have encoun-tered. One has only to consult the pre-classification reports on research in almost any American province (outside the Southwest, where a special classification has been developed), noting the indefinite use of the word "culture" to denote anything from the manifestation of a general pattern influential over an area a thousand or more miles in extent, to the highly specialized manifestation of a culture apparent at a cluster of closely localized sites, and noting the confusion of unstandardized cultural terminology, to appreciate the need for simplifying the complexity of cultural data and concepts through the establishment of systematic order. In men's affairs, chaos does not reduce itself to order without a plan. The accomplishments of science stand as a monument to planned orderliness. (McKern 1939: 303)

The "planned orderliness" of the midwestern taxonomic method was created by linking archaeological components into increasingly larger units—focus, aspect, phase, pattern, and base—on the basis of shared traits. The method expressly kept separate the commonly used term *trait* and what McKern called "determinants." Traits could be determinants, but only if they were diagnostic, that is, only if they were unique to one cultural manifestation (the sum of artifacts from a given site or group of sites that indicates that one cohesive culture once existed in that space). If traits were "linked" to two or more manifestations, then they were "useless as determinants" (McKern 1939: 305). McKern and others recognized that the method of classification they were proposing was entirely arbitrary and that the determinants selected from the infinite array of possibilities were timeless and spaceless units. This was the real beauty of the system, as opposed to being its weakness: cultural manifestations were classified by means of unique characteristics; then a search was made to determine which characteristics could be deleted in order to leave meaningful groups of related manifestations. This process then was repeated several times to create groups that were more inclusive. When the process was completed, there was, for example, a horticultural-pottery *base* that contained two *patterns*—Mississippi and Woodland—each of which contained a number of classes known as *phases,* each of which contained two or more *aspects,* each of which contained two or more *foci.* Finally, each focus comprised a number of components, which were the "Manifestation[s] of any given focus at a specific site" (McKern 1939: 308).

Did proponents of the method abandon time as an important analytical consideration? No. What they did do was place it in a parallel analysis, the same spot they reserved for space. McKern was very specific in urging that any grouping of cultural divisions that grew out of attempts to use the method not be viewed in any evolutionary sense: "A common historical origin may be suggested, but the implication should be considered as an indicator, guiding further research, rather than as proof in itself. . . . A chronology independently constructed from available time criteria may later be determined as a parallel development and correlated with a culture classification to establish or refute evolutionary sequence" (McKern 1939: 312).

McKern's article was published well after midwestern archaeologists had begun using the method. In 1935 Thorne Deuel published a taxonomic integration of cultures in the Mississippi River valley, more or less in a manner that paralleled the midwestern taxonomic method (Willey and Sabloff 1974: 121), but there is little evidence that the synthesis had much of an effect on subsequent literature. More important was Fay-Cooper Cole and Deuel's *Rediscovering Illinois: Archaeological Explorations in and around Fulton County* (1937). This book was one of several state or regional compilations to appear in the late 1920s and 1930s. The difference between it and its competitors was its adherence to a well-organized set of principles. The main objective of the work was to develop a chronological ordering of cultures that made up, to use the midwestern-taxonomic-method nomenclature, the Woodland and Mississippi patterns—in other words, to take the next analytical step once various cultural manifestations had been classified. Cole and Deuel (1937: 33) viewed this next step—chronological ordering—as only one of many in a long analytical process that could be accomplished "only when there is a definite recognition of types of artifacts, and when a specific terminology makes it possible to class similar materials together." In other words, classes of artifacts first had to be grouped together *regardless* of time. Using those artifacts to tell time was a separate, though obviously important, task. Based on materials generated by three seasons of excavation and surface collection in north-central Illinois, Cole and Deuel established a cultural sequence that would stand for years. As we will see later, much of that sequence would soon be imported wholesale into Missouri.

Before leaving *Rediscovering Illinois,* I should point out that in an appendix to the work, Deuel (1937) labored to define what he termed *Middle Mississippian,* which became a catchall phrase for a cultural unit. This was, as I noted in Chapter I, an unfortunate choice of wording and one that has caused confusion ever since. Holmes (1903a) first coined the term *Middle Mississippi* in his "Pottery of the Eastern United States" to refer to the shell-tempered pottery found in such abundance throughout the Mississippi River valley. By the beginning of the 1940s, "This division of eastern ceramics [had] come to be accepted as a term applying to the entire cultural complex which usually accompanies this characteristic pottery" (Ford and Willey 1941: 348). Deuel's Middle Mississippian unit is still in use today, though it is rapidly disappearing.

Although this chapter deals with the period 1911–1940, I will include here a major synthesis of the prehistory of the eastern United States that appeared in 1941 and that was the source of the quote just given. That year Ford and Gordon Willey published "An Interpretation of the Prehistory of the Eastern United States," which viewed time and artifacts in terms of a series of sloping stages that reiterated the concept of time lag from region to region—a time lag that was clearly identified with the process of diffusion. For example, Ford and Willey used the introduction of conical burial mounds as the distinguishing characteristic between what they termed the Archaic stage and the Burial Mound I stage. They saw the introduction of conical mounds as having begun in Louisiana around A.D. 700 and spread up the Mississippi River, not reaching St. Louis until approximately 100 years later. Likewise, the introduction of temple mounds, which marked the interface between the Burial Mound II and Temple Mound I stages, began in Louisiana around A.D. 1150 and finally reached St. Louis around A.D. 1450. Work conducted since their synthesis has demonstrated that the dates selected by Ford and Willey are much too late and that the notion that mound building was introduced from Mexico (diffusion of cultural traits was the centerpiece of the Ford-Willey scheme) is inaccurate. On the other hand, the relative sequence of certain archaeological traits in their scheme is correct—a sequence provided by stratigraphic excavation, cross-dating, and seriation. The sequence looks all the more remarkable to us because of the absence of the means to assess absolute dates. For example, Ford and Willey correctly equated the Tchefuncte complex in Louisiana with the Red Ochre complex in Illinois, and Marksville in the South with Hopewell in the North. They also correctly equated Baytown (Griffin 1941) with both Marksville and Hopewell and placed the Tennessee-Cumberland material late in the sequence.

Culture Areas

One important outcome of this and other regional archaeological syntheses was the recognition of culture areas and the correspondence of traits within the various areas to physical-environmental variables. Early proponents of native culture areas included Otis T. Mason (1896, 1907) and William H. Holmes (1919), though the schemes they proposed became "obsolete soon after they were developed" (Meltzer 1985: 258). Later schemes included those by Wissler (1938) and Kroeber (1939), the latter's *Cultural and Natural Areas of Native North America* being a widely cited classic. Culture areas were defined on the basis of trait associations, similar to the rationale behind the midwestern taxonomic method. Unlike McKern's system, however, culture-area formulations were time-bound. In fact, time, along with environment, played key roles in such formulations:

> One of the major approaches to interpreting cultural activities was the recognition of culture areas with a strong emphasis on the effect of environment on the development of material-culture traits. . . . Along with the identification of the area center went the identification of marginal tribes within and between areas. Trait associations were perceived as important factors. Since many traits were assumed to have originated in or near the culture-area center and to have spread outward, the age area hypothesis came into use. This concept is basic to the proposition that the Mississippian phenomenon originated in the central Mississippi Valley and spread outward from there, and is only one instance where anthropological theory led archaeologists astray. (Griffin 1985a: 269)

The key mechanism by which culture traits moved was, again, *diffusion*. "Diffusion was . . . accomplished in some instances by borrowing from neighboring groups. . . . Diffusion accounted for the spread of maize and other agricultural crops. Trade and exchange were regarded as mechanisms for diffusion, and migration was a form of diffusion. Finally, conquest and colonization also resulted in the diffusion of new ideas and behavior" (Griffin 1985a: 270). As we will later see, colonization and other forms of population movement have figured prominently in interpretations of the archaeological record of Missouri.

The Founding of National and State Archaeological Societies

By 1935 there were seven universities offering a Ph.D. in anthropology—four in the East (Harvard, Yale, Columbia, and Pennsylvania), two in the upper Midwest (Chicago and Michigan), and one in the West (California) (Griffin 1985a: 265)— and a significant percentage of students being trained in those programs were in archaeology. Still, as Griffin (1985a: 265) notes, "The [total] output was small and archaeological training in any real sense was abysmal. People learned by working in the field, from the literature, talking with colleagues, and appealing in appropriate language to the supernatural." Learning from one's colleagues had always been the practice in archaeology, and to put this learning on a bit more formal basis, archaeologists such as Kidder had established regional conferences (in his case the Pecos Conference) so that everyone working in a particular region had the opportunity to stay abreast of developments in the field. Several regional conferences were sponsored by the National Research Council (an arm of the National Academy of Sciences), the first of which, on midwestern archaeology, was held in St. Louis in 1929 (National Research Council 1929). Despite the slowly growing number of archaeologists in the field and the realization that there were philosophical as well as political concerns that potentially affected all archaeologists, there was no national organization devoted solely to Americanist archaeology.

Prior to 1934 archaeologists were members of various anthropological societies such as the American Anthropological Association and the anthropology section of the American Association for the Advancement of Science (AAAS). Certain archaeological societies existed at the time, but for the most part they were localized groups—more clubs than societies—or national organizations whose leanings were more to classical archaeology (e.g., the Archaeological Institute of America). One important organization during the 1920s and 1930s was the Committee on State Archaeological Surveys, which was established by the National Research Council in 1920 (Guthe 1930; see also Griffin 1985a). One of the programs proposed by the committee was for a survey of Illinois, Indiana, Iowa, and Missouri, which would extend the coverage of statewide archaeological surveys that were beginning to spring up across the East—for example, in Alabama, Ohio, New York, and Kentucky. The committee published the results of state surveys in the *American Anthropologist* from 1921 to 1933, helped form state archaeological societies, and sponsored archaeological meetings.

Late in December 1934, following a meeting of the anthropology section of the AAAS, the Society for American Archaeology was founded (Griffin 1985a: 261; Guthe 1967). Contrary to some lore, the SAA was not formed as a splinter group of the American Anthropological Association but rather as an organization to carry on the work begun by the Committee on State Archaeological Surveys. By the end of World War II, the SAA was the dominant organization in Americanist archaeology, and its official publication, the quarterly *American Antiquity*, was the dominant periodical in the field.

The winds of change that affected archaeological method and technique in the 1930s, much of it brought about through a growing sense of professionalism among archaeologists, caused a chill in the relations that had evolved over the last three-quarters of a century between prehistorians and what might best be termed avocational archaeologists. Prior to the founding of departments of anthropology and the subsequent rise of archaeology as a university-based discipline in the 1920s and 1930s, the dividing line between avocationalists and professional prehistorians was not very clear. Anyone with the time and inclination could, in essence, "do" archaeology and get his or her name in print. Formal training was not much of a concern because there was nowhere to go to receive it. The group of prehistorians that Powell and later Holmes assembled for the Bureau of American Ethnology had little or no formal training in archaeology, and they in turn relied on relatively untrained personnel to conduct fieldwork and on the general public for information on the whereabouts of archaeological sites and material. This arrangement worked well for a time, but it probably was inevitable that as soon as formal training became available status differences would begin to appear. Individuals who spent a significant part of their lives in classroom study followed by several years of apprenticeship were hardly going to view persons without such training as their equals.

There was another distinction that apparently was as real in the 1930s as it is today, that is, the distinction between avocational archaeologists—individuals who, while they might collect antiquities, have serious interests in knowing more about the past—and pothunters—individuals who churn through archaeological deposits for artifacts to keep or sell. Often the line between the two is extremely fine, since the sources of materials for avocational archaeologists often are the pothunters. (I might add that the hands of museum directors and curators have not always been clean in this regard either.) We have seen that as early as the nineteenth century archaeologists (e.g., C. Thomas 1894) were worried about the future of the prehistoric record. Clarence B. Moore (1910), you may recall, complained about the wholesale looting of archaeological sites that had been going on in northeastern Arkansas for years (he did not envision his work as looting). This worry continued into the mid–twentieth century:

> The present actual status of archeological conservation in the United States, however, is deplorable. . . . From motives of mere curiosity or greed, dealers and relic hunters in practically every state are steadily destroying an irreplaceable heritage. The Antiquities Act of 1906 forbids unauthorized archeological excavation on public lands, but the law is difficult to enforce and, so long as archeological specimens can be sold on the open market, can have at best a very limited effect. This annihilation of our readable past which, due to the great popularity of relic hunting, is steadily growing worse, indicates the need for a carefully planned archeological program before it is too late. At present a race between the scientist and the curio seeker is on. Scientists are relatively few in number and must work slowly and carefully, whereas relic hunters are extremely numerous, and loot sites with great rapidity. The probable outcome, unless definite action is taken very soon, is only too obvious. . . . It is a sad paradox that at this time, when trained men are becoming available and new techniques for determining archeological history are reaching a high pitch of development, the materials themselves should

be vanishing like snow before the sun. It is even more tragic since an enlightened national policy in this regard could save them for all time. (Setzler and Strong 1936: 308–9)

Setzler and Strong set up a rigid dichotomy between scientist and curio seeker, but what about those individuals who fell somewhere in the middle? Were they to be ostracized? McKern (1935: 81–82) didn't think so:

> Unfortunately, there is a classification that divides those who rise to the name archaeologist into two distinct and separate groups: students and collectors. I believe that such a classification is fundamentally wrong. . . . Unquestionably, the activities of amateurs, when motivated by the purpose to find the truth at any price, and when conducted with studious care and according to methods which insure accurate and complete data, can be of inestimable value to the professional student. In fact, it is difficult to see how the work of the specialist can progress satisfactorily, if indeed it can survive, without the support of a constantly growing element of amateur student.

One means of reaching interested amateur archaeologists was through a national organization such as the SAA, and from its inception that organization comprised avocational as well as professional archaeologists. Indeed, as Griffin (1985a: 265) noted,

> The idea of including nonprofessionals as Society Affiliate members was based not only on a desire to inform them of better methodology and the aims of archaeology, but also was economically necessary. The small number of "professionals" meant that their dues would have had to be prohibitively high to publish a journal if the membership was not open to amateurs. There was also the recognition that amateurs were excellent guides to many sites; and that their collections, if studied, could be of considerable value, and might eventually be donated to professional institutions.

An even more direct means of reaching interested nonprofessionals was through the establishment of state organizations that could unite professionals and amateurs residing and working in the same general region. By 1940 archaeological societies had been established in 17 eastern states, though "Not all of these societies were of equal strength, nor did they all develop with equal rapidity" (Guthe 1952: 4). One state organization, founded in 1934, was the Missouri Archaeological Society. Carl Chapman (1985a: 241–42) noted that the groundwork for the society's formation was laid in 1931 by two University of Missouri professors, Jesse Wrench (Figure 4.15), a historian with some background in biblical archaeology, and Brewton Berry, a sociologist.

Wrench and Berry applied to the Civil Works Administration in 1934 for funding to survey Missouri counties and were granted two weeks' worth of

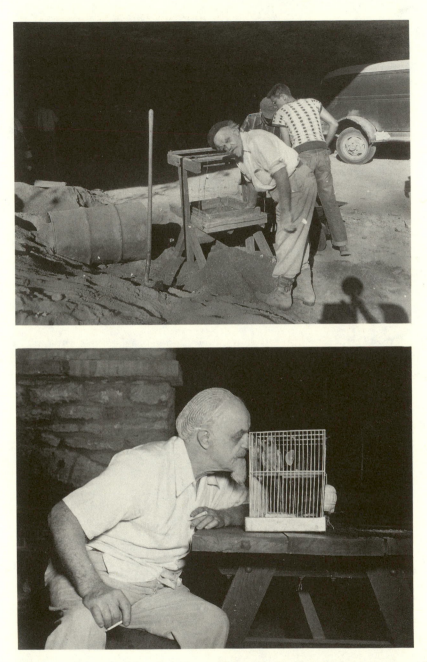

Figure 4.15. Jesse E. Wrench (1882–1958) (top) at Graham Cave, Montgomery County, Missouri, ca. 1944 and (bottom) at Van Meter State Park, Saline County, Missouri, ca. 1950. Wrench was well known at the University of Missouri as an eccentric professor who often wore a hair net (see bottom photograph) and a long, flowing cape as he bicycled to class. Apparently on more than one occasion he cut his lawn wearing nothing but his underwear, which caused some consternation to the church-goers across the street attending Sunday services. Wrench and his wife, Jane, also served as "parents" to numerous foreign students at the university and were proponents and financial backers of cooperative grocery stores and cooperative student housing.

support. Given the success of the project, they received additional funding from the Federal Emergency Relief Administration to survey additional counties and to contact artifact collectors. When the survey closed at the end of the year, Wrench and Berry got in touch with a number of individuals about forming a permanent organization to continue the work. The meeting resulted in the formation of the State Archaeological Society of Missouri (changed to the Missouri Archaeological Society in 1946), with Wrench as president and Berry as secretary. The aims of the society were "to preserve the remains of the prehistoric peoples of Missouri; to study those remains scientifically; to publish information about them; to provide amateurs and professionals with opportunities to discuss their common interests; and to arouse public opinion to the appreciation of Missouri's antiquities" (Chapman 1985a: 242). The society immediately began publishing *The Missouri Archaeologist* and over the years added new publications as needed.[9]

The opening article in the inaugural issue of *The Missouri Archaeologist* was entitled "The Task of a State Archaeological Society" and was written by J. C. Harrington of the University of Chicago, which was at that time a training ground for virtually all archaeologists working in the Midwest. Harrington had some sage advice on the goals and future direction of the fledgling society, as well as on potential pitfalls:

Missouri's belated entry into the field of American prehistory may be more fortunate than would appear on the surface. A survey of the results achieved by similar organizations in other states emphasizes the need of most careful planning if our efforts and money are to be spent to the greatest advantage. Can we learn from these other instances just what such an organization can hope to accomplish; how it can best proceed, both in planning a sound program and in carrying it out, avoiding the pitfalls and errors which have so frequently negated the results of these others? The writer sincerely believes that such is possible, provided we "get off on the right foot." . . .

Look back at the work of other states again and see what they have done. We find altogether too many instances of files and desks and basement shelves cluttered with masses of unorganized references to sites, too inaccurate and insufficient ever to be of any great value. A site which cannot be re-located for careful excavation at a later date is of little value to anyone attempting to work out the archaeology of a region. Look again at the records of the collections. We find occasional photographs of excellent arrow-heads and weird objects, but seldom the exact site from which they came. Once you have tried to work out the very intricate movements and overlappings of the many tribes which inhabited the Mississippi Basin during the past few centuries, you will immediately realize that

9. *The Missouri Archaeologist* came about because, as Berry (1975: 6) remembered later, "we had to give [the members] something for the $1 dues they were paying."

one must know the exact provenance of every object. . . . (J. C. Harrington 1935: 1–2 [unpaginated])

After admonishing new society members to keep precise and organized records, Harrington moved quickly to the topic that was foremost in everyone's mind:

> You will ask at this time, no doubt, "Where does *our* fun come in? Is it to be all work and no play?" We picture the "romance" of archaeology as pertaining solely to the unearthing of the unexpected. Has this second phase of archaeology— excavation—a place in the program of a state archaeological society? To a considerable extent, YES, but we may as well face the issue at the outset and realize that *proper excavation is a highly technical and exacting procedure* and should be indulged in only by those who are properly trained. . . .
> But all the glamor of archaeology is not in excavating. To me, and I believe to every member of the Society, the real thrill comes in carrying on a piece of independent work as carefully and systematically as one is capable of doing. Tracing down an old village site which we have come across in our reading; following out an obscure Indian trail; or trampling over fields looking for surface finds, house pits, earthworks, and mounds; accurately locating and describing these finds; classifying and describing the objects picked up on the surface—all this can be, and is much more, thrilling than toiling in the heat of the sun with a pick and shovel. (J. C. Harrington 1935: 2–3 [unpaginated])

I would guess that Harrington's appeal, though novel in the way he approached amateur excavation, did not seriously curtail such activities in the state. But membership in the society grew annually through intensive membership drives and, just as importantly, through the society's sponsorship of projects on which members could work. Wrench and Berry learned early on that publications were nice, but what people really wanted was to become involved in fieldwork. They also realized, presumably, that despite their own personal interest in archaeology they were not trained archaeologists.

On the inside of the back cover of the first issue of *The Missouri Archaeologist* they included the following note: "Mr. J. C. Harrington, Director of Archaeological Field Work, University of Chicago, has been added to the faculty of the University of Missouri for the summer session. He will teach two courses in archaeology and direct the excavations which will be undertaken in the vicinity of Columbia." Harrington (Figure 4.16) was one of Fay-Cooper Cole's students at the University of Chicago, and his addition to the summer teaching staff at the University of Missouri was an important turning point in the institution's credibility. Berry (1975: 52) later reminisced: "Neither Wrench nor I deluded ourselves into thinking that we were archaeologists. We knew that we needed to learn much, much more about the techniques of the science. . . . We decided to bring the archaeologists to us. . . . Wrench and I also took the course." The excavation of a small mound south of Columbia occurred as planned and was written up by Harrington (1938) in *The Missouri Archaeologist* (Figure 4.17).

The inaugural issue of *The Missouri Archaeologist* also contained two notices that are of historical interest: one stated that the Society for American Archaeology had just been formed and that annual membership dues were $3 (in 1993 the dues were $75), and the second announced, "An excellent article on 'Stone-Age Men of Crawford County', by Mr. Carl H. Chapman, appeared in the Feb. [1935] issue of *The Missouri Magazine,* published by the Missouri State Chamber of Commerce, Jefferson City."[10] If there is an earlier article written by Carl Chapman, I am unaware of it. What got Chapman interested in the archaeology of his local county was a love of artifacts; what allowed him to receive a modest amount of training that eventually would place him at the forefront of Missouri archaeology was the availability of federal grants-in-aid, small even for those days, and the willingness of Wrench and Berry to support the young man from Crawford County. That initial support gave rise to a remarkable

Figure 4.16. J. C. Harrington, summer instructor of the University of Missouri archaeological field school, 1935.

10. The article apparently was republished as "Stone Age Man of Crawford County" in the *Missouri Resources Museum Bulletin* 16: 1–9 (1935).

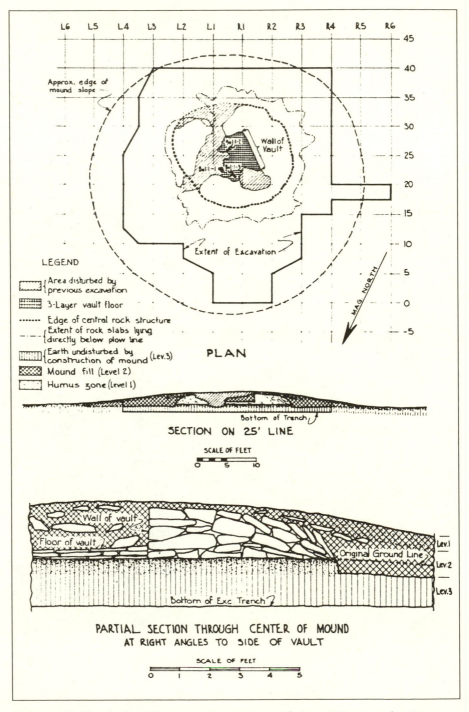

Figure 4.17. Plan and profile views of excavations of site 23BOI, mound I, Boone County, Missouri (from J. C. Harrington 1938, courtesy Missouri Archaeological Society).

relationship between the University of Missouri and Carl Chapman that would span portions of six decades.

The Growth of Federally Sponsored Archaeology

One of the great hallmarks of American archaeology in the 1930s was the infusion of funding for federal programs, many of which were established as part of President Franklin D. Roosevelt's attempts not only to jump-start the economy but to provide for the millions of people who were out of work and who faced little or no possibility of employment. A significant portion of that funding went to archaeology, especially fieldwork connected with the construction of large public works such as dams and reservoirs. The years 1933–1936 were important because of the large number both of projects that were undertaken in the southeastern United States and of archaeologists who were hired to run the projects. Dozens of archaeologists received their first significant field training on those projects and by 1940 were beginning to branch out to different institutions, taking with them a battery of field methods and techniques that had been developed and refined in the reservoirs.

It is interesting that in their *History of American Archaeology,* Willey and Sabloff (1974) do not even mention the great projects that were undertaken during the heyday of federal archaeology, especially since they treat in detail the earlier accomplishments of federally funded research undertaken by units such as the BAE (the authors added material about these projects in the third edition). It is a well-known adage that history repeats itself, and, as I note later, the second great wave of federal archaeology—that undertaken in the 1970s—was viewed in some circles in the same way that the work conducted during the 1930s was often viewed—as emergency excavations undertaken in haste and without much thought as to program orientation or research questions. There were, to be sure, drawbacks to the earlier federal programs, as Jennings (1986: 56) points out, but, as Griffin (1985a: 269) comments, "the benefits far outweighed the deficiencies."

Largely in response to what was widely perceived in archaeological circles as massive destruction of the archaeological record, professional and amateur archaeologists had long lobbied Congress for laws and enabling legislation to protect sites on public lands, but the results were disappointing. The Antiquities Act had been passed in 1906, in theory offering protection to archaeological properties on federal lands, but in practice little was done to protect sites from land-modifying activities and pothunting. Through the Committee on State Archaeological Surveys, some federal money was made available to combat the loss of information, and in 1928 the Smithsonian Institution received $20,000 to use as matching money "to cooperate with any state, educational institution, or scientific organization in the United States for continuing ethnological research among the American Indians and the excavation and preservation of archaeo-logical remains, provided the monies appropriated be matched by the institution to whom the grant was made and not more than $2,000 be allocated to any one state" (Guthe 1952: 5). As Haag (1985: 273) notes, "These were significant sums in 1928."

The first benchmark of the 1930s federal archaeology program was the creation of the Tennessee Valley Authority in 1933, although to the "everlasting dismay, vexation, and frustration of archaeologists, the Act contained not a word per-taining to investigation or protection of archaeological remains destined to be covered by the impounded waters of the several proposed dams" (Haag 1985: 274). Finally, through the lobbying efforts of archaeologists, a plan for surveying the reservoirs was drawn up, but it was abandoned because dam construction was proceeding at such a pace that the time could not be spared (Lyon 1982). Instead, attention shifted to massive excavation projects, the first being in Norris Reservoir (Tennessee) in January 1934.

Congress created numerous relief agencies to address the declining economic situation, including the Federal Emergency Relief Administration, followed by the Civil Works Administration, the Works Progress Administration, and the Civilian Conservation Corps. Using labor provided by these agencies, several large reservoirs—the best known being Norris Reservoir and Chickamauga Basin in Tennessee, Pickwick and Guntersville basins in Alabama, and Kentucky Basin in Kentucky—witnessed excavation projects in the 1930s (Figure 4.18). It is difficult to overestimate the importance of those excavations in terms of how they changed the prevailing perceptions of the prehistoric past as well as added a much-needed infusion of precision to fieldwork. Many of the excavations may have been "criminally inept" (Jennings 1986: 56), but others were models of excellence. Relative to the importance of the excavations in terms of new views on culture history, Griffin (1985a: 269) states:

> The cultural sequence for northern Illinois published in 1937 (Cole and Deuel 1937) was recognized by 1930 and was well known to archaeologists in the Midwest before the public works program began. This sequence and that in Ohio were major influences in the identification and segregation of archaeological complexes in the Midsouth. However, it was the excavation of the large deep shell middens in northern Alabama that effectively shifted the emphasis in the Eastern United States to the stratigraphic identification of successive complexes and indications of continuity or cultural change from the archaic to the protohistoric and historical assemblages.

Missouri never enjoyed the massive amounts of federally sponsored archaeo-logical excavation that some of the southeastern states received, and the state of knowledge about Missouri's prehistory suffered as a result:

Figure 4.18. Photograph of excavations of Mulberry Creek shell mound, Colbert County, Alabama (Pickwick Basin), 1937 (from W. S. Webb and DeJarnette 1942).

The importance of the state of Missouri in the study of American archaeology is generally recognized. She derives this importance from her position with respect to the Mississippi, Missouri, Ohio, Illinois and other rivers. . . .

It is not surprising, in view of her location, to find that Missouri is rich in prehistoric remains. A century ago Squier and Davis reported this fact . . . and since their time there have been not a few pioneers in Missouri archaeology. Most of these pioneers, however, failed to produce anything of permanent value. They collected bones, pottery, and stone artifacts, which are now to be seen in most of the museums of the state; but they did not keep adequate records of their excavations, and as a consequence their work is of little use to the modern student.

In the meantime archaeology had been making rapid progress in states not far distant from Missouri—Illinois, Iowa, Nebraska, Kentucky, Tennessee, Oklahoma, Arkansas, to mention only the nearest. Missouri, however, remained a blank page in the story of prehistoric America. (Berry et al. 1938: 3)

Berry et al., of course, were familiar with the work of Thomas, Fowke, Bushnell, and others in Missouri, but they were more or less correct in their assessment: in 1930 if you had held up what was known of Missouri prehistory against what was known of the prehistory of the neighboring states, Missouri would have paled in contrast.

In 1931 Wrench and Berry set out to change that situation:

> Recognizing this fact [that archaeological work in Missouri lagged behind that in other states], the two senior authors of this report (Wrench and Berry), professors at the University of Missouri, began in 1931 to make a study of the state's archaeology. Due to conditions at the time they were unable to secure funds for research, and for several years they could do no more than locate a few sites and conduct some library investigations. In 1934 they were given the services of a number of CWA workers for the brief space of two weeks. Although these people were entirely unacquainted with archaeology, the attempt was made to give them a modicum of training, and they were sent out to locate antiquities and to report them on a form especially prepared for such untrained workers. . . . The results of that brief survey were encouraging, and a few months later a more ambitious project, under the FERA, was inaugurated.
>
> This second project enlisted the services of about eighty-five men, and extended over a period of approximately three months. A number of these workers were competent and interested, and a great deal of valuable information was collected. . . .
>
> The establishment of the [National Youth Administration], in the fall of 1935, provided another opportunity for archaeological work. It was decided to use a few NYA students at the University in exploring Boone County, in which Columbia and the University of Missouri are located. The project has been continued each year up to the present time [1938]. Two students, Carl Chapman and Wilber Seitz, have worked on the project throughout their four years at the University, while a third, James Lowe, was associated with the work three years.
>
> The purpose of the project was to locate the Indian remains of the county, to make a record of the collections of local amateurs, to gather specimens from the surface at each site, to determine the nature of the prehistoric civilization, or civilizations, which had existed in the county, and to reconstruct as much as possible of the history of the county prior to the coming of white settlers. (Berry et al. 1938: 3, 5)

Although neither Wrench nor Berry had had extensive archaeological training, they established a fairly methodical system of survey:

> The method adopted was that of following, on foot, the various courses of the streams, even the smallest, searching for chert chips, artifacts, pottery, and other evidences of occupation. At the same time a thorough house-to-house canvass was conducted, resulting occasionally in excellent clues, and often revealing interesting local collections. Care was taken to record the exact location of every site. . . . Photographs or sketches were made of all collections of relics, along with information as to where they were found. A representative sample of the surface material was gathered from each site, which has been carefully catalogued and stored at the University. (Berry et al. 1938: 5)

The report in which the above comments appeared was entitled "Archaeo-logical Investigations in Boone County, Missouri" and appeared in vol. 4, no. 3 of *The Missouri Archaeologist*. It was authored by Berry, Wrench, Chapman, and Wilber Seitz (1938) and represented the first comprehensive statement on the distribution of prehistoric sites that resulted from the statewide survey established by Wrench and Berry. Apparently the surveyors moved rapidly, since Berry et al. (1938: 9) stated that by April 1938, "half of Boone County's 688 square miles have been thus combed . . . [and] 653 sites have been located in the county." In addition to the survey results, the report contained summaries of the excavation of two mounds and a "village site." The excavation plans that accompanied the report (Figure 4.19) were professionally done (lettered in the same hand [probably that of Wrench] as the plan map of J. C. Harrington's excavation of mound BO1 [Figure 4.17]), and the descriptions of the excavations and artifacts were clear and concise.

By 1938 membership in the Missouri Archaeological Society had grown to 253 (*Missouri Archaeologist* 5[1]: 22–24). By 1940 numerous counties had been surveyed by students and avocational archaeologists, and the society had become firmly established, with several chapters scattered throughout the state. Regional-chapter meetings gave members the opportunity to compare notes on the progress of the various surveys that were underway and to view collections (Figure 4.20). When possible, students or staff from the University of Missouri would attend the meetings to demonstrate support for what the members were doing. Weekend excavations directed by Wrench and students gave members an opportunity to experience what fieldwork was like (Figure 4.21). Although the MAS fulfilled a social as well as an educational niche in the state, its primary purpose in those early years was to provide a base of support for continuing the statewide survey begun in 1931. Wrench and Berry established what came to be known as the Archaeological Survey of Missouri (ASM), which was housed on the University of Missouri campus. When society members discovered a site, they were to complete a survey form, which asked for a variety of information on location, ground conditions, and so forth, and send the form to the ASM office in Columbia.

In reading the early site forms, one is struck by the fact that there was little in the way of standardized practice relative to how to complete the forms. The categories remained standard, but the responses varied widely in terms of usefulness. For example, legal locations, that is, section, township, and range, often were not included, though the forms asked for that information. There also were spaces for information on the nature of the archaeological remains—for example, whether sherds and projectile points were found—but only in rare instances was such information recorded. There also were places on the forms in which to draw maps that would help others find the sites, but in most cases these were either left blank or the maps were so crude that the sites cannot be relocated. Some of the inaccuracies or deletions of pertinent

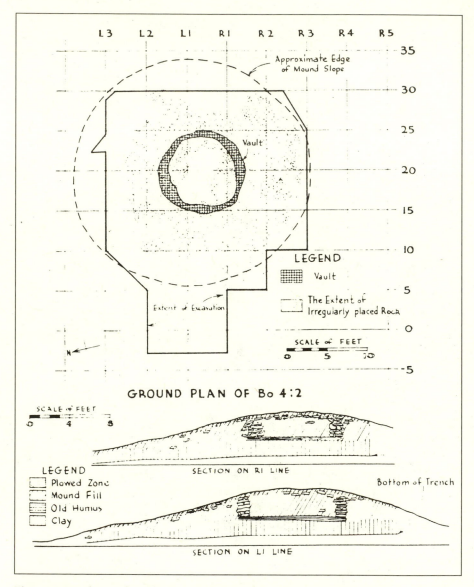

Figure 4.19. Plan and profile views of excavations of site 23BO4, mound 2, Boone County, Missouri (from Berry et al. 1938, courtesy Missouri Archaelogical Society).

information undoubtedly were because the recorders, while wanting to help the society and the university, were not particularly interested in having other people find out where their favorite collecting spots were located. On the other hand, most society members had never filled out survey forms, and they needed direction. Looking at some of the forms completed by the university staff

From the Hannibal Courier–Post,
October 31, 1939

PLAN CLUB FOR
ARCHAEOLOGY

WILL MARK INDIAN SITES
AND DISCOVERIES—
HURLEY DESCRIBES TRIP

Organization of a chapter of the Missouri Archaeological Society is scheduled to be completed at a meeting of local archaeological hobbyists and persons interested in Indian lore at a meeting at the home of Allen Eichenberger, 523 North Fifth street, on Tuesday night, November 14.

Preliminary plans for forming the chapter were discussed Tuesday night at a meeting at the home of Joe Hurley, 2607 Chestnut street.

The club plans to mark off authentic Indian sites such as burial mounds and camps in Marion and Ralls counties. Official maps of the two counties will be used in marking the sites and records of artifacts found in each place will be kept.

According to present plans, the chapter will make one major field trip each year and conduct one major project of research.

Dues paid by members will provide for individual membership in the Missouri Archaeological Society and club membership in state archaeological societies of neighboring states.

At Tuesday's meeting Joe Hurley gave a comprehensive report of a meeting and field trip he attended with members of the Missouri society to the King Mounds, an ancient buried city at Wickliffe, Ky., near Cairo, Ill., on October 14–15.

The burial mounds of pre-historic Indians at Wickliffe have yielded 116,831 artifacts which have been cleaned, marked as to location, classified, tabulated and recorded.

Archaeologists of Missouri, Illinois, Kansas, Indiana and Kentucky took the recent field trip to the mounds.

Reprinted with permission from the Hannibal Courier–Post.

From the Hannibal Courier–Post,
November 14, 1939

EICHENBERGER
TO HEAD CLUB

ARCHAEOLOGICAL SOCIETY
FORMED HERE TO SEEK
INDIAN TRACES

J. Allen Eichenberger, well known as a researcher on Indian lore and archaeological subjects, was elected chairman of the Marion–Ralls Archaeological Society at an organization meeting held last night at his home, 523a North Fifth street. Joseph Hurley was elected secretary–treasurer.

As one feature of the meeting, Hugh Dysart gave a talk on the Indian burial mounds at Lewiston, Ill., which he visited recently. The next meeting of the two-county group will be held at Dysart's home, 1217 Park avenue, on December 12.

The local groups will be a chapter of the Missouri Archaeological Society.

Using official maps of Marion and Ralls counties, the group plans to mark off authentic Indian sites such as burial mounds and camp grounds.

The society also will trace an old Indian trail which years ago started at Cincinnati Landing on Salt river in Ralls county, ran north through the famous Spalding salt springs and then through Marion county to the bay north of Hannibal. The trail passed near the site where Hannibal-LaGrange College is now located.

The trail is said to have been used by Mathurin Bouvet, a French explorer–settler who established a salt factory at Spalding in 1795 and transported salt to a shipping point on the Mississippi river above Hannibal.

The first major project of the local society will be to explore a large Indian mound on the Arch Sims farm in Ralls county, Hurley said.

The group will keep a record of all artifacts found by members in the two counties.

Formation of the society grew out of the individual interest and research in Indian lore and the group will coordinate the activities of its members.

The secretary said the members will be glad to confer with persons owning property on which Indian sites are believed to be located.

Reprinted with permission from the Hannibal Courier–Post.

Figure 4.20. Newspaper clippings from the *Hannibal Courier-Post* for October 31 and November 14, 1939, announcing the formation of the Marion-Ralls Archaeological Society (reprinted courtesy *Hannibal Courier-Post*).

Figure 4.21. Missouri Archaeological Society field party (site unknown), ca. 1954.

during the same period, one begins to understand the source of some of the problems.

It is easy to look back and spot mistakes made by one's predecessors, and in so doing I would have to say that the early surveys did not produce the kinds of information that we would like to have today. Those surveys were, however, products of the time, and as one looks at the fieldwork conducted during the late 1930s, one gets the feeling that what was being done in Missouri was no worse than what was being done in other states that had initiated statewide surveys. At least for some sections of Missouri, one could use the ASM site files, incomplete as they were, and plot the locations of sites in space. One might even be able to begin to develop an understanding of the distribution of sites by time period. There is no indication that anyone in Missouri was particularly concerned about the inherent biases contained in the records, but neither is there much evidence that archaeologists generally worried about such things. It appears the feeling was that some information was better than none, and Wrench and Berry did everything they could to obtain that information before it was lost.

5

Understanding Time, Space, and Form

1941–1960

The period 1941–1960 was a significant one in Americanist archaeology generally and, for different reasons, in Missouri archaeology particularly. It would be a
relatively simple task to devote this entire volume to the expansion in fieldwork
as well as in method that took place in Americanist archaeology during this
period, but even then I would have to bypass numerous interesting examples.
There were, however, several themes that characterized the 1940s and 1950s, and I
focus attention on three of them: (1) the construction of chronological orderings
of archaeological materials and by extension the supposed ordering of cultures
that made and used the materials; (2) the development of typological systems
for artifact categorization; and (3) the integration of archaeological information
into discussions of geographic regions.

None of the three issues—chronology, typology, and regional-information
integration—can be separated from the others, which presents me with an
organizational problem. The problem stems from the fact that up until roughly
1940 Americanist archaeology had enjoyed a relatively slow growth, uncluttered
with many methodological, let alone theoretical, issues. Thus I have found
it a relatively simple matter to chronicle the development of archaeology in
the United States, and thereby in Missouri, during the 80 years prior to 1940.
Chronicling the growth of archaeology during the 20 years after that date is
nowhere near as easy. During the 1940s and 1950s Americanist archaeology came
of age, not only in terms of its outlook but also in terms of its methods. And no
issue played as vital a role in the development of the discipline as the formulation
of a system or systems that could be used to keep track of time, space, and form
on a large scale. The midwestern taxonomic method was still used throughout
the 1940s, but chronological ordering became an increasingly important aspect
of archaeological analysis. By 1950 the method that McKern and others had taken
such pains to develop was largely ignored, as archaeologists began developing
systems that placed a premium on time and space as well as on form. By

1958 these systems had been formalized and would remain the cornerstone of archaeological systematics for decades.

The historical development of these various systems forms the outline of the following discussion, but I must tell you that the headings I use to introduce various topics obscure the fact that there was no orderly progression in how archaeologists came around to developing and using various frameworks for the study of time, space, and form. Archaeology often grew in a dozen directions at once, slowing only occasionally to take stock of where it was headed. The sharp increase in the number of archaeologists ensured that there were competing schemes, and it took a while for one or more to rise to the top.

No area of archaeology prospered more during the period 1941–1960 than did chronology. The breakthrough in chronological ordering that archaeologists had long awaited occurred in the late 1940s and early 1950s, with Willard Libby's development of radiocarbon dating, which almost at once answered age-old questions that had haunted archaeology.[1] For example, radiocarbon dating gave a time depth to the Archaic period—that murky temporal unit that had long separated the makers and users of Clovis and Folsom points from the chronologically later pottery-making peoples. Perhaps most important to archaeologists working in the eastern United States, especially the Mississippi River valley and environs, radiocarbon dating allowed the precise ordering of pottery-making traditions. Two of those traditions, "Hopewell(ian)" and "Mississippian," were well known, but the amount of time over which each had existed was not.

The 1940s were nothing if not the decade of types. The earlier work of James Ford and a few others mushroomed into a cottage industry as numerous archaeologists joined in creating and naming ceramic types and projectile-point types. The major impetus for this development was an exponential increase in fieldwork during the 1940s: as archaeologists began to identify the vast amount of variation contained in the archaeological record of the eastern United States, they created new types to keep pace with newly identified variation. Ceramic types had long been used, for the most part implicitly, to assign time to archaeological deposits or to track movements of cultural groups, but it was only after 1940 that

---

1. I should note here a word about radiocarbon dates. They won't play a major role in any of the discussion, but I want to point out a few things to avoid confusion. Radiocarbon was a boon to archaeologists, who suddenly had a means of dating archaeological deposits in terms of absolute time. However, it soon became clear that some of the dates being produced were problematic—some were too recent, while others were too old. Leaving aside the technicalities of the problems (see Browman 1981 for a readable review), techniques were developed to correct for age discrepancies, primarily by using tree-ring dating as a cross check. These techniques, however, were not developed until after thousands of dates had already been produced. Therefore, archaeologists routinely report dates as "corrected" or "uncorrected." Further, it is important to cite which correction technique one is using, since several are available.

midwestern archaeologists began to formalize their positions as to what types implied and how they could best be used.

Certainly no time period prior to 1941 had witnessed anywhere near the volume of well-integrated information that began flowing out of the eastern United States after that date. The trend began with Cole and Deuel's *Rediscovering Illinois* in the late 1930s and accelerated in succeeding years. Almost without exception these were much more than simple compilations of work that had been done in a region. Rather, they were treatments of fairly massive amounts of information that had been gathered over the decades—information that, with rare exceptions, had never been distilled into single publications.

As a final prefatory note, I should point out that despite my emphasis on studies that were centered around the questions of time, space, and form, few projects undertaken between 1941 and 1960 focused specifically on those issues. Instead, most programs were designed to address the description of a specific set of archaeological remains. On one hand, archaeologists took it for granted that what they were doing related to the delineation of those three dimensions, and they saw no need to spell it out in so many words. This fairly well characterizes most of the archaeology that was carried out in Missouri after 1941, though as we will see below, there were some notable exceptions. During the period in question, Missouri archaeologists were never at the forefront of the discipline and were more beneficiaries of, rather than contributors to, improvements in method and technique. Neither were they participants to any serious degree in debates on the issues of the time.

On the other hand, in terms of sheer volume, the amount of survey and excavation undertaken by personnel at the University of Missouri, usually in conjunction with volunteers from the Missouri Archaeological Society (Figure 5.1), was enormous. Survey work was initiated in the locations of all the major reservoirs that had been slated for construction, and by 1960 dozens of sites had been excavated. From the reports that were produced as a result of that work came an outline of Missouri prehistory prepared by Carl Chapman, a master craftsman whose expertise was in constructing culture histories. Chapman's work represents one man's blueprint for fleshing out time, space, and form and deserves to be treated in some detail. To some readers, this will be the most interesting part of the book, since it begins to chronicle Missouri archaeology as they remember it.

Integrating Form with Time and Space

One work from the post-1940 period that would have an impact on Missouri archaeology was *The Fort Ancient Aspect,* by James B. Griffin, published in 1943 (though the work was completed long before the publication date). Griffin's

Figure 5.1. Carl Chapman and Missouri Archaeological Society volunteers at Graham Cave, Montgomery County, Missouri, 1950.

objective in undertaking the analysis of Mississippi-period (not Mississippian tradition) materials from southern Ohio and adjacent regions was clear: "A review of the literature on the archaeology of the eastern United States and an examination of the pottery collections in the Ceramic Repository of the Eastern United States in the Museum of Anthropology at the University of Michigan indicated that the group of sites constituting the Fort Ancient culture would offer a profitable field for comparison of cultural and ceramic materials in the light of the recently suggested McKern classification" (Griffin 1943: 1).

Griffin (Figure 5.2) was also interested in ordering the material chronologically, as were Cole and Deuel in *Rediscovering Illinois,* and both volumes serve to dispel the myth, as Spaulding (1985: 304) notes, that the midwestern taxonomic method was only a prelude to the "real" task of archaeology, which was the construction of cultural chronologies. Instead, these works represented attempts

to create a new archaeology, a scientific archaeology, in a context of an earlier prescientific, intuitive, and speculative archaeology. The earlier archaeology was characterized by hit-or-miss descriptions of archaeological excavations and materials and by frequent loose behavioral reconstructions including routine appeals to incoming migrations to explain any marked difference between two kinds of culture in a region. For Cole and Deuel and for Griffin, such tactics were

Figure 5.2. James B. Griffin, longtime director of the Museum of Anthropology at the University of Michigan, 1988. During the 1940s, Griffin became the recognized expert on pottery from the eastern United States and contributed his expertise to most of the large federally sponsored projects in the Southeast. Perhaps of all the lasting contributions Griffin made to Americanist archaeology, it was the long-term survey of portions of the lower Mississippi River valley, which he carried out during the 1940s with Philip Phillips and James A. Ford, that was the most important.

inadequate. A scientific archaeology first acquired a finely textured sampler of cultural variety in a region of interest . . . and then objectively determined "degrees of likeness" for the prehistoric entities and placed them in the proper chronological relationship by any means possible. (Spaulding 1985: 302–3)

Spaulding (1985: 303–4) points out the inherent weaknesses in the midwestern taxonomic method (see also Kroeber 1940), but these do not undermine the importance of either *Rediscovering Illinois* or *The Fort Ancient Aspect*. Both studies were regional in nature and recognized that time and space were as important as form in creating archaeological classifications. Carl Chapman borrowed heavily from both in creating a culture classification to organize archaeological remains from Missouri.

Carl Chapman's Approach to Culture Classification

Chapman used his classification as the basis of his master's thesis and then published it in a four-part series in *The Missouri Archaeologist* entitled "A Preliminary Survey of Missouri Archaeology" (Chapman 1946, 1947, 1948a, 1948b). His was the first general overview of Missouri prehistory ever to appear, and it deserves a close examination if for no other reason than to understand how in the 1940s the man most intimately connected with the archaeology of the state viewed prehistory. I go into much more detail on Chapman and his career in Chapter 9; here my emphasis is strictly on how he classified archaeological units. Chapman obviously saw his efforts as preliminary, but he also saw an opportunity to try out the midwestern taxonomic method on an untapped set of data:

> There is not enough information to make a complete or final inventory of the Indian cultures that existed in the State, but there are enough data to make a preliminary outline of the archaeology and to indicate the probable interrelationships of the Indian groups. All the cultures cannot be classified definitely and often the exact sequence and full distribution cannot be determined. Most Missouri cultures can be placed tentatively within a taxonomic system by comparing their traits with trait lists of cultures already classified elsewhere. Distribution is sometimes suggested rather than accurately stated, and sequence is arbitrary in some instances. The series is by no means a final outline of the archaeology of Missouri but is presented as a basis for further research. It is intended to serve as a framework to be added to, when correct, and torn down and rebuilt when found to be incorrect. (Chapman 1946: 5–6)

Chapman's method of analysis followed that of Cole and Deuel (1937) and McKern (1939):

> Trait lists obtained from particular archaeological sites or groups of seemingly related sites first are compared with lists of determinants . . . to place the cultures within the more generalized divisions of pattern and phase. The same lists are compared with aspect and focus lists, when available, to determine the more specific divisions. If the traits compare favorably with more than half of the determinants for pattern or phase, the culture is placed tentatively in the division to which it is most similar. . . . A like method is used to place the culture in the division of . . . aspect or focus. . . .
>
> The taxonomic system does not within itself take into consideration the factors of time and areal distribution of the Indian cultures. Therefore, after a brief

description of each culture, their distribution will be outlined (in Missouri) and they will be placed in approximate sequential order. (Chapman 1946: 6–7)

Chapman dealt with the cultures in reverse chronological order, beginning with the historical-period Osage and Missouri Indians in part 1 (Chapman 1946) and following with the Middle Mississippi and Hopewellian cultures in part 2 (Chapman 1947), the Woodland cultures and the Ozark bluff dwellers in part 3 (Chapman 1948a), and "ancient cultures" in part 4 (Chapman 1948b). One interesting question Chapman raised relative to using the midwestern taxonomic method was what to do with cultures that existed during the historical period: "There was some question whether it should be attempted to place the Osage culture within the Midwestern taxonomic system, because the culture was late in time, had a name and was already classified linguistically. . . . In spite of these facts, a classification was attempted for the sake of giving some indication of the things to be looked for in tracing the Osage by means of archaeology" (Chapman 1946: 24–25).

In constructing trait lists, or lists of various qualities found in groups of artifacts taken from sites, Chapman used only items made of "native" materials, such as stone and bone, as opposed to objects obtained through contact with Euro-Americans. He compared Osage traits with those of the Woodland pattern compiled by Byers et al. (1943) and Deuel (1937), as well as with traits of the Mississippi pattern (Cole and Deuel 1937), finally classifying the Osage within the latter (Figure 5.3). Further examination placed the Osage within the Upper phase of the Mississippi pattern (Cole and Deuel 1937). Placing the Osage within a broader context, Chapman (1946: 26) also noted similarities between, on one hand, Osage traits, and on the other, those of neighboring archaeological manifestations such as the "top-layer culture" of the western Ozark Highland (Griffin 1937; M. R. Harrington 1924a, 1924b), the Neosho focus in Oklahoma (Baerreis 1939), and the Oneota aspect of the Upper Midwest. Chapman also classified the Missouri culture under the Oneota aspect of the Upper phase of the Mississippi pattern.

Chapman's (1947) classification of Middle Mississippi culture into five units— the New Madrid focus, the Steed-Kisker component (a unit with extremely limited spatial distribution), the Plattin focus, the Kimmswick focus, and the Monks Mound aspect (Figure 5.3)—was based in large part on several years of excavation that had been undertaken in eastern Missouri south of St. Louis. The New Madrid focus, named by Winslow Walker and Robert McCormick Adams (1946) in their excavation report on the Matthews site in New Madrid County, was in the 1940s the best-known Mississippi(an) manifestation in eastern Missouri and one of the most often referenced units in the entire central Mississippi River valley. Walker and Adams's work at Matthews, conducted in 1941 and 1942, had been funded by the WPA and sponsored by both the Academy

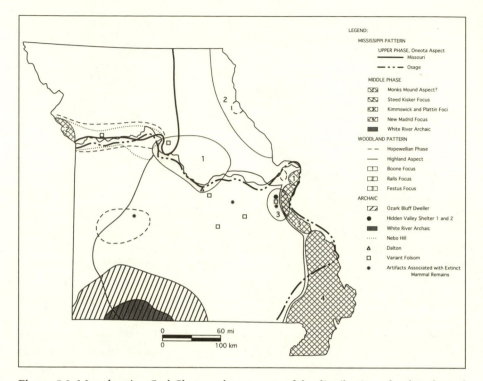

Figure 5.3. Map showing Carl Chapman's summary of the distribution of archaeological cultures in Missouri. The map does not agree in several respects with Chapman's text. For example, in the text (Chapman 1947) he classifies Middle Mississippi culture into five units, one of which, Steed-Kisker, he refers to as a component. In the map he refers to it as a focus. Also, in the text he refers to Ozark Bluff Dweller as a Woodland culture (Chapman 1948a), primarily because he knew some sites associated with that unit contained pottery, but on the map he placed it under the heading "Archaic" (after Chapman 1948b).

of Science of St. Louis and the Missouri Resources Museum in Jefferson City (see also Adams and Walker 1942). During the course of work at the site, they excavated a portion of the large mound, part of the palisade, and several houses and burials. The Kimmswick and Plattin foci were named by Adams (1941; see also Adams and Magre 1939 and Adams et al. 1941) based on WPA-funded survey and excavation in Jefferson and Ste. Genevieve counties. The Monks Mound aspect was based on artifacts found in St. Louis County that resembled those from across the Mississippi River at Cahokia; the Steed-Kisker component was based on artifacts from Clay and Platte counties north of Kansas City that resembled artifacts from Cahokia (Wedel 1943).

Chapman's identification of Hopewellian culture in Missouri was based on numerous artifacts, especially pottery, from diverse parts of the state—Ralls

County (Eichenberger 1944), St. Louis County (Blake 1942), the Kansas City area (Wedel 1938), and southwest Missouri along the Osage River (Mack 1942)—that resembled materials from west-central Illinois (e.g., Cole and Deuel 1937). What at that time was referred to as Hopewell pottery was easily identified by the distinctive incised and stamped decorations it carried (Figure 1.4). However, the lack of stratified sites that carried the full complement of pottery traditions made its chronological positioning problematic. While Hopewellian pottery clearly preceded shell-tempered Mississippian pottery, no one was sure by how much. Chapman's classification of Hopewellian culture as part of the Woodland pattern followed standard archaeological practice in the Midwest (e.g., Anonymous 1943; Cole and Deuel 1937; McKern 1939).

Chapman (1948a) subdivided Woodland cultures (not to be confused with the Woodland *pattern*) into the Highland aspect, the Ozark bluff dwellers,[2] and the Boone, Ralls, and Festus foci. The Highland aspect covered an enormous area of south-central Missouri, from the Missouri River on the north well into Arkansas on the south. Chapman (1948a: 100) believed that the Highland aspect was the latest Woodland-pattern culture found in Missouri. By the mid-1940s numerous rock shelters had been examined (e.g., L. Adams 1941; Fenenga 1938; Fowke 1922) and several small surveys had been conducted (e.g., Berry et al. 1940; Lowe 1940), but none of the work was systematic. Also, the lack of visible stratigraphic separation in the deposits led to their being excavated as single units. Chapman's assignment of the Highland aspect as the "latest Woodland pattern culture" was based in part on a lack of stratigraphic positioning of diagnostic markers but also, I suspect, on the *apparent* lack of mounds in the Ozark Highland—a determination that within a decade had been shown to be erroneous. In his discussion of the Highland aspect Chapman never mentioned mounds; instead, he stated that burials "were apparently made at random on the village sites or in occupied caves or shelters" (Chapman 1948a: 101). On the other hand, the Boone, Ralls, and Festus foci were discussed under the general heading "Mound-Building Cultures of the Woodland Pattern." Chapman was working under the unstated assumption that the mounds connected with those foci must have been a continuation of a practice begun by earlier Woodland-pattern, Hopewellian peoples. Therefore, if the Highland aspect did not contain mounds, it must have been later than the Boone, Ralls, and Festus foci.

The tripartite division of Boone-Ralls-Festus foci was an outgrowth of work by Wedel (1943), who, in attempting to place the Hopewellian mounds in Platte

2. Note that Figure 5.3 shows the Ozark bluff dwellers under the heading "Archaic." This particular unit apparently presented Chapman with a problem: some Ozark bluff dweller sites contained pottery, and others did not. As discussed below, by the time he wrote part 4 (Chapman 1948b), he was beginning to arrange units by time period, and he finally placed the Ozark bluff dwellers at the end of the Archaic period and the beginning of the Early Woodland period.

Figure 5.4. Photographs of burial vault in the Pearl group, mound C, Platte County, Missouri (from Wedel 1943).

and Clay counties in a regional perspective, had identified three mound-building centers in Missouri—the Kansas City area (Figure 5.4), the mouth of the Osage (Chapman's Boone focus), and the Ralls and Pike counties area of northeastern Missouri (Chapman's Ralls focus). The Festus focus, south of St. Louis, originally was named by R. M. Adams (1941) based on limited excavation in Jefferson County. The majority of mound excavations that Chapman used to establish the Boone phase were those undertaken by Fowke in the early twentieth century. Some mounds contained central stone crypts, several had individual stone boxes, and others had no central chambers. A few contained grave pits excavated beneath the mounds. Four other central-chamber mounds were excavated by the University of Missouri in the 1930s—three in Boone County and one in Montgomery County (Chapman 1941). Excavation of sites, primarily mounds, used to define the Ralls focus had been conducted, with few exceptions, in the nineteenth century (e.g., Hardy and Scheetz 1883; Watkins 1883). The only twentieth-century work noted by Chapman was Allen Eichenberger's excavation of a mound near Saverton (Eichenberger 1939) and Chapman's own unpublished excavation of a mound in Lincoln County. Chapman (1948a) made a case for separating the Boone and Ralls foci, but it was at best a halfhearted gesture, given the marked similarities in mound construction and interment practices between the two (see Denny 1964).

Embedded in the southwestern corner of the state, and overlapping spatially with the Highland aspect, was the archaeological manifestation known as the Ozark bluff dwellers (Figure 5.3), a name assigned by M. R. Harrington (1924b) based on his excavations of several rock shelters in northwestern Arkansas. A unique feature of these rock shelters was that they were dry, and hence perishable items such as textiles remained preserved in them in considerable quantities (Figure 5.5). These included cradles, baskets, woven bags, sandals, mats, feather robes, spear shafts, and mummified human remains (Bushnell 1915; Dellinger 1932, 1936; Dellinger and Dickinson 1942; Gilmore 1931; M. R. Harrington 1924a, 1924b). Interestingly, Chapman did not attempt to place the Ozark bluff-dweller culture into the midwestern taxonomic method, though in part 4 (Chapman 1948b: 157) he speculated, "The end of the early or Archaic Period is perhaps represented by the Ozark Bluff Dwellers at the time they began using pottery" (see Hoebel 1946).

Chapman also placed in the Archaic period several cultures that—based partly on stratigraphic evidence but more on similarity in artifact style—he believed were similar to ancient cultures in the Plains and Southwest: "Numerous variants of Folsom projectile points have been found at different places throughout Missouri which suggests the possibility that an early hunting culture similar to the Folsom complex in the Southwest once inhabited the State" (Chapman 1948b: 137). We now recognize the forms to which Chapman was referring as Clovis points, which predated Folsom points by several hundred years. Chapman (1948b: 137–38) recognized the danger inherent in equating similarity in form with similarity in age: "The evidence for the presence of a Folsom culture in Missouri is typological and it is risky to assume that the culture existed in the State from that evidence alone."

Several other early cultures were recognized, including Dalton and Nebo Hill. The former was named for the type site east of Jefferson City that produced the concave-base, serrated-blade forms that became hallmarks of the late Paleo-Indian period (see Chapter 1). The pieces described by Chapman were all surface finds, but he judged their relative chronological placement correctly. The Nebo Hill culture was based on lanceolate bifaces found near Kansas City (Shippee 1948), though Chapman expanded the range east to central Missouri to include lanceolate forms that currently would be placed in the Sedalia type. Chapman (1948b) placed Nebo Hill chronologically later than Dalton, though he clearly favored an early date for the culture.[3]

3. Nebo Hill is now known to date to the Late Archaic period (3000–1000 B.C.) (see Chapter 8).

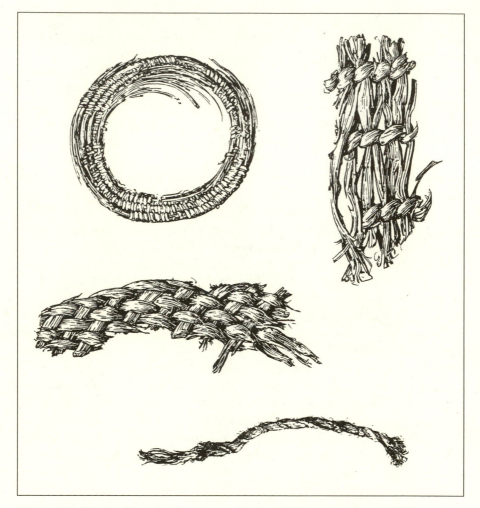

Figure 5.5. Textiles from Jacobs Cavern, McDonald County, Missouri (after Bushnell 1915).

The master chronological chart developed by Chapman (1948b: 155) is reproduced in Figure 5.6. For the time it represented a reasonable attempt to arrange the known archaeological manifestations chronologically. The time estimates were erroneous, which would not become evident for several more years, and several "cultures" were out of place. For example, we now know that the Boone and Ralls foci mounds are Late Woodland in age and postdate the Hopewellian tradition by several hundred years. Note that Chapman's chart does not contain a Late Woodland period. In fact, he used the term "late prehistoric period" to encompass the Steed-Kisker component, the Highland aspect, and the foci in the Middle Mississippi phase.

PERIOD	TIME ESTIMATE	CULTURES			CURRENTLY ACCEPTED DATES
		NORTH MISSOURI	SOUTHWEST MISSOURI	SOUTHEAST MISSOURI	
EUROPEAN CONTACT AND PROTO-HISTORIC PERIOD	A.D. 1830 / 1800 / 1600	Missouri Indians / Little Osage Indians	Great Osage Indians / Ozark Top-Layer Culture	Illinois Tribe?	A.D. 1541
LATE PRE-HISTORIC PERIOD	1500 / 1400 / 1300	Steed-Kisker Focus / Highland Aspect	White River Middle Mississippi / Highland Aspect	New Madrid / Kimmswick and Plattin Foci and Monks Mound Aspect / Festus Focus and Highland Aspect	A.D. 450
MIDDLE WOODLAND PERIOD	1200 / 1000	Unnamed Woodland Cultures / Hopewellian	Hopewellian / Unnamed Woodland Cultures	Hopewellian / Unnamed Woodland Cultures	250 B.C.
EARLY WOODLAND PERIOD	800 / A.D. 500	Ralls Focus / Boone Focus	Pottery Horizon Ozark Bluff Dwellers	Hidden Valley Shelter Two	600 B.C.
ARCHAIC PERIOD	8000 B.C	Nebo Hill / Dalton Culture Variant Folsom?	Non-pottery Ozark Bluff Dwellers and White River Archaic culture / Nebo Hill / Dalton culture Variant Folsom? / Association with extinct mammal remains.	Hidden Valley Shelter Ore Variant Folsom? / Association with extinct mammal remains.	Late — 3000 B.C. / Middle — 5000 B.C. / Early — 7500 B.C.

Figure 5.6. Carl Chapman's tentative sequence and dating of archaeological cultures of Missouri (after Chapman 1948b) compared to, along right margin, currently accepted dates.

In summary, Chapman's scheme was the first attempt to apply elements of the midwestern taxonomic method to the archaeological record of Missouri. His treatment was in no respect as detailed as Griffin's (1943) work on the Fort Ancient aspect, but in fairness Griffin was treating only one unit. Chapman in 1946 had seen numerous collections from Missouri locales and had a fairly good command of the available literature. Given the nature of much of that literature—sketchy at best, for the most part—Chapman formulated a comprehensive temporal and spatial outline of Missouri prehistory. I should emphasize, to the annoyance of readers who have already figured this out, that his model went well beyond the midwestern taxonomic method. Unlike the work of R. M. Adams (e.g., 1941), from which Chapman drew much of his classification of late-period cultures, Chapman's framework introduced the term *period* as a chronological unit in which to place various foci and aspects that were roughly contemporaneous. Use of the term would accelerate during the late 1940s and early 1950s.

Before leaving Chapman's culture classification, I need to make another point—one I will return to in Chapter 9. Chapman obviously realized that he was stepping outside the midwestern taxonomic method when he added the dimensions of time and space to his analysis, but I doubt he realized that he had violated the basic tenet of McKern's system. McKern (1939) made every effort to underscore the distinction between traits (qualities of artifacts) and determinants (qualities of artifacts that serve to place them in certain periods or traditions), and in fact he noted that traits could be determinants *only if they were unique to one cultural manifestation.* According to McKern, if traits are "linked" to two or more manifestations, then they are "useless as determinants" (McKern 1939: 305). Chapman, however, used traits exclusively. His failure to distinguish between traits and determinants paved the way for considerable frustration as he began to search for the archaeological signatures of groups that were later known as the Osage.

Another hallmark publication of the period, from the standpoint both of Americanist archaeology and of Missouri archaeology, was Griffin's edited volume *Archeology of Eastern United States* (Griffin 1952e), which was a compilation of papers by former students of Fay-Cooper Cole at the University of Chicago. The volume—often affectionately referred to as the "Green Bible" because of the color of the binding, the attention the book received, and the authority it had—stands as a state-of-the-art summary of the archaeological record of the eastern United States as it was interpreted in the late 1940s. Each chapter focused on a different area of the East, with an introductory chapter by Guthe (1952) and a summary chapter by Griffin (1952b). Among the chapters was Chapman's (1952) submission, "Cultural Sequence in the Lower Missouri Valley," which was a summary of archaeological remains along the Missouri River from Kansas City to St. Louis, though he also included a brief discussion of remains from the

Ozark Highland. The headings he used to organize his presentation represented a significant departure from how he organized his four-part series in *The Missouri Archaeologist*. For example, one heading reads "Hopewellian Phase—Middle Woodland Period," but another heading reads simply "Early Mississippi and Late Woodland." Chapman clearly was still trying to adhere to some of the standard terminology of the midwestern taxonomic method, but his expanding interest in time-and-space systematics was disrupting his ability to do so. There can be no doubt that by 1950 the sun had almost set on McKern's method.

As he had in his earlier synthesis, Chapman still viewed migration as the primary cause of the myriad changes evident in the archaeological record of Missouri. For example, he viewed differences between the Boone focus of the Early Woodland period and the Hopewellian phase of the Middle Woodland period in terms of a western movement of Illinois groups:

> The period following the early development of the Boone Focus saw a large scale migration of people and ideas into the area. Extensive travel and trade marked the times. One of the far western outposts of the Hopewellian sphere of influence seemed to lie in the center of the lower Missouri Valley. The Hopewell mode of life appears to have been carried through to this place from the center of Hopewell culture in Illinois. However, it could be that in some instances Woodland peoples already established in the region, added to their culture new ideas and customs derived from the eastern Hopewellian. If such was the case, the period saw the overriding of some of the less complicated Woodland cultures until they possessed a striking similarity to the Illinois Hopewell. (Chapman 1952: 141–42)

Here Chapman was clear about the role of migration as well as diffusion in helping to shape the archaeological record. Chapman in this instance set up an either-or situation: maybe migration or, on the other hand, maybe diffusion caused the spread of traits. Such waffling was typical of many cultural schemes of the time, in which archaeologists mixed and matched the two possibilities to suit their particular interpretations of the record.

Chapman's comment about the "overriding of some of the less complicated Woodland cultures" also was not unique to him. For decades the view had been widely held that there were two "capstone" cultures in the East—Hopewellian and Mississippian—that represented the pinnacle of cultural achievement in the prehistoric past. Contemporary cultures that did not exhibit the trappings of their more advanced neighbors obviously were "simpler" and thus could easily be assimilated into the spheres of influence of advanced cultures. Chapman wove the elements of migration and assimilation into his explanation of the post-Hopewellian archaeological record in Missouri:

> After the influx of Hopewellian people was an interval of the culture history of the Lower Missouri Valley during which there were movements of new people

and ideas into the area but on a smaller scale. Mississippi people were well entrenched at the mouth of the Missouri River in late prehistoric times and some had succeeded in making establishments quite far up the Missouri River. It seems these people were on the march, spreading new ideas and new ways of living wherever they penetrated. The Lower Missouri Valley appears to have been a frontier of the Mississippi people and was never thoroughly converted to the new trend of living. A culture close to the Cahokia Area was located on the western edge of the Lower Missouri Valley which indicates that migrations had penetrated that far west. Cultures of the same general period on the southern tributaries of the Missouri River were Woodland peoples with a smattering of Mississippi traits suggesting a spread of ideas rather than people. (Chapman 1952: 143)

Chapman's article in the Green Bible was much clearer and more concise than was his earlier four-segment presentation, in large part because he handled time in a more straightforward manner. The last sentence in the above quote demonstrates that by 1952 Chapman recognized that people exhibiting Late Woodland–period traits were in some areas of Missouri living next to groups exhibiting Mississippian traits. For example, he cites R. M. Adams's (1941) excavations in Jefferson County as evidence of contemporaneous Woodland-Mississippian presence in eastern Missouri and cites Bennett and Maxwell's (1942) similar conclusions based on work in Illinois. Chapman (1952: 150) concluded that "it seems that there was a Late Woodland Complex in much of Missouri and Illinois which was contemporaneous with Middle Mississippi cultures in some places and later or earlier in others. It is probable that the Highland Aspect in the Lower Missouri Valley was contemporaneous with Steed-Kisker, a marginal Middle Mississippi culture."

Excavations of stratified deposits in several regions of Missouri also contributed to Chapman's ideas on cultural chronology. For example, Chapman cited (a) work at the "Old Fort" in Saline County by the University of Missouri as the key to separating later, Oneota-aspect materials from earlier, Hopewellian artifacts[4] and (b) excavations at the Givens site, also in Saline County, as the key to separating Hopewellian materials from Early Woodland materials. Hopewellian was placed earlier than Steed-Kisker because "Wedel [1943] notes a case of intrusive Middle Mississippi burials in a probable Hopewellian burial mound. Wedel also cites no evidence that Steed-Kisker and Hopewellian were contemporaneous and in fact indicates that the Hopewellian was the earlier of the two. He points out that such a sequence is in line with previous findings and interpretations in the Mississippi Valley" (Chapman 1952: 150). The lack of

---

4. Subsequent excavations at the Old Fort (Wood 1973) showed Chapman's assignment of a portion of the deposit to "Hopewellian" was incorrect.

excavation of stratified village sites connected with Boone-focus burial mounds led Chapman to maintain (erroneously) that focus as an Early Woodland unit.

The other chapter in the Green Bible in which Missouri prehistory was discussed was one by Griffin (1952a), "Prehistoric Cultures of the Central Mississippi Valley." He summarized what little was known at the time regarding pre-Mississippian cultures, but he devoted the major part of the paper to a discussion of later-period foci and complexes, including the New Madrid focus of southeastern Missouri (Adams and Walker 1942).

The most important paper in *Archeology of Eastern United States* was Griffin's (1952b) summary article, "Culture Periods in Eastern United States Archeology." It was and still is a landmark article in Americanist archaeology because it represents a discussion of the archaeological record of a large region principally in terms of time (see also Griffin 1946). Griffin's general goal was to present a broad overview of prehistoric life in the East, and to order the discussion he divided the archaeological record into six chronological periods (he often substituted the term *stage* for *period*)—Paleo-Indian, Early Archaic, Late Archaic, Early Woodland, Middle Woodland, and a hybrid unit termed *Mississippi and Late Woodland*. The last unit is of interest here because Griffin states that in some regions there was a Late Woodland period between Hopewell and Mississippi while in other areas Late Woodland groups "seem to have existed along with and to have participated to some degree in the development of Early Mississippi" (Griffin 1952b: 362). This was one of the first, if not the first, statements that perhaps whatever "Mississippi" was had grown out of a Late Woodland base. This statement would have a profound effect on how the critical period A.D. 450–1000 was later viewed by several generations of archaeologists.

Griffin's summary chapter to the volume was accompanied by maps that showed the distribution of culture units for the various time periods, but most remarkable of all is his figure 205, which is a chronological chart that not only places the various units in geographic and temporal order but assigns absolute dates to them. As Griffin stated in the figure caption, the unit alignment reflected ideas of the late 1940s, that is, the pre-radiocarbon era, but one cannot help but be struck by both the correct relative positioning of the units and the accuracy of some of the absolute dates. Some cultural units, such as Ohio Hopewell and Adena, were hopelessly miscalculated, but many of the later ones, including the Boone focus and the Highland aspect in Missouri, were on target. Griffin moved the Boone focus out of the Early Woodland period (where Chapman had placed it) and placed it after Hopewell. By the time the volume was produced, three laboratories—one at the University of Michigan, one at Columbia University, and Willard Libby's laboratory at the University of Chicago—had begun to produce radiocarbon dates, and these were presented by Griffin (1952c) in the final chapter of *Archeology of Eastern United States*.

The Addition of Formal Types to the
Study of Time, Space, and Form

It could be argued that the most important work relative to the archaeology of Missouri—and to that of the entire southeastern United States—produced between 1941 and 1960 was *Archaeological Survey in the Lower Mississippi Alluvial Valley, 1940–1947,* coauthored by Philip Phillips, James Ford, and James Griffin (1951). It is difficult to underestimate the impact the volume has had on the archaeology of the Mississippi River valley or to deny its seminal position in anticipating many later trends in the discipline. The volume is, as Dunnell (1985a: 299) states, "a frank and penetrating discussion of state-of-the-art archaeology in the late 1940s and in rereading it, one finds the 1940s to be less distant than the date suggests. The book deserves the respect of history and will reward the modern reader abundantly."

The volume summarized the results of the "Lower Mississippi Archaeological Survey," a multi-institutional project that was initiated in 1939 and completed in 1947. The authors were clear about the objectives of the project:

> The purpose of the Survey was to investigate the northern two-thirds of the alluvial valley of the Lower Mississippi River—roughly from the mouth of the Ohio to Vicksburg, Mississippi [Figure 5.7], an area long regarded as one of the principal blind spots in the archaeology of the Southeast. This is not altogether due to lack of work in the area, or to the character of such work, but rather to the fact that it had so far failed to reveal anything concerning the earlier pre-Mississippian cultures. The need for a comprehensive survey had been repeatedly voiced at Midwestern and Southeastern conferences and various suggestions made for carrying out such a project. (Phillips et al. 1951: v)

During the course of the eight-year project, which was interrupted on several occasions, various crews spent a total of seven months in the field finding and mapping sites, making surface collections, and conducting test excavations.

Although the authors were interested in finding traces of pre-Mississippian cultures, they were particularly interested in those that perhaps had given rise to Mississippian culture:

> There is general agreement among students of Southeastern archaeology that the climax of the late prehistoric cultures is the archaeological facies long recognized under the designation "Middle Mississippi." At a comparatively late date— A.D. 1400–1500 is probably not too late for its peak of development—this culture was firmly established over an immense area. . . . By 1939, when the present Survey was first discussed, an immense amount of data on Middle Mississippi had accumulated, but the problem of its origins and development appeared to be as far from resolution as ever. There was a general impression, shared by many students of Southeastern culture, that this was because the "central" Mississippi

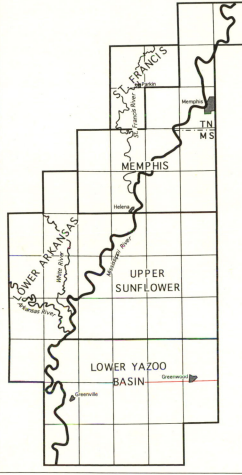

Figure 5.7. Map of the central Mississippi River valley showing the 50 survey quadrangles (each about 17 miles north–south by 14 miles east–west) and the 5 analytical units employed during the Lower Mississippi Valley Survey (after Phillips et al. 1951).

Valley, the assumed center of distribution of the culture, had not been sufficiently investigated. It was primarily to make good this lack that the present Survey was undertaken. (Phillips et al. 1951: 39)

The amount of data compiled for the final report was, and still is, truly impressive. It would be difficult to find a more comprehensive discussion of ceramic types—Griffin's specialty as director of the Ceramic Repository at the University of Michigan—or a more thorough correlation of ceramic types by excavation level—Phillips's specialty. Two sections of the report deserve special mention because of the careful manner in which the analyses were handled. The first is the section on the identification of archaeological sites from documentary sources. Of particular importance to the prehistory of southeastern Missouri and northeastern Arkansas was the account by Phillips, Ford, and Griffin of the de Soto expedition, which reached the region in 1541, and the projected route the expedition took in crossing the Mississippi River into Arkansas (see Swanton 1939). The question of de Soto's route through the region has long been a topic of intense debate among archaeologists (see D. F. Morse and P. A. Morse 1983), who would like to be able to link archaeological sites to places mentioned in the de Soto chronicles. Phillips et al.'s discussion is both thorough and detailed and set a standard against which to measure later work.

The other section of the report that set a standard was the correlation of archaeological sequences with the recent drainage history of the Mississippi alluvial valley. The basis for the correlation was the plotting of archaeological sites against channel maps prepared by Harold Fisk in his monumental report *Geological Investigation of the Alluvial Valley of the Lower Mississippi River* (Fisk 1944), which was prepared for the U.S. Army Corps of Engineers. The centerpiece of Fisk's report was a series of multicolor maps showing not only the positions but also the ages (in absolute terms for the younger channels, in relative terms for the older channels) of 26 former courses of the Mississippi in what is known as the meander-belt region, which extends from just south of Cape Girardeau, Missouri, to Donaldsonville, Louisiana. This reconstruction was recognized as a boon to archaeologists, since any site situated in a former channel had to postdate abandonment of that channel by the Mississippi. Although we now know that Fisk's reconstructions are grossly inaccurate (e.g., Saucier 1981), Phillips et al.'s use of the method was appropriate. Their attempt to date the sites by means of channels also spawned similar studies in Missouri (e.g., Hopgood 1969; Scully 1953) and elsewhere.

The most significant contribution—in fact a legacy—of the Phillips, Ford, and Griffin report was the extraordinary number of ceramic types that were described, most for the first time. It is difficult in retrospect to comprehend that for all the work that had been undertaken in the Mississippi alluvial valley up to 1951, few ceramic types had been formulated to partition the vast array of pottery that had been recovered from especially the late portion of the archaeological record. Beginning with the rather nonscientific investigations of the 1870s and 1880s and continuing up through the work of Cyrus Thomas (1894) and into the twentieth century, thousands of vessels and many times that number of sherds had been excavated from sites in southeastern Missouri, but none of these materials—nor those from northeastern Arkansas—had been systematically sorted into types. To be sure, Holmes (1903a) described considerable variation in what he labeled "Middle Mississippi" pottery, but he made no attempt to categorize that variation systematically.

The first effort to categorize ceramics from southeastern Missouri—and apparently from Missouri in general—in terms of type nomenclature was Griffin's work on surface material collected in New Madrid County by R. M. Adams and

Walker (1942) and on material excavated by Walker and Adams (1946) from the Matthews site in that county. But it was in *Archaeological Survey in the Lower Mississippi Alluvial Valley* that Griffin, with Phillips and Ford, kicked typological classification into high gear. Presentation of the pottery types in that volume is arranged in chronological order from the earliest to the youngest groups, but, interestingly, the groupings with few exceptions run in more or less geographic order from south to north. This phenomenon is in part attributable to the fact that the early portion of the ceramic record in Louisiana had received much more archaeological examination by trained professionals such as Ford than had the contemporaneous portion of the record in Missouri. Given the quantity of information available from Louisiana, it was natural that more early period types would be formulated for the region. On the other hand, the late portion of the archaeological record of northeastern Arkansas, and to an extent that of southeastern Missouri, had been explored in depth for years and the late-period pottery had been well described by Holmes (1903a) and others. Not coincidentally, that portion of the Mississippi Valley had supported literally hundreds of late-Mississippian-period communities, the populations of which had the habit of burying exquisite vessels with their dead.

Phillips, Ford, and Griffin (1951: 426) acknowledged the usefulness of their system—"Our classification cannot be too bad or it would not have produced the consistent patterning of types through time that is shown in the seriation and stratigraphic analyses"—but they also acknowledged dissatisfaction:

> The archaeologist who thinks he has achieved a final classification of anything is a rare and probably untrustworthy individual. Most of the shortcomings of our classification have been fully exposed in the type descriptions. Our guess is that very few of our types will stand up when more and better material is available. Many of them will break down into more specialized groups, a few (we may hope) will be combined into more general groups. It is not likely that the total number of types will be reduced. The outlook for the Southeast as a whole, so long as present typological methods remain in favor, is not pleasant to contemplate. Where we are now counting types in tens, they will be counted in hundreds. (Phillips et al. 1951: 426)

The authors could have had no way of knowing how well they predicted future developments in the archaeology of the central and lower Mississippi Valley, for while they had reason to anticipate a proliferation of typological nomenclature, they had no way of knowing that literally hundreds of types and (later) varieties would be devised to account for the massive decorative, technological, and functional variation evident in the ceramic vessels from the region. And nowhere would this proliferation occur more than in Missouri.

The method adopted by Phillips, Ford, and Griffin in constructing types and type descriptions stemmed directly from Ford's earlier work, especially his

Birmingham Conference paper (Ford 1938a; see also Ford 1938b). The reason for constructing types was unchanged from Ford's earlier work: types were considered to be constructs useful in assigning temporal order to archaeological deposits. If they served some other purpose—for example, if the traits used to sort the pottery "correspond[ed] to characters that might have served to distinguish one sort of pottery from another in the minds of the people who made and used it" (Phillips et al. 1951: 63)—then so much the better. But chronological ordering came first. Phillips et al. (1951: 64) recognized types as composites of various separate *characters*—paste, vessel form, surface, and decoration—and they reasoned that each character had its own history. It was viewed as "unreasonable" to assume that one character was always more useful than another in assigning time or to insist that all pottery should be sorted consistently on the basis of the same characters. However, they also recognized that, to decrease confusion, one should

> select the most sensitive—and at the same time most recognizable—characters as guides or "constants" in the process of classification. In Southeastern pottery generally, these are features of surface treatment and decoration, and thus it has come about that what may for convenience be called the Southeastern classification employs a binomial system of nomenclature in which the second term or "constant" is descriptive of surface treatment or decoration, as in Mulberry Creek *Cord-marked* or Indian Bay *Stamped*. (Phillips et al. 1951: 64–65)

Just as selecting the "characters" around which to construct a typological system was viewed as arbitrary, so was the decision about where to draw the line on one type and construct another. To place this problem in perspective, we need to examine a bit of the philosophy behind Phillips et al.'s concept of what a type implied:

> Each community that had reached a certain level of sophistication in pottery-making will be found to have been maintaining side by side several different vessel styles [read *types*]. . . . Between these centers, styles vary and trend toward those of other centers in rough proportion to the distances involved, subject of course to ethnic distributions and geographic factors.
>
> Thus we have in mind the concept of a continuously evolving regional pottery tradition, showing a more or less parallel development in and around a number of centers, each of which employs a number of distinct but related styles, each style in turn being in process of change both areally and temporally. With this remarkably unstable material, we set out to fashion a key to the prehistory of the region. Faced with this three-dimensional flow, which seldom if ever exhibits "natural" segregation, and being obliged to reduce it to some sort of manageable form, we arbitrarily cut it into units. Such *created units of the ceramic continuum* are called *pottery types*. (Phillips et al. 1951: 62–63)

This was, and in many respects still is, the standing philosophy behind the creation of the ceramic types used to bring chronological ordering to the vast archaeological record of the Mississippi alluvial valley. In the 1960s the techniques used to create those units changed somewhat, as did the nomenclature system itself—a topic we explore a bit later—but the legacy had been firmly established. However, the legacy did not turn out as Phillips et al. planned. They clearly recognized the inherent problems in the typological system they had constructed and constantly warned archaeologists of the dangers in blindly accepting the system. They also provided one of the most insightful comments on ceramic typologies ever written:

> Exigencies of language require us to think and talk about pottery types as though they had some sort of independent existence. "This sherd *is* Baytown Plain." Upon sufficient repetition of this statement, the concept Baytown Plain takes on a massive solidity. The time comes when we are ready to fight for dear old Baytown. What we have to try to remember is that the statement really means something like this: "This sherd sufficiently resembles material which *for the time being* we have elected to call Baytown Plain." Frequent repetition of this and similar exorcisms we have found to be extremely salutary during the classificatory activities. (Phillips et al. 1951: 66)

Here Ford, with Phillips and Griffin, clearly called attention to the problem that Dunnell (1986: 173) suggests weakened Ford's earlier work—the differences between the type as a class and the objects that are assigned to the type. Unfortunately, archaeologists since the time Phillips et al. published their monograph have forgotten to repeat the "exorcism" quoted above. Continued reliance on the modal concept of types, without the continued refinement encouraged by Phillips et al., has resulted in a stagnation of analysis beyond chronological positioning of archaeological assemblages. In addition, what Phillips et al. elected to call Baytown plain in 1951 is, for all intents and purposes, still labeled Baytown plain. No real attempts have been made to go beyond simple type descriptions of Baytown or any other of the myriad types and to define the type in terms of the specific traits, or *characters,* as Phillips et al. termed them. We are still very much in the same shape as we were in in 1951: as we move farther away (in time and/or in space) from the "centers" that produced the archetypal pottery used by archaeologists to construct the type,

> the characters that we have selected as determinants for the type gradually shift, the all-too familiar phenomenon of "creep," until at some point we can stretch our original type definition no further and to consider whether material "X" more closely resembles Type "B," already established at another center, or whether it is not sufficiently like either "A" or "B" and must be given an independent status as Type "C." These wretched hair-line decisions beset the classifier at every step. (Phillips et al. 1951: 65)

Phillips et al. would not have taken consolation in the fact that things have not changed much in the four decades since they wrote their report.

One interesting feature of the Phillips et al. report is that the authors took pains to point out areas of disagreement among themselves, especially on how to interpret mixed pottery complexes. In fact, they foreshadowed one of the more significant discussions in the archaeology of the 1970s and later, namely, the distinction between style and function and which set of "characters"—those that are stylistic or those that are functional—is appropriate for placing things in chronological order (Dunnell 1978b). The lack of distinction between the two would have severe consequences on how the archaeological record of southeastern Missouri and neighboring regions would come to be interpreted (O'Brien 1993, 1994). Given the magnitude of the problem, the disagreement between Ford on one hand and Phillips and Griffin on the other merits at least brief examination. Basically, Ford's position was that pottery

> was developing in a continuum throughout its entire history in the Mississippi Valley, that whether new types evolve by modification of older ones or come in as new ideas from the outside, they take their place in an uninterrupted cultural flow. The logical consequence of such a view is that, in most cases a "mixed" pottery complex represents a single brief span of time on the continuum, an "instant" for all practical purposes, when both elements of the mixture were being made and used side by side. The importance of this postulation for the seriation method can hardly be exaggerated. Ford does not deny that mixed complexes sometimes do result from reoccupation of sites. Such collections he frankly banishes from his graphs and says so. . . .
>
> Griffin and Phillips, on the other hand, while not rejecting the general theory of continuity, are inclined to feel . . . that there are more instances of mixture through reoccupation of sites than Ford has recognized. In particular . . . they have tended to see indications of at least one significant break in the otherwise placid stream of pottery continuity at the point where the tempering material shifts from clay to shell, in other words between the Baytown and Mississippi periods. They feel that, by including mixed collections on the graphs, Ford has effected a spurious transition that seems to prove his continuity hypothesis, but in reality leaves the question open. (Phillips et al. 1951: 427)

Several decades of excavation in the meander-belt portion of the Mississippi alluvial valley would demonstrate that the abrupt change from clay-tempered pottery to shell-tempered pottery is real (Figure 5.8), as is the abrupt change from sand-tempered pottery to shell-tempered pottery along the western margin of the valley. Interestingly, the mechanism for the temporal changes was commonly viewed as migration—a mechanism that only recently has begun to be challenged seriously.

In summary, it is not an overstatement to note that with the publication of *Archaeological Survey in the Lower Mississippi Alluvial Valley* Americanist archaeology was elevated to a different level. The authors were forthright, of-ten blunt, about problems not only in their data sets—for example, biases in

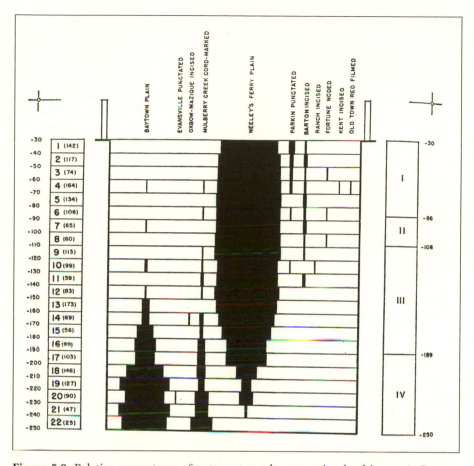

Figure 5.8. Relative percentages of pottery types by excavation level in cut A, Rose Mound, Cross County, Arkansas. The negative numbers on the left correspond to depth (in cm) below the top of the excavation stakes (upright rectangles at the edges of the graph). The numbers in boxes refer to 10-cm excavation levels; the numbers in parentheses indicate the total number of sherds recovered from each level. The Roman numerals at the right represent idealized strata obtained by averaging the four walls of the 2-m² excavation unit. Note the pronounced stratigraphic shift from clay-tempered pottery (the four types on the left) to shell-tempered pottery (used by permission from Phillips et al. 1951 [copyright 1951 by the President and Fellows of Harvard College]).

the sherd collections—but in their analytical methods as well. They dramatically overhauled the chronological position of archaeological cultures, especially Hopewell, which was pushed farther back in time so that there was at least 500 years between it and the beginning of the Mississippi period—enough time in which to fit, at least in the Mississippi Valley, the Middle and Late Baytown periods. Hopewell itself was no longer thought of as a panregional phenomenon but rather, as Griffin (1946) had earlier suggested, as one of several Middle

Woodland manifestations. For the Mississippi Valley sequence, they used the designation Early Baytown for the Middle Woodland, aligning it with Marksville to the south (Ford and Willey 1941). If it did nothing else, the massive synthesis compiled by Phillips et al. indeed demonstrated that "the archaeology of the Lower Mississippi Valley, and eastern North America generally, is even more interesting, and perhaps more important" (Phillips et al. 1951: 457) than even they thought. Griffin (1985b: 7) later commented that his collaboration with Phillips and Ford was fruitful, "even if some lemons appeared in the publication."

The volume by Phillips et al. was followed by a number of studies that extended coverage of the survey area. They had originally intended to completely cover the entire valley south of Cape Girardeau, Missouri, but they scaled back considerably during the course of the project. Project organizers had subdivided the valley into a series of 15-minute quadrangles (each approximately 14 miles east–west by 17 miles north–south) using the grid system established by the Mississippi River Commission (e.g., Fisk 1944). Phillips et al. included 171 quadrangles in their survey area but examined only 49 of those; these 49 were collapsed into five geographical units for regional comparisons (Figure 5.7) (Phillips et al. [1951: 40] state that they surveyed 49 quadrangles, but their map of the geographical units [figure 16] shows 50 quadrangles). In 1949 the University of Michigan established the Central Mississippi Valley Archaeological Survey to investigate the area between the mouth of the Illinois River and a point in southeastern Missouri where the earlier survey had stopped (Griffin and Spaulding 1952). In 1954 Stephen Williams completed a doctoral dissertation (Yale University) entitled *An Archeological Study of the Mississippian Culture in Southeast Missouri*, which was a compilation of information gathered during several field seasons of surface collection and excavation in several areas of southeastern Missouri, undertaken as an outgrowth of Griffin and Spaulding's project. Williams generated enough data to establish a series of time-space units for southeastern Missouri, and as D. F. Morse and P. A. Morse (1983: 27) note, "Williams's cultural sequence interpretations are the basis for those still used in southeast Missouri today." I examine some of those units later, not so much for their content as for the rationale behind their establishment. Williams's work is an example of how Americanist archaeology was changing in the 1950s relative to time-space systematics.

Remember that time was not of primary consideration in the midwestern taxonomic method—not that it was considered unimportant, but it was handled separately from the units created by comparing trait lists. We have also seen that by the early 1950s the midwestern taxonomic method was used by fewer and fewer archaeologists, so that by the time of the Phillips et al. monograph, the terms *focus* and *aspect* were being replaced by terms such as *period* and *phase*. In fact, Phillips et al. (1951) make few references to focus or aspect, preferring to substitute the term *period*. They note, "The 'periods' derived from seriation are not as different conceptually from 'foci' as one might think" (p. 427), though this was an overstatement of fact. Periods and foci were about as far apart as two units could be. The first was nothing but a temporal unit; the second was anything *but* a temporal unit, though by the late 1940s foci were being placed in time. Given that the midwestern taxonomic method was falling into disuse, it was natural that archaeologists would invent a new system of nomenclature to categorize variation in the archaeological record.

A Standardized System for Time, Space, and Form

The new system was laid out in two papers in *The American Anthropologist*—Phillips and Gordon Willey (1953) and Willey and Phillips (1955)—that later were combined and reissued under the title *Method and Theory in American Archaeology* (Willey and Phillips 1958). The papers, and later the book, had a tremendous influence on how archaeology was practiced, in essence providing a cookbook approach to carving up the archaeological record in terms of time, space, and form. In fact, the framework became so firmly attached to its formulators that it quickly became known as the Willey-and-Phillips system, a parallel event to what had happened with McKern 20 years earlier, despite his protestations.

Willey and Phillips identified four types of units: (1) spatial units—locality, region, and area; (2) formal units—component and phase; (3) temporal units—local sequence, regional sequence, and period and area chronology; and (4) integrative units—horizon style and tradition. Here I discuss only phases, since, of all the units, it has received the widest usage. The phase in the Willey-Phillips system more or less replaced the focus as the unit of analysis above the component and was defined as "an archaeological unit possessing traits sufficiently characteristic to distinguish it from all other units similarly conceived, whether of the same or other cultures or civilizations, spatially limited to the order of magnitude of a locality or region and chronologically limited to a brief span of time" (Willey and Phillips 1958: 22). They pointed out that a phase has "no appropriate scale independent of the cultural situation in which it is applied . . . phases may have very considerable and highly variable spatial and temporal dimensions" (pp. 23–24). In other words, phase A might include materials from a 300-year span of time and from an area of 400 square kilometers. Phase B, on the other hand, might include materials from a 150-year time span and from an area of 200 square kilometers. Phases are constructed from components with similar artifact assemblages. This is how it works: an artifact assemblage from a component is examined relative to its similarity to artifact assemblages from other components; if the analyst feels the assemblages are similar enough, the components—one from each site—are placed in the same phase. The assignment is based strictly on impressions of *similarity*, as opposed to McKern's (1939) emphasis on *dissimilarity*.

At one level, phases are "practical and intelligible unit[s] of study" (Willey and Phillips 1958: 22), but once they take on lives of their own they are difficult to modify. One of the problems in Missouri archaeology has been the incredible growth in phase names since the 1950s—a growth that has not followed the slow, deliberate procedure envisioned by Willey and Phillips (this rapid growth was, to a degree, anticipated by Earl Swanson in 1959 [Swanson 1959]). Instead, the nomenclature has grown like Topsy, with the vexing result that the literature is replete with phase names that have lasted only a short time before being replaced.

Stephen Williams (1954) applied the initial formulation by Phillips and Willey (1953) to his materials from southeastern Missouri, stating, "It is, to the writer's knowledge, the first attempt to apply the method to an entirely new body of data which had not previously been ordered by another conceptual scheme" (p. 24). This probably is a correct statement, at least with regard to materials from Missouri. Williams delineated 13 phases from 4 geographic regions of southeastern Missouri and arranged them in chronological order. The regions— the Cairo Lowland and the Little River Lowland in the meander-belt system of the Mississippi River and the Malden Plain and Crowley's Ridge to the west—each had their own series of phases, with some overlap among them. Assignments of individual components (sites, in this case) to the phases were based almost exclusively on the occurrence of sherds of various ceramic types.

Williams (1954: 200) clearly stated that he was in the Phillips camp as opposed to the Ford camp when it came to the concept of type, noting that types should have a correspondence to "characters that might have served to distinguish one sort of pottery from another in the minds of the people who made and used it"—a quote from Phillips et al. (1951: 63) that Williams assigned to the hand of Phillips. Although Williams made use of the Phillips et al. typological system, he also introduced numerous ceramic types not previously described. These were important additions to the list of types because they were in most cases created to sort out significant variation that previously was either unrecognized or left unseparated. For example, he separated red-slipped, shell-tempered material on the basis of shell-particle size, creating the type Varney red-filmed to distinguish vessels tempered with coarse particles from those tempered with fine particles (Phillips et al.'s Old Town red-filmed). He also recognized a distinctive pre–Mississippian period sand-tempered ware—Barnes plain and Barnes cordmarked—and was, apparently, the first archaeologist to notice a difference in its distribution relative to contemporaneous clay-tempered pottery: "The Barnes wares tend to have a westerly distribution along the St. Francis River on the Malden Plain while the [clay-tempered] Baytown wares are most important along the Mississippi. This is not a hard and fast rule but the purest sites of each type seem to lie at these extremes" (S. Williams 1954: 203).

Williams's work in southeastern Missouri set the stage for subsequent phase development, primarily by archaeologists from the University of Missouri who became alarmed by the rapid destruction of sites in the region through agricultural activities, especially land leveling. Williams, like Phillips, Ford, and Griffin, never intended his phases to remain unrefined, but later archaeologists for the most part accepted his designations uncritically. The constructions became so ingrained in archaeological thinking over the next several decades that they became the centerpieces of two syntheses of regional chronology for the central Mississippi River valley—that by Phillips (1970) and that by D. F. Morse and P. A. Morse (1983). The first serious challenge to the validity of the phases was by Gregory Fox (1992), almost four decades after the publication of Williams's dissertation.

The Development of Projectile-Point Types

By 1950 typological classification of ceramic materials had far outdistanced the classification of stone artifacts. This is not to imply that the objects typically referred to as projectile points had not in some cases been named (e.g., Folsom, Clovis, Dalton), but the nomenclature for lithic tools had not yet matched that for pottery. Ceramic material had always figured prominently in Americanist archaeology, reaching a descriptive peak with the work of William Henry Holmes and an early analytical peak with chronological work in the Southwest. Hence, later archaeologists such as Ford and Griffin were preconditioned to regard pottery as integral to descriptive archaeology as well as to the chronological ordering of archaeological deposits. In addition, pottery is abundant on sites in the central and lower Mississippi River valley (as it is in the Southwest), and it was natural that it would assume a place of primacy in archaeological analysis. Projectile points, on the other hand, are rarer occurrences on most sites. I should point out that any piece of pottery, no matter how plain and inelegant, can be placed in a type. Broken projectile points, because of the features used to create types, are more difficult to place.

Early articles in *The Missouri Archaeologist* probably were typical of many in the United States relative to the manner in which the classification of what I will term for convenience' sake *projectile points* was handled. Groups of points were identified in some cases by specific form-related criteria, such as location of notches, but in many cases the characteristics were more general in nature and were imbedded in general descriptions of groups of objects. In other words, a rather inclusive description of a group was put forth, and all objects that generally fit that description were included in that type.

In Missouri, the clearest statement from the 1930s on projectile-point classification came not from a professional archaeologist but rather from a banker, J. Allen Eichenberger, a member of the Missouri Archaeological Society. In a short paper entitled "Notched Chipped Implements Classified" (Eichenberger

1937), he made a number of insightful comments regarding the classification of chipped-stone implements. Eichenberger used two traits to classify what are commonly thought of as projectile points—pattern and technique of fashioning—with the hope of eventually creating a series of types that integrated both of them. In his 1937 paper he discussed only the former and reached the conclusion that "the most important basis for classification as to pattern is the notch, or provision for hafting" (p. 4). The eight general patterns that Eichenberger derived were based on combinations of stem, base, and notch characteristics. He developed a hierarchical taxonomic system to distinguish variations evident in his sample (Figure 5.9) and arranged his eight master patterns to show "a gradual evolution from the notchless, but polished edged Fishtail Type . . . to the heavily barbed pattern, Stem Type, Barbed" (p. 4). What I find most interesting about his classification is that he went on to state, "This evolutionary arrangement is for convenience of handling alone and should not be interpreted as representing an evolutionary development of the patterns" (p. 4). This was a warning that some professional archaeologists should have heeded. In a later paper, Eichenberger (1944) added technique of fashioning (flaking technique) to his classification system, employing that dimension as the

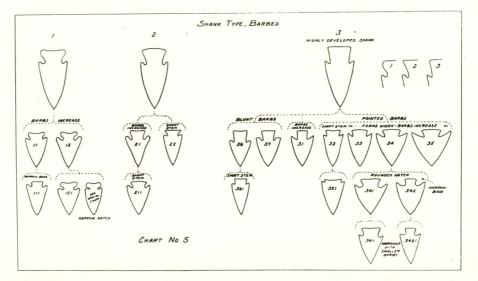

Figure 5.9. One part of the categorization of projectile points developed by J. Allen Eichenberger. The system is a hierarchical taxonomy—the portion shown here includes barbed specimens of the "shank type." The three main types (1–3) can be divided into other types as more defining attributes are included. Eichenberger, though an amateur, created quite a sophisticated system and one that rivaled any classifications in existence at the time (from Eichenberger 1937, courtesy Missouri Archaeological Society).

basis for subdividing specimens into four types, with "pattern" used as a basis for subdividing the specimens within each type.

One of the first efforts to standardize projectile-point categorization on a large, regional scale was "An Introductory Handbook of Texas Archaeology," which appeared as volume 25 of the *Bulletin of the Texas Archeological Society* (Suhm et al. 1954). The volume, which contained synopses and trait lists of the recognized cultural complexes of Texas as well as descriptions of pottery and projectile-point types, quickly sold out and was reissued as "Handbook of Texas Archeology: Type Descriptions" (Suhm and Jelks 1962). The handbook not only reorganized an expanding list of named pottery and projectile-point types from Texas and neighboring regions into coherent units, but it also listed the known geographic range of the types and, where known, included date ranges. The success of the handbook can be linked directly to its appeal to amateurs and collectors as well as to professionals. In fact, it probably sold 10 copies to collectors and amateurs for every copy sold to professionals. The reason for the appeal lay in the book's simplicity. Anyone who wanted to know what kind of point a certain specimen was could open the book and find a similar, named specimen among the photographs. What could be easier? The authors had drastically cut down on the confusion in the literature over what a specimen of a particular shape should be called—a confusion created in part by the proliferation of point-type names that was occurring in the late 1940s and early 1950s (e.g., Bell and Hall 1953; Krieger 1947), as more archaeologists started creating their own types without searching the literature to see if similar points had already been named. By 1960 at least two other guides to projectile-point types had been published, incorporating Suhm et al.'s (1954) types and adding new ones (Bell 1958, 1960). Those volumes also became best-sellers.

Remarkably, given the large amount of archaeological fieldwork that was done in Missouri during the 1950s by professional and amateur archaeologists, the growing standardized system of named projectile-point types was not used. Rather, archaeologists invented their own typological systems to incorporate materials found during various survey and excavation projects (Figure 5.10). By 1960 two systems had emerged as favorites: Chapman's (1954) system, which was based on his survey of the Pomme de Terre Reservoir in west-central Missouri, and that of his student Robert Bray (1956) (Figure 5.11), which was based on Bray's work at the Rice site in southwestern Missouri. Chapman developed his system for "convenience in description" (Chapman 1954: 26), although he raised several interesting issues in his discussion—points that are still not resolved completely. One issue revolved around why classification is done, the other around the issue of form and function:

> The prevalent tendency in classification of projectile points has been to select certain characteristics, usually of shape, and to separate the artifacts into classes

Figure 5.10. University of Missouri field crew sorting projectile points found during survey of Table Rock Reservoir, 1955.

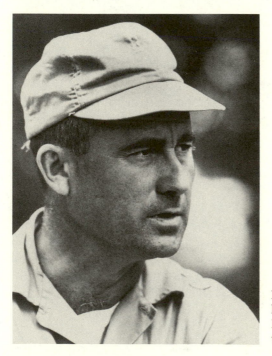

Figure 5.11. Robert T. Bray, longtime staff member in the Department of Anthropology at the University of Missouri, 1964.

upon the basis of these. Some have taken the stand that the association of a particular group of artifacts roughly similar in characteristics within a definable cultural complex of a particular time horizon should be the basis for classification. Others advocate a standardized, purely descriptive method. . . .

Several things appear to be stumbling blocks in the classification of tools of various kinds and projectile points in particular. These are the determination of the techniques involved in the manufacture of the implements, the use of the tool and the part it played in the culture complex. These would seem to be the most important aspects since, if known, they open the way to a fuller interpretation of the culture. (Chapman 1954: 26)

Here Chapman was echoing the sentiments heard earlier from Walter W. Taylor (1948), who criticized various archaeological programs for their failure to incorporate functional studies into overall, supposedly comprehensive, statements on prehistoric cultures. Chapman underscored several points made earlier by Steward and Setzler (1938) but also presaged some of the statements that would appear later as part of the platform of the so-called new archaeology (see Chapter 6):

Each class of objects would have cultural meaning. Traditional methods of manufacture and use in a specific activity would both be inherent in the classification. Isolated objects completely out of context could not be compared with others on the basis of form alone. A ceremonial knife in one complex is not comparable with a hunting spear point in another regardless of their similarity in form. Their meaning is entirely different. They are elements in two separate complexes. Classes of objects of known manufacture and use are needed in order to make comparisons that establish cultural relationships. This might lead to a break from the cold, lifeless comparison of bits and pieces of cultural complexes based on superficial likenesses and eventually lead to comparisons of life-like cultural combinations that would give a clearer picture of the interdependences or relationships of living cultures within space and time. If the classification aims at interpreting the particular cultural complex and its interrelationship, the bases for comparisons with other complexes has been established. (Chapman 1954: 27)

The classification technique chosen by Chapman was, however, based strictly on formal properties since, as he noted (Chapman 1954: 27), "the cultural objects were from too many sites widespread in time. Also the knowledge was not available in most instances to ascertain the techniques of manufacture and the use of the tool." He termed the projectile-point groups "descriptive types or categories" (Chapman 1954: 27) and used combinations of letters and numbers to denote types and subtypes, similar to the system established by Bell and Baerreis (1951) in Oklahoma and one he had used during a preliminary survey of the proposed Table Rock Reservoir (Chapman et al. 1951).

The typological system developed by Bray (1956) was based on his excavation of the Rice site in Stone County (Figure 5.12). The system was similar to that

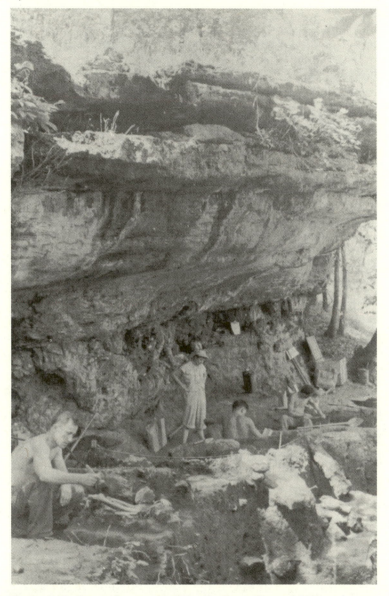

Figure 5.12. Excavations at the Rice site, Stone County, Missouri, 1952.

designed by Chapman (1954), though it was somewhat easier to use because Bray's type names were mnemonic devices. For example, CN1 referred to corner-notched-type 1, and CS1 referred to contracting-stem-type 1. Note the asymmetry involved in the system: one type is based on the shape of the stem, the other on notch location. Although Bray's system was easier to use than Chapman's, the ability to use either system was based strictly on one's familiarity with it. In other words, without a key and a description, especially for Chapman's system, the reader would have no idea about the nature of the type. To overcome this potential drawback and to place his work in a broader context, Bray actually made comparisons between his types and previously published types. Regardless, by the early 1960s, home-grown typological systems (e.g., Marshall 1958, 1960, 1963b) had for the most part been completely abandoned in favor of the type-naming system popularized by Suhm et al. in "An Introductory Handbook of Texas Archaeology" (1954).

Federally Sponsored Archaeology in Missouri

Research by Chapman and Bray in southwestern Missouri was conducted under contracts to the University of Missouri from the National Park Service. It is difficult to overemphasize the important role the work conducted under those contracts had in pushing ahead an understanding of Missouri's prehistory. Never before in the long history of archaeological work in the state—including that reported by Thomas (1894)—had so much information come from such large areas, nor had it been reported in such detail. During the period 1946–1951, the University of Missouri and the Missouri Archaeological Society began a long series of investigations in the west-central and southwestern portions of the state in areas that were slated for reservoir construction. The results of those efforts, submitted to the National Park Service in the form of reports but almost without fail published in abbreviated form in issues of *The Missouri Archaeologist*, were significant in several respects. They not only demonstrated the extensive nature of the archaeological record, but they also established a chronological ordering of much of that record. However, to really understand the significance of those projects, one has to step back and place them in a nationwide perspective, for the reservoir projects marked a turning point not only in Missouri archaeology but in the archaeology of several states. To develop this perspective we need to go back in time a bit, to the late 1930s, and pick up the story of federally sponsored archaeology that we left earlier.

Recall that one of the largest archaeological undertakings of the 1930s had been the program sponsored by the Tennessee Valley Authority (TVA) in the Southeast. As a result of large-scale efforts by several universities, an enormous amount of information had been gathered during construction of reservoirs on the Tennessee River and some of its major tributaries. Archaeologists had rallied around the program, and many of them went on to have outstanding careers in the discipline. But the Southeast was not the only part of the country in which reservoir construction was slated. It may have been where the money for archaeological investigation was, but it did not have a monopoly on a rich and diverse archaeological record in imminent danger of destruction. Missouri was another of those areas:

> The most pressing problem confronting those working on the archaeology within Missouri during the period 1938 to the present [1954] has been the salvage of cultural and historical information from the stream valleys that were planned to be dammed for reservoir areas. The University of Missouri, with its limited funds for Archaeological Research, began surveys under the direction of the Sociology Department in one of the proposed reservoir areas, the Wappapello Reservoir, in 1938. This work was closed with the construction of the dam in 1939. Survey work in reservoir areas was resumed after World War II. It was not until the fall of 1946 that it was possible to organize a program of salvage archaeology for the state. The cooperation of the Missouri Archaeological Society was obtained at that time and the University of Missouri Archaeological Research Division [later changed to American Archaeology Division] was oriented almost entirely toward salvage archaeology in proposed reservoir areas. (Chapman 1954: 10)

Reservoir archaeology in the 1940s was in one respect a continuation of TVA-related efforts of the 1930s, but in another respect it was an entirely new creature, the offspring of a close working relationship between universities and the federal government. The scale was also completely different. Whereas the number of federally sponsored projects in TVA reservoirs (basins) can be counted, no one knows the exact number of reservoirs eventually surveyed in the 1940s and 1950s during the heyday of what was termed the Inter-Agency Archaeological Salvage Program (IAASP), though J. O. Brew (1968) listed the number as 500-plus. It also is impossible to calculate the precise number of reports that grew out of the work, though it must have been over a thousand, based on Petsche's (1968) estimate of the number of reports that grew out of all salvage archaeology in the United States between the mid-1940s and mid-1960s. Some 150 or so state and private institutions participated in the interagency program at some point during its history.

The program was the result of a coordinated effort on the part of archaeologists across the United States to prevent the wholesale loss of information as a result of impoundments planned or under construction by federal agencies such as the Corps of Engineers and the Bureau of Reclamation. Through the efforts of prominent ethnologists and archaeologists such as Frank H. H. Roberts (Figure 5.13), Julian Steward, and Frank Setzler,[5] various federal agencies—primarily the

---

5. These were not the only archaeologists/ethnologists who worked diligently to address the threat from progress. As Jennings (1985: 282) chronicles, by June 1945 the American Council of Learned Societies had appointed four archaeologists (William S. Webb, A. V. Kidder, J. O. Brew, and Frederick Johnson) to the newly created Committee for the Recovery of Archaeological Remains. The committee was formed to lobby Congress for funds, to help devise a plan to address the emergency, and

Corps of Engineers, the Bureau of Reclamation, the National Park Service, and the Smithsonian Institution—signed an agreement on October 9, 1945, to work together in conducting a massive recovery program (Jennings 1985: 282) and created the IAASP. And it grew at a rapid rate, especially as it related to the archaeological record in the Missouri River basin. In fact, the Missouri River portion of the River Basin Surveys (RBS), which itself grew out of the IAASP, became the archaeological centerpiece of the entire program, partly because of the enormity of the projects but also because of the unique nature of the prehistoric remains. Some of the largest dams and reservoirs, especially Garrison, Oahe, and Fort Randall, were being built along a stretch of the Missouri that extended from western North Dakota into southern South Dakota; when filled they flooded literally hundreds of prehistoric villages, many of which either were not excavated or were barely examined because of time constraints and lack of funding (Figure 5.14).

Crew chiefs had to contend with complex logistical problems, such as how to mobilize personnel, how to lodge and feed workers—especially crews working in the middle of nowhere (Figure 5.15)—and get them paid, and how to get the archaeological materials back to the central laboratories that had been established around the United States. Various institutions involved in the River Basin Surveys handled matters differently, but one thing noticeable from the late 1940s forward was the increase in the number of permanent archaeological laboratories and field schools that sprang up as a result of an institution's affiliation with the RBS (Corbett 1961). Also, it is apparent that many institutions continued to concentrate on certain geographical areas long after having completed the technical reports under the auspices of the RBS. It is also fair to say that involvement with the RBS projects radically changed the way many archaeologists approached field methods. For one thing, even though crews in some areas—such as North Dakota and South Dakota—faced horrendous time constraints, many reservoir locations received a fairly high percentage of survey coverage, something not seen in the TVA basins, where oftentimes no survey was conducted. Thus RBS archaeologists had at least a modicum of information about the sites they were supposed to sample through excavation. Decisions about which sites to excavate might have been made on the basis of incomplete information, but it was much better than making them on the basis of no information.

---

generally to mobilize the archaeological community to assist in the effort. Later, Henry W. Hamilton, a farmer from Saline County, Missouri, was appointed to the committee—the only nonprofessional archaeologist ever appointed (although, technically, Webb might belong in that category, since he was not trained as an archaeologist but rather came to the profession from physics). Hamilton was an active voice in the Missouri Archaeological Society (he served a long tenure as president, beginning in 1958) and was a well-respected figure in Americanist archaeology.

Figure 5.13. Frank H. H. Roberts (1897–1966), assistant chief of the Bureau of American Ethnology and, from 1945 to 1964, director of the River Basin Surveys within the bureau (courtesy W. R. Wood).

Figure 5.14. Rising water from the Oahe Reservoir encroaches on site 39SL10-2, Sully County, South Dakota, ca. 1960 (courtesy W. R. Wood).

Figure 5.15. River Basin Survey field camp, Dewey County, South Dakota, ca. 1960 (courtesy W. R. Wood).

Excavation methods changed as well, as archaeologists realized they did not have the leisure of slowly excavating sites by hand. In some areas crews used heavy equipment to remove overburden so that houses, pits, and burials could be outlined and then hand-excavated. Readers interested in the early use of heavy equipment should read the exchange in Wedel's (1951) article on the subject. Because of its "efficiency, far lower cost (as opposed to hand labor) in both time and money" (Jennings 1985: 293; see also Jennings 1963), the practice of using equipment to remove overburden was officially adopted by the Smithsonian Institution in 1948 (Wedel 1953).

Technically, administration of the salvage program rested with the Bureau of American Ethnology, which was part of the Smithsonian, though, as Jennings (1985: 283) points out, the National Park Service was required to submit and defend the annual budget. It probably would have been more efficient to house the program within the park service, though at the time the service simply was not capable of mounting the kind of program required. Universities began helping out, in some cases diverting their archaeological plans to regions where

Figure 5.16. W. Raymond Wood and colleagues on the bank of Garrison Reservoir (Lake Sakakawea), McLean County, North Dakota, 1960: standing, Walter Birkby; seated (left to right), Jon Muller, Robert Neuman, Wood, Fred La Rocque (photograph by B. Weinreich, courtesy W. R. Wood).

the RBS was shorthanded, such as the Missouri Basin (Figure 5.16). To attract the assistance of even more institutions, the park service in 1949 hatched a new plan:

> This was the NPS cooperative agreement or contract program, that is still in use today. The scheme, as well as the document and its implementation, was simple. When a specific emergency situation arose, varying from a single site to an entire reservoir (and those existed in half the states), some local institution was invited to enter into a cooperative agreement with the NPS to perform the specified tasks. The institution committed the time of a principal investigator, space, facilities, equipment, and sometimes clerical help; the NPS committed funds. The document specified the contributions of each party, the components of the assignment, and due dates for both preliminary and scientifically acceptable reports. . . . The NPS agreements offered the institutional archaeologists a host of incentives. These included funds for field work and pursuit of what may have been, or could become, a personal research interest, and the individual archaeologist's incentives for research and publication were strengthened by the knowledge that

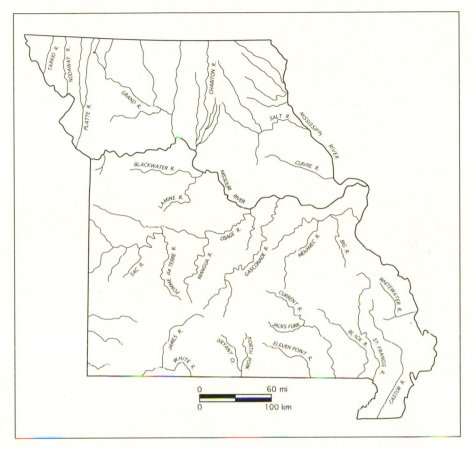

Figure 5.17. Map showing locations of major rivers in Missouri.

research through the contracts improved an individual's chances for tenure and promotion. Many people received an early record in research. (Jennings 1985: 286–87)

One of those people was Carl Chapman, who, as we have seen, was involved in salvage archaeology in Missouri as early as 1938. Between 1946 and 1961, Chapman and his associates and students turned out literally thousands of pages of reports on Missouri prehistory that resulted from archaeological activities conducted in various parts of the state, primarily in the major river valleys (Figure 5.17). Many of these projects were sponsored through cooperative arrangements between the University of Missouri and the National Park Service. I will focus here on three of the larger projects—those in the Pomme de Terre, Table Rock, and Joanna reservoirs (Figure 5.18)—as examples of contract archaeology in Missouri in the 1940s and 1950s.

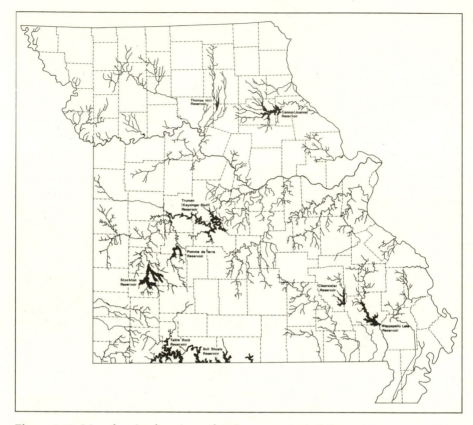

Figure 5.18. Map showing locations of major reservoirs in Missouri.

I can only speculate that in 1946, not many years after his return to the United States from a German prisoner-of-war camp and fresh from graduate work at the University of New Mexico, Chapman was faced with a dilemma: where to turn next? Everywhere he looked, portions of the archaeological record either were being destroyed or were threatened with destruction. Lake Wappapello, just north of Poplar Bluff, had inundated an unknown number of sites when the dam gates were closed in the 1930s. Even greater destruction had occurred when, in 1931, Union Electric finished construction of Bagnell Dam and the Lake of the Ozarks, which backed water up the Osage River for over 100 river miles. Chapman realized that only modest efforts at recording any archaeological information had been expended at Wappapello (Berry et al. 1940)[6] (Figure 5.18), and, worse yet, no survey or excavation had been conducted before the creation

6. James Lowe accompanied Chapman on a survey of the St. Francis River in Wayne County in 1938 and wrote a wonderful recounting fifty years later (Lowe 1988).

Figure 5.19. Table Rock Dam under construction, 1956.

of the Lake of the Ozarks by Union Electric. This couldn't be allowed to happen again. But where to start?

As early as 1946 Chapman realized that a planned dam and reservoir (Table Rock [Figure 5.19]) would destroy an untold number of sites along the White River and its major tributaries in Stone County and eastern Barry County, in southwestern Missouri (Chapman 1956: 16). At the same time, construction plans were proceeding for (a) the Pomme de Terre Reservoir in Polk and Hickory counties in west-central Missouri, which would flood sites along the Pomme de Terre River (a tributary of the Osage River) and one of its tributaries, Lindley Creek, and (b) Bull Shoals Reservoir, located downstream from Table Rock, primarily in Arkansas but extending northward into Missouri (Figure 5.18). None of the areas was well understood archaeologically, though preliminary reconnaissance of Pomme de Terre in 1946 by members of the Missouri Archaeological Society had yielded some information on prehistoric sites (Chapman 1961: iii). Apparently that work was never published.

Rather than concentrating on one proposed reservoir site immediately, Chapman continued to mobilize his amateur forces to salvage what information they could from southwestern and west-central Missouri. The university and the MAS conducted some survey of the Pomme de Terre area during 1948, but apparently their major push was in Bull Shoals Reservoir (Chapman 1954: 10). Lee Adams, an MAS trustee from Monett, Missouri, who was familiar with the White River valley, conducted a preliminary survey of the Table Rock region (L. Adams 1950), and in 1949 the Ozarks Chapter of the MAS organized a committee to coordinate surveys in the proposed Pomme de Terre Reservoir area (Chapman 1954: 10). Activities in the region accelerated rapidly throughout the 1950s. In 1950 Chapman held one of his annual summer field sessions in the Pomme de Terre Reservoir, re-locating previously recorded sites and updating the information on the site forms. This was followed by more MAS-sponsored survey and in 1952 by the signing of a cooperative agreement between the university and the park service for archaeological survey and the testing of six sites. The university transmitted the final report to the NPS late in 1953, and Chapman summarized the findings in *The Missouri Archaeologist* (Chapman 1954).

Table Rock Reservoir

Meanwhile, Chapman was also heavily involved in work along the White and James rivers in advance of completion of Table Rock Reservoir. In 1951 students in his summer field session conducted the first organized reconnaissance of the Table Rock locality (Chapman et al. 1951). Chapman (1956: 17) later noted, "Evidences indicating a long period of Indian occupation were recovered from 57 sites. At least three periods of occupation, 2 non-pottery and 1 pottery were suggested. It was pointed out that the area probably contained some of the best evidence of the Ozark Bluff Dwellers and data on the related problems of the development of agriculture in the region."

The survey of the area scheduled to become Table Rock Reservoir continued through 1955, with excavation beginning in 1952. Chapman and his students tested 17 sites during the initial phase of the project, and the findings set the stage for the next, larger phase. The project report was 683 pages long but was quickly boiled down for inclusion in *The Missouri Archaeologist* (Chapman 1956). Bray's report on excavations at the Rice site in the reservoir area (Bray 1956), an important site in terms of establishing a chronological framework for southwestern Missouri, was left fairly intact from the original report. Survey in the region continued through the mid-1950s, primarily through the efforts of Lee Adams, whose excellent report (L. Adams 1958) demonstrates the immeasurable contributions that amateurs made to furthering archaeological knowledge of the region.

In 1955 the University of Missouri signed another agreement with the park service to carry out full-scale excavation of sites in the Table Rock Reservoir location, the end result of which was a 1,179-page report (Chapman 1960c) that summarized the archaeological survey—during which almost 900 sites were recorded—and the excavation of numerous rock shelters and open sites. Among the open sites excavated were Loftin and Cantwell. Loftin was an important site if for no other reason than that it contained an 80-foot by 60-foot earthen mound; it was one of only two sites in the region that contained mounds (D. R. Henning 1959, 1960a, 1960b). Five small, presumably residential, structures were excavated, along with a larger structure that was beneath the mound (Wood 1958; Wood and Marshall 1960). The Cantwell site also produced house outlines (Chapman 1960b).

Pomme de Terre Reservoir

While the Table Rock project was in various stages, work began anew in the Pomme de Terre Reservoir area—a program formalized through a series of three one-year agreements between the University of Missouri and the park service. Chapman, being pulled in a dozen different directions, turned over management of the project to one of his research associates at the University of Missouri, W. Raymond Wood, who was responsible for compiling the final report and producing a synopsis for *The Missouri Archaeologist* (Wood 1961). The work included excavations at open-air sites and rock shelters, but one of Wood's primary objectives was the close examination of burial cairns that were ubiquitous in the Pomme de Terre Valley. His analysis followed in large part Rouse's (1955) prescribed method for correlating phases, which consisted of what Rouse termed descriptive, distributional, and historical techniques to distinguish between what might best be called analogous and homologous traits.

Wood described several archaeological complexes and foci (Figure 5.20) in an effort to sort out the apparent long occupational span evident in the region, the bulk of his work being aimed (a) at subdividing the Highland aspect, which since Chapman's (1948a) earlier formulation had remained an elusive entity, and (b) at identifying cultural units dating to the Late Archaic (labeled "preceramic" in Figure 5.20) period. Dating of the sites and components in the reservoir was done through cross-correlations based on projectile-point types, which was made all the more difficult because of the paucity of stratified deposits and, where such deposits occurred, their shallow nature.

Despite such problems, Wood's categorization has withstood the test of time. Nebo Hill, Sedalia, and Afton are still recognized as Late Archaic–period manifestations; the burial mounds that formed the basis for creating the Boone focus, the Fristoe burial complex, and the Lindley focus are still recognized as Late Woodland–period features; and Steed-Kisker is still regarded as a Mississippian-period manifestation. In essence, radiocarbon dating has allowed us to refine the chronological placement of various archaeological units, but their positions relative to each other have not changed. In retrospect, Wood's approach to taxonomic classification of archaeological units, which was much more formalized than Chapman's (1946, 1947, 1948a, 1948b) earlier attempt, represented a historical point of introduction of a formal methodological approach to Missouri

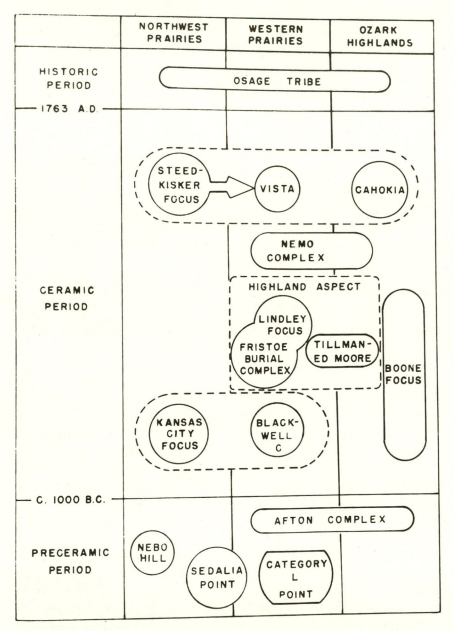

Figure 5.20. W. Raymond Wood's tentative correlation of taxonomic units in western and central Missouri. Wood's formal approach to the categorization of units was a major advance over previous schemes. His chronological placement of the units remains essentially unchanged today (from Wood 1961, courtesy Missouri Archaeological Society).

archaeology (ignoring for the moment the much broader lower Mississippi Valley survey of Phillips et al. [1951])—one that would carry over to one of the most significant projects ever undertaken in Missouri, which I will discuss in Chapter 6.

Joanna Reservoir

Research in the Joanna Reservoir, on the Salt River in northeastern Missouri, began in 1959, and the final report (Chapman and Henning 1960) was submitted to the NPS in June 1960. Construction plans for Joanna lagged behind those for Table Rock and Pomme de Terre, and Chapman and his colleagues had time to initiate a site survey instead of immediately embarking on a program of excavation. The only previous research in the Salt River basin that was even remotely systematic had been a survey conducted by members of the Marion-Ralls Archaeological Society in the early 1940s (Eichenberger 1944). The university survey, conducted by Dale Henning (Figure 5.21), located 118 sites, 23 of which were labeled as mounds (D. R. Henning 1961). Chapman (1961: iv) viewed the Salt River basin as having been a potentially important corridor for "the transmittal of culture from the Mississippi to the Missouri valley," probably based on the fact that a Middle Woodland "Hopewell" site near the point where the Salt exited the Mississippi River bluffs had been excavated by a joint university-MAS field party (Eichenberger 1944) (Figure 5.22). Until the 1980s this site, 23 MA3, was the only documented location in the Missouri portion of the Mississippi River valley north of St. Louis that had produced the stamped Havana-like pottery so common in western and west-central Illinois.

In summary, the joint work conducted by the University of Missouri and the MAS in the three reservoirs, Table Rock, Pomme de Terre, and Joanna, radically changed the way in which archaeologists began to view the prehistory of Missouri. The work in southwestern Missouri—until then almost an archaeological void—established "an 8,000–10,000 year sequence of human use of the region, a sequence hitherto unsuspected" (Jennings 1985: 290). No longer were archaeologists forced to rely on M. R. Harrington's (e.g., 1924a, 1924b) accounts of "bluff-dweller" occupations; instead, the picture began to emerge of various groups of people moving throughout the area and occupying open sites as well as rock shelters. At least along the Pomme de Terre River, some groups at different times in the past buried their dead in mounds, though their methods of disposing of the bodies differed significantly through time (Wood 1961). It also became apparent that the Ozarks were not the marginal area that archaeologists (e.g., Chapman 1948a) had thought they were. For example, Wood (1961, 1968) found shell-tempered pottery at Vista Shelter that was identical to pottery recovered by Wedel (1943) from Steed-Kisker near Kansas City (see Figure 5.20). Many

Figure 5.21. Dale R. Henning at the Hoecake site, Mississippi County, Missouri, 1966 (photograph by G. Gardner, courtesy D. R. Henning).

Figure 5.22. Members of the Marion-Ralls Chapter of the Missouri Archaeological Society excavating site 23MA3, Marion County, Missouri, 1948.

Figure 5.23. Excavations at Standlee Shelter, Barry County, Missouri, 1955.

of the projectile points found in Table Rock and Pomme de Terre reservoirs were similar in form to points from the Mississippi River valley, especially the arrow points that today would be placed in the Nodena and Madison types and which date late in the Mississippian period. Other forms were similar to Middle Woodland points from Illinois that were then termed "Hopewell" points.

In looking back over the early reservoir work in Missouri and attempting to judge whether it was "good" archaeology, the answer arrived at is a resounding "yes." The goals, similar to those of reservoir projects undertaken in other states, were to find sites as quickly as possible, select some for excavation, and then excavate them. The objectives that guided the selection were mainly related to time: when was a particular site occupied, and did it exhibit significant time depth? Excavations at Rice (Bray 1956; Marshall and Chapman 1960a) (Figure 5.12), Lander Shelter (Bray 1957), Lander Shelter 2 (Marshall 1963a), Jakie Shelter (Chapman 1960a; Marshall and Chapman 1960b), and Standlee Shelter I (Bray 1960) (Figure 5.23) in the Table Rock Reservoir location were prime examples of sites that were selected because of their potential for establishing regional chronological controls. In short, the projects did what they were intended to do.

The projects also were completed on time, and, even more importantly, the *reports* were completed on time. This was not the case with the River Basin Survey projects in general (see Jennings 1985; Lehmer 1965 [cited in Jennings 1985]; and Wedel 1967 on problems relative to the RBS projects). In addition, the work was inexpensive, even ignoring inflation. For example, initial survey of the Joanna Reservoir was accomplished for $2,800, half of which was supplied by the University of Missouri (Chapman 1961: v). I estimate that all the work in Table Rock Reservoir was accomplished for under $50,000. Even the harshest critic of salvage archaeology might be stunned to know that the cost of *all* projects conducted under the auspices of the RBS between 1946 and 1967— including the massive work in the Missouri River basin—was under $10 million (Jennings 1985)—an average annual cost of less than $500,000. It would be anyone's guess how many archaeological projects with that price tag currently are let in this country each *month*. Chapman certainly thought the projects were successful, judging from his letter to the park service accompanying the Pomme de Terre Reservoir report (reproduced in Chapman 1961):

> All those, present and future, interested in the heritage of the past should be grateful for the preservation of this irreplaceable knowledge and these antiquities never before revealed. Another chapter in the cultural history of Missouri and another segment of the fascinating past of the United States have been added to the store of human knowledge. We would prefer it to be a fuller chapter, a broader picture, but time was too short. Your excellent cooperation and aid made possible the fullest study within the limits of time available.

Whether or not Chapman realized it at the time, the role that salvage archaeology had played in the archaeology of Missouri was only a portent of things to come, as more and more of the interagency funds were poured into Missouri. Whatever one wishes to call it—contract, salvage, rescue, or emergency archaeology—that particular brand of archaeology had made a name for itself, not only in Missouri but across the United States. Some of the most well known archaeologists were involved heavily in it, and the funding for it was being used to provide a modest income for thousands of students. It would not be too many years before the name "contract archaeology" would become a derogatory term, as the discipline attempted to shift its focus from the perceived "old archaeology," with its attendant focus on things such as chronology and culture history, to a so-called "new archaeology" that focused on the processes of culture and culture change.

6

Salvage Archaeology and the Emergence of Environmental Studies

1961–1976

Throughout the 1960s archaeological work continued at the sites of Missouri's proposed reservoirs under the direction of staff from the University of Missouri.[1] Much of the work was carried out in a fashion more or less similar to previous investigations, although by 1966 excavation projects in the reservoirs far outnumbered survey projects. One gets the feeling from reading various reports written in the late 1960s that investigators felt that most of the sites in the large reservoirs had already been discovered during earlier surveys and that their time could be spent most profitably in excavating a sample of those sites. This was not a phenomenon that was unique to Missouri. Few archaeologists prior to 1960 ever questioned whether the sites they were excavating adequately reflected the range of variation present in a region—a fact that could only be established through some kind of ordered sampling. And if archaeologists didn't worry too much about the representativeness of the sites they were excavating, they certainly didn't worry about how representative the artifacts were that they were analyzing. But they did, on occasion, worry about other things, especially if those "other things" were controversial.

Americanist archaeology had always had its controversies, in part because the field seems to attract people who are a little contentious to start with, people who, when their pet propositions come under fire, can come out swinging. One such controversy had occurred in 1948 with the publication of Walter W. Taylor's *A Study of Archeology* in the American Anthropological Association Memoir series. The book was an outgrowth of Taylor's Harvard dissertation, and in

---

1. I should point out, for the sake of accuracy, that in the mid-1960s the University of Missouri became a four-campus system (Columbia, Rolla, St. Louis, and Kansas City). For purposes here, however, I ignore the distinction and refer to the Columbia campus as the university.

it he lambasted a sizable percentage of practicing Americanist archaeologists. Researchers panning the work of their contemporaries was nothing new, but rarely had a fresh Ph.D. attempted to make a name for himself by attacking some of the most prominent people in the field. Taylor had some legitimate points to make, but his form of presentation unfortunately overshadowed those points, and few people took him seriously. At one level, he argued for the formalization of fieldwork and the completion of archaeological reports, and he excoriated archaeologists such as Alfred Kidder for flitting from project to project while producing nothing in the way of synthetic treatments of the excavations. But Taylor's most important point was that archaeologists were simply paying lip service to cultural context as opposed to integrating archaeological objects within that context.

Archaeology, to Taylor, was supposed to be the study of past cultures, but he was of the opinion that archaeologists had tended to concentrate instead on constructing chronological frameworks and making ill-advised comparisons between site assemblages. Where were the studies of cultural processes and human behavior, especially studies of function? Taylor's emphasis on function bore considerable resemblance to points made previously by other archaeologists, even as early as 1913 (e.g., Bennett 1943; Childe 1946; Steward and Setzler 1938; R. B. Dixon 1913), but he hammered the points home in a way that others had not. The study of function and functional relations between and among archaeological phenomena is not an easy task once one moves beyond rhetorical exercises. And, as Trigger (1989: 279) points out, Taylor himself was unable to incorporate "a functional view of prehistoric cultures to promote a new understanding of cultural change . . . or introduce any major innovations into archaeological interpretation." Taylor also held tightly to the belief "that much change occurs as a result of fortuitous contacts between human groups" (Trigger 1989: 278), which certainly was not a novel view.

Despite his shortcomings, Taylor, in my opinion, made several important points. He argued vigorously that the only way archaeologists were going to make sense out of the archaeological record in terms of cultural reconstruction was to completely overhaul the manner in which sites were excavated and reported. He argued that archaeologists should pay more attention to things such as food remains and less attention to fancy objects. They should also quantify their data, he asserted, as opposed to relying on laundry lists of cultural traits that were either present or absent (i.e., the midwestern taxonomic method). And above all, archaeologists should develop some means of verifying their conclusions (or of proving them false). The reaction to Taylor's suggestions (e.g., Watson 1983; Woodbury 1954) was largely negative, again because of the acerbic tone of his presentation and his ponderous style of writing. Whether archaeologists thought he was right or wrong was immaterial; no one liked to see their friends and acquaintances skewered by a relative novice, and for the most part the profession ignored him. This is not to say that culture and behavior as archaeological topics were completely ignored in the years following the publication of Taylor's book, but there was not the wholesale change in focus for which Taylor pleaded. The revolution in archaeological thinking was still several years away.

Radical change in a discipline's direction does not take place in a vacuum, nor does it happen because someone mandates it. Thus in many respects the type of change that Taylor argued for probably could not have occurred in the 1940s, even if he had been more temperate in his presentation, for the simple reason that Americanist archaeology was not preconditioned for the change. Although some investigators, for example, Albert C. Spaulding, were interested in such things as the meaning of archaeological types and whether they could be used to monitor changes in certain kinds of behavior, the majority of attention in archaeology was firmly fixed on matters of chronology and cultural taxonomy. This fixation must have upset at least some cultural anthropologists of the day (including Taylor's mentors at Harvard), who viewed the archaeological record as a gold mine from which to extract behavior-related tidbits about past cultures. By the mid-1950s, things began to change.

In the United States—unlike in Canada and Great Britain—archaeologists are trained in departments of anthropology and, although they take more course work in archaeology, they also receive fairly rigorous training in physical anthropology, linguistics, and especially cultural anthropology. Cultural anthropologists on staff in American departments of anthropology have always far outnumbered archaeologists, and they and other nonarchaeologists have dictated the curriculum that students take during their graduate careers. This arrangement usually is met with little resistance by archaeologists for a variety of reasons, not the least of which is the fact that most archaeologists consider themselves anthropologists first. This acceptance has naturally led archaeologists to assume the theoretical and methodological trappings of their cultural-anthropology colleagues and, invariably, to the inclusion of the concept of *culture* into their repertoire of topics worthy of consideration.

We can begin to see the effects of this inclusion in the late 1930s (e.g., Steward and Setzler 1938), but they became much more obvious sometime in the mid-1950s, when numerous articles and monographs appeared that borrowed concepts and principles from anthropology and applied them to archaeological situations. Central to all these applications was the notion of culture change and continuity, with decided emphasis on mechanisms of change such as diffusion, acculturation, and migration—a renaissance of the same mechanisms that had figured prominently in the ethnology and archaeology carried out by the Bureau of American Ethnology. Importantly, these mechanisms were still seen as *explanations* of why culture change had or had not occurred. Change in the archaeological record meant that cultures themselves had changed; no change meant that cultures had remained stable. Willey and Phillips (1958: 5) labeled this type of reasoning "processual interpretation," which is an appropriate term since archaeologists really weren't explaining anything.

In the face of a lack of any kind of theory in archaeology that could be drawn upon to *explain* the formal, spatial, and temporal variation evident in the archaeological record, archaeologists turned to their cultural-anthropology colleagues for help. Unfortunately, the help that was offered wasn't much good for the study of living human groups, and it certainly wasn't appropriate for explaining the archaeological record. This was not immediately obvious to either anthropologists or archaeologists in the late 1950s, and certainly by 1960 there was a growing belief in archaeology that what archaeologists should be studying was the same thing their departmental colleagues were studying—culture—though it was far from clear exactly how to make this change.[2]

A New Approach to the Archaeological Study of Culture

An integrative approach to the study of the past appeared suddenly on the horizon. The author of this approach, Lewis R. Binford (Figure 6.1), was a hybrid of two of his professors at the University of Michigan, evolutionary anthropologist Leslie White and archaeologist James B. Griffin (with a little of Albert Spaulding thrown in). Between 1962 and 1965 Binford published three articles that had profound effects not only on how archaeology came to be practiced but also on how the discipline viewed itself. In short, Binford produced the revolution in archaeological thinking that Taylor had attempted in 1948. Many people have attempted to answer the question of why Binford was successful whereas Taylor was not, setting aside the question of Taylor's arrogant presentation. One common response is that by the 1960s the nation's university campuses were beginning to call for change, especially in terms of making the curriculum "relevant" to everyday life. At the same time, war was being declared on segregation and poverty, and, of course, war would soon be unofficially declared in Southeast Asia. The nation itself was in for radical changes in the 1960s, and in some instances people didn't much care where it came from.

I wouldn't say that this argument is completely without merit, but I would look more toward the five to ten years in archaeology prior to Binford's first article for the answer. If anything, archaeologists had become preadapted for a shift toward an integrative study of the past through their exposure in graduate school to the writings of anthropologists such as White and especially Julian Steward, who argued for the consideration of physical-environmental variables in evolutionary schemes (see also Steward and Setzler 1938). A generation of young archaeologists

2. For an overview of the culture-history vs. cultural-process debate, see Flannery 1967.

Figure 6.1. Lewis R. Binford at Tierra del Fuego, Argentina, 1994. Binford, a leading figure in the so-called new archaeology movement of the 1960s and 1970s, was influenced significantly by Leslie White, one of his professors at the University of Michigan and the preeminent proponent of cultural evolution in the twentieth century. Binford extended White's notions of culture to the archaeological record, demanding that archaeologists use that record to test various propositions about past cultural processes. If archaeologists of the 1970s and 1980s had been polled to find out whom they considered the leading figure in Americanist archaeology, and if those archaeologists had put personalities aside and answered honestly, Binford undoubtedly would have topped the list (photograph by L. A. Borrero, courtesy L. R. Binford).

had already cut their teeth on the brands of evolutionary anthropology espoused by White and Steward,[3] and in them they saw the salvation of their discipline. It was toward this end that Binford introduced his first article, "Archaeology as Anthropology" (Binford 1962a).

Binford was not subtle in his attack on traditional archaeology, as the first paragraph of his abstract illustrates:

> It is argued that archaeology has made few contributions to the general field of anthropology with regard to explaining cultural similarities and differences. One major factor contributing to this lack is asserted to be the tendency to treat artifacts as equal and comparable traits which can be explained within a single model of culture change and modification. It is suggested that "material culture" can and does represent the structure of the total cultural system, and that explanations of differences and similarities between certain classes of material culture are inappropriate and inadequate as explanations for such observations within other classes of items. Similarly, change in the total cultural system must be viewed in an adaptive context both social and environmental, not whimsically viewed as the result of "influences," "stimuli," or even "migrations" between and among geographically defined units. (Binford 1962a: 217)

Read the last sentence again and think back to some of the things archaeologists such as Chapman were saying. Binford was voicing his dislike of archaeological explanations tied to ill-defined external mechanisms that could be invoked when the evidence for any other type of explanation was lacking. It was White's kind of anthropology that Binford later stressed should be practiced by archaeologists: "Archaeologists should be among the best qualified to study and directly test hypotheses concerning the process of evolutionary change, particularly processes of change that are relatively slow, or hypotheses that postulate temporal-processual priorities as regards total systems. The lack of theoretical concern and rather naïve attempts at explanation which archaeologists currently advance must be modified" (Binford 1962a: 224). At its simplest level, Binford's argument was that archaeologists had ignored the roles played by artifacts in cultural systems; if one could not sort out the differences between form and function relative to the artifacts, then the discipline had little hope of understanding the social processes of which the artifacts were a part. In short, archaeologists had no chance of *explaining* culture process. I argue in Chapter 9 that archaeologists *are* in an excellent position "to study and directly test hypotheses concerning the process of evolutionary change," but it is not through adopting Binford's approach that they are able to do it. In actuality what Binford was advocating

---

3. See articles in *Evolution and Culture* (1960), edited by Marshall Sahlins and Elman Service, for an introduction to the evolutionary views of White and Steward.

was a more rigorous approach to interpreting the past, not explaining it. But we're getting way ahead of the story.

Binford's second article, "A Consideration of Archaeological Research Design" (Binford 1964), had an even more pointed message for archaeologists: "It is argued that the methodology most appropriate for the task of isolating and studying processes of cultural change and evolution is one that is regional in scope and executed with the aid of research designs based on the principle of probability sampling" (Binford 1964: 425). In advocating a regional approach, Binford noted:

> Under current programs of salvage archaeology and increased foundation support for archaeological research, we are being given the opportunity to study major regions intensively. In spite of the opportunities currently available, it is my impression that very little thought has been given to research design. Methods and approaches utilized in such investigations seem to be little more than expanded or greatly enlarged field sessions of the type that has traditionally characterized American archaeological data collection. To be sure, the work may be neater, more attention may be given to stratigraphy, more classes of phenomena may be observed and collected than in the field work of years past; yet the general methods of data collection and observation remain unchanged. (Binford 1964: 426)

This was a devastating statement if true, since archaeologists assumed that their data-generating methods were changing in order to keep up with new advancements in theory. Was Binford saying that archaeological *theory* itself had not changed? Was he implying, as Taylor (1948) had two decades before, that archaeologists were in actuality only paying lip service to the explanation of culture process?

It was in his third article, "Archaeological Systematics and the Study of Culture Process" (Binford 1965), that Binford moved in for the kill: "It is argued that the normative theory of culture, widely held among archaeologists, is inadequate for the generation of fruitful explanatory hypotheses of cultural process. One obvious shortcoming of this theoretical position has been the development of archaeological systematics that have obviated any possibility of measuring multivariate phenomena and permit only the measurement of unspecified 'cultural differences and similarities,' as if these were univariate phenomena" (p. 203). By "normative theory" Binford meant the view held by many archaeologists and anthropologists that culture is an abstraction from behavior and, although it can be divided practically into units for ease of analysis (e.g., Ford 1954), culture is actually a cohesive whole. In addition, standard belief held that culture is transmitted as a whole across time and space. Changes in trait frequency through time were seen as results of diffusion, drift (Ford 1954), or migration, all viewed as being quite natural and regular occurrences (Caldwell 1958: 1):

Cultural differences and similarities are expressed by the normative school in terms of "cultural relationships" which, if treated rigorously, resolve into one general interpretative model. This model is based on the assumption of a "culture center" [the culture-area concept discussed in Chapter 4] where, for unspecified reasons, rates of innovation exceed those in surrounding areas. The new culture spreads out from the center and blends with surrounding cultures until it is dissipated at the fringes, leaving marginal cultures. Cultural relationships are viewed as the degree of mutual or unilateral "influence" exerted between culture centers or subcenters. (Binford 1965: 204)

Binford was especially critical of what he termed the "aquatic view" of culture:

Interpretive literature abounds with phrases such as "cultural stream"[4] and in references to the "flowing" of new cultural elements into a region. Culture is viewed as a vast flowing stream with minor variations in ideational norms concerning appropriate ways of making pots, getting married, treating one's mother-in-law, building houses, temples (or not building them, as the case may be), and even dying. These ideational variations are periodically "crystallized" at different points in time and space, resulting in distinctive and sometimes striking cultural climaxes which allow us to break up the continuum of culture into cultural phases. (Binford 1965: 197–98)

The cultural phases to which Binford referred were archaeological complexes based on shared traits—outgrowths of the midwestern taxonomic method (McKern 1939) via the Willey and Phillips (1958) reformulation. About the use of these "normative" constructs that served to cement the idea that culture is a cohesive whole, Binford made a point that, although archaeologists paid lip service to it, had never been tackled head on: "This emphasis on shared traits in our system of classification results in masking differences and in lumping together phenomena which would be discrete under another taxonomic method. . . . *We should partition our observational fields so that we may emphasize the nature of variability in artifact populations and facilitate the isolation of causally relevant factors*" (Binford 1965: 205; emphasis added).

Why should this statement have been seen as novel? Generations of archaeologists had argued that their types, foci, and phases were not end-alls in themselves but rather the seemingly best ways to partition the data at the time. As new data came in, the units could be corrected to incorporate the data. Binford, however, was not advocating new types or phases but rather a different way of examining the data for variation. And that new way was derived directly from

4. Witness Chapman's (1980: 262) quote: "Cultural change stemmed from the broad streams of cultural evolution taking place in the eastern half of the North American continent, Mesoamerica, and northern South America."

one's theoretical perspective on change, which for Binford involved the use of a multivariate approach—one that recognized that each piece of information would have independent variables—to understanding how artifacts functioned in the societies of which they were a part (see also Binford 1962a).

Binford (1965), based on his firsthand knowledge of midwestern archaeology (e.g., Binford 1962b; Binford et al. 1970), used as an example perceived similarities between cooking pots from west-central Illinois (Havana tradition) and those from southern Ohio (Scioto tradition). Traditional archaeological accounts lumped the traditions into "Hopewell," with each unit sharing traits of the Hopewell "culture." Binford asked on what grounds this association was being made. Certainly not on vessel shape and size, since those were different. Rather, the association was being based on design similarity. Pots from both areas contain zoned, incised and/or stamped designs, which was enough for archaeologists to lump them together under the term *Hopewell*. Ignored in this categorization was the fact that differences in vessel shape and size might be a function of the number of people being fed, which might be tied to differences in residential-group size. The ramifications of this perspective could have led to a complete reappraisal of the Hopewell problem, not only in Illinois and Ohio but also in Missouri, where pottery similar to that in the two proposed "Hopewell centers" (Havana and Scioto) had been found in four areas: eastern Missouri (Blake 1942; Eichenberger 1944), central Missouri (McKinny 1954), the Kansas City area (Roedl and Howard 1957; Wedel 1943, 1959), and sporadically across the Ozarks. However, no such rethinking occurred.

With two major exceptions (I discuss one shortly and the other toward the end of the chapter), there is no evidence that what Binford and eventually others were clamoring for had much if any effect on Missouri archaeology during the 1960s. This lack of effect, evident in the literature by an absence of references to Binford or the dozens he influenced, is surprising given the literally hundreds of articles that were written during the 1960s and early 1970s on how to restructure archaeological inquiry so as to understand past cultural processes. Certainly much of what was written in those halcyon days was unintelligible except to those who had written it, and much of it was little more than polemical statements and posturing, but embedded in the discussion were many excellent discussions of method and technique. Lost among the various pseudophilosophical arguments about the nature of scientific inquiry (see Chapter 9) was the significant fact that very little archaeological inquiry had ever been formulated according to rigorous standards that allowed working propositions to be proved false (see Chapter 8). Rather, archaeologists had an idea of the way things worked in the past and they set out to demonstrate that that is how things actually *had* worked.

Scientific standards demand that one try and disprove assumptions, not "prove" them. Archaeologists in the 1960s—the so-called new archaeologists—began steeping themselves in the philosophy-of-science literature and from it learned that any serious scientific inquiry (at least this is what the philosophers said) went through sequential steps: (1) formulate a proposition, (2) decide what the testable implications of that proposition are, and then (3) determine not the validity of the implications but rather whether the data generated from analysis of the archaeological record supports the original proposition. I examine the love affair that archaeologists of the 1960s and 1970s had with the philosophy of science in Chapter 9. Here I want to call particular attention to the term *implications* because that term was not always understood by archaeologists, even by those who espoused a hypothesis-testing approach to archaeological inquiry. In fact, it is impossible to test a hypothesis (a better term for most archaeological "hypotheses" is *propositions*). Few archaeologists understood that what one actually tests are the on-the-ground implications of a proposition—tests that should either negate the validity of the proposition or provide support for it.

By way of example, suppose we want to determine whether several of the rock shelters found in southwestern Missouri were occupied year-round by a group of Late Woodland people—the projectile points found there indicate it was occupied between ca. A.D. 400 and 900—or whether they were occupied only intermittently, perhaps on a seasonal basis. How would we structure our research to determine this? For starters, we might propose that if the shelter had been occupied year-round we would find a range of materials that would not be found if the shelter had been occupied seasonally. If the shelter had been used by hunting parties as a temporary stop-over, we might find only hunting gear. If it had been used as a game-processing station, then we would expect to find tools associated with that activity (unless the tools had been removed by any number of natural or cultural processes). It might have been used as a temporary shelter for a hunting party that also returned there to process game. Each activity should leave an archaeological signature. It would be up to the archaeologist to decide what the different signatures would be—these are the testable implications drawn from each proposition—and to structure analysis accordingly.

If our first proposition is that the rock shelter served as a permanent base camp, but upon excavation we find no pottery, milling stones, storage pits, or any of the other things that might indicate some degree of permanent residence, then maybe we should conclude that the shelter served another purpose. We also could conclude that our implications were erroneous, that is, that permanent occupants of Ozark rock shelters (a) either didn't know how to make pottery or at least didn't make it, (b) didn't eat plant foods and thus didn't use milling stones, and (c) didn't store food. Any of these alternatives is possible, and we need to examine the archaeological record carefully to determine if other supposedly contemporary sites in the region contain those items. It makes little sense to base an argument in part on the presence/absence of ceramic vessels if no groups in the area used pottery.

Perhaps the key question that archaeologists began asking themselves in the early and mid-1960s was how to construct the bridge between proposition and data. Where could one go to get information on what the artifact content of a hunting camp would be versus that of a permanent base camp? Did we simply guess what might be present, based on an intuitive feel for what hunters and gatherers would have needed in the past? Could we examine modern hunting-and-gathering societies and get clues to the past, or had things changed so much that there were no modern analogs? One of the great debates that grew out of the new archaeology, with Binford at the fore, was over the appropriateness of what came to be known as *ethnoarchaeological* research—using archaeological remains of modern peoples as analogs of the past. The debate was not simply about the appropriateness of it as a method of understanding the past but also how best to use ethnoarchaeological data and how to avoid the pitfalls of spurious analogy. Some argued (e.g., Ascher 1961) that the only useful analogs were those that were close in time and space to the archaeological case—an offshoot of the direct historical approach; others argued that only groups with technologies similar to the archaeological case could be used.

These debates would continue well into the 1980s; the point here is that apparently few, if any, archaeologists working in Missouri paid much attention to the debates. Much of the archaeology undertaken in Missouri continued to be primarily an inductive exercise—more of an exploratory endeavor than a problem-oriented one. This does not mean that archaeology slowed appreciably during the 1960s. In fact, the frenetic pace of the late fifties, where field crews were employed across the state in advance of reservoir construction, quickened during the sixties, as more and more reservoirs came under construction.

The Height of Reservoir Surveys

Site survey, which forms the backbone of any kind of regional analysis, has been around in a variety of forms since the beginning of archaeological research. Basically, it entails walking across a landscape, searching for evidence of past human use of the landscape, and documenting locations where such evidence exists in three-dimensional space through the use of some type of coordinate system. As we saw in Chapter 4, the Archaeological Survey of Missouri (ASM) was the brainchild of Jesse Wrench and Brewton Berry and was formed as a clearinghouse for information on site locations in the state. Wrench and Berry initially hired individuals to conduct surveys in various areas of Missouri, but they soon realized that a wider network of people, acting in regulated fashion, could significantly increase the number of sites reported to the central survey office. Thus the Missouri Archaeological Society (MAS) was founded, in large part as a way of increasing survey coverage through the efforts of interested artifact collectors. Collectors were encouraged not only to report their sites but also to photograph their collections and prepare short reports on the nature of the collections—a plan that had been around since the 1800s, when the Smithsonian Institution had issued circulars requesting the same.

Perusal of issues of *The Missouri Archaeologist* from the 1950s and 1960s leads one to conclude that Wrench and Berry's brainchild was in many ways successful. Thousands of site forms had been turned in by 1960, most of them by nonprofessionals. Through the efforts of Carl Chapman, who worked constantly to upgrade the skills of MAS members, numerous workshops on how to conduct site surveys and fill out site-survey forms were held annually. Chapman's efforts gradually had some effect on the quality of the information, though most forms still were lacking in detail. For example, most forms did not contain information on what kinds of artifacts were found at a site or how dense the artifact scatters were, making it impossible to even guess at the age or function of a site.

As critical as these problems are for those who later want to use the information to interpret the prehistory of a locality, there are ways around them. For example, sites that are not well reported can be reexamined to supply missing information. Although such efforts are labor-intensive, it is not an impossible task—provided the original recorder listed enough locational information that the site can be found again. Correspondence in the ASM files indicates that Chapman and his staff spent considerable time attempting to verify and augment the information that came in from surveyors. Those problems, however, pale in comparison to another problem—one that had no effect on the business of archaeology in the 1960s but that would dramatically affect archaeology a decade later. That problem, which I introduce here and return to in Chapter 8, is one that completely undermines any attempt to discuss the relationship between humans and their landscape. The issue, which sounds strange at first, is not where sites *are* located but rather where they are *not* located.

How can one understand changes in prehistoric occupation of a region if all that exists is a list of site locations? Without knowing where sites are *not* located, based on surveys that have turned up no evidence of human use, how can we begin to examine *why* they are located where they are? None of the surveys undertaken in Missouri prior to the 1970s were aimed at understanding the distribution of sites across space except in the most cursory of fashions. For the most part surveys were directed toward high-probability areas, that is, areas that archaeologists decided beforehand should contain archaeological sites. Areas that were assumed to be low-probability locales were either written off or given low priority during surveys. This statement applies to surveys both within and outside construction areas such as reservoirs; it also applies as much to surveys conducted by professionals as to those conducted by nonprofessionals. This lack of attention to the distribution of sites across the landscape is surprising, given the interest in settlement archaeology—literally, how and why settlements are distributed the way they are across the landscape—that arose during the 1950s and grew exponentially during the 1960s (see Chapter 7).

Specific techniques used in site survey never varied. Surveys for the most part were carried out on foot, usually by two or more persons in a survey party, though nonprofessionals usually worked alone. Surveyors would walk over terrain until pottery, projectile points, flakes, or some other evidence of human use of the locality was noted. At that point the surveyors might attempt to determine how large a site was, based on the amount of area containing the scatter of artifacts, but usually a dot on a map would be all that was recorded. Grab samples of artifacts might be made, and off the survey party would go to another site. Even in bounded sampling universes, such as reservoir areas, it was rare for survey parties to keep track of *where* they had searched for sites and found none. All that was turned in at the end of a project was a map—either a topographic map or a county-road map—showing site locations.

One notion that has changed considerably over the years is the notion of *site*, not that this was even considered an issue in the 1960s. No one asked questions such as: What constitutes an archaeological site? Ten artifacts? Five? An isolated mound? Is a better definition so many artifacts per unit of area, such as 5 flakes per 100 square meters? The question of what constitutes a site became important in the 1980s (but see D. H. Thomas 1975 for an earlier statement), as a few archaeologists began to realize that the normative concept of *site* was too restrictive. This evolution in thinking was intricately tied to a realization that survey methods and the mind-set of what constituted a site were causing a substantial portion of the archaeological record to go unreported. At least through the 1960s the working definition of *site* used by archaeologists in Missouri was any place that contained a substantial (never specified) number of artifacts. This was an acceptable definition as long as the objective of archaeological survey was to find sites—preferably large, deep sites—for excavation. Archaeologists looked for sites that produced significant quantities of material on the surface, the rationale being that the subsurface portions of the sites should likewise contain large numbers of artifacts. Why would that be of such importance? Because large sites, especially deep, well-stratified sites, were the best ones to use in cultural-chronological orderings and culture histories, especially in the pre-radiocarbon era. In plain language, deep sites meant lots of artifacts, from which you derived lots of artifact types. Thus you could compile long trait lists, which could then be used to construct phases.

Until the late 1970s, there was no appreciation among Missouri archaeologists of the fact that surface materials were a legitimate source of data in their own right and not simply indicators of what lay below the surface. Numerous articles written prior to that time certainly discussed surface artifacts from Missouri sites, but they were by and large chronological in orientation. None of them asked whether surface materials could be used as a proxy for excavated remains.

Binford and others (e.g., Ford in Phillips et al. 1951) had raised these issues, which by 1969 were being vigorously debated in the leading archaeological journals, but the debates, for the most part, appear to have bypassed Missouri.

One of the longest-running projects undertaken in Missouri began in the early 1960s in the area of the proposed Kaysinger Bluff reservoir in Benton, Hickory, St. Clair, and Henry counties. By the time the reservoir (subsequently renamed the Harry S. Truman Reservoir)[5] began to fill in the late 1970s, flooding a portion of the Osage River and the lower reaches of the Pomme de Terre and South Grand rivers, the area had received more intensive examination than any other single area in Missouri. Several institutions and government agencies contributed significant amounts of funding and manpower to the project, and as a result we have a prehistoric record that is incredibly rich and detailed, especially for the Archaic period. We also have an extensive record of floral and faunal suites for different periods over the last 4,000–5,000 years. Work undertaken in the reservoir in the late 1960s and early 1970s was of such importance to Missouri archaeology that it deserves extended treatment. Because I don't want to divide the discussion into the earlier and later work, I delay discussion of the work in the Kaysinger Bluff Reservoir until later in the chapter.

Stockton Reservoir

Stockton Reservoir, located in Cedar, Dade, and Polk counties (Figure 5.18), impounds water of the north-flowing Sac River and its major tributary, the Little Sac River. The earliest coordinated archaeological work in the basin began in 1961 under a cooperative agreement between the University of Missouri and the National Park Service. During the first two years, the future reservoir area was surveyed and six sites were tested (Chapman et al. 1962). A second cooperative agreement, covering the years 1962–1964, was subsequently signed, leading to a series of extensive excavations at rock shelters, burial cairns, and open sites (Chapman et al. 1963; McMillan 1966a; Wood 1965a). Two open sites, Dryocopus (Calabrese et al. 1969) and Flycatcher (Kaplan et al. 1967; Pangborn et al. 1971), produced house patterns, which at the time were rare in the western Ozarks (see discussion of Loftin and Cantwell in Chapter 5).

Excavations of rock shelters in Stockton for the most part were not as extensive as those in the Table Rock Reservoir shelters, though McMillan (1966a) recovered a full sequence of materials ranging from the Middle Archaic period at least through the Late Woodland period. He also documented a wide range of pottery-temper types, including shell, bone, clay, limestone, sand, and grit.

---

5. Harry Truman's middle name was "S" and carried no period. However, a period was inadvertently inserted when Congress passed legislation authorizing the reservoir that carries his name.

Stratigraphic mixing severely limited clear vertical separation of temper types, though McMillan (1966a: 183) stated that at several sites limestone- and shell-tempered sherds tended to occur slightly above sherds that were tempered with other materials. He also documented the presence of a clay-tempered sherd with decoration (e.g., cross-hatching on the rim) that he saw as "reminiscent of Hopewellian wares" (McMillan 1966a: 182).

The presence of "Hopewellian" ceramics in the Ozarks had long been noted by archaeologists (e.g., Chapman 1947), though with few exceptions only a few sherds were known from the sites. In 1965 these included Woody Shelter (Sudderth and Chapman 1965), Rodgers Shelter (McMillan 1965a), and Brounlee Shelter (Chapman and Pangborn 1965) in the proposed Kaysinger Bluff Reservoir area (discussed below), Blackwell Cave (Wood 1961) in the Pomme de Terre Reservoir, and scattered sites in the southwestern corner of the state (L. Adams 1958; Marshall 1963c). Two exceptions to the low occurrence were Tater Hole Shelter and Griffin Shelter, both in Stockton Reservoir. During initial testing of the sites in the early 1950s, Marshall (1954) recorded the presence of numerous "Hopewellian" sherds. McMillan (1966a: 188) noted that the material analyzed by Marshall (1954) was similar to the type Ozark zoned stamped, named by Baerreis (1953) for material from the Cooper site in northeastern Oklahoma.

The centerpiece of archaeological work in the Stockton Reservoir area was Wood's (1965a) analysis of burial structures similar to those in the Pomme de Terre Reservoir area (Wood 1961). The structures were small earth-and-rock mounds averaging 20 feet across and 1.5 feet high that were erected as protective coverings for human burials. Burial types included primary inhumations, in which the body was placed in the ground soon after death; bundle burials, in which the flesh was removed from the bones and the bones gathered together and buried; cremations; and broadcast burials, wherein the defleshed bones were pulverized and then cast over an area. By the mid-1960s, 48 burial structures had been excavated in west-central Missouri (Bradham 1963; Bray 1963a, 1963b; Chapman and Pangborn 1962; Falk 1969; Falk and Lippincott 1974; McMillan 1968; Marshall 1956; Wood 1961, 1967; Wood and Pangborn 1968). Based on the excavation results, Wood (1965a) identified four burial complexes: Afton, Bolivar, Fristoe, and Stockton.

The Afton complex, named for the pentagonal Afton point that was found with several inhumations, was primarily a Late Archaic–period manifestation, followed by the Late Woodland–period Bolivar and Fristoe complexes and then by the Late Woodland–Mississippian–period Stockton complex. Except for the Afton complex, Wood was tentative about the dates of the complexes as well as about the relations of the complexes to each other. The Fristoe complex was the first unit named (Wood 1961); later, the Bolivar complex (Wood 1965a) was devised to separate burials containing charred plant foods, Scallorn points, Cupp points, turtle-carapace bowls, and butted spatulas made of elk bone from those that did not contain those items. The Stockton complex was established to include burials that contained more than a few sherds of shell-tempered pottery.

Excavations in Stockton Reservoir yielded further evidence of material created by Caddoan peoples (or at least materials that looked Caddoan) in the southwestern quarter of the state. A vessel containing eight horizontal incised lines around the rim had been found in association with burned and unburned bone at the Vaughn site in Table Rock Reservoir, which Chapman and Bray (1960) viewed as evidence of a colonization of the region by Caddoan peoples. McMillan (1966a) found bone-tempered sherds in several of the Sand Bluff shelters in Stockton Reservoir, and Wood and Pangborn (1968; see also Pangborn 1966) found a Spiro-engraved bottle in the Eureka mound in Stockton Reservoir.

I couldn't chronicle the history of archaeological work in southwestern Missouri, especially in Stockton and Pomme de Terre reservoirs, without dedicating a paragraph to Rolland E. Pangborn (Figure 6.2), of Humansville, Missouri, one of the more interesting characters in the annals of Missouri archaeology (Kay 1981). Pangborn had an intense interest in archaeology but had no formal training in the subject. His interest and common sense heavily outweighed his lack of formal training and led to his employment with the University of Missouri's American Archaeology Division as a research assistant. Pangborn worked on most of the university's projects in southwestern Missouri from the late 1950s through the middle 1970s, quickly becoming Wood's right-hand man in the field. He developed an excellent knowledge of the archaeological record of the region and authored or coauthored several articles on various aspects of his and Wood's research.

Joanna Reservoir

While fieldwork was progressing in the reservoirs in the west-central portion of the state, work resumed in the proposed Joanna (later renamed Clarence Cannon) Reservoir on the Salt River, in the northeastern portion of Missouri. The first phase of work (Chapman and Henning 1960) had been a small survey that relocated sites found by the Marion-Ralls Archaeological Society and extended the survey further west into the proposed reservoir area. The rationale for the subsequent phase of work appears in Chapman's introduction to the report to the National Park Service (Chapman 1962: v): "The emphasis of the research was directed toward the recovery of a local cultural sequence within the Salt River Valley, expanding the knowledge of as many of the cultural periods as possible, and with special emphasis placed upon the recovery of information concerning the ceremonies associated with the mound structures so prevalent within and adjacent to the proposed Joanna Reservoir." Chapman believed that the work carried out prior to submission of the report had been successful:

Figure 6.2. Rolland E. Pangborn (1916–1981), longtime archaeological field assistant with the University of Missouri, ca. 1964 (photograph by G. Gardner, courtesy D. R. Henning).

> Although a full cultural sequence was not determined, and many questions were left unanswered concerning the ceremonial activities of those building the mounds in the area, it is felt that within the limits of the time and funds available that a fair insight into these problems was obtained. Another necessary step in progressing the overall goals of obtaining the full sequence of cultural development of the Joanna Reservoir area was accomplished. Furthermore, many new insights into ceremonial activities of both the Archaic and the Woodland period were obtained. (Chapman 1962: v–vi)

A third cooperative agreement between the university and the park service led to another round of excavation in 1962 and 1963, primarily of burial mounds. The report was submitted to the NPS in 1964 (D. R. Henning et al. 1964).

The burial mounds in the Joanna Reservoir area were similar in many respects to those Fowke (1910) had excavated in central Missouri—rock-lined crypts with burials placed in and around them (Heldman 1962; A. E. Henning 1964; A. E. Henning and D. R. Henning 1964; D. R. Henning 1961). The most extraordinary feature was the Hatten I mound, located on the South Fork of the Salt River. The mound contained three separately prepared areas: (1) a 2.5-by-2-meter central chamber constructed of limestone slabs; (2) a 3-meter-diameter chamber of limestone slabs; and (3) a mound of alternating layers of limestone slabs and chert cobbles. Each area contained different types of burials—extended primary, bundled, and cremations. At least 118 bodies had been placed in the mound over its long period of use.

Several open-air sites were also excavated in the early 1960s (e.g., K. W. Cole 1964; D. R. Henning 1962, 1964), including one, the Ross site, that produced postmolds of at least two houses (Heldman 1962). These were the first prehistoric houses in northeast Missouri to be excavated.

In 1967 the University of Missouri returned to the Joanna Reservoir, by which time Congress had authorized its name to be changed to the Clarence Cannon Reservoir in memory of Missouri's powerful congressional representative. Excavation of several sites occurred during 1967 and 1968 under the direction of Walter Klippel (Klippel 1968, 1969b, 1972; Klippel et al. 1972). Klippel's research interests were varied, but a considerable portion of his work focused on a hypothesis formulated in 1964 by D. R. Henning, who suggested that tradition lag in terms of stone-artifact types existed in the Salt River basin, resulting in "the survival and retention of Archaic stone tool technology with the addition of pottery making in the Late Woodland" (D. R. Henning 1964: 106). Klippel (1968: 1) discussed this possibility and linked it to evidence from other supposedly preceramic sites in the Salt Basin: "The collation of these uncoordinated data has fostered interest, not only in the local Archaic manifestations themselves, but also in the potential the area might have for unraveling many general problems of cultural trends and development in the Midwest during the Archaic period."

Henning's notion of stone-tool lag was based in large part on the absence of projectile-point types that clearly and unmistakably dated to the Early Woodland and Middle Woodland periods. As I pointed out in Chapter 5, much of the chronological ordering of cultural components and sites in Missouri was a reflection of the way such orderings were accomplished in places outside the state, especially Illinois for the Woodland periods. For example, one hallmark of the Middle Woodland period in western and west-central Illinois was the presence of elaborate stamping and incising on vessel exteriors. Griffin (1952d) and others developed numerous types to partition the enormous variation evident among the vessels, which normally are referred to collectively as Havana-tradition pottery. Another hallmark of the Middle Woodland period was the so-called Hopewellian point, a broad, rounded, corner-notched form that today typically is referred to as a Snyders point. Few Snyders points have been found in the Salt River valley, and the number of classic Middle Woodland Havana-tradition pottery sherds similar to those from Illinois but found in the Salt River valley would fit comfortably in one's hand. In addition, the early surveys produced no projectile points similar in form to Early Woodland points (e.g., the contracting-stem Belknap type or the square-stem Kramer type) in Illinois, nor did they produce the classic grit-tempered Black Sand pottery that also occurs in abundance on Early Woodland sites in Illinois.

In the absence of these markers, Henning concluded that human population in the basin had declined drastically after the Late Archaic period, had remained low throughout the Early Woodland and Middle Woodland periods, and then had risen dramatically during the Late Woodland period. Without stratified deposits and some of the classic chronological markers, it was difficult to separate components and to develop an independent set of markers for the Salt River area. What Henning viewed as tradition lag—the holdover of point styles from the Late Archaic period to the Late Woodland period—was actually more apparent than real. The shallowness of most of the sites, the absence of markers for some time periods, and the fact that many sites had been reoccupied over a long period of time created the effect of tradition lag. Later work showed that the Salt River valley had indeed been occupied during the Early Woodland and Middle Woodland periods.

Klippel's work in the Cannon Reservoir is important because he began to examine sites that appeared to represent single-period occupations. One site he selected for excavation during 1967, the Booth site, produced a large quantity of Late Archaic points, other tools, and associated stone-carving material, which allowed for the first time a detailed study of an encampment along the Salt River dating ca. 3000–1000 B.C. (Klippel 1968, 1969b). Klippel's second season of work was even more focused, this time on the nature of occupations at around 1000 B.C., the dividing line between the Late Archaic and Early Woodland periods. One location he picked for excavation, the Collins site, proved much more interesting than even Klippel had expected. In addition to the usual lithic, ceramic, and faunal debris, the site produced carbonized plant material, the most significant being charred sumpweed *(Iva annua)* seed coats. Detailed analysis demonstrated that the size of the seed coats was well beyond that seen in wild specimens, leading Klippel (1972; see also Klippel and Mandeville 1972) to suggest that the plants had been domesticated.

The issue of plant domestication is deeply rooted in archaeology, but until the late 1960s and early 1970s normal archaeological procedures did not allow for the recovery of most plant materials. In many instances excavators did not screen dirt from deposits to catch fine bits of material, such as plant remains, and even when they did, the wire mesh was too large to catch seeds and other small plant parts. Even if larger fragments had been present, they would have been crushed by the weight of the dirt being pushed through the screen. The pre–ca. 1970 literature on eastern United States archaeology does contain some descriptions of vegetal material from archaeological sites, but for the most part these were based on remains from rock shelters in areas such as the Ozarks and the eastern Kentucky Appalachians. Preservation of uncarbonized remains is often excellent in rock shelters, which on the one hand is a bonanza to archaeologists but on the other presents a significant bias in favor of one particular kind of site.

I take up the notion of plant domestication again in Chapter 8, but it is important to note here that most field projects in the 1960s were not designed to recover plant remains (few archaeologists were interested in plant remains when they had lithic and ceramic artifacts to study), nor did they have the requisite equipment to do so. By the late 1960s, however, prehistoric diet was becoming an important component of archaeological analysis, and flotation was beginning to be used more and more as a means of recovering small, carbonized plant parts (Struever 1968); by the early 1970s water-separation machines had been introduced. Flotation is a simple procedure in which sediments are broken up in water, often helped along through the addition of a deflocculent such as sodium silicate, which breaks up clumps of material. As the clay lumps break up, they release any carbonized plant parts, which float to the surface and can be collected in small-mesh screens. Water-separation machines work on the same principle (Watson 1976), but they agitate the sediment samples from below. The carbonized plant remains float to the surface of the barrel and are caught on an overflow screen. Not surprisingly, after archaeologists became more interested in prehistoric diet and started using flotation, evidence of widespread use of dozens of different wild plants by prehistoric groups soon flooded the literature.

For now we leave the Cannon Reservoir, though we will pick the story up again in Chapter 7. I create this hiatus for one very important reason: the next phase of work was in many respects based on a new orientation and certainly on a new set of field and analytical methods. By the time the next round of fieldwork was being planned for the Salt River (in the mid-1970s), Americanist archaeology was beginning to go through radical changes on several fronts. That story is interesting enough that I don't want to preempt it here.

The Federal Highway Salvage Program

Reservoir-construction projects were not the only programs to begin receiving federal funding in the 1950s and 1960s. Perhaps inspired by the perceived effectiveness of the River Basin Surveys in mitigating the damage to threatened archaeological sites in reservoir locations, the U.S. government initiated the highway salvage program in New Mexico in 1954 (Jennings 1985; Ritchie 1961). In 1956 Congress passed the Federal Aid Highway Act, which authorized states to expend federal funds on archaeological survey and testing in advance of interstate-highway construction. The first project in Missouri was a study of archaeological sites in two southeastern Missouri counties—New Madrid and Pemiscot—that lay in the proposed corridor of Interstate 55, one of the major midcontinental north–south arteries. Thirty sites were found in the corridor, and two of them were tested during 1964 and 1965 (Marshall 1965, n.d.-a).

One site, Kersey, forms the basis of much of what is known of early-Mississippian-period life in the meander-belt portion of the central Mississippi River valley. Richard Marshall (Figure 6.3) excavated a complex series of burials at Kersey, including a stockaded area that contained numerous bundle burials. One feature of Kersey was the diversity of temper types found in the pottery from in and around the burial areas, including clay, shell, sand, and various combinations of the three. Based on his examination of the Kersey materials, Marshall (1965, n.d.-a) named two new phases for extreme southeastern Missouri—Kersey, which was a very late Late Woodland–period[6] unit, and Hayti, which was a very early Mississippian-period unit.

For several years following Marshall's work, no additional highway-related salvage operations were carried out in Missouri. The situation began to change in the 1970s as the Federal Highway Administration began putting increasing pressure on the states to comply with archaeological legislation. The Missouri Highway and Transportation Department hired its first archaeologist in the early 1970s, which meant that the department could carry out in-house archaeological

Figure 6.3. Richard A. Marshall (right) excavating skeletons at the Murphy site, Pemiscot County, Missouri, 1956.

---

6. Most archaeologists who work in the Mississippi River valley do not use the temporal unit "Late Woodland period." Following Phillips et al. (1951), they substitute the term "late Baytown."

surveys in advance of road design. However, the small size of the staff precluded in-house personnel from undertaking large excavation projects, which were contracted out to universities and private firms on an as-needed basis. By the late 1970s the MHTD had become the third-largest (behind the St. Louis and Kansas City districts of the Corps of Engineers) sponsor of archaeology in Missouri.

Southeastern Missouri Land-Leveling Salvage Project

One thing that was evident in the 1960s about sites and site locations was the increased destruction of the resource base through land-modifying activities. This realization was nothing new; Fowke (1922) had noted earlier in the twentieth century that rock-shelter deposits in the Ozarks were being destroyed at a rapid rate through their removal for fertilizer. J. C. Harrington (1935), in his call for participation in the newly formed Missouri Archaeological Society, noted that the task of the members was to gather as much information as possible from sites slated for destruction. The society and the University of Missouri had long heeded the call to save archaeological information threatened by reservoir waters, and in the early 1960s they had added to their venue sites slated for destruction by federal-highway construction. In 1966 the university added another set of threatened sites to its list, those in southeastern Missouri that faced destruction through land leveling for agricultural purposes:

> The effects of agricultural and commercial progress are damaging to the archaeology of Southeast Missouri. Expanding cities and highways do their usual damage, but the major problem in Southeast Missouri is land forming, or the use of mechanical equipment to reform the lay of the land for agricultural purposes. Land forming consists of two major types of land manipulation. One is "smoothing" or "planing" [Figure 6.4, top]. The other is land-leveling [Figure 6.4, bottom]. Another process which accompanies either of these or may be done separately is chisel plowing. Depending on the present grade and condition of the land one or the other, or both procedures may be used.
>
> The least destructive type is smoothing or planing . . . and consists of using a land plane to fill in depressions. . . . Within the seven county delta region of Missouri, it is estimated that twelve thousand and one hundred acres were planed in 1966 and that 171,171 acres have undergone planing since 1955. . . .
>
> Land leveling . . . consists of using large "buckets" to move soil from one part of a field to another to bring it to grade. . . . Between 1955 and 1965, 49,206 acres were brought to grade in the delta of Southeast Missouri. In 1966 alone, twenty-one thousand three hundred acres were leveled. All figures indicate a continued increase in leveling in the future. For example, the sale of landforming equipment has increased from sixty pieces in 1962 to 125 pieces from January to September, 1966. It was estimated that two hundred pieces would be sold by December, 1966. . . .

Figure 6.4. Two major types of equipment used in land alteration in southeastern Missouri: land plane (top) and land leveler (bottom). The photographs were taken in Pemiscot County, Missouri, in 1965, but they could have been taken anywhere in the meander-belt region of the Mississippi River valley. The land being planed or leveled is fairly flat to begin with, but these machines remove all traces of elevational differences, including swales, natural levees, point-bar deposits, and prehistoric mounds (from J. R. Williams 1967).

All of these practices are expensive. For example, it costs an average of approximately fifty dollars an acre to land level. Crop production as well as the value of the land is raised however, and within a few years, little of the arable land will remain untouched. (J. R. Williams 1967: 1–5)

This statement was correct. The destruction of archaeological sites in southeastern Missouri and northeastern Arkansas (Medford 1972) has been of massive proportions, with little nonurban land remaining unaltered. Compounding the problem in southeastern Missouri has been the excavation of a complex system of large ditches to drain the essentially flat terrain. An unknown number of sites has been affected, though it undoubtedly is in the thousands. McGimsey and Davis (1968) estimated that by the middle of the 1960s over 25% of the known archaeological sites in the Arkansas portion of the Mississippi alluvial valley had been destroyed by land leveling.

Between 1966 and 1968, the University of Missouri, under the Inter-Agency Archaeological Salvage Program, conducted a salvage operation in the southeastern Missouri counties of Mississippi, New Madrid, and Pemiscot. J. Raymond Williams (1967, 1968, 1972) directed the three-year program, during which 22 sites were examined. These included Denton Mounds and Cagle Lake in Pemiscot County and Hoecake in Mississippi County. I mention these three sites in particular because of their prominence in the literature. Denton Mounds and Cagle Lake are very late Mississippian-period sites located along Pemiscot Bayou, an ancient crevasse channel of the Mississippi River. Both sites have long been favorites of pothunters, who have unearthed an impressive array of elaborately decorated vessels that were incorporated with burials. The sites are 2 of about 13 communities in the Pemiscot Bayou locality that existed until at least the sixteenth century, an estimate based on Spanish goods found at several of them. Analysis of the materials produced through decades of pothunting has given us some understanding of the range in variation of material items (O'Brien 1994), but J. R. Williams's (1968, 1972) excavations produced the only information on architectural details. Also, with the exception of Chapman and Anderson's (1955) work at Campbell, another late-Mississippian-period site, Williams's detailed and thoughtful analyses of excavated sherds have produced the only baseline data that exist on ceramic-type frequencies from excavated midden deposits at Pemiscot Bayou sites.

It was J. R. Williams's (1967) work at Hoecake (Figure 6.5), however, that was perhaps his most important contribution to our understanding of Missouri prehistory. The site, located in Mississippi County, derived its name from the cone-shaped mounds (resembling cornmeal "hoecakes") that once dotted its surface. In the early part of the twentieth century Houck (1908) noted the importance of the site and stated that at the time there were 54 mounds, some of which were 25 feet high. As I noted in Chapter 3, however, field verification

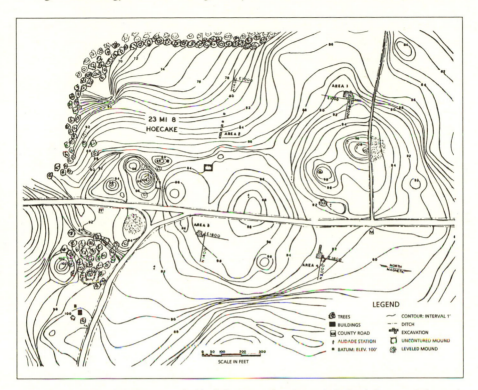

Figure 6.5. Map of the western half of the Hoecake site, Mississippi County, Missouri (from J. R. Williams 1967).

of some of Houck's recorded 20,000 mounds in Missouri has consistently shown that many of his supposed mounds were in actuality natural-levee remnants or prairie mounds, so we might rely more on J. R. Williams's (1967) estimate that there were originally 31 mounds, not 54. In 1966 archaeological materials were spread over an area of roughly 200 acres, and Williams (1967: 24) states that only 1 mound was left undisturbed. In 1963 a house and 2 mounds on the site had been excavated (Anonymous 1964; Marshall and Hopgood 1964), 1 of which produced 3 tombs containing 14 individuals. The tombs were lined with split cane and covered with logs. Williams's excavations uncovered the remains of 11 houses plus numerous other architectural features.

Of particular interest from a historical point of view was J. R. Williams's documentation at Hoecake of a phenomenon mentioned earlier by Stephen Williams (1954) relative to southeastern Missouri pottery-bearing sites—the paucity of "pure" shell-tempered or "pure" clay-tempered ceramic assemblages (see also Hopgood 1969). What typically is found instead are sherds of each temper type and, frequently, sherds that contain both types of temper. S. Williams (1954: 272) had in mind the former when he stated that "this mixture is a result of dual occupation by two different components at different times" and "the sites are transitional and show the change from one tempering [clay being the earlier] to the other." If the first proposition is correct, he asked, why did it occur so frequently? And if the second proposition is correct, why are there so few "pure" sites? "Surely," he asked, "not every site in the area is transitional?"

In the 1960s and early 1970s (and indeed even in some quarters today), a key issue in archaeology was the documentation of movements of people and ideas from region to region. For example, the presence of a handful of stamped pottery at scattered sites in the western Ozarks was taken to be evidence of the penetration of the region by Hopewellian peoples. Likewise, the first occurrence of shell-tempered pottery in a locality was often regarded as signaling incursions by Mississippian groups bent on colonizing the clay- or sand-tempered-vessel users. J. R. Williams did not exhibit this syndrome. Perhaps suppressing the urge to view Hoecake as chronicling a thousand years of population movements into the area—after all, in addition to both shell-tempered and clay-tempered pottery it also contained log tombs similar to "Hopewellian" examples in Illinois and Ohio—he stated simply, "We know nothing about possible human migrations or cultural diffusion into and out of the area" (J. R. Williams 1967: 156; see also J. R. Williams 1971). Such cautious statement of opinion was rarely repeated in much of the later archaeological work in the central Mississippi River valley.

Reading J. R. Williams's accounts of the land-leveling projects, one quickly understands the real nature of salvage archaeology during the 1960s. Finding out who was going to level which piece of property was a grave concern of the field crews, as was obtaining the cooperation of landowners. As land-leveling activities changed in response to the weather, crews were shuttled from site to site, never having enough time to complete the needed work at any one location. These problems notwithstanding, Williams produced excellent reports in which he attempted to integrate the findings into emerging pictures of prehistoric life in the alluvial valley (see J. R. Williams 1964, 1974 and Klippel 1969a). In fact, the reports are among the best ever produced on Missouri prehistory. Without them our knowledge of particularly the Mississippian-period occupation of the meander-belt portion of the Mississippi River valley would not be nearly what it is, since few projects in the region were undertaken after 1968. Unfortunately, the land-leveling-related salvage program in southeastern Missouri was terminated in the late 1960s as funding within the National Park Service was shifted to other projects.

Humans and Their Physical Environment

It would be difficult to pick up an archaeological research report from the 1950s and 1960s and not find a substantial section dedicated to a discussion of the physical environment of the locality being examined. Archaeologists have long recognized the effects of environment on human actions, but by the 1950s a good portion of the discipline had escaped the environmental determinism of earlier decades (e.g., Wissler 1926) and were clinging either to an environmental "possibilism"—a kind of indeterministic process in which the physical environment is seen not so much as limiting cultural outcomes but rather as setting limits on cultural development—or to the cultural ecology of Julian Steward (e.g., 1949, 1955), whereby certain relational links between technology and environment, regardless of geographic locale, created similar cultural outcomes.

Included in the list of topics addressed in archaeological reports of the period were the physiographic and geological setting of the locale, its water sources, vegetation, climate, soils, and often the fauna native to the region. The authors generally included tables listing such things as soil associations or series, monthly fluctuations in temperature and rainfall, and stream discharge. Usually the authors also included a sentence or paragraph acknowledging that the environment changed over time and that what was being reported was based on modern observations and did not necessarily hold for the past. For example, climate has not remained constant even throughout the Holocene; rather, it has fluctuated dramatically. Such changes in temperature, especially if lower or higher temperatures persist for prolonged periods of time, affect vegetation as well as animals. Disruptions of vegetation can, over time, lead to changing distributions of soil types, which are conditioned in part by the kinds of vegetation that decay to help form the soils. Available moisture, in turn, conditions stream discharge, which in turn determines the amount of sediment left by the stream and the amount of sediment it removes. Like a domino effect, all these changes act in turn to finally create a new arena to which humans respond.

What is missing in these reports, in addition to attempts to understand changes in the physical environment, are attempts to understand concomitant changes created in the human populations residing in the environments. Thus the environment is really being viewed as a more or less static backdrop against which human interactions are carried out. This analogy was not lost on Phillips et al. (1951: 36):

> The environmentalist view, if we interpret it correctly, is that culture can only be understood in terms of environment. It seems no less true that environment can only be understood in terms of culture. The concept of environment as a background, therefore, is inept, unless we have in mind the sort of background that one sees in a well-constructed museum diorama, in which a three-dimensional model is projected upon a two-dimensional background so cleverly that the eye cannot distinguish where one leaves off and the other begins. In short, it appears that culture and environment must be comprehended simultaneously, if either is to be understood in all its bearings.

The lack of integration of archaeological methods with those useful in examining paleoenvironments was one of Walter Taylor's (1948) major complaints and was brought into sharp focus at a meeting of the National Research Council's Committee on Archaeological Identification, held in Chicago in 1956. The report that was subsequently issued (W. W. Taylor 1957) called for closer coordination of work between archaeologists and paleoenvironmentalists.

It was not entirely coincidental that the meeting was held in Chicago, because by the late 1950s the University of Chicago, through its Oriental Institute, was becoming a leader in environmental archaeology. The driving force behind the study of human-environment interaction was Robert J. Braidwood, whose efforts were joined by Robert McCormick Adams[7] and others. The 1960s witnessed phenomenal growth in large-scale survey-and-excavation projects in the Near East, a significant number of which were directed by Braidwood, Adams, and their students (e.g., R. McCormick Adams 1962, 1965; Braidwood 1958, 1960; Flannery 1965; Hole 1966; Hole et al. 1969; Kraelin and Adams 1960). These interdisciplinary archaeological studies, which focused on the role played by the physical environment in the development of settled life, agriculture, and eventually urban areas, led to a series of conceptual changes in how archaeologists approached the topic of human-environment interactions (especially by archaeologists trained at the universities of Chicago and/or Michigan [e.g., Lewis Binford, Richard MacNeish, Frank Hole, and Kent Flannery]) and spawned a whole generation of similar studies in semiarid regions of the Western Hemisphere, such as Highland Mexico (e.g., Byers 1967; Flannery 1966, 1968; MacNeish 1964; MacNeish et al. 1967, 1970, 1975). The Highland Mexico projects would eventually play an indirect, though very significant, role in structuring interdisciplinary work in Missouri.

One of the obvious problems facing archaeologists interested in understanding how aspects of the physical environment have changed through time—a preliminary exercise to understanding human *responses* to the changing environment—is finding the data necessary to pinpoint the changes. The basic mechanics of landscape evolution have been well known since the middle of the nineteenth century. Certainly by that time it was evident that the North American continent had undergone successive climatic changes, including periodic "ice ages." Recall that one of the burning issues of nineteenth-century prehistory was whether ice-age humans had been present to hunt the large animals recovered from mid-continental bogs; by the late nineteenth century the issue had been expanded as archaeologists attempted to determine whether there had been a North American Paleolithic period.

---

7. This Robert McCormick Adams is the cousin of the Robert McCormick Adams whose work in eastern Missouri was sponsored by the Works Progress Administration (Chapter 5).

It was one thing to ask whether humans had been here during the last glacial period, but it was another to ask the calendar age of that glaciation. Stratigraphic sequences and cross-correlation of strata yielded a relative sequence of events, but even after it had been demonstrated that humans and now-extinct fauna had been contemporaries, the absolute ages of the associations of humans and animals such as large bison remained undetermined. With the dawn of the radiometric era came answers to many of these questions. We often think of radiocarbon dating as being solely the province of archaeologists, but its development was also a boon to paleoclimatologists, who could then date their pollen sequences and, like archaeologists, begin to focus on finer and finer units of time. It no longer was enough to place a terminal date on the last glacial episode and then lump the last 11,000 or so years, from then to the present, into a single unit. It was clear that this current period—the Holocene—had witnessed considerable climatic variation and that if the proper data were available, the period could be subdivided into finer units.

Archaeologists quite naturally were interested in such research since the data would allow them to understand something of the past environments in which their subjects had lived. Some of the earliest work on paleoenvironments of the late Pleistocene and early Holocene was done in the western United States and the Mississippi alluvial valley. Research done in various parts of the West, including the Rocky Mountains (e.g., Matthes 1951), the Great Basin (e.g., Antevs 1948; Heizer 1951), the Southwest (e.g., Bryan 1950; Sayles and Antevs 1941), and the Great Plains (e.g., Antevs 1950; Moss 1951; Schultz et al. 1951), incorporated a variety of data such as the positioning of glacial moraines (Antevs 1950; Matthes 1951), rates of varve—layers of deposit in lakes and ponds—buildup (Antevs 1950), cross-correlation of terrace sequences (Moss 1951), sediment analysis (Heizer 1951; Sayles and Antevs 1941; Schultz et al. 1951), and floral analysis (Schultz et al. 1951). Many of the paleoclimatic interpretations that grew out of this early research have been shown to be incorrect or at best outdated, but that is beside the point. What is important is that by 1950 archaeologists had begun to team up with geomorphologists and paleoclimatologists in an effort to document the myriad landscape and climatic changes that various locales had witnessed during the tail end of the Pleistocene and throughout the Holocene.

Farther east, most of the work carried out in the Mississippi alluvial valley was by Harold Fisk (e.g., 1944) or by those influenced by him (e.g., Saucier 1964, 1968). Fisk realized the Mississippi Valley was a chronicle of geomorphological responses to changing climatic episodes that had affected the continent. His lofty goal was to reconstruct the history of landscape development, especially during the terminal Pleistocene and Holocene epochs, in the Mississippi Valley from Cairo, Illinois, to the Gulf of Mexico. During the Pleistocene the Mississippi River transported huge amounts of glacial outwash from the north, spreading it laterally throughout southeastern Missouri in the form of thick terrace-train deposits. During the early Holocene, the Mississippi, which had moved progressively eastward, captured the meander-belt system of the Ohio River. From then until the present, the history of the Mississippi River system has been one of constant movement as the stream migrated across the landscape, leaving in its wake hundreds of abandoned channels and cutoff chutes.

Fisk (1944) developed a relative chronological ordering of these features, which was viewed as a boon by archaeologists, who suddenly had an added means of dating their sites. Although subsequent work (e.g., Saucier 1968, 1974, 1981) has shown Fisk's chronology to be grossly inaccurate, the importance of his work is unquestioned. He was the first researcher to tie the landscape evolution of the lower alluvial valley to climatic change and to the corresponding rates of water and sediment discharge in the upper reaches of the Mississippi system. Again, the timing of these events as well as the magnitude of certain of the processes that Fisk postulated have subsequently been corrected, but the importance of the work as a landmark study still stands. The region in which Fisk was working— an active floodplain setting—is no match for the West in terms of preservation of landscape features, and many of the problems that Fisk encountered in his attempt to document the evolution of the Mississippi alluvial valley would have been foreign to researchers such as Ernst Antevs, who was doing the same kind of work but in environments that were more stable. The semiarid and alpine regions of the continent were free of the erosional and depositional force connected with a river such as the Mississippi, which continuously eradicates previous landforms and creates new ones in their place. Thus it is quite understandable that the majority of paleoenvironmental research conducted in the 1940s and 1950s took place in the West.

Sustained interest in the midwestern Holocene climate and its relation to other aspects of the physical environment dates at least to the 1950s. The upper Midwest in particular was viewed as an excellent laboratory for the study of environmental change because of its unique vegetational composition—a mixture of forest and prairie. Stretching eastward from the Great Plains to central Indiana is a complex mosaic of tall-grass prairie and deciduous forest known as the Prairie Peninsula (Transeau 1935) (Figure 6.6). The peninsula of interlocking fingers of prairie upland and forested river valleys formed early in the Holocene and throughout its history has been vulnerable to climatic change. This vulnerability shows up not only in the pollen record but in such things as soil composition, valley-fill sequences, and archaeological site locations.

In the mid-1950s the first boreal pollen record in the midcontinent was recognized at Muscotah Marsh in northeastern Kansas (Horr 1955; see also Wells 1970, in which Wells reidentified the "fir" pollen as being from spruce); the zone containing the boreal pollen was subsequently dated to 13,000 ± 1500 B.C. Here was evidence that during the close of the Pleistocene spruce forests were growing where now there were tall-grass prairies. By the 1960s pollen from other parts of

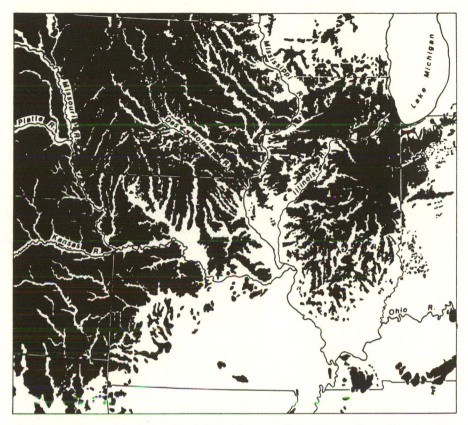

Figure 6.6. The Prairie Peninsula of the midwestern United States (from Warren 1982a, courtesy Academic Press).

the Midwest supported the long-held proposition that boreal forests had been far south of their current latitudes during the terminal Pleistocene and that, as they retreated northward as temperatures rose, they were replaced in some areas by hardwood forests and in other areas by prairies. What happened next, that is, how climate changed throughout the Holocene, was open to question. And it was this broad time period, which encompassed the major occupation of the midcontinent by humans, that was of most interest to archaeologists.

In 1960 James Griffin advanced the notion that climatic change contributed to the growth and decline of northern Hopewellian groups through its effects on their crop cycles (Griffin 1960). The importance of that paper was not whether Griffin was correct (we now know that the situation was much more complex than he suspected) but that he tied the disappearance of a major archaeological tradition to climatic change. The view that climate directly affected cultural development was widely held during the 1960s. Some archaeologists maintained what we might term the hard-line position that climate dictated cultural responses; others held to a middle-ground position that climate set parameters for cultural development—the environmental "possibilism" mentioned earlier.

Examination of the relation between climatic change and human settlement and subsistence practices was the basis for a long-term study of late-ceramic-period cultures in the upper Midwest entitled "Climate, Ecology, and the Oneota Culture" under the direction of David Baerreis of the University of Wisconsin–Madison. That National Science Foundation–supported program involved intensive study not only of archaeological materials from Oneota and Mill Creek sites in Iowa, Missouri, Minnesota, extreme southeastern Nebraska, and western Wisconsin, but also of paleoclimatic indicators, such as plant and animal remains, snails, and pollen. Baerreis's collaboration with Reid Bryson, also of the University of Wisconsin–Madison, led to a series of reports and monographs (e.g., Baerreis and Bryson 1965, 1967; Bryson 1966; Bryson et al. 1970; D. R. Henning 1970) that modeled Holocene climate in the upper Midwest and examined the archaeological record, especially the late portion, in terms of the documented changes in climate (see also Bryson 1966 and Bryson and Wendland 1967). The site-specific analyses built on work that was more extensive in area (e.g., Borchert 1950; Deevey and Flint 1957; H. E. Wright 1968) and produced a concise set of data that would repeatedly be incorporated into later work in the Midwest (e.g., Baerreis et al. 1976; Webb and Bryson 1972; Wendland 1978; Wendland and Bryson 1974).

With this all-too-brief introduction to studies of humans and their environment, I now turn attention to the lower Pomme de Terre River valley, located in western Missouri, and examine in considerable detail the first truly interdisciplinary study ever conducted in Missouri that focused on humans and their changing physical environment. To clarify, this study, although it focused on the lower Pomme de Terre River valley, was not connected with the Pomme de Terre Reservoir project discussed in Chapter 5. The study area I examine here was located downstream of the Pomme de Terre Reservoir, in that portion of the valley to be flooded by the proposed Harry S. Truman (formerly Kaysinger Bluff) Reservoir. The decade-plus of work produced a wealth of paleoenvironmental data that are unparalleled in terms of the breadth and depth of what they cover. You won't find any mention of a "new archaeology" in the myriad reports, books, and articles that flowed out of the Pomme de Terre program, though the principal investigator, W. Raymond Wood, well understood Lewis Binford's program (Wood 1970). What you *will* find is tacit agreement among a diverse group of highly qualified researchers that the only way to examine 11,000 years of human-environment interaction is through detailed excavation and analysis and tight control over both content and context. In short, what you will find is good science carried through to its logical conclusion.

Humans and Their Environment in the Lower Pomme de Terre Valley

The work in the Pomme de Terre Valley, even before the various portions of the project had been completed, had spawned several clones that eventually became important projects in their own right. (I examine two of these—the Harry S. Truman Reservoir Archaeological Project and the Cannon Reservoir Human Ecology Project—in Chapter 7.) It is not unusual to find in the annals of archaeology certain projects that were copied for the field techniques and methods that were employed, but it is rare to find one that was widely copied because of its methods *and* its overall perspective. The Pomme de Terre project was heavily grounded in ecology, meaning that the interest of the investigators lay in understanding various interactions that past human groups had had with their social and especially physical environment. As opposed to the then-usual role played by most environmental specialists on archaeological projects—that is, they were viewed as ancillary staff—specialists on the Pomme de Terre project were active participants in helping to structure both fieldwork and analysis.

I have to backtrack in time a bit to the early days of work in the region in order to put the later work in proper chronological as well as methodological perspective. It will be clear that the work in the Pomme de Terre River valley did not begin as an interdisciplinary program established to examine human-environment interactions. Rather, the initial project was designed on the order of all the other reservoir projects of the 1950s and 1960s, with the guiding objectives being to locate sites and to excavate portions of those that held some promise of adding to the cultural sequence. And for several years that was the way the project ran—but that was before Ray Wood became involved and changed forever the way in which midwestern archaeologists approached the question of how humans got along with their physical environment. The way he did it was to assemble a top-notch team of scientists, each of whom brought his or her expertise to bear on a common problem in a truly interdisciplinary fashion.

Work conducted during the early 1960s in the Kaysinger Bluff Reservoir area (Figure 5.18), combined with the work in the Stockton Reservoir discussed earlier in this chapter, yielded a wealth of information on the prehistoric occupation and use of the middle and lower reaches of the Pomme de Terre River valley and that portion of the Osage River valley in and around its junctions with the Pomme de Terre and the South Grand rivers. Surveys and excavations conducted in the proposed reservoir (Chapman 1965; Falk 1966, 1969; Wood 1965b) added substantially to a growing appreciation for the breadth and time depth involved in the prehistoric use of the region. Altogether, the sites covered the span of prehistoric human occupation in Missouri from the Paleo-Indian period up through the Late Woodland period (9250 B.C.–A.D. 900).

By 1963 test pits excavated at numerous open sites and rock shelters in the western Ozarks demonstrated that the sites contained components that dated to one or more time periods, but none offered even the remotest possibility of spanning the entire cultural sequence that had been pieced together for the Ozarks region. The cultural sequence as it was then known was a patchwork of pieces from various sites in the Ozarks, with considerable cross correlation between material from those sites and material from stratified sites outside the region.

From the excavations of Fowke, through the work of Bushnell, Wissler, and Nelson, and finally to the work directed by Chapman, Ozark rock shelters held a special lure for archaeologists working in Missouri. Such interest should not be particularly surprising. Rock shelters, if the limestone in which they formed is not riddled with fissures and if they open away from the prevailing-weather directions, offer the potential of housing perishable materials such as textiles and plants, which rapidly deteriorate in open sites. Also, rock shelters are bounded spaces that accumulate human debris at rates that tend to far exceed the rates at open sites, where the debris is subject to wider scattering. Deposits tend to build up rapidly in rock shelters, and hence artifacts are sealed in place rather quickly. The end result is better stratification than is normally encountered at open sites. Thus some archaeologists view rock shelters, especially those with deep deposits, as the answer to their prayers.

On the other hand, rock shelters are nightmares to excavate properly. The fact that there are limits to the amount of living floor that can be used contributes to the buildup of material within a shelter, but it also means that that particular space probably is subjected to much more intensive use than a floor at an open site might receive. Instead of moving over a few meters to build a new hearth, a person occupying a rock shelter, because he or she doesn't *have* a few meters to move over, might scrape away the previous hearth and construct the new one in its place. Likewise, the option of where to excavate a storage pit is limited, whereas at an open location one has an almost unlimited choice. Centuries or millennia of reoccupation of rock shelters can result in deposits that are so riddled with storage and burial pits that the strata in places appear reversed, with older materials on top of younger items. And humans were not the only creatures attracted by the thought of using a rock shelter for protection. Pack rats and voles, as well as a host of other burrowing rock-shelter denizens, equal or surpass their human counterparts in the ability to churn archaeological deposits.

These problems notwithstanding, substantial efforts were expended during the 1950s and 1960s in excavating Missouri rock shelters. I examine a few of the efforts briefly as an introduction to the excavation of the most important rock shelter in Missouri archaeology, Rodgers Shelter. One of the earliest projects was Wilfred Logan's (1952) work at Graham Cave in Montgomery County (Figure 6.7), which became a favorite site for excavations by Wrench, Chapman, and members of the Missouri Archaeological Society (Figure 6.8). This work was

Figure 6.7. Missouri Archaeological Society field crew leaving Graham Cave, Montgomery County, Missouri, 1955.

followed by J. Mett Shippee's (1966) excavations[8] at Arnold Research Cave in Callaway County (Figure 6.9) (supplemented with help from MAS volunteers [Figure 6.10]), Richard Marshall's (n.d.-b) work at Verkamp Shelter in Phelps County, and Bruce McMillan's (1965c; see also Roberts 1965) excavations at Tick Creek Cave and Merrell Cave in Phelps County. These excavations provided excellent stratigraphic summaries of changes in temporally diagnostic items such as projectile points, and in the case of Arnold Research Cave an abundance of woven items (Figure 6.11), but none of the work was without its problems. Tick Creek Cave and Arnold Research Cave, for example, contained fairly shallow and highly mixed deposits, and although the projectile-point forms indicated the sites had been occupied over approximately 7,000–10,000 years, it was difficult, or in the case of Arnold Research Cave impossible, to sort the strata chronologically. Because of the depth of the deposits at Verkamp Shelter, Marshall was able to present a reasonable assessment of stratigraphic change, but Logan was faced with the same problem at Graham Cave that Shippee had faced at Arnold. One look at Logan's stratigraphic section (Figure 6.12) should convince even the most skeptical reader of the interpretive problems posed by rock shelters.

---

8. Mett Shippee, like Rolland Pangborn, was a nonprofessional archaeologist who became a longtime research associate in Chapman's American Archaeology Division at the University of Missouri.

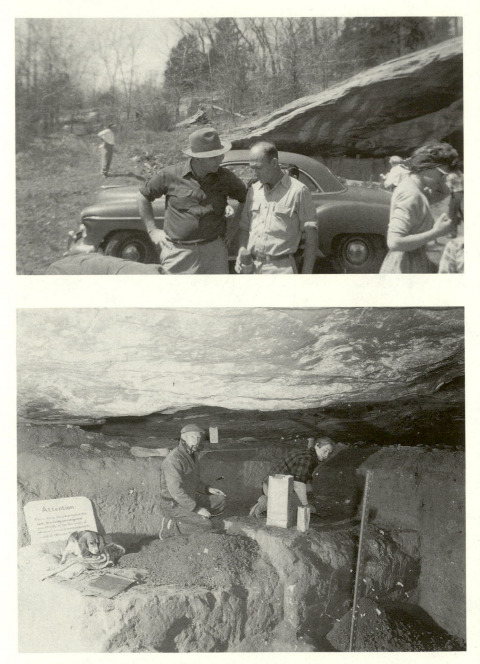

Figure 6.8. Missouri Archaeological Society members at Graham Cave, Montgomery County, Missouri, 1955; top, Henry Hamilton (left) and Carl Chapman; bottom, Harry and Florence Collins.

Figure 6.9. J. Mett Shippee excavating at Arnold Research Cave, Callaway County, Missouri, 1956.

Figure 6.10. Missouri Archaeological Society members helping out in the excavation of Arnold Research Cave, Callaway County, Missouri, 1955.

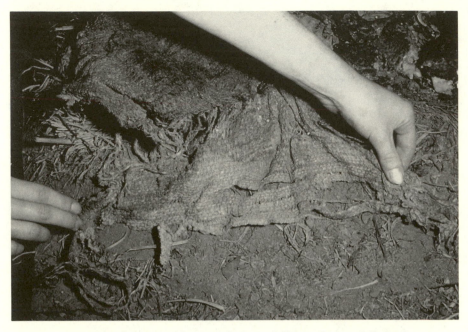

Figure 6.11. Textiles from Arnold Research Cave, Callaway County, Missouri, 1955.

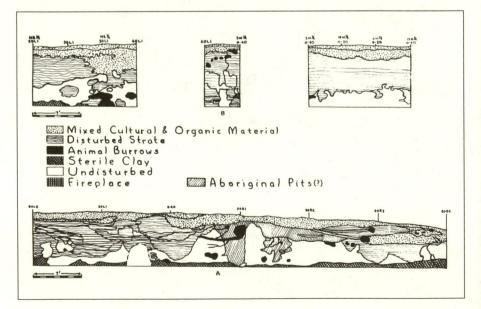

Figure 6.12. Excavation profiles from Carl Chapman's and Wilfred Logan's work at Graham Cave, Montgomery County, Missouri, in 1949–1951 (from Logan 1952, courtesy Missouri Archaeological Society).

Rodgers Shelter

It was in this tradition of rock-shelter archaeology that the springtime survey of Kaysinger Bluff Reservoir was initiated in 1962. A number of promising shelters were located, including a small recess in the base of a high limestone bluff on the right-hand (looking downstream) side of the Pomme de Terre River in Benton County (Figure 6.13). There appeared to be nothing particularly unusual about the site. It was larger than most rock shelters in the lower Pomme de Terre Valley but certainly paled in comparison to some of those in other parts of the Ozarks. The mouth of the shelter, which faced south, was 70 ft long and had a maximum overhang of about 25 ft. Surface artifacts within the confines of the overhang indicated that humans had used the recess at some point in the past, and plans were made to test the depth of the deposit, along with those of several other shelters, the next summer. A 35-ft-long trench oriented along the short axis of the overhang was placed in the floor of the shelter in 1963 and carried to an average depth of 4 ft, where the excavators encountered a gravelly clay layer that they took to be the base of the artifact-bearing deposit. The test trench was backfilled, and the excavation crew moved on.

In 1965 Carl Chapman passed the reins of the Kaysinger Bluff project to Ray Wood. Plans were made to continue the excavations at Rodgers Shelter, since the 4 ft of deposit found the previous summer was better than nothing when trying to develop a chronological ordering of cultural units. The deposit was deeper than other rock-shelter deposits in the immediate vicinity and appeared to have less mixing. McMillan (Figure 6.14) was selected as field director, and the first thing Wood told him to do "was to carry the excavations to bedrock" (McMillan 1992: 3).[9] This was sage advice, since by the close of the 1965 field season, McMillan (1965a) had determined that the deposits on the slope in front of the shelter extended to a depth of at least 25.5 ft (Figure 6.15), at which point the deepest excavation level intersected the water table. He recognized four depositional strata, including a terrace gravel deposit that extended from the 9-ft mark to the water table. Within this stratum were several chert tools, including a point segment with the bilateral flaking typical of Paleo-Indian points. The majority of these materials lay between 18 and 25 ft below the ground surface, with an essentially 9-ft-thick sterile zone toward the top of the gravel terrace deposit (Figure 6.15). Overlying the gravel deposit was a 5-ft-thick stratum containing Early and Middle Archaic points, followed by a 2-ft-thick sterile deposit, followed by a 2-ft-thick stratum containing Late Archaic points,

9. After I wrote this section, Bruce McMillan kindly sent me a copy of his Plains Conference paper in which he discussed Wood's role in the Pomme de Terre project. I found that I had independently used many of the same sources he cited, but in subsequently revising this section I have borrowed heavily from his excellent paper (McMillan 1992).

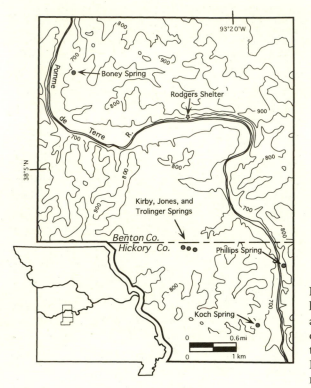

Figure 6.13. Map of the lower Pomme de Terre River area, showing the locations of major sites excavated by the Western Ozark Research Program (after C. V. Haynes 1976).

followed by an upper foot of deposit that contained Woodland-period points and pottery.

The most significant aspect of Rodgers Shelter was the deep, sealed deposit that McMillan (1966b) suggested dated to the Paleo-Indian period. Paleo-Indian artifacts were not rare in west-central Missouri, but they had never been found in a sealed context. That the proposed Paleo-Indian component was overlain by a thick, essentially sterile deposit and that the stratum was overlain by Early and Middle Archaic materials indicated that the earliest component might be unmixed and could date to a fairly short span of time. The Early Archaic–Middle Archaic stratum contained lanceolate points (including small, reworked Dalton points) similar to those from the earliest occupation of Lander Shelter I (Bray 1957) and the Rice site (Bray 1956) in Table Rock Reservoir. It also contained Graham Cave side-notched, Rice lobed, and Jakie stemmed points, which by 1965 were widely recognized as good pre–5000 B.C. time markers. These point types had been identified not only in the Table Rock Reservoir rock shelters (Bray 1956, 1957) but also in Graham Cave (Logan 1952) and Arnold Research Cave (Shippee 1966) in central Missouri and in Tick Creek Cave (McMillan

Figure 6.14. R. Bruce McMillan (left) and Marvin Kay at Rodgers Shelter, Benton County, Missouri, 1967 (photograph by G. Gardner, courtesy D. R. Henning).

1965c; Parmalee 1965; R. G. Roberts 1965) and Merrell Cave (McMillan 1965c) in the Gasconade drainage of south-central Missouri (see also McMillan 1963, 1965b). Based on the stratified nature of the deposits and the considerable vertical spread over which they occurred, Rodgers Shelter was selected for more intensive examination.

To archaeologists who have entered the profession in the last 20 years or so, Wood's order to punch a test unit down through a nonartifact-bearing layer probably does not appear too noteworthy. Archaeologists now routinely excavate considerably deeper than the bottoms of artifact-bearing levels or at least probe underlying deposits by means of coring devices. But in 1964, it was a rare occurrence for archaeologists to excavate deeper than the supposed bottom of material-bearing strata. As one of Wood's contemporaries, James Brown, noted later:

> The beginning of the new perspective toward midwestern archaeology began in 1964 when buried archaeological strata were discovered at Rodgers Shelter in southwestern Missouri. Up to that time, it was routine to regard sterile sediments underlying surface sites as the bottom of the occupation. But, after this discovery, one could no longer be content that this was so, especially with regard to sediments in shelters and on floodplains that have been subject to aggradation since the

Figure 6.15. Standing at the base of the trench into the terrace deposits in front of Rodgers Shelter, Benton County, Missouri: top, 1966, Earl Neller, with rod, and Marvin Kay; bottom, 1968, Rolland Pangborn (photographs by G. Gardner, courtesy D. R. Henning).

Pleistocene. What had once been treated as a safe presumption had now to be treated very differently. The so-called sterile layers below an occupation began to be subject to careful reexamination. (J. A. Brown 1983: 5)

Wood's directive to McMillan was based on an understanding of physical-environmental processes and the ability to visualize dramatic landscape changes. Wood realized that the gravelly clay that had been reached in 1963 was hillslope wash that had spread out over the surface of the terrace containing the rock shelter. The fact that artifacts did not occur in the deposit implied nothing about underlying strata. If the recess had been occupied during the early Holocene but then not occupied for some period of time, the slopewash would have effectively sealed the underlying deposits. This is precisely what had occurred, but then-conventional wisdom overlooked the fact that cultural deposits could be interrupted by several meters of alluvial (deposited by running water) or colluvial (deposited at the foot of a slope) deposits.

Wood's interest in the environment, as McMillan (1992: 1) points out, stemmed from his graduate career at the University of Oregon, where his adviser was Luther Cressman. The latter is often remembered in the annals of anthropology more for his tumultuous three-year marriage to Margaret Mead than for his fieldwork, but this is a terrible oversight. Cressman conducted several studies of human adaptation in the northern Great Basin (e.g., Cressman 1942), and his examination of archaeological materials from the Dalles on the Columbia River (Cressman 1960) is excellent. McMillan (1992: 1) also points out that Wood (Figure 6.16) perhaps was preadapted for an interest in human interactions with the physical environment, a point alluded to by Wood himself: "those of us who were born and raised in the continental climate that characterizes the Great Plains[10]—no less than those who have been introduced to -40° F temperatures and 100 mph winds, having come to the Plains from elsewhere—tend to be sensitive to ecological matters" (A. E. Johnson and Wood 1980: 42).

Wood well understood the potential of the Rodgers Shelter deposits to answer questions regarding not only the environmental history of the western Ozarks—a history encapsulated in such things as pollen and environmentally sensitive snail species—but also the history of humans' adaptation to, and modification of, their physical environment there. In 1966 he and McMillan applied to the National Science Foundation for funding to continue excavations at Rodgers Shelter and to bring in a team of recognized specialists in various subfields of environmental analysis (Wood 1966). They received the funding, and excavations continued from 1966 to 1968. In their report to the NSF, Wood and McMillan stated their reasons for continuing work at Rodgers Shelter:

10. Wood was born in the western Nebraska town of Gordon.

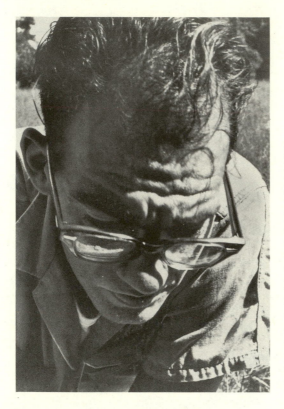

Figure 6.16. W. Raymond Wood at Rodgers Shelter, Benton County, Missouri, 1966. Wood began his career in Missouri working exclusively in southwestern Missouri. With the opening of the deep deposits in front of Rodgers Shelter, his interests migrated to the lower Pomme de Terre River valley, where, during the 1960s and 1970s, he assembled a truly interdisciplinary team of scientists interested in the terminal late Pleistocene and Holocene landscape (photograph by G. Gardner, courtesy D. R. Henning).

Once [the 1965] excavations had established that Rodgers Shelter . . . contained one of the longest cultural sequences in the Midwest, the site locality was conceived as a laboratory for the study of cultural change and stability in an area where man was adapting to a hilly, forested environment: the Ozark Highlands. The heuristic value of the study area is enhanced by the fact that the Ozarks are bounded on the north and east by two of the major river valley systems in the United States: those of the Missouri and Mississippi rivers. These large alluvial valleys provided environmental potentials strikingly different from those of the Ozarks, and saw the rise of at least two of the major cultural traditions of the Eastern United States. West of Rodgers Shelter are the great prairies of the Southern Plains, another major ecological entourage to which man has been adapting since the end of the Wisconsin, and which saw yet another evolutionary trend that contrasted to that in the Ozark Highland.

Broadly defined, the hypotheses to be tested with the data from the shelter, and with archeological data from the Ozark Highland in general, are concerned with the articulation of culture and environment through time, viewed in contrast to the cultures developing in the great river valleys to the north and east, and the grasslands to the west. Viewed in this framework, insights are sought into the effect of the hilly environment of the Ozarks vis-à-vis those developments in adjoining regions, especially where cultural and environmental variables are recognized. (Wood and McMillan 1969: 1–2)

Enlarging the Pomme de Terre Project

Those were far-reaching goals proposed by Wood and McMillan—goals that required a truly *inter*disciplinary research approach, as opposed to the *multi*disciplinary approach typical of some archaeological projects of the time. *Multidisciplinary* means that a group of investigators from several disciplines have been assembled to work on a problem; *interdisciplinary* implies that the specialists are actually working *together* on a common problem using complementary methods. Each specialist knows what the others are doing because he or she is involved with the project on a daily basis; each learns more from the others' specialized knowledge than he or she would have learned working alone. Archaeologists often found out the hard way that you can't legislate cooperation and integration; rather, successful integration depends entirely on how well a team works together and, importantly, how the project is managed by the principal investigator.

Wood expanded his goals to include more than Rodgers Shelter and assembled an excellent team to work in the Pomme de Terre Valley. Most of the archaeologists were graduate students at the University of Missouri who had little or no fear of working in 20-ft-deep holes (Figure 6.17). Specialists included Peter Mehringer (Figure 6.18) and James King (Figure 6.19), then both of the University of Arizona, who examined pollen samples from Rodgers Shelter as well as from several bogs in the area; Everett Lindsay of the University of Arizona, who studied the Pleistocene fauna from the springs; Paul Parmalee of the Illinois State Museum, who described the vertebrate fauna from Rodgers Shelter; William Bass, then of the University of Kansas, who studied human skeletons from the shelter; and C. Vance Haynes, then of Southern Methodist University, who undertook a geomorphological analysis of the shelter and several spring localities in the valley (Figure 6.20). Each had established (or was in the process of establishing) a national reputation in his specialty, and each provided a level of expertise not commonly seen on archaeological projects.

The title Wood selected for the project was "The Archeology and Paleoecology of the Western Ozark Highlands," though the project became known informally as the Western Ozark Research Program. The term *ecology* is normally defined as the study of relations between and among organisms; where the two-legged variety is involved, the term *human ecology* (an outgrowth of the term *cultural ecology,* which had been used by Robert Lowie, Julian Steward, and others) has been adopted. Unfortunately, the general public, through lapses in Latin skills (the suffix *-ology* means, literally, "the study of"), has treated ecology as a physical entity and, further, an entity that is synonymous with *environment.* Some archaeologists (e.g., Chapman 1975) have fallen into the same trap. Although it is true that ecological relations take place within physical environments—and actually may be conditioned to some degree by environmental variables—we

Figure 6.17. Jim Simpson at the bottom of the initial test pit into the sealed deposits at Rodgers Shelter, Benton County, Missouri, 1965 (courtesy R. B. McMillan).

Figure 6.18. Peter Mehringer extracting pollen from mastodon tusk cavity, Boney Spring, Benton County, Missouri, 1968 (courtesy R. B. McMillan).

Figure 6.19. James E. King collecting pollen samples, Koch Spring, Hickory County, Missouri, 1971 (courtesy R. B. McMillan).

Figure 6.20. C. Vance Haynes examining stratigraphic profile at Rodgers Shelter, Benton County, Missouri, 1967 (courtesy R. B. McMillan).

can in no way speak of "the ecology" of an area. From a semantic standpoint, speaking of "the ecology" of an area makes about as much sense as speaking of "the archaeology" of an area. What is meant by these shorthand notations is the examination of ecological relations in an area and the study of the archaeological record of an area.

Seven seasons of work at Rodgers Shelter were spread over a 14-year period—1963–1968, 1974, and 1976—during which time comprehensive studies of other localities were undertaken. One can gain worthwhile insights into how an archaeological project progresses—especially in terms of the interplay among goals, interpretations, and field techniques—by reading the various reports that were produced between 1965 and 1982, especially those assembled in Wood and McMillan (1976). The first major statement on the archaeological record of the rock shelter was in McMillan's (1971) dissertation (University of Colorado), "Biophysical Change and Cultural Adaptation at Rodgers Shelter, Missouri," followed by two articles five years later (McMillan 1976b, 1976c). McMillan's basic working proposition when he began his analysis was that since Rodgers Shelter reflected a more or less complete (with a few minor absences) record of Holocene prehistory, it should also contain evidence of the changing physical environment in the lower Pomme de Terre locality. Specifically, periods of cool, wet conditions and periods of hot, dry conditions should be reflected by changes in the faunal, floral, and sedimentological records. Once paleoclimatic changes were documented and the directions of those changes were fixed, the artifact record could be examined for evidence of changes in form and function that paralleled paleoenvironmental changes.

Large block excavations undertaken in 1966 and 1967 were aimed at recovering materials needed to address the issue of Holocene climatic change and human response (McMillan 1971, 1976b). The mass of material that was recovered from the four major strata defined in the earlier excavations was subdivided into finer stratigraphic units and examined from the standpoints of temporal change across the shelter and terrace. For example, could different activity areas be delineated? To answer such questions, Parmalee et al. (1976) examined faunal and floral remains, and McMillan (1971) and Ahler (1971; see also Ahler and McMillan 1976 and Ahler 1979) undertook analyses of chipped-stone tools.

Ahler's (1971) analysis of bifacially flaked tools that were once hafted to bone or wooden handles or shafts was the first detailed, formal treatment of tool function that was based on Missouri materials. Basic to his analysis were five explicitly stated assumptions, the most important one being that within the broadly based category "projectile point" there exist multiple functional classes. Ahler was not the first to recognize that so-called projectile points served myriad functions, but he was among the first to formalize the criteria used to separate objects according to the suspected functions they served. Ahler also was apparently the first to use replicative use-wear experiments—in which a scientist uses a new

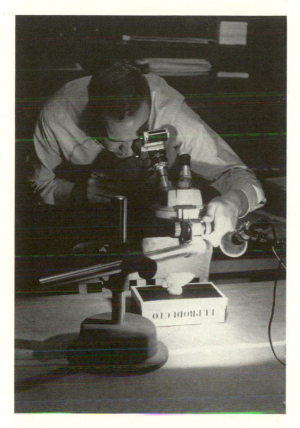

Figure 6.21. Stanley Ahler at work on his analysis of projectile-point function, 1969 (courtesy R. B. McMillan).

stone tool in different ways and then determines which of those ways leaves use marks that match those on the artifact—and microscopic examination of use-wear on Missouri materials (Figure 6.21). Microscopic examination of wear patterns on tools to determine how they were used goes back at least to the work of Sergei Semenov (1964), though by the early 1970s the technique was becoming fairly widely used in Americanist archaeology (e.g., Keeley 1974; D. F. Morse and Goodyear 1973; Nance 1971; Wilmsen 1968).

Key to understanding the depositional history of the Rodgers Shelter locality was the ability to correlate a massive amount of information into a coherent picture of environmental change. Central to this work were C. V. Haynes's (1976, 1985; see also G. R. Brackenridge 1979, 1981) geomorphological interpretations of the lower Pomme de Terre Valley and physical-chemical analysis of sediments within the shelter and on the slope below the shelter (Ahler 1973a, 1973b; McMillan 1971). A summary of the sedimentary structure of the deposit is presented below; suffice it to state here that stratigraphic changes were interpreted in terms of the availability and lack of availability of sediments throughout the Holocene caused by fluctuations in climate and the resultant effects on the Pomme de

Terre River and on hillslope vegetation. Rates of sedimentation were suspected to have averaged as high as 17.8 centimeters/100 years at ca. 8500–6000 B.C. and as low as 1.9 centimeters/100 years at ca. 4300–1000 B.C. This drop, together with an increase in the bones of prairie-dwelling taxa and a corresponding decrease in white-tailed-deer bones in Archaic-period levels in Rodgers Shelter, led McMillan (1971, 1976c) to conclude that effects of the mid-Holocene Hypsithermal, or Atlantic, climatic episode were being witnessed. As this warmer and drier climate began to prevail ca. 6500 B.C., the vegetation pattern in the region changed from one of mixed prairie and timber to one dominated by grasses. Forests moved to positions farther downslope to take advantage of shrinking water supplies. Concomitant with this change in vegetation would have been a shift in dominant taxa from edge species such as white-tailed deer to grassland taxa such as bison, prairie chicken, and antelope. As the climate returned to more moderate conditions after about 1000 B.C., edge species rebounded at the expense of grassland species. McMillan (1976c: 230) noted, "There was also increased use of aquatic resources, although it is not known if this is related to changes in the stream itself following the hypsithermal."

As detailed as the Rodgers Shelter data were, there was a definite need for new data to answer questions raised by earlier analyses. In certain areas field techniques had improved greatly over those in use in the late 1960s, resulting in the standard practice of recovering classes of items that were previously overlooked. For example, the flotation method for recovering seeds and other carbonized plant parts (Struever 1968) was becoming standard practice by 1970, and the increase in native and tropical plants being recovered from archaeological sites in the eastern United States was logarithmic. Also, the physical-chemical analyses of the shelter and terrace deposits were completed well after the last excavation season, a point noted by Ahler (1976: 123): "Perhaps the discussion here will suggest hypotheses to be investigated while future work is in progress, although it was obviously of no aid in structuring the field research design at Rodgers Shelter." Clearly, more excavation was needed.

Work resumed at Rodgers Shelter in 1974 through a grant to the Illinois State Museum from the National Park Service. By that time McMillan had become director of the museum, and his objective was to continue the long-term study begun by Wood and to fill in several gaps in the emerging picture of the paleoenvironment of the lower Pomme de Terre Valley. The NPS contract was originally for excavations at Phillips Spring, located a short distance upstream from Rodgers Shelter, but the contract was amended to continue work at Rodgers. Excavations at both sites continued in 1975 through a contract with the Kansas City District of the U.S. Army Corps of Engineers, which also supported several years of analysis. Marvin Kay (Figure 6.14, right), who had been with the program from the beginning and was responsible for the later years of excavation at Rodgers Shelter, noted the importance of continuing the work begun earlier:

[I]n reviewing these [earlier] conclusions, we (McMillan, Ahler, and I) were basically of two minds. First, we felt that there was a real need to evaluate all of the data from Rodgers Shelter. Or, if this proved impossible, at the very least to examine the major classes of finished artifacts and tools, to review their geo-morphic and stratigraphic contexts, and their configurations in space—the latter in attempts to define "macroactivity areas" insofar as these could be interpreted without reference to architectural features. Second, we realized that sampling would be needed to further examine ideas on chronology, environmental change and subsistence at Rodgers Shelter. As illustrations, there were no radiocarbon dates for the Late Archaic and Woodland units of Rodgers Shelter, the effects of an unconformity dated about 7500 B.P. on debris distributions and densities were unknown, diachronic change in artifact style had not been explored, and there were gaps in the subsistence and environmental records. (Kay 1982a: 4)

The three-volume final report (Kay 1982f), which was published several years after the work was completed, was a compilation of studies conducted primarily by the staff of the Illinois State Museum. Based on data from the 1976 excavations, Kay (1982b, 1982c) recalibrated the correlation of strata across excavated portions of the Rodgers Terrace and reexamined the depositional history of the terrace fill. New radiocarbon dates were added to the sequence, and the timing of various depositional episodes was recalculated. One interesting feature of Kay's (1982c) analysis was the separation of natural rock that occurred in the deposits into one of two categories—roof spall (small chips of stone) and alluvial deposit—to better understand the depositional sequence within and in front of the shelter. Concentrations of angular roof spall, caused by recurring periods of freezing and thawing, might indicate cooler and/or wetter winters, whereas deposits of more-rounded rocks might indicate increased upland erosion as a result of vegetation loss. Kay (1982c: 118) warned that these data should be used in conjunction with other information, since there could be several processes responsible for such concentrations of angular or rounded rocks, but his attention to those types of detail is noteworthy in itself.

Kay devoted considerable attention to an analysis of projectile-point form (Kay 1982d) and functions (Kay et al. 1982). The depth of the archaeological deposit, coupled with the amount of fill removed during excavation, led to the creation of a very significant set of chronological markers for the western Ozark Highland that probably never will be equaled.

Frances King's (1982a) reconstruction of the early historical-period vegetation of Benton County through the use of General Land Office records established a baseline against which to examine Holocene climatic and vegetation change using pollen, plant macrofossils, and vertebrate- and invertebrate-animal re-mains. The recovery of carbonized seeds from Rodgers Shelter was low (F. B. King 1982b), which was vexing given the lengthy occupation represented at the site. Analysis of gastropods (Baerreis and Theler 1982) from the standpoint of determining microclimatological change produced mixed results, as did the analysis of freshwater mussels (Klippel et al. 1978). As with the floral remains, the low numbers of specimens in several key stratigraphic layers precluded the ability to use the methods to their maximum potential.

On the other hand, because of the large number of vertebrate faunal remains, Purdue (1982) was able to examine the critical points of McMillan's thesis: that the Rodgers locale experienced significant environmental change during the Hypsithermal and that the change to hotter and drier conditions was reflected in a large increase in grassland animals such as bison and antelope and a decrease in forest-edge animals such as white-tailed deer. After examining the 1976 data, Purdue concluded that the information generally supported McMillan's thesis but that there were differences in detail. For example, some open-habitat species appeared at Rodgers Shelter in levels when the region was supposed to be forested, perhaps a result of patchy local environments.

The most significant aspect of Purdue's analysis, however, entailed examination of the body size of gray squirrels and eastern cottontails from various levels at Rodgers Shelter and of gray squirrels from Graham Cave (Klippel 1971). In all three cases early (pre-Hypsithermal) body size resembled the size of specimens found today in moister areas of the eastern United States. During the Hypsithermal, body size declined to a point equal to that found in modern specimens farther west. After the Hypsithermal, body size increased, but the animals were still smaller than those evident in pre-Hypsithermal times. Purdue's findings established an important baseline that was incorporated into many subsequent faunal analyses conducted in the Midwest.

Phillips Spring

Concurrent with the 1974 and 1975 excavations at Rodgers Shelter was the excavation of Phillips Spring, located approximately 5.5 km upstream from Rodgers (Figure 6.13). Backhoe trenches placed in the edge of the active artesian spring in 1973 demonstrated that at least two buried components were present, one at 1.5 m that dated 2330 ± 50 B.C. and another at 3 m that dated 5920 ± 90 B.C. Excavations in 1974, funded by the NPS, identified three Late Archaic components and a Late Woodland component (Chomko 1976, 1978). Of particular importance was the presence of seeds and rind of bottle gourd (*Lagenaria siceraria*) and seeds of squash (*Cucurbita pepo*) (Chomko and Crawford 1978; Kay et al. 1980), along with wooden digging sticks, in a sealed Late Archaic horizon that dated 2272 ± 57 B.C. (F. B. King 1982c; Robinson and Kay 1982). Funding from the Corps of Engineers allowed Kay to return to Phillips Spring in 1976, 1977, and 1978 to uncover more of the deposits, with an emphasis on two of the Late Archaic components that contained lanceolate Sedalia points and Sedalia "diggers" (Seelen 1961), the latter actually having served as adzes, we now know.

The 1978 excavations demonstrated the presence of no less than five separate Sedalia components above the squash-and-gourd zone (Kay 1982e).

Phillips Spring would be an important site regardless of its location, if for no other reason than that it contained stratified Late Archaic horizons and large quantities of material remains. Sedalia-complex sites are not rare occurrences in the southern Prairie Peninsula; what made Phillips Spring unusual was the sealed nature of the components and the clear separation of different occupation floors. However, it was the preservation environment, that is, water-logged deposits, that made the site unique. The presence of near-surface water led to the preservation not only of uncarbonized gourd fragments and wood, but of pollen, which was not preserved at Rodgers Shelter nor in the upper 4 m of deposits at Boney Spring, located approximately 5 km downstream from Rodgers Shelter. The pollen record confirmed the existence of an essentially modern flora throughout the late Holocene use of the spring by human groups (J. E. King 1982).

The Pleistocene Springs

Work in the lower Pomme de Terre Valley was not limited to the Holocene nor to examination of evidence of human occupation. Space precludes more than a brief account here of an entirely different—though related—focus, namely, the late Pleistocene vertebrate-faunal and palynological (pollen and spore) record of the western Ozark Highland. One of Wood's original goals was to establish a series of baseline data on late Pleistocene climate and to determine whether there existed in the numerous bogs in the valley any definite evidence of association between humans and Pleistocene fauna (Wood 1976b). Koch Spring is located south of Phillips Spring in Hickory County (Figure 6.13); recall from discussion in Chapter 2 that Koch Spring was the site of Albert Koch's work in 1840 that produced mastodon bones (Koch 1857). Several other springs in the area—Kirby, Jones, and Trolinger on the Benton–Hickory County line and Boney Spring, downstream of Rodgers Shelter—were also known to have produced faunal remains.

The sites were investigated during the 1960s and 1970s, first as part of Wood's NSF-funded project, later with funding provided to J. E. King by NSF, and finally under the Illinois State Museum's contract with the Corps of Engineers (J. E. King 1973, 1975; Saunders 1975, 1977a). Wood (1976a: 7) notes that the original intent of the excavations in the springs was to explore whether there was evidence of human associations with extinct mammals but that the reasons changed prior to the testing of Boney Spring in 1966 and Trolinger Spring in 1967. By that time it was evident that fossil pollen was not preserved in the Rodgers Shelter deposits, so the springs were cored for pollen (Figure 6.22). Work soon expanded to include major excavation of Boney Spring in 1971, Trolinger Spring in 1978 and 1979, and Jones Spring in 1971, 1973, and 1975–1977, with miscellaneous work carried out at Koch Spring and Kirby Spring in 1971. No single spring deposit contained an unbroken sequence of pollen, macrobotanical remains, or extinct mammals. Rather, sequences were punctuated—a condition Jeffrey Saunders (Figure 6.23), the primary excavator of the spring deposits, likened to the contents of time capsules of known approximate but different ages (Saunders 1983b: 8). Taken together, individual deposits and their associated faunal and floral spectra were correlated and radiometrically tied to specific chronological periods.

One interesting facet of the work at the springs was the logistics involved in working in wet environments. Early attempts to excavate the deposits at Boney Spring were fraught with difficulties because of the heavy artesian discharge. Later, excavators sunk wells at various intervals around the spring and used pumps to lower the water table to a level below the bone bed. Eventually, a 7-m-deep trench was cut to bedrock. Similar operations involving wells and excavated sluices drained water out of the other sites (including Phillips Spring) so that they also could be excavated. None of the excavations produced evidence of contemporaneity between humans and extinct animals, but the faunal and floral records that were recovered are unparalleled in the midcontinent. Not only did the excavations document a changing environment through time, as seen in the

Figure 6.22. Members of the Western Ozark Research Program pulling a sediment core from Boney Spring, Benton County, Missouri (photograph by G. Gardner, courtesy D. R. Henning).

Figure 6.23. Jeffrey J. Saunders with mastodon femurs, Boney Spring, Benton County, Missouri, 1971 (courtesy J. J. Saunders and the Illinois State Museum).

Figure 6.24. Main bone bed, Boney Spring, Benton County, Missouri (courtesy J. J. Saunders and the Illinois State Museum).

various materials recovered, but they contributed substantial information on the nature of bog formation and on the fossilization processes that structured the bone deposits over time.

Saunders's (1983b) description of the series of events that led to the formation of Boney Spring and its faunal deposits (Figure 6.24) can be generalized, recognizing differences in timing, to the other springs and deposits in the lower Pomme de Terre Valley:

> 1) reworking of older terrace gravel before 28,000 years [ago] to form the aquifer for spring activity; 2) a period of clay deposition and terrace building from 28,000 to 26,000 years ago; 3) a period of stability and peat formation from 26,000 to 23,000 years ago; 4) a second period of clay deposition and renewed terrace building from 23,000 to 20,000 years ago; 5) a second period of stability and moss mat formation from 16,500 to 13,000 years ago; 6) a third period of terrace building from perhaps 9000 to 4200 years ago; and 7) a third and Recent period of stability and peat formation from 4200 years ago to the present. . . .
>
> . . . Sometime after 20,000 years ago, the spring under pressure worked through the clays represented by the second period of terrace building and emerged upon the ground surface. Here a pond formed, trees and a moss mat grew and presumably animals came to water. At approximately 16,000 years ago discharge to the spring was disrupted and a decrease in flow occurred. The environment became [drier], organic mat vegetation ceased to develop and began to decay and animal visitation at the site became more intense. The climatic factor that seems to tie these events together best is drought, at first perhaps unpronounced and unnoticed but growing in intensity and by 13,500 years ago becoming extremely severe. It was during the severe stages of this drought that the remains of animals accumulated in and around the spring. By this stage Boney Spring had diminished to a mere trickle of water that quickly evaporated at the surface. During this interval, based on evidence of the bone bed in Boney Spring, large numbers of animals, particularly mastodons and ground sloths, were attracted to the locality and it was here, 13,500 years ago, that many of them perished. Their remains lay littered on the surface of the ground around the spring until buried in clay by the third and final phase of terrace building no later than 9000 years ago. (Saunders 1983b: 6)

The combined faunal and floral records contained in the springs were impressive and allowed the formulation of a fairly comprehensive model of the late Pleistocene environment of the lower Pomme de Terre Valley.[11] Jones Spring contained the oldest sediments of all the bogs, with initial deposits being about 49,000 years old. Botanical evidence indicated that for several thousand years after the deposits began forming the climate was mild and moist, perhaps more so

---

11. The following summary is derived from Saunders 1975, 1977b, 1983a, 1983b; J. E. King 1973; J. E. King and Lindsay 1976; and Mehringer et al. 1968, 1970.

than that of today. Vegetation consisted of deciduous trees, and animals included alligator *(Alligator mississipiensis)*, mastodon *(Mastodon americanum)*, and giant bison *(Bison latifrons)*. Prior to 40,000 years ago, this warm environment gave way to one that was cooler and drier. Pine woodlands, mixed with some stands of oak, dotted the landscape, and animal taxa included mastodon, mammoth *(Mammuthus jeffersonii)*, Harlan's ground sloth *(Glossotherium harlani)*, and large forms of bison *(Bison antiquus)*. The remains of mammoths and mastodons are not common occurrences in Missouri, though their discovery in Jones Spring was by no means a unique event. What was unique was that they were found together, since their diets came from two different kinds of environment. Mastodons' tooth structure shows that they were browsers as opposed to grazers, meaning that they ate leaves, branches, and twigs. Mammoths were grazers, and their remains usually are found with the remains of other grazers, such as bison and horses. The presence of mammoths and mastodons together in the Jones Spring deposits indicates that the vegetation pattern was a mosaic of coniferous forest and open grassland.

This environment was not long-lasting. By 38,000 years ago, as the Trolinger Spring deposit indicated, the grassland had expanded and the coniferous forest had disappeared, to be replaced by deciduous forests that were greatly reduced in extent, probably relegated to river bottoms and spring margins. The flora supported a variety of animals, including an extinct form of the black bear *(Ursus americanus amplidens)*, mammoth, two species of horse *(Equus complicatus* and *E.* cf. *scotti)*, and a smaller version of the bison than that from Boney Spring. Evidence from higher up in the Trolinger Spring deposit indicated that around 34,000 years ago the climate became cooler and more moist, and once again pine dominated the landscape. Contemporary fauna included muskoxen *(Symbos cavifrons)*, the stilt-legged deer *(Sangamona fugitiva)*, and large numbers of mastodon. Deposits at Koch Spring that were equivalent in age also yielded the remains of ground sloths.

Botanical evidence from Trolinger, Boney, and Koch springs indicated that an abrupt shift from pine to spruce occurred around 23,000 years ago, suggesting the onset of a full glacial period, with its colder and drier climate. The earliest part of the period might have witnessed the coldest climate in over 50,000 years. No remains of animals were found in those levels, likely a result of the animals' southward migration in the face of the changing climate. The final piece of the puzzle was represented in deposits at Boney Spring. Plant macrofossils and pollen, some of which were recovered from the pulp cavities of mastodon tusks, documented the presence of spruce between 16,500 and 13,500 years ago, along with several deciduous taxa such as willow, poplar, and elm. The diverse fauna included mastodon, Harlan's ground sloth, giant beaver *(Castoroides ohioensis)*, tapir *(Tapirus veroensis)*, horse, and, because the deposits were so recent, numerous small modern taxa. Within a short time, certainly by 11,000 years ago, the deciduous oak-hickory forests and grasslands would completely replace the spruce forests, signaling an end to the North American continent's last ice age. The large browsers and grazers would be replaced by smaller but certainly more diverse fauna, which humans would become very adept at hunting.

In summary, the faunal assemblages from the lower Pomme de Terre springs are unparalleled in terms of what they tell us not only about the environment of the region over the last 50,000 years but also about the animals that roamed the forests and grasslands that covered the landscape prior to human occupation. The large size of the mastodon sample—featuring the remains of 71 individuals— makes the collection unique in terms of information on the population dynamics of these large browsers during the late Pleistocene. For example, the overall larger size of animals that lived in spruce forests as compared to those in pine forests (Saunders 1983a) indicates that in terms of available food supply versus energy expenditure, the former was a superior habitat. Also, the late Pleistocene samples contained a higher proportion of prime individuals than did other samples, leading Saunders (1983a) to suggest that by the end of the Pleistocene mastodon populations had become self-regulating—a situation that would soon change with the onset of warmer Holocene temperatures. Failure to maintain any sort of population regulation led to rapid extinction of animals not only in western Missouri but across the midcontinent.

The Project's Legacy

It is difficult to overestimate the importance of the decade-plus of work carried out in the lower Pomme de Terre Valley under the auspices of the Western Ozark Research Program. Wood, McMillan, and their associates (Figure 6.25) were able to effectively maintain over a long period of time a scientific interest in one particular locale—something that before that time had not been accomplished in Missouri. Prior research in the state, while it would be unfair to call all of it hit-or-miss, was rarely sustained in any particular locality for more than a few field seasons. There were various reasons for this, one perhaps being Chapman's eclectic interests and another his realization of how much there was to be done. Short of time and money, he decided to get the most widespread overview rather than more detail from fewer places. Wood's interests were not limited only to paleoenvironments or to the cultural record of the lower Pomme de Terre Valley—he had, after all, already established a national reputation in Plains prehistory and worked for several seasons in Arkansas before coming to the University of Missouri—but he recognized an excellent opportunity when he saw one and took it to its natural conclusion.

The results of the program begun by Wood and completed under McMillan and Kay speak for themselves. No other program in the Midwest comes close

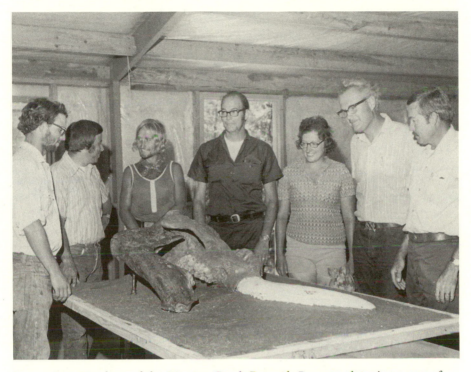

Figure 6.25. Members of the Western Ozark Research Program donating a cast of a mastodon mandible and maxilla to the Fristoe, Missouri, museum, 1971: from left to right, Louis Jacobs, R. Bruce McMillan, Jeffrey J. Saunders, W. Raymond Wood, Frances B. King, James E. King, C. Vance Haynes (courtesy W. R. Wood).

to the Western Ozark Research Program in terms of the kind of data it generated relative to understanding human responses to changing paleolandscapes.[12] Work at Rodgers Shelter produced what was at the time the longest cultural sequence for Missouri and yielded an unparalleled view of changes in artifact form and function. Excavations at Phillips Spring added information on Late Archaic–period use of the region and contributed evidence of some of the oldest cultigens in the eastern United States. Almost as an added bonus, the project also generated important data on late Pleistocene fauna that were indigenous to mixed-vegetation parklands and then to glacial-period spruce forests.

Perhaps equally important was the training that the numerous students who took part in the project received. Students at the University of Missouri, dating back to the days of Wrench and Berry and continuing through the decades

12. Most published reviews of the project were positive (e.g., Krause 1977), though one (Newton 1978), ranks in my opinion as the most vicious, ad hominem attack I have ever seen.

that Chapman directed archaeological research in the state, had taken active roles in running archaeological projects and writing the final reports. Chapman's first three graduate students—Wilfred Logan, Robert Bray, and Richard Marshall—graduated in the 1950s, and all went on to productive careers in archaeology: Logan with the National Park Service, Bray first with NPS and then with the University of Missouri, and Marshall first with Missouri and then with Mississippi State University. Wood continued this tradition, placing a significant number of students in the NPS and various universities and museums. When McMillan became director of the Illinois State Museum (ISM), he hired numerous Wood students in the Quaternary Studies Program, several of whom (e.g., Walter Klippel and Marvin Kay) have gone on to have distinguished careers at various universities.[13] McMillan (1992: 8) credits Wood as being the impetus for the development of the internationally known program in Quaternary studies housed at the ISM: "I am in the unique position to know, that if it had not been for the vision of Ray Wood in 1965 who instilled in some of us the importance of interdisciplinary research, the program . . . in which I am so intimately involved, would not be here today."

There was another legacy left behind by the Western Ozark Research Program —one that is much more subtle than the outstanding scientific merits of the program or the training that it provided students, but nevertheless one that had a direct bearing on the future of Missouri archaeology. This was the involvement of institutions from outside Missouri in archaeological programs undertaken in the state. The involvement of the ISM in an archaeological project in the western Ozarks of Missouri made perfect sense from a variety of standpoints, not the least of which was the fact that McMillan, the museum director, had been with the project since its inception. McMillan's leaving Missouri for Illinois certainly did not carry with it a requirement that he turn over his license as a Missouri archaeologist,[14] nor was there a stipulation that he had to surrender his interest in Missouri prehistory. In fact, McMillan strengthened his hand substantially through the addition of more Missouri archaeologists to his staff (e.g., Klippel and later Kay), in the process picking up Jeffrey Saunders and James and Frances King, all three of whom had been involved with the Ozarks project for years. By the mid-1970s, McMillan had a formidable staff, and it was natural that the National Park Service would turn to the museum to continue the excavations at Rodgers Shelter and to expand research to include Phillips Spring. The Kansas City District of the U.S. Army Corps of Engineers continued

13. Although McMillan, Klippel, and Kay technically were Chapman's students (meaning he served as chairperson of their graduate committees), they obviously were greatly influenced by Wood.

14. Although I am using *license* in a metaphorical sense, there were movements in the 1970s to license archaeologists in certain states or to require national certification (see Chapter 7).

this contractual arrangement in 1975, though the University of Missouri was awarded a concurrent contract for additional survey and excavation in Truman Reservoir.

The presence of the ISM in Missouri signaled a definite end to the University of Missouri's monopoly on archaeology in the state, but that monopoly had been slowly disappearing for a number of years. Archaeological work by non-Missouri institutions had certainly occurred throughout the twentieth century, but most projects—such as the sporadic excavations in Jacobs Cavern—were short-term endeavors that never seriously threatened the centrality of the university. Even the lower Mississippi Valley survey conducted by Phillips et al. (1951), as well as subsequent spin-off surveys (e.g., Griffin and Spaulding 1952; S. Williams 1954), were rather short-term affairs. There was, however, one project that shifted the spotlight away from the university, and that was the Powers Phase Project, a University of Michigan–sponsored program (funded through grants from the National Science Foundation) in the late 1960s that focused on the examination of Mississippian-period occupation in the Western Lowland (primarily Butler and Ripley counties) of the Mississippi alluvial valley. During the course of its life, the project became the training ground for a score of archaeologists who since have made significant contributions to the discipline. The project rightfully deserves an important place in the history of Americanist archaeology in terms of its goals and accomplishments, especially the almost total excavation of several Mississippian-period communities.

Mississippian-Period Prehistory and the Powers Phase Project

Most of the fieldwork connected with the Powers Phase Project was completed in the late 1960s and early 1970s, though publication dates of articles and monographs that resulted from the project date several years later. So much material was excavated by project personnel that only now, with enhanced analytical capabilities provided by computing equipment, are many of the artifacts being examined for the first time. The significance of the Powers Phase Project will be more easily understood if I place it and its subject matter—the ca. A.D. 1100–1350 portion of the archaeological record in the Western Lowland of the central Mississippi alluvial valley—in a broader geographical and historical context.

Despite the prominence of numerous southeastern-Missouri Mississippian-period sites in the archaeological literature (e.g., Chapman 1980; D. F. Morse and P. A. Morse 1983), our knowledge of the archaeological record of most of those sites is woefully inadequate. As D. F. Morse and P. A. Morse (1990: 166) note, "The Cairo Lowland region is more complex than the remainder of the Central Valley in terms of the identification of a progressional sequence of events after A.D. 1000.

Most sites are multicomponent and have received only minimal excavation or analyses." Morse and Morse singled out the Cairo Lowland because it has received considerable archaeological investigation, though there is little reason to judge it any differently than any of the other named lowlands in southeastern Missouri. Few "progressional sequences" in any of them are well understood.

Excavation of Mississippian-period sites in southeastern Missouri indeed has been minimal, unless one includes the antiquarian-oriented work undertaken at numerous sites during the late nineteenth century. What lured many of those early investigators to the region were the impressive mounded (Rich Woods) and mounded and/or palisaded settlements (Peter Bess, Lakeville, Sandy Woods, County Line, Beckwith's Fort, Matthews, Sikeston, East Lake, and Lilbourn) (see J. R. Williams 1964 for a summary of the sites) located throughout the Eastern Lowlands. Most of the centers, at one time or another, have been lumped in the Cairo Lowland phase, a term coined by S. Williams (1954) after he completed his survey of southeastern-Missouri sites (Chapter 5) and his excavations at Crosno, a large, fortified site in Mississippi County. Williams described the Cairo Lowland phase—what he termed "the typical Mississippian manifestation in this region" (S. Williams 1954: 31)—in the following manner: "It may be characterized as having rather compact and well laid out sites often surrounded by a wall and a ditch. A medium sized mound usually adjoins a well-defined plaza area" (S. Williams 1954: 273). Phillips (1970: 925) considered the Cairo Lowland phase to be the "most profusely documented phase in the Lower Mississippi Valley, if not the entire southeast." However, that statement reflected more on the two dozen or so antiquarian-oriented publications detailing unprovenienced ceramic mortuary assemblages from Cairo Lowland–phase sites than on the status of rigorous classificatory-historical research.

Excavations at several of the fortified communities in the Eastern Lowlands, though not extensive, give us some idea of the layout and dates of occupation of the communities. The largest center is Beckwith's Fort (which the state of Missouri renamed Towosahgy after purchasing the site for a state park) in Mississippi County (Figure 6.26). Houck (1908) claimed that at one time artifacts were scattered over 300–400 acres and that the site contained 20 mounds, though this apparently was an inflated figure. Today, a continuous spread of artifacts covers an area in excess of roughly 50 acres, and remnants of 7 mounds are evident within the palisade line and fortification ditch (J. E. Price and Fox 1990; see also Chapman et al. 1977). Most radiocarbon dates fall between A.D. 1100 and 1300, but there is also evidence (radiocarbon and ceramic) that the center may not have been abandoned until the 1400s. Healan's (1972) surface collection of Beckwith's Fort documented several spatially discrete clusters of Baytown-period (the term used to encompass both the Middle Woodland and Late Woodland periods in the Mississippi alluvial valley) and Mississippian-period sherds, though the majority of collection units contained sherds of both periods.

Figure 6.26. Aerial photograph (looking north-northeast) of Beckwith's Fort, Mississippi County, Missouri (date unknown). The trees mark locations of mounds; the circular band of lighter colored sediments mark the location of the ditch and fortification wall that encircled part of the community (from Chapman 1980).

Lilbourn, perhaps the second-largest center (Figure 6.27), received extensive excavation in 1970 and 1971 prior to destruction of part of the site in advance of expansion of a vocational-technical school (Chapman et al. 1977). Excavations revealed a complicated archaeological signature, with numerous examples of houses having been erected on top of other houses and burial pits placed through earlier burials. Few of the tens of thousands of artifacts (Figure 6.28) have been analyzed, though available data suggest that the center was contemporaneous with other large fortified communities in the Cairo Lowland. Radiocarbon dates span the period ca. A.D. 1100–1370.

If the excavations that have been undertaken at these large centers (Figure 2.10)—including those at Matthews (Croswell 1878; Walker and Adams 1946), Sikeston (Potter 1880), Sandy Woods (Potter 1880; Rust 1877), and Lakeville (C. Thomas 1891)—have demonstrated anything, it is that the sites are complex in terms of stratigraphy and layout. In addition to the examples given above, Fox's (1992) reanalysis of S. Williams's (1954) stratigraphic cuts at Crosno demonstrates the extremely homogeneous nature of the midden deposit, despite the depth of the midden and the fact that the site appears to have been occupied for several hundred years.

Figure 6.27. Aerial photograph (north to the top) of the Lilbourn site, New Madrid County, Missouri, 1941. The large mound excavated by G. C. Swallow is in the grove of trees slightly below the center of the photograph; the fortification walls and some of the house outlines are clearly evident (from Chapman 1980, courtesy U.S. Soil Conservation Service).

Figure 6.28. Skeleton with chipped-stone mace from the Lilbourn site, New Madrid County, Missouri (from Chapman 1980). The skeleton was one of many excavated at Lilbourn by the University of Missouri in the mid-1970s (see Chapman and Evans 1977).

The genesis of the large, fortified centers is unknown (but see below), though it is clear that sometime after ca. A.D. 1000 populations in the Mississippi alluvial valley underwent a change in how they distributed themselves across the landscape. Instead of residing in small, dispersed communities, at least some segments of the population nucleated in certain localities and constructed palisades around their centers. It also seems clear that this was a rearrangement by local populations as opposed to a settlement pattern effected by intrusive groups—a statement based on the fact that all the centers contain earlier components that exhibit artifact suites not unlike the later assemblages. The reasons for the disruption in settlement pattern are unknown, though the literature is rife with speculation. It is equally clear that not all of the population of southeastern Missouri lived in the fortified settlements. Literally hundreds of other communities (some quite large) appear to have been in use at the same time as the big centers, but the relation of the nonfortified settlements to the fortified ones is unclear.

D. F. Morse and P. A. Morse (1983: 264) speculate that the following sequence of events led to the development of at least one of the centers, Beckwith's Fort (Towosahgy):

> A ceremonial center developed after the Hoecake site [located just north of Beckwith's Fort] was largely abandoned and the population concentrated more upon the meander belt soils of this portion of the Cairo Lowland. Towosahgy at this time was a dispersed site of mounds and residential areas over an area of perhaps up to several hundred hectares. At some time during the twelfth century a fortified civic-ceremonial center that was more restrictive in area was constructed within the dispersed mound area. . . . Such a center would have provided refuge to the population dependent upon the center.

The question that is unanswerable at present is why the population would have sought refuge. If we take the sudden development of the fortified centers to be an indication of increased intergroup hostility—a consideration without much support from other evidence (a few skeletons from Turner, in the Western Lowland, had arrow points embedded in them [Black 1979])—then perhaps the population relied on the center for defensive purposes.

This is exactly the scenario that has been used to explain the development of the centers—defense from neighboring groups—and it is closely related to the explanation archaeologists have developed relative to the rise of Mississippian society in general, namely, the formation of powerful, and often competing, chiefdoms. It is almost impossible to pick up an article or book on the Mississippian period (e.g., Chapman 1980; D. F. Morse and P. A. Morse 1983; J. E. Price 1973, 1978; Smith 1990b) and not find repeated reference to the evolution of chiefdoms during the middle portion of the period. Views are split over the precise nature of the chiefdoms. Chapman (1980) viewed each fortified community as the apex of a chiefdom, with outlying settlements ranked below the central community. D. F. Morse and P. A. Morse (1983), on the other hand, argued that some of the smaller fortified centers, such as Crosno (S. Williams 1954), were subsidiary to the larger sites (in the case of Crosno, to Beckwith's Fort). Based on the results of survey and excavation carried out during the Powers Phase Project, James E. Price (1973, 1978; see also J. E. Price and Griffin 1979) proposed that the single fortified community in the Western Lowland portion of Missouri, Powers Fort, was at the apex of a settlement system that included at the next level several pairs of communities that contained substantial populations, followed by much smaller communities, followed by single-family farmsteads (Figure 6.29). This hierarchical model has been extended by a number of archaeologists (e.g., Chapman 1980) into the Eastern Lowlands to account for the settlement systems connected with the fortified communities there.

The genesis of the Powers Phase Project initiated by the University of Michigan was the discovery by Price, while an undergraduate student at the University of Missouri, of several Mississippian-period sites near the Little Black River in western Butler County, just southeast of the town of Naylor. Price subsequently excavated a small portion of one site, Turner, in 1966 and found that the village had burned, which appeared to have effectively sealed the house floors and everything that was on them at the time. The remarkable state of preservation of Turner—a phenomenon suspected to exist at other Mississippian-period communities in the area—and its potential for addressing numerous questions about Mississippian life in the central Mississippi Valley was not lost on Griffin when he visited the locality in 1966. Through the Museum of Anthropology at the University of Michigan, Griffin supplied funding for continued excavations at Turner during 1966 and 1967, during which time Griffin and Price wrote a successful NSF grant to continue excavations at several other Mississippian-period sites in the region.

The centerpiece of the University of Michigan's work was the excavation of Turner and Snodgrass, another burned Mississippian-period village. Both were situated on the crests of sand ridges, which are typical topographic features in the Western Lowland—that expanse of Pleistocene-age Mississippi River floodplain and terraces bounded by the Ozark Escarpment on the west and Crowley's Ridge on the east. One interesting feature of Turner and Snodgrass is that they were located only about 150 meters apart. The research design established by Griffin and Price called for the almost complete excavation of the two communities and the testing of several others, which was carried out between 1966 and 1976. They also surveyed over 200 square kilometers of the Little Black River drainage and located 80 Mississippian-period sites.

Burned Mississippian-period houses were not unique to Turner and Snodgrass; what set them apart from other occurrences was the state of preservation of the structures and related artifact-bearing deposits. The sites' location on large sand ridges connected with the Pleistocene-age braided-stream channels of the

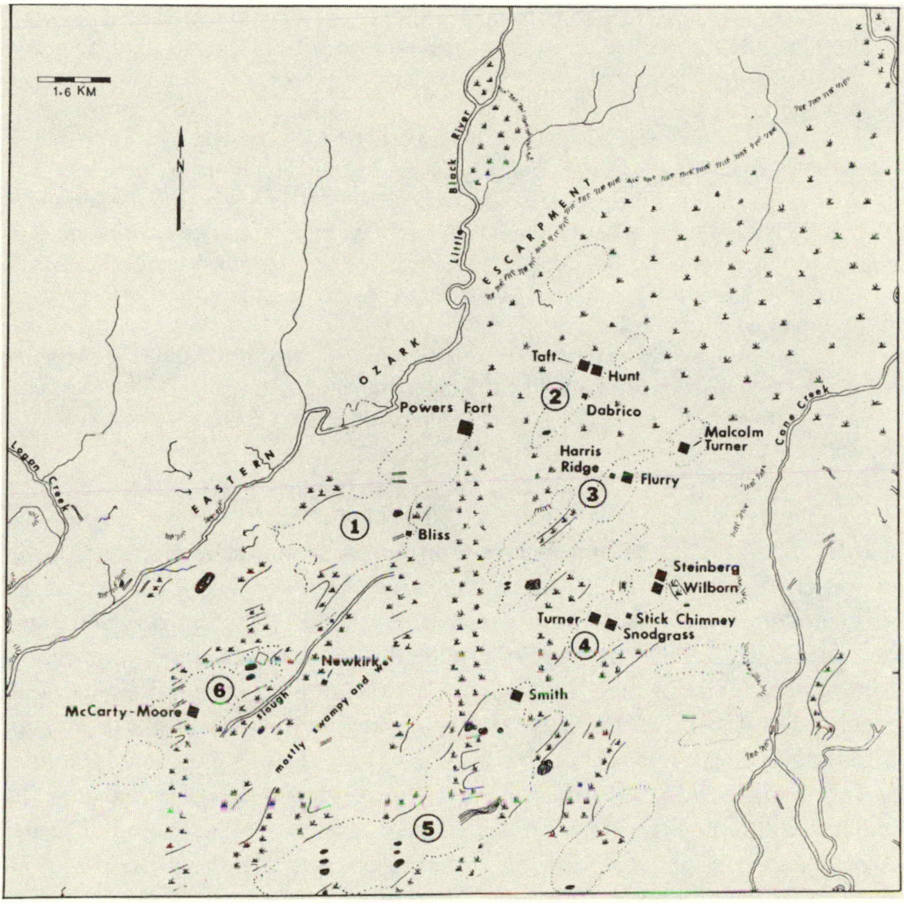

Figure 6.29. Map showing distribution of Powers-phase settlements, Butler County, Missouri. Numbers refer to sand ridges, which comprise sediments associated with braided-stream channels of the ancestral Mississippi River. The relative sizes of settlements are designated by the sizes of the blocks (from J. E. Price 1978, courtesy Academic Press).

Mississippi River—logical places for habitation and agriculture in a low-lying region susceptible to frequent flooding—insured their survival. Coarse sediments, which are constantly being reworked by wind and rain, spread over the villages from higher-elevation areas on the ridge network and created an effective barrier against erosion and destruction through modern plowing and disking.

However, the nature of the sand ridges made survey difficult, and the number of sites missed during the survey is unknown. Price's comments on the biasing effects of the sandy surface are of more than passing interest because they represent one of the most succinct assessments ever to appear in print:

Perhaps the most frustrating factor for site detection in the lowland zones of the Little Black River area involves a surface-obscuring phenomenon we do not fully understand. Sites on the sandy loam ridges in the area are sometimes obvious and at other times are completely obscured. Large village sites, the Steinberg site being an example, were discovered in areas that had been repeatedly surveyed several times by at least three individuals. If surface conditions are not exactly right, no evidence of prehistoric occupation is visible. Two weeks later the surface may be littered with cultural materials. A slight shifting of surface sand by wind is probably responsible for this phenomenon. We have observed the Turner site when only about five sherds could be collected from the surface even after it had been plowed and rains had fallen on it.

There is a possibility that some sites are buried beneath duned sand. The Flurry site was first discovered in a road cut, and subsequent subsurface reconnaissance revealed that most of the western side of the site was buried under several feet of drifted sand. (J. E. Price 1978: 212)

Despite the biasing effects of the sedimentological environment, Turner and Snodgrass were not the only burned communities found on the sand ridges of western Ripley County. Some of the others were similar in size to Turner and Snodgrass, and some were considerably smaller (Figure 6.29). In fact, there appeared to be a size hierarchy, with Powers Fort at the top, followed by communities of 40 or more houses, then by communities of 10–12 houses, and finally by tiny 1- or 2-house sites (J. E. Price 1973, 1978; Price and Griffin 1979). Interestingly, at least 3 and probably 4 other sets of "paired communities" similar to Turner and Snodgrass existed on surrounding sand ridges (Figure 6.29). The paired communities themselves appeared to be of two sizes. For example, Turner covered an area of about 1.5 acres, while Snodgrass was about 2.5 acres in size—a size dichotomy noticed in other pairs, as well.

J. E. Price (1973, 1974, 1978) and Price and Griffin (1979) labeled the aggregate settlement array the Powers phase, characterized as "a Mississippian influx into the Western Lowland of Southeast Missouri as a colonization effort that failed" (Price 1978: 225). I doubt seriously that there was ever a "colonization." Whether or not the effort failed, there is no question that the communities were short-lived. Radiocarbon and thermoluminescence dates (Lynott 1987) from Turner, Snodgrass, and Powers Fort place the sites between ca. A.D. 1200 and 1350. For whatever reason, the Powers-phase communities "were consumed by fire, bringing the cultural activities to an abrupt and instantaneous halt" (J. E. Price and Griffin 1979: 7). All the communities around Powers Fort appear to have burned either at the same time or within a short period of time. This does not appear to have been the fate of Mississippian communities in the Eastern Lowlands, which, while showing scattered evidence of burning, do not exhibit the amount of destruction seen in Powers-phase communities.

The excavations of Turner and Snodgrass (J. E. Price 1969, 1973; J. E. Price and Griffin 1979), as well as minor excavations at several other sites such as

Taft and Flurry, yielded numerous insights into what "villages" from the middle portion of the Mississippian period looked like in the Western Lowland. Based on the slightly earlier mean of the radiocarbon dates from Turner (A.D. 1308 [corrected][15] as opposed to A.D. 1343 [corrected] from Snodgrass), that village may have been occupied before Snodgrass.[16] It contained 48 structures arranged linearly, with a supposed plaza area between two of the rows. Supposedly when Turner was abandoned and Snodgrass was founded, the Snodgrass inhabitants buried their dead in the small plaza area at Turner, where 118 children and adults were interred in 54 graves (Black 1979). Snodgrass contained 90 houses, 38 of which were located inside a walled area (Figure 6.30), with the rest arranged outside the wall and within a ditch that encircled the village. Significant differences in house size were evident at the site, with the largest houses, which averaged 30 square meters, located within the inner walled area. Only 6 adults were found interred at Snodgrass, though numerous infant burials were found beneath house floors.

In a historical sense, the excavation of Turner and Snodgrass represented a turning point in Mississippian-period archaeology. As Griffin (1985b: 15) noted, there had been no Mississippian sites anywhere in the eastern United States excavated almost in their entirety (Figure 6.31) before those two sites. Griffin raised another point about the excavations that I should insert here because it was characteristic of the 1960s, namely, that researchers used the latest method or technique being espoused in the literature of the new archaeology. One of those techniques was random sampling. A person might not have understood *how* to use it, but they knew they were *supposed* to use it:

> At that time random sampling was the golden key to unlocking the door to many archaeological questions, and some number of graduate students, when we initiated the field program, were insistent that random sampling should be the procedure followed. However, we already knew where an adequate number of sites were located, their dimensions, the locations of house structures, and that surface finds demonstrated rough contemporaneity. . . . I thought it was more important to deviate from a then popular acceptable archaeological approach. (Griffin 1985b: 15)

Another component of the Powers Phase Project entailed excavation of one of the smallest sites found during survey to gain a better understanding of the role played by suspected "farmsteads" in the Powers-phase settlement system. The candidate selected for excavation was Gypsy Joint, located on a sand ridge

15. Corrections were made using Damon et al. 1974.

16. All artifacts from Turner and Snodgrass are undergoing systematic analysis by Bruce Smith of the National Museum of Natural History. One goal of the work is to develop a better understanding of the timing of the founding and abandonment of the two communities.

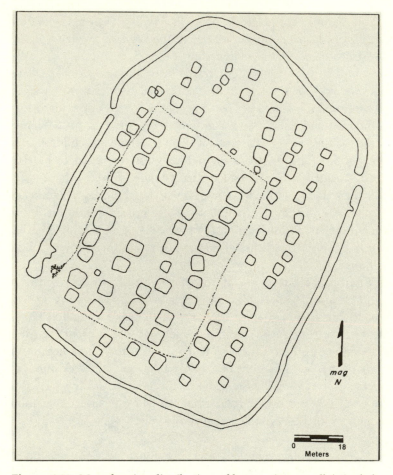

Figure 6.30. Map showing distribution of houses, inner wall (stippled line), and palisade ditch at the Snodgrass site, Butler County, Missouri (from J. E. Price 1978, courtesy Academic Press).

a few kilometers southwest of Powers Fort. The small site (360 square meters) contained two structures, a burial, eight pits, and a concentration of charred maize (Figure 6.32). The house structure, which measured approximately 5 meters on a side, had been constructed of single posts set in a shallow basin. Excavation and analysis of the site was carried out by Bruce Smith (Figure 6.33), one of Griffin's graduate students at the University of Michigan. Readers interested in the role formal, processual studies played in the development of Americanist archaeology during the 1960s and 1970s should read Smith's (1978) analysis of the materials from Gypsy Joint.

Smith produced what is in my mind the best-reasoned report on a Mississippian-period site published in the 1970s. This statement is not intended to

Figure 6.31. Mechanically stripped area and excavated features at the Snodgrass site, Butler County, Missouri (courtesy B. D. Smith).

denigrate the other reports that came out of the Powers Phase Project, but all of them were descriptive as opposed to analytical statements. Smith had the luxury of dealing with a fairly small assemblage compared to the hundreds of boxes of material from Turner and Snodgrass, and he used the opportunity to undertake a detailed analysis of what happened over a few years at a small site. The basic problem he staked out was to define the niche of the site in the overall cultural system of the Powers phase (Smith 1978: 16). To address this problem, he asked five questions: (1) During which season(s) was the site occupied? (2) What was the duration of the occupation(s)? (3) What was the size of the occupying group? (4) What activities were carried out? and (5) What ties did the users of the site have to other Powers-phase groups? Smith had considerable experience in dealing with faunal remains from Mississippian-period sites in the immediate region (Smith 1974a, 1974b, 1975, 1976), and he saw that answers to some of the research questions probably lay in detailed analysis of the numerous animal bones from Gypsy Joint.

To answer the questions in as straightforward a manner as possible, Smith proposed a series of mutually exclusive propositions (he used the term *hypotheses*) and then established a series of predictions drawn from each—predictions that provided a link between the propositions and what would be expected to occur in the artifact assemblage (see also Smith 1977). He then evaluated each

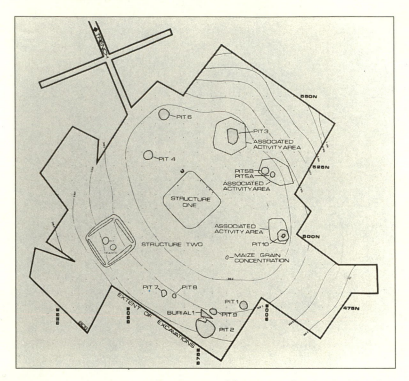

Figure 6.32. Map showing distribution of features at the Gypsy Joint site, Butler County, Missouri (from Smith 1978).

proposition against a wide range of material remains, especially animal bones and carbonized seeds, in an exhaustive assessment of the relative strength of alternative propositions. The conclusion Smith drew from the analysis was that Gypsy Joint had been occupied for about three years by a nuclear family. In one of the most carefully crafted caveats ever placed in an archaeological report, he quickly added, "It should be clearly kept in mind that this account does not consist of conclusions that are known to be factually correct. Rather it represents a set of interrelated conclusions that are supported by explicitly stated inductive arguments within the framework of the full scientific method. It is of course up to the reader to decide whether or not these conclusions are reasonable and, in fact, supported by the arguments presented" (Smith 1978: 196). This is about as honest a statement as one could possibly hope for.

Smith successfully bypassed much of the posturing of the new archaeology that was in vogue during the 1960s and early 1970s, as archaeologists attempted to convince the discipline that to do science one had to subscribe to the "hypothetico-deductive" school of reasoning. Much of what had been said (and published) had been so polemical—all talk with little product—that it turned

Figure 6.33. Bruce D. Smith (standing, center) and field crew in the Advance Lowland of southeastern Missouri, 1979. Smith is better known for his work on the Powers Phase Project in Butler and Ripley counties, Missouri, but in 1979 he initiated a large-scale survey of the northwestern corner of the Mississippi Embayment—that section of the Mississippi River valley that stretches from just south of Cape Girardeau, Missouri, to the Gulf of Mexico (courtesy B. D. Smith).

off more than a few archaeologists who might otherwise have benefited from a solid exposition on the differences between empiricism and intuition (see Chapter 8). Smith, on the other hand, took it for granted that the only way to arrive at a reasonable answer—and he knew it would be reasonable only for the time being—was by operating empirically, which simply means, as I discuss in Chapter 9, that the evidence cannot at the moment fit any other conclusion than the one put forward. But to demonstrate this, all competing propositions have to be shown to be false. It can't be demonstrated by creating a "just so" story that appears to accommodate the available data. Unfortunately, Missouri archaeology in the late 1960s and 1970s was replete with just-so stories.

7

Archaeology as Big Business

The Late 1970s

Despite the archaeological interest that the University of Michigan's Powers Phase Project sparked, and the wide coverage that it received, one could arguably claim that it did little to diminish the University of Missouri's place at the center of Missouri archaeology. The university's monopoly on the archaeology of the state might have been weakened a bit, but the presence of an outside institution did not undermine the university's share of the fieldwork that was available since the university already had more work than it could possibly handle. The Powers Phase Project was funded by the National Science Foundation, while the University of Missouri received the vast majority of its funding for archaeological research from the National Park Service; as long as the NPS funds were available, the university was more than able to keep its archaeologists employed. If the University of Michigan wanted to apply for NSF funds to work in southeastern Missouri, so much the better, since the University of Missouri wouldn't get around to excavating those sites anyway. As long as an institution from outside the state did its own thing without horning in on the university's federal-contract operation, everyone was welcome.

The early work in the lower Pomme de Terre Valley was similarly sponsored by NSF, first through a grant to the University of Missouri but later through one to the Illinois State Museum (ISM). Again, this did not disrupt the university's ability to receive federal-contract funds and in fact was a plus for the university, since some of its archaeologists were major players in the ISM program. Everything changed in 1974, when the NPS awarded the contract for additional work in the lower Pomme de Terre Valley not to the university but to the ISM. For the first time, an institution other than the university—and one from outside the state, to boot—was involved in contract archaeology, that is, non-NSF-sponsored archaeology, within Missouri. Worse yet, the university was on the verge of losing the biggest contract that it had ever hoped to receive—funding from the U.S.

Army Corps of Engineers for long-term survey and excavation in the Cannon Reservoir, which was worth hundreds of thousands (perhaps millions) of dollars. What had happened to the monopoly that the university once had on archaeology in the state? More importantly, where did all this competition suddenly come from?

Where did it come from, indeed. The answer was that the competition stemmed in large part from the efforts of one man who was concerned that not enough money was being spent on contract archaeology in the United States. That one man was none other than Carl Chapman, who was ultimately responsible for opening the floodgates of federal support for archaeology not only in Missouri but in every other state as well. The only thing was, the money spent in Missouri didn't all go where he thought it probably would. It didn't all go the University of Missouri. Chapman couldn't have anticipated this in 1969 and 1970, when he began setting in motion his dream of big-buck archaeology. He undoubtedly realized it in 1974, when the park service contracted with the ISM for continued work in the lower Pomme de Terre Valley.

Contract archaeology—literally, the performance, for a fee, of an archaeological investigation under a set of conditions agreed upon by two or more parties—has been around in one guise or another for decades. We've already seen its influence on the archaeology of the 1930s—during the height of the New Deal era—and later during the days of the River Basin Surveys. By the late 1960s archaeologists had been conditioned to working with state and federal agencies on various highway and reservoir projects, and some of the most prominent and influential American archaeologists had taken active roles in the research. Few archaeologists of the time, I suspect, ever turned down contracts because they weren't of the "pure" research type. Rather, they took them because there literally was no difference between the type of archaeology called for in the contract and the type they had been doing for years. In Missouri, for example, surveys and excavations in Table Rock, Stockton, Pomme de Terre, Kaysinger Bluff (Harry S. Truman), and Joanna (Clarence Cannon) reservoirs were carried out in the same fashion that they were outside the reservoirs: one looked for sites, recorded their locations, and selected the most promising ones for excavation. "Most promising" usually meant the ones that would produce the most artifacts and/or the longest cultural sequence.

Contract work during the 1950s and 1960s was a bonanza for archaeologists at the University of Missouri, both in terms of expanding their knowledge of the archaeological record and in terms of generating sorely needed funding for the support of students. The reservoirs, which were the foci of most of the federal funds expended during that period, contained large numbers of sites, and large numbers of sites meant that the chances of finding rich sites to excavate rose appreciably. Chapman was able to mobilize his staff in the American

Archaeology Division, which he had established in the late 1940s as a research wing of the Department of Sociology and Anthropology,[1] and set off to explore new areas.

Even by 1960 large areas of Missouri had never been investigated from the standpoint of archaeological potential, especially some of the rugged terrain in the western Ozarks, and this was where many of the reservoirs were going to be constructed. This must have seemed like it was manna from heaven—cash from the National Park Service to spend exploring the archaeological potential of relatively unknown regions. All that was required was to find the sites, report their locations, and then apply for more money to excavate some of them. What could be easier? Probably nothing, although there was a catch: the NPS didn't have the kind of money that it took to excavate a Rodgers Shelter or to perform the exacting work required to examine the depositional history of a Pleistocene bog.

As long as the archaeologist's interests were focused on surveys of likely site locations and on quick excavation, the funding level was adequate. But when those interests turned to painstakingly slow excavation and analysis, the latter of which could easily consume one-half to three-quarters of the budget, something had to give. As we saw with Rodgers Shelter, what gave was dependence on NPS funding, with a shift to National Science Foundation support. However, suppose that, despite the obvious importance of the site, NSF had declined to fund the project? After all, NSF receives more deserving proposals each year than it can possibly fund—a point I will return to later. Suppose it had also had to turn down specialists Everett Lindsay and James King, who submitted proposals to study pollen samples and fauna in the Pomme de Terre Valley? What would we know about the cultural sequence of the region or about the Pleistocene vegetative and faunal records? The answer is that we would know where some sites were located and to what periods they dated, but we wouldn't know much more. This situation bothered a lot of archaeologists, who witnessed similar ironies in other states. The funding was there to do archaeology, but if one sunk all the available funds into a single site, there was no money left to take care of all the other sites. Of course, this problem had been around since at least the early days of the River Basin Surveys (e.g., Wedel 1967)—too little money and often too little time.

One might ask, weren't there laws that protected the sites until they could be investigated? The answer is that yes, there were a variety of laws, but none of them provided protection for the lengths of time that would have been required if excavation were to be put off until archaeologists could reach all threatened sites, nor did they really provide the level of funding necessary to conduct intensive investigations, particularly of the interdisciplinary kind that was becoming more

1. The department split into separate sociology and anthropology departments in 1965.

important during the late 1960s. Laws pertaining to federal responsibility vis-à-vis archaeological properties on federal lands had been around since 1906, when Congress, at the urging of archaeologists in the Southwest, passed the Antiquities Act to protect against vandalism of ruins, monuments, and anything else of antiquity on lands owned or controlled by the federal government. Passage of the Historic Sites, Buildings, and Antiquities Act of 1935 strengthened the provisions of the earlier act and led to the eventual formation, in 1945, of the Inter-Agency Archaeological Salvage Program (Chapter 4).

It was in the 1960s, however, that the most wide-ranging and probably the most important protective legislation was passed, beginning with the Reservoir Salvage Act of 1960, which continued the Department of the Interior's lead role in addressing the loss of archaeological information to reservoir construction. The act was intended to remedy the chronic underfunding of reservoir-salvage projects (Reaves 1976), but no enabling legislation was ever passed to provide funding. A more significant piece of legislation was the National Historic Preservation Act of 1966. No one at the time had the slightest idea of the nightmare that the act would impose on archaeology, because in concept the legislation was extremely appealing. It placed considerable authority with the secretary of the Department of the Interior and directed him or her to create a National Register of Historic Places that would list significant archaeological and historical sites. Note the word *significant;* we will return to it shortly. The act also called for establishing a President's Advisory Council on Historic Preservation, which, through section 106 of the act, was given a review-and-commentary function in instances where National Register properties were to be affected adversely by federally funded activities.

At the close of the decade came what Bob McGimsey (1976) called the most important piece of archaeological legislation ever passed—the National Environmental Policy Act of 1969. This act called for the compilation of environmental-impact statements before any project is undertaken by a federal agency. The statements were specifically to include reports on archaeological, historical, and cultural resources. As important as this legislation was in addressing up-front adverse impacts that federally funded activities would have on archaeological sites, it did *not* require that those adverse impacts be mitigated. In other words, federal agencies had to identify the damage that would be done to archaeological sites, but they did not have to do anything about it. In 1971 President Richard Nixon signed into law Executive Order 11593: Protection and Enhancement of the Cultural Environment, an attempt to pull together the diverse pieces of legislation on the books, especially those pertaining to the National Register of Historic Places. One key component of the order was a directive to the National Park Service to develop criteria and policies for evaluating the potential of properties for inclusion on the National Register. The register had been created under the

National Historic Preservation Act of 1966, but no formal set of guidelines for site inclusion had ever been compiled.

Federal Archaeology in the 1970s

It was in this confusing arena of legislative acts and executive orders that archaeologists and government agencies found themselves in the early 1970s. The National Park Service was still the key agency relative to archaeological investigations, and by all accounts other federal agencies were willing to have the park service continue to shoulder the responsibility. But it was becoming more and more difficult for the other agencies to ignore archaeological properties on their lands. For example, agencies were now required to submit environmental-impact statements for each proposed project—a headache that many of them simply did not know how to address. Previously, if the Corps of Engineers wanted to build a reservoir, they would work through the Inter-Agency Archaeological Salvage Program, administered through the NPS, to have the archaeological work done. Now the law was requiring *them* to ensure that the work was accomplished. It was during the early 1970s that government agencies other than the NPS (e.g., the Bureau of Land Management, the Forest Service, the Bureau of Reclamation, and the Corps of Engineers) started hiring large numbers of archaeologists, most of whom were recruited to compile inventories of sites on federal lands and to write environmental-impact statements.

In effect, the legislation created unheard-of opportunities for archaeology students, though many of them soon found out that the opportunity came with a severe price. Some prospered in government positions, becoming accustomed to the regimentation and paperwork, but others did not. Many of the early crop of archaeologists to take government positions either had their doctorates or were doctoral-level students. They had been brought up in the doctrine of the new archaeology and were interested in things other than the compliance process. Many of them took government positions as a stop-gap measure until they could find a teaching-and-research position at a university, but they soon found that it was extremely difficult, for a variety of reasons, to leave government service and return to a university setting. For one thing, college and university positions were scarce, and there was a glut of recent graduates with Ph.D.'s in hand ready to compete for the positions. Also, government employment paid well, and even if federal archaeologists wanted to leave, they often could not afford it. In addition, the security of federal employment was as good as the tenure that colleges and universities offered their faculty—a fact with all the more impact because there was no guarantee that one would be awarded tenure if one did leave for a teaching position. Faced with the realities of life, well-trained archaeologists who had been attracted to government positions either had to stay and try to make a difference in how federal archaeology was done, or they had to find positions outside of archaeology. What they didn't know, however, was that another option, courtesy of the American free-enterprise system, was waiting for them right around the corner. In fact no one in the early 1970s could have guessed what was about to happen to Americanist archaeology, unless that person were Carl Chapman.

The Archaeological and Historic Preservation Act of 1974

Chapman was a busy person in the late 1960s. Not only was he directing archaeological projects across the state, teaching courses at the University of Missouri, coordinating the Missouri Archaeological Society, overseeing the Archaeological Survey of Missouri, and compiling reports of investigations, he was hatching a plan to force government agencies to expend the proper amount of funding for the mitigation of adverse effects to archaeological resources. By the late 1960s archaeologists agreed that the funding available was too small to accomplish the kind of work needed and that something had to be done to increase the level of support. Bob McGimsey of the University of Arkansas, Chapman's eventual partner in rousing legislative support, pinpointed the start of what turned into a grassroots movement on the part of archaeologists:

> Our presence in Washington can be traced directly to the three Mississippi Alluvial Valley Conferences, which had been convened by Jimmy Griffin [University of Michigan], Hester Davis [University of Arkansas], and me in 1968. From those conferences (attended by over 50 archaeologists who were active in the Valley at the time) came three things: a basic regional research design, the pamphlet "Stewards of the Past" 60,000 copies of which were distributed nationwide [published in 1970 through the Extension Division, University of Missouri–Columbia], and the conviction that federally sponsored activities other than dam building posed a serious threat to archaeological resources nationwide, and, therefore, that some solution must be developed on a national level. Legislation must be introduced that would authorize any federal agency whose actions adversely affected archaeological resources to expend agency funds to mitigate this adverse effect. At that time agencies were contending, correctly, that their appropriations did not permit such expenditure. Hence Carl's and my trip. (McGimsey 1985: 326)

The trip to which McGimsey referred happened in July 1969, when, as he says, "Carl Chapman took me in hand and led me to Washington to talk to members of Congress" (McGimsey 1985: 326). That trip was only the first of many that Chapman and McGimsey would make over the next five years. McGimsey noted that during that time he spent over 200 days in Washington and talked with the legislative staff of every senator and every congressman from every state. The task was grueling:

> I would normally start a day on the top floor of a particular congressional office building explaining the purpose and appropriateness of the legislation to each congressional staff on that floor, and then work my way down to ground level. Wherever possible, I attempted to identify myself with an archaeologist from that state or territory. . . . Thanks to the organization in the various archaeological societies and the intense interest of most archaeologists it was almost always possible for me to say that I was speaking for "so and so" who was not able to be present. . . . After making basically the same presentation dozens of times, I became very appreciative of the signs most members maintained in their offices telling what State I was "in." (McGimsey 1985: 328)

The "intense interest" on the part of archaeologists to which McGimsey referred enabled the proposed legislation to be seen as coming from a larger segment of society than two archaeologists. The Society for American Archaeology urged its members to write their congressional representatives and senators and to urge other societies to get behind the proposed legislation. The effort eventually paid off handsomely. The draft bill was jointly sponsored by Senator Frank Moss of Idaho and Congressman Charles E. Bennett of Florida in 1969, but it was not signed into law until 1974. The final legislation was entitled the Archaeological and Historic Preservation Act of 1974 (Public Law 93–291), although few archaeologists ever knew it as anything other than the Moss-Bennett Act. If there is an archaeological hall of fame, the plaques of Moss and Bennett should be placed alongside those of Chapman and McGimsey, for it was those four individuals who finally pried open the government coffers and fed a generation of archaeologists. As we will see, some ate better than others.

The key element in the Moss-Bennett Act that was missing from previous legislation was that it established guidelines for how to spend federal money on archaeology and even went so far as to suggest how much should be spent. This was innovative legislation, but the end result was not necessarily what archaeologists had hoped for. Because of the important role one of the stipulations played in American archaeology during the 1970s and 1980s, I present it in some detail. This stipulation, almost a magic word in archaeological— and eventually in public—circles, was what we might call *the 1% solution*. To understand the evolution of this term, we again call on McGimsey:

> While the law was being drafted, it was assumed by all involved that the Department of [the] Interior, as the only federal agency with a staff of professional archaeologists, would assume administrative responsibility for conducting essentially all of the research. It was, therefore, appropriate that a provision be made in the legislation for the transfer of funds from other agencies to the National Park Service, and that it administer the conduct of research. During early drafting, it was pointed out to those of us involved that there was no possibility for the passage of legislation that authorized unlimited transfer from one federal agency to

another. . . . we were challenged to come up with some percentage that would . . . be acceptable by the archaeological profession and the federal agencies. . . . in the final version, 1% became the guideline. *The intent was for this to be a limiting guideline only for the funds transferred by another agency to the National Park Service.* Shortly after passage, a Corps of Engineers lawyer interpreted the 1% limitation to apply to the *total funds expended by the agency for all archaeology on a project,* not just as a limit on transferred funds as had been intended. (McGimsey 1985: 330, most emphasis added)

Most archaeologists, I believe, still do not understand that, as written, the Moss-Bennett Act did not exclude agencies from spending more than 1% of project costs on archaeological work, it only limited the amount of money that an agency could transfer to the park service. Regardless, most agencies began contracting directly with archaeologists instead of going through the park service, thus reducing the role of that agency in non-park-service projects. In addition, agencies weren't going to pay more than they were forced to, and they all began to see 1% of project costs as a ceiling on archaeological funding. Even if they had understood the nuances, archaeologists wouldn't have complained, given the fact that they had just come into more money than they had ever seen. The only question was, how did one get the machine to start cranking out money? The answer came immediately: you put in a bid, along with everyone else. Gone were the days when a university worked as a sole-source contractor through an arrangement with the NPS. Now, universities could read the *Commerce Business Daily,* as other government contractors did, to find out about upcoming projects.

Even before Moss-Bennett was signed into law, private archaeological firms began springing up around the country, but the number was nothing compared to that after 1974. As government agencies began taking over responsibility for projects, they soon found that the number of projects outstripped the capabilities of their in-house archaeologists, and they were forced to go outside to get the work completed. Agency archaeologists became less archaeologists and more managers, since it fell to them to write scopes-of-work, to select contractors, and to ensure that the contractors who had been selected stayed in compliance and on schedule. The early days under the Moss-Bennett Act were complicated by the fact that few archaeologists, including those in the government, understood the law, especially how one piece of legislation dovetailed with another. Their work was further complicated by the fact that the drafters of the Moss-Bennett legislation forgot to reference the National Historic Preservation Act of 1966, especially with regard to the National Register of Historic Places and the role played by the Advisory Council on Historic Preservation. The earlier act had established the register and carried the provision that before any government agency could destroy a property on the register it had to consult with the council and receive advice about how to proceed. This oversight was easy enough to remedy through amendment, but that amendment did not come along until 1980.

The Agony of Contract Archaeology

In the meantime, archaeology was beset with a series of dilemmas. First, ever since the signing of Executive Order 11593 in 1971, the NPS had been struggling to develop guidelines for determining which sites should be included on the national register. These guidelines came to be known as "criteria for determination of significance," or, simply, "eligibility criteria." The park service solicited the help of the archaeological community in constructing criteria, but as Michael Schiffer and John House (1977a: 64) noted in the late 1970s, "The topic of significance . . . is by far the most controversial issue" in American archaeology. The problem was that everyone had his or her own notion of what constituted a significant resource. The number of articles that appeared on the subject within a short span of time was staggering (e.g., Barnes et al. 1980; K. A. Dixon 1977; Grady 1977; House and Schiffer 1975b; T. F. King 1978, 1983; Klinger and Raab 1980; McGimsey and Davis 1977; Moratto and Kelly 1978; Raab and Klinger 1977, 1978; Schiffer and House 1977a, 1977b; Scovill et al. 1972; Sharrock and Grayson 1978). Some archaeologists argued that sites should be determined significant or not significant based on their actual significance, that is, their ability to produce data relevant to current archaeological problems (e.g., House and Schiffer 1975b; Schiffer and House 1977a). Others (e.g., Lipe 1974) argued that representative portions of the resource base should be left for future investigation, since no one can predict future theoretical and methodological directions.

Robert Dunnell's (1984: 67) position on significance was extreme: "the single most important source of conflict in making significance assessments lies in the apparently widespread notion that resource identification, significance assessments, and mitigation efforts . . . are research." Dunnell's position, at least as stated then, was that the goals of archaeology and those of cultural-resource management (CRM [technically, compliance-related archaeology, often referred to simply as contract archaeology]) are so fundamentally distinct that the question of significance as asked by archaeologists bears little or no resemblance to the question as asked by land managers. The points Dunnell raised are worth considering. If one sets out to examine an archaeological problem, one must be able to collect information that is free from bias and is as complete as possible. CRM, because of its areal restrictions (e.g., the boundaries of a reservoir or the right-of-way of a highway), immediately imposes a bias on the portion of the archaeological record to be sampled. If, for example, one is interested in trace-element analysis of pottery to determine whether it is of local as opposed to nonlocal manufacture, pottery samples from myriad localities might have to be examined, including samples from outside the project area. Here archaeological goals conflict with management goals. Determinations of significance could be made on the basis of which sites contain potential pottery samples, but Dunnell (1984) was asking whether such a criterion meshes with why the federal government is spending money to mitigate a site. Obviously to him it does not. I return briefly to Dunnell's point a little later.

Regardless of how one approaches the problem of significance and the criteria used to establish the significance of a site, the national register—the place where sites determined to be significant are placed—was never intended to be a planning document but rather to be a preservation tool (Grady and Lipe 1976; Schiffer and Gumerman 1977). However, the opinion was often voiced (e.g., Aten 1974) that only those sites eligible for inclusion on the register should be considered eligible for federal funding to mitigate damage to them. This, unfortunately, became the "official" opinion of federal agencies: no determination of eligibility, no money. I say "unfortunately" because the endless bureaucratic red tape that one went through to receive determinations of eligibility created some nightmarish situations. First, forms had to be filled out stating precisely why a certain site was eligible. The archaeologist might have hundreds of sites with which to contend— say, in a large reservoir area—but no one wanted to complete hundreds of federal forms. Some of the sites might have received a small amount of excavation to determine such things as depth of deposit, presence of prehistoric features, and the like, but in essence the archaeologist often was being asked to do what was nearly impossible, that is, to make determinations of significance based on very little information. What if the initial excavation units just happened to hit the only subsurface features on a site? Or, suppose the few initial excavation units happened to miss the dozens of features on the site? The former site probably would have been declared eligible where the latter would not. One could argue that more work should have been done during this "testing" phase to determine more about the sites, but when an archaeologist was faced with a large number of sites and not enough time and money, added work became impossible.

Archaeologists quickly figured out that eligibility meant funding. Since agencies were not going to spend money on sites that were not eligible for inclusion on the national register, determinations of eligibility became important considerations. This did not necessarily lead to more sites' being determined eligible than otherwise would have been; what sometimes occurred was that only one or two sites would be forwarded to the advisory council as being significant, but the nomination forms would make the sites out to be second only to Pompeii in terms of significance. Most archaeologists, however, conscientiously attempted to plow through the regulations and to devise statements of significance that fairly represented the resource base. Others did not (see Barnes et al. 1980 and Klinger and Raab 1980 for additional discussion). Some recognized that their hands would be tied by their initial selection of sites, and they attempted to cover the bases accordingly by nominating as many sites as possible. What was needed was flexibility during the mitigation stage of a project. In short, if, upon closer examination, a site did not yield the kind of information for which it had received its eligibility status, there should have been a way to "declassify" it as an eligible site and move the work elsewhere. Eventually, these kinds of tradeoffs were built into the memoranda of agreement that were signed by the advisory council, the state historic-preservation offices, and the funding agencies, but in the early years of Moss-Bennett no one had worked out such arrangements.

On a personal note, I entered the field of archaeology as contract-funded work was about to make its meteoric rise, and, like many other archaeologists of the period who were fresh out of graduate school, my first professional position was as director of a large federally funded project, which I discuss later in this chapter. Being somewhat acquainted with the ins and outs of contract archaeology, especially the endless red tape and bureaucratic hurdles that seemed to confront most archaeological projects during the early days, I used to wonder if the archaeology of the seventies was at all like it was in the days of the Works Progress Administration or River Basin Surveys (RBS) projects. Archaeologists of those days might not have worried whether the government limited their area in which to survey, but I wondered about other problems that might have hampered their work. More than one archaeologist who had lived through all three periods said they had never seen anything like the 1970s. In the days of the RBS the bottom line was on getting material out of the ground as quickly as possible, analyzing it, reporting the information, and then moving on to another site. There was little or no competition between institutions involved in salvage operations, since there were plenty of opportunities for everyone to become involved.

On the other hand, the 1970s brought about a change not only in how salvage archaeology was carried out but also in how it was viewed from within the profession. Jesse Jennings, who was deeply involved in RBS archaeology, stated his perceptions of the differences:

> CRM and its inventories require a work force of specialists far larger than the salvage operation ever mustered, but the contributions to archaeological knowledge remain scandalously small for funds expended. Even worse and far more serious are the losses the CRM contract archaeologists themselves suffer. Those include reduced self-esteem, loss of autonomy and independence of action, and eroded scientific integrity, as bureaucrats and contracting officers reduce archaeology to numbers and even prescribe the procedures to be used in the field. The salvage model is clearly superior to CRM if the goal is enrichment of knowledge of the American heritage. (Jennings 1985: 293)

Those are harsh words, and I would venture to guess that not even Jennings would apply them across the board to all contract-archaeology programs. But there is a very real element to what he was saying, both in terms of product and the effect on archaeologists.

In assessing the early contributions made by cultural-resource management, Schiffer (1975a: 1) pointed out, "It is hardly necessary to document in any detail the dismal research record of contract archaeology. A glance at the bibliography of any compendium of method and theory . . . will attest to the negligible impact of contract 'research' on modern archaeological thought." Schiffer was correct, although one might have supposed that it would take a few years for contract archaeology to make its mark on archaeological thought. The more chilling statement Schiffer could have made was that modern archaeological thought had little or no impact on contract archaeology. Given where archaeological method and theory was in the 1970s, failure on the part of the majority of contract archaeologists to at least reference it was due either to ignorance or to a conscious effort on their part to separate what they did from what methodologists and theorists did. As we will examine below, archaeologists interested in "pure research" did little to heal the wounds.

A few years later, Schiffer and Gumerman (1977: 9) noted, "The dramatic up-surge in contract-supported archaeological activity, generated primarily through [the National Environmental Policy Act], has precipitated a second crisis in American archaeology, far different from the initial crisis of a rapidly dwindling resource base. . . . Even the casual observer of the bulk of contract reports cannot help but note that there has been a marked indifference to standards of quality research." The feeling that substandard work was being performed was not restricted to a few archaeologists. Members of the Society for American Archaeology spurred its leadership for guidance, and in 1974 the SAA sponsored a series of seminars aimed at various CRM topics, including guidelines for report preparation. This document, known as the "Airlie House Report" (McGimsey and Davis 1977), identified nine categories of information that should be addressed in a report, perhaps the most important one being the theoretical base of the research, that is, the assumptions underlying the archaeological problem and an explicit statement of how propositions and testable implications were derived from the theoretical base (Vivian et al. 1977). The "Airlie House Report" also called for peer review of reports. Despite the existence of these guidelines, and the acceptance of them by many archaeologists and state historic-preservation officers, there was still a feeling (e.g., Longacre 1981 [see Hester 1981 for a reply]) that the reports contributed little of a useful nature to archaeology at large.

The seminar series raised the awareness of the archaeological audience in attendance and perhaps contributed to the gradual improvement of reports, but one of the things that acted to reduce its effectiveness was the long delay in publication. By the time the "Airlie House Report" was published in 1977, the profession had begun to live with bad CRM reports or, at best, with reports that were never to be published or had only limited distribution (see Brose 1985; Raab et al. 1980). As an aside, it should be mentioned that there was a segment, actually a rather large segment, of archaeologists that formed a new society in 1976, the Society of Professional Archaeologists, partly in response to the black eye that archaeology was receiving and partly in response to the worry that agencies and firms soliciting work from archaeologists were going to start requiring them to be licensed. The thought was that if archaeologists got out ahead of this call and began licensing themselves, it would appear to the agencies (and to the public) that archaeologists were finally putting their house in order. The backlash to this movement was swift, with many archaeologists at the 1976 Society for American Archaeology meeting in Dallas sporting pins that read "Register sites, not archaeologists." SOPA membership has held constant over the years, but it has never been a dominant force in American archaeology.[2] Self-policing has never worked in archaeology, and it never will.

The meteoric rise in funding available during the 1970s was a double-edged sword for some archaeologists, as Jennings (1985: 293) noted. Taking the money meant that an archaeologist could practice his or her profession, but taking it also might put one under immediate suspicion of being greedy. By the mid-1970s, taking the money might have indicated that the archaeological research one was conducting was theoretically and morally bankrupt. Contract archaeologists were looked upon as incapable of competing with the rest of the profession for National Science Foundation funding and the like, and in some circles they became second-class citizens in every sense of the word. This happened in colleges and universities throughout the United States, where CRM archaeologists were looked upon as sources of income but not as equal members of the faculty. Mark Raab (1982) likened the situation to hiring a bounty hunter, which is not a bad analogy: the bounty hunter is somebody you need but not someone you would ask over for Sunday dinner. Advertisements for university-level CRM positions usually would read something like the following:

> Seeking archaeologist to head cultural resource management program in department of anthropology. Opportunity for part-time teaching. Responsible for developing and administering contracts. One-half (or none of) salary provided by departmental funds, other half to be secured from contracts and grants. Non-tenure-track position. (Raab 1982: 126–27)

Contract-archaeology programs were excellent sources of revenue that could be used to train graduate students, to purchase equipment, and to help meet general administrative costs, and the person hired to direct the program had

---

2. Carl Chapman believed deeply that professional archaeologists should be licensed, and he was elected president of SOPA in 1979.

to be a jack-of-all-trades. To attract a good person, universities dangled part-time teaching as a lure. The University of Missouri never did this. Chapman, who for years had directed the American Archaeology Division, was a tenured member of the department, and his successors in the position—Richard Krause, William Marquardt, and I—were hired as members of the department first and as directors of the division second. None of us was ever on a "soft-money" appointment, that is, one dependent on outside income. Other universities in Missouri had vastly different types of programs. Whereas the program at the University of Missouri was not dependent on outside support, others were, and all fell on hard times when the competition for contracts heightened during the 1980s. Staff and part-time faculty who had been around for years were suddenly informed that they had no positions because of the decline in revenues. Similar situations occurred around the country with alarming regularity as a result of an economic slow-down and increased pressure from private-contracting firms, which had sprung up during the 1970s to take advantage of the CRM bonanza. No longer was archaeology monopolized by universities. Between about 1974 and 1981, at least 20 private firms, many of them based in other states, conducted archaeological investigations within Missouri. The precise number is difficult if not impossible to determine since some firms were either one-person operations or short-term partnerships that lasted through one or two projects.

Some of the wounds caused by the increased alienation that CRM archaeologists felt from the rest of the profession were self-inflicted by the contract archaeologists themselves, who in some cases deserved the reputation they received. But part of the alienation, I suspect, was a result of jealousy, not only on the part of archaeologists who considered themselves "pure" researchers but also on the part of nonarchaeologists who worked beside the archaeologists in university anthropology departments. And I suspect also that the reasons behind this jealousy had everything to do with money. Federal funding for pure research—that is, research unencumbered by contract stipulations—has always been difficult to receive because there are more qualified applicants for funding than there is money available to fund them. We can use data from the NSF as a guide, since it has continued to be the major source of archaeological funding since it was founded in 1950.

John Yellen and Mary Greene (1985; see also Casteel 1980 and Yellen et al. 1980) state that between 1954 and the close of the government fiscal year 1983, the Anthropology Program at NSF, which grew out of the earlier Anthropology and Related Sciences Program, had awarded slightly under $42 million to archaeological projects (not including dissertation-improvement awards) out of the roughly $96 million spent on all anthropology projects combined. In other words, archaeology projects had garnered about 44% of the money, with the remaining 56% split among other subfields such as cultural anthropology and linguistics. The average award to archaeological projects was about $33,000.

Yellen and Greene show that although the amount of funding to archaeological projects grew over time, the level of support in terms of "real dollars"—funding level adjusted for inflation—declined dramatically. For example, the 1983 level fell to a point where it was only one-third what it had been in 1968.

Equally interesting is the geographic location of the projects that were being funded. Within the 30-year period between 1954 and 1983, 40% of the projects funded were carried out in the United States and Canada. But breaking the 30-year period down into smaller increments shows that the level of funding for projects in the United States and Canada fell by 14% between 1979 and 1983, while levels for Middle America, Europe, Africa, and South America rose 3–6%. In an earlier article, Yellen et al. (1980) argued that the decrease in support for United States research was probably a result of the rise of CRM archaeology, their logic being that since CRM money was easier to obtain, fewer archaeologists were approaching NSF. Yellen and Greene (1985), however, later backed off of this explanation in light of their data, which showed a relatively continuous decline in funding for United States projects since 1962.

If one really wants to understand the source of frustration in the 1970s for archaeologists who were unaccustomed to, or disinterested in, doing contract archaeology, look at the amount of federal money that was spent on contract projects in any given year. Even as early as the mid-1960s, Heizer (1966: 58) estimated that in California there was $100 of contract funding available for every dollar of noncontract money. The best, and probably the most accurate, statement available relative to the dramatic increase in CRM funding is that by McGimsey (1985: 330): "A study I made in 1971 indicated that approximately one million dollars of public money on the state and federal level was spent to recover or preserve archaeological resources. Ten years later that figure had increased to an unknown total, but estimates range from *one hundred to two hundred million dollars*" (emphasis added). In other words, even if we take McGimsey's lower figure, and I have no doubt that the estimate is well within the ball park (see Fitting 1979 [p. 231] for figures for Michigan), more money was spent on contract archaeology in *one* year than NSF had passed out to *all* anthropology—not only to archaeology—programs since its inception! Given that level of funding, it is little wonder that so many archaeologists became willing to accept not only a battery of regulations and restrictions on the kinds of work they could do but also the disdain of their colleagues.

If money—or more precisely, jealousy over money—played a role in fueling the controversy over the legitimacy of CRM, it shared the stage with basic philosophical arguments over how archaeology should be done. These arguments had little or nothing to do with funding but everything to do with how one structured one's entire research process. The "new archaeology" that started in the early 1960s might have covered a lot of ground over the years, but nothing was as sacred to it as the difference between inductive reasoning (generating conclusions from observations) and deductive reasoning (formalizing research into "if-then" statements), the latter being touted by the new archaeologists as the only way to structure scientific inquiry and the former being seen as the outdated thought process of culture historians. And no self-respecting new archaeologist could be seen even associating with culture historians.

Perhaps the clearest discussion of the conflict that naturally arose in the face of controversy over the appropriateness of contract archaeology as a legitimate enterprise is in Tom King's (1971) article "A Conflict of Values in American Archaeology," which was updated as "Resolving a Conflict of Values in American Archaeology" (King 1977). King is an interesting case of someone who shifted from a university research position—where he served as chief archaeologist with the UCLA Archeological Survey—to a government agency—as an archaeologist with the National Park Service. His sense of frustration in trying to do contract archaeology in a university setting—in essence trying to do scientific archaeology for government agencies who didn't want scientific archaeology—was typical of the time:

> In 1969/70, as chief archaeologist at the UCLA Archeological Survey, I was keenly aware of the pragmatic difficulties engendered by this conflict. The Survey was heavily involved in salvage, but the shadow of Louis [*sic*] Binford, who had left UCLA in 1968, lay long across the minds of graduate students. . . . We at the Survey felt a need to make our operations scientifically relevant, and this need was often hard to square with our equally serious obligations to the agencies for whom we did free or contract salvage. (T. F. King 1977: 87)

King noted that contract archaeology is basically incompatible with a deductivist approach—formation of propositions, recognition of test implications, and construction and implementation of tests. Thus, "Fieldwork in the context of this approach is a tool employed after the archaeologist has recognized and defined a problem, framed hypotheses relevant to the problem, and designed tests of the hypotheses to which fieldwork is found to relate. The kinds of field techniques employed are determined by the test requirements, within limits of feasibility" (T. F. King 1977: 89). On the other hand, the inductivist method "is based on the assumption that a valid and worthwhile body of fact will have been attained when enough data have been gathered to permit synthesis and inference. . . . According to an inductive ethic, every bit of information can be used in synthesis; presumably, *all* information can be and should be gathered" (T. F. King 1977: 89). Doesn't this sound like the strategy behind the earlier surveys in Missouri, where every shred of available evidence was important to support the case being made? Unfortunately, "available evidence" was an output directly linked to the predilections of individual investigators.

It should have come as no surprise that government agencies in the 1960s were not particularly impressed with either the new archaeology or with the new archaeologists: "To the agency or industry supporting an archaeological project . . . the outcome and indeed the existence of the research is truly 'incidental'. . . . Government and business do important things other than archaeology, and the public archaeologist, like it or not, must be a part of their doing" (T. F. King 1983: 156). The agencies that controlled the purse strings—particularly the NPS—had established policies and administrative structures that were consistent with doling money out on an as-needed basis for archaeology (T. F. King 1977), and the agencies were used to receiving nice, fat, descriptive reports that listed all the sites found and the artifacts recovered. They were not used to hearing about sampling design, problem formation, and "hypothetico-deductive" reasoning. For their part, archaeologists and their institutions, who/which were

> dedicated to the strategies of induction could easily handle, and intuitively justify, piecemeal salvage. Such work was justified on the basis of the familiar jigsaw analogy: When we have enough pieces, the picture will become clear. It was not necessary to wonder on what basis we perceived the shape of the pieces, and there was no need to worry about what phenomena we would like to see most clearly pictured when we got through. The central definitive focus of the archaeologist's life, and the measure of one's adequacy in relation to one's professional peers, was fieldwork; the more of it one did, the further one would advance the discipline. . . . Further, it was entirely proper for students to spend vast amounts of time in the field doing salvage and in the laboratory doing analyses and writing, toward no other goal than the preparation of "descriptive site reports" that proceeded through standard stages to present the collected data for future reference (Swartz 1967)—another piece added to the puzzle! (T. F. King 1977: 90–91)

Such an approach was logically inconsistent with the goals of a deductivist archaeology, as King (1977) pointed out. Standard site reports, thick with artifact description, were not the product of choice of the deductivists, who might not even be interested in the removal of artifacts from a site. If one was drawn to contract archaeology, with its inductivist approach and procedural guidelines, one ran the risk of being "branded . . . as a mere technician unsuitable to the cloisters of academia" (T. F. King 1977: 91). There was a way out of the dilemma, though in retrospect no one could have predicted how quickly a change in attitude would come about. And, happily, the change suited almost everyone, regardless of intellectual predilection. Ironically, especially in light of the above comments about CRM's being anathema to the deductivist approach, the change occurred when some of the new archaeologists dropped their preoccupation with polemical statements about deductivist archaeology and started doing CRM. One such archaeologist was Michael Schiffer (Figure 7.1), a product of the University of Arizona and a former student of Lewis Binford's at the University of California, Los Angeles. Schiffer had been steeped in the deductive method and knew the ins and outs of the new archaeology. He also knew how to apply some of the new archaeology to a contract situation.

Figure 7.1. Michael B. Schiffer (sitting) in the Cache River basin, northeastern Arkansas, 1974. Schiffer received his doctorate from the University of Arizona in 1973 and took a position with the Arkansas Archeological Survey, where he became codirector of the Cache River Archeological Project. In the late 1970s and 1980s his name became synonymous with the investigation of formation processes of the archaeological record. Interestingly, Schiffer, who had been one of Lewis Binford's students at the University of California, Los Angeles, later became one of Binford's most outspoken critics, especially with regard to Binford's dismissal (in Schiffer's view) of formation processes (courtesy M. B. Schiffer).

The Cache River Archeological Project and Regional Sampling

In 1973 the Arkansas Archeological Survey signed a contract with the Memphis District of the Corps of Engineers to examine archaeological remains in the Cache River basin in the Western Lowland of northeastern Arkansas. The contract required a survey of the entire basin, an assessment of site significance, and recommendations for mitigating the impact of channelization of the Cache River on the archaeological record. The 699-page (single-spaced) report that summarized the findings in the Cache Basin, authored by Schiffer and his colleague John House (Schiffer and House 1975), was hailed in some quarters as a landmark CRM report. Incredibly, the archaeological part of the project cost the Corps of Engineers only $48,000, although Schiffer and House (1977a: 63) note that the actual cost of the project was closer to $80,000–100,000 if donated services were figured in. There can be little doubt that the Cache River Archeological Project set the standard for CRM. Even two decades later, despite the fact that archaeology has witnessed significant theoretical and methodological advancements, few CRM programs (or non-CRM, for that matter) have equaled the Cache River project in terms of quality and attention to detail.

One significant feature of the project was its multistage research design, a concept that had been widely discussed in archaeology (e.g., Redman 1973) but not widely applied. Multistage meant literally what the name implied: fieldwork and analysis were structured in a series of stages, with each stage building on the one before it. The important difference between the Cache project and previous salvage and CRM projects was that each stage in the Cache project actually fed results back into previous stages so that subsequent work could be modified accordingly—a strategy that was widely adopted by agency archaeologists for their scopes-of-work. The basic sequence of the previous salvage model, on the other hand, which comes through loud and clear in reports from work in areas such as Table Rock and Stockton reservoirs, is that a survey was conducted, some sites were discovered, and some of those were excavated. This is a linear format: step B is not started until step A is completed. The Cache model, in contrast, was a series of research designs prepared by experts on particular topics. Although the individual research designs suggested areas of potential investigation, they also contained enough flexibility so that if one avenue didn't produce anticipated results, another suggested avenue was there to take its place and researchers didn't have to start over in the fund-seeking department.

One methodological area in which the Cache project provided innovation was in the initial inspection of an area for potential excavation sites, or areal survey (House and Schiffer 1975a). It was not the first project to confront the issue of regional sampling (see Plog 1976), and it certainly would not be the last, but the various topics that Schiffer and House considered in setting up their survey project had rarely been mentioned in the CRM literature. Sampling on a regional scale was a topic of considerable interest in the late 1960s, especially the most appropriate techniques for obtaining representative samples and the rate at which a region should be sampled. The issue became immediately germane in CRM because archaeologists realized that, despite the protestations of federal agencies, reservoirs and other similar-size project areas were too large to survey completely and intensively.

The agencies, on the other hand, were operating under the National Environmental Policy Act and Executive Order 11593, the provisions of which called for determining which sites were eligible for inclusion on the national register. In fact, the executive order, signed in 1971, called for an inventory of all sites on federal lands by July 1, 1973. After that date, federal agencies would be out of

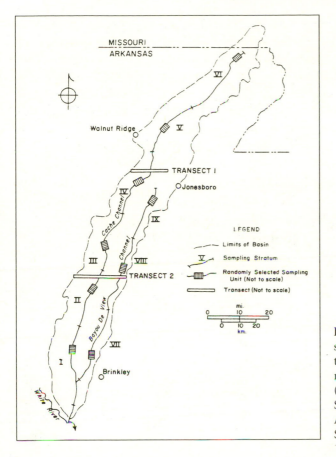

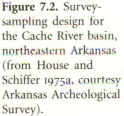

Figure 7.2. Survey-sampling design for the Cache River basin, northeastern Arkansas (from House and Schiffer 1975a, courtesy Arkansas Archeological Survey).

compliance. Of course, the date was unrealistic—any date would have been un-realistic, since no agency could ever hope to identify every site on the lands under its jurisdiction. In light of strict interpretation of the law, the original contract for work in the Cache Basin called for a complete survey of the 65-square-mile direct-impact zone as well as an estimate of resources in the secondary-impact zone. Schiffer and House convinced the Corps of Engineers that they had neither the time nor the funding to attempt such a survey and that a representative sample of sites in the region would yield the needed information. The corps agreed, and an 11% survey was conducted in direct-impact and secondary-impact areas through a mix of different-sized sampling units (House and Schiffer 1975a) (Figure 7.2).

The significance of the Cache project was not simply in its novelty in sampling or in its demonstration that appropriate archaeological method and theory could be applied in a CRM situation. Rather, it was the demonstration that appropriate archaeological method and theory could be used as intelligent management tools (for criticism of the project on this point see Windmiller 1977). Most archaeologists never doubted that good archaeology could be practiced under the rubric of CRM; what was entirely unclear in the 1970s was how to mesh the goals of archaeology with the goal of managing the resource base. The Cache project was one of a number of CRM projects that by the middle 1970s were beginning to demonstrate that the two sets of goals could, at least conceivably, be meshed with a minimum of conflict. Probably the majority of such projects were in the Southwest (e.g., Canouts 1972; Goodyear 1975; Raab 1976a), though another project by the Arkansas Archeological Survey (Pine Mountain [Raab 1976b]) deserves consideration.

Research Goals versus Management Goals—A Question of Ethics?

Despite the hope that these projects provided for quieting the fears that research goals and management goals were naturally at odds with one another, the problem of how to determine whether a site was significant and thus eligible for mitigation-related funding never was completely resolved. And, for all practical purposes, it never will be resolved until archaeology develops a new perspective on the archaeological record. Dunnell's (1984) rather gloomy statements about the natural differences between CRM and research imply that the incompatibility is irreversible (a position that comes close to the earlier position of Fitting [1978]):

> Archaeological research begins with a problem. In an attempt to solve the problem, potential data sources are selected and variables identified for documentation. The *choice* of analytic methods, collection techniques, areas, sites, etc., is necessarily predicated on the initial problem. When the formulation of the problem or the approach to problem-solving is not explicit, there is almost inevitably both a failure to obtain necessary information and inclusion of irrelevant data. . . .
>
> CRM is not so constituted. . . . The generation of a CRM project has nothing whatsoever to do with an archaeological problem. CRM is generated by nonarchaeologists and concerns potential impact on a particular piece of real estate. The initial input is spatial. The archaeologist is thus deprived of the rationales that are used, implicitly or explicitly, to make all of the decisions known to influence the quantity, quality, and nature of the archaeological data. The notion of relevance that guides the selection of resources in problem-oriented research is replaced by a less well-defined notion of significance. (Dunnell 1984: 67–68)

Dunnell's comments center around an ethical issue: "If we accept the overriding purpose of CRM as conservation of the archaeological record for humanistic and scientific use, is the problem-oriented research approach to assessing significance ethical and moral?" (Dunnell 1984: 68). The matter of ethics in archaeology has been around since at least 1935, the year the Society for American Archaeology was founded, and in 1961 the society passed a series of guidelines addressing proper behavior of archaeologists.[3] The topic heated up again in the early 1970s, with literally hundreds of journal pages devoted to such issues as client-archaeologist relations, price-gouging, and the like. In 1976 the newly formed Society of Professional Archaeologists published a code of ethics and a set of standards of research performance (see E. L. Green 1984). But despite the interest in ethics over the years, few people had explicitly asked whether it is ethical to use a problem-oriented approach to assess archaeological significance.

In a very real sense, determinations of significance in the seventies and eighties—and to be honest, those made today—were not all that different from those made in the previous decades. The criteria differed, keeping in step with some theoretical and methodological reorientations, but areas were still surveyed, sites were selected for excavation, and artifacts were analyzed. The reasons for which sites were slated for excavation differed from previous reasons, and eligibility forms were filled out—a new wrinkle—but many of the old assumptions were left intact. For example, the "site" was still viewed as an adequate unit of analysis, despite the increasing attention paid to regions. As I discuss in Chapter 8, the concept of site is revered in Americanist archaeology. But why should areas with dense concentrations of artifacts play more of a role in regional analysis than areas of lower density? Why should excavation play such a key role in managing cultural resources when it is a destructive process? What role, if any, should sampling play in CRM projects? Dunnell's (1984) position was that almost everything archaeologists do systematically biases the archaeological record—both the part that is sampled and the part that is left. We decide where to survey, where to excavate, what to collect, what to leave, and what to report.

Contemporary theory does little or nothing to alleviate this bias, and if anything it heightens it. Contemporary theory provides our propositions about the way prehistoric groups conducted their business, and it governs the way we structure our field and analytical research to examine the validity of our propositions. This certainly is problem-oriented archaeology, but does it have a place in CRM? Recall T. F. King's (1977: 89) statement, "According to an inductive ethic, every bit of information can be used in synthesis; presumably, *all* information can be and should be gathered." If this dictum is true, then the CRM ethic and the inductive ethic are the same. But does this imply that one can not

---

3. The Committee on Ethics and Standards, headed by John L. Champe, published "Four Standards for Archaeology" in *American Antiquity* 27:137–38 (1961). Henry W. Hamilton, the nonprofessional from Missouri who served on the Committee for the Recovery of Archaeological Remains, was on the committee.

think deductively while trying to *save* as much information as possible? The basic question is this: Can we examine a series of well-thought-out research questions and at the same time fulfill our ethical responsibility to preserve a representative portion of the resource base? I believe the answer is yes, although, as Dunnell stated a decade ago, such a wedding would take a complete reorientation in perspective on the archaeological record.

The Cache River project and a few others similar in outlook were steps in the right direction and served as prototypes for programs that came after them. Two such programs were carried out in Missouri, one in the Harry S. Truman Reservoir and one in the Clarence Cannon Reservoir. I examine these two projects in some detail, with an emphasis on research orientation and how well they met their goals. Both were innovative from the standpoint of sampling—why it was done and how it was done—but of key concern is how the sampling processes were used to address not only management goals but also research goals. The fits and starts that the two projects went through in wrestling with the mesh of preservation and research—and I tend to focus more on the Cannon Reservoir project because I have firsthand knowledge of it—were probably little different from those that affected other large-scale CRM projects in the 1970s and 1980s. However, I also discuss the Truman project in some detail because it was the first archaeological program in Missouri to employ a rigorous survey-sampling design at the regional level. The Cannon project used the Truman survey design as a starting point but evolved into a much more complex examination of human use of the Salt River valley throughout the Holocene. That project also became a laboratory for testing and using a variety of strategies designed specifically to mesh the dictates of CRM with problem-oriented archaeology. Both projects, I believe, fulfilled Schiffer's (1975a: 6) admonition "to abandon the stereotype of contract archeology as a suspect, perhaps illegitimate activity that is no more than a necessary obligation to be grudgingly fulfilled."

The Harry S. Truman Dam and Reservoir Project

Work in the lower Pomme de Terre Valley by Ray Wood and Bruce McMillan produced a massive amount of data on the Holocene environment and on human use of two localities in the valley, Rodgers Shelter and Phillips Spring, but missing was a more regional perspective on changing land-use patterns. By the early 1970s several surveys had been conducted in the proposed Truman (originally Kaysinger Bluff) Reservoir area (Chapman et al. 1965; Falk and Lippincott 1974), and several sites other than Rodgers Shelter had been excavated (e.g., Chapman et al. 1965; Falk 1969; Lippincott 1972; Wood 1965b), though the surveys were spotty and the excavations were fairly limited in scope. Truman Reservoir (including easements) was slated to cover 166,000 acres (259 square miles), but most of the archaeological work had been confined to the lower Pomme de Terre Valley, which was only one portion of the large project area. What about archaeological resources in other areas of the reservoir?

In 1975 the Kansas City District of the Corps of Engineers recognized the deficiency and invited proposals from interested contractors for additional survey of the reservoir. Ray Wood and Donna Roper submitted a proposal to the corps (Roper and Wood 1975) and ultimately were selected to perform the work. Roper and Wood's interests mirrored in some respects those of most archaeologists, that is, they wanted to know where sites are located, when they were occupied, what functions were carried out at the sites, and so forth. But some of their concerns were not the usual ones that had been asked on dozens of previous surveys in Missouri, and the way in which they structured the survey bore little resemblance to previous endeavors. What they needed in order to address the questions they posed was an intensive investigation of where sites were located as well as where they were *not* located—a concern not previously addressed in Missouri. What was *not* needed was a hit-or-miss type of survey that tended to concentrate attention on high-probability areas at the expense of other localities.

Roper received her Ph.D. from the University of Missouri in 1975, using as her dissertation an archaeological survey of a portion of the Sangamon River valley in central Illinois (Roper 1975a). Her dissertation addressed formal modeling of site locations in the Sangamon Valley relative to several environmental variables such as proximity to water, landform on which a site was located, and so forth. In reading both her dissertation and the research design drawn up for the Truman Reservoir survey, one notices the new perspective in survey procedure and rationale that Roper, a product of the 1970s, introduced into Missouri archaeology. The seventies were nothing if not the decade of realization that site survey was an integral part of archaeology. The development of a rationale for large-scale surveys in the Americas rested with pioneering projects such as Phillips et al.'s (1951) survey of the lower Mississippi River valley, Gordon Willey's (1953) survey of the Virú Valley, Peru, and William Sanders's (1956) survey of a portion of the Valley of Mexico (see also other papers in Willey 1956), but the 1970s witnessed an exponential investment in archaeological-site survey, as summaries written at the close of the decade attest (e.g., Dunnell 1979; Goodyear et al. 1978; Plog et al. 1978; Schiffer et al. 1978).

By the mid-1970s, large areas of the American Southwest (e.g., Judge 1973; Layhe et al. 1976; Reher 1977; Whalen 1977) and especially Highland Mesoamerica (e.g., Blanton 1972; MacNeish et al. 1975; Parsons 1972, 1976; Sanders 1967, 1970; Sanders et al. 1979) had been surveyed intensively. The rationale for conducting the surveys differed little among projects, all more or less having five goals in common: (1) assessment of environmental variation and relative productivity of the study area; (2) location of sites; (3) classification of sites into analytically meaningful taxa; (4) assignment of temporal affiliation to sites; and (5) evaluation of functional differences among sites (O'Brien and Warren 1982a: 20). These studies came to be known as "settlement-pattern" analysis—in short, examination of the "manner in which a people's cultural activities and social institutions are distributed over the landscape" (Rouse 1972: 96), or, as Bruce Trigger (1967: 151) put it, identifying and explaining "functioning systems of economic, political and effective relationships."

There is little in the archaeological literature for Missouri in the 1950s and 1960s to suggest that these goals of settlement-pattern analysis had much of an effect on the way surveys were structured. It sounds rather damning, but it appears that site-survey programs were designed to do little more than find the best places to dig: "The [1959–1960] survey and testing [of Kaysinger Bluff Reservoir] was aimed in great part at the location and evaluation of mounds, cairns, caves, and rock shelters. . . . Open campsites with heavy concentrations of refuse were also sought, and all sites of possible importance in evaluating and interpreting the archaeology of the proposed reservoir were located" (Keller 1965: 219). In fact, in the dozens of survey reports prepared for the National Park Service, I didn't find even a single reference to any consideration of settlement pattern or the types of information that could be learned through settlement-pattern analysis. This is unfortunate, given the devastation that large portions of the archaeological record received between 1956, when Willey's edited volume on settlement patterns appeared, to 1975, when Roper and Wood drew up plans to survey Truman Reservoir. Because of the manner in which earlier site-location information was collected, it could not be used to make reliable statements about patterns of settlement across the landscape.

Despite the conceptual and methodological advances that were made in settlement-pattern studies during the 1950s and 1960s, some archaeologists began to realize some of the limitations of the concepts and definitions that were being used. As Parsons (1972: 132) noted, one significant contribution to the reassessment that followed was the concept of the *settlement system,* a refinement of Chang's (1962) *annual subsistence region.* Parsons (1972: 132) suggested that Howard Winters (1967) may have been the first Americanist archaeologist to use the term formally. Winters (1969: 110) later distinguished between settlement pattern—"the geographic and physiographic relationships of a contemporaneous group of sites within a single culture"—and settlement system—"the functional relationships among the sites contained within the settlement pattern . . . the functional relationship among a contemporaneous group of sites within a single culture." For Winters, cultural limits were defined by the distribution of distinctive stylistic traits (Parsons 1972: 132), more or less along the same lines as the criteria used to establish the units in the midwestern taxonomic method and later the Willey-and-Phillips (1958) system.

As early as 1956 Sanders was bringing into sharp focus the distinction between the characterization and analysis of differences between sites and differences within sites. The former he termed zonal settlement patterns and the latter community settlement patterns (Sanders 1956). Community patterns have as units of analysis single sites; zonal patterns "are concerned with the distribution of community sizes, distances between communities, density of population, and the symbiotic interrelationship between communities" (Sanders 1956: 116). Trigger (1967, 1968) took the division one step further and subdivided settlement structure into (a) microstructure, consisting of individual households; (b) macrostructure, the community; and (c) the distribution of communities across the landscape.

Some of the issues mentioned here were addressed by Roper and Wood (1975, 1976) in their research design for the Truman Reservoir survey (see also Roper 1975b), but the more telling document is the final report of the 15-month-long survey undertaken in 1975 and 1976 (Roper 1983). In it Roper discusses topics that previously had been either ignored by archaeologists working in Missouri or glossed over as being relatively unimportant. For example, she examines the issue of ground-cover variation and how it affected the ability of surveyors to see the ground surface and also mentions possible bias in the survey results introduced by variation in how different individuals see things in the field. An honest appraisal of biases that could have affected the analytical results of a survey project had never been high on anyone's list of topics to discuss in the final report—primarily, I believe, because the biases were never recognized as problematic. If, for example, ground cover was thick in a particular locality, one simply looked somewhere else.

As I have pointed out several times, prior to the Truman survey archaeologists working in Missouri were not particularly interested in where sites were *not* located. The later Truman survey, however, couldn't be structured in the same manner as previous surveys because Roper and Wood *were* interested in where sites were not located. Part of this interest most assuredly came about as a result of intellectual curiosity, but part of it came about because of federal law. Management of cultural properties implied that one knew what properties were there to manage, and to acquire such data meant that localities had to be surveyed intensively. And the next level up, *intelligent* management, dictated that one knew where the sites were *not* located as well as where they *were* located.

One interesting problem with which archaeologists wrestled in assisting with the management of cultural properties was how to adequately survey large areas such as the Truman Reservoir. As Roper (1983: 215) states in her summary of the survey program,

Very early in the survey it became obvious that, given available time and funding, it would be impossible to completely walk all of the 166,000+ acres being acquired by the Corps of Engineers. Further, it would be completely naive to assume that even if all of the acquisition area were walked that all sites would be recorded. For any of a variety of reasons, including site burial and invisibility of sites under certain ground cover conditions (not to mention the problem of defining what is to be called a site), the archeologist never records *all* the sites in an area. . . . The decision to be made in the Truman Reservoir survey was not whether or not to sample, but rather *how* to sample.

Roper (1983: 216–17) presented one of the more concise statements regarding the need for sampling that appeared during the 1970s:

Frequently, the archeologist is in a position to want to estimate parameters of the population of sites in the region of interest. For example, if it is of interest to know the distribution of sites of various sizes, or perhaps the relation of a particular size of site to the drainage system, or even simply to estimate the number of sites in a given area, it is necessary to have some knowledge of the reliability of the sample of sites used to estimate these parameters. In some cases, there may be enough information already available to do so with conventional survey techniques or data already at hand.

In other cases, so little is known about the archeology of a region that there is no way to evaluate how a conventionally drawn sample of sites estimates the parameters of interest. . . . The basic issue is not always how many sites one can record in a given unit of time, however, but how much *information* can be recorded in the same period of time. It is for this reason that many archeologists carrying out regional surveys in which it is impossible to survey the entire area have found it efficient and informative to use some sort of probability sampling design. Such a design may well record fewer sites, but it will do so in a manner which will permit the archeologist to make supportable statements about the cultural resource base of the region.

Binford and others had made some of the same statements in the early and mid-1960s, a point not lost on Roper, who quoted Binford's (1964) article on archaeological research design:

I recently wanted to demonstrate that most of the sites in a particular area were located adjacent to streams. This was impossible because I had no data as to where the archaeologist reporting on the area had concentrated his survey efforts. Was the failure to report sites in areas not adjacent to streams the result of sites being absent, or was it simply a lack of investigation in those areas not adjacent to streams? (Binford 1964: 427)

Roper, in assessing the previous decade's worth of survey in the Truman Reservoir area, summarized the situation facing many archaeologists of the period who were being asked to evaluate the significance of sites on federal lands—evaluations that would be used to decide whether further archaeological work would be undertaken relative to the sites or, conversely, whether they would be "written off":

> The lack of a single unified survey goal in all of these surveys, other than that of recording sites prior to inundation, hampers an evaluation of their significance. The period 1959 to the present happens to span one of the most explosively productive periods in American archaeology . . . and to criticize surveys done in 1959 because they do not conform to the standards of 1975 is unwarranted intellectual arrogance. Yet to be asked in 1975 to assess the significance of sites recorded in 1959 *is* to be asked to judge these surveys by modern standards and to evaluate their potential for shedding light on currently defined problems and goals.
>
> The answer, of course, is that the previous survey information will be useful for some purposes, but not for others. At the time of the first surveys in the reservoir, the overriding concern in American archaeology was with culture history. Information was collected that would inform on descriptive interpretations of the culture sequences of an area. . . .
>
> For other present survey goals . . . many of the previous surveys are not useful and it is impossible to evaluate the significance of the sites. Except for Lippincott's 1967 and 1968 survey in the Thurman site vicinity [Falk and Lippincott 1974], no survey recorded what areas were surveyed and no sites found. . . . Thus, it is impossible to evaluate areas surveyed and the kinds of ground cover encountered. (Roper 1975c: 6–7)

Roper and Wood, whether they knew it or not, were the first archaeologists in Missouri to establish a systematic sampling strategy for a survey project. The program was carried out in two stages, the first a traditional, "purposive" survey of the reservoir area, especially borrow areas (areas from which dirt is hauled for use elsewhere, as in road construction) and highway-relocation corridors (Roper 1975c), and the second a "probabilistic" survey (Roper 1983). The latter had as its underlying concern the derivation of a representative sample of sites across the 166,000-acre survey area. But what was the sample supposed to be representative of? Roper (1983) was not specific on this point, though she noted that "the emphasis of the survey design was to answer questions concerning differential use of the reservoir area over time and space. . . . The behaviorally realistic concept of human interaction with the natural environment cross-cutting zonal boundaries was also to be incorporated" (Roper 1983: 70).

Given this orientation, and realizing that "Human adaptations are not to single resource zones but rather to a series of such zones" (Roper 1983: 70), the decision was made to employ "transects"[4] as sampling units, the idea being that they would cut across different environmental zones, thus ensuring that all zones were

---

4. Transects are lines; the survey actually used long, narrow rectangles to outline survey areas.

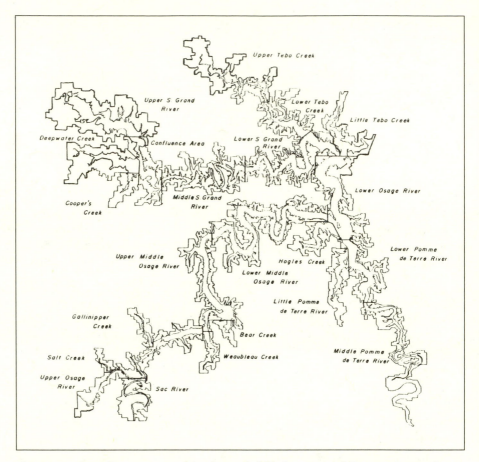

Figure 7.3. Sampling strata used in the probabilistic survey of Truman Reservoir, west-central Missouri (from Roper 1983).

sampled. To examine different environments throughout the entire project area, the reservoir was subdivided into 22 units (Figure 7.3), each defined by a stream (e.g., Salt Creek) or a stream segment (e.g., upper middle Osage River). Transects were laid out north–south or east–west within each unit so as to run roughly perpendicular to a stream (Figure 7.4). Transects were of variable length but of a standardized width of one-eighth of a mile. Ten percent of the transects within each unit were selected for survey, with the selection of units being random. This rate was based on pragmatic considerations, such as available time and money.

One of the problems encountered by the field crews was dense ground cover (e.g., grass and bushes) in some areas—a problem certainly not unfamiliar to previous survey crews working in Missouri. But instead of ignoring those areas and moving to areas with better ground visibility, Roper's crews employed

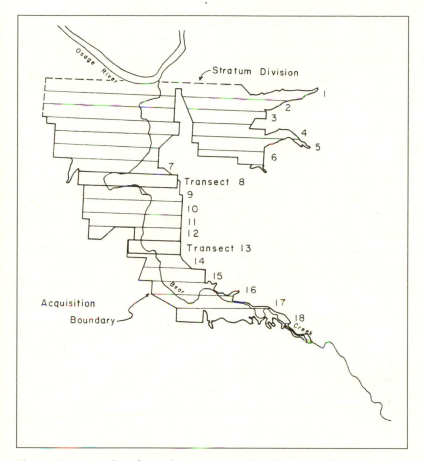

Figure 7.4. Examples of sample transects used in the probabilistic survey of Truman Reservoir, west-central Missouri (from Roper 1983).

"shovel testing," or the excavation of small holes at regular intervals to determine whether artifacts were present. Today's students of archaeology might be surprised to learn that shovel testing, which is now standard practice in low-visibility areas, was not typical procedure a few decades ago. In fact, it was not until the mid-1970s that the method was discussed in the literature (e.g., Lovis 1976). One drawback to the method is its low rate of return, even on sites that are known to contain large quantities of artifacts. Debates arose over its use, with one side saying it was all that was available for low-density areas and the other that it was essentially a useless procedure. The debate still crops up in the literature from time to time (e.g., Lightfoot 1986, 1989; Shott 1989).

Roper and Wood's survey produced 1,363 new sites, roughly two-thirds of which were found during the traditional walk-over and one-third during the transect survey. Site locations were measured relative to 18 environmental variables, 8 of which were related to water (e.g., distance to river), 8 to topography (e.g., site elevation), and 2 to vegetation (e.g., amount of forest within 1 mile). Analysis demonstrated that some differences in site location over time could be detected, such as perhaps a trend toward locating communities near greater expanses of bottomland (Roper 1983: 209). In discussing her analysis, Roper (1983) raised an interesting point regarding the correlation or lack of correlation between the sites and several of the environmental variables, especially those of a topographic nature. This is an important point, because it emphasized one of the major differences between contract and noncontract archaeology—the freedom or lack of freedom to survey beyond a set limit, a difference that became all too obvious to some archaeologists in the 1970s—and because it anticipated predictive modeling of site locations, which within a few years became an important component of CRM.

Traditionally, archaeologists were free to establish the geographical boundaries of their survey projects. No one, for example, told Gordon Willey that he could not survey areas above a certain elevation in the Virú Valley or Bill Sanders that his coverage was limited to the lower piedmont zone of the Teotihuacán Valley. These were surveys that were funded by grants, and the grantees were fairly free to spend the money as they saw fit. This was not the case with the majority of archaeological surveys conducted in the United States after 1975. Archaeologists were working, either directly or indirectly, for the federal government, and the law only pertained to archaeological resources that were being adversely affected by government-funded activities. Thus, relative to the Truman Reservoir, Roper's investigation was limited to lands that were at or below 706 feet above average mean sea level (AMSL). What about the higher-elevation areas outside the pool, especially areas in the rugged uplands to the east? Suppose there were special kinds of sites—for example, nut-processing localities—located in those areas during the Late Archaic period and again during the Middle Woodland period? How would those be factored into the overall model of prehistoric settlement systems? The obvious answer is, of course, they would not. Archaeologists either accepted the conditions set out in the scopes-of-work prepared by federal agencies or they often did not receive the contracts. Some, as we will find out later, extended areal coverage by surveying the areas outside the boundaries on their own time, but these appear to have been rare occurrences.

In retrospect, the Truman Reservoir survey established for Missouri a model of regional archaeological analysis that was without precedent. It expanded the scope of a decade of environmental archaeology that itself had been without precedent in the state and provided a larger context in which to view the dynamics of prehistoric occupation and use of the western prairie–timberland border by prehistoric groups throughout the Holocene. Running concurrently with the survey were studies of regional history and architecture (Linderer 1983;

Miller 1983; Synhorst 1983a, 1983b), analyses of lithic and ceramic artifacts (e.g., Roper and Piontkowski 1983), and test excavations (e.g., Chomko 1983; Novick and Cantley 1983). Based on the survey and testing information, several sites were selected for large-scale excavation, the results of which were published in a three-volume report (Roper 1981). Later surveys concentrated on federally owned land and easements above the normal-pool elevation of 706 feet AMSL (Iroquois Research Institute 1980; R. L. Taylor et al. 1986), using more or less the same field methods used by Roper.

The Cannon Reservoir Human Ecology Project

The Truman project was not the only large survey-and-mitigation project in Missouri during the mid and late 1970s. The St. Louis District of the Corps of Engineers had won the go-ahead from Congress in the early 1970s to begin construction of the Clarence Cannon (earlier named Joanna) Dam and Reservoir (Figure 7.5), and corps personnel estimated it would be in operation by the late 1970s. This meant that any archaeological work that was being contemplated would have to be completed in fairly short order, and the district hired its first archaeologist to begin planning that operation. By 1974 the University of Missouri had spent portions of seven field seasons working along the central portion of the Salt River, and university personnel looked forward to many more seasons of work. Carl Chapman had served as principal investigator on previous projects in Cannon Reservoir, and he began planning for future work there.

The Corps of Engineers had earlier contracted with the Missouri Botanical Garden in St. Louis to compile an environmental assessment of the Cannon Reservoir region (Missouri Botanical Garden 1974), which took into account some of the impacts that construction would have on archaeological resources. The botanical garden asked Dale Henning, then of the University of Nebraska–Lincoln, to review the archaeological section of the report, since he had conducted much of the original survey and excavation during his tenure at the University of Missouri. The assessment report prepared by the Missouri Botanical Garden reiterated that numerous archaeological sites would be adversely affected by construction-related activities, although the precise number was unknown because the region had never been rigorously surveyed. The first step in any archaeological program would have to be a survey of the reservoir area to find out how many sites were there and which ones were going to be either destroyed or damaged.

Interestingly, the question of how much damage reservoir construction does to archaeological sites had never really been addressed, though one might have thought that if federal law turned on the question of "adverse impact," someone should have figured out what some of those long-term impacts might be. For

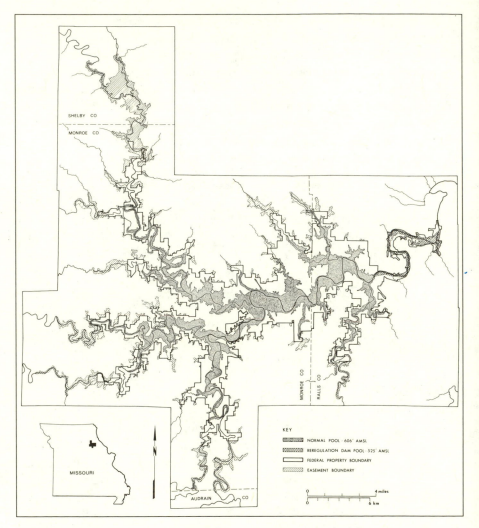

Figure 7.5. Map showing boundaries of Cannon Reservoir and of the Cannon Reservoir Human Ecology Project area, northeastern Missouri (from O'Brien and Henning 1982, courtesy Academic Press).

example, burying a site under 60 feet of water does not necessarily mean that the site will be destroyed, though in the 1970s it was unclear what happened to sites when they were at the bottom of a reservoir (e.g. Padgett 1978).[5] For all intents

5. Both the Arkansas Archeological Survey (Padgett 1978) and the American Archaeology Division at the University of Missouri (Garrison et al. 1977, 1979) were engaged in measuring the effects of inundation on archaeological sites. In the case of the Missouri study, unprovenienced artifacts were

and purposes, those sites would never be seen again, since they would be covered with deep deposits of silt, but that did not mean, under some interpretations of the law, that they had been adversely affected. Clearly, however, other sites, such as those located near the shoreline of a reservoir, would be subjected to severe erosion as a result of wave action and fluctuations in water level behind the dam. Sites in recreation areas, parking lots, and concession areas would be destroyed during construction, as would those lying in the path of highway relocation. The most damaging of all activities is the bulldozing of trees, which tears sites to pieces as the trees are uprooted. Thus it could be argued that in terms of adverse impact, sites in areas to be tree cleared would be most affected, and the ones out in the middle of the reservoir would be least affected. In the 1970s, however, the prevailing view was that most types of impact should be treated in similar fashion.

Based on the assessment report, the St. Louis District drew up a series of recommended steps to address the impact on archaeological sites in Cannon Reservoir and then went looking for someone to do the work. Three institutions appeared to be viable candidates: the University of Missouri, the Missouri Botanical Garden, and the University of Nebraska–Lincoln (UNL). The first two were obvious choices, but why UNL? The reason was simple: Dale Henning had joined the faculty there and had assumed the directorship of the Division of Archeological Research, which was a well-funded training ground for the university's archaeology students. As Bruce McMillan had done when he moved to the Illinois State Museum, Henning had kept his interest in Missouri prehistory. His knowledge of the ins and outs of the contract business and his grounding in Missouri prehistory gave the University of Missouri a serious competitor for the contract.

All three institutions were invited to submit brief proposals of how they would approach the development of an inventory of prehistoric properties owned (or soon to be owned) by the corps, with the implication that the inventory was only the first step in an overall program of cultural-resource management (CRM). In plain language, each party recognized that whichever institution received the contract for survey and assessment would, in all likelihood, receive additional contracts for excavating sites deemed eligible for inclusion on the National Register of Historic Places. In plainer language, the institution the corps selected probably would be awash in cash for the next several years. The botanical garden realized that it did not have the staff to handle a project the size of the one

---

placed under the waters of Table Rock Reservoir to monitor the effects of such things as siltation and underwater disturbance. Similar efforts were sponsored by the National Park Service nationwide. My impression of such studies is that they were a waste of time. Even if siltation "preserves" a site, I can't imagine that in a few hundred years—the average life expectancy of a reservoir—someone will go to the trouble and expense of removing tens of meters of sediment to investigate an archaeological site.

that loomed on the horizon, and they withdrew from consideration, leaving the universities of Nebraska and Missouri to compete for the contract. The corps selected Nebraska, a decision based in large part on Henning's reputation as someone who could see large projects through to completion.

The loss of the contract was a blow to Chapman, who had shelved some of his duties at the University of Missouri to lobby in Washington for increased federal support for archaeology. He had succeeded, all right, but now he had nothing to show his home institution for all the time he had been gone. If the university could lose the Cannon contract, which at one time it had appeared to have a lock on, how many more might it lose in the coming years?

UNL formed the Cannon Reservoir Archaeological Project in 1974, and several of its personnel began surveying the 65,000-acre reservoir area (Figure 7.5) late that year. Henning (1979: 8) reflected on those early days:

> In 1974, I estimated that 400 sites would be located within the 65,000 acre tract. It was upon this estimate that our projected means for controlled surface collections, subsurface testing, and ultimate mitigatory measures were conceived. By the end of the first year of survey and testing, we were in serious trouble; nearly 1,000 sites were recorded in the normal pool area, each of which could contribute in some way to our knowledge of northeast Missouri prehistory. Further, our efforts were becoming dissipated; construction of recreational facilities threatened destruction of many sites. We were forced by time and having to play "catch up" into doing several intensive subsurface tests each season, which slowed the survey and the ultimate accumulation of testable data and selection of sites for mitigation. Obviously the more sites we located, the less the percentage of sites which could be mitigated. Further, we were criticized for lack of a comprehensive design following review of our first full annual report; the negative reviews were justified.

Any of a number of archaeologists of that period could have written similar comments about the first year of a large contract program—too little time and too much work. Also, the vagaries connected with such a large project were maddening. As soon as work began on one site, another site would be located that commanded immediate attention before it was destroyed. Just about the time work was switched to the new site, another site would be found, and so on. Even working out the logistics of keeping various crews in the field—finding housing, keeping vehicles running, purchasing supplies—was a full-time job. A new generation of archaeologists began to learn what their forebears connected with the River Basin Surveys had learned: large-scale archaeological projects could be nightmares to run.

While the survey was proceeding, crews began to excavate several sites in 1975 and 1976. The rationale for excavation varied from site to site, ranging from imminent destruction of a site by construction activity to more traditional

Figure 7.6. Burial pits in the cemetery area at the Cave site, Monroe County, Missouri (from O'Brien and Warren 1982c, courtesy Academic Press).

archaeological considerations, such as establishing typological systems for pottery and projectile points. Field procedures consisted primarily of excavation and a small amount of surface collecting. At most sites the plow zone was removed by mechanical stripping, and subsurface features (storage pits, post molds, burials, etc.) were excavated by hand (Figure 7.6). Backhoe trenches were excavated at several sites to obtain stratigraphic information. The reports that were produced (e.g., Angus 1976, 1977; Hunt 1976a, 1976b, 1977a, 1977b) were site-specific descriptions of the subsurface features that were present and of the artifacts that were recovered during excavation. As part of the large 1976 annual report, Henning included Robert Warren's (1976) summary of survey data and structure—a point I will return to shortly.

The Corps of Engineers sent the reports out for peer review, meaning that several people in the archaeological profession were handpicked to provide written assessments of the reports, both in terms of quality of reporting and, more importantly, in terms of quality of the research framework. The reviews, as Henning (1979: 8) noted, were critical, especially of the project's design. Michael Ruppert, who wrote the original research design for the project, had stated that "the major research orientation of this project will be the definition and study of settlement-subsistence systems" (Ruppert 1975: 2). Once a working taxonomy of site types was formulated, at least two endangered sites of each type were to be chosen for excavation (Ruppert 1975: 13–14): "The emphasis of major excavations should be toward recovery of data which will increase knowledge about settlement types and systems." These were satisfactory goals for a project of its size; the only problem was, the project didn't live up to the goals it set for itself: the rationale that was adopted for the actual selection of sites to be tested did not follow the research design, and sampling and analytical procedures did not meet the stated goals. In short, "there was no multistage strategy that permitted analysis at the testing level in order to structure larger excavations" (O'Brien and Henning 1982: 8). Reviewers recognized the incongruity between goals and product and blasted the project.

Peer review was not a new concept in contract archaeology, but in the 1970s it became standard practice since agencies entrusted with large sums of federal money to spend on archaeological projects wanted to ensure that the work being performed met with the general approval of the archaeological community. Although the reviewers of the Cannon annual reports were on target with most of their criticisms, at times the tone they adopted was too strident. My guess is that some of them had never tried to run a large contract project and thus had never been pulled in a dozen directions at once, nor had they had to operate under fuzzy federal regulations that, while creating a monster, did not carry instructions on its proper care and feeding. The early Cannon project showed all the symptoms of a program that had the best interest of the resource base at heart but didn't know how to watch out for those interests. The four supervisory archaeologists (as well as many other staff members) were graduates of Nebraska's master's program, which has long been recognized for producing quality archaeologists. Although the training they had received at Nebraska served to orient them toward anthropological archaeology, the fact that the group was inbred meant that fresh ideas were slow to be infused into the project.

Before the Corps of Engineers would award another contract to the university, they required completion of a comprehensive research design, a plan of action, and determinations of eligibility for all the sites found during survey. I was hired as project director in 1977 and given those assignments to complete in two months' time. This was my first exposure to big-dollar archaeology, and I was much too naive to realize the enormity of running what became (for a while) the largest federally sponsored archaeology program in the United States. After several months I realized that I needed help in organizing and carrying out the myriad tasks associated with the project, and I hired Robert Warren, who had designed the original survey, and Dennis Lewarch, with whom I had worked previously, as associate project directors. Warren received his master's degree at

Nebraska before going to the University of Missouri to study with Raymond Wood; Lewarch was in the Ph.D. program at the University of Washington, and Robert Dunnell was his adviser. There is an old adage that says good managers hire people who are smarter than they are, and I followed this advice.

All of us had been greatly influenced by three articles that were published in the 1970s—Stuart Struever's "Problems, Methods and Organization: A Disparity in the Growth of Archeology" (1971a) and "Comments on Archaeological Data Requirements and Research Strategy" (1971b) and Charles Redman's "Multistage Fieldwork and Analytical Techniques" (1973)—and took to heart the issues raised therein when we restructured the project. Struever's argument was that despite an insistence on the part of the new archaeologists that processual studies—literally, studies designed to investigate the processes by which cultures change—were the direction in which the field should be heading, actual research strategies seldom if ever were designed and carried out to maximize the recovery of information pertinent to that goal. Most strategies were the same tried-and-true procedures that had been standard archaeological procedure for years. However, to develop an in-depth understanding of things such as how and why people distributed themselves over the landscape or how they made changes in the ways they obtained their food necessitated a change in procedure.

Struever's immediate archaeological problem was to describe and explain culture change in the lower Illinois River valley from ca. 300 B.C. to A.D. 200. Struever proposed that changes evident in subsistence and social organization during that period were adaptive responses to various selective pressures. His task was to describe the subsistence and organizational basis of the earlier and later systems and to demonstrate how changes in the earlier system were responses to those pressures. Struever (1971a) stated that to accomplish his objective, the following procedures would be followed. First, the paleoenvironment would be reconstructed, with delineation of significant microenvironmental zones. Second, each microenvironment would be sampled systematically by surface survey to locate representative samples in the various zones. Third, surface collections would be made and analyzed with an eye toward identifying temporal placement and site function. Fourth, a series of randomly selected test units would be placed across a site to sample the population of artifacts and subsurface features. Fifth, large-scale excavations (by hand) would be carried out in areas of sites where the units defined activity areas. Sixth, large sections of the sites would be exposed (by heavy equipment) to provide sufficient samples of artifacts in association with features to control for sampling error. Struever's six-step procedure echoed the procedure outlined by Binford (1964) several years before.

The physical environment in which Struever was working was very similar to the central Salt River valley (less than 70 miles separate the two localities), and, like him, we were interested in human adaptations to a midwestern riverine environment. In many respects, Struever's goals coincided with ours, and we adopted the basic elements of his six-stage framework. We also realized that, as Redman (1973) had proposed, a four-stage research design offered the best chances of maximizing recovery of information and especially of articulating research objectives with field and analytical methods. The stages were (1) the use of both inductive and deductive reasoning in formulating a research design and in analyzing the data; (2) the use of programmatic and analytic feedback between different stages of research; (3) the use of probability sampling; and (4) the formulation of analytic techniques appropriate to the subject matter (O'Brien and Warren 1982a: 23).

Three projects had a significant bearing on the structure and goals of the re-formulated Cannon project: Wood and McMillan's work in the Pomme de Terre Valley, Richard MacNeish's Tehuacán Archaeological-Botanical Project (Byers 1967; MacNeish 1964; MacNeish et al. 1967, 1970, 1975), and Kent Flannery's Valley of Oaxaca Human Ecology Project (Flannery 1976; Flannery et al. 1970). The latter two projects were formed to investigate 10,000 years of human adaptation in semiarid highland valleys in south-central Mexico and, for their time, were visionary programs that, like the Pomme de Terre project, had integrated the work of specialists in fields such as geomorphology, agronomy, and ethnobiology with the work of archaeologists instead of treating the results of those specialists as ancillary data. I had worked in Oaxaca and Tehuacán for five field seasons while at Rice University and the University of Texas at Austin and had seen firsthand, especially in Oaxaca, how archaeological projects with a human-ecology slant were put together. Three other members of the Cannon project also had worked in Oaxaca and were greatly influenced by the experience. Because of that influence, we made the decision in 1977 to change the name of the project from the Cannon Reservoir Archaeological Project to the Cannon Reservoir Human Ecology Project, reflecting not only a change in name but a complete reorientation (O'Brien 1977). Besides, we found the acronym of the original name to be less than flattering.

The orientation of the reorganized project was highly ecological (O'Brien and Warren 1982a; Warren and O'Brien 1982a, 1982b) in scope, with a concise set of expectations drawn from our understanding of how organisms—in this case humans—exploit patchy environments, that is, those comprising complex, intersecting floral communities. In fact, patch ecology was the central focus of the Cannon project. Although Lewarch, Warren, and I were not novices in the field of ecology, I need to mention an intellectual debt owed Alan Osborn and Carl Falk, both then of the University of Nebraska–Lincoln. They had coauthored a manual (Osborn and Falk 1977) for use by their field-school students who were working along the Niobrara River in north-central Nebraska, and we borrowed heavily from their insightful analysis of how to put into operation a research strategy centered around the concept of human use of patchy environments.

As I noted in Chapter 6, the southern Prairie Peninsula, which includes the Salt River valley, is a mosaic of environments that was formed during early postglacial times by a unique set of climatic factors (Kuchler 1964; Transeau 1935). At a macroscale, the two most obvious biomes are the tall-grass prairie and the deciduous forest, peninsulas of which interdigitate—or interlock like fingers on folded hands. The southern Prairie Peninsula is an ideal laboratory in which to examine human response to intersecting environmental subsets, each of which comprises different geomorphological and floral characteristics. The importance of this spatial variation on the organisms (including humans) that use these patches is noted by Wiens (1976: 90): "A variety of attributes or adaptive responses of populations develop within the selective regimes associated with this heterogeneity."

Of particular concern was how human groups had distributed themselves across the landscape at different times in search of food and other resources. The physical environment of the region, especially vegetation patterns, had changed dramatically throughout the Holocene, and to understand changing land-use patterns, we needed to be able to model what environmental changes had occurred. This point was made by Struever (1971a), but he used the term *environmental reconstruction*. Past environments, however, cannot be reconstructed. We can never hope to know precisely where the edge between the forest and prairie was at ca. 5000 B.C., but we *can* model what previous environments might have looked like. For example, we can use General Land Office (GLO) records to map vegetation patterns from the early nineteenth century. In laying out township and range lines, GLO surveyors faithfully recorded understory and overstory observed along section lines. Field notes also document the common names, diameters, and distances and directions from corner posts of "bearing trees"—trees that were marked to enable the relocation of section and quarter-section corners. These data, although they have their biases (Warren 1976; Wood 1976c), allow the delimitation of prairie and forest communities and can be used in studies of the compositions, diversities, densities, and resource potential of forests.

As important as they are, GLO data give us a view of vegetation zones only for the early nineteenth century (or later, as in some areas of Missouri). What do we do about the remainder of the Holocene? As Wood and his colleagues showed in the Pomme de Terre Valley, there are other data that can be used to model previous environments. For our model of Holocene environmental change in the central Salt River valley, we made generous use of a variety of existing information from the Midwest (Warren 1982a; Warren and O'Brien 1982a, 1982b). For example, pollen and accompanying radiocarbon dates have shown that around 5000 B.C. much of the Midwest was affected by dry, westerly winds that dominated weather patterns during progressively longer portions of the year. By that date changes in vegetation patterns were pronounced, with prairies reaching their maximum eastward extent—well beyond their modern limits. Evidence from the Pomme de Terre Valley and elsewhere (Ahler 1973a, 1973b; Butzer 1977, 1978; Klippel 1970, 1971) indicates that rates of hillslope erosion increased significantly as a result of the retreat of forests to wetter positions along stream courses. All these developments would have had profound effects on animal populations, causing changes in body size, population density, and geographic distribution (McMillan 1976c; McMillan and Klippel 1981; Purdue 1980). As Warren (1982a, 1984) pointed out, aquatic resources would have been affected as well: stream discharge decreased in Missouri and Illinois (Hill 1975; Klippel et al. 1978), lake levels dropped in at least portions of the upper Midwest (Brugman 1980; Van Zant 1979), and swamps became desiccated in the Mississippi River floodplain of southeastern Missouri (J. E. King and Allen 1977).

All of the above data were used to construct a model of what the environment might have been in the Salt River valley during the Hypsithermal. Similar lines of evidence were used to fill out the model for the remainder of the Holocene. We then examined the archaeological record from neighboring portions of the Midwest for information concerning the timing of certain human responses to the changing physical environment. These data were used to construct a model of how groups in the Salt River valley made use of the landscape and its resources through time. We then derived from the model a series of expectations that could be examined archaeologically through survey and excavation.

At this point you might ask why we had to be so formal in our modeling. Couldn't we simply have gone out, found where sites were and were not located, and let it go at that? We certainly could have, but our opinion was that without developing a formal model and a set of predictions, there was little chance, given the size of the region to be examined, of maintaining any semblance of order during the investigation. In other words, we could easily have shot off in a dozen directions at once, spending several years and several million dollars to generate a warehouse full of artifacts that were not adequate to address what we saw as the really important and interesting research questions. To constantly remind ourselves of what it was that we were doing, and *why* we were doing it, we needed a formal research statement that guided everything we did. It did not *control* the research—we could always add to or subtract from the statement—but it helped keep our research operations on course. When a particular site was selected for excavation, it was because we had reason to suspect it would yield information relative to human adaptation to the changing Holocene environment. When a site was surface collected intensively—as numerous sites were—it was because we had good reason to believe that it contained artifacts that could be used to understand different functions that were carried out at that locality (e.g., resource extraction, food processing).

Perhaps the most significant feature of the Cannon project was the site survey, which allowed us to examine large-scale patterns of how prehistoric groups used the central Salt River valley. Here we were immediately faced with the conflict in values that Tom King (1971, 1977) spoke of. On the one hand, our responsibility to the Corps of Engineers was to document the sites that would be affected by construction activities. On the other hand, we had drawn up a reasonable research design, which centered around the changes that groups had made in their relation to the physical environment throughout the Holocene. And, it stood to reason, those groups had not limited their activities to the area of the Salt River valley below 606 feet AMSL, the normal pool level of Clarence Cannon Reservoir, nor even to the 65,000-acre "take area"—which included the pool area, a shoreline easement, and preserves designated as public-access areas, recreation areas, and conservation areas (Figure 7.5). Archaeological survey conducted prior to 1977 was restricted to this take area, which included bottomland and terraces—the heart of the oak-hickory biome. Our interest lay in the higher elevations as well—steep valley sides, ridge tops, and flat uplands—the latter the heart of the tall-grass-prairie biome. Although we could never hope to know precisely the territories over which prehistoric human groups had roamed during their economic pursuits, we could be sure that the higher-elevation areas, especially the upland prairie, had figured prominently in those activities.

We approached the Corps of Engineers with a solution to the problem of how to include nonfederal lands within our survey, and they agreed to it. We would structure a survey that would examine a much larger area than was included in the take area, but we would use nonfederal funds to cover that portion that lay outside the reservoir lands. The extended project boundary, which conformed to the area examined by the Missouri Botanical Garden (1974) during their environmental-impact study, encompassed 1,149 square kilometers (Figure 7.5). In reality, we used two approaches to the survey, each with different goals and designs (Warren 1979, 1982b).[6] The *purposive survey,* a continuation of the efforts begun by Henning in 1959 (D. R. Henning 1961) and continued by Warren in 1974–1976 (Warren 1976), was designed to locate and record archaeological sites lying in the direct-impact zone (federal lands). But to examine the region as a whole with as few biases as possible, we used a doubly stratified *probabilistic survey.*

Probabilistic survey, in various guises, was nothing new to archaeology in 1977, though it was still far from clear how best to sample a region for this type of survey. Archaeologists in the 1960s and 1970s were heavily influenced by spatial geographers such as Peter Haggett, whose book *Locational Analysis in Human Geography* (Haggett 1965) became almost a sampling bible. They quickly learned the sampling buzz words, such as "stratified random sample" and "stratified systematic unaligned sample," but some of the literature of the

6. The following discussion of survey strategies is adapted from Warren 1982a, 1982b.

period makes it clear that it was not always evident *why* one chose one type of sampling procedure over another.

There are several ways in which a survey sampling design can be structured, though I highlight only two here. Regardless of which method is selected, the first decision is to select the percentage of the region one wishes to sample and what the size and shape of the sampling units will be. The latter consideration presents a whole set of methodological considerations that could easily fill the rest of this chapter (see Plog 1976 for an overview); suffice it to say that the size of the units is tied directly to myriad variables, not the least of which is sampling rate. Once these two decisions have been made, the remaining decision concerns how to select which units get sampled. In simple random sampling, the units are, as the name implies, located randomly. For example, as shown in the top set of blocks in Figure 7.7, if we wish to survey 10% of a region, we could divide the region into 100 equal-sized units, number them 1–100, and draw 10 numbers out of a hat. We then would survey those units. We could also divide the region into 200 units and survey 20 of them. The results might be dramatically different—hence my comment about unit size and sampling percentage being linked. I might also add that we could, after pulling a number, survey that unit and then put the number back in the hat, perhaps to be selected again. This is called sampling with replacement.

We could also stratify the sampling area based on environmental features that we view as having conditioned the location of human settlements and use areas. In the bottom set of squares in Figure 7.7, 25% of the survey region is composed of prairie and 75% of forest. The sampling units are the same size as they were previously, and we select them randomly, but we ensure that three-quarters of them are located in forested areas and one-quarter in prairie areas. Thus, the result would be proportionate samples from each topographic area.

Each method has its drawbacks, but the stratified random sample has the advantage of ensuring proportional coverage, whereas simple random sampling does not. There is no guarantee with simple random sampling that all 10 units might not be located in one corner of the survey area. Stratifying the region minimizes the chance that sampling units will be clustered. The question, of course, is how to stratify the region. There is no right or wrong answer to this question; for the Cannon Reservoir survey we used five slope-position categories, or *drainage classes,* as the first set of sampling strata. Each drainage class correlated with a discrete set of landform types and with a number of other important environmental variables (Warren and O'Brien 1981), and together they partitioned the study area into a series of five ribbon-like zones that roughly paralleled the courses of major streams or capped upland interstream divides (Figure 7.8). The classes contained distinct arrays of topographic features, and tests showed that they significantly reflected patterned variation of dominant

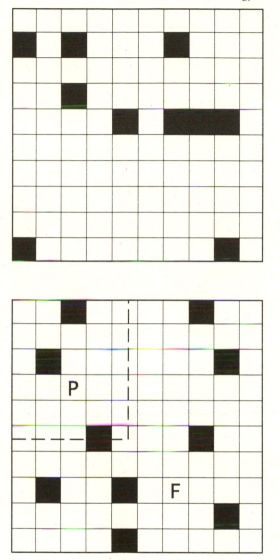

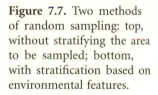

Figure 7.7. Two methods of random sampling: top, without stratifying the area to be sampled; bottom, with stratification based on environmental features.

biome distributions, forest species compositions, tree diversities and densities, soil characteristics, and prehistoric and historical-period site locations.

The study area was also stratified into five geographic areas, and we sampled each one independently to ensure dispersion of survey units across the sampling area. We also controlled for land areas falling within different drainage classes in order to increase the likelihood that survey units were proportionately representative of environmental variation in the region. To survey the doubly stratified study area, we used legal quarter-section units (160 acres each) as sampling quadrats; we then surveyed 10% of the possible 1,766 units. We used a variety of techniques, including shovel testing, to find sites within the sample quadrats.

In retrospect, the survey of the Cannon Reservoir was a success from several standpoints, not the least of which was the integration of the goals of cultural-resource management with those of solid research into the changing cultural and physical landscape in the Salt River valley throughout the Holocene. Importantly, as with the Truman Reservoir survey, we were able to document where sites did not occur. Almost 100% of federal lands in the Cannon Reservoir were surveyed between 1974 and 1979, giving us an excellent sample of floodplain and bottomland-terrace sites from which to select candidates for excavation. In addition, we were able to extend our knowledge base into the upland areas that surrounded the valley, though we were able to carry out only limited weekend testing of a few of those sites.

One of the most interesting, and at the time vexing, problems that we faced with respect to excavation was in actuality not an archaeological problem at all but rather a bureaucratic one. Even as the probabilistic survey was getting under way, we were forced to excavate some sites in order to keep pace with construction activities. Ideally, one would like to delay excavation until the survey has been completed and the data analyzed, but this was impossible. Thus, decisions about which sites to excavate were sometimes made before we

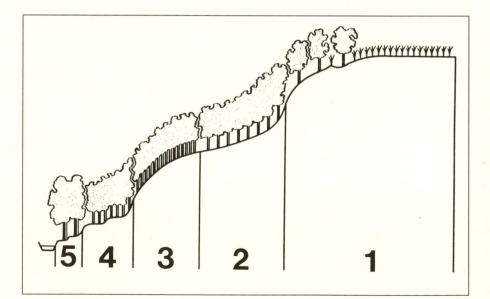

Figure 7.8. Idealized transverse section of the central Salt River valley, showing drainage classes and associated floral and topographic characteristics (from Warren and O'Brien 1981).

knew how a particular site stacked up against others in the larger sample. In some cases we got lucky. For example, the Pigeon Roost Creek deposit turned out to be over 3 meters deep and to contain an almost unbroken record of occupation from the Dalton period through the Mississippian period (Figure 7.9). Its geomorphological setting indicated that it might be a deep site, but so did the settings of 200 other endangered sites. We did not have time to test them all, but as I said, we got lucky.

The nonarchaeological problem we faced was that federal regulations required that before funds could be expended to excavate a site, it had to be declared eligible for inclusion on the national register. It did not actually have to be placed on the register—why place it on the register if it was going to be destroyed?— but the Advisory Council on Historic Preservation had to concur with the case being made for the site's eligibility. As I asked previously, how could a site be determined eligible if you didn't have much information on it—information about the depth of deposit, the date and nature of components that were present, and so forth? These kinds of information obviously could only come through excavation, but excavation had to wait for determinations of eligibility. How did one get around this catch? After considerable delay, a mechanism was finally installed in the federal regulations that provided for *some* excavation—but not too much—as a means of making determinations of eligibility. Regulations were drafted that divided archaeological fieldwork into three sequential segments: (1) site survey, (2) site testing (minimal excavation), and (3) mitigation (large-scale excavation).

These regulations might have worked for small projects, but the individuals who drafted them had never worked on a project the size of Cannon. There simply was no way of sequentially (a) completing the survey, (b) assessing several thousand sites in terms of eligibility criteria, (c) testing a sample of the site population, (d) further evaluating those sites in terms of eligibility criteria, (e) completing individual site forms, (f) waiting for the advisory council's concurrence, and (g) finally excavating the sites determined eligible. If we had followed such a course, we might by now, over a decade after the floodgates were closed, be at the point of submitting the forms. And what about the sites that were being destroyed while we waited for approval? Surely some mechanism was needed to circumvent the red tape associated with the entire process.

Through the persistent urging of the Corps of Engineers, such a mechanism was devised, although it was almost too late in coming. The mechanism, which actually may have been tried out for the first time with the Cannon project, involved submitting what the advisory council called "district nominations." These allowed for the submittal of a number of sites at once, all under a "thematic heading." Our thematic heading was "time." We put together four units, each representing a very large slice of time, and listed as many sites as possible in each unit. If we had no temporally diagnostic artifacts from a site, we

Figure 7.9. Photograph showing Dalton-period artifacts and hearths at the Pigeon Roost Creek site, Monroe County, Missouri.

guessed at its temporal affiliation based on such things as topographic setting— anything to get as many sites listed as possible. The more sites we listed, the more opportunity we had of including a site that down the road might become a prime candidate for excavation. The advisory council accepted our nominations, and a memorandum of agreement between the council and the Corps of Engineers was signed in late 1977.

By the close of fieldwork in the summer of 1979, 48 prehistoric sites had been excavated (including those excavated by University of Missouri personnel) and 39 had been subjected to intensive, systematic surface collection (O'Brien 1985a). Excavations at most sites combined mechanical removal of the plow zone with hand excavation of underlying deposits. Two overriding concerns were (1) delineation of the structure of prehistoric communities—how the communities were laid out (O'Brien and Warren 1982c)—and (2) recovery of faunal and floral remains from sealed contexts (e.g., pits) that could be dated securely, either by radiocarbon dating or through association with pottery and projectile points. Preservation of carbonized seeds ranged from fair to poor (F. B. King 1982d), but bone preservation usually was excellent (Bozell and Warren 1982). Thus we were able to construct quantitative profiles of the animals that composed the human diet and to examine how the diet had changed through time. We were also fairly successful in developing a chronological ordering of ceramic materials from the region (Donham 1982; Donham and O'Brien 1985) and were even more successful in developing a classification and ordering of projectile points, both of which were based in large part on 186 points from the 3.3-meter-deep deposits at Pigeon Roost Creek (O'Brien and Warren 1982b, 1983, 1985).

There certainly were far more sites in the project area than could ever have been excavated, and to augment our recovery program we added a method that had been used in archaeology for a variety of purposes but had rarely been used to its full potential. That method was surface collection. All archaeologists collect artifacts from site surfaces, some to create type collections, others to gain a preliminary idea of when a site was occupied, still others to pinpoint areas of a site for future excavation. Techniques for performing surface collections are variable, as are recovery rates, with each depending on the purpose for which the collection is intended. The type of collection strategy I discuss briefly here is *intensive, systematic* surface collection, which sets it apart from haphazard (uncontrolled) grab sampling. By *systematic* I mean that there is a system to how artifacts are collected; by *intensive* I mean that either all artifacts or all of a particular kind of artifact are collected. Systematic surface collection is applied routinely today both in CRM and non-CRM projects, though, like numerous other methods that appear to be commonplace today, this is a fairly recent phenomenon. I consider the issue of surface collection in more depth in Chapter 8, especially with reference to experimental data; here I briefly examine some of the history behind the method and its place in the Cannon project.

One early use of systematic surface collection was by Binford et al. (1970), who employed the method at Hatchery West in Carlyle Reservoir, Illinois, to predict where subsurface house patterns would be located (the proposal being that rich surface deposits would overlay houses). To make the collection, Binford and his associates plowed the site, gridded it into a series of squares 6 meters on a side, and then waited for the rain to settle the soil and expose the artifacts. The team collected all material from each square, placing the material in separate bags by square. This probably was not the first time (the work was done in 1963) that a team of archaeologists had gridded off a site and collected surface materials by unit, but no other example had a larger impact on Americanist archaeology. Soon, intensive systematic surface collection was routinely used to guide the placement of excavation units. Interestingly, Binford et al. began their work under the assumption that dense concentrations of surface materials could be used to predict the locations of house outlines, but what they found, in many instances, was a lack of congruence between the two. High surface-artifact density predicted not where the houses were but rather where the dump areas were. Houses were located in areas of extremely light surface debris, which led Binford et al. to investigate the depositional history of the site further.

Similar studies were conducted by Charles Redman and Patty Jo Watson (1970) in Turkey and by Paul Tolstoy and Suzanne Fish (1975) in the Valley of Mexico, and both revealed that the relation between what is on the surface of a site and what lies below the surface can be exceedingly complex. These studies, especially their examinations of how deposits are formed, paved the way for a host of similar studies during the 1970s (see Lewarch and O'Brien 1981a for examples), including Dan Healan's (1972) study of intrasite structure at Beckwith's Fort, the large, fortified Mississippian-period center in Mississippi County, Missouri.

Concurrent with the emphasis in Americanist archaeology on surface materials as guides to excavation came a separate realization that *"the surficial distribution of artifacts constitutes an appropriate source of archaeological data independent of subsurface remains"* (Dunnell and Dancey 1983: 270; emphasis in original). Part of this realization undeniably came about as cultural-resource managers began dealing with large numbers of sites and soon realized that excavation alone was not adequate to address the myriad issues raised by CRM. Archaeologists integrating surface collection with other field methods (Lewarch 1979; O'Brien and McDaniel 1982) began to create data bases that were useful in solving a number of site-specific problems, such as predicting the presence or absence of subsurface features such as pits and hearths; defining "site" boundaries (see Chapter 8); determining intrasite growth patterns; locating functionally distinct areas; locating residential versus nonresidential areas; and defining site function (Lewarch and O'Brien 1981a). These were the uses we made of most controlled surface collections from the Salt River valley.

Successful integration of intensive surface collection with other methods also developed regional data sets for determining land-use patterns, dating cultural components across a region, and determining relations between and among sites in terms of how they functioned in settlement systems (Lewarch and O'Brien 1981a: 320). In short, intensive surface collection allowed for the controlled comparison of form and function through time and across large expanses of space. The point accepted by a growing number of archaeologists was made by Dunnell and Dancey (1983): If recurrent patterning in a set of surface artifacts can be attributed to the activities of prehistoric groups rather than to postdepositional processes (see Chapter 8) or collection biases introduced by the archaeologist, then any given body of surface material is potentially useful for research. This does not imply that *every* surface collection is going to yield the kind of information desired—for example, Alan Downer (1977) failed to detect significant patterning in surface materials from Phillips Spring—but often the analyst fails to take into account various biases or unique properties of the specific situation during analysis (Lewarch and O'Brien 1981a: 318).

Related to the issue of intensive, systematic surface collection is the issue of what constitutes a site. This contentious issue in Americanist archaeology came into sharper focus as a result of CRM (Dunnell 1992; Klinger 1976), and I defer in-depth discussion of it until Chapter 8. But we might pause here to look at the questions involved: What *does* constitute a site? A single artifact? Ten artifacts? Or is a site defined by density—so many artifacts per unit of area? Sites to a certain degree are bookkeeping devices used by archaeologists to keep track of artifacts and space. The term *site* immediately connotes a locality that contains artifacts, but the term implies nothing about the number of artifacts or the amount of area over which they are spread. Sites can range in size from many hectares down to a few square meters or even down to the occurrence of a single artifact. How we record these phenomena—in essence, how we define *site*—is problematic. It is unfair to say that archaeologists have always paid little or no attention to small sites, but the archaeological literature is clear that there has always been a bias against localities that did not produce enough artifacts to assign the sites to particular time periods or that did not hold out the promise of containing subsurface features. And pedestrian survey is not really designed to locate low-density artifact scatters.

With the advent of CRM, archaeologists were forced to confront the issue of small sites, since they were part of the resource base and therefore were potentially eligible for protection. Concurrently, as we have seen, archaeologists were beginning to shift their attention to landscape archaeology—how prehistoric groups interacted with the physical environment during their economic pursuits. During the 1970s numerous projects were specifically designed to investigate the settlement systems of mobile hunters and gatherers, and the field procedures that grew out of those projects revolutionized how archaeologists examined the distribution of artifacts across a landscape, resulting in the new method called "siteless survey." Foremost among those projects were William Dancey's (1973, 1974, 1976) survey of the Priest Rapids area of eastern Washington; David Thomas's (1969, 1971, 1973, 1975) survey of the Reese River valley in Nevada; Emma Lou Davis's (1975) survey of China Lake, California; and Robert Bettinger's (1975) survey of Owens Valley, California. Characteristic of all the surveys was the systematic search for artifacts within explicitly defined sample units. While sites were, in some cases, located, recorded, and collected in traditional fashion, the surveyors accorded these no more importance than isolated artifacts between clusters. By plotting the locations of individual artifacts across the various landscapes, surveyors detected patterns in artifact distribution that would have gone undetected using traditional survey methods, which obviously are geared to locating high-density artifact clusters. The results of surveying the distributions of artifacts across a landscape are excellent in terms of information yielded on differential human use through time of that landscape. In terms of the dictates of CRM, "siteless survey" allows the investigator to make much better judgments regarding the significance of the resource base than do traditional survey methods.

To better understand the nature of human use of the central Salt River valley and to estimate the number of "sites" that were being missed by our traditional survey, we undertook a siteless survey of a 43-hectare portion of the bottomland

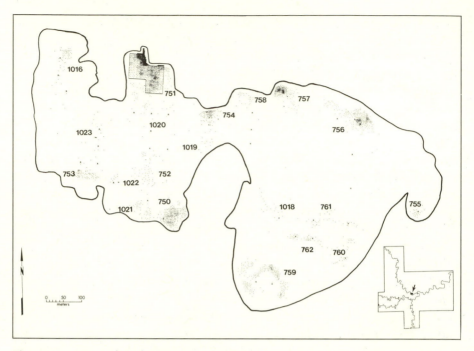

Figure 7.10. Map of artifact scatter in Putman Bottom in the Salt River valley, Monroe County, Missouri (after Warren and Miskell 1981).

along the North Fork of the Salt River—a locality known locally as Putman Bottom. Survey teams walked every furrow of the plowed bottom and flagged each artifact that was noticed. The locations of the artifacts were then shot by transit and the readings converted to points on a map. When fieldwork was completed, 15,969 artifacts had been plotted, the distributions of which indicated that artifact concentrations varied widely in size, density, and location (Figure 7.10). There also were hundreds of artifacts that lay outside concentrations, some of which undoubtedly had been displaced by plowing. But other pieces, such as isolated small projectile points, probably were in more or less the same position as when they were lost or discarded.

For comparative analysis, artifact concentrations were consolidated into 20 cases on the basis of the spatial contiguity of artifacts as shown on large-scale distribution maps. In the course of analysis (Warren and Miskell 1981), different kinds of technological patterns were recognized among the concentrations. Two kinds of sites were represented: (1) proposed residential sites, which had high artifact densities indicative of intensive and/or recurrent occupations and artifact assemblages that represented light domestic activities; and (2) proposed procurement-processing sites, which had low artifact densities indicative of infrequent and/or temporary utilization and artifact assemblages that represented resource-extraction and/or heavy-processing activities. These results were consistent with the expectations of the settlement model: that functional diversity was high among sites in Prairie Peninsula bottomlands containing varied and dispersed resources and that settlement locations in narrow, banded environments were conditioned as much by domestic requirements as by strategic-resource needs.

Interestingly, Putman Bottom had been surveyed several times prior to 1978, during which 13 of the 20 concentrations had been recorded as sites. The 7 concentrations that were missed ranged from low- to high-density scatters. This told us that the traditional survey that was being undertaken probably underestimated the true number of "sites" by as much as 30–40%. When one took into account that the survey had been conducted in a plowed bottomland, where surface visibility was not obscured by ground cover, the underrepresentation of all sites undoubtedly was much higher.

Historical-Period Archaeology at Cannon Reservoir

I mentioned in the Preface that because of space limitations I would not discuss projects that focused on the historical period unless that focus was part of a larger examination of a regional archaeological record. Probably few contract-archaeology projects have expended the amounts of time and money on historical-period archaeological investigations that were expended by the Cannon project, the reason being that the Salt River valley was an ideal laboratory in which to examine the processes of colonization and spread of human settlement in a frontier environment. The majority of immigrants to the Salt River valley came from the Bluegrass region of Kentucky between ca. 1820 and 1850, bringing with them what Mitchell (1972, 1978) termed an *upper South culture*, based on tobacco, hemp, and slaves. This culture was transplanted almost immediately upon arrival in the Salt Valley (R. D. Mason 1982, 1983; R. D. Mason et al. 1982). Our interest was in determining what cultural- and physical-environmental factors influenced such things as where colonists made their land purchases, how many acres they purchased, and how their holdings grew or shrank through time as colonists accumulated or lost wealth.

Some of the requisite information needed to address these issues can be derived from excavation, but the archaeological record is no substitute for documentary information when trying to understand who the colonists were, where they came from, and to whom in the region they were related. We discussed with the Corps of Engineers the possibility of expanding our research into archival sources to gain a better perspective on the people behind the sites, and they agreed. We then spent almost five years in various archives in Missouri and Kentucky making detailed use of land-entry records, population- and agricultural-census records, probate records, marriage records, poll books, and the like. By the end of that time, we had a fairly extensive set of information on 1,041 families that we used to examine the implications of a formal model of historical-period settlement that Hudson (1969) had originally devised and that we subsequently modified (Mason et al. 1982; Warren and O'Brien 1984; Warren et al. 1981, 1984); the model viewed movement of Euro-American groups across the landscape in terms of three processes—colonization, spread, and competition—each resulting in a unique spatial distribution of farmsteads.

It would be an overstatement to claim that prior to CRM archaeologists never paid much attention to the historical-period record, though it probably is safe to say that most of the attention was paid to sites such as mills, fur-trade posts, military facilities, and the residences of historical figures. The dictates of CRM, however, forced managers and archaeologists to consider all resources, down to such things as small farmsteads. Thus, the Cannon site survey inventoried all standing architecture as well as known sites where structures had once stood. Thirty-four sites, from a list of over 350, were nominated to the National Register of Historic Places and were determined to be eligible for inclusion. Eventually, 7 farmsteads were excavated, and an additional 14 were mapped and surface collected systematically. Several houses and farm buildings were drawn by an architectural team associated with the Historic American Buildings Survey.

Our preliminary assessment of the completeness of the documentary information for a particular farmstead was one important criterion for making a request for eligibility; the other was the integrity of the standing architecture and/or the surrounding site. We used a classification system to subdivide the large sample of standing buildings (Figure 7.11), which assisted us in tracking variation across the sample and identifying redundancy (O'Brien and Lewarch 1984; O'Brien et al. 1980). The farmsteads were excavated in the same manner as the prehistoric sites, with all archaeological deposits being waterscreened and all visible artifacts left in place until the site was mapped (Figure 7.12). Of particular interest were British and American ceramic items that could be used to examine topics such as social position and the availability of durable goods in a midwestern frontier locale (Majewski 1987; Majewski and O'Brien 1984, 1987; O'Brien 1984b; O'Brien and Majewski 1989; O'Brien, Mason, and Saunders 1982).

I leave it to others to judge the merits of the Cannon Reservoir Human Ecology Project, though I believe it more than fulfilled the legal requirements of cultural-resource management. In fact, that point was never really at issue. What was at issue was how to blend the dictates of contract archaeology with solid research into changing human adaptation to a midwestern riverine environment. One difference between the Cannon project and other large contract programs was that the results (admittedly some were preliminary) were published in book form (O'Brien 1984b; O'Brien, Warren, and Lewarch 1982). This point was made by Don Fowler, who reviewed one of the volumes:

Figure 7.11. The Matthew Mappin house, Monroe County, Missouri. The Greek Revival house, constructed of heavy frame members, was built shortly after 1840 by a family that had immigrated to the Salt River valley from Bath County, Kentucky (drawn in 1978 by the Historic American Buildings Survey [from O'Brien and Lewarch 1984]).

The volume is comparable in purpose to hundreds of other reports generated by "contract archaeologists". . . . The difference is that the present report is published as one of the hardcover Academic Press archeological series, in contrast to the usual practice of *issuing* a limited number of soft-cover (or no cover) reports that usually molder in the files of the contracting agency and are circulated one copy at a time through the copy-machine grapevine. The volume is apparently designed to be a "model" CRM report—to demonstrate that "contract" research can produce results as scientifically useful as "pure" research. The contract–pure research dichotomy is an oversimplification, but it highlights a long and often bitter debate in U.S. archeology [over] whether the results of legally required contract research have really been worth the vast amounts of money, time, and effort poured into them since about 1970. The present volume appears to justify an affirmative response to this question. (Fowler 1984: 196)

Figure 7.12. Photograph of the completed excavation of the Mappin-Vaughn house site, Monroe County, Missouri (from O'Brien, Mason, and Saunders 1982, courtesy Academic Press).

We were criticized in various quarters (e.g., Shay 1987) for certain conclusions that we drew from analysis, and I believe many of those criticisms had merit. William Green (1984) argued that the first volume, though informative, had been written before all the data were analyzed, a point on which all of us agreed (O'Brien 1984a). Many of the data still are unanalyzed. The subsequent volume (O'Brien 1984b), which was dedicated solely to an analysis of the historical-period occupation of the Salt River valley, was designed to present a more complete picture of that topic, but reports continued to flow from the project years after its official completion date. They will continue to appear as more analysis is done. That is, after all, the way science operates.

Closing the Circle

Life is full of little quirks and twists (most of which are too small and insignificant to be rated as full-fledged ironies), one of them being that in the end the University of Missouri once again became involved with the Cannon project. I was hired by the university in 1980 and brought with me the massive data sets that resulted from the years of work in the reservoir. In fact, the majority of what was written on the work conducted from 1977 onward was compiled by University of Missouri students and faculty through a subsequent contract between the university and the St. Louis District of the Corps of Engineers. Thus, although the University of Missouri did not receive the enormous amount of money that was poured into the fieldwork, it did realize some of the fruits of the labor put in by the University of Nebraska.

If the Cannon project had been completed a few years earlier, the book on the years of work in the reservoir would have been closed in the early 1980s. After all, fieldwork had been completed, except for a few clean-up operations; the reservoir was filling; and reports and monographs had been written. The agency was happy with the way the project had turned out, and the two universities involved had received payment for the services of their archaeologists. What more was there to do? As I said, had this been the 1970s, the book would have been closed. But it wasn't. When the project shifted back to the University of Missouri, it wasn't only mountains of data that came to the university. It was also over 1,500 boxes of archaeological materials of all kinds—an enormous amount by anyone's standards. The University of Nebraska did not want the responsibility of housing the material, but Carl Chapman did, believing that Missouri artifacts belonged in Missouri. As I point out in the next chapter, he signed an agreement with Nebraska and the St. Louis District in 1979, and the University of Missouri became the proud recipient of several million artifacts.

Having such a tremendous array of materials certainly was important from a research standpoint, but would the university really be able to provide for their protection? Few people in museums and universities were asking that question in the 1970s, but one of those people was Chapman. As we will see, by 1979 he had begun to plan for the protection of the archaeological collections at the university. Unfortunately, the level of care provided did little to get at the root of what was fast becoming a national disgrace. Of course, those were still the fast-paced days of cultural-resource management, when most archaeologists were more worried about getting artifacts out of the ground than they were about preserving the materials for the future. It would not be too many years, however, before the issue of collections preservation and management became a central focus in Americanist archaeology. Ironically (this one was a full-fledged irony), the centrality of the issue did not result from any concerted effort on the part of archaeologists; rather, to a significant degree it came from American Indians.

8

Archaeology as the Science of Artifacts

The 1980s and 1990s

This chapter should have been the easiest to write, since one always finds it comparatively simple to write about things that are familiar, and here it is no different for me. I became heavily involved with archaeological fieldwork across the state after becoming director of the American Archaeology Division at the University of Missouri in 1980, and thus I can personally chronicle what has occurred in Missouri archaeology since that time. However, the logarithmic growth in archaeological fieldwork during the 1980s—and the 1990s are no different—makes it almost impossible to provide even a brief glimpse of projects and analyses that occurred during that period. I warned you in the Preface that I would forget to include or would be forced to leave out some important sites and excavations. Unfortunately, omissions here are at a scale well above those in previous chapters, as I have had to delete mention of numerous projects that produced significant and interesting results.

Even after deciding what to include, I faced a major problem in how best to organize the chapter. Given the myriad different directions that fieldwork in Missouri has assumed since 1980, it is almost impossible to organize the work into a coherent series of topics. Much of the work, especially on the analysis side, has become so diverse and at the same time so detailed that the limits of some of the categories I tried to establish were stretched beyond the point of usefulness. To complicate matters, a series of events transpired in American archaeology during the 1980s that actually had nothing to do with fieldwork or analysis but had dramatic effects on the ways in which archaeology in the United States is currently practiced and will be practiced long into the future. Those events surrounded the related issues of who actually owned archaeological remains and how the remains were being stored.

In the end, I decided to focus the discussion on two analytical topics—surface archaeology and the physical properties of artifacts—and on two ethical and legal issues that were of growing concern in Americanist archaeology generally during the 1980s—the curation of archaeological collections and the movement toward repatriation of human remains and funerary items. I conclude the chapter with a discussion of what I consider to be the most significant archaeological find made in Missouri during the 1980s—the discovery at Albert Koch's Sulphur Springs (Kimmswick) site in Jefferson County of in situ Clovis points alongside the remains of mastodons.

Although it doesn't characterize everything I present in this chapter, the title "Archaeology as the Science of Artifacts" is appropriate for what I view as a critical research development not only in Missouri archaeology but also in Americanist archaeology during the 1980s. My use of that title in no way implies that work done prior to 1980 was necessarily nonscientific, nor am I suggesting that earlier work somehow viewed artifacts as being unimportant considerations in archaeological inquiry. Obviously, neither of those things is true. Rather, my purpose in using it is to call attention to the fact that several theoretical and methodological reorientations occurred in Americanist archaeology after 1980 that changed in a significant way how the archaeological record is approached. Several projects undertaken in Missouri typified this trend and in some cases actually were path-setting programs for archaeology generally. The age-old tried-and-true objectives of archaeology—for example, the writing of culture histories—were still around in the 1980s, but in certain quarters there was a growing interest in creating an archaeology grounded in an empirical context. And it is this empirical context that established the basis for scientific inquiry and began to set that kind of inquiry apart from other kinds.

Archaeology in an Empirical Context

Of all the definitions of science I have seen, Dunnell's (1988b: 9; see also Dunnell 1982b) strikes me as one of the best:

> Science is a particular kind of sense-making system that is distinguished by the use of theory to explain phenomena and which employs an empirical standard of truth as the ultimate arbiter of the correctness of its conclusions. Science has an explicit, self-constructed set of propositions which serve as the terms of observation and the means of relating those observations to one another; it is theoretical. In consequence of this property, cause is rendered in mechanistic terms, i.e., it is always located in the relational propositions of theory, usually termed "laws." Cause is attributed, not observed.

Dunnell's definition calls immediate attention to the fact that science is, at base level, nothing more than a way of making sense out of the world. Importantly, it is not the *only* way of making sense out of things but rather only *one* way. Scholars connected with the arts and humanities, for example, have ways of making sense out of the world around them that are every bit as appropriate as the sense-making systems used by scientists. Science is set apart from these other systems by its components: (a) a body of theory that is supposed to *explain* how and why things operate the way they do and (b) a coherent body of methods and techniques that are useful in determining the validity of logical implications that derive from the theory. It is strict reliance on the construction of propositions that can be proved false that sets science apart from other sense-making systems. In short, science is based on the ability to determine whether our conclusions are wrong.

If we accept this view of science, then we have to conclude that much of what has been passed off (often implicitly) as scientific endeavor in Americanist archaeology does not exactly fit the bill. Certainly if we examine most of the archaeological fieldwork carried out in Missouri over the last few decades, we would have a difficult time arguing that the conclusions drawn from that work could be proved false. Most work was never structured in such a way that its conclusions *could* be falsified. Rather, work actually was designed to *confirm* the conclusions. The result of these exercises was, as I noted in the Preface, the creation of stories that seemingly accounted for the facts as then known. These are what are called *post-facto accommodating arguments*—they accommodate the data to previously conceived notions of the way things ought to be. And they certainly don't *explain* the data in terms of any theory. Cause, if it is attributed to anything, is viewed as the result of such things as diffusion, acculturation, and group movement—the old anthropological standbys that have seen considerable duty over the last 150 years.

As I pointed out in Chapter 6 in the briefest of detail, much of the so-called new archaeology of the 1960s took aim at the supposed outdated goals of archaeology and attempted to replace such things as culture history with what were widely perceived as "scientific" goals, the most important of which was understanding culture process. Embedded in this called-for change in direction was the dictum that to be scientific, that is, to be able to "explain" the nature of the archaeological record (why things happened as they did), archaeology needed to figure out what the laws are that govern human behavior (J. J. Reid et al. 1975; Schiffer 1975b, 1976). If we only knew what the laws were—and there was no shortage of competing schemes to discover those laws (e.g., Binford 1985; Gould 1980, 1985; Gould and Watson 1982)—then perhaps we could answer the "why-type" questions—Why did agriculture develop when and where it did? Why did Mississippian peoples build pyramidal mounds? and so forth.

This emphasis on laws was rather curious in light of archaeology's deep and abiding interest in understanding culture change. How can laws be used to understand change, unless the properties of the subject matter are so invariant that change will *always* produce unidirectional and thus *predictable* outcomes? For example, we know that if we heat water to 212°F at sea level, it will boil and change to steam. And, importantly, water will boil at that temperature today, tomorrow, and the next day because there are invariant and essential properties of the molecule H_2O that cause it to react in a certain way when heat is applied. Do people always (re)act in a certain way to a particular stimulus? They must if there are laws that govern their behavior. We know, however, that they do not. All organisms—humans included—are *structured* by empirical laws—chemical and physical laws, for example—but they are not *governed* by them. The one law that does apply to organisms and their evolution is the law of contingency, that is, what happens at any point in an organism's life or within a lineage's evolution is *contingent* on but not *determined* by what happened at previous points. In other words, change is *stochastic,* or probabilistic, as opposed to *random.* And it *certainly* is not predetermined. As I point out in more detail in Chapter 9, some archaeologists unwittingly adopted a philosophy of science that deals exclusively with the physical-chemical side of the world, not the life-history side.

Archaeology's gradual emergence from the search for laws that govern human behavior was not in a unified direction. Rather, Americanist archaeology of the 1980s and early 1990s contained numerous competing ways of viewing the world, the majority of which need not concern us here. For example, one position (in reality, several related positions)[1] was grounded in the belief that somehow the archaeological record could be read like a text, but only through the combined efforts of numerous eyes, each pair bringing a different perspective to the issue. Specifically, the archaeological record could yield answers to questions of gender, race, and so on, but such analysis required the expertise of those sensitive to such issues (e.g., Conkey and Gero 1991). Such "paradigms" (to use the word loosely) demonstrated once again that in the absence of theory, archaeologists would borrow anything on the market, even goods offered by social historians.

Empirical Consequences

Despite these forays into the nonempirical world, the 1980s also marked the emergence of a small but increasingly growing segment of the archaeological community that attempted to phrase scientific conclusions so as to have empirical consequences—"those ultimate features upon which the acceptance or rejection of the conclusion rests" (Dunnell 1988b: 10). In Missouri, earlier work in the Pomme de Terre Valley had shown that such a concept certainly was applicable, and to a certain degree the Cannon Reservoir Human Ecology Project had furthered the notion. No sediments and artifacts from a site in the Midwest received more extensive treatment than those from Rodgers Shelter.

---

1. See Stark 1993 for a particularly lucid account of these positions, which are often lumped under the rubric "post-processual" studies (Hodder 1985).

Ahler's (1973a, 1973b, 1976) detailed analysis of sediments in the shelter, coupled with C. V. Haynes's (1976) geomorphological work, led to conclusions with empirical consequences that could then be examined with future data. Likewise, Ahler's (1971; see also Ahler and McMillan 1976) exhaustive work on the form and function of hafted, pointed bifaces—especially his microscopic use-wear analysis—was a model examination that paved the way for similar studies in the United States (Hayden 1979; Keeley 1980; Keeley and Newcomer 1977; Odell and Odell-Vereecken 1980). Importantly, Ahler's conclusions were testable because of the scientifically sound protocol employed. Although much of the work of the Cannon project involved detailed analysis of edge wear on stone artifacts (e.g., Curry 1979; Lewarch 1982; Warren and Miskell 1981), the data sets were so large that many analyses similar to those conducted on materials from Rodgers Shelter were not completed. Consequently, the results in many cases were preliminary estimates as opposed to concise empirical statements.

What set these projects apart from others was a rigorous adherence to a blueprint—a research design—that set forth both the issues to be addressed and the methods and techniques that were designed specifically to address the issues. For the Cannon project, considerable time was spent in outlining the theoretical underpinnings of the program (O'Brien 1977; O'Brien and Warren 1982a), in formulating propositions relative to how prehistoric and historical-period groups had used the landscape (Warren and O'Brien 1982b, 1984), in deriving testable implications from the propositions, and in describing how certain methods would be employed to examine the implications. Wood and McMillan (e.g., Wood 1966, 1976a; Wood and McMillan 1969) did the same relative to their work in the Pomme de Terre Valley, though perhaps in not such formal detail. The point I am leading up to is that it was not the fact that the personnel connected with these projects rigorously studied artifacts that made the projects scientific. It was, rather, the rigorous approach to fieldwork and analysis, as laid out in research designs, that made them scientific.

The Study of Formation Processes

As Dunnell (1988a) points out, increasing attention during the 1980s to formation processes—processes that create the archaeological record (e.g., daily activities involved with the manufacture, use, and discard of tools) and subsequently act to disrupt it (e.g., erosion, rodent activity, and modern plowing)—assisted greatly in the development of an empirical archaeology. Schiffer's early work on identifying formation processes (e.g., Schiffer 1972, 1976) led to a number of studies that not only expanded the list of processes (e.g., Stein 1987; Wood and Johnson 1978) but also treated such issues as modeling and replicating the effects of various processes on the archaeological record (e.g., Camilli 1988; Dunnell 1990a; Jermann 1981; Lewarch and O'Brien 1981a, 1981b; O'Brien and

Lewarch 1981; Odell and Cowan 1987; Wandsnider 1989). Importantly, Schiffer (1972, 1976, 1983, 1987) separated formation processes into two kinds—cultural and noncultural—a division that forced archaeologists to at least pay attention to the fact that all disturbances were not of the same origin and that different processes left variable imprints on archaeological signatures. Interestingly, the greatest impact that the study of formation processes had in archaeology was in the realm of cultural-resource management, which is not surprising given that federal guidelines required environmental-impact statements to take into account archaeological resources and that more archaeologists than not were engaged in CRM.

It is difficult to overestimate the effect that the examination of formation processes had on the redirection of archaeology toward an empirical end. By themselves, the types of modeling and experimentation used in investigating the effects of formation processes on archaeological signatures did not create a scientific archaeology, but they were a step in the general direction. As I discuss below, attention in some quarters began to shift away from associational units such as site and more toward the artifacts themselves and the kinds of modification they received during their manufacture, use, and discard, as well as toward cultural and natural disruptions to artifact patterns. In a very real sense, archaeologists were becoming predisposed to science by developing a scientifically defensible understanding of how the archaeological record is generated (Dunnell 1988a: 27).

Cultural-Resource Management in the 1980s

Ironically, it was never intended in any of the massive federal legislation pertaining to CRM that archaeological projects be "scientific." It *was* intended— in fact it was demanded—that archaeologists provide a plan of research that would be followed during a project and that they employ accepted standards in the conduct of fieldwork and analysis. However, there was always debate in archaeological circles over the place of "science" in CRM (e.g., see papers in E. L. Green 1984). This discussion was somewhat problematic, given the fact that federal agencies often required that CRM reports pass through peer review, including, in some cases, review by archaeologists totally opposed to CRM who viewed the whole exercise as "nonscientific." This requirement was akin to a declaration of open season on archaeologists involved in CRM work, and in more than a few cases the reviews were devastating. In many instances, however, a reviewer's complaint that a particular piece of CRM work was not scientific was really a thinly veiled gripe that the work was funded by the Corps of Engineers as opposed to the National Science Foundation.

To place in proper context the role that empirical studies began to play in archaeology, it is important to provide a bit of historical background, in effect picking up the story of CRM in Missouri that we left in Chapter 7. One of the lasting legacies of the large-scale CRM projects such as those conducted in Cannon and Truman reservoirs in Missouri and the Cache River basin in Arkansas was the development of methods and techniques—both field and analytical—to manage the archaeological record. Given the enormous size of some of the data bases with which managers and archaeologists had to contend, it was reasonable that efforts would be directed toward developing recovery and analytical techniques that would yield needed information at a lower cost than excavation. An equally important topic to anyone involved with a multistage archaeological project was the time required to analyze materials and to incorporate the results into succeeding levels of research (Goodyear et al. 1978; Schiffer et al. 1978). Thus it was natural that many of the methodological and analytical advances made in the application of surface-derived data, which were relatively inexpensive and quick to generate, were made in the 1970s and early 1980s.

By at least 1980, the complexion of CRM had begun to change in Missouri, as it had across the nation. The number of large-scale projects had declined significantly, though there were still several large projects in operation—perhaps the two best-known being the Dolores Archaeological Project in southern Colorado (e.g., Breternitz et al. 1986; Peterson and Orcutt 1987; Petersen et al. 1985) and the FAI-270 Project (e.g., Bareis and Porter 1984) in the American Bottom of western Illinois. These and other projects still employed large numbers of field and laboratory workers, but the number of large programs was well down from the level witnessed during the mid to late 1970s. Rising to take their place were the mitigation efforts of archaeologists in advance of literally tens of thousands of small jobs that ranged anywhere from road and street repair and construction, to runway-extension projects, to the construction of public housing. Anytime federal money was involved, and in most instances this consisted of federal pass-through funds to the states, archaeological resources had to be taken into account.

Although I have no hard figures to back up this claim, I would guess that the number of private archaeological-contracting companies that sprang up in the 1980s represented at least a fourfold increase over the number of companies active during the 1970s. There was still plenty of money to be made, and in fact the scale-down in size of the projects made it easier for the smaller firms to exist. They had found their niche, and it was defined by the $10,000 survey project and the $100,000 testing project. Many of the larger companies active in the highly competitive archaeology market of the 1980s were engineering and environmental-assessment firms, which had expanded their staffs in the 1970s to include archaeologists. They could withstand some of the heat generated from the fierce competition for archaeological projects and carry their archaeologists through dry periods. However, many of the firms whose only business was archaeology could not weather such periods and either folded or attached themselves to other private concerns. Many small colleges and universities that had geared up in the 1970s for what appeared to be an unending supply of outside funding also were hard hit as a result of the fierce competition, and most of them abandoned their contract-archaeology programs in the 1980s.

The adjustment in scope of archaeological projects in the 1980s significantly lowered the number of sites that any one project had to address, but in many cases the amount of money spent in mitigating impending damage to any particular resource rose appreciably over previous levels—an excellent situation if you were fortunate enough to be awarded a contract. Part of the reason for this phenomenon was simply good business on the part of archaeologists. If you were awarded a survey project, there was a fairly good chance that your "insider" position would net you the next phase of work, technically termed the "testing and determination-of-eligibility" phase (explained in Chapter 7). Successful completion of that phase, which included filling out determination-of-eligibility forms for submittal to the Advisory Council on Historic Preservation, increased one's chances of receiving the phase-III "mitigation" contract. Not a few archaeologists figured out that by increasing the number of potentially eligible sites, they could guarantee a higher per-site expenditure of funds during the excavation phase—as long as the advisory council concurred with their recommendation. I realize this sounds cold and calculating, but the plain fact of the matter is that CRM was (and still is) a business just like any other. And no one stays in business without incoming work.

There is, however, nothing that says business and science can't mix—witness, for example, the number of Nobel laureates who have come out of Bell Labs—and archaeology is no exception. The 1980s produced numerous archaeological advances, in part because archaeologists usually had more than adequate funding and fewer sites per project. Also, keen competition probably played no small role in forcing archaeologists to create a better product. Along the way, they began to pay much more attention to what for the most part had been an overlooked part of the archaeological record. They came to the realization that much of the record consists of small artifact scatters—a class of phenomena that, as I mentioned in Chapter 7, had always been overlooked in favor of sites that were "homogeneous artifact mines," as Dunnell (1992a: 26) put it. These mines were places where chronological orderings could be constructed and typological systems formulated, which meant that as long as those were the goals of archaeology, small sites would be bypassed completely.

The Maturing of Surface Archaeology

The search for artifact mines has a long and proven history in Americanist archaeology, but there is no doubt that many such mines still rest undiscovered. In chapters 5 and 6 I discussed various survey projects that have been undertaken in the Mississippi alluvial valley in southeastern Missouri, beginning with Phillips et al.'s (1951) megaproject in the 1940s and S. Williams's (1954) follow-up survey in the early 1950s, and continuing into the 1960s with surveys in advance of land leveling (J. R. Williams 1967, 1968, 1972) and highway construction (Marshall 1965, n.d.-a). These surveys were general in nature, meaning that survey parties covered considerable areas in relatively short periods of time. That they missed sites is beyond question, as recent resurveys have demonstrated. For example, Lafferty (1993; see also Lafferty et al. 1991) reported the occurrence of over 200 prehistoric sites in the 7,000-acre New Madrid Floodway in the Cairo Lowland, though earlier surveys (e.g., S. Williams 1954) had discovered a much smaller number of sites. Similarly, Whittaker (1993) and Dunnell and Whittaker (1990) reported a much more extensive Late Archaic–period archaeological record than earlier surveys had documented.

The earlier projects yielded valuable information on site location and content —information that in some instances is irreplaceable because of site destruction —but it is interesting that no work was ever done to determine the effects of agricultural processes and natural disturbances such as erosion and sedimentation on site recognition in an active floodplain setting (see Ferring 1986). Archaeologists (e.g., J. R. Williams 1967, 1968, 1972) make frequent mention of the fact that alluvial-valley landscapes change from year to year as a result of sedimentation, erosion, and man-made modifications such as plowing and land leveling, but rarely have they attempted to determine quantitatively the effects of such biases on archaeological-signature recognition and artifact recovery (but see Medford 1972).

How best to survey for "sites" has been a sticky issue in Americanist archaeology for decades, especially since the advent of settlement archaeology in the 1950s. An even stickier issue has been how best to use resulting survey data. There can be no real answer to the first question, since the answer resides in the types of questions being addressed by the survey. If, for example, all we want to know is how many prehistoric mounds are left in Pemiscot County, we probably are safe in driving up and down county roads and peering through a pair of binoculars. We could, upon spying a mound, get out of our vehicle and walk over to see if it was artificial or natural (we'll assume we could distinguish between the two). Such an exercise might seem trivial, but the question of how many mounds are left in Pemiscot County is legitimate. Given this question, and the way it was answered, we can't then turn around and use the results of the survey to answer a different question, such as how many Mississippian-period sites there are in the county. We didn't look for Mississippian-period sites, we looked for mound sites. Even though the vast majority (if not all) of mound sites in Pemiscot County date to the Mississippian period, what about contemporary sites that don't contain mounds (and there are literally thousands)? The point is that research questions cannot overreach the limitations of the data base. Yet attempts to do just that are commonplace in archaeology.

The above example is not as contrived as you might think. It is becoming increasingly evident that our understanding of the late prehistoric record in the Missouri portion of the Mississippi Valley is highly biased in favor of mound-containing localities. Much of that bias stems from the fact that surveys in the region, with few exceptions (e.g., Lafferty 1993; Lafferty et al. 1991; Whittaker 1993), have been undertaken rapidly and with no attempt to ensure systematic coverage. Despite this bias, not a few authors (e.g., D. F. Morse and P. A. Morse 1983; S. Williams 1980, 1983, 1990) have posited that after ca. A.D. 1350 much if not all of the Cairo Lowland portion of the valley was abandoned, with resident populations moving out of the area, perhaps to northeastern Arkansas and along Pemiscot Bayou in extreme southeastern Missouri (D. F. Morse and P. A. Morse 1983). This is what has come to be known as the "vacant-quarter" hypothesis (S. Williams 1983, 1990), and it is based in large part on the absence of late-Mississippian-period pottery types at the large mound communities in the Cairo Lowland. Thus, according to the scenario, an absence of late pottery indicates an absence of inhabitants. But suppose, for the sake of argument, that (a) we aren't recognizing local late-period ceramic types, which might be different from those from northeastern Arkansas and the southeastern corner of Missouri, or (b) the populations dispersed during the late portion of the Mississippian period and lived in very small communities—which left very small archaeological signatures. Could we be overlooking an important part of the record because our scale of analysis, with its emphasis on large sites, biases our view? How can we, at this point, know what to believe, given the manner in which the Cairo Lowland has been surveyed?

The types of field methods used to survey the Mississippi River valley were not unique to that region, nor were the biases that resulted from the procedures. Some of the most extensive surveys ever undertaken in North America were centered in the semiarid highland valleys in Mexico, especially the valleys of Mexico (e.g., Blanton 1972; Parsons 1971, 1972, 1976; Sanders 1970) and of Oaxaca (e.g., Blanton 1978; Blanton et al. 1982). Between the middle 1950s and roughly 1980, tens of thousands of hectares were surveyed by crews working seasonally, and the resulting information was used in myriad analyses (see O'Brien et al. 1989 for a summary). Given the amount of land that survey teams had to cover, they often moved at rates of 10–20 square kilometers weekly (Kowalewski 1990; Lewarch and O'Brien 1981)—a rate of coverage that precludes the discovery of small-scale archaeological signatures and creates a systematic yet unquantifiable bias in the survey sample. Data generated from the surveys, like those generated from surveys of the Mississippi alluvial valley, have given us a fairly clear picture of where the major prehistoric "sites" are located, and, similarly, the data have been used to derive population figures for different prehistoric periods, to discuss the role of exchange in the development of complex societies, and to examine the development of political hierarchies—all subjects that would appear to require more-exacting types of data than are at hand. Few criticisms of the ill-advised use of survey data from Mexico have appeared (but see O'Brien 1988; O'Brien et al. 1989; Santley 1983), the most interesting being those by Parsons (1990) and Sanders et al. (1979), who criticized their own earlier work. Similarly, few criticisms of the Mississippi Valley surveys have appeared (but see Fox 1992 and O'Brien and Fox 1994a, 1994b), in large part because of blind acceptance of the data.

Most such criticism takes aim not at the use of surface-derived data to address questions of archaeological interest but rather at the scale at which the surveys were carried out and at the types of data produced. For the most part, pedestrian surveys produce aggregate data—meaning data generated for a large, spatially bounded surface, that is, a "site"—as opposed to continuous data. With rare exceptions, little more than passing interest is taken in segmenting the bounded surface into smaller units to account for chronological, functional, or depositional variations. Where finer segmentation occurs (e.g., Blanton 1978), the data are still too coarse-grained to address the fine-grained questions put to them (O'Brien and Warren 1982a; O'Brien et al. 1989). As Parsons (1990: 29) points out, neither is there more than passing interest in the systematic study of formation processes that create and affect surficial archaeological records.

Perhaps as a result of the ways in which scopes of work related to CRM projects were written by government agencies—which in many cases required archaeologists to consider recovery bias—large-scale surveys conducted in the United States during the 1970s and 1980s began to pay more attention to site-formation processes as well as to various formation processes that affect the integrity of artifact distributions. One class of processes that received consider-able treatment was the mechanical tillage of archaeological deposits. Intensive, systematic surface collection as a field method grew exponentially during the 1970s, though early in the decade there was little or no archaeological literature that suggested how plowing and related activities affected archaeological signa-tures. This situation began to change as archaeologists began to perform exper-iments designed to reveal the direction and magnitude of change induced by agricultural—as well as nonagricultural—activities. These experiments caused some archaeologists, especially those involved in CRM, to develop the attitude that small, "disturbed" sites were important components of the resource base and thus warranted attention (Talmage and Chesler 1977). Indeed, Executive Order 11593 mandated that literally *all* archaeological resources be considered, and it did not exclude "disturbed" sites. One now *had* to do something with small assemblages as opposed to writing them off as being insignificant to the grander goals of archaeology.

What, Exactly, Is a Site?

We saw in the last chapter how the Cannon project had employed intensive, systematic surface collection as one of its key methods. Most collections were made at large, dense sites as a means of understanding internal variation and as a way of generating data on such things as site function, date(s) of occupation, and so forth. In the case of Putman Bottom, survey was directed toward generating a picture of changing land use by piece plotting the locations of individual artifacts across space, regardless of "site" boundaries. In essence, the concept of site was abandoned, and attention was focused instead on surveying the spatial distribution of artifact densities. For analytical purposes, some artifacts were regrouped into concentrations to examine the internal composition of the clusters and to contrast differences among clusters. But as interesting as this work was, there was little consideration of what has since become an important philosophical issue in Americanist archaeology. The Cannon project still relied on the concept of "site" not only as a bookkeeping device but also as an analytical unit. In hindsight, such an emphasis was questionable.

Obviously, the notion of site is deeply embedded in Americanist archaeology, and no one is going to rid the discipline of such a favorite concept, despite the fact that it has flaws. Federal regulations are built around the concept of site, which means that archaeologists involved in CRM cannot all of a sudden decide that they will no longer deal with sites—even though it has been pointed out with increasing frequency (e.g., Brooks 1979; Wandsnider 1988) that what we are managing is arbitrary and highly skewed. Dunnell (1992a: 25–26) points out several logical problems with the concept of site, dividing them into problems that are ontological (e.g., are sites "real," empirical archaeological entities?), those that are epistemological (e.g., how do we define such units on the ground?), and those that are theoretical (e.g., what role should the concept play in our explanations?). Dunnell's views on the inadequacy of the concept of site have not gone uncontested; for a particularly pointed criticism, see Binford (1992).

The most insidious problems are ontological in nature, because how we approach the "reality" of sites as entities in turn conditions the methods we use to look for them and how we employ them in our explanations. We might begin this discussion by asking why we should believe that sites are *really* things as opposed to *real* things. As Dunnell (1992a: 29) points out, "sites are difficult to 'define' because they are not really things or qualities but rather concentrations or quantities." On the other hand, sites are *real* things, at least given our perceptions of reality, because they can be seen. Given our inherent mind-set, the presence of a mound or a scatter of pottery indicates the location of a "site"—a place that contains evidence of past use.

No archaeologist would take the position that zones between sites were not used by prehistoric peoples, though it was not until the 1970s that there was a significant appreciation for what came to be known as the "off-site" archaeological record—isolated artifacts and low-density artifact scatters that lie between larger artifact clusters (Foley 1981 [see D. H. Thomas's (1975) earlier statements]). The usual procedure was to record the "sites" first and then to survey the intervening areas to see how light the artifact densities were. Some researchers termed this approach to the low-density portion of the record "siteless survey" or "nonsite survey," but it did not conform to what Dunnell and Dancey (1983) and Thomas (1975) had in mind when they referred to siteless or nonsite survey, that is, surveying the distribution of artifacts across the landscape, with little or no attention paid to the notion of "site." Clearly, the majority of operations were carried out with the notion of site intact. In short, no amount of methodological rigor could mask the fact that no wholesale change had taken place in the manner in which the archaeological record was conceived.

If formation studies consistently demonstrate the dynamic nature of the archaeological record, why should we believe that sites are anything more than simple observational units, created by the act of observation at a particular moment in time?

> Materials are added, removed, and rearranged continuously in the archaeological record. No one would contest that settlements, camps, villages, activity loci, and the like can produce what we see today as more or less dense clusters of artifacts, but there is no necessary relation between such ethnographic concepts, many of which are themselves suspicious as units of ethnographic observation, and high-density clusters of artifacts. Not all such clusters are the product of behaviors implied by the ethnographic categories, nor do all such ethnographic units leave high-density artifact clusters. Settlement, occupation, and activities are not agents of deposition; at best they are highly interpretive summaries of relations among such agents. The historical relatedness of their pieces is highly variable and not directly correlated with spatial proximity. (Dunnell 1992a: 27)

If we are interested in activities (in the sense that Schiffer [1976] uses the term), for which I prefer the label *specific behaviors*, then it seems ill-advised to use "site" as an interpretive unit. It would appear to be more appropriate to bypass the notion of site and to define those behaviors in terms of the composition and distribution of individual archaeological records, along the way attempting to understand the effects of cultural and noncultural formation processes on artifacts. Through time, "sites" grow in size as people add more trash, artifacts are displaced as a result of human as well as animal activities, and even after a location is abandoned, erosion and other natural processes can greatly alter the so-called integrity of the record. In essence what we are left with is an archaeological record that does not directly reflect the behaviors that were responsible for the artifacts' positions in the first place.

If we use materials from site surfaces in archaeological analysis, we should at least understand something about the variable nature of such surfaces. I don't personally know any archaeologists who would claim that site surfaces have *not* been subjected to numerous processes that have affected the distribution of materials. Archaeologists routinely make reference to processes such as plowing and its effects on the archaeological integrity of a site, though few have conducted the kinds of experiments necessary to address the nature and degree of disturbance. Experiments conducted as part of the Cannon project (Lewarch 1979; Lewarch and O'Brien 1981b), which I discuss below, were a step in this direction, as were those conducted by Roper (1976), Trubowitz (1978), Ammerman (1985 [see also Ammerman and Feldman 1978]), and Odell and Cowan (1987), but to date there remain too few data to allow us to accurately model such things as artifact populations and artifact displacement across a large number of cases. Furthermore, the handful of cases we currently have available cannot be used in any sort of meaningful predictive fashion because of the limited environmental situations in which the studies have been conducted.

Regardless of our lack of knowledge concerning the effects of myriad kinds of processes that shape the distribution of archaeological materials across a surface, intuition tells us that not all surfaces are the same. For the sake of convenience, this lack of isomorphism, or fit, can be reduced to two kinds of cases: surfaces that approximate what Dunnell (1988a: 29) terms "independent interpretive populations" and those that are samples of what he terms "larger, agglomerate populations." Archaeology has long recognized both, but in few instances has the distinction been formalized. The two kinds of cases require, in fact *demand*, recognition.

No one would surface collect the floor of a site such as Rodgers Shelter, knowing the site was 9 meters deep, and declare that the surface sherds and projectile points tell the history of the locale's use, even if the artifact sample were extremely large and diverse. We would, rather, recognize that a 9-meter-deep site could scarcely exhibit the full range of functional and historical markers on its modern surface. We might use the surface artifacts to infer something about the *last* use of the site but certainly not about its earliest use. Even if the shelter contained only a meter of deposit, the surface artifacts might be only a sample of a much *larger, agglomerate population* of artifacts deposited by more than one group of past residents in the location. The second kind of surface—the one comprising an *independent interpretive population*—is a much rarer occurrence. In the case above, if a group of people deposited tools on the floor of a cave and no group before or after them ever used the cave, then that artifact assemblage would be an independent interpretive population. However, such an event was a rare occurrence; hence, most archaeological deposits are agglomerations of materials that were made, used, and discarded over time spans of variable length

Figure 8.1. Photograph showing plowed portion (upper 25 cm or so) and deeper, unplowed portion of the archaeological deposit at the Muskrat Run site, Ralls County, Missouri.

by different groups of people. If we are going to sample these deposits, we ought to know what kind of sample we're obtaining.

If there is such a thing as an "average site" in Missouri, it comprises both Archaic and Woodland materials in a 20-centimeter-thick plow zone and in an underlying artifact-bearing zone that varies in thickness from 20 to 60 centimeters (Figure 8.1). There are, obviously, as many exceptions to this rule as there are cases that apply, but the archaeological literature is replete with this kind of "multicomponent site." Given that many midwestern sites have been subjected to agriculturally related activities such as plowing and disking, one might think that considerable attention has been paid to the effects of such operations on artifact deposits. However, this has not been the case. Some studies have been done—several in Missouri—but they have only scratched the surface of what is a very complicated issue.

Plow-Zone Mechanics

To begin to examine some of the effects of plowing on archaeological signatures, Dennis Lewarch and I conducted a series of experiments during the Cannon project aimed at modeling how artifacts move in three dimensions as they are subjected to mechanical tillage (Lewarch and O'Brien 1981b). Basic to these experiments was the construction of artifact scatters of different sizes and shapes using size-graded chert flakes. In essence, we constructed a site by placing known quantities of flakes in 2-square-meter grid units (Figure 8.2). The scatters were then subjected to different kinds and durations of tillage (Figure 8.3), after which the grid was reestablished and the visible flakes collected and their frequencies compared to the original frequencies for each size class. We found that the surface assemblage reached a point at which further plowing had little effect on it, but we used only lithic artifacts and only one type and depth of plowing. Based on the results of the experiments, we devised analytical techniques that reduced tillage "noise" and accounted for longitudinal spread of artifacts by tillage implements (Lewarch and O'Brien 1981b; O'Brien and McDaniel 1982).

Results indicated "that there was little transverse displacement but variable amounts of longitudinal displacement, which was influenced by artifact size, duration of tillage, and the number of artifacts in a pattern" (Lewarch and O'Brien 1981b). These conclusions were in large part at odds with some of the assumptions widely held among archaeologists that plowing and disking either cause severe disruption of pattern or affect the pattern in an unknown (and unknowable) manner. Unbeknownst to us (and to them), George Odell and Frank Cowan (1987) were carrying out experiments almost identical to ours in the bottomlands of the Illinois River valley. They found support for several propositions Lewarch and I put forward, a major exception being that they found that duration of tillage has a profound effect on the amount of tillage-related displacement. We, on the other hand, found that tillage had little or no effect on distribution after about three plowings (see below). Dunnell (1990a) questioned Odell and Cowan's conclusions because they failed to take into account the relation between artifact size and lateral displacement, when in fact a positive correlation had been noted (Lewarch and O'Brien 1981a, 1981b).

One drawback to the experiments was that we did not re-collect the locations after an extensive number of tillings to see how artifact composition and patterning changed. Rather, we simulated what would happen over time. Basically, our notion was that with increased plowing, the "size effect" (Baker 1978; Baker and Schiffer 1975) segregation process sets in—larger artifacts tend to stay near the surface and smaller ones migrate downward—which results in greater discrepancies between recovery rates of size classes. Over time, this segregation can dramatically alter relative proportions of each size class of artifact in a surface assemblage. Small artifacts did appear to behave like soil particles, and we predicted that they could be used to provide a stable measure from which to calibrate tillage effects on surface assemblages. However, we did not actually test that proposition.

Modeling the long-term effects of tillage on archaeological deposits was perhaps an important step toward understanding plow-zone mechanics, but it was only an initial step. In fact, it left many important research questions

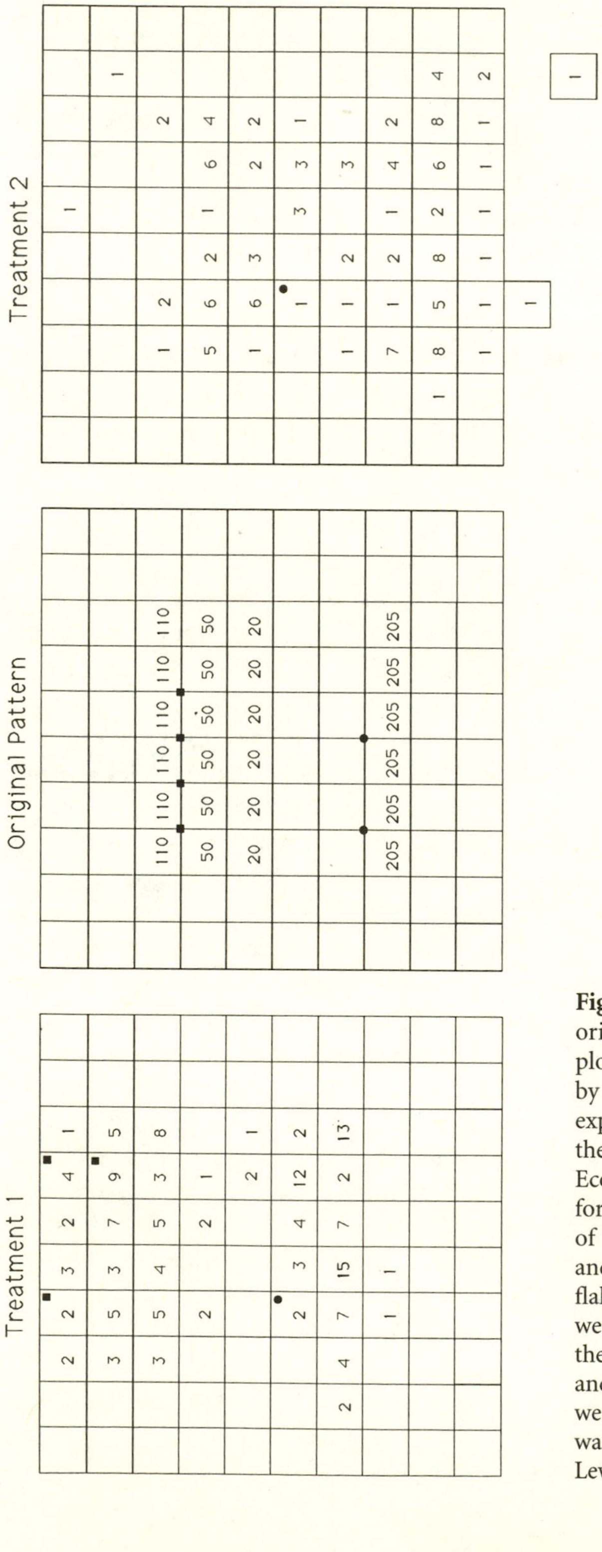

Treatment 2

Original Pattern

Treatment 1

Figure 8.2. Diagrams showing original frequencies and post-plowing frequencies of flakes by 1 m² unit in two tillage experiments conducted during the Cannon Reservoir Human Ecology Project (see Figure 8.3 for directions of plowing in each of the two treatments). Circles and squares represent bifacially flaked tools; all flakes and tools were placed on the surface. Note the longitudinal displacement and the reduced frequencies that were recovered when the surface was collected after plowing (after Lewarch and O'Brien 1981b).

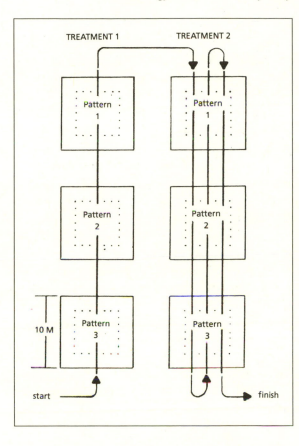

Figure 8.3. Direction of plowing through six patterns created for the Cannon Reservoir tillage experiment. Treatment 1 consisted of a single pass through the center of each pattern; treatment 2 consisted of three passes through each concentration. Compare the resulting artifact patterns shown in Figure 8.2 to the direction of plowing and the number of passes (after Lewarch and O'Brien 1981b).

unanswered. Archaeologists began to answer certain of these questions, however, during the 1980s as they developed a better understanding of plow-zone mechanics and of the important role of systematic surface collection in archaeological inquiry. Several projects undertaken since Lewarch and I conducted the original experiments have greatly increased our understanding of how plow-zone artifact assemblages are modified and how better to realize the analytic potential of surface assemblages from plowed fields. I discuss below four such projects from Missouri, each of which was undertaken for slightly different reasons but all of which have added significantly to our knowledge of the origin and development of surface- and plow-zone-artifact assemblages.

Cold Water Farm

With regard to assemblage composition, the plowing experiment suggested that one means of controlling for certain directional biases was to subject an archaeological surface to repeated systematic collections. The results of the experiment indicated that small objects could be used to generalize about the larger artifact population that produced the recovered sample, but it was clear that rare classes of objects, regardless of size, would more than likely be substantially underrepresented or absent entirely in samples collected at any one time. As part of a long-term effort at understanding changing patterns of land use on the highly dissected Pleistocene–early Holocene surface of western Dunklin County (the Malden Plain), Dunnell in 1983 initiated a six-year collection of a tract termed Cold Water Farm (Dunnell 1985b, 1988a, 1992a).[2] The same protocol was used during each of the six collections, and ground conditions were essentially the same. He was interested in the two questions mentioned above: (1) How biased was the surface sample of artifacts? and (2) How did the concept of "site" hold up after six seasons of collection?

The tract selected for the experiment had produced evidence of use by prehistoric groups, though site surveyors had overlooked the artifact scatter in the 1950s because of its low density of material. The tract bordered an ancient slough that had formed on the braided-stream surface, and visual inspection indicated that the heaviest prehistoric use of the tract had bordered that watercourse. Basic field strategy was to walk every fifth row of the plowed field and to flag every visible artifact not connected with Euro-American use of the property; surveyors left the artifacts in place. Given the sedimentary history of the region—an alluvial landscape with no naturally occurring rock— every scrap of stone, unless it was obviously brought in as fill or was modern construction material, was considered an artifact and thus was plotted. When artifact clusters were encountered, only the edges were marked (clusters were defined as the occurrence of 2 artifacts within 10 meters of each other). Clusters were collected as a unit or, in the case of one large cluster, through the use of a 4-x-4-meter grid.

Figure 8.4 (top) illustrates the results of the collections for four of the six years. Notice the change in shape of the large polygon labeled 23DU272, which lies on the western edge of the slough. It was fairly large in 1983, contracted in size during 1984, changed shape in 1985, and expanded again in 1987—the year in which it spread to the edge of the former watercourse. To the south, two clusters that were not apparent in 1983 appeared in 1984, changed location in 1985, and expanded to form a larger cluster in 1987, when a new cluster appeared just to the north. When a composite of the four seasons' worth of work is examined (Figure 8.4 [bottom]), several more clusters are formed, and our overall impression of the artifact distribution changes dramatically.

Throughout the 11,000 or so years the stable surface was exposed, there were numerous instances of artifacts' being used (presumably) and abandoned both

2. This discussion is a distillation of information in Dunnell 1988a, 1992a.

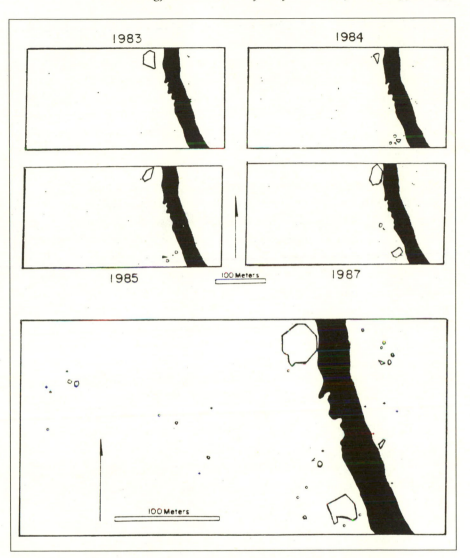

Figure 8.4. Distribution of artifacts and artifact clusters in the Cold Water Farm tract, Dunklin County, Missouri, plotted by field seasons (top) and by the four field seasons combined (bottom). Open polygons and localities marked "C" represent clusters; dots represent isolated finds. The dark band marks the location of a former slough (from Dunnell 1992a, courtesy Plenum Press).

near the slough and away from it. Use and discard (or loss) of artifacts was much higher adjacent to the slough, yielding the two large clusters evident in Figure 8.4. They contained ceramic and lithic artifacts that date the clusters to ca. A.D. 500; the density of pottery, debris from tool manufacture, and burned earth point toward "domestic" activities having taken place. And what of the isolated artifacts? Can they be best explained as isolated losses or discarded members of one of the two large clusters, or were they dragged out of one of the clusters by plowing, even though they were small? To answer this question, Dunnell made extensive collections of sediments around each isolated find (Madsen and Dunnell 1989; Vance 1989), and his reasons for doing so are as important as his findings. If it can be determined that year-to-year variation in what is collected is not attributable to extraneous systematic error (e.g., walking different rows from one year to the next), then the bulk of the variability must arise either from the archaeological record itself or from the effects of sampling only the plow zone.

How do we determine how much variability (if any) is being controlled by each source of that variability? Intuitively, we at least can understand some of the effects of plowing and disking on an artifact scatter, not the least of which is the burial of some artifacts and the exposure of others. Some experiments have been conducted on the way in which materials sort themselves vertically after disturbance (e.g., Baker 1978; Baker and Schiffer 1975; Lewarch and O'Brien 1981b; Stockton 1973), though much more experimentation is needed. But how do we assess the variability that arises from the archaeological record itself? Dunnell reasoned that isolated lithic artifacts might have reached their destination as a result of isolated activities carried out across the sampling area. Sherds, on the other hand, are difficult to interpret as isolated artifacts. Not only are they associated, at least intuitively, with more sedentary and complex activities than implied by isolated occurrences, they also are fragments of much larger artifacts. Thus, as Dunnell (1988a: 35) notes, "the presence of one sherd implies the presence of others, unless the sherds were used as artifacts in their own right" (or were disposed of differentially, i.e., piece by piece). Not surprisingly, sediment samples collected from around each isolated artifact exhibited different contents. Sediments surrounding lithic artifacts contained little or no microdebitage (tiny flakes that result from tool manufacture and use). Sediment samples taken around isolated sherds, however, contained microdebitage in frequencies not unlike those associated with the "domestic" clusters.

Despite the insights generated concerning the archaeological record of Cold Water Farm, there remained ambiguities, even after the surface was examined six times. For example, the dilution that resulted from plowing made it difficult to separate low-density artifact clusters from isolated deposition events. Also, isolated artifacts might have represented isolated depositional events or the effects of plowing on larger aggregates of artifacts. Finally, no one inspection of a plowed surface is likely to take in more than a fraction of the elements of a low-density archaeological record. Importantly, CRM decisions that employ simple walk-over surveys of plowed fields and the haphazard collection of artifacts will systematically destroy key pieces of the record, and we will, as Dunnell (1988a:

37) notes, return to the days in which size was the only determinant used to assess archaeological significance.

Does this mean that every plowed surface has to be rechecked for artifacts on a regular basis? Not necessarily, although repeated surveys would be helpful in contributing to our understanding of prehistoric land use (e.g., Ammerman and Feldman 1978; Frink 1984). More importantly, we need a better understanding of plow zones and their mechanics so that eventually it will be possible to assess the biases inherent in typical pedestrian surveys and to develop new techniques that overcome those biases (Dunnell 1988a: 37). If there is a take-home message in Dunnell's work at Cold Water Farm, it is simply the well-known axiom that any archaeological deposit—even deeply buried and well-stratified deposits—started life as *surface* deposits. At every step of their lives, the deposits are subject to modification through a variety of formation processes that affect not only the distribution of artifacts but also the composition of the deposits. As well-known as this axiom is, a glance at the archaeological literature would suggest that we tend to ignore it from time to time.

Sites, if they are anything, are fuzzy historical settings that have witnessed the deposition, removal, and redeposition of artifacts. They are not units of formation and really have "no legitimate role as units of observation. . . . Objects found in spatial proximity . . . may have, and frequently do have, entirely unrelated histories that preclude a simple equation between spatial proximity and systemic relevance. Their composition and organization is *strictly modern and archaeologic*" (Dunnell 1992a: 29; emphasis added). It is fair to say that Americanist archaeologists are not going to throw out the concept of site, but we might do well to understand its systematic deficiencies.

Burkemper

Because Lewarch and I used only lithic items in our plowing experiments, it was questionable whether our results applied to other materials such as pottery, which is a component of many midwestern archaeological deposits. Stone flakes are for the most part not degradable items, meaning that they usually are not broken by plowing and disking. Pottery is, however, friable and subject to reduction, as are other materials such as bone and shell. Our modeling of the long-term effects of plowing suggested that over time an equilibrium would be reached and that subsequent plowing would have little effect on the surface assemblage. However, we were using only flakes. We also were holding the type of plowing, the direction of plowing, and the depth of plowing constant. Clearly, this rarely happens in the real world. We also suggested that the sizes of lithic items on the surface of an archaeological deposit can give us some indication of how long a deposit has been plowed, but, once again, we were using only nonreducible items. We needed a plowed surface that contained large quantities of pottery and preferably bone and shell in addition. We found such a locality, the Burkemper site, located in southern Lincoln County, Missouri. Work was structured to examine not only the effects of plowing on artifact distributions but also the representativeness of the surface-artifact assemblage relative to the plow-zone assemblage.

Burkemper is located on a low floodplain terrace of the Cuivre River in eastern Missouri, 0.5 kilometers west of the junction of the Cuivre and Mississippi rivers. The locality was recorded in 1980 by Missouri Highway and Transportation Department (MHTD) personnel during a survey in connection with the proposed relocation of Missouri Route 79 to the west of the town of Old Monroe. In 1980 personnel from the University of Missouri assisted MHTD archaeologists in designing and implementing a controlled surface collection of that portion of the site to be affected by construction activity (Crampton 1983; O'Brien 1985b). The university then used the distribution of surface materials to structure the large-scale excavation it conducted in 1984 and 1985.

Burkemper was an important archaeological resource from numerous standpoints. Its most noticeable feature was the abnormally large quantity of surface archaeological materials. After heavy rains, especially those following periods of cultivation, the surface was literally paved with artifacts. Animal and human bone, fresh-water-mussel shell, pottery fragments, and lithic items occurred with frequencies rarely encountered in the Midwest. The majority of pottery and projectile-point types present on the surface indicated a Middle Woodland–period occupation of the locality.

Several decades of intensive work in the lower Illinois River valley, just to the east of Burkemper, have yielded a remarkable understanding of the archaeological record there, especially as it relates to the history of plant use, ceramic technology, and mortuary practices (summarized in Braun 1977 and O'Brien 1986, 1987). We viewed anticipated work at Burkemper as an opportunity to build on the work in western Illinois and to determine whether Middle Woodland peoples on the west bank of the Mississippi River were doing similar things and at roughly the same time as their neighbors to the east. Later in this chapter I examine some of the analyses that were aimed at developing an understanding of those similarities; here I concentrate on the surface phenomena.

Based on visual inspection in 1980, the artifact scatter containing at least 5 artifacts per square meter covered an area of approximately 2.8 hectares, but that figure was only an estimate. Our interest in undertaking the systematic surface collection was twofold. First, the surface collection would be, areally, the most extensive collection of materials from the locality. The assemblage was viewed not only as an important data set in its own right—especially as it related to later occupations—but also as a guide to the placement of test units. Density-distribution plots resulting from an intensive, controlled surface collection would at least allow us to horizontally stratify the site and to test areas of high and low surface-artifact density. Second, differences in the kinds and sizes of artifacts apparent across the terrace suggested that the locality was an excellent laboratory in which to examine the effects of agricultural activity on artifact assemblages.

Prior to collection in 1980, the surface had been cultivated and subsequently had received over an inch of rain. The area to be collected was divided into 2-x-2-meter units, and because of the size of the artifact scatter and the amount of archaeological material present, the surface was sampled at a 50% rate by collecting units in a checkerboard fashion. Standard categories—lithic material, bone, shell, pottery, burned earth, and unmodified limestone and sandstone—were used to subdivide the artifact collection (Crampton 1983; O'Brien 1985b). Lithic and ceramic artifacts were sorted into four size classes—greater than 1 inch (artifacts did not pass through a screen with 1-inch mesh), less than 1 inch but greater than 3/8 inch, less than 3/8 inch but greater than 1/4 inch, and less than 1/4 inch. A series of density maps was produced for each artifact class (all sizes combined), two of which are illustrated in Figure 8.5. Despite decades of repeated tillage, the surface-artifact distribution maintained a structure that appeared to result in large part from cultural deposition (see O'Brien 1985b and O'Brien and Lyman 1996 for details), though some was a result of continuous east–west plowing.

Of more interest here were comparisons made between surface-artifact assemblages and those from the 24–26-centimeter-thick plow zone. As expected, plow-zone assemblages contained incredibly large numbers of artifacts. For example, one 2-x-2-meter unit contained 1,754 sherds, 2,578 grams of animal bone, and almost 40,000 grams of limestone. Interestingly, although the surface assemblages gave a rough approximation of the relative order of magnitude of the plow-zone assemblages, there often was little or no consistent relation between the two. A surface assemblage might rank in the uppermost quartile in terms of number of sherds or weight of shell, bone, and limestone, but its corresponding plow-zone assemblage would rank in the second or third quartile for each class. When class compositions were summed, that is, weights of all artifact classes were combined, the relation between surface and plow-zone assemblages was much more straightforward. It also was obvious that the exposed surface contained (by frequency for sherds, by weight for shell, bone, and limestone) approximately 3–4% of the combined plow-zone-and-surface assemblage. This percentage range held up over 2 plowings.

We were also interested in the effects of plowing and other agricultural activities on artifact size. Because of the mechanical and natural processes that operated on the artifact scatter over the centuries, materials such as pottery, bone, and shell should have been greatly reduced in size. Further, we might suspect that, regardless of original size ratios, within each class of material smaller pieces should outnumber larger ones. Indeed, this assumption was found to be correct relative to pottery. Two areas along the eastern margin of the collected area were selected for ceramic size-class analysis using frequencies of sherds in two size

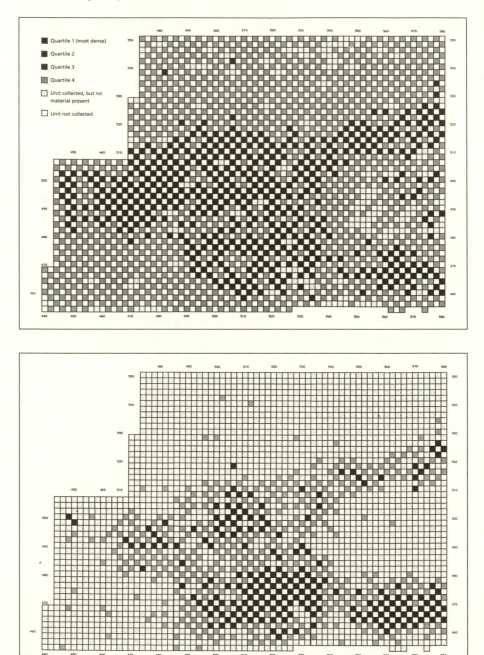

Figure 8.5. Densities, by quartile, for limestone (top) and shell (bottom) collected from the surface of the Burkemper site, Lincoln County, Missouri (from O'Brien and Lyman 1996).

classes: size-class 1—sherds that did not pass through a 1-inch-mesh screen—and size-class 3—sherds that passed through 3/8-inch mesh but not through a 1/4-inch mesh. As expected, the size distribution within each area was skewed significantly toward smaller sherds. Sherds are extremely vulnerable to plow-induced breakage, which in the case of Burkemper was exacerbated by disking, annual manuring, and fertilizing. In addition, the site was collected heavily for decades, and undoubtedly some of the breakage was caused by constant trampling.

Lee Lyman and I used faunal remains to further examine the extent of agriculturally related damage inflicted on the assemblage (Lyman and O'Brien 1987). Animal bone, because of its porous nature and, in some cases, its shape, is a potentially sensitive marker of postdepositional damage to an archaeological deposit. I say "potentially" because the analyst must be able to distinguish between signs of postdepositional modification and culturally induced damage. In the only other study of surface/plow-zone zooarchaeology of which we were aware, Hesse and Wapnish (1985: 26–27) assumed that sherds are more resistant than bone to agriculturally induced modification and that low frequencies of identifiable animal bone indicate heavy attrition through postdepositional processes.

Numerous bones and bone fragments from Burkemper displayed fresh breaks (clean, unstained fracture surface). Inspection of deer astragali—very dense, compact elements—indicated that animal bones were modified extensively. It was assumed that cultivation-related activities would affect only those specimens above a certain minimum size and that specimens smaller than that minimum size would escape breakage. Because the astragalus is low in food value (Binford 1978) relative to other skeletal elements, we suspected plowing and not prehistoric use accounted for the majority of breakage. Certain prehistoric butchering processes, especially marrow extraction and grease production, would have yielded many broken bones that would show evidence of staining and dirt encrustation on the broken surfaces. Mechanical processes associated with cultivation should further fragment the larger pieces and be signified by fresher breaks. There may, then, be little difference in the size of specimens with fresh breaks and those with old breaks because cultivation would reduce the size of large pieces to some minimum size similar to the minimum size of pieces resulting from butchering. This appeared to be the case with the Burkemper surface collection; only 3 of the 8 deer elements we used, comprising 180 specimens, showed statistically significant differences between the size of specimens displaying fresh breaks and the size of specimens with old breaks.

Robards

Robards is a tract of land in Dunklin County that lies adjacent to the Varney River (actually a slough), a relict braided channel of the ancestral Ohio-Mississippi River system that formed during the Pleistocene. The tract was collected by Dunnell throughout much of the 1980s as part of his long-term effort to examine human-land relations on the Pleistocene-age Malden Plain. As opposed to the protocol he used to collect Cold Water Farm, Dunnell established a grid system of 4-square-meter units across the tract and collected all materials larger than about 2 millimeters (Dunnell and Simek 1995). Resulting artifact-density maps (Figure 8.6) illustrate the distribution across the tract of sherds of sand- and shell-tempered pottery. The sand-tempered assemblage comprised approximately 500 sherds distributed across 6 or more clusters as well as sherds scattered more thinly across the tract. The shell-tempered assemblage (most sherds were red-slipped) comprised 1,960 sherds, and they also occurred in clusters and as scattered occurrences. Very few sherds were larger than 2 centimeters on a side, and without systematic and intensive examination of the ground, the archaeological signature of the locality in all probability would never have come to light. Or if it had, it probably would have been seen as insignificant. Dunnell and Simek (1995: 24) report that the landowner, upon seeing the ceramic assemblage, quipped, "This ain't no site; an Indian carrying a red pot tripped and fell, that's all." Some archaeologists might have felt the same way.

The composition and distribution of surface materials was important for understanding prehistoric use of the tract, but the controlled manner in which the materials were collected also allowed Dunnell and Simek to examine the relation between object size and plowing history—in short, to understand an important aspect of the formation history of the deposit. Basic to their argument is the proposition that duration of tillage should correlate positively with the size of reducible items such as sherds—the longer a deposit is plowed, the smaller the sherds should be, until a point of no further reduction is reached. This proposition assumes that plow zones are fixed in depth and therefore that no new items are added to the plow zone by deeper plowing. But plow zones are not static entities. They can be removed by erosion, and they can be expanded through deeper plowing. Such additions can be detected by simple statistical procedures and their origins resolved by spatial analysis.

For example, the few large sand-tempered sherds recovered were, with one exception, located within the densest clusters of sherds and thus probably represented outliers of the plow-zone artifact population. Thus, there were no substantial deposits of subplow-zone sand-tempered pottery that were occasionally being hit during deeper plowing. On the other hand, the largest shell-tempered sherds occurred on the edges of the shell-tempered-sherd clusters, indicating that there were pits or middens that ringed the surface concentrations and that were producing large sherds. Test excavations indicated that pits were producing the larger sherds.

The value of Dunnell and Simek's work lies in what it tells us about the use of object size as an important analytical tool. Tillage-degraded materials such as bone and pottery, though often written off by archaeologists as being

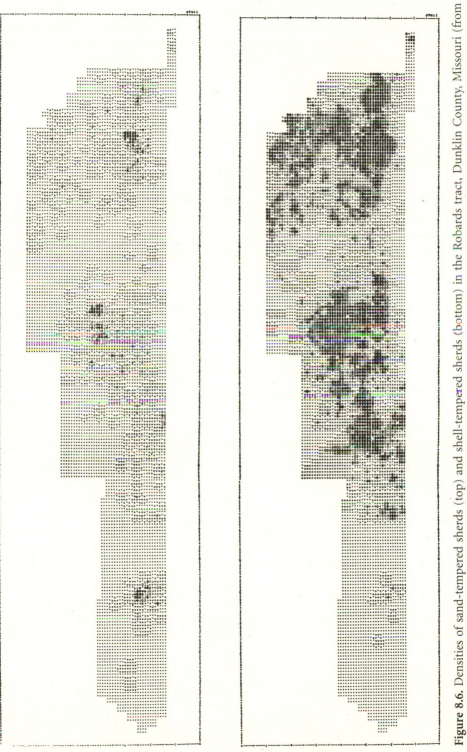

Figure 8.6. Densities of sand-tempered sherds (top) and shell-tempered sherds (bottom) in the Robards tract, Dunklin County, Missouri (from Dunnell and Simek 1995).

insignificant, are major sources of information on the structure of archaeological deposits and the history of disturbance. What should appeal to most archaeologists is the fact that these kinds of information are obtainable without the cost of excavation or damage to the subplow-zone deposit.

Common Field

Another type of formation process that would appear to be important to keep in mind when evaluating the structure of surface signatures, especially those in an active floodplain setting, is sediment removal. The combined effects of sediment removal and agriculturally related disturbance have never been examined in controlled tillage experiments, to my knowledge, but a fortuitous (depending upon how you look at it) event in 1979–1980 created a situation in which it was possible to compare an archaeological surface before and after an extreme erosional episode to determine the combined effects of disking and sediment removal on an archaeological signature. Common Field (also known as Big Field) is a 17-hectare fortified Mississippian-period mound site located in the Mississippi River floodplain in Ste. Genevieve County. The site has been cultivated since the middle of the eighteenth century and received its name from the common usage of the floodplain by French agriculturists. In December 1979 levees that protected the field from the Mississippi River broke during a prolonged period of high water and scoured roughly 40 centimeters of topsoil from the field, exposing articulated burials, pits containing charred corn, carbonized house posts, complete ceramic vessels, and large quantities of sherds and animal bones. University of Missouri personnel undertook work at the site in March 1980, by which time the surface had been hunted intensively for complete artifacts by local collectors and had been disked twice.

Interestingly, although the site has been known for years (R. M. Adams et al. 1941; Bushnell 1914; Keslin 1964), few artifacts were ever visible on the surface. For example, Keslin (1964: 26) examined the site in 1958 after an episode of plowing and subsequent rain and found 20–30 small sherds. Alluviation in the Mississippi Valley can be extremely heavy, and sedimentation rates have probably increased throughout the historical period. Moffat and Anderson (1984) report that during the historical period as much as a meter of alluvium has been deposited on Kaskaskia Island, just south of Common Field, while other estimates range higher (e.g., Voigt and O'Brien 1981). One would guess that the creation of the levee system, while channeling the river, has on occasion (when the levees failed) led to increased erosion.

It was evident that the water that poured through the levee break late in 1979 washed away the ca. 26-centimeter-deep plow zone at the site, scoured another 14–15 centimeters of sediment (Figure 8.7), and left a pavement of artifacts in its wake. Were these artifacts in more or less the same horizontal locations as

Figure 8.7. Photograph of the Common Field site, Ste. Genevieve County, Missouri, after the flood of 1979.

they were before the levee broke, or had they been washed into low areas? Also, what effect did subsequent disking have on the artifact distribution? To address these questions, a mix of aerial photography, systematic surface collection, and computer enhancement of images was employed. The photographs were used to produce a topographic map and to record locations of archaeological features such as house stains and pits.

The use of aerial photographs in archaeological fieldwork dates at least to the 1920s, when they were used to map Cahokia (Rowe 1953: 907–8). That same decade, Alfred Kidder used the services of Charles Lindbergh during his Carnegie Institution–funded surveys in the Yucatán. Aerial photography as a remote-sensing method has been used extensively in Europe to identify the remains of Neolithic earthworks and in the American Southwest to identify road networks and related features. The National Park Service developed an appreciation for aerial photography as a means of documenting cultural resources and issued a number of general source books (e.g., Limp 1989, 1993; Lyons 1981; Lyons and Avery 1977; Lyons and Mathien 1980) and case studies (e.g., Wood et al. 1982) designed to acquaint archaeologists with its potential. In the Midwest, aerial photography has been used extensively to locate structural elements such as mounds, palisades, ditches, and houses and to monitor disturbances to archaeological surfaces. Missouri sites examined extensively through aerial photography include Rich Woods in Stoddard County (Leeds 1979), Lilbourn in Mississippi County (Cottier 1977) (Figure 6.27), County Line in Stoddard County (Teltser 1992), Beckwith's Fort in New Madrid County (Figure 6.26), and Langdon in Dunklin County (Dunnell 1993, Dunnell n.d.).

At Common Field, some features were easy to spot both on black-and-white and on false-color-infrared photographs. For example, the clay composition of some of the smaller mounds showed up nicely in contrast to the outlying sediments, allowing us to plot their original sizes fairly precisely. Because of the time that would be involved in performing on-ground mapping of the several hundred houses that could be seen in the field, we wanted to map them from the photographs. However, the photographic contrast between cultural signatures and slightly depressed areas of wet soil was often negligible, making even field verification difficult in those instances where large amounts of charcoal from wall posts were not present to assist in identification. To circumvent this problem, we scanned the photographic images, converted them to digital images, and used a series of enhancement techniques to reduce interference from noncultural pixel (picture element) intensities and to quantify the range of pixel values of cultural features (O'Brien et al. 1982). In-field mapping of 7 known house stains and numerous wet areas across a 25-x-27-meter control block gave us an independent means of verifying the digital boundary limits that separated houses from wet areas. Once we derived the ranges of pixel values of cultural features, we applied the technique to other areas of the site.

We placed 9 blocks of 2-x-2-meter collection units across the site in areas containing structural remains and dense concentrations of lithic, ceramic, and faunal debris, and we expanded the units to include areas of lower artifact density. We collected slightly more than 1,400 units, representing about 3.3% of the area of the artifact scatter.[3] Artifact density was extremely high over large portions of the scatter, and we collected over 14,000 sherds, nearly half of which could be placed into published types. Ferguson (1990) documented spatial variation in the provenience of pottery types and linked the variation to differential use of various localities throughout the life of the community. There was a distinct, positive correlation between dense concentrations of pottery and house stains, with the concentrations tending to occur around the outer edges of two or more house walls—a trend also noted by Trader (1992) with respect to lithic debris.

In summary, the work at Common Field allowed us to examine a previously buried surface and to gauge the effects of severe sediment erosion on spatial patterning of artifacts and cultural features. The contrast between the pre- and

---

3. The scatter was confined to a sandy levee remnant adjacent to what appeared at the time to have been either an active channel of the Mississippi River or a cutoff chute.

postflood surfaces was striking in terms of artifact and feature visibility, but perhaps more striking was the integrity of the artifact patterning relative to features. Certainly many of the artifacts evident in early 1980 were brought to the surface by the two postflood disking episodes that preceded archaeological work, but many also were exposed through soil erosion. Importantly, stripping of the plow zone by the river did not greatly alter the horizontal distribution of plow-zone artifacts and instead dropped them on the newly created surface. This conclusion was based in part on the presence on the new surface of approximately 20 human skeletons, many of which exhibited bones in articulated position. The only disturbance of the skeletons was through recent disking, which fractured some long bones and crushed several skulls. In several instances, grave goods, including intact ceramic vessels, were found in their original positions alongside the skeletons. Also, numerous refits of surface sherds that exhibited old breaks— and thus had not been broken by postflood disking—were made using specimens from the same and adjoining collection units.

The projects discussed above, although only a small portion of the archaeological work undertaken in Missouri during the 1980s, show the increasing emphasis in Americanist archaeology on empirical studies. Did such studies represent a clear break with all the traditional concerns of archaeology? I think not. Chronological placement of artifacts and determinations of the functions served by various artifacts were still important analytical issues, but certainly absent from discussion were topics such as cultural diffusion and assimilation. At least in some quarters attention was shifted away from culture history and toward such things as formation processes and the varied nature of artifact distributions. Given this shift in analytical focus, it was perfectly natural that the artifacts themselves would begin to come under increased scrutiny.

The Physical Properties of Artifacts

Archaeologists have varied interests, but it is probably safe to assume that the one interest they all share is artifacts. Most professional archaeologists enter the field because of a fascination with prehistoric objects, and it is this fascination that gives them at least one thing in common with avocational archaeologists. The two broad artifact classes most studied in archaeology are those made from stone and those made of clay. In Chapter 5 I touched on the development of typological systems for what commonly are termed "projectile points," and in Chapter 6 I briefly mentioned Ahler's (1971) classic analysis of the function of pointed, hafted bifaces from Rodgers Shelter. Despite these discussions, throughout the book I have given much more coverage to ceramic-artifact studies, and you might be left with the impression that analyses of lithic raw materials and artifacts have somehow played a minor role in the development of Americanist archaeology. Such is decidedly not the case, nor is it true that lithic-artifact analysis has played little or no role in the archaeology of Missouri. Again, I was faced with the decision of what to focus on most heavily, and I chose pottery.

Relative to Missouri archaeology, I believe this was an appropriate decision, as I hope to convince you shortly. But I call your attention to numerous excellent studies that have been conducted on lithic materials from Missouri or that bear directly on the use and alteration of lithic resources by prehistoric peoples in Missouri. Topics include (a) sources of raw materials used by prehistoric peoples to fashion their tools (e.g., House 1975 [Pitkin chert]; Griffin 1965 [obsidian]; Griffin et al. 1969 [obsidian]; Ives 1984, 1985 [Crescent Hills chert]; Luedtke and Meyers 1984 [Burlington chert]; Meyers 1970 [lower Illinois Valley cherts]; Southard 1973 [chert tools from Beckwith's Fort]; see especially Ray 1985 [Missouri cherts]); (b) heat-treatment of chert (Bleed and Meier 1980; Mandeville 1973; Rick 1978; see especially Dunnell et al. 1994); and (c) lithic-reduction sequences (e.g., various papers in Johnson and Morrow 1987; Morrow 1984).

One topic that has been of long-standing interest to archaeologists in the Midwest is the role played by lithic raw materials and finished products in trade networks. In one form this interest extends well back into the nineteenth century, when it became obvious that some of the items recovered from the ubiquitous mounds in the eastern United States were not manufactured from local raw materials. The items had come from somewhere, though it was not immediately obvious whether the actual items were brought in or whether the raw materials were brought in and the items were made locally. Source areas for some of the raw materials were difficult to identify, while the sources of others were fairly easy to find. Archaeologists long assumed, for example, that much of the obsidian found in midwestern sites was from flows in the Rocky Mountains, especially those in Yellowstone National Park, though it was not until the 1960s (Griffin 1965; Griffin et al. 1969) that this source was confirmed through methods such as neutron-activation analysis.

The empirical basis underlying such source determinations, however, was quickly transcended by archaeologists who, in typical fashion, began to concoct stories about the role played by trade in the prehistoric social and political arena. No doubt trade networks existed at least by the Middle Archaic period in the midwestern United States, though the most dramatic expressions date to the Middle Woodland period (e.g., Carr and Sears 1985; Griffin 1965; Seeman 1979; Struever 1964; Struever and Houart 1972). By A.D. 300 some groups in the Midwest, especially those in western and west-central Illinois and in southern Ohio, were receiving items such as obsidian and grizzly-bear canines from the West, mica from the Appalachians, marine shells from the Gulf Coast, and copper from the Great Lakes. The presence of these goods not only in Illinois and Ohio but in various portions of the East led to formulation of the concept of the Hopewell interaction sphere (e.g., Caldwell 1964; Struever 1964; Struever and Houart 1972), which I discussed in Chapter 1. The presence of an interaction sphere meant that someone had to control and operate the system, and the obvious choices were local elites who desired to improve the social and political standings of themselves and their families. There certainly was no shortage of ethnographic parallels from which to draw (various Melanesian groups have always been popular), and soon the archaeological literature was full of references to such things as Hopewellian "Big Men" (e.g., Chapman 1980). The work of ethnologist Marshall Sahlins, especially his article "Poor Man, Rich Man, Big-Man, Chief: Political Types in Melanesia and Polynesia" (Sahlins 1963), was and continues to be a favorite of archaeologists in need of a model for Hopewellian socioeconomic organization. Big Men put on elaborate shows of wealth, including throwing parties and giving away goods, in order to attract and keep followers. Parenthetically, two other works by Sahlins, *Social Stratification in Polynesia* (Sahlins 1958) and *Stone Age Economics* (Sahlins 1972), have also been favorites of archaeologists. It is not coincidental that the work of Sahlins has figured so prominently in the archaeology of the last several decades, especially in the search for culture process. He was heavily influenced by Leslie White (as he was by Julian Steward) and while at the University of Michigan either trained or influenced a generation of "new archaeologists" (including Lewis Binford). Carl Chapman, who received his Ph.D. from Michigan, apparently also was influenced by Sahlins (e.g., Chapman 1980: 76).

Trafficking in lithic items continued throughout the Late Woodland period, but by A.D. 900 one commodity, the chert "hoe," had outstripped all other goods in terms of sheer volume. With few exceptions, hoes were manufactured from either Mill Creek chert, which occurs in southern Illinois, or Dover (Fort Payne) chert, which occurs in northwestern Tennessee. Hoes were traded in finished form as opposed to the raw materials for them being traded (Cobb 1989; Dunnell et al. 1994); further, there is no convincing evidence (contrary to some speculations) that specialists were involved in the production and distribution of the implements (Cobb 1988, 1989). The ubiquity of Mill Creek and Dover hoes— Dunnell et al. (1994) suggest the former preceded the latter chronologically, with Dover hoes becoming the dominant type in southeastern Missouri after ca. A.D. 1350—to the virtual exclusion of hoes of other chert types suggests that they offered an advantage that was evident to users. Neither chert is particularly easy to flake unless heat-treated, but electron-spin resonance of samples from the Malden Plain (Dunnell et al. 1994) indicates hoes were not heat-treated, presumably because heat-treatment would weaken their resistance to impact damage. On the other hand, small hoe fragments and flakes removed during hoe sharpening were often heat-treated before being recycled as arrow points and other tools (Dunnell et al. 1994).

By far the most common lithic raw material on Mississippian-period sites in southeastern Missouri is chert found in gravel deposits on Crowley's Ridge, which abuts the Malden Plain along its western edge. However, Teltser's (1991) work at County Line (Stoddard County) is one of the few studies that have attempted to quantify the types of raw materials used in the region and the reduction strategies that were employed in tool manufacture. Ongoing analysis by McCutcheon and Dunnell (1993) is aimed at understanding the physical properties of Crowley's Ridge chert nodules.

Pottery Technology and Function

As important as some of the above studies of stone tools and raw lithic materials are, I believe the studies that best characterize the movement in archaeology toward an empirical understanding of the past are those that have centered on the analysis of pottery from the standpoints of how it was made and used. In the remainder of this section I focus attention on several studies of prehistoric pottery from Missouri localities that have attempted to show how and why Woodland- and Mississippian-period potters made their vessels the way they did and what effects, if any, changes in such things as subsistence and settlement systems had on vessel manufacture. Importantly, these studies have addressed the question of *why* certain changes took place as opposed to simply documenting when and where they took place.

Pottery, as Braun (1983: 108) points out, "is an archaeologist's delight. Its brittleness guarantees frequent breakage and disposal; its crystalline structure virtually guarantees preservation." Given that pottery manufacture is an additive process (as opposed to stone-tool manufacture, which is a subtractive process) and thus can generate infinite variation, it is no surprise that pottery has figured prominently in culture-historical studies and in fact is second to none as a tool that has been used to understand the past. Pottery can serve any number of functions and undoubtedly did so in prehistoric cultural systems. For example, it could have served as a medium of exchange as well as a symbol of a certain status, though such uses probably would have left no archaeological signatures. But the main function of a pot, we would suppose, was as a container in which to cook, to store, and/or to transport any manner of materials. And those uses *did* leave signatures.

As Braun (1983: 108) notes, prehistoric pots were tools. And as with any other tool, they were created using available technologies and for specific purposes. Our interest is in knowing what those purposes were and how well the tools did their intended jobs—an interest that, as we have seen, certainly was well established among prehistorians before the turn of the century (Chapter 3). Holmes (1886b), for example, recognized the link between the function of a pot and how it was made and thus focused some of his attention on the technological aspects of shell-tempered pottery from the central Mississippi River valley (see also Holmes 1903a).

Numerous publications on ceramic function appeared in the Americanist literature during the first half of the twentieth century; among the more widely cited are March (1934), Bennett (1943), Linton (1944), and, slightly later, Colton (1953). But it was the publication of Anna Shepard's *Ceramics for the Archaeologist* in 1956 that opened an entirely new vista in archaeological examination of prehistoric pottery. Shepard demonstrated not only that pots were used as tools by prehistoric peoples but that they could also be used as tools by the archaeologist. Encouraged by Shepard's straightforward approach to understanding prehistoric ceramic engineering, archaeologists began to literally tear into sherds to understand such things as paste composition, firing temperature, type of tempering materials used, and so forth. As important as this orientation was, however, it did not signal a complete shift in theoretical perspective, and many of the studies conducted after the introduction of Shepard's volume still focused on such things as group movement, trade, and the like.

I am doing a great disservice to an important body of work by skipping ahead several decades, and I do not want to leave the impression that archaeologists completely dropped the issue of pottery technology and function during the 1960s and 1970s. The fact that Shepard's book was in the fifth edition by 1968, only 12 years after it was first published, amply demonstrates a continued interest on the part of archaeologists in how prehistoric ceramic vessels were made and used. It was, however, a paper published in 1983—David Braun's "Pots as Tools"— that radically altered the manner in which archaeologists routinely handle the analysis of pottery. Braun pointed out two common conditions in archaeology that in many ways also typified the state of ceramic analysis in the early 1980s: (1) the lack of integration of analytical techniques with a body of interpretive theory and (2) a sophistication in measurement that was way out in front of any sense of what the measured variation means. The article was only one in a series of papers (cited below) in which Braun detailed the results of his analysis of Woodland-period cooking jars from western Illinois—an analysis that had as its central premise "measurements of ceramic technical variation routinely used for culture-historical purposes can also inform us about variation in whole-vessel use" (Braun 1983: 115).

The Mechanics of Woodland-Period Cooking-Vessel Walls

Of the myriad dimensions of vessel manufacture on which he could have focused, Braun (1983, 1985a, 1987) selected wall thickness and temper-particle size. Examining the wall thickness of cooking vessels would appear to be an excellent analytical entry point, since the decision of how thick to make a wall affects at least three aspects of a vessel's mechanical performance: (1) thermal conductivity (how well a vessel conducts heat into its contents [everything else being equal, the thinner a wall, the greater its ability to conduct heat]); (2) overall strength (the ability to withstand mechanical stress); and (3) resistance to thermal shock (how well a pot can withstand sudden and extreme changes in temperature [on average, the thinner the wall, the better a pot can withstand thermal shock]). Vessel-wall thickness, in many respects, is a compromise that a potter makes, given available technologies and the intended purpose of the vessel. A potter might want to create a large cooking vessel with thin walls, but perhaps he or she does not have the technological ability to make such a vessel and keep it from collapsing under its own weight. Throughout the Woodland period, vessel size and wall thickness must have been competing priorities, with the final product being a compromise. Of immediate archaeological interest is how prehistoric potters wrestled with those compromises and how the compromises shifted through time as technological limitations changed.

Braun (1985a, 1987) eventually plotted the wall thicknesses of sherds from 64 well-dated contexts from 32 sites in west-central Illinois to determine both the direction and magnitude of change.[4] His resulting time-series curve (Figure 8.8) illustrates that a thickening of vessel walls occurred between ca. 200 B.C. and A.D. 50, after which time the walls became thinner. Specifically, mean wall thickness ca. 200 B.C. was approximately 7.7 mm and increased to a maximum of approximately 8.2 mm by the start of the Christian era. After approximately A.D. 50, wall thickness declined at a rapid rate until ca. A.D. 300 (mean wall thickness of 6.1 mm), at which point it decreased at a slower rate until A.D. 550 (mean thickness of 5.8 mm), when the rate of decrease again accelerated, such that by A.D. 750 mean wall thickness was 5.3 mm. Braun (1985a: 526) also found that after ca. A.D. 450, vessel diameter had less and less influence on wall thickness, so that by A.D. 800 thickness actually tended to decrease with increasing vessel diameter—a phenomenon he interpreted as further evidence of increasing demand for thermal conductivity and thermal-shock resistance.

The same trend in wall thickness noted by Braun occurs in other ceramic assemblages, including those from the Saline Valley of southern Illinois (Hargrave 1981; Hargrave and Braun 1981) and from Burkemper, in Lincoln County, Missouri (Hoard 1992; O'Brien and Hoard 1996; O'Brien et al. 1994). Interestingly, Hargrave's (1981) analysis of Saline Valley materials showed that on average vessel-wall thickness was 5 mm thicker than averages for contemporary materials 60 km away. Similarly, Hoard and I (1996 [see also Hoard 1992]) demonstrated that Burkemper materials were on average 2 mm thicker than Braun's (1985a, 1987) averages for contemporary materials from west-central Illinois (Figure 8.8).

---

4. Braun 1985a discusses 56 contexts; he included 8 additional samples later (Braun 1987). I am greatly simplifying Braun's analysis. See his extended discussion (Braun 1985a).

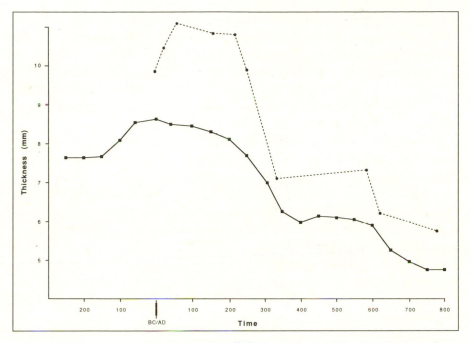

Figure 8.8. Time trend of mean vessel-wall thickness for Middle Woodland– and Late Woodland–period sherd samples from western Illinois (solid line) and from the Burkemper site, Lincoln County, Missouri (dotted line) (from O'Brien and Hoard 1996 [Illinois curve adapted from Braun 1985a]).

In addition to wall thickness, Braun (1982, 1983) also examined the size of temper particles (primarily angular pieces of feldspar and quartz, commonly referred to as "grit") in his Illinois samples. He found that over time there was a reduction both in the density of particle sizes greater than 1 mm in average diameter and in average particle size: "These tendencies suggest both an increasing use of temper to manipulate flexural strength, and an increasing concern for stresses resulting from differential thermal behavior of the temper. Viewed alongside the changes in wall-sectional shape, then, the changes in tempering characteristics also indicate an engineering trend of increasing attention to the accommodation of use-related thermal stresses" (Braun 1983: 124–25). The relation among temper type, temper-particle size, and thermal stress is anything but straightforward (O'Brien et al. 1994). For example, temper can add strength to a clay body, both before and after firing, but different types of temper exhibit different expansion coefficients when heated, and without care, their use could lead to vessel failure. The size of temper particles also contributes to the success of a vessel. As Bronitsky and Hamer (1986) found, smaller temper size leads to a reduction in failure from *mechanical stresses.*

What are we to make of these trends in Woodland-period cooking vessels? As Braun (1983) noted, it does us little good to be able to measure minute changes in things such as vessel walls and the size of temper particles if we can't then *explain* the variation that we measure. What *performance characteristics* (Braun 1983; O'Brien et al. 1994; Schiffer and Skibo 1987) did Woodland potters look for when they manufactured their pots, and why were they looking for them? What explains the trend in larger, thinner-walled pots through time? The possible answer to this intriguing question was provided by a decade's worth of integrated work, primarily in the lower Illinois River valley, that produced considerable insights into the settlement and subsistence systems of Middle Woodland– and early Late Woodland–period peoples. Widespread evidence from midwestern riverine settings in Illinois and eastern Missouri (e.g., D. L. Asch and N. B. Asch 1978, 1985a, 1985b; D. L. Asch et al. 1979; N. B. Asch and D. L. Asch 1981; Pulliam 1987) indicated that around the beginning of the Christian era Woodland groups increased their dependence on the seeds of native oily and starchy plants. There is also evidence that the frequency of juvenile dental caries increased significantly between A.D. 1 and A.D. 600 in west-central Illinois (Buikstra 1977; Cook 1979; Cook and Buikstra 1979), suggesting that seeds were being boiled until they were gelatinized and then fed to infants (Braun 1983).

Thus it appears that the trend in decreasing vessel thickness was tied to evolving food-preparation systems: "This parallel [between decreasing wall thickness and increasing appearance of starchy and oily seeds in the archaeobotanical record] strongly suggests that these ceramic changes all reflect increasing attention to the cooking of seed broths in meal preparation, increasing nutrient extraction and possibly improving palatability" (Braun 1987: 164). Localized differences in vessel manufacture probably varied in relation to the demands placed on the vessels by the users. Braun (1985a: 527) noted that the differences in wall thickness between his sample and the one from the Saline Valley paralleled paleobotanical evidence for a much lower importance of edible starchy and oily seeds in the Saline Valley diet (Lopinot 1982: 804–6). Evidence of the role played by vessels in cooking seeds is provided by hundreds of sherds from Burkemper, which exhibit thick (often up to 1 mm) carbonized residues on the interiors.

The trend toward thinner cooking-vessel walls and the rise in the use of seeds as dietary staples led bioarchaeologist Jane Buikstra to propose that these changes could have led directly to changes in fertility of Woodland-period women. Infants could have been weaned at an earlier age and placed on a seed-based, carbohydrate-rich diet. The shortening of the lactation period in Woodland mothers, coupled with a corresponding resumption of ovulation, could have led to a rise in fertility. As it turned out, Buikstra was correct (Buikstra et al. 1986; see also Holland 1989); evidence of increased fertility during the early Late Woodland period (ca. A.D. 400–750) was found in skeletal series from western Illinois.

Buikstra's proposition was clearly a result of using one trend evident in the archaeological record to posit, in logical fashion, the existence of another. The work of Buikstra and Braun, when coupled with faunal analysis from localities in western Illinois (e.g., Styles 1981; Styles et al. 1985; Styles and Purdue 1986) and eastern Missouri (e.g., O'Brien 1995; Purdue et al. 1989) produced a wealth of information on the strategies Woodland-period groups used to procure and process their food. Analysis of some of the physical properties of Woodland ceramics provided not only a means of chronologically ordering depositional contexts (Braun's wall-thickness curve) but also of monitoring changes in several aspects of Woodland-period life. By the end of the 1980s, numerous archaeologists had taken heed of Shepard and Braun's notion that pots were indeed tools for the archaeologist and had extended research in innumerable directions (see Rice 1987).

Pottery Temper as an Analytical Focus

Braun's initial work on temper-particle size among Illinois samples and Hoard's similar analysis of Missouri materials were only two steps in a long series of interesting and highly significant studies of ceramic tempers conducted during the 1980s and 1990s and in many respects typify the growing movement toward the creation of a science of artifacts. Archaeologists have long recognized that not all pottery from the eastern United States was tempered with the same material and that even within a single class of temper there were major differences in the size of particles from vessel to vessel (e.g., Holmes 1886b). Throughout the twentieth century archaeologists have used temper inclusions as a means of partitioning the archaeological record into spatial and temporal units—a use that makes sense because it is easily demonstrable that tempering materials replaced each other through time and across space.

Fiber-tempered pottery is the earliest type of clay container found in the United States, dating to the third millennium B.C. in the Southeast (Sassaman 1993). In the Midwest, fiber-tempered pottery was found at the Late Archaic Nebo Hill site near Kansas City (K. Reid 1984a, 1984b; Skibo et al. 1989), with dates that fall in the 2600–1500 B.C. range. Nebo Hill sherds are soft, and pastes contain 5–15% silt-sized particles and no sand. By ca. 500 B.C., thick-walled, mineral-tempered pots became common over large portions of the mid-latitude United States east of the Mississippi River. Localized type designations—Marion thick in the upper and central Mississippi Valley—belie similarities in ceramic technologies and shapes that extend from Missouri to New York. Temper varies regionally, but sherds of Marion thick usually contain large angular to subangular pieces of crushed igneous (and sometimes metamorphic) rock. D. T. Morgan et al. (1986: 212) describe the 5,000-plus Marion thick sherds from the Mississippi floodplain Ambrose Flick site (western Illinois) as "on the order of 9–18 mm in thickness with a cordmarked or fabric-impressed interior. . . . Temper particles, which may be as large as 5 mm in diameter,[5] are typically an abundant inclusion. Commonly the paste is soft, and in many instances surfaces are highly eroded, with temper protruding through the surface." This description is typical of contemporary materials from other sites in the Midwest (e.g., Begg and Riley 1990; Harn 1986).

Beginning around 400 B.C. and in some areas of the Midwest overlapping with Marion thick, a new, thinner, hard-paste ware—commonly referred to as Black Sand incised in Illinois and Missouri—became predominant in portions of the central and upper Mississippi Valley. Incised-over-cordmarked vessels were tempered with large amounts of sand and/or finely crushed igneous rock, often to the point where sherds have an extremely sandy feel. In some areas, other minerals occur frequently in pastes (in the lower Illinois River valley chert was a significant addition [Farnsworth and Asch 1986: 370]).

These Early Woodland mineral-tempered wares are important for examining the beginnings of sedentary life in the central Mississippi Valley and neighboring regions (e.g., Braun 1985a, 1987; Farnsworth and Asch 1986; O'Brien 1987; Styles 1981). Across the Midwest, the period 600–200 B.C. witnessed the development of dozens of ceramic industries. Potters in widely separate localities produced wares that were remarkably uniform, leading to suggestions such as "It is speculated that either ceramic reproduction at this early stage of the craft in the Midwest was rote, or that a small interaction 'sphere' occurred in Marion Culture which distributed potters or the ideas of their craft over a large, diffuse territory" (Begg and Riley 1990: 250). In other cases, regional variation is plainly evident, and the usual explanation invoked is group intrusion. Munson (1982, 1986) argues that producers of Marion thick and Black Sand vessels were from different groups, with the latter living to the northwest and west of the former.

A similar explanation is presented for the occurrence of two Early Woodland ceramic traditions in the American Bottom—the Florence phase (Emerson et al. 1983) and the Columbia complex (Fortier 1985), where the primary temper was crushed sherds (grog), not minerals (Emerson 1986; Emerson and Fortier 1986). Vessels assigned to the Florence phase, which appears to be contemporary with the Black Sand tradition to the north and perhaps with the late stages of the Marion-thick tradition, are, in contrast to Black Sand vessels, tempered with crushed sherds. Judging from reported ranges and means of sherd thickness (Emerson et al. 1983), Florence vessels are thinner than Marion vessels and probably are thinner than most mineral-tempered Black Sand vessels. Columbia-complex vessels are similar to Florence vessels but may date slightly later. Fortier

5. Some particles in sherds from eastern Missouri and western Illinois actually range as high as 10 mm in diameter.

et al. (1984: 76) believe that the "Florence phase ceramics would appear to have their antecedents in the grog-tempered, zonally decorated ceramics of the Midsouth and lower Mississippi River valley, rather than in the ceramics of the northern Marion phase."

By 200 B.C. pottery in the midwestern United States was being tempered with a variety of materials, including the aforementioned angular pieces of feldspar, crushed limestone, crushed bits of fired clay (including sherds), or sand. There was significant geographic variation, and not surprisingly the ranges correspond fairly well with the availability of local materials. For example, in the Mississippi alluvial valley of southeastern Missouri, where there are no igneous- or metamorphic-rock outcrops, Middle Woodland– and Late Woodland–period pottery was tempered with sand or fired clay. Limestone occurs frequently in late Middle Woodland–period (ca. A.D. 300–450) vessels (the Baehr and Pike series) from western Illinois (e.g., D. T. Morgan 1985; Struever 1960) and became one of the dominant tempers in the American Bottom (Kelly et al. 1984) and throughout much of Missouri (e.g., Chapman 1980; Vehik 1978; Wedel 1943), excluding the Mississippi River valley, during the Late Woodland period.

By at least A.D. 900, perhaps significantly earlier in some areas, much of the sand- and clay-tempered pottery was replaced by shell-tempered pottery. The cultural-temporal unit used to designate this appearance is *Emergent Mississippian*, a term first used for variously tempered materials from the American Bottom of western Illinois (e.g., Kelly et al. 1984). Locations in the eastern Ozarks of southeastern Missouri have produced large quantities of shell-tempered materials dated directly through thermoluminescence or indirectly through radiocarbon assays at around A.D. 600 (Lynott 1982, 1986; Lynott and Price 1989; J. E. Price 1986). James Price and Mark Lynott view the region as the heartland of shell-tempered ceramics, with adjacent regions receiving the requisite technological knowledge at later dates through diffusion.

Some investigators (e.g., D. F. Morse and P. A. Morse 1990) believe these dates to be invalid markers for the beginning of shell-tempered pottery in the central Mississippi Valley, though there is at present no reason not to believe that shell-tempered pottery could have been produced in the eastern Ozarks by late in the seventh century. However, outside the eastern Ozarks, Hoecake, in Mississippi County, is the only other Missouri site that has yielded a seventh-century date for shell-tempered pottery (J. R. Williams 1974). The preponderance of dates from shell-tempered-pottery contexts in the region (e.g., Zebree, in northeastern Arkansas [D. F. Morse and P. A. Morse 1980; P. A. Morse and D. F. Morse 1990] and Robards, in Dunklin County [Dunnell 1982a]) fall in the ninth and tenth centuries.

Early shell-tempered pottery occurs in several vessel forms, the three most prominent being bottles, restricted-neck jars, and low, wide bowls and pans (Dunnell and Feathers 1991; P. A. Morse and D. F. Morse 1990). Many of the vessels were red-slipped on the interior, the exterior, or both. The generic name given to this early shell-tempered pottery is *Varney*, named by S. Williams (1954) after the Old Varney River site in Dunklin County. The development of shell-tempered pottery out of earlier clay-tempered or sand-tempered pottery has long been of interest to archaeologists working in the central Mississippi Valley, who often have turned to "explanations" such as group intrusion to account for the presence of a new type of pottery after ca. A.D. 800 (e.g., Lynott and Price 1989; D. F. Morse and P. A. Morse 1983). Consistent reliance on a typological approach to ceramic analysis has kept attention from being focused on the life histories of various technologies such as shell-tempered-pottery manufacture (Feathers 1989b: 79) and on scenarios centered around group migration and diffusion.

The archaeological literature is fairly straightforward in how the appearance of shell-tempered vessels is viewed: shell tempering signifies the end of the Late Woodland period and the beginning of the Mississippian period. In other words, shell-tempered pots replaced mineral- and/or clay-tempered pots. Nowhere in the literature is there more than passing mention that a ceramic vessel might be tempered with more than one material. However, several studies from Missouri (e.g., Feathers 1988, 1989b; Teltser 1988, 1993), including the Phillips et al. (1951) survey, have shown that the shift from sand or grog to shell initially was not one of complete replacement. Where extensive archaeological work has produced large ceramic assemblages, such as the American Bottom of western Illinois and the Cairo Lowland of southeastern Missouri, clearly limestone-, sand-, and/or grog-tempered pots were being manufactured several hundred years after the advent of shell-tempered pottery, and combinations of temper can occur in the same vessel.

James Feathers (1990a), on the other hand, reports very few sherds from the Malden Plain of southeastern Missouri and northeastern Arkansas tempered with both sand and shell. Studies emphasizing dimensions of vessel form and paste characteristics (e.g., Dunnell and Feathers 1991) suggest that, at least on the Malden Plain, indigenous Late Woodland peoples were responsible for both traditions. There, the

> earliest shell-tempered pottery is quite distinctive from the sand-tempered pottery it replaced. The shell temper is abundant (up to 40%) and coarse (ranging up to 2 mm in diameter). A red slip was often applied to one or both surfaces which were first smoothed by scraping. The pottery is quite porous (about 45% apparent porosity) and soft (between 2.0 and 2.5 on the Mohs scale). In contrast, the sand-tempered ware is rarely slipped, the exteriors are roughened with a cord-wrapped paddle, and the pottery is less porous (about 23%) and harder (2.5 to 3.0 on the Mohs scale). The sand is rounded quartz, ranging from 20% to 40% of the body with only occasional grains larger than 1 mm in diameter. (Feathers and Scott 1989: 554)

Feathers's (1988, 1989a, 1989b, 1990a, 1990b; Dunnell and Feathers 1991; Feathers and Scott 1989; compare Bronitsky and Hamer 1986) work on shell-tempered pottery from floodplain contexts in southeastern Missouri extends our understanding of ceramic manufacture and use in the Mississippi Valley. Feathers (1989b: 78–79) asks

> whether shell tempering was a technique already known and therefore part of the pool of available variability at the time it began to predominate in the manufacturing process or whether its rapid spread is due to diffusion of a technique that once available quickly outcompeted alternatives.
>
> While this question is largely historical in nature, the two alternatives require different functional arguments. In the first case, shell tempering was already known but was not selected earlier because the advantages it bestows did not outweigh the disadvantages, because of the way pottery was used or made (e.g., poor control over firing). In the second case there is no question the advantages outweighed the disadvantages. The question is simply one of availability. Once introduced it spread rapidly.

The question arises, What, if any, advantage did shell-tempered vessels offer over those tempered with various minerals? Indeed, the broader question applies to the shift from fiber to various minerals as well. Various scenarios have been discussed in the literature to account for the various temper shifts, but it was only during the 1980s that in-depth experimentation was undertaken to examine the performance characteristics of pottery of different tempers. One important set of experiments was conducted by Michael Schiffer and James Skibo (1987; see also Skibo et al. 1989) on fiber- versus mineral-tempered ceramic products. Schiffer and Skibo conducted the experiments in the belief that comparison of "design priorities for Archaic and Woodland pottery furnishes a basis for exploring changes in the societal contexts of these ceramics that might have promoted the technological change" from Archaic to Woodland pottery (Schiffer and Skibo 1987: 602). They examined three sets of 8-square-centimeter briquettes (one set untempered, one set tempered with fiber, and one set tempered with mineral) relative to six performance characteristics: ease of manufacture, heating effectiveness, portability, impact resistance, thermal-shock resistance, and abrasion resistance. Their results indicated that "Archaic technology placed a high priority on ease of manufacture and portability, whereas Woodland—especially Late Woodland—technology stressed heating effectiveness and characteristics that promote longer uselives (e.g., impact resistance, thermal shock resistance, and abrasion resistance)" (Schiffer and Skibo 1987: 607). Whatever the advantages were of producing and using fiber-tempered pottery, it would appear that the containers did not have wide and long-lasting appeal. No other midwestern pottery contemporary with that from Nebo Hill has been recovered, and a large temporal gap existed in the area between its production and the earliest manufacture of mineral-tempered ware.

The use of limestone—or any calcium-carbonate-based material—as a temper is problematic, though its widespread use in the Midwest suggests that it offered certain advantages under prescribed conditions. It has been suggested that calcium-carbonate temper offers two advantages: its chemical composition ($CaCO_3$) increases the workability of clay (Million 1975; Stimmell et al. 1982) over other tempering agents, and its expansion rate is similar to that of most clays, thus reducing the rate of failure during initial firing. On the other hand, it is well known that lime spalling occurs as an end process of heating calcium carbonate, which converts to calcium oxide (CaO) and carbon dioxide (CO_2) during heating. The gas dissipates, and on cooling the CaO hydrates to form calcium hydroxide $Ca(OH)_2$. Stresses related to the volume expansion of the particles cause popping and cracking of the clay body. There are methods of controlling the degree of damage: reducing the size of the temper particles (Laird and Worcester 1956); "docking" the fired items (plunging them into cold water while they are still hot) (Klempter and Johnson 1986); adding salt to the prefired paste (Klempter and Johnson 1986); firing the composite above 1000°C or below approximately 700°C (both in an oxidizing atmosphere) (Rice 1987); or firing the composite in a reducing atmosphere (Rice 1987).[6]

Although more experimental work needs to be done before we thoroughly understand the successful technologies that produced limestone-tempered pottery in Missouri and adjoining regions, it is evident from recent experiments (Hoard and O'Brien n.d.; Hoard et al. 1995) that the addition of limestone temper produced vessels that were stronger than either grit- or fired-clay-tempered vessels when fired at 600°C. Test bars made of dry clay from a Boone County, Missouri, deposit were tempered with each of the three materials (35% by dry weight), allowed to dry for 24 hours, and then fired in an oxidizing atmosphere at 600°C for an hour. Each bar was then tested for the amount of force needed to initiate cracking (peak load) and then to cause complete failure. The results demonstrated that less force was needed to break the bars tempered either with grit or fired clay than the limestone-tempered bars, though the latter had less capacity for deformation before rupturing. In other words, it took more force to create cracks in limestone-tempered specimens, but once cracks began to develop, the limestone-tempered specimens failed more rapidly than did the clay- or sand-tempered bars. Thus, the increase in resistance to mechanical (as well as perhaps thermal) stresses offered by limestone-tempered

6. Exactly how Woodland potters fired calcium-carbonate-tempered pottery is still undetermined. As Rice (1987: 98) points out, successful firing probably involved careful monitoring of time, temperature, *and* firing atmosphere.

wares may explain in part why some Woodland-period potters used such a risky temper.

In a similar study, which actually was the impetus for the above-mentioned experiment, Feathers (1989a) measured the "toughness" of fine- and coarse-shell-tempered test bars against that of sand-tempered bars. Figure 8.9 illustrates not only that it took longer for shell-tempered specimens to break but also that there was considerable time lag in the shell-tempered specimens between crack initiation and failure. Feathers also found differences among shell-tempered specimens by fine versus coarse grain and by percentage of temper. Coarse-tempered specimens with 45% shell outperformed specimens of all other classes. Similar performance tests conducted by Feathers and Scott (1989) yielded quantitative differences between shell- and sand-tempered specimens. They found that coarse-shell-tempered pieces were tougher than those tempered with sand and that the shell-tempered replicates did not break catastrophically, in contrast to sand-tempered replicates. They suggested that the large, platelike structures created by crushed shell are better deterrents to crack propagation than are sand particles:

> The higher strength and toughness of the shell-tempered samples can be explained by the nature of the calcite grains. When viewed under high magnification (160x), the particles appear as bundles of longitudinal fibers. When these fibers are aligned parallel to the direction of stress, they increase strength because of the greater force required to break them as compared to the force required to break through the clay matrix. . . . Because of the difficulty in propagating a crack across the fibers, the particles tend to be pulled out from the matrix rather than broken. This pulling action absorbs considerable energy. (Feathers 1989a: 5)

Given the added strength afforded by shell as a temper, why was it not used earlier, if indeed vessel strength was a favorable feature? It is not very enlightening to suggest that earlier Woodland potters did not realize some advantages afforded by crushed shell, so we might have to seek other reasons for its late development. Mussel shell is a combination of organic material and a crystalline carbonate, aragonite, and has a hardness of 3.5–4.0 on the Mohs scale. Burning the shell at 200–400°C, which Mississippian-period potters apparently did (Feathers 1989a: 581; Million 1980), removes organic material and converts the crystalline structure from aragonite to calcite, which has a hardness of about 3.0. Without burning, shell not only is harder to crush, but an increase in particle volume during the aragonite-to-calcite transition can cause pots to fail during firing. Bronitsky and Hamer (1986) suggested that Mississippian-period potters burned raw shell at temperatures that exceeded the point of carbonate decomposition (650°C or higher), but if this were the case the platelets would have been reduced to a fine powder and we would not recognize the temper

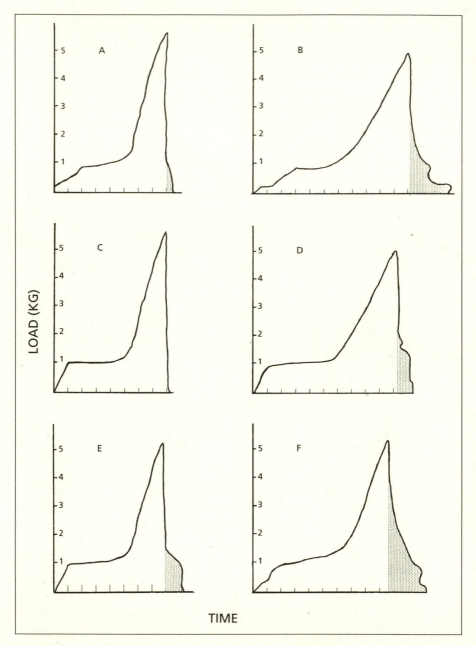

Figure 8.9. Graphs of load versus time for test bars tempered with (a) sand (composite of multiple samples), (b) shell (composite), (c) 25% fine shell, (d) 25% coarse shell, (e) 45% fine shell, and (f) 45% coarse shell (c–f, single samples) (redrawn from Feathers 1989a).

as shell. Hence the presence of visible shell platelets indicates the shell was burned at temperatures below the carbonate-decomposition point and that pots were fired at temperatures below the critical temperature or, as Feathers (1989a: 581) suggests, at higher temperatures but in a reducing atmosphere (perhaps for shorter periods [Dunnell and Feathers 1991: 31]).

Dunnell and Feathers (1991) noted that there are two disadvantages of oxidized shell-tempered pottery: its softness and its porosity. The failure of vessels from abrasion might not have been an important consideration, but porosity certainly could have affected the manner in which vessels were used. J. W. Foster (1873a: 95) thought that shell-tempered vessels were intentionally porous so as to allow liquids to cool through evaporation, a notion debunked by Holmes (1886b). Dunnell and Feathers (1991: 34) found that early oxidized shell-tempered pottery from the Malden Plain was twice as porous as local sand-tempered pottery. Not coincidentally, early shell-tempered vessels, not only those from the Malden Plain but those from other regions in the central Mississippi Valley as well, often were covered on the interior (and occasionally on the exterior) with a thin, reddish slip. Earlier sand-tempered vessels also were occasionally slipped, but this probably had little to do with function. Slipping appears to be, as Dunnell and Feathers (1991: 34) note, an example of a trait that starts out "as a component of stylistic variation ('decoration') in [sand-tempered] Barnes ceramics, shifting to function (reduction of permeability) in the early shell-tempered ceramics in a new selective environment (shell tempering), and ending up once again as style in Middle and Late Mississippian when wholesale and unrelated changes in ceramic technology [including firing in reducing atmospheres] decrease porosity to earlier levels."

The Materialist, or Evolutionary, Perspective

The work on various aspects of prehistoric pottery discussed above in many ways characterizes the radical changes in approach that Americanist archaeology has gone through in the last several years. One could argue that it was only with the advent of new and complex analytical machinery that such studies are possible, but surely this is not the case. The means of conducting such studies have been around for decades in one form or another; it simply took someone to ask the appropriate questions. There are now enough signs, however, to suspect that archaeology will not soon retreat from its newly found materials-oriented approach. Part of my reason for saying this is that this materials-oriented approach is being conducted under a *materialist* perspective—not materialist in the sense that anthropologists (e.g., Harris 1968b, 1979) typically use the term but in a completely different sense. The sense to which I refer is that upon which Darwinian evolution is based—a perspective that views (a) relations between and among phenomena as being time- and spacebound and (b) variation between and among objects as change rather than simply as difference (Dunnell 1982b). This view contrasts with essentialism, which assumes that things have an "essence," hence the name. It is the "essential properties" of an object that dictate whether the object is grouped as A or B; variation is viewed as an "annoying distraction" (Lewontin 1974: 5).

It is clear that throughout its history archaeology has maintained an essentialist perspective. For example, at the root of most archaeological analysis is the splitting and lumping of materials into kinds (types) based on perceived similarities and differences. Change, when it is mentioned, is viewed as the transformation of one type into another. Archaeologists have done the same thing with time-space units such as phases and with sociopolitical units such as tribes and chiefdoms, where central tendencies in data sets become the center of analytical attention and variation is relegated to the position of "annoying distraction." But it is on this variation that the Darwinian process of selection works—something that biologists routinely take for granted but which until fairly recently has escaped the attention of archaeologists. Does selection actually "select" one pot over another because it has a thinner or thicker wall? No, of course not, but it *does* "select" among human users of the pots. If users of limestone-tempered pots having wall thicknesses of 5–6 mm are more successful in the long run than the users of slightly thicker pots tempered with grit—and if you think this is farfetched, think back to the decrease in wall thickness and the concomitant rise in births during the Woodland period—then why should we not view thinner-walled, limestone-tempered pots as adaptations? Most biologists view such things as birds' nests and beavers' dams as adaptations; what keeps us from viewing pots or projectile points the same way?

A growing number of archaeologists—many of whom work or have worked in Missouri—are becoming convinced that an "evolutionary archaeology," or, as Holland and I have labeled it, a "selection-based" archaeology (O'Brien and Holland 1990), not only is possible but also represents the most effective use of the archaeological record. Dunnell, in a long series of articles (Dunnell 1978b, 1980, 1982b, 1988b–c, 1989, 1990b, 1992b) began to lay the groundwork for such an approach, which was subsequently picked up and expanded by others (e.g., Braun 1987; Feathers 1989b, 1990a–b; Leonard and Jones 1987; Neff 1992, 1993; O'Brien and Holland 1990, 1992, 1995a–b; O'Brien et al. 1994; Rindos 1984, 1985, 1986, 1989).[7] The approach is based on the premise that objects in the

---

7. It would be practically impossible to find the first reference by an archaeologist to natural selection and the archaeological record, but certainly one clear statement was made by the British prehistorian Grahame Clark (1970: 61–62): "The thesis I would seek to propound is quite simply that man and his way of life as this has developed down to the present day are both ultimately the product of natural selection. . . . In saying this one has, of course, to make many reservations. . . . Natural selection could nevertheless operate on cultural variations as well as on genetic mutations."

archaeological record were parts of past human phenotypes in the same way that any bodily feature was and that some of those objects were shaped by selection—in other words, they were adaptations (O'Brien and Holland 1992). The best way to understand the role played by those adaptations, that is, to understand what their functions were, is through engineering-design analysis. In essence, one does what Schiffer, Skibo, Feathers, and others have done: tear the sherds (in the case of pottery) apart, see how pots were made, and compare as many variants as possible to determine the differences among them quantitatively. Then, suggest *explanations* for those differences that are founded on mechanical and engineering principles.

Such experiments produce empirical data; perhaps more importantly, they are replicable. Perhaps even more importantly, there is a coherent body of theory that produces the methods and techniques and guides analysis. That theory is Darwinian evolution. My purpose in pointing out the role that evolution has begun to play in Missouri archaeology is not to convert you to such a position but rather to point out that, in my mind at least, archaeology has finally reached the point where it can become a science. Evolution, of course, has been around in Americanist archaeology for a long time. In the nineteenth century it was evolution as espoused by Lewis Henry Morgan and others to which most Bureau of American Ethnology archaeologists subscribed, at least in part. Later, it was evolution according to Leslie White and Julian Steward and slightly later evolution as written by ethnologists Morton Fried, Marshall Sahlins, and Elman Service.

The trouble was, these brands of evolution—specifically, cultural evolution—were (and still are) nothing more than unidirectional, progressive formulations grounded in the notion of transformation (Dunnell 1980). Change is viewed simplistically as an outcome of need: if a group was facing food shortage, they simply formed alliances with other groups or developed a different means of obtaining food. In most anthropological schemes, groups (and, by extension, individuals within the groups) always come out as winners, as opposed to how it is in real life. Selection plays no role in most evolutionary scenarios concocted by anthropologists and archaeologists, since evolution becomes little more than a set of invented solutions to problems posed by the environment (Lewontin 1983). In other words, humans go out and get whatever it is they want or need. What archaeologists have done, unwittingly or not, is to interpret what it was that prehistoric humans needed. In essence, the archaeological record becomes little more than a proving ground for those interpretations.

In a reflective essay on the state of archaeological interpretation in the mid-1980s, Patty Jo Watson, technically another Missouri archaeologist through her position at Washington University in St Louis, notes, "I take *interpretation* to mean what the archaeologist does to or with archaeological data to make sense of them, both particularistically (*explaining* a specific piece of a specific site) and generally (*explaining* the past)" (P. J. Watson 1986: 440; emphasis added). I agree with Watson that interpretation is a sense-making system. For example, when Chapman examined the role of the green-corn ceremony in Hopewellian life (Chapter 1), he was trying to make sense out of what he saw archaeologically. Likewise, the midwestern taxonomic method was a way to make sense out of perceived similarities and differences in the archaeological record. I cannot agree with Watson that interpretation equals explanation.

Watson was one of three authors of a small but highly influential book—*Explanation in Archeology: An Explicitly Scientific Approach*—that appeared at the height of the "new archaeology" (P. J. Watson et al. 1971). The book proved to be so popular that it was revised and published several years later as *Archeological Explanation: The Scientific Method in Archeology* (P. J. Watson et al. 1984). Watson and her coauthors argued that archaeology could and should be a science and that explanation was the desired end product. Further, they argued that explanation could only come about through rigorous adherence to the scientific method: "Archaeologists should begin with clearly stated problems and then formulate testable hypothetical solutions. The degree of confirmation of conclusions should be exhibited by describing fully the field and laboratory data and the reasoning used to support these conclusions. This is what we mean by an explicitly scientific archeological method" (P. J. Watson et al. 1984: 129).

Who could argue with their statement that archaeologists should state their problems clearly and describe the data fully? And who could argue against testing hypotheses, though as I pointed out in Chapter 6 what we are really doing is examining the *testable implications* of a hypothesis (see especially the discussion in Chapter 6 of Bruce Smith's work on Gypsy Joint). Watson et al. were explicit on their definition of science:

> science *is* based on the working assumption or belief by scientists that past and present regularities *are* pertinent to future events and that under similar circumstances similar phenomena will behave in the future as they have in the past and do in the present. This practical assumption of the regularity or conformity of nature is the necessary foundation for all scientific work. Scientific descriptions, explanations, and predictions all utilize lawlike generalizations hypothesized on the presumption that natural phenomena are orderly. (P. J. Watson et al. 1984: 5–6)

A few pages later they continued:

> The ultimate goal of any science is construction of an axiomatized theory such that observed regularities can be derived from a few basic laws as premises. Such theories are used to explain past events and to predict future ones. Good theories lead to prediction of previously unsuspected regularities. Logical and mathematical axiomatic systems are essential as models of scientific theories, but

no empirical science has yet been completely axiomatized. As Hempel indicates, it may ultimately turn out for any science, or for all sciences, that the goal is actually unattainable. (P. J. Watson et al. 1984: 14)

For background, you need to know that Carl Hempel became a favorite philosopher of the new archaeologists of the 1960s and 1970s (e.g., Fritz and Plog 1970). Hempel's views on science and how it operates formed the basis of the reintroduction into philosophy of nineteenth-century empiricism, though the term usually applied to Hempel's paradigm is *logical positivism*.[8] One of his books, *Aspects of Scientific Explanation, and Other Essays in the Philosophy of Science* (Hempel 1965), became as widely cited in the archaeological literature of the 1970s as it did in the philosophical literature of the 1960s. His view of science is what Watson et al. (1971, 1984) abstracted as their view (see above quote): the use of "an axiomatized theory such that observed regularities can be derived from a few basic laws as premises." Watson et al. eventually were joined in their endeavor to make the philosophy of science more accessible to the archaeological community by other neopositivists, such as Merrilee and Wesley Salmon (e.g., M. H. Salmon 1975, 1982; M. H. Salmon and W. C. Salmon 1979). Central to all their arguments was the Hempelian account of how one arrived at explanation— what Hempel termed the "deductive-nomological" approach. Despite his use of unusual terms, Hempel's basic tenet is simple: whatever is to be explained (he used the term *explanandum* to refer to the "whatever") is derived logically from one or more universal statements, or laws, keeping in mind that certain boundary conditions might apply—hence, Watson et al.'s (1984: 5) above-cited definition of science as the "belief by scientists that past and present regularities *are* pertinent to future events and that under similar circumstances similar phenomena will behave in the future as they have in the past and do in the present."

There are still philosophers around who view science in Hempelian terms, but by the middle of the 1970s it was becoming clear that the deductive-nomological approach was dying a natural death. There were attempts to keep it alive, for example by linking it to the "bridging-law" concept of philosopher Ernest Nagel (e.g., 1961), but these also died out—except among archaeologists, who began making bridges between the archaeological present and the archaeological past through such things as ethnographic analogy and ethnoarchaeology (see Fritz 1972). In other words, archaeologists were using the present as an analog of the past. In fact, they *had* to resort to analogy; how else were they going to find the laws that Hempel said were there—the very laws that, once discovered, led to the formulation of "axiomatized theory" and thus ultimately to explanation?

8. Interested readers should see Guy Gibbon's (1989) *Explanation in Archaeology* for an in-depth discussion of positivism and its role in archaeology.

What a blessing it was that archaeologists now had access to the past through the present. They could find patterning in their archaeological data sets and interpret it in terms of modern analogs, or, conversely, they could use present behavior as a guide to what to look for in the prehistoric archaeological record. If one found enough corollaries between the past and the present, then surely laws could be constructed to account for the similarity in pattern. Any slight deviations could be explained away in terms of slightly different "boundary conditions," to use Hempel's term, that had impinged on the creators of what became archaeological signatures. The end result of this exercise was scientific explanation—defined as interpretation by way of law formulation. This is why Watson (1986: 452) equates archaeological interpretation with "describing and explaining the real past."

There are, however, some archaeologists, myself included, who do not agree with this equation of interpretation with explanation nor with the belief that the Hempelian view of science can be applied to the study of organisms, including humans. The type of science Watson has in mind—a predictive, law-driven science—will not work in archaeology. Hempelian science is not particularly useful for studying humans—or any other organism—because of the assumptions it makes relative to laws. No one has ever denied that chemical-physical laws don't apply to organisms, but at the level that concerns most archaeologists—behaviors (why we do what we do) and the products of those behaviors—they do not appear to play a deterministic role. And determinism—that is, the intrinsic properties that something has that make that something predictable—is the basis of Hempelian explanation (again, within reason—remember Hempel's "boundary conditions"). Deterministic laws work well for physical things such as elements and molecules and their chemical interactions, but they do not work well for organisms. There are deterministic laws that govern how carbon atoms interact with other atoms. For example, burning H_2 in O_2 *always* produces water. We can make that bet today, tomorrow, or 10 years from now and we'll win it (as long as we hold conditions the same)—just as Hempelian science says we will. The safety of the bet resides in our knowing what the laws are that govern the behaviors of atoms and in our understanding of the various chemical-physical mechanisms that carry out the dictates of the laws. Those laws apply to invariant properties of *inanimate* objects, but they don't work on such things as the behavior of organisms (O'Brien and Holland 1995a). They are, however, precisely the kinds of laws archaeologists wanted to apply to humans: "A statement of relation between two or more variables which is true *for all times and places*" (Fritz and Plog 1970: 405; emphasis added).

Invariant physical laws are not the only kind of laws around. What about the law of contingency, which says that whatever happens at point D is conditioned in part by what happened at points A, B, and C? Point D is not *determined* by what happened at the other points but rather is *contingent* on what happened at those points. Whatever is manifest at point D is *stochastic* as opposed to *random*—meaning that the expression of D is derived from a limited, rather than an *infinite,* number of possibilities. The theory of Darwinian evolution is built around contingency as a historical process. Organisms evolve, and in the process usually change shape, but there isn't an unlimited number of shapes into which they can change from generation to generation. There are certain forms that hang on for hundreds, thousands, or millions of generations, with very little variation evident from the first generation to the last. In other words, forms are *channeled* in certain directions because of their history (Mayr 1988: 108). Few of those knowledgeable in natural science would argue that Darwinian evolution isn't a theory or that in its modified form (modified in the sense that we now understand genetic transmission, embryonic development, and the like) it is not capable of providing *explanations* for how and why we are the way we are. It's not a perfect theory—theories aren't judged on degrees of perfection—but it's a damn good one because it works. Darwinian evolutionary theory has made its way into the archaeological arena, and I predict that it is here to stay. It offers a powerful means of examining variation, whether that variation be in skin color, stature, or stone tools.

I am not implying that the only chance Americanist archaeology has of becoming scientific rests with the application of Darwinian evolution to archaeological problems, but I believe such an option offers the best chance (see Dunnell 1982b, 1988b for a similar view). Hopefully, the archaeology of the 1990s and beyond will bury the notion of intent as the cause of anything. In the meantime, reliance on empirical data will at least keep the number of stories to a minimum.

The conduct of materials-science studies such as those described in this chapter relies on the availability of archaeological materials. But what if there weren't any materials left to study? Archaeologists have long assumed that the archaeological record is a limitless resource; if you need more material, you simply go out and excavate some more. In one sense, the record *is* limitless, since every day modern artifacts are entering the ground, but these materials scarcely help us understand the physical properties of ceramic items made ca. A.D. 1300. Unfortunately, urban expansion, agricultural activities, and the like are destroying large pieces of the archaeological record on a daily basis. There often is no opportunity to return to a locality and surface collect or excavate a new sample because the locality has been modified to such an extent that the archaeological signature has been obliterated. Oftentimes, the only sample of a particular assemblage comprises materials collected in the distant past. At least we can use those collections, hopefully employing new analytical methods and techniques. But what if the older collections weren't available either? What then? Such questions might have seemed absurd 20 years ago, when museums and universities were at the height of the cultural-resource-management boom. Archaeologists would not have paid much attention to the thought that the portions of the archaeological record they were storing in attics and basements could disappear out from under them. However, they soon began paying attention, as it became clear that American archaeology was in a state of emergency. The state of emergency had several fronts, but the one word that united them was *responsibility,* which took on legal as well as ethical complexions. I examine two issues here, the curation of archaeological materials and the repatriation of Native American skeletons and grave goods, and though I divide the issues for ease of presentation, you will immediately see connections between the two.

Archaeological Materials: A Question of Conservatorship

Most of us assume that museums and institutions are holding tanks for the nation's antiquities, much in the way that libraries are reservoirs of the printed word. Thus, when we want to know about a particular artifact, all we have to do is find out which university or museum holds the material and then ask the appropriate personnel for permission to study it. We assume that museums, like libraries, carefully curate their collections and label their artifacts for easy retrieval. That point of view is reasonable, given the view that most of us have of how museums operate. But that doesn't mean that the view is correct. In truth, the public would be shocked to learn of the state of archaeological collections housed in museums and institutions across the country. Not only are many of them unorganized and uninventoried, but their physical condition has not been protected and many items have deteriorated to the point where they are unsuitable for research or exhibit purposes. Museums and repositories of archaeological materials have been plagued with these problems for decades, but some of them began facing up to the problem only recently. Some still haven't faced up to it.

I note somewhat parenthetically that during the boom period of cultural-resource management, archaeologists were so busy trying to save bits and pieces of the archaeological record from bulldozers that little time, thought, or energy was expended on learning how to protect those very materials from destruction through inadequate curational processes. Lee Lyman pointed out to me how ironic it was that archaeologists, who were well versed in Schiffer's (1976) delineation of cultural and noncultural transformation processes vis-à-vis the portion of the archaeological record that is in the ground, never made the next logical step: the recognition of postrecovery transformations (what we might term "museum transforms").

At the 41st annual meeting of the Society for American Archaeology (SAA) held in St. Louis in 1976, William Marquardt, then director of the American Archaeology Division at the University of Missouri, chaired a symposium entitled

"Regional Centers in Archaeology: Prospects and Problems." Papers were read and commented on by several persons who have figured prominently in our discussions up to this point, including Carl Chapman, Bob McGimsey, Stephen Williams, and Stuart Struever. Over and over the same story was heard: our national archaeological collections are in a terrible state of disrepair, the condition is worsening, and no one really knows what to do about it. This was one of the first public forums in which the extent and magnitude of the curation problem was documented (Marquardt 1977b), and it pointed out the paradox in American archaeology that there was money available to get artifacts out of the ground, but there was little money available to do anything with the artifacts afterward.

The SAA symposium was held at the height of the CRM frenzy, when archaeologists were all too happy to take money for field projects. They didn't particularly like the federal guidelines under which they had to operate in structuring their fieldwork and analysis, but they accepted them as the price of doing business. They certainly did not want the federal government dictating how collections and records were to be maintained. Don't read this the wrong way; archaeologists didn't mind receiving federal money for curation—in fact, they clamored for it—as long as it did not come with strings. And it was obvious that archaeologists were not going to attach their own strings. Marquardt (1977a: 38) summed up the dilemma beautifully: "Thus, it seems to me that many of us feel a certain ambivalence toward federal funding and the attendant federal bureaucratization of yet another formerly academic pursuit. On the one hand we fear the loss to a federal superstructure of our local and regional institutional initiative, and on the other hand we realize the futility of attempting to analyze, curate, and manage our artifacts and data without some substantial federal assistance."

The question of how much money the federal government was supposed to furnish for the safe-keeping of archaeological collections was rarely addressed. On the one hand, various pieces of legislation dating as far back as the Antiquities Act of 1906 carried provisions for the curation of archaeological records (maps, photographs, and field records) as well as artifacts. Subsequent legislation (e.g., the Historic Sites Act of 1935, the Reservoir Salvage Act of 1960, the National Historic Preservation Act of 1966, and the Archaeological Resources Protection Act of 1979) broadened the scope regarding the care to be given artifacts and records. One problem with those acts was the lack of precise standards and procedures to be followed in providing care. Neither did the acts impose penalties for failing to comply with the broad guidelines. Institutions, for their part, ignored the provisions—what few there were—completely. When entering into agreements with federal agencies to conduct archaeological work, the last thing on anyone's mind was to set aside enough money to properly house the collections and documents that would result from the work.

University space is always at a premium, and what usually happened was that a university, after signing a large government contract, would designate a leaky, dimly lit corner of a basement as its curation center. Staff archaeologists, especially if they had any curation experience, might not be too happy with the arrangement, but the decision not to spend money on the collections meant more funding for employment during the fieldwork and analysis stages. It is not difficult to see that in such situations, the collections were going to lose.

Universities weren't the only culprits behind the scandalous treatment of collections and accompanying documentation; museums and private firms shared equally in trying to shove the problem under a rug. Museums, especially, should have performed better, but they, too, had their priorities, and caring for hundreds of boxes of sherds and animal bones often was not at the top of the list. Museums inadvertently contributed to the problem in another way, by not teaching the public about the importance of strong research collections. The public knows that archaeological items form the basis of what we know about the past, but they overlook the role played by collections in the *reformulations* that we make of that past. If the public completely misses the point about the value of conserving collections, it should come as no surprise that the funds needed to address the problem are difficult to obtain.

The University of Missouri was not immune to the problems of what to do with large collections of archaeological materials, just as it had not been immune to the lure of big money offered by CRM. The large projects with which university personnel had been involved from the 1950s on had generated literally tens of millions of artifacts, all of which had been stored in whatever quarters happened to be available at the time. The size of the collections ranged from extremely small—perhaps a few sherds donated by a collector—to extremely large—hundreds of boxes from projects such as that conducted in the Truman Reservoir. In fact, addition of the Truman material completely outstripped the university's ability to house collections. Chapman and Marquardt realized this, and they approached the Kansas City District of the Corps of Engineers with a novel idea: they wanted to use a small portion of the contract funds to build a structure to house the material. The district was receptive to the idea, and the university erected a small, metal-frame building at Sinclair Farm, one of its research facilities on the edge of Columbia. Chapman also convinced the university administration that a new building was needed to house the thousands of other boxes that had been stored around campus, and a larger metal building was erected next to the Truman-collection building.

This was a turning point for archaeological curation at the University of Missouri. Chapman and Marquardt had realized the deteriorating state of collections and had done what they could to ensure that the materials were put into some kind of coherent order and placed in better surroundings. The university, for its part, had made modest funding available for a storage building, and the corps had provided for the storage of the Truman collection. When the Cannon project wound down in 1979, the University of Nebraska approached the St. Louis

District of the corps to see if they would be amenable to erecting an additional building at Missouri to house the collections from work on the Salt River. Corps personnel were amenable, and in 1980 another metal structure was added to the Sinclair Farm facility.

The willingness of the corps to spend money on curation represented a significant departure from previous practices of most federal agencies. In an internally contradictory statement, National Park Service archaeologist Doug Scovill noted in 1976,

> Federal archaeology is trying to shift from the now dominant concept of "specific-site salvage archaeology" to a philosophy of conservation archaeology within the framework of cultural resources management concepts. This shift is infinitely difficult. Federal managers do not (and *rightfully* should not) see archaeological research as a mission-oriented objective; it is mission supportive. Like any support activity, it represents a cost which must be borne, but which should prudently be kept to a minimum consistent with compliance requirements. (Scovill 1976: 23)

Scovill's views, in my opinion, are dead wrong. How could archaeology ever be a support operation for the construction of a dam? Archaeology and dam construction are two *entirely unrelated* programs. Scovill completely missed the fact that even as early as the middle 1970s some federal agencies were toying with the idea of putting archaeology on more of an equal footing with such activities as dam construction. In other words, they were beginning to make archaeology, to use Scovill's words, "a mission-oriented objective." And if it were not for a few federal archaeologists, along with a few enlightened Corps of Engineers officials, who eventually made archaeology a mission-oriented objective for the St. Louis District (see below), the future of archaeological collections in the state of Missouri would be grim. But this is getting slightly ahead of the story.

Everyone was delighted with the arrangement made between the University of Missouri and the two corps districts for the construction of storage buildings to house federal collections. Unfortunately, there was a certain amount of naïveté on both sides relative to the adequacy and permanence of what had been provided in the way of safekeeping. As I mentioned earlier, we often think that because an object is in a museum collection, it must be out of harm's way. But museum storage ensures nothing relative to the likelihood that an object will exist for any extended period of time in a reasonable condition. Rather, the likelihood of extending the life of most objects found in typical collections is tied directly to an ability to provide a stable environment for the objects, but even then success is not assured. Many objects are their own worst enemies. Specimens made from organic materials (e.g., bone, shell, and wood) can decay, and often the procedures routinely used to retard decay in themselves affect the specimen adversely. Metal objects can break down over time regardless of whether they are in humidity-controlled environments. The point is that archaeological specimens require periodic examination and treatment for their preservation. The science that has developed to address such problems of stabilization is the field of conservation.

Conservation, however, is only one aspect of the problem of collections care. The legal and ethical responsibility that a museum or other institution has to its collections centers around taking all actions necessary to preserve objects, at least theoretically, in perpetuity; to gain intellectual control over them (by acquiring and recording information about them); and to make them accessible to students, faculty, outside researchers, and the interested public. Care, the essence of the word *responsibility*, includes providing controlled environmental conditions, ensuring adequate security, maintaining necessary catalog records, and repairing damage to individual objects. What had been done at the University of Missouri was to erect several inexpensive metal buildings over the collections. Individual collections could be located among the thousands of boxes, and a crude inventory system allowed researchers to get a preliminary sense of what was in a box, but this hardly constituted intellectual control—or, as it turned out, a safe environment.

To understand the magnitude of its curation problem, the American Archaeology Division began in 1987 to count the number of boxes in its holdings—not only what was at Sinclair Farm but also what was housed at its two field stations (one in Saline County, the other in Ripley County) and in various buildings on campus. The count ran over 13,000 boxes. In 1988 the AAD wrote a proposal to the National Science Foundation to inventory the collections from 7 southeastern Missouri counties in order to gain "intellectual control" over at least a portion of the materials. Three years and $113,000 later, we had finished inventorying 2,345 boxes (each containing roughly 1.2 cubic feet) of material, from 276 sites in only 5 of the 7 counties (O'Brien et al. 1992). It appeared that it was going to be a slow process to catalog the remainder of the collection from the other 109 Missouri counties. This was a grim prospect, made all the worse by the fact that the metal buildings housing the collections had begun to deteriorate badly. Putting newly packaged collections back into leaky buildings without climate control was only prolonging the inevitable.

At about the same time that the university was undertaking its detailed inventory of its archaeological collections, the Department of the Interior published proposed curation guidelines for the proper housing of government collections. These guidelines (36 CFR 79) were far-reaching and outlined what the responsibilities were of government agencies that produced archaeological materials. Under the provisions of the rule, it became an agency's responsibility to monitor the repositories housing the materials and to determine their adequacy for providing care. The rule was very specific about the meaning of the word *adequate*. Collections facilities had to maintain complete and accurate records; they had to store records in such a manner that they were safe from theft and fire; they had to make the collections and records available for study; they had to meet local building-code requirements; and they had to be operated by trained staff. At that time, and even today, few facilities in the United States housing federal collections could meet those requirements.

It became apparent that the rule would soon become law (which it did) and that federal agencies would be required to meet the provisions. The Corps of Engineers became one of the first agencies nationwide to begin an assessment of facilities, and the St. Louis District in particular took the lead in developing evaluative procedures. That district maintains several lakes in Missouri and Illinois and has jurisdiction over a long stretch of the Mississippi River. During the 1960s–1980s, the district had sponsored numerous archaeological projects on its landholdings, though no one was sure exactly how many. In 1988 the district began the long process of tracking down its collections, inventorying them, assessing their condition, and determining whether curation activities were consonant with federal rules.

What the district staff found was not surprising, nor was it much different from what was happening around the country. They discovered they owned 92 collections, totaling over 3,400 cubic feet of artifacts and records, stored at 10 different repositories. The following are excerpts from the report (Trimble and Meyers 1990):

> Most buildings functioning as repository facilities are woefully inadequate. . . . They are neither designed for nor adapted to the requirements of a modern curation center. In most cases, institutions make do with whatever space they can acquire from their governing bodies. (p. 11)

> In most cases, the repository rooms are dirty and shelving and collection boxes are covered with dust. (p. 11)

> Environmental monitoring is nonexistent in all but one repository. (p. 11)

> Portions of two repositories have already been destroyed by fire[9]. . . . Three repositories are experiencing major water damage from leaking roofs, and collections in two other facilities have experienced water damage from internal failures. (p. 12)

> Only six of the ten repositories could produce all collections they are responsible for curating. . . . A number of collections cannot be accounted for and an unknown number of artifacts have been misplaced or destroyed. (p. 12)

> Time is taking its toll on collections. Those excavated 15 to 20 years ago are showing serious signs of neglect and deterioration. Boxes are frequently over-stacked, sagging, over-packed, and torn. . . . Containers rarely conform to a standard

---

9. Including one building on the University of Missouri–Columbia campus that was destroyed by fire in 1977. The building, an old two-story house, contained artifacts and fieldnotes from several archaeological projects.

size. . . . Labels and binding tape are loose [Figure 8.10]. . . . Paper bags are torn and their contents scattered. . . . Bag labels written in pencil are fading. Many artifacts were never cleaned or labeled. Even more recently excavated collections are showing the results of inadequate care. In fact, most new collections were never properly prepared for long-term curation. (p. 12)

In some cases the documentation has been lost. Some collection managers in the past did not consider collection documentation a part of their curatorial responsibilities [Figure 8.11]. As a result, the records for some collections were never turned over to curation facilities. (pp. 12–13)

In short, the corps staff found not only that their collections were being housed in ill-suited environments but that they also were being mismanaged. To address the deficiencies, they recommended that several procedures be implemented, the most important being that the collections be coalesced into two repositories—one at the Illinois State Museum and one at the University of Missouri—and that cooperative agreements be signed with both institutions spelling out exactly what steps would be taken in the future to upgrade the status of the collections. In July 1990 the St. Louis District signed such an agreement with the university, which I view as perhaps the most important landmark in the history of Missouri archaeology—one that would have tremendous impact on the future of the archaeology of the state. For its part, the corps offered to pay the university over a million dollars to prepare all of the Missouri portion of the district's collections for state-of-the-art curation. This entailed not only repackaging and labeling the materials but also cataloging all the materials and preparing a master information-retrieval system. The project was envisioned to take about 7 years to complete. The university, in turn, agreed to construct a state-of-the-art curation and conservation center where *all* archaeological and ethnological collections would be housed. The St. Louis District–University of Missouri partnership resulted in the construction of the 23,000-square-foot Museum Support Center on the university campus in Columbia, which opened its doors in the spring of 1994 (Figure 8.12). The curation center is capable of handling about 25,000 cubic feet of material, given current shelving arrangements, which should solve the state's curation needs well into the twenty-first century.

The university is not the only institution in Missouri that curates material from the state, but since the mid-1980s it has taken on more responsibility for collections generated by state and federally sponsored activities. For example, it accepts (for a set fee) collections from projects funded by the Missouri Highway and Transportation Department, without regard to which institution or firm did the work. Most agencies are happy to establish curation agreements with major research institutions because of the permanence factor. In other words, major universities probably will be around forever, whereas private firms (as well as some smaller colleges) may not. No agency wants to pay money for curation only to find itself back in possession of the artifacts a few years later. For an

Figure 8.10. Decomposing collection boxes at the Sinclair Farm collections repository, University of Missouri, 1990.

Figure 8.11. Archival-storage room in Swallow Hall, University of Missouri, 1990.

institution's part, acceptance of collections means acceptance *in perpetuity,* a phrase most university lawyers abhor. The phrase has been around since the inception of CRM, but more than a few institutions did not live up to the moral and ethical, not to mention legal, responsibilities for which they were signing on. This is beginning to change, but in a way it is unfortunate that it took legislative action to bring it about.

The proper care of federal collections was not the only archaeological concern that came under legislative action during the 1980s and 1990s. A parallel development hit universities and museums much harder than any provisions in the Department of the Interior guidelines had and sent them scrambling to save many of their collections not from the hands of time but from the hands of the descendants of the very people who once had made and used the artifacts in the collections.

Archaeological Materials: A Question of Ownership

Imagine someone walking into a museum and politely saying, "I'd like to take possession of your human skeletons, and while you're at it, I would also like to have all the pottery and other grave objects associated with the human remains." When asked why, the person responds, "Because your museum is showing disrespect for the remains of my ancestors." If this sounds farfetched,

Figure 8.12. Museum Support Center, University of Missouri, constructed in 1993–1994.

just ask someone at your local museum; the odds are that he or she either has been involved with such a confrontation or knows someone who has.

Unlike a lot of issues in American archaeology, the question of artifact ownership is a fairly recent one. When ownership of artifacts *has* become an issue, it has revolved around patrimony laws of other countries and whether antiquities housed in museums in the United States were obtained illegally. Archaeologists, for the most part, have supported agreements between the United States and other countries to deter international trafficking in antiquities, but then comparatively few archaeologists work abroad. If they do, most countries will allow archaeologists either to work on the collections there or to apply for a permit to take a collection out of the country temporarily. But archaeologists were not so willing to support cultural-patrimony laws when it suddenly dawned on them that the very things they study were going to be reburied. Largesse is easy to dispense when it doesn't cost anything, but in the 1970s when Native American groups began demanding the return not only of skeletal remains but also of associated funerary items, the price became too high. Naturally, archaeologists and physical anthropologists mounted a resistance movement, and the collision between the two sides was often unpleasant.

What caused all the furor in the first place? This is a difficult question to answer, but part of the answer can be found in how museums had long treated human-skeletal material, which really was no different than how they treated all other archaeological materials—not very well. Some Native Americans didn't take too kindly to the remains of their presumed ancestors being shoved into cardboard boxes, being thin-sectioned for analysis, or being put on exhibit. And they were horrified (as were archaeologists) over incidents of wholesale looting and desecration that routinely took place across the country (Figure 8.13). In the mid-1970s American Indians against Desecration (AID) was formed to deal with the situation, which was summed up in 1985 by its director, Jan Hammil, as follows:

> As we crossed the country and visited the universities, museums and laboratories, we found the bodies of our ancestors stored in cardboard boxes, plastic bags and paper sacks. We found our sacred burial places stripped and desecrated, the bodies and sacred objects buried with our dead on display for the curious and labeled "collections," "specimens" and "objects of antiquities." A.I.D. estimates that between three and six hundred thousand Indian bodies have and continue to be so treated, most, as a result of federal projects, using federal monies and stored at federally supported institutions.[10]

---

10. Statement read by Jan Hammil before the Interior and Insular Affairs Committee's Subcommittee on Public Lands, U.S. House of Representatives, July 30, 1985, Washington, D.C.

Figure 8.13. A looter of an archaeological site on federal lands in New Mexico showing off his trophies. Ironically, the photograph, taken by another looter, was used to successfully prosecute the two (courtesy U.S. Forest Service, Region 3, Albuquerque [the original photograph was dark and grainy; hence the poor reproduction]).

Hammil noted in her statement that AID had "attempted to isolate the causes leading to Indian bodies being desecrated and offer methods to avoid compounding the problem by additional bodies being added to the already intolerable situation." She noted that there was a need for federal policy aimed at avoiding "significant archaeological sites including sacred Indian burial sites" and emphasizing "consideration of traditional cultural values and the effect of federal projects on those values."

Hammil's comments were delivered in 1985, but by then the "reburial" issue, as it came to be known, was at least 15 years old. It would be impossible to pinpoint the birth of the reburial controversy, but the one case that I would support as a candidate to mark the beginning of the movement was the discovery in Iowa of the remains of a young Indian female and 26 Euro-Americans during highway construction in 1971 (Anderson 1985). In typical fashion, the Euro-American skeletons were reburied immediately, but the Indian skeleton was shipped to a laboratory for analysis. After a storm of protests from Native Americans, church organizations, and students, the state archaeologist declared the remains to be nonsignificant from a scientific standpoint and ordered them to be reburied. This was followed in 1975 by the excavation of a burial area in Council Bluffs, Iowa, and the reburial of the skeletons after a nine-day examination period. Then, in 1976, the inevitable happened: the Iowa legislature passed a law requiring the reburial of *all* Native American skeletal remains. In addition, the law made it illegal for anyone—archaeologists or not—to disturb or remove burials. Archaeologists were stunned by the passage of the Iowa law, but by then it was too late; the floodgates were wide open, and other states began following suit. Could Missouri be far behind?

As it turned out, Missouri was not far behind, and in 1987 the 84th General Assembly passed RS Mo. 194.400–410, disarmingly entitled "Unmarked Human Burial Sites." The bill was signed into law by Governor John Ashcroft in July 1987 and changed forever the face of Missouri archaeology. The law, in terms of most of its inclusions, was a boilerplate version of language adopted in other states (see H. M. Price 1991 for a lengthy treatment of state-specific legislation). The intent of the law was simple: No one could tamper with graves, regardless of the age of the grave, without proper authority. This applied to graves located anywhere, but the law was directed at those on private property. As Marcus Price, a lawyer as well as an anthropologist, noted, the "legislation was inspired by worthy motives, but unfortunately the text employed imposes significant and largely unintentional burdens on Missouri's farmers, property owners, developers, taxpayers, and scientists" (H. M. Price 1988: 4). Price homed in on the fact that as written, the law didn't apply only to *known* graves but also to cases where there was reason to believe that human remains *might* exist—such as in practically any agricultural field in Missouri. The law forbade any ground-disturbing activity to take place within a 50-foot radius of a *known or suspected* burial until the proper authorities were consulted.

The law stated further that any person knowing or with "reason to know" that unmarked human remains are being disturbed or destroyed "shall immediately notify" either the state historic-preservation officer (SHPO) (the director of the Department of Natural Resources) or the local law-enforcement officer with jurisdiction for the area in which the remains occur. If you read the law specifically, I and every other archaeologist in the state should have immediately written the SHPO and informed him that at that very moment literally thousands of Missourians were breaking the law by plowing and disking their fields. Farmers in some sections of southeastern Missouri probably were breaking it at least once a minute.

The law directs the SHPO (or his/her designee) to make reasonable efforts to identify and locate persons who can establish direct kinship with or descent from the individual represented by the remains (a very unlikely event). Failing this, the SHPO is to determine which group has ethnic affinity with the deceased and to seek their input on the disposition of the remains. If group affinity cannot be determined, the SHPO, in consultation with the "unmarked-human-burial consultation committee," shall determine the disposition, which in Missouri has meant reburial, in some cases preceded by analysis. The law even prescribes the composition of the consultation committee: the SHPO (or designee), two archaeologists or skeletal analysts, two Native Americans from tribes recognized by the federal government, one member who is a non-Indian minority, and one non-Indian, non-minority member who is neither a professional archaeologist nor a skeletal analyst. One could not ask for a more politically correct committee.

While Missouri and other states were passing local legislation to protect unmarked human burials, the federal government also was at work. In 1989 Senator Daniel Inouye of Hawaii introduced a bill in the U.S. Senate that would far surpass any law passed by individual states in terms of its effects on American archaeology. The bill, termed the Native American Repatriation of Cultural Patrimony Act, went through only minor changes before being signed into law by President George Bush on November 16, 1990. The law became known officially as the Native American Graves Protection and Repatriation Act (NAGPRA). The government published proposed regulations for implementing provisions contained in NAGPRA in May 1993.

Basically, NAGPRA did for human burials on federal lands what the state laws did for those on private lands, that is, forbade unauthorized excavation. But the law was much more sweeping in that it also directed all federal agencies and museums and repositories that receive federal funding to conduct two inventories of their holdings. The first inventory, which was to have been completed by November 16, 1993, was to be a summary of all collections that contained unassociated funerary objects, sacred objects, or objects of cultural patrimony, that is, objects that probably came from burial contexts but for which no skeletal remains exist in the collection. The purpose of the summary was to provide information about the collections to lineal descendants and culturally affiliated Indian tribes that might want to request repatriation of the objects. The second inventory, which was to be completed by November 16, 1995, was to be a listing of all human remains and associated funerary items in order to facilitate repatriation by groups having affiliation with the remains and objects.

Repatriation is not a new issue; perhaps the most (in)famous case involving it occurred in the late 1960s, when the New York State Museum was asked to return 26 Iroquois wampum belts that the museum had had for decades (Arnet 1970). But that event and others like it were only small brush fires compared to the inferno set off by the passage of NAGPRA and the publication of its implementing language. Few museums were exempt from the legislation because of the wording of the implementing rules (36 CFR Part 10, Sec. 10.2):

> *Museum* means any institution or State or local government agency (including any institution of higher learning) that has possession of, or control over, human

remains or cultural items and receives Federal funds. The phrase "receives federal funds" means the receipt of funds by a museum after November 16, 1990, from a Federal agency through any grant, loan, contract (other than a procurement contract), or other arrangement by which a Federal agency makes or made available to a museum assistance in the form of funds. Federal funds provided for any purpose that are received by a larger entity of which the museum is a part are considered Federal funds for the purposes of these regulations.

Clearly, the thousands of skeletons and related artifacts held by the joint Museum of Anthropology–American Archaeology Division at the University of Missouri fell under NAGPRA regulations.

One aspect of NAGPRA to which archaeologists and physical anthropologists have always had a particularly violent reaction is the "lineal descent and cultural affiliation" clause. How, they have asked, could anyone establish descent from groups of people who had died a millennium ago? For example, because a historically documented group had been in an area during the nineteenth century, did that mean that a Late Archaic–period burial from that same area was of an ancestor to that group? Could the modern group claim "lineal descent" and repatriate the remains? Using an example from Missouri, could the Osage or Missouri tribes claim the remains of an Oneota burial from Saline County? NAGPRA is not very specific about what rules of evidence are to be used to establish claims.

Of course, the major complaint that archaeologists and physical anthropologists had against NAGPRA, as well as against the state laws, was that it removed materials from the research arena. As of this writing, five years since NAGPRA became law, it is much too early to determine the effect of the legislation on archaeological and bioarchaeological analysis. Somebody well into the twenty-first century should do a detailed examination of how much material actually went back into the ground and what kinds of information were lost as a consequence. However, it is clear from what has transpired to this point that hundreds if not thousands of skeletons from sites across the United States have been reburied and thus will not be available when new techniques and methods are developed to address such things as prehistoric health and diet.

Archaeologists and physical anthropologists have argued from the beginning that it is extremely shortsighted to think that we now know everything there is to know about the demographic profile and health of prehistoric populations. They cite example after example of current research in bioarchaeology that makes use of collections that have resided in museums for decades (Buikstra and Gordon 1981; Ubelaker and Grant 1989). There is no reason to suspect that similar analyses will not take place in the future. Indian groups counter with the claim that the vast majority of the remains have sat on dusty shelves for years and have never been examined, and they see little prospect that the remains will ever be examined. Some state further that the fact that American scientists, most of whom are of Euro-American descent, view the remains of the ancestors of Native Americans as "museum specimens" is an extension of the bias against Indians that has always existed in this country.

Is there a right and a wrong point of view? Not really. Could there have been a better solution than to legislate one? Probably, and in some quarters that solution has worked quite well. For example, in 1989 the University of Missouri opened a series of talks with the Osage Nation to reach an understanding that would be sensitive to the feelings of the Osage—which the university and the state officially recognize as Missouri's original citizens—and at the same time preserve the skeletons housed at the university. The proposal called for treating the remains with dignity by constructing within the new curation center a mausoleum area and limiting access to the skeletons to researchers with legitimate research projects. A committee comprising university archaeologists and physical anthropologists as well as members of the Osage Nation would vote on the legitimacy of the projects. Also, the Museum of Anthropology removed all human remains from public display.

I began this chapter by talking about archaeology as a science, and I am firmly of the opinion that that is what archaeology should be. This doesn't mean, however, that along the way there isn't room for an archaeologist to be a bit of a humanist as well. Legislation took over when all else failed, but the future of archaeological research on human remains will still rest heavily on our ability to educate Native Americans about what can be learned through the examination of bones and on our ability to accommodate the concerns they have about such examinations. In retrospect, there must have been better ways to spend the tens of thousands of hours and the millions of dollars that went into trying to figure out who owns the past.

Mastodons and Humans—Again

It wasn't human bones but rather those of a mastodon that made the biggest splash in Missouri archaeology in the 1980s. Finds of mastodon bones are not all that common, though as we have seen, there have, over the years, been several finds made in Missouri. What made such news was the discovery of an indisputable association of mastodons and Clovis points—the first clear association found in the New World. The key word here is *clear,* meaning beyond any doubt. Other occurrences have been postulated, but none has unimpeachable associational integrity. Ironically, the finds were made at the one locality where over a century earlier Albert Koch had *not* found what he was convinced was human-mastodon association—Sulphur Springs. In Chapter 3 we left the story of Albert Koch and his hunt for associations of Pleistocene-age fauna and humans—a hunt that had taken him from the Bourbeuse River of the eastern Ozarks, to the Sulphur Springs locality in Jefferson County, and finally to the lower Pomme de Terre River in Hickory County. At two of those localities, the ones on the Bourbeuse and the Pomme de Terre, Koch satisfied himself that he indeed had found good associations. What he had found, it turned out, were mastodon bones and artifacts but not the slightest bit of evidence that the two were contemporary.

Excavations at the various localities continued sporadically throughout the nineteenth and twentieth centuries, especially at Sulphur Springs. Even William Henry Holmes visited the locality, which by then was known as the Kimmswick bone bed, shortly after the turn of the century (Figure 8.14).[11] The remains of mastodons and other Pleistocene animals turned up in excavations there on a regular basis, as did stone artifacts. In fact, there is a letter from Matthew Stirling of the Bureau of American Ethnology to Ashley Montagu (cited in Montagu and Peterson 1944; see also Montagu 1942) in which Stirling recalls a comment made by Holmes in 1927 or 1928 that upon a trip to the Missouri Historical Society he had been shown a projectile point that, he was told, had been found by Koch at Sulphur Springs. Montagu and Peterson erroneously presumed that this was incorrect and that the point had come from Koch's excavations on the Pomme de Terre, but it probably *was* from Sulphur Springs, and it was *not* excavated by Koch. The artifact, which is in the Field Museum of Natural History in Chicago (catalog number 205526), is obviously a Clovis point. I think it probably came from the excavations of one C. W. Beehler, who around the turn of the century leased the bone beds for excavation purposes.[12] A short report (probably inserted by Stephen Peet) in Volume 23 (1901) of *The American Antiquarian and Oriental Journal* that was "Quoted from the Local Paper" stated:

> A miner and explorer by the name of C. W. Beehler, who was for a long time searching for silica in the neighborhood of Kimmswick, Mo., finally came upon a large number of bones and pottery which he has put into a museum. These bones

11. Holmes visited the site in late September or early October of 1901 (Holmes 1903c: 237). The photograph shown in Figure 8.14 was used in the 1904 Louisiana Purchase Exposition held in St. Louis.

12. Bruce McMillan pointed out to me that the piece was donated to the Field Museum in 1931 by Byron Knoblock, a well-known artifact collector from Illinois. Knoblock had obtained the specimen from Dr. W. F. Parks of St. Louis, who, according to Knoblock, had seen the point in place shortly after it had been discovered. Parks gave it to Knoblock eight years after it was found, which apparently was sometime between 1903 and 1907. This range is based on the recollections of Parks, who, in a letter quoted to me by McMillan, stated that "the excavations near Kimmswick, Missouri were carried on about 1903 to 1907. The flints I gave Mr. Knoblock were found associated with the bones of mastodon, *Equus Complicatus*, and ground sloth, *Megalonyx*, and other bones of prehistoric animals. I visited the place very often during the excavation." Was this Beehler's excavation? We will never know for certain, but it probably was.

Figure 8.14. Kimmswick bone bed, Jefferson County, Missouri, 1901; left to right: Walter Miller (hired digger and son of the landowner, Fritz Miller, who leased the bone beds to the Humboldt Exploration Company), W. J. Townsend, William Henry Holmes (National Museum of Natural History [NMNH]), C. W. Beehler (excavator of the bone beds), and De Lancey Gill (NMNH) (photograph by George Stark, courtesy Missouri Historical Society).

were in stages of petrification; many of them were bones of a mastodon. It is said that they were taken out from under the hole from which Dr. Koch took the mastodon whose bones are now in the British Museum in London. The animals were said to be huddled together under the lee of a hill, and that they were covered with the accumulation of ages, with a soft loam at the top. Several museum men have visited the spot. One gentleman thinks that there was here a salt lick spring, as there was in the Big Bone Lick; that the animals, driven, gathered here to drink of the spring, and as the ground was miry around the springs, they were mired and were covered up in a short time. The one nearest the surface was found by Dr. Koch, and Mr. Beehler was fortunate to discover others on the same spot.

Holmes was one of the "museum men" to whom the article refers:

Setting out for the West on September 26 [1901], I stopped a few days at St. Louis to visit the fossil mastodon beds at Kimmswick, 25 miles south of the city, and, in company with Mr. C. W. Beehler and Mr. T. D. Townsend, who are interested in the property and engaged in its exploration, spent a very instructive day at the site. The question of the association of human remains with those of the mammoth and mastodon has been raised at this place also, but up to the present time the evidence collected is not at all conclusive. It is believed that the bones found, which so closely resemble the humerus of man, may be portions of the fibulae of young mastodons, and that the flint implements reported as occurring with the fossil remains may have been recently introduced, since identical forms are plentiful on the surface of the site. At any rate, it seems wise to suspend judgment in the case until more critical and exhaustive studies have been made. (Holmes 1903c: 237)

Numerous excavations of the bone bed occurred after Holmes's visit, including those of Gerard Fowke (1928). The most informative report is that by R. M. Adams (1953), who worked at the site in 1940–1942 under the sponsorship of the Academy of Science of St. Louis and the Missouri Resources Museum. Adams excavated four test units in higher ground above the saline, sulphurous springs that gave the locality its original name. He noted that the bones of mastodon and other Pleistocene animals (e.g., ground sloth and bison) occurred in a horizontal band, intermixed with boulders and gravel. The bone-bearing deposit was capped with a layer of what Adams termed loess—"windblown soil deposits . . . made up of finely ground rock dust which accumulated during and after glacial periods. . . . It is only under the intact loess deposits that fool-proof evidences of undisturbed levels containing the bones are found. Excavations which extended farther under the bluff, beneath the deeper deposits of loess, produced fewer animal bones. This may have been due to the fact that such bones were sealed off from the sulphur/salt water seepage which tended to preserve the bones wherever it came in contact with them" (R. M. Adams 1953: 46). Adams, as well as several geologists who examined the locality, believed the loess to be a primary deposit that had formed over the last 1,000–5,000 years, though it is clear that the deposit was not a primary one but rather consisted of redeposited loess from the 20-meter-high bluff top to the north. Concerning the contemporaneity of humans and mastodons, Adams (1953: 54) stated that "the evidence is incomplete and tantalizing, but does tend to strongly suggest this contemporaneity." As it turned out, Adams's suggestion was correct.

In 1979 Russell Graham of the Illinois State Museum began a new round of excavations at the Kimmswick locality—work that paid off later that year and in 1980 with the recovery of two Clovis points and several other tools in direct association with mastodon remains. The bones and artifacts were in three small, ponded basins in the surface of the colluvial deposit noted by Adams. The overlying deposit—Adams's "loess" layer—contained Early Archaic points, including one of the St. Charles type (Graham et al. 1981: figure 2j). The two Clovis points were discovered in what Graham et al. referred to as zone C3; the points were 1.25 meters apart horizontally. The basal ear of a lanceolate point, a basal fragment of a projectile-point preform (exhibiting a hinge fracture), and chert flakes were recovered from the underlying C1 level. The basal ear

Figure 8.15. Russell Graham and Carl Chapman unearthing a Clovis point at Kimmswick, Jefferson County, Missouri, 1980 (courtesy R. Graham and the Illinois State Museum).

was manufactured from the same chert as the Clovis point found at the turn of the century. Also present were thousands of small flakes that resulted from the resharpening of stone tools (Graham and Kay 1988). Kay's (1986) analysis of microwear on the Clovis points indicated that they had been used only as projectile points and not as cutting implements.

Graham's excavation extended the list of fauna at Kimmswick begun earlier by Hay (1924); at least two genera of ground sloth were present (*Glossotherium harlani* in the Clovis levels and *Megalonyx jeffersonii* in one of the underlying levels), along with rabbit (*Sylvilagus* sp.) and white-tailed deer (*Odocoileus virginianus*). The main mastodon elements recovered were from the extremities (phalanges, metapodials, tarsals, and carpals), along with two teeth of an adult individual and one tooth of a juvenile. None of the bones was articulated, in contrast to Adams's discovery of the semi-articulated vertebral column of a juvenile mastodon.

Graham's discovery was of tremendous archaeological importance in that it secured the association between humans and mastodons in North America—an association that had long been suspected but never demonstrated with, to use Adams's (1953: 46) phrase, "fool-proof evidence." Graham called in specialists in the field to view the points and mastodon remains in the ground (Figure 8.15), which became standard practice beginning with the Folsom discovery (see Meltzer 1991). Remarkably, it took 52 years after the discovery of indisputable evidence of Pleistocene-age humans in the United States for the evidence of their association with mastodons to appear. Even more remarkable is the fact that what up to this point is still the only documented occurrence was made at a site that had been excavated for nearly a century and a half.

9

Interpretation versus Explanation:

A Reflection on Missouri Archaeology

A book that covers a topic as large and diverse as Missouri archaeology should, in the concluding chapter, not only answer questions posed earlier but also summarize trends that emerged in the preceding discussions. In the following sections I provide what I hope is a useful road map through the confusing streets and alleys of the who, what, where, and when of Missouri archaeology. Summaries are important, but I am not sure that in and of themselves they give us the means to examine the question of *why* things turned out the way they did.

One of the issues I set out to address in this book was how closely Missouri archaeology mirrored developments in the field of Americanist archaeology as a whole. Was there a close parallel, or did investigations into Missouri's past tend to be idiosyncratic? How did the broader development of theory and method in Americanist archaeology affect the study of Missouri prehistory? And what role, if any, did Missouri archaeologists play in the development of the theories and methods that have influenced Americanist archaeology? If you have made it this far, you undoubtedly have formulated your own opinions as to how these questions can best be answered. Likewise, I have my own opinions, and I will lay out some of my arguments later. However, my main objective in this chapter is to assess not only why Missouri *archaeology* took the road that it did but also why our understanding of the *archaeological record* of Missouri has developed as it has. The issues clearly are related, and to address them we once again will have to confront the differences between interpretation and explanation and examine the roles they play in archaeology.

Trends in Missouri Archaeology

Missouri archaeology, as you can now well appreciate, is a confusing amalgam of researchers as well as of research agendas. The list of archaeologists who have worked in the state is long; there are too many projects to keep track of; and the intricacies of various methods that have been developed to keep track of time, space, and form are confusing. There are several ways to divide Missouri archaeology into categories that make sense from a historical perspective, any one of which brings some order to the who, what, where, and when of the subject. For example, we can subdivide it in terms of *who conducted the work*— whether the persons were from outside the state or were Missouri natives. Or we can subdivide it in terms of the *nature of the questions asked*—for example, culture-historical-type questions versus strictly time-related questions. We can also subdivide it in terms of *local versus nonlocal issues*. For example, were artifacts from Dunklin County used to address an issue that was specific to the prehistory of that locality, or did the use transcend the fact that the material was from Dunklin County?

We don't have to go back through 150 years of Missouri archaeology and slavishly pigeonhole all the research that has been done to see examples of each category. In fact, we can for now look just at the work that was done prior to 1920. We'll start with the work of Albert Koch, whose exploits brought national attention to Missouri's archaeological record. Koch was a Missourian when he became interested in excavating the fossilized remains of extinct animals, which led to his discovery at two localities in the state of what he thought was indisputable evidence of human-mastodon contemporaneity. But it is a mistake to categorize Koch as a Missourian who was interested in the prehistory of the state. He lived in St. Louis and thus perhaps knew the state better than he did other areas, but geographic location, that is, where the evidence was found, was of no importance. All that apparently mattered to Koch was excavating fossils— wherever they occurred—and demonstrating their contemporaneity with the material record left by humans.

Missouri figured prominently in another issue of the nineteenth century, namely, the attempt to determine who was responsible for constructing the earthen mounds across the eastern United States. Cyrus Thomas's crews spent considerable time in Missouri inspecting earthworks in the Mississippi Valley, the results of which were incorporated into his final overview (C. Thomas 1894). Thomas also gleaned information from several published accounts on Missouri mound excavations for his report. But it wasn't the fact that the mounds were in Missouri that brought Thomas's crews to the state; in fact, wherever mounds happened to occur was where Thomas's parties worked. Their job was to extract information that could be used to demonstrate a continuity between the groups responsible for mound construction and the American Indians.

Aleš Hrdlička's work falls in the same category as Thomas's, for even though Hrdlička analyzed human-skeletal material from Missouri, his agenda was certainly more broad-based. He was, as we saw in Chapter 4, vociferous in his opposition to evidence of great human antiquity in North America, and he saw it as his duty to pass judgment on the nature of human remains, regardless of place of origin. The fact that some of the material he analyzed was from Missouri mounds and rock shelters excavated by Gerard Fowke was strictly secondary to his goals.

However, the work of Koch, Thomas, and Hrdlička is only part of the story. Thomas, for example, may have been using information from Missouri to examine larger issues, but what about all the other Missouri mound investigators of the late nineteenth century whose work was discussed in Chapter 3—persons such as W. B. Potter and Spencer Smith? Were they interested in using Missouri mounds and artifacts to address larger problems, or were they prehistorians using information from Missouri to address what we might loosely term "local" issues? Smith was interested in recording as carefully as possible the interior of the Big Mound in St. Louis and the artifacts it produced. Similarly, Potter was concerned with mapping the remains of some of the large fortified settlements on and near Sikeston Ridge in New Madrid County. Potter, being a member of the Academy of Science of St. Louis (as was Smith), must have read the literature and known various opinions about the identity of the mound builders, but that larger issue was secondary to his direct interests. Simply put, persons such as Smith and Potter were Missourians who were interested in the archaeological record of their state. Given the richness of that record, they saw no need to go outside their own backyard to satisfy a curiosity about the past.

There is even a third category of research and researchers for this early period. For example, Clarence B. Moore was neither a Missourian interested in the prehistory of a particular locale nor a prehistorian interested in using information from Missouri to solve a particular problem. Rather, he was interested in searching for antiquities to excavate and send back east and in preparing beautifully illustrated reports for the Academy of Natural Sciences of Philadelphia. Charles Peabody and Warren Moorehead of the anthropology department at Phillips Academy in Andover, Massachusetts, had similar motives. They were interested in anything and everything from the prehistoric period, regardless of where it was found. The strategy they adopted to satisfy their curiosity about the past was what the Smithsonian Institution had done years earlier: publicize your interests—Peabody and Moorehead used local newspapers across the country—and wait for people to respond. When E. H. Jacobs notified Phillips Academy that he knew the whereabouts of rock shelters containing traces of human habitation, Peabody and Moorehead came immediately.

I didn't say much about Moorehead in Chapter 4, although in many respects he typified the prehistorian whose work falls in this third category. By the time he came to Jacobs Cavern in 1903 he had already conducted extensive investigations in southern Ohio (e.g., Moorehead 1892, 1897) and would go on to work in several other states, including Maine (Moorehead 1922) and Illinois (Moorehead 1927). In between, he even had time to write a plea for social justice regarding the treatment of Native Americans (Moorehead 1914). From what I know of Moorehead, his interests were eclectic, and from his platform as director of the anthropology department at Phillips Academy he was able to pursue those interests wherever they led him. Jacobs Cavern was simply another place in the vast reaches of the eastern United States in which he could ply his trade.

Gerard Fowke was another peripatetic traveler who worked in numerous states, though certainly one of his longest tenures was in Missouri. Throughout his career he aligned himself with various institutions and groups such as the Missouri Historical Society—recall his work with the St. Louis "Knockers" (Chapter 3)—but, as with most of his associations, it was intermittent. Fowke clearly was someone who didn't put down roots, preferring instead to search the eastern United States for another site to excavate or another collection to catalog.

In summary, it would appear that at least through the first two decades of the twentieth century, the case can be made that there were three kinds of investigations that made use of Missouri's archaeological record. First, there were those in which the remains were part of larger sets of information used to examine non-geographic-specific questions. Second, there were those made by individuals living in Missouri who were interested in the archaeological record of their local area. Third, there were those made by persons from outside the state who were fascinated with the past and who saw Missouri sites as having the potential to satisfy their fascination.

By now you're probably anticipating what my next point will be—that the work conducted in Missouri after about 1920 can also be placed into one of these three categories—and you are correct. What came after that date certainly mirrored in many ways what went before it. Take the work of Jesse Wrench and Brewton Berry in the mid-1930s, as they attempted to inaugurate a statewide survey of archaeological sites and to catalog artifacts that lay in private hands. I would place their work in the second category—an emphasis on Missouri prehistory by Missourians. They used surveys and excavations in Missouri as a means not only to examine questions of culture history but also to train students and members of the Missouri Archaeological Society in fieldwork (Figure 9.1).

For the next four decades, Missouri archaeology was, with few exceptions, in the hands of Missourians. They would be the ones who would do the lion's share of the work with little interruption from the outside. Most archaeologists working in Missouri were of the home-grown variety, trained in the early years by Wrench and Berry and from the late 1940s on by Carl Chapman. As we saw in Chapter 5, this was the period of large-scale involvement of members of the MAS in numerous activities ranging from reservoir surveys (Figure 9.2) to excavations. Every activity in which Chapman and his students and staff were involved became an occasion to engage the services of amateur forces, and the latter responded with enthusiasm. Chapman created an army of volunteers

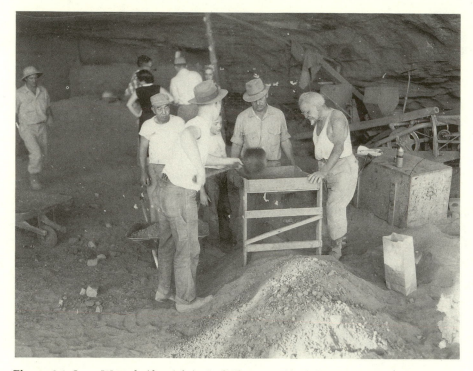

Figure 9.1. Jesse Wrench (far right), Carl Chapman (far left), Henry Hamilton (facing front, at sifter), and Missouri Archaeological Society volunteers at Graham Cave, Montgomery County, Missouri, 1955.

to keep the mission of the University of Missouri alive in as many areas as possible.

The exceptions to the hold that Missourians had on the archaeology of the state were important—for example, the survey of the Mississippi River valley by S. Williams (1954)—but these forays were only brief interruptions in an otherwise monopolistic period. Importantly, these intrusions by outside expeditionary forces met with no resistance in Missouri, unlike the situation in Arkansas, where investigators such as Phillips et al. were accused by University of Arkansas zoologist–artifact collector Samuel C. Dellinger (D. F. Morse and P. A. Morse 1983: 23) of coming into the state and "skimming the cream" (Phillips et al. 1951: 40). Rather, Missouri was an open state as far as Chapman and others were concerned, and they welcomed the expertise that archaeologists such as James Griffin, James Ford, and Philip Phillips brought to bear on culture-historical problems that involved Missouri.

By the mid-1960s, another project appeared on the horizon that would use information from Missouri to examine an issue that transcended state boundaries—the "Climate, Ecology, and the Oneota Culture" project conducted

Figure 9.2. Surveying the upper reaches of Bull Shoals Reservoir, southwestern Missouri, ca. 1947.

by David Baerreis of the University of Wisconsin–Madison. Recall from Chapter 6 that the program involved intensive study not only of archaeological materials from late prehistoric-period (Oneota and Mill Creek) sites in Iowa, Missouri, Minnesota, extreme southeastern Nebraska, and western Wisconsin but also of paleoclimatic indicators such as plant and animal remains, snails, and pollen. Although the project was directed by an investigator located outside the state, it involved two University of Missouri archaeologists, Dale Henning and Amy Henning (Harvey), both of whom were also Ph.D. students at the University of Wisconsin–Madison. Material from Missouri served as the basis of Dale Henning's dissertation (D. R. Henning 1970), and, if we want to pinpoint the first occurrence of a professional archaeologist from Missouri using the archaeological record of the state to address issues that went far beyond the state's boundaries, I suggest it was Henning's work.

The excavation of Rodgers Shelter under Raymond Wood's direction is another example of a Missouri archaeologist's examining a problem specific to Missouri, but the way he put together his research team, which comprised specialists from institutions in other states, represented a significant departure from the way archaeology in the state had been organized previously. In addition, although the excavation of Rodgers Shelter was initially intended to examine the culture history of the lower Pomme de Terre River valley and to help sort out chronological issues, the project was quickly redesigned to investigate human-environment interactions on a much broader scale. Importantly, Wood and Bruce McMillan designed the excavations and analyses to build on previous work conducted not only in Missouri but in the Midwest generally, and as a result, the data generated by the project had implications that extended far beyond the Pomme de Terre Valley.

The long-running Powers Phase Project that began in the late 1960s was a case of a Missouri archaeologist, James Price, with direct influence from a non-Missouri archaeologist (Griffin) taking an in-depth look at the culture history of a specific locality. The work was important from a historical perspective because it represented the first time that a university outside of Missouri took the lead role in a project that was centered in the state. Also, the results of the project had implications for archaeological research in areas other than just the Western Lowland. For example, the time-space-form unit that Price and Griffin devised, the Powers phase, was used as a model of Mississippian-period interaction in other southeastern-Missouri localities by Chapman (1980) and others (e.g., D. F. Morse and P. A. Morse 1983).

Work undertaken in Missouri during the 1970s–1990s also can be placed in the categories already discussed. The University of Missouri continued to play a major role in Missouri projects, but it was joined by institutions from outside the state, such as the University of Nebraska-Lincoln and the Illinois State Museum. The museum continued the earlier investigations of Wood and McMillan in the lower Pomme de Terre Valley, and Nebraska launched, in 1975, an in-depth examination of human occupation of the Salt River valley. Both projects were broadly based and yielded data that have had significant impact on how human adaptation in the greater Midwest has been viewed.

The explosion in opportunities for fieldwork provided by the arrival of cultural-resource management ensured that more institutions and private concerns would take an active part in Missouri archaeology. Some of the work has been accomplished by Missourians and some by those outside the state. There also has been a decided growth in studies that use Missouri materials to address nonlocal issues. For example, Robert Dunnell's examinations of aspects of the archaeological record of the Malden Plain, while providing insights into the culture history of the area and adding to the chronological ordering of segments of the record, have been conducted under an entirely different perspective than most projects in the state—an issue that I touched on in Chapter 8 and will discuss in more detail later.

What are we to make of these trends that have characterized archaeological work in Missouri? Are they unique, or could we find them in the archaeology of other states? Undoubtedly, I think we *would* find them elsewhere because these are the trends that have characterized Americanist archaeology throughout the last 150 years. For example, in the early and middle nineteenth century numerous eastern states had scientific societies, and their members were naturally more interested in the prehistory of their locales than they were in larger archaeological concerns. Later, these larger concerns became manifest through the efforts of various government-sponsored investigators such as Cyrus Thomas, William Henry Holmes, and Aleš Hrdlička. As long as there were persons such as Clarence Moore, Warren Moorehead, and Gerard Fowke around, local archaeological records were sure to be sampled by nonresidents lured by the chance to recover artifacts and publish a scientific paper or two.

The integration of anthropology, and by extension archaeology, into university curricula, which began primarily in the East but by the second decade of the twentieth century had spread into the upper Midwest and California, ensured not only that there would be a continuous supply of prehistorians but that the practice of archaeology would be canonized. The practice fields of the students in those programs varied significantly; some universities used their own backyards, others went into other people's backyards. Various federally sponsored programs of the 1930s were a boon to archaeological training in that they provided not only funds for educational assistance but also the opportunity to conduct archaeology on a large scale. Later, the River Basin Surveys and cultural-resource management would provide similar opportunities.

No, Missouri archaeology does not present a special case; the details of its development, of course, are different from those of other states, but some of the same trends are there. Missouri was not investigated by Bureau of American Ethnology personnel to the extent that other states were, but it did witness a share of the activity. "Outsiders" such as Clarence Moore didn't spend as much time in Missouri as they did in other states, but they made their search-and-seizure raids nonetheless. Missouri saw few Works Progress Administration projects, but it later made up for it in its high number of reservoir-salvage projects. Archaeology became a part of the University of Missouri curriculum at a later date than it did in many other eastern and midwestern states, but once it came in through the efforts first of Wrench and Berry and then of Chapman, it quickly found its niche. Archaeology developed its own strong leader in Missouri, Chapman, as the field did in so many other states—people whose names became synonymous with archaeology in their states. And Missouri led most other states in developing a strong and active society comprising interested nonprofessionals. Certainly the broad types of research agendas that characterized archaeology in other states—agendas that had chronological ordering, culture history, human-environment relations, and so on as their central focus—were as prevalent in Missouri as they were elsewhere. Missouri archaeologists may not always have been in the forefront of developments in method and theory, but they knew about them nonetheless and incorporated them (not always correctly) into their analytical repertoire.

Given this summary, I am left with the feeling that Missouri archaeology more or less followed in step with archaeology as it was being developed and practiced in other states, the end product of which was a composite Americanist archaeology. As I completed the research for this book I became less and less interested in comparing Missouri archaeology to Americanist archaeology and more interested in using the former as a case study of the latter. The *really* interesting issue is not chronicling *how* Missouri archaeology developed but *why* it developed the way it did. The basis of my argument rests squarely on the fundamental dichotomy I outlined in Chapter 1—the manner in which we approach the archaeological record. Do we interpret it or do we try to explain it? Missouri archaeology offers classic examples of both.

Interpretation versus Explanation in Missouri Archaeology

How one approaches the archaeological record—literally, how one *does* archaeology—is a product of myriad factors, not the least of which is who one's mentors were and where one received one's training. And, importantly, the approach that one uses at any moment relative to understanding the archaeological record is subject to change. The rate at which we change our approaches, as well as our opinions, is a product not only of the type and amount of fieldwork we do but also of how current we stay in the literature and how involved we are with other professionals. On one hand, there are archaeologists who, upon completing their graduate training, never pick up a journal again. They assume the training they received in school prepared them to be archaeologists and that the learning process is over. The approach they learn as students is the one they keep with them throughout their professional careers. On the other hand, there are archaeologists who read 10 books a week and change their approach at the drop of a hat. Whatever they see as the hottest product on the market is what they will adopt as their perspective.

I want to make it clear that what I am talking about here are *kinds* of approaches—things that are qualitatively as opposed to quantitatively different from each other. The *kind* of approach one takes in archaeology does not come from doing more fieldwork or from reading more archaeological reports; it goes much deeper than that. Let me see if I can make this distinction clearer. It stands to reason that someone with 10 years of experience working in Missouri will know more about the temporal and spatial distributions of archaeological remains than someone with considerably less experience. Experience here has nothing to do with whether or not one has a professional degree. There are dozens of amateur archaeologists in Missouri with more knowledge about specific aspects of the archaeological record than I have, and I seek their advice constantly. This kind of knowledge is cumulative, that is, the more you work on something and are exposed to its intricacies, the more you know. However, more work will not necessarily effect a *qualitative* change in how a person views something. Note that I am not using *qualitative change* as a synonym for *interpretive change*. For example, I am not suggesting that because someone changes his or her mind over the type of sociopolitical organization that he/she thinks Mississippian peoples had, a qualitative change has taken place. That is simply a change in interpretation.

The type of qualitative change I have in mind is one that is much more profound and refers to a complete shift in how a person views the archaeological record itself—in essence a change in paradigm. Because I use the term *paradigm* in a manner that will baffle some readers, I need to define it. Dictionary definitions of the term mention such things as verb conjugations or noun declensions; some dictionaries define *paradigm* as "an example or archetype." Neither definition is what I have in mind. In science, more specifically the philosophy of science, a paradigm is taken to mean, in simple terms, one's view of how the world operates. In short, it constitutes the intellectual grounds upon which one meets experience (Kuhn 1977). A paradigm is not a theory, since it explains nothing, but it conditions the types of theories that one sees as being important, that is, the types of theories one draws on to *explain* something. More to the point here, paradigms directly condition how we view the archaeological record and, most importantly, *how we use that record to examine the past.* For some archaeologists, including Carl Chapman, the ticket to accessing the past is purchased through great increases in quantitative knowledge of the archaeological record. The paradigm that guides their work is interpretation. To Chapman, the past was a mystery, but like all mysteries it could be solved; all it took was hard work and more information. Certainly no one ever accused him of not working hard or of not generating more information. Chapman's entire life was devoted to finding out more about the prehistory of Missouri, regardless of time or space. When he died in 1987, his knowledge of Missouri archaeological sites and artifacts was encyclopedic. It is safe to say that no one will ever come close to matching what he had learned over the half century that he participated in and, for most of that period, directed archaeological activities in the state.

In contrast, there are archaeologists who do not hold to an interpretive paradigm and who do not try to access the past through great cumulative leaps in knowledge. They believe that certain aspects of the archaeological record can be viewed profitably, but they hold out little encouragement that we'll ever be able to understand, let alone reconstruct, things such as social organization and kinship systems. I'm drawing some pretty hard boundaries here, but I will call these archaeologists empiricists (I put myself in this category). In Chapter 8 I noted that one hallmark of the 1980s was a movement toward empirical research, especially with regard to the analysis of artifacts. What I did not point out was that the term *empiricist* is still often used pejoratively to refer to researchers who, according to some, are so narrowly focused on the evidence and on the rules of evidence that what they end up saying is trivial. There is no doubt about it; in archaeology it is much easier to interpret than it is to explain. You get to pick and choose the information you want, and you can change your interpretation at any point. If, on the other hand, you follow the rules of evidence, you walk a very narrow path, always running the risk of getting your case thrown out of court because you didn't follow the rules precisely. Conversely, there are no rules governing interpretation. As I noted earlier, the ultimate arbiter of an explanation— and yes, I will argue that explanation can *only* come about through empirical research—is the degree of conformity between results and expectations. In other words, explanation is dependent upon both theory *and* performance criteria.

In this section I examine the work of two Missouri archaeologists—Carl Chapman and Robert Dunnell—to give you some idea of how those two diametrically opposed paradigms—interpretation and explanation—have been employed and what the products of those efforts have been. Some readers are going to object strenuously to this presentation on the grounds that these represent extreme positions and that few archaeologists actually adhere to either one. Archaeologists who follow an interpretive approach in analyzing the archaeological record are going to say that even Chapman was much too speculative for them. More empirically minded archaeologists are going to say that Dunnell is too much of an archconservative for them and that even he lapses into an interpretive mode on occasion. To be fair, most archaeologists *do* fall somewhere in the middle between interpretation and explanation. They see themselves as objective interpreters of the past who rely on the best evidence available at the time; as new evidence comes along, they use it to modify their interpretations. The important point here is *not* that explanation is *better* than interpretation—although in my opinion it is—but that the two are entirely separate. Archaeologists have tended not to understand this distinction and have moved back and forth between the two with relative ease and confidence, in the process creating a vast middle ground in archaeology. Knowing this should make it easier to understand why what we've seen in the preceding chapters has played out the way it has.

Carl H. Chapman: Interpreting the Past from the Archaeological Record

Of all the research Carl Chapman conducted during his career, it was the archaeological record and historical documents connected with the Missouri and Osage tribes that offered him the most tantalizing lure. His work on these groups, I would argue, was his crowning achievement, and it was that work that would have been featured in the third volume of *The Archaeology of Missouri,* had Chapman lived to write that volume. One issue that intrigued Chapman throughout his career was where to look for the roots of both groups—how to identify archaeological materials as being Osage or Missouri. Chapman's position (actually, *positions*) on this point exemplifies both the role of interpretation in archaeology and how interpretations of the archaeological record are subject to change. To place the discussion in a comprehensible context, I need to provide a bit of background.

Two Siouan groups are important here: Chiwere-Siouan speakers, comprising the Winnebago, the Missouri, the Ioway, and the Oto; and Dhegiha-Siouan speakers, comprising the Kansa, the Osage, the Quapaw, and the Omaha-Ponca. The linguistic subgroups (Chiwere and Dhegiha) began to diverge by ca. A.D. 1000. Legends of the Chiwere-speaking groups (Dorsey 1886: 221–22; W J McGee 1897c: 191–96) suggest the Ioway, Oto, and Missouri separated from the Winnebago near Green Bay, Wisconsin, and moved south. Legend has it that the Ioway settled on the Iowa River somewhere near its confluence with the Mississippi and that the Oto and Missouri moved farther south, establishing villages near the confluence of the Grand and the Missouri rivers in central Missouri. Supposedly, the Oto eventually quarreled with the Missouri and moved farther up the Missouri River.

Traditions of the Dhegiha speakers (Dorsey 1886: 215) state that they had once been a single group living in the Ohio River valley. They then supposedly moved into the Mississippi Valley, where the Quapaw separated from the others and moved into eastern Arkansas. The other groups eventually moved to the mouth of the Missouri River. Those groups then ascended the Missouri River to the mouth of the Osage River. There the Osage separated and moved upstream to the headwaters of the Osage River in western Missouri, while the Kansa moved on to establish themselves along the lower Kansas River in present-day Kansas. The Omaha and Ponca continued up the Missouri River to what is now northeastern Nebraska.

European trade goods have been used to identify contact-period sites, and ethnohistorical information has been used to pinpoint the locations of eighteenth-century Osage and Missouri villages (Figure 9.3) (Berry and Chapman 1942; Bray 1991; Chapman 1952, 1959; D. R. Henning 1970, 1993). It was on the Osage that Chapman focused the majority of his attention.

Over the last 50 years or so, various archaeological units have been identified as Osage. One of those units is Oneota (see Chapter 6), which has been identified as "Siouan" for over half a century (Griffin 1936 [Griffin specifically referred to the Chiwere-Siouan groups]). In his four-part overview of Missouri prehistory, Chapman (1946) placed the Osage, along with the Missouri, in the Oneota aspect of the Upper Mississippi phase of the Mississippian pattern—a placement

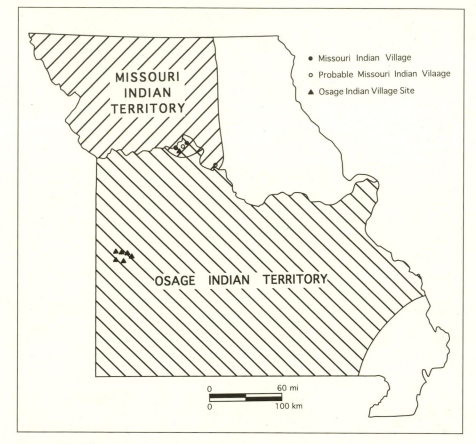

Figure 9.3. Carl Chapman's proposed distribution of Osage and Missouri groups during the protohistoric period (after Chapman 1946).

accomplished through comparison of trait lists (I will return to the issue of trait lists later). But Oneota was not the only archaeological unit that Chapman viewed as being "ancestral" to the Osage. Since Griffin (1936) had already suggested that Oneota was related to the Chiwere-Siouan groups (e.g., the Missouri), Chapman was left with the possibility that his own assignment of Oneota as proto-Osage was incorrect. Thus, in the same volumes of his four-part series (Chapman 1946, 1948b) in which he made the link between the Osage and Oneota, Chapman also toyed with linking the Osage to three other archaeological units, including the Neosho focus of Oklahoma (Baerreis 1941) and the Top-Layer culture of southwestern Missouri and northwestern Arkansas (M. R. Harrington 1924a). This was not unreasonable, since archaeologists such as Griffin (1937) and Baerreis (1941) viewed material in those units as being in the Oneota aspect. As I only alluded to in Chapter 4 but as Yelton (1991) points out in detail, Chapman's interpretive efforts were doomed. For example, in matching trait lists (Chapman 1946: 49), Chapman found a match in house form between those of the Osage and those in the three archaeological units, though none of the latter had ever produced evidence of houses. Chapman's contention of a match between Osage burial practices and burial-related information derived from the three archaeological units likewise was an attempt to shoehorn the evidence into a preconceived interpretive framework.

By the early 1950s Chapman had abandoned the notion that Oneota was "proto-Osage," perhaps because, as Yelton (1991: 139) suggests, Griffin and others had abandoned the notion that the Neosho focus and the Top-Layer culture were Oneota.[1] In its place Chapman inserted a three-part interpretation, the details of which changed slightly over time (Chapman 1952, 1974, 1980). First, he suggested that the Osage and their linguistic kin had once been Mississippian peoples living in the central Mississippi River valley of southeastern Missouri. Then, sometime between ca. A.D. 1350 and 1500, those peoples dispersed, except for the people who became the Quapaw. The non-Quapaw groups drifted either northward up the Mississippi Valley or westward into the Ozarks. It was the latter "bands, clans, extended families, or other scattered social units" that became the Osage (Chapman 1980: 228). They were the ones responsible for the artifacts in caves and rock shelters that were given the archaeological-unit designations of Neosho focus, Top-Layer culture, and Jakie aggregate. Finally, the newly constituted Osage culture lost most of its original Mississippian characteristics and acquired those of the Oneota tradition, which was shortly to give rise to the Missouri Indians.

Yelton (1991: 142–52) takes Chapman's points one by one and places them in perspective. First, he provides ample evidence that the archaeological units from southwestern Missouri (the Neosho focus, the Top-Layer culture, and the Jakie aggregate) are poorly delineated. It is difficult to find traits (primarily artifact forms) in one unit that do not occur in the other units (often in both other units). Chapman knew of the problematic nature of the units, but he clung tenaciously to his belief that "It is just as likely that the people from the expanding centers in the Mississippi alluvial valley penetrated the headwaters of the White River and its tributaries on hunting, gathering, and trading expeditions" (Chapman 1980: 228). This tenacity, however, was not equaled by evidence.

Yelton (1991) offers the following discussion of the problems with Chapman's line of reasoning, and I quote from it at some length because of the insightfulness of his comments:

1. I base the synthesis of Chapman's model presented below on Jeffrey Yelton's (1991) dissertation, in which he argues, correctly I think, that if there is an archaeological precursor to the Osage, it is Oneota. Yelton was a student of Chapman's in the early 1980s, first helping to analyze animal bone from Osage sites, then analyzing Oneota and Osage ceramics, the latter of which formed the basis of his dissertation.

If [the "Oneota look" of Osage artifacts resulted from diffusion from the Missouri and Oto], one could expect to find protohistoric and early Osage sites with little or no Oneota influence. This has not occurred. Chapman (1952: 145) dismissed this lack of evidence in a unique way. Apparently, it is "probable" that early Osage villages "were in the rough country bordering the Osage and Gasconade rivers. Unfortunately, the heart of the Osage territory was sealed from archaeological investigation by the building of Bagnell Dam in 1932. None of the sites were studied before coverage by waters of the Lake of the Ozarks." Thus the lack of non-Oneota, protohistoric Osage sites is linked with a non-falsifiable proposition. No evidence is given to show that the "heart of the Osage territory" sites were flooded; it only is assumed that they are there, because they are not found in other areas.

In contrast, Chapman argued that a proponent of an Oneota-Osage genesis must produce definite Oneota–Osage sites. "If it were assumed that the Osage archaeological assemblages were Oneota culture originally, it would be necessary to find European contact and precontact sites of the Oneota culture from which the Osage assemblages might have derived. The only Oneota sites that fit this description are the ones that have been identified as Missouri Indian" [Chapman 1974: 195–96]. This is a circular argument. We know that only the Missouri lived at Oneota sites, because the Osage Tribe is not derived from the Oneota tradition; we know that the Osage Tribe is not derived from the Oneota tradition, because we have identified all Oneota sites as having been occupied by Missouri Indians. . . .

It is not parsimonious to explain Osage origins by using Chapman's model. . . . The best available model is that Osage culture is derived from the Oneota tradition, rather than from a non-Oneota group that received Oneota influence. Ironically, this was the original position of Griffin (1937) and Chapman (1946, 1948[b]). (Yelton 1991: 151–52)

There is no question that Chapman's efforts, throughout his long career, were tied directly to interpreting the archaeological record, specifically by creating cultural sequences that were based on the dozens of sites he and his associates excavated. Jeff Yelton once told me that Chapman compared chronological ordering to building a wall: You stacked your bricks (cultures) course by course, until the wall was completed. Obviously there would be gaps in the wall, so you had to fill them in by imagining (Chapman's word, according to Yelton) what was most likely. Later, when you found a brick that was of the right size, you could fill the gap permanently.[2] In this respect Chapman was like many of his contemporaries. He used the McKern method as mortar until a better product—the Willey and Phillips system—came along, at which point he switched to the new product. Of course, we've come a long way since Willey and Phillips, and

2. Yelton provided me his perceptions (pers. comm. 1993) of how Chapman viewed archaeology in general and how this view led to Chapman's constantly changing his mind over the years regarding the Osage-origins question.

their method has declined in use. However, simply because fewer archaeologists today make use of Willey and Phillips's temporal-spatial units than they did 30 years ago gives us no reason to criticize either the method or those who made intelligent use of it. The decline in use was simply a product of how perspectives change—as we understand more, we modify our methods.

From the start there was a fatal flaw in Chapman's wall of cultures, and here I disagree with Yelton's assessment of the situation. He says that Carl could never tear down a wall once he had built it. I would argue that he never built a wall that would last because the mortar he used to join the bricks never set. And it never set because he didn't read the directions that came on the bag. Obviously he had read McKern's (1939) article on the midwestern taxonomic method, but he did not follow the procedures involved in logically constructing phases, foci, and aspects. He used McKern's *terms,* as he did those of Willey and Phillips (1958), but he did not understand the key point that McKern was making when the method was formulated—the difference between traits and determinants. As I discussed in Chapter 4, McKern expressly kept separate the commonly used term *traits* and what he called "determinants." Traits could be determinants, but only if they were diagnostic, that is, only if they were *unique to one cultural manifestation, not found in two or more different manifestations.* Traits that were "linked" to two or more manifestations were "useless as determinants" (McKern 1939: 305). Chapman, however, used the archaeological units devised by David Baerreis (Neosho focus), M. R. Harrington ("Top-Layer" culture), and others as if *those* archaeologists had employed the midwestern taxonomic method correctly, which they had not. He then constructed trait lists and compared the traits across the board to arrive at the conclusion that the Ozark Highland was full of proto-Osage peoples after ca. A.D. 1350.

Later, in the second volume of *The Archaeology of Missouri,* Chapman did the same thing for the central Mississippi River valley section from which the proto-Osage supposedly had migrated. Now he divided the archaeological record of the early portion of the Mississippian period (before the migration) into phases, based on the success he saw in James Price's efforts to establish the Powers phase in the Western Lowland of southeastern Missouri (J. E. Price 1973; J. E. Price and Griffin 1979) (see Chapter 6). Chapman's procedure was to identify a phase for every large fortified site in the region, with each phase including not only the large settlements but also their "satellites." This resulted in the naming of 14 phases (he labeled Hunze as an "aggregate"). These, according to Chapman (1980: 185), were better than earlier phase designations for the region, which "are confusing and not consistent in that they are not based on the same type of information." Although Chapman admitted that some of the

fortified towns might have been interrelated through alliances, the working hypothesis . . . is that each fortified civic-ceremonial center with its satellite villages

can be classified as a phase (Willey and Phillips 1958). Therefore, it is proposed that there is a greater number of phases in the Southeast Riverine Region of Missouri and Arkansas than has been previously suspected or proposed. Before the hypothesis can be tested, several of the fortified towns need to be investigated, as do the villages, farmsteads, and collecting stations that are within a reasonable radius of towns and might be satellites. (Chapman 1980: 185)

However, some of those "towns" *had* been investigated, a few of them extensively (see Chapter 6), as Chapman discussed at length later in the volume. One thing is evident from his treatment of the artifacts from the different "towns" (as it is to anyone with firsthand knowledge of the materials): the artifacts are consistently similar across the region. I am *not* saying that variation isn't present, but you could never see it by using standard typological procedures, which was Chapman's approach to artifact analysis. How then, could you define separate phases? And *why* would you cite Willey and Phillips as a reference for this perspective on phases, when they defined a phase as "an archaeological unit possessing traits *sufficiently characteristic to distinguish it from all other units similarly conceived*" (Willey and Phillips 1958: 22; emphasis added)? The inescapable answer is that archaeological method took a backseat to loose interpretation—a phenomenon not limited to Chapman and his work (see Fox 1992 and O'Brien and Fox 1994a for other examples). Appeals to methodological constructs— foci, aspects, phases, or whatever—shrouded the interpretations in a mantle of archaeological respectability, but underneath was a kind of homespun story that even the methodological constructs, which ironically were developed to *guide* interpretation, could not support.

Chapman rarely used the term *explanation* in his articles and books, but the term *interpretation* occurs repeatedly. It is clear from the context in which *interpretation* appears, however, that he intended it as a synonym for *explanation*, which, as we will see below, was not unique to Chapman. It is also clear that his explanations of culture change were made in terms of prime movers such as diffusion and group movement. Accordingly, throughout his two volumes (Chapman 1975, 1980) terms such as *borrowed, cultural stream,* and *imposed* take center stage. Similarly, he viewed a perfect match between humans and their environment as being the reason for cultural stasis, that is, periods of no change. Most of his interpretive efforts were geared toward identifying which traits moved where and how the movement changed through time.

Robert C. Dunnell: Deriving Explanations from the Archaeological Record

In contrast to Chapman's attempts to arrive at what he termed explanation is the work of Robert Dunnell (Figure 9.4), who has been the driving force

Figure 9.4. Robert C. Dunnell in Dunklin County, Missouri, 1980.
Dunnell emerged during the 1980s as a central figure in archaeological
method and theory, in large part a result of his work on classification
and his attempts to integrate a Darwinian approach into archaeology.
Archaeologists who were more inclined to interpretation found his
strict adherence to a "physics-of-artifacts" approach too stultifying
and prescriptive; some scientific-minded archaeologists applauded his
no-nonsense approach to the archaeological record (photograph by
D. J. Meltzer, courtesy D. K. Grayson and M. D. Dunnell).

behind the application of Darwinian evolutionary theory to archaeological
problems. From several standpoints, a historical perspective on Dunnell's work
is as enlightening as that on Chapman's. You probably could not find two more
polar opposites in Americanist archaeology: Chapman the weaver of elegant
interpretations, Dunnell the archconservative who rarely (if ever) has used the
word *interpretation*. Chapman spent all of his career and Dunnell has spent a
large part of his career so far doing archaeology in Missouri, yet it is clear that
neither had much if any influence on the other.

Although Dunnell is perhaps best known as a theoretician, it is difficult to understand how his theoretical perspective applies to empirical data without examining his work on "the hard phenomena of the archaeological record" (Dunnell 1978a: 195). I reviewed some of Dunnell's work in Chapter 8—work that, for the last 15 years or so, has centered almost exclusively on the collection and analysis of materials from Dunklin County, Missouri, specifically that portion of the county that lies on the Pleistocene-age Malden Plain. Dunnell's ties to Missouri stem from his marriage in 1966 to Mary Davidson, the daughter of Wilburn and Laverne Davidson of Kennett, both longtime members and trustees of the Missouri Archaeological Society. Dunnell was born in Wheeling, West Virginia, in 1942, and as soon as he finished high school he headed south to escape a life in the coal mines. He landed a job as a laborer on the Barkley Reservoir construction project in western Kentucky but soon saw a notice that the University of Kentucky was hiring people for archaeological work to be carried out in advance of the reservoir. Following that initial exposure to archaeology, he enrolled at the university in the fall of 1960, served as a museum and research assistant during his student years, and received his bachelor's degree in anthropology in 1964.

The University of Kentucky had long been an active participant, often a leader, in federally sponsored archaeology in the eastern United States (see Milner and Smith 1986 for an excellent review), and by the mid-1960s it was involved in numerous survey-and-excavation projects across Kentucky and West Virginia. Also by the mid-1960s the university had begun to shift much of its attention to the narrow valleys of eastern Kentucky, and Dunnell, though he had moved on to Yale for his Ph.D., continued to take an active part in the work, including survey and excavation in Fishtrap Reservoir in Pike County. His dissertation, *The Prehistory of Fishtrap, Kentucky: Archaeological Interpretation in Marginal Areas,* was completed in 1967. That same year, he and Mary, who also was a Yale-trained anthropologist, moved to Seattle, where he became an assistant professor in the University of Washington's anthropology department.

The discussion of Dunnell's work in Chapter 8 was more or less from the standpoint of methods and techniques—primarily those that could be used to understand the structure of surface-artifact distributions—though I mentioned the work that he and James Feathers did to better understand the properties of shell- and sand-tempered pottery. This latter work fits neatly in the "physics-of-artifacts" category, which I would define as understanding how material properties affect the various uses to which a tool can be put—what Dunnell (1978a: 195) termed "performance standards" and Schiffer and Skibo (1987: 600) termed "performance characteristics." Archaeologists have long had an interest in the material properties of artifacts (see Chapter 7)—an interest that has accelerated as more and more machines have come along that allow us to probe and tear apart materials, to view their components with previously unattainable resolution, and to measure minute variation in such things as how tools were made and used.

Americanist archaeology has witnessed a proliferation of journals devoted exclusively or in large part to the physics of artifacts, and, in reading through the extensive literature, one cannot help but be impressed with the detail that has gone into the analysis of the physical properties of such things as clays, tempers, and slips. Dunnell and his students (e.g., Dunnell and Feathers 1991; Dunnell and Jackson 1992; Dunnell et al. 1994; Feathers 1989a; Feathers and Scott 1989) certainly have contributed to the literature, but there is, in my opinion, a major difference between Dunnell's motives and those of other archaeologists who do physics-of-artifacts studies. In short, his proximal motive is to characterize materials—this is really no different than the motive most if not all archaeologists have—and to use the resulting data to isolate variation—again, a motive most archaeologists have.

At that point, however, there is a divergence. Dunnell attempts to explain variation in terms of Darwinian theory (see Chapter 8) instead of interpreting what the variation means. This divergence in purpose was not lost on Watson (1986; see also P. J. Watson et al. 1984), who reviewed Dunnell's outlook in a stridently critical tone in her article "Archaeological Interpretation, 1985." Watson's characterization of Dunnell as a "dogged and dogmatic" empiricist (P. J. Watson 1986: 445) is right on the money. The gist of her argument is that there is a small but vocal minority in Americanist archaeology composed of people who feel that their access to the "real" past (Watson uses the term repeatedly but never defines it) is either limited or nonexistent. One gets the feeling in reading the article that Watson wanted to place Dunnell in the category of people who do not believe the past is accessible but at the last minute placed him in with those whom she labeled "narrow empiricists," that is, those who have an "extreme skepticism about access to the real past" (P. J. Watson 1986: 446). Actually, Watson should have placed Dunnell in with the other group, since he believes the past is *not* accessible.

Dunnell's position is "disquieting" to Watson (1986: 444), and she places him on or near what she terms "the 'artifact physics' horn of the archaeologist's dilemma" (P. J. Watson 1986: 445), a term she borrowed from DeBoer and Lathrap (1979), who defined "artifact physics" as a methodologically sound but trivial analytical procedure for measuring "the form and distribution of behavioral by-products . . . in a behavioral vacuum" (DeBoer and Lathrap 1979: 103). Watson (1986: 446) has a difficult time understanding how "one can say anything about the archaeological record without covertly if not overtly employing a reconstructionist [read *interpretive*] approach to some nontrivial degree." Watson raises an interesting point and obviously one with which archaeologists must wrestle. The problem is, as archaeologists asked throughout the 1960s and into the 1970s, how do you go about "reconstructing" past cultures? The "new archaeology" provided numerous answers to this question, but none was particularly satisfying to some archaeologists, including Dunnell. Interestingly, Dunnell's reaction was similar to that of Irving Rouse, who had been the chair of his doctoral committee at Yale. Rouse (1964: 465) had earlier commented that archaeologists should focus on the *products* of evolution and leave the *process* of evolution to ethnologists.

Dunnell's (1982b, 1988b, 1992b) arguments against cultural reconstruction— that is, against our ability to access the past—are based on the belief that we lack the means to sort through various plausible reconstructions and pick the correct one. In other words, the past must remain inaccessible because we have no means of assessing the strength of a reconstruction. Any particular reconstruction (interpretation) might be *plausible,* but plausibility isn't truth. What recourse do we have? Should we vote on which scenario is most plausible? Scientists don't sit around and vote for their favorite scenario. They argue over explanations, but they don't argue over the *rules* of explanation. Not so with some archaeologists, who act more like jurors than scientists. Archaeologists still adhere to the notion that stories can be confirmed, as witnessed by the quote from Watson et al. (1984: 129) I used in Chapter 8: "The degree of *confirmation of conclusions* should be exhibited by describing fully the field and laboratory data and the reasoning used to support these conclusions. This is what we mean by an explicitly scientific archeological method" (emphasis added). This may be an explicitly *archaeological* method, but it is decidedly not scientific.

Our lack of access to the past, however, does not mean that things in the archaeological record cannot be *explained.* But how, you might ask, can something such as the appearance of shell-tempered pottery be explained? We might *interpret* the appearance of shell-tempered pottery in terms of invention or diffusion, but this doesn't qualify as an explanation. We want to know *why* something occurred, not simply *how* it occurred. Explanations stem from theory, not from common sense, though as Dunnell (1982b) pointed out, most archaeology has been and continues to be guided by common sense. In Dunnell's case the theory that guides the explanation is Darwinian evolution. In fact, once you buy into Darwinian evolution as a theory, it even dictates *how* things such as artifacts should be examined. The place to start is function. We accept the fact that things such as prehistoric pots, regardless of the material used as temper, were parts of human phenotypes (see Chapter 8). Now, just because some feature is phenotypic does not mean that it automatically is subject to selective control. Just as with the somatic (bodily) parts of the phenotype, it is the *functional* objects, or features, that are shaped by selection. Neither artifacts nor their attributes carry labels that tell us whether they were functional or stylistic (nonfunctional), just as bodily features don't. It is up to the archaeologist, as it is to the biologist, to determine whether a feature was functional and *how* it functioned (there are several archaeological approaches to this problem [see Dunnell 1978b, 1980;

O'Brien and Holland 1990, 1992]). If objects such as pots and projectile points came under selective control, that is, if they were functional, then evolutionary theory tells us that they were true adaptations. Importantly, it is the specific *properties* (attributes) of artifacts in which we are interested—properties such as shell tempering—and *how* those properties changed through time as a result of selection. Observed variation in artifacts, and how that variation changes over time, is what we are tracking analytically.

Few papers on artifact function don't at least cite Dunnell's (1978b) article entitled "Style and Function: A Fundamental Dichotomy" (see also Dunnell 1978a). The paper was an attempt to point out the intrinsic difference between features of the archaeological record that were functional in terms of the roles they played in past cultures and those that were stylistic. Based on a reading of the literature after that paper appeared, archaeologists missed Dunnell's point, perhaps in part because of his counterintuitive claim that stylistic features are neutral, that is, that they carry no adaptive value and hence do not affect the fitness of the possessor. The key to understanding which features were functional and which were stylistic lies in the examination of the life histories of the features in question. Dunnell apparently was the first archaeologist to note that when we plot the frequency of some archaeological features over time, say, a particular method of creating a haft on a projectile point, we get curves that resemble those shown by somatic features that are under natural selection (Dunnell 1978b; O'Brien and Holland 1990, 1992) (Figure 9.5). When we plot the frequency of other features over time, we get curves that resemble those shown by somatic features that are neutral, that is, that are not under selective control (Figure 9.5).

Clearly, traditional artifact types are inappropriate for examining functional aspects of the archaeological record. Simply put, many traditional types were devised to address issues such as time or cultural connectedness and thus were not devised to address functional issues. One cannot form a type for one purpose and then decide a priori that it also can be used for another purpose, such as tracking minute changes in things such as edge angle on a projectile point or the wall thickness of a ceramic vessel. In fact, even most so-called functional types, which usually are based on analogy (similar forms equal similar functions), are not suitable for empirical studies of function. The ability to track what often is minute change is a prerequisite to being able to explain that change. In other words, if we can't quantify change, we certainly can't explain it.

Dunnell entered the classification debates fairly late (see Chapter 5), though the fact that Rouse was the chair of his doctoral committee at Yale meant that he had considerable exposure to the issues involved in the debates. His first contribution to the subject was a short book, *Systematics in Prehistory* (Dunnell 1971; see also Dunnell 1986), in which he introduced the notion of *paradigmatic classification* as a means of objectifying the variation within groups of objects. The book was widely used as a text in graduate seminars, but it is apparent, at

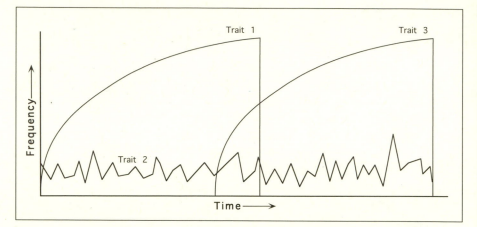

Figure 9.5. Hypothetical changes in frequency of two traits under selective control (1, 3) and of a trait not under selective control (2). The former exhibit a rapid increase in frequency, followed by an abrupt decline because of their rapid replacement by other traits. Traits not under selective control "drift" along.

least to me, that one of two things occurred: either most archaeologists did not understand what Dunnell was saying or they rejected it. I base this proposition on the fact that even in the years immediately following publication of the book, few archaeologists employed paradigmatic classification on a routine basis. The method produces a very different result than what typological systems produce, and it bears at least brief discussion because it has been performed on a variety of kinds of objects from Missouri, including rural Euro-American architecture (O'Brien and Lewarch 1984; O'Brien et al. 1980), stone items (Curry et al. 1985; Lewarch 1982), and pottery (Teltser 1988).

Suppose we have a pile of projectile points in front of us and we want to make some sense out of the variation that exists among them. We could rely on common types that have been proposed, but many of them are not rigorously described. We could, alternatively, create classes of projectile points based on certain features that we deem to be of importance to whatever problem we have at hand. We'll call each feature a dimension. Let's say that dimension A refers to the location of notching on a projectile point. Under that dimension we could have an infinite amount of variation, but for our analysis we'll use four attribute states. We'll call "side notching" attribute state (AS) 1, "corner notching" AS 2, "basal notching" AS 3, and "no notching" AS 4. We'll make base shape our second dimension and assign three possible attribute states to it: AS 1, "straight base"; AS 2, "concave base"; and AS 3, "convex base." The classes, which are already defined for us, are the cells that result from the 3-x-4 matrix (Figure 9.6). We'll call the upper left-hand cell class 1, which is defined as a side-notched point with a convex base; class 2 is defined in our scheme as a corner-notched

		Dimension 1			
		side	corner	basal	none
	convex	1	2	3	4
	concave	5	6	7	8
	straight	9	10	11	12

Dimension 2

Figure 9.6. Two-dimensional paradigmatic-classification matrix for projectile points.

point with a convex base; and so on. The fact that there are 12 possible classes that result from our scheme does not ensure that every class will be represented in our sample. Theoretically, they *could* be represented, but they might not be. In fact, they might not be represented in *any* sample. This is not a flaw in the system, and in fact the absence of a particular class of artifact might lead us to ask why it is *not* represented—a question that is not so apparent when traditional methods of categorization are used.

In short, paradigmatic classification gives us an objective means of examining variation. We know what a particular class is simply by looking at the definition. We don't have to worry about whether what we are calling Bell plain pottery is what someone else is calling Bell plain or whether our Marshall point looks like someone else's. Once we've quantified the variation present in a group of artifacts, we still, of course, have two avenues open to us: we can interpret the variation, or we can attempt to explain it. The point is, precise quantification and the identification of variation don't make what we do scientific. It's what we do with the data that dictates whether the outcome is scientific or not.

At this point you still might not be entirely sold on the notion that interpretation and explanation are all that different, though I have tried to convince you that they are. Explanation, by its very nature, is tied both to theory and to a set of performance criteria derived *from* that theory. You do not have to understand all the intricacies of evolutionary archaeology or of classification to realize that there is a difference between how archaeologists like Carl Chapman have approached Missouri's archaeological record and how those like Robert Dunnell have approached it. One interpreted the record, the other forms explanations for the question of why it is the way it is.

Why the Wide Disparity in Approaches to the Archaeological Record?

As I noted, the worldview that someone brings to bear on a problem is conditioned by many things, not the least of which is educational experience—where one went to school, under whom one studied, and who one's colleagues are. I did not start out to write this book with the idea of examining much in the way of the backgrounds of archaeologists who have worked in Missouri, but the more I got into it the more I became convinced that it is impossible to understand the development of archaeology without some understanding of the people involved. At this point I'm not sure that backgrounds in and of themselves *explain* anything, but I *am* sure that they help us understand the directions Missouri archaeology has taken over the last several decades.

It is tempting in a discussion of why things happened the way they did to invoke what is usually termed the "Big Man" proposition, meaning that (a) one person controlled or influenced an outcome and (b) things would have turned out differently had that person not existed. You know the story: World War II wouldn't have happened without Adolf Hitler, there would be no communism without Karl Marx and Friedrich Engels, and so on. Likewise (admittedly on a less-important front), in archaeology there would have been no "new archaeology" without Lewis Binford, no move toward incorporation of a Darwinian evolutionary perspective without Dunnell, and no cultural-resource management without Chapman and Bob McGimsey. We could argue at length the validity of this view, as some anthropologists did early in the twentieth century,[3] but I don't see that as being particularly useful. There is every reason to suspect, for example, that the "new archaeology" would have happened regardless of whether Binford had been around to write "Archaeology as Anthropology." Why? Because by the late 1950s some archaeologists were becoming bored with culture history and chronological ordering; the making of archaeology into something anthropological was not the intellectual domain solely of Binford.

3. Alfred Kroeber, in his article "The Eighteen Professions" (Kroeber 1915), stated that the only historical value individuals have is as examples. Edward Sapir (1917) was among those who rebutted this claim.

But to say that the "Big Man" proposition doesn't explain *everything* in no way implies that it explains nothing. It would be difficult to find a better example of the Big Man in archaeology than Carl Chapman. Chapman was not a contributor to archaeological method and theory, but he was an avid reader of the archaeological literature. He was also an active field person. What he read and what he saw in the field conditioned his views of archaeology, and, in turn, it was his views that conditioned how the record of Missouri's past would come to be known. Not only did he personally conduct much of the archaeological work undertaken in Missouri between 1940 and 1975, but he also trained several generations of students to assist him in his quest for more knowledge about Missouri's past. In addition, he either wrote or edited much of what found its way into print. Most importantly, he was the person who finally pulled together bits and pieces of the archaeological record that had been gathered over nearly a century and made that synthesis available to thousands of people. He deserved the title of Big Man, and he wore it well. Anyone who came into contact with Chapman for more than a brief period could attest that his approach to archaeology was no less dogmatic than that of any Bureau of American Ethnology prehistorian.

For those who never interacted closely with Carl, I cannot give you a better description of the man than what Dale Henning said in a piece published in the *Iowa Archeological Society Newsletter* shortly after Carl and Eleanor were killed: "Field work [with Carl] was fast, exciting and fun. We learned fast and tended to . . . argue the finer points of what was being found. Then, Carl would search his memory, bringing to recall items seen in collections, in the field or laboratory and, with eyes fixed squarely to yours, would drive home his interpretations of reality. One never won an argument with Carl, but could learn from it" (D. R. Henning 1987: 5). Compare Henning's description of Chapman to Griffin's (1974: vi) description of William S. Webb, the chairman of the anthropology department at the University of Kentucky who in 1934 assumed responsibility for the massive Tennessee Valley Authority archaeological program: "Webb was a man of very strong opinions, both personal and professional; having once made up his mind that a given research path or idea was correct, he followed it with drive and determination. He was able to develop or accept a new notion, work on it, worry over it, and finally convince himself that it must be true. Thereafter, no amount of argument or contrary evidence was likely to sway him." If I didn't know better, I would swear Griffin was describing Carl Chapman.

And interpret the record Carl did, from his first article—"Stone Age Man of Crawford County," published in 1935—to the last of his great efforts—*Osage and Missouri Indian Life Cultural Change: 1675–1825*, published in 1985. Despite Carl's standing in the field, I have always been perplexed as to why someone he respected did not point out to him that through much of his interpretation he was muddying the waters of archaeological taxonomy. There were numerous archaeologists who could have done this—especially Griffin, who obviously was a strong influence on Chapman. They were more or less of the same generation, although Griffin was about 10 years older and had seen much more in the way of archaeology across the eastern United States than Carl had. But Carl Chapman was, in just about every sense of the word, a self-made man, and I think he learned at an early age to depend on his own abilities to get by. Other people's opinions might be taken into account, especially those of people he respected, but in the end, it was his intuition that he followed. Chapman came out of Crawford County, Missouri, during the Great Depression and, if the story is true, sold his car for $10 just to have enough money to live on after he arrived in Columbia.

When he came to the University of Missouri in the fall of 1935, he had an intense desire to be an archaeologist, but where was he supposed to receive the training? The nearest thing to an archaeologist the university had was Jesse Wrench, a historian of the ancient world, and Brewton Berry, a sociologist. Berry taught a few anthropology courses in the sociology department, but neither he nor Wrench would have been capable of teaching Chapman much about archaeological methods, much less about archaeological theory. In fact, as I pointed out in Chapter 4, Wrench and Berry hired J. C. Harrington of the University of Chicago to direct a field school near Columbia so that they, along with the students, could learn proper excavation methods. But knowing how to remove a skeleton from the ground without breaking it says nothing about how one is going to gain an understanding of the archaeological record. It is clear from reading the few articles that Wrench and Berry wrote that they were more preoccupied with getting material out of the ground and cataloging it than they were with interpreting it.

Chapman completed his undergraduate degree in sociology at the University of Missouri in 1939, and the following year he was appointed the first director of American archaeology at the university (Figure 9.7).[4] He took a leave of absence in 1941 to work on a master's degree at the University of New Mexico, but the war came along, and, like so many other young men, he put his formal education on hold and enlisted in the Air Force. It was in Albuquerque that he met and fell in love (there was never any doubt about that) with Eleanor Finley. She soon became Eleanor F. Chapman and one day the proud wife of the dean of Missouri archaeology and superb illustrator of almost every book, pamphlet, and article on Missouri archaeology that was published between about 1946 and 1980.

It was not until 1946, following a stint in a German prisoner-of-war camp, that Chapman completed the requirements for his master's degree in anthropology.

---

4. Chapman was a master at creating titles, most of which never received university approval. He eventually deeded the university title "director" to others who came after him, in the process adopting the title "Research Professor in American Archaeology."

Figure 9.7. Carl Chapman (1915–1987) in the field, ca. 1946.

Figure 9.8. Carl Chapman in his office at the University of Missouri, 1948.

That year he returned to the University of Missouri as assistant professor of sociology and anthropology (Figure 9.8). Chapman was one of several professional archaeologists that Griffin invited to the University of Michigan in the late 1940s to complete course work toward a doctorate in anthropology. He completed a year's worth of course work in Ann Arbor in 1949–1950 and returned to the University of Missouri in the summer of 1950.[5] He finished his dissertation in 1959. A year of formal training is not much time to spend on any subject, regardless of the caliber of the school and of the instructors—and Michigan rated highly on both counts—but I wouldn't be surprised if Carl had viewed it as simply an interruption of what he loved the most, which was doing Missouri archaeology.

Except for his forays to Washington, D.C., in the 1970s, for the next three decades Carl would turn his attention to countless aspects of the archaeological record of his state and would churn out an incredible amount of information, in the process training dozens of students and involving hundreds of interested laypersons in his day-to-day affairs. This was all part of his plan to make the past as accessible to everyone else as it was to him—an accessibility made through a literal, as well as liberal, interpretation of the archaeological record. The final interruption to his lifelong passion occurred on the evening of February 18, 1987, on a highway in Kissimmee, Florida.

On the surface, Carl might have appeared quite similar to a host of other archaeologists of his generation, but I have come to the conclusion that in some ways he was enigmatic. Other archaeologists of that time worked long hours, published the results of their work, and trained graduate students, but the passion and dedication that he brought to the pursuit may be unsurpassed in the annals of Americanist archaeology. He dedicated a considerable portion of his career to securing federal legislation for funding cultural-resource management, which probably was motivated as much by what it could do for Missouri as it was out of concern for a national need. Regardless of whether he was working for the state, the country, or both, what he did was selfless.

The important point, I believe, is that when he graduated from the University of Missouri in 1939, the field of Missouri archaeology was wide open. He had quickly gone beyond what his two mentors could give him in the realm of formal training, and when, in 1940, he was given the university title of Director of American Archaeology, the field was almost his alone. The war years slowed the pace of Missouri archaeology, but by 1950, when Chapman returned from his one-year stay in Ann Arbor, the pace quickened exponentially. So much was happening at once—only a small portion of which I discussed in Chapter 5—

5. Another faculty member in the then Department of Sociology and Anthropology, Robert F. G. Spier, filled in for Chapman as director of the American Archaeology Division and secretary of the Missouri Archaeological Society in 1949–1950.

that I'm not sure Carl ever had time to catch his breath. Whole new vistas into Missouri's past were being opened before his eyes, and with his army of students, staff, and lay volunteers, he could reach those vistas in a way that had never before been possible.

I know from personal experience that when you involve hordes of students and lay volunteers in an archaeological project, they constantly bombard you with questions about what it all means. As I noted in the Preface, they want to know what group of people left the artifacts; they don't particularly want to know that you and other archaeologists have placed the materials in the Neosho phase. They want to know where the group came from, and where they came from before that; they want to know what language the group spoke; they want to know a million things. And it is much easier to interpret the archaeological record for them than it is to use the record as an explanatory device. The latter takes more time, and time was something that Carl didn't have much of.

Once you start an archaeological society, once you start traveling across the state to give lectures or to examine someone's artifact collection—in short, once you get people fired up about archaeology—you can't stop. People constantly want more, and they feel let down if you're not there to provide it. You have to be at people's beck and call—after all, you said you wanted their help in the first place—and you have to give them something to do. That means more weekend excavations, more site surveys, more workshops. You have to try and educate them through archaeological literature, and that means more newsletters and more monographs. Someone has to write the monographs and edit the reports that come in from your volunteer army. Someone has to photograph the artifacts, and someone has to prepare the site plans and drawings for publication (thank God for Eleanor [Figure 9.9]). Last but certainly not least, someone has to teach the students and write the proposals to the funding agencies to keep the students and staff employed. Archaeological vistas, Carl Chapman found out, often come at a steep price.

I'm not sure, as I said at the beginning of this section, that this brief summary provides much in the way of an explanation of the development of Missouri archaeology from 1940 on, but I certainly think it provides a basis for understanding the development. And I know what you're thinking—is this simply my *interpretation* of what happened? I don't think so; rather, I think the evidence is fairly clear on the matter. But what about the other archaeologists who worked in Missouri? Didn't their training and other prior experiences play a part in how they viewed and used the archaeological record? Most assuredly. I noted in Chapter 6 that Raymond Wood had been trained at the University of Oregon by Luther Cressman, who was someone with an intense interest in the topic of humans and how they interact with their physical environment. Part of Wood's interest came from that influence, and he passed that interest on to Bruce McMillan, Marvin Kay, and Robert Warren. Dunnell was a student of Irving

Figure 9.9. Eleanor Chapman replicating the copper plates from the Spiro site, eastern Oklahoma, ca. 1955.

Rouse's at Yale and needless to say was influenced by him, especially in the area of typology and classification (Rouse ties with Albert Spaulding in the number of articles or books cited [four each] in Dunnell's [1971] *Systematics in Prehistory*). Dunnell, in turn, influenced his students—Dennis Lewarch (Figure 9.10), Lee Lyman, Patrice Teltser (Figure 9.11), James Feathers, Patrick McCutcheon, Fran Whittaker, and Mark Madsen—who have worked in Missouri.

Intellectual genetics do not work only from professor to student. For example, I hired both Warren and Lewarch as associate directors of the Cannon Reservoir Human Ecology Project in 1977 and learned a good deal from both of them. Having Warren on the project was the next best thing to having Wood there in terms of his knowledge of environmental archaeology, especially as it related to Holocene climatic history and vegetation change. Having Lewarch on the project was the next best thing to having Dunnell around. He understood the intricacies of artifact classification, from a philosophical as well as from a practical point of view, and he had been influenced by Dunnell as to the importance of surface artifacts for defining such things as site structure and function. Warren and Lewarch in many ways introduced me to these topics and helped turn what might have been a good project into an excellent one, and one that was in many ways unique.

Intellectual transmission is not limited to interests but, more importantly, also includes such things as the way the world is perceived. It should come as no surprise that many of Chapman's students (e.g., Robert Bray, Richard Marshall,

Figure 9.10. Dennis Lewarch in Home Valley Park, Skamania County, Washington, 1974 (courtesy D. L. Lewarch).

Figure 9.11. Patrice Teltser surface collecting in Scott County, Missouri, 1993 (courtesy L. Wandsnider).

and Raymond Williams) became proficient at interpreting the archaeological record or that Dunnell's students (e.g., Feathers, Teltser, and McCutcheon) and my students (e.g., Thomas Holland and Robert Hoard) have adopted an evolutionary perspective. And no one should be surprised that students who worked with Wood (e.g., McMillan, Ahler, Kay, and Warren) have an in-depth understanding of how empirical science operates. None of these individuals, however, is a clone of his or her mentor (the last thing archaeology needs is clones), and all would undoubtedly argue that several other persons provided significant intellectual direction at various points in their lives.

A Brief Personal Perspective

For a variety of reasons I have not used the words *right* or *wrong* in discussing the approaches that have been employed in Missouri archaeology, primarily because I would rather the reader judge for himself or herself which is the more useful strategy. Of course, if we mention the word *useful,* then we are forced to ask, "Useful for what?" For my purposes, I prefer taking a stab at using the archaeological record as an explanatory tool. I'm interested in explaining why things happened the way they did in the past and in understanding what the consequences were when things happened that way; I draw my conclusions from how the empirical data stack up against certain expectations derived from evolutionary theory. In other words, I find explanation to be a "useful" approach. You have probably come to the conclusion that I am not a fan of archaeological interpretation, and you are absolutely correct. My problem is, unless there is a body of theory to guide the formulation of certain expectations that can then be examined in light of empirical evidence, how do I judge the merits of an interpretation? How do I know, for example, that your story is superior to someone else's? The basis of Rudyard Kipling's "Just So Stories" was the line "Things were so, just so, a little time ago." The same line could be applied to archaeological interpretations, as I have pointed out elsewhere (O'Brien 1994).

I thought of several ways to end this book, and I picked one that not only summarizes a bit of Missouri archaeology but, for what it's worth, gives you my perspective on the subject. I am going to pretend you asked me for a short list of subjects that somehow encapsulate not only the development of Americanist archaeology but also how archaeology, in all its different guises, has come to be practiced in the United States. Further, I will pretend that you want this view to emanate from work that has been done in Missouri. And by the way, don't be annoyed because I deleted your favorite piece of work; remember, you asked for a short list.

I would start with Cyrus Thomas, whom I've always admired because of his use of the deductive approach in archaeology. He had an idea (through the influence of John Wesley Powell) about how things had operated in the past that was based on his reading of the evidence available up to that point. He reasoned that if his reading was correct—that the mounds had been constructed by the American Indians and not by an extinct race of mound builders—then he should find further evidence in unexplored sources (primarily as-yet-untouched mounds). If for some reason he hadn't found that evidence, I suspect he would have expanded his search. Then, at that point, if he hadn't found the evidence, I assume he would have said so (and probably would have been fired by Powell). I doubt he would have gone through all the contortions of someone such as Stephen Peet, who by the time Thomas published his final report (1894) saw the evidence for what it was and should have thrown in the towel on the mound-builder issue. However, Peet couldn't quite shake his preconceived notion that, as Lewis Henry Morgan had proposed, there was a nice, steady, orderly progression to cultural development. Thomas didn't destroy the notion of order, but he showed that there was a distinctly different way in which it had made itself manifest. I like the idea of a person's going against accepted dogma.

I also admire the way Nels Nelson handled the Jacobs Cavern mastodon engraving. His arguments against both its authenticity and the antiquity of deposits in the cavern are excellent examples of how to rebut propositions that spring out of sloppy fieldwork and intense speculation. In many ways, his arguments foreshadowed those made today against work that purportedly demonstrates the presence of humans in North America during any time earlier than the Pleistocene/Holocene boundary (see Meltzer 1991 for a summary). I would assign Nelson's papers to any introductory or graduate-level archaeology class as an example of how good science operates.

As an introduction to the myriad issues that confronted archaeologists in the 1940s, there is no better statement than what Phillips et al. (1951) had to say in *Archaeological Survey in the Lower Mississippi Alluvial Valley, 1940–1947*. As Dunnell (1985a) remarked, it is a landmark study. Their discussion of the prehistory of the Mississippi Valley is interesting in and of itself, but, as I pointed out in Chapter 5, the most interesting feature is the running commentary among Phillips, Ford, and Griffin as they attempt to bring order to the archaeological record. If you want a solid introduction to issues such as typology, seriation, and the like—especially an introduction that demonstrates that the issues are not as cut-and-dried as the textbooks indicate—then this is the book for you.

Likewise, I would urge you to explore thoroughly Wood et al.'s Pomme de Terre research in all its aspects, because it is an excellent example of how the inductive half of science works. Too often we train students (this certainly was the case in the 1960s) that deductive reasoning produces "good" science, while induction is for those who are interested only in mundane details. The new archaeologists who perpetuated this view somehow forgot that they were not born with the general propositions that they so eagerly sought to test but rather induced them from the empirical world of "facts" as they knew them—facts that others had derived by means of painstaking attention to detail. And few if any Missouri archaeologists ever paid as much attention to detail as Raymond Wood. Russell Graham's detailed examination of the Kimmswick bone beds is another excellent example of empirical research, in his case made all the more difficult because of the subject matter and its importance to American archaeologists.

Since it is one of the few examples in Missouri archaeology of formal testing of hypothetical implications, I suggest you examine Bruce Smith's work at Gypsy Joint, the small site in the Western Lowland that was excavated as part of the Powers Phase Project. As I pointed out in Chapter 6, formalized testing of the implications derived from hypotheses and propositions became standard practice in the late 1960s and early 1970s. What set Smith's (1978) work apart from similar studies in Americanist archaeology was that he actually did what he said he was going to do, and he did it with almost no polemic.

Some of the literature that emanated from the Cannon Reservoir Human Ecology Project, especially the summary volume on the prehistoric period (O'Brien, Warren, and Lewarch 1982), would give you a fairly accurate assessment of where cultural-resource management was in the late 1970s. You might also find the ecological approach that the project adopted of some interest.

As an introduction to the materials-science approach in archaeology, you should look at some of James Feathers's work on pottery from southeastern Missouri. More importantly, his work is an excellent rebuttal against the argument that the physics-of-artifacts approach is a cold, sterile exercise that has nothing to do with prehistoric human behavior. Grounded as it is in evolutionary theory, his work has *everything* to do with monitoring changes in specific human behaviors. If you are starting to develop the opinion that culture historians and artifact physicists have nothing in common, you should also take a careful look at Dunnell and Feathers's article (1991) "Late Woodland Manifestations of the Malden Plain, Southeast Missouri." This article, more than any other I can think of, should change your mind.

You of course must read Chapman's two-volume set, *The Archaeology of Missouri*. Unless you're intensely interested in the details of what was found where, just read it for what it tells you about the way he viewed the archaeological record. The volumes represent Chapman's final great vision of what the past must have been like, and they do it at a scale that will never be duplicated. Chapman can be justly criticized for his speculative approach to the archaeological record but not for his knowledge of that record.

There is another aspect of archaeology that you might want to look at, and it is one that, although not unique to the state, is exemplified in Missouri to a degree perhaps not equaled elsewhere. That aspect is the fact that nonprofessionals have made numerous contributions to our understanding of the past. Other states have had individuals who, although they carried no professional credentials, made outstanding contributions in the field, but Missouri has consistently produced a contingent of people who earned considerable respect for their accomplishments. I have tried to highlight some of their many accomplishments throughout the book, though I have tended to include to this point works that pertain only to Missouri.[6] I should point out here the contributions made by several nonprofessionals to the broader field of Americanist archaeology. People who quickly come to mind include Frank Magre, who worked with R. M. Adams; Leonard Blake (Figure 9.12), who became a nationally recognized authority on prehistoric corn and other domesticated plants (Blake 1981; Cutler and Blake 1973; see especially Voigt and Pearsall 1986); Allen Eichenberger (Figure 9.13), who became an expert at replicating artifacts in plastic and whose casts of Paleo-Indian material are in hundreds of research collections around the country;[7] Ted Hamilton (Figure 9.14), who became an internationally recognized authority on trade guns (Brain 1988; T. Hamilton 1960) and Native American bows (T. Hamilton 1982); and Ted's brother, Henry Hamilton (Figure 9.15), who, as I pointed out in Chapter 5, was a member of the prestigious Committee for the Recovery of Archaeological Remains created in 1945. Henry was a prolific writer who probably is best known for his work on tobacco pipes (H. W. Hamilton 1967; H. W. Hamilton and J. T. Hamilton 1972) and on copper artifacts from the Spiro site in eastern Oklahoma (H. W. Hamilton et al. 1974), which he coauthored with his wife, Jean Tyree Hamilton (Figure 9.15), and Eleanor Chapman.

This brief list of topics and publications should at least give you a picture of the development of Missouri archaeology, but the picture will sharpen the deeper into the subject you go. I hope by now you will agree that the subject is a fascinating one, full of colorful people and interesting issues. It definitely bears your closer inspection. You will, of course, form your own opinions about such things as explanation and interpretation, why archaeologists did what they did, and how they reached the conclusions they did. Don't take my opinions as anything more than what they are; read the primary literature yourself.

If I have learned one thing from this study, it is that at any point in the past it would have been difficult to predict where archaeology would be 20 years in the future. You might have been right some of the time, at least in a very general sense, but the field is so broad and has developed at a such a rapid rate that one's predictive accuracy would fall off dramatically when plotted against time. But there is one thing about which I am sure: 20, 50, 100 years down the road, archaeologists will still be haggling over what certain data mean, they will still be looking for the oldest this or that, and most of them will be interpreting

6. For an excellent discussion of the contributions made by nonprofessionals in the St. Louis area, see Pool 1989.

7. The master copies are in the National Museum of Natural History, Smithsonian Institution.

Figure 9.12. Leonard E. Blake, 1955.

Figure 9.13. J. Allen
Eichenberger lecturing at
Van Meter State Park, Saline
County, Missouri, ca. 1961.

Figure 9.14. Ted and Leone Hamilton, ca. 1961.

Figure 9.15. Henry and Jean Hamilton excavating at the Murphy site, Pemiscot County, Missouri, 1955.

Figure 9.16. Visitors at a University of Missouri archaeological field-school open house, Jakie Shelter, Barry County, Missouri, 1956 (photograph by Perry J. Morris).

the archaeological record. In other words, there is no reason to suspect that archaeologists in the future will not be engaged in the same argument in which our forebears a century ago were engaged and in which we are engaged today. And that, quite simply, is one long argument about the past.

Regardless of how we choose to formulate that argument, perhaps we should remember something else about archaeology—something that transcends differences in approach and that I assume underlies our common interest in the past. Griffin (1985b: 21) summarized this "something else" in an exchange he heard between A. R. Radcliffe-Brown, a British social anthropologist, and Alfred Kroeber:

I am reminded of a presentation given by Alfred Kroeber to anthropologists at the University of Chicago in the mid-1930s. . . . After Kroeber's talk there were a number of questions, and then Radcliffe-Brown took Kroeber to task for his interests in cultural history when he could be doing much more meaningful studies such as those Radcliffe-Brown did. He asked Kroeber "Why do you continue to do hypothetical reconstructions of cultural history?" Kroeber's reply was, "Because I enjoy it. Do you mind?"

There can be no doubt that most people enjoy knowing more about the past. They have a natural curiosity about what happened centuries and millennia ago, and they look to archaeologists to help them understand it (Figure 9.16). Most of us entered the profession because we have more than a passing interest in the past; like Kroeber, we enjoy doing archaeology, which is, after all, what got us hooked in the first place. However, I am not convinced that that enjoyment can be purchased with little or no regard for how we educate the public. I firmly believe that we have a responsibility to be honest about what archaeology can and cannot do with respect to answering questions about the past. If nothing else, I hope I have made you a bit more wary of some of the little stories you've undoubtedly heard about Missouri's prehistoric past.

REFERENCES

Abbott, C. C. 1872. The stone age in New Jersey. *The American Naturalist* 6:144–60, 199–229.

―――. 1876. The stone age in New Jersey. *Smithsonian Institution, Annual Report* (1875), 246–380.

―――. 1877. On the discovery of supposed Paleolithic implements from the glacial drift in the Valley of the Delaware River, near Trenton, New Jersey. *Tenth Annual Report of the Trustees of the Peabody Museum of American Archaeology and Ethnology* 2:30–43.

―――. 1881. *Primitive industry.* Salem, Mass.: Bates.

―――. 1888. On the antiquity of man in the Valley of the Delaware. *Proceedings of the Boston Society of Natural History* 23:424–26.

Adams, L. 1941. Rockhouse Cave. *The Missouri Archaeologist* 7(2):18–27.

―――. 1950. *The Table Rock Basin in Barry County, Missouri.* Missouri Archaeological Society, Memoir no. 1.

―――. 1958. Archaeological investigations of southwestern Missouri. *The Missouri Archaeologist* 20.

Adams, R. M. 1941. Archaeological investigations in Jefferson County, Missouri. *Transactions of the Academy of Science of St. Louis* 30(5).

―――. 1953. The Kimmswick bone bed. *The Missouri Archaeologist* 15(4):40–56.

Adams, R. M., and F. Magre. 1939. Archaeological surface survey of Jefferson County, Missouri. *The Missouri Archaeologist* 11(3–4):1–72.

Adams, R. M., F. Magre, and P. Munger. 1941. Archaeological surface survey of Ste. Genevieve County, Missouri. *The Missouri Archaeologist* 7(1):9–23.

Adams, R. M., and W. M. Walker. 1942. Archaeological surface survey of New Madrid County, Missouri. *The Missouri Archaeologist* 8(2):1–23.

Adams, R. McCormick. 1962. Agriculture and urban life in early southwestern Iran. *Science* 136:109–22.

―――. 1965. *Land behind Baghdad: A history of settlement on the Diyala Plains.* Chicago: University of Chicago Press.

Ahler, S. A. 1971. *Projectile point form and function at Rodgers Shelter, Missouri.* Missouri Archaeological Society, Research Series no. 8.

―――. 1973a. Post-Pleistocene depositional change at Rodgers Shelter. *Plains Anthropologist.* 18:1–26.

―――. 1973b. Chemical analysis of deposits at Rodgers Shelter. *Plains Anthropologist* 18:116–31.

―――. 1976. Sedimentary processes at Rodgers Shelter. In *Prehistoric man and his environments: A case study in the Ozark Highland,* ed. W. R. Wood and R. B. McMillan, 123–39. New York: Academic Press.

―――. 1979. Functional analysis of nonobsidian chipped stone artifacts: Terms, variables, and quantification. In *Lithic use-wear analysis,* ed. B. Hayden, 301–28. New York: Academic Press.

Ahler, S. A., and R. B. McMillan. 1976. Material culture at Rodgers Shelter: A reflection of past human activities. In *Prehistoric man and his environments: A case study in the*

493

Ozark Highland, ed. W. R. Wood and R. B. McMillan, 163–209. New York: Academic Press.

Allison, V. C. 1924. Quaternic and tertic chronology. *The Pan-American Geologist* 42:199–217.

————. 1926. *The antiquity of the deposits in Jacob's Cavern.* American Museum of Natural History, Anthropological Papers 19:293–335.

————. 1928. In re Jacob's Cavern. *American Anthropologist* 30:544–49.

Ammerman, A. J. 1985. Plow-zone experiments in Calabria, Italy. *Journal of Field Archaeology* 12:33–40.

Ammerman, A. J., and M. W. Feldman. 1978. Replicated collection of site surfaces. *American Antiquity* 43:734–40.

Anderson, D. C. 1985. Reburial: Is it reasonable? *Archaeology* 35(5):48–51.

Andrews, E. 1875. Dr. Koch and the Missouri mastodon. *American Journal of Science and Arts* 110:32–34.

Angus, C. 1976. Descriptive analysis of materials recovered from the Murphy site (23RA224) and sites 23RA202 and 23RA204. In *Cannon Reservoir Archaeological Project Report,* Appendix 3, part 2, ed. D. R. Henning. University of Nebraska, Department of Anthropology, Technical Report no. 76–05.

————. 1977. The Shinn site (23MN222). In *Cannon Reservoir Archaeological Project Report,* vol. 1, ed. D. R. Henning. University of Nebraska, Department of Anthropology, Technical Report no. 77–02.

Anonymous. 1863. The antiquity of man. *Westminster Review* 79:517–51.

————. 1943. The first archaeological conference on the Woodland pattern. *American Antiquity* 8:392–400.

————. 1964. Excavation of a Baytown period house at the Hoecake site. *Missouri Archaeological Society Newsletter* no. 179:2.

Antevs, E. 1948. Climatic changes and pre-white man. Vol. 3, The Great Basin, with emphasis on glacial and postglacial times. *University of Utah, Bulletin* 38:168–91.

————. 1950. Postglacial climatic history of the Great Plains and dating the records of man. In *Proceedings of the Sixth Plains Archaeological Conference, 1948.* University of Utah, Anthropological Papers 11, 46–50.

Arnet, C. 1970. The Constitution and the custody law. *The Indian Historian* 3(2):11–12.

Asch, D. L. 1976. *The Middle Woodland population of the lower Illinois Valley: A study in paleodemographic methods.* Northwestern University Archeological Program, Scientific Papers no. 1.

Asch, D. L., and N. B. Asch. 1978. The economic potential of *Iva annua* and its prehistoric importance in the lower Illinois River valley. In *The nature and status of ethnobotany,* ed. R. I. Ford, 300–341. University of Michigan, Museum of Anthropology, Anthropological Papers no. 67.

————. 1985a. Prehistoric plant cultivation in west-central Illinois. In *Prehistoric food production in North America,* ed. R. I. Ford, 149–203. University of Michigan, Museum of Anthropology, Anthropological Papers no. 75.

————. 1985b. Archeobotany. In *Smiling Dan: Structure and function at a Middle Woodland settlement in the lower Illinois Valley,* ed. B. D. Stafford and M. B. Sant, 327–401. Center for American Archeology, Kampsville Archeological Center, Research Series no. 2.

Asch, D. L., K. B. Farnsworth, and N. B. Asch. 1979. Woodland subsistence and settlement in west central Illinois. In *Hopewell archaeology: The Chillicothe Conference*, ed. D. S. Brose and N. Greber, 80–85. Kent, Ohio: Kent State University Press.

Asch, N. B., and D. L. Asch. 1981. Archeobotany of Newbridge, Carlin, and Weitzer sites—the White Hall component. In *Faunal exploitation and resource selection*, by B. W. Styles, 275–91. Northwestern University Archeological Program, Scientific Papers no. 3.

Ascher, R. 1961. Analogy in archaeological interpretation. *Southwestern Journal of Anthropology* 17:317–25.

Aten, L. E. 1974. Comments. In *Proceedings of the 1974 Cultural Resource Management Conference*, ed. W. D. Lipe and A. J. Lindsay Jr., 93–97. Museum of Northern Arizona, Technical Series no. 14.

Atwater, C. 1820. Description of the antiquities discovered in the state of Ohio and other western states. *Transactions and Collections of the American Antiquarian Society* 1:105–267.

———. 1833. Description of the antiquities discovered in the western country. In *The writings of Caleb Atwater*, 1–165. Columbus, Ohio: published by the author.

Babbitt, F. E. 1884a. Exhibition and description of some paleolithic quartz implements from central Minnesota. *American Association for the Advancement of Science, Proceedings* 33:593–99.

———. 1884b. Vestiges of glacial man in Minnesota. *The American Naturalist* 18:594–615, 697–708.

Bacon, W. S., and W. J. Miller. 1957. Notes on the excavation of a burial area in northeastern Missouri. *The Missouri Archaeologist* 19:19–33.

Baerreis, D. A. 1939. Two new cultures in Delaware County, Oklahoma. *The Oklahoma Prehistorian* 2:2–5.

———. 1941. Recent developments in Oklahoma archaeology. *Oklahoma Academy of Science, Proceedings* 21:125–26.

———. 1953. Woodland pottery of northeastern Oklahoma. In *Prehistoric pottery of eastern United States*, ed. J. B. Griffin, 4–53. Ann Arbor: University of Michigan, Museum of Anthropology.

Baerreis, D. A., and R. A. Bryson. 1965. Climatic episodes and the dating of the Mississippian cultures. *The Wisconsin Archaeologist* 46:203–20.

———, eds. 1967. *Climatic change and the Mill Creek culture of Iowa*. University of Wisconsin–Madison, Archives of Archaeology no. 29.

Baerreis, D. A., R. A. Bryson, and J. E. Kutzbach. 1976. Climate and culture in the western Great Lakes region. *Midcontinental Journal of Archaeology* 1:39–57.

Baerreis, D. A., and J. Theler. 1982. Habitat and climatic interpretation from terrestrial gastropods at Rodgers Shelter. In *Holocene adaptations within the lower Pomme de Terre River valley, Missouri*, ed. M. Kay, 177–98. Report submitted to the U.S. Army Corps of Engineers, Kansas City District.

Baker, C. M. 1978. The size effect: An explanation of variability in surface artifact assemblage content. *American Antiquity* 43:288–93.

Baker, C. M., and M. B. Schiffer. 1975. Archeological evidence for the size effect. In *Arkansas Eastman Archeological Project*, by C. M. Baker, 117–22. Arkansas Archeological Survey, Research Report no. 6.

Bareis, C. J., and J. W. Porter, eds. 1984. *American Bottom archaeology: A summary of the FAI-270 Project contribution to the culture history of the Mississippi River valley*. Urbana: University of Illinois Press.

Barnes, M. R., A. K. Briggs, and J. J. Nielsen. 1980. A response to Raab and Klinger on archeological site significance. *American Antiquity* 45:551–53.

Beck, L. C. 1823. *A gazetteer of the states of Illinois and Missouri.* Albany, N.Y.: Webster.

Beckwith, T. 1887. Mounds in Missouri. *The American Antiquarian* 9:228–32.

Begg, C., and T. J. Riley. 1990. Petrographic analysis of Marion thick ceramic sherds from the Plum Island site, Illinois. *Midcontinental Journal of Archaeology* 15:250–64.

Bell, R. E. 1958. Guide to the identification of certain American Indian projectile points. *Oklahoma Anthropological Society, Special Bulletin* no. 1.

————. 1960. Guide to the identification of certain American Indian projectile points. *Oklahoma Anthropological Society, Special Bulletin* no. 2.

Bell, R. E., and D. A. Baerreis. 1951. A survey of Oklahoma archaeology. *Texas Archeological and Paleontological Society, Bulletin* 22:1–100.

Bell, R. E., and R. S. Hall. 1953. Selected projectile point types of the United States. *Oklahoma Anthropological Society Bulletin* 1, 1–16.

Bennett, J. W. 1943. Recent developments in the functional interpretation of archaeological data. *American Antiquity* 9:208–19.

Bennett, J. W., and M. Maxwell. 1942. Archaeological horizons in southern Illinois. *Transactions of the Illinois State Academy of Science* 35:50.

Berry, B. 1975. Looking backward. *Missouri Archaeological Society Newsletter* no. 296:1–8.

Berry, B., and C. Chapman. 1942. An Oneota site in Missouri. *American Antiquity* 7:290–325.

Berry, B., J. E. Wrench, C. Chapman, and W. Seitz. 1938. Archaeological investigations in Boone County, Missouri. *The Missouri Archaeologist* 4(3).

Berry, J. B., J. E. Wrench, and C. H. Chapman. 1940. The archaeology of Wayne County. *The Missouri Archaeologist* 6(1).

Bettinger, R. L. 1975. The surface archaeology of Owens Valley, eastern California: Prehistoric man–land relationships in the Great Basin. Ph.D. diss., Department of Anthropology, University of California, Riverside.

Binford, L. R. 1962a. Archaeology as anthropology. *American Antiquity* 28:217–25.

————. 1962b. *Archaeological investigations in the Carlyle Reservoir, Clinton County, Illinois, 1962.* Southern Illinois University Museum, Archaeological Salvage Report no. 17.

————. 1964. A consideration of archaeological research design. *American Antiquity* 29:425–41.

————. 1965. Archaeological systematics and the study of cultural process. *American Antiquity* 31:203–10.

————. 1978. *Nunamiut ethnoarchaeology.* New York: Academic Press.

————. 1985. "Brand X" versus the recommended product. *American Antiquity* 50:580–90.

————. 1992. Seeing the present and interpreting the past—and keeping things straight. In *Space, time, and archaeological landscapes,* ed. J. Rossignol and L. Wandsnider, 43–59. New York: Plenum Press.

Binford, L. R., S. R. Binford, R. Whallon, and M. A. Hardin. 1970. *Archaeology at Hatchery West, Carlyle, Illinois.* Society for American Archaeology Memoirs no. 24.

Black, T. K., III. 1979. *The biological and social analyses of a Mississippian cemetery from southeast Missouri: The Turner site, 23BU21A.* University of Michigan, Museum of Anthropology, Anthropological Papers no. 68.

Blake, L. W. 1942. A Hopewell-like site near St. Louis. *The Missouri Archaeologist* 8(1):2–7.

————. 1981. Early acceptance of watermelon by Indians of the United States. *Journal of Ethnobiology* 1:193–99.

Blanton, R. E. 1972. *Prehistoric settlement patterns in the Ixtapalapa Peninsula region, Mexico.* Pennsylvania State University, Occasional Papers in Anthropology no. 6.

————. 1978. *Monte Albán: Settlement patterns at the ancient Zapotec capital.* New York: Academic Press.

Blanton, R. E., S. Kowalewski, G. Feinman, and J. Appel. 1982. *Monte Albán's hinterland. Part I: The prehispanic settlement patterns of the central and southern parts of the Valley of Oaxaca, Mexico.* University of Michigan, Museum of Anthropology Memoirs no. 15.

Bleed, P., and M. Meier. 1980. An objective test of the effects of heat treatment of flakeable stone. *American Antiquity* 45:502–7.

Boas, F. 1896. The limitations of the comparative method of anthropology. *Science* 4:901–8.

Bohannan, P., and M. Glazer. 1988. *High points in anthropology.* 2d ed. New York: McGraw-Hill.

Borchert, J. R. 1950. The climate of the central North American grassland. *Annals of the Association of American Geographers* 40:1–39.

Boucher de Perthes, J. 1847. *Antiquités celtiques et antédiluviennes.* Vol. 1, *Mémoire sur l'industrie primitive et les arts à leur origine.* Paris: Treuttel and Wurtz.

Bozell, J. R., and R. E. Warren. 1982. Analysis of vertebrate remains. In *The Cannon Reservoir Human Ecology Project: An archaeological study of cultural adaptations in the southern Prairie Peninsula,* ed. M. J. O'Brien, R. E. Warren, and D. E. Lewarch, 171–95. New York: Academic Press.

Brackenridge, G. R. 1979. The impact of climatic change on floodplain sedimentation, soil formation, and eolian activity in southern Missouri. Master's thesis, Department of Geological Sciences, University of Arizona.

————. 1981. Late Quaternary floodplain sedimentation along the Pomme de Terre River, southern Missouri. *Quaternary Research* 15:62–76.

Brackenridge, H. M. 1814. *Views of Louisiana; together with a journal of a voyage up the Missouri River, in 1811.* Pittsburgh: Cramer, Spear and Eichbaum.

Bradham, J. R. 1963. The Simmons mound, 23CE104, a rock and earth fill mound in Cedar County, Missouri. *The Missouri Archaeologist* 25:69–85.

Braidwood, R. J. 1958. Near eastern prehistory. *Science* 127:1419–30.

————. 1960. *Excavations in the Plains of Antioch, an archeological survey.* University of Chicago, Oriental Institute, Publication no. 61.

Brain, J. P. 1988. *Tunica archaeology.* Harvard University, Peabody Museum of Archaeology and Ethnology, Papers 78.

Braun, D. P. 1977. Middle Woodland–early Late Woodland social change in the prehistoric central midwestern U.S. Ph.D. diss., Department of Anthropology, University of Michigan.

————. 1979. Illinois Hopewell burial practices and social organizations: A reexamination of the Klunk-Gibson mound group. In *Hopewell archaeology: The Chillicothe Conference,* ed. D. S. Brose and N. Greber, 66–79. Kent, Ohio: Kent State University Press.

————. 1981. A critique of some recent North American mortuary studies. *American Antiquity* 46:398–416.

————. 1982. Radiographic analysis of temper in ceramic vessels: Goals and initial methods. *Journal of Field Archaeology* 9:183–92.

———. 1983. Pots as tools. In *Archaeological hammers and theories,* ed. J. Moore and A. Keene, 107–34. New York: Academic Press.

———. 1985a. Absolute seriation: A time-series approach. In *For concordance in archaeological analysis: Bridging data structure, quantitative technique, and theory,* ed. C. Carr, 509–39. Kansas City: Westport.

———. 1985b. Ceramic decorative diversity and Illinois Woodland regional integration. In *Decoding prehistoric ceramics,* ed. B. A. Nelson, 128–53. Carbondale: Southern Illinois University Press.

———. 1987. Coevolution of sedentism, pottery technology, and horticulture in the central Midwest, 200 B.C.–A.D. 600. In *Emergent horticultural economies of the Eastern Woodlands,* ed. W. F. Keegan, 153–81. Southern Illinois University at Carbondale, Center for Archaeological Investigations, Occasional Paper no. 7.

Braun, D. P., and S. Plog. 1982. Evolution of "tribal" networks: Theory and prehistoric North American evidence. *American Antiquity* 47:504–25.

Bray, R. T. 1956. The culture-complexes and sequence at the Rice site (23SN200), Stone County, Missouri. *The Missouri Archaeologist* 18(1–2):46–134.

———. 1957. Lander Shelter I, 23SN189, Stone County, Missouri. *The Missouri Archaeologist* 19(1–2):22–51.

———. 1960. Standlee Shelter I, 23BY386. In *Archaeological investigations in the Table Rock Reservoir,* by C. H. Chapman and others, 485–532. Report submitted to the National Park Service, Lincoln, Neb.

———. 1961. The Missouri Indian tribe in archaeology and history. *Missouri Historical Review* 55:213–25.

———. 1963a. The Button cairn, 23HI208, Hickory County, Missouri. *The Missouri Archaeologist* 25:41–54.

———. 1963b. Site 23HI30b, Indian Hill mound. *The Missouri Archaeologist* 25:55–61.

———. 1978. European trade goods from the Utz site and the search for Fort Orleans. *The Missouri Archaeologist* 39:1–72.

———. 1991. The Utz site: An Oneota village in central Missouri. *The Missouri Archaeologist* 52.

Breternitz, D. A., C. K. Robinson, and G. T. Gross, comps. 1986. *Dolores Archaeological Program,* final synthetic report. Report submitted to the Bureau of Reclamation, Denver.

Brew, J. O. 1968. Foreword to *Bibliography of salvage archeology in the United States,* comp. J. E. Petsche. Smithsonian Institution, Publications in Salvage Archeology, River Basin Surveys no. 10:1–11.

Brinton, D. G. 1881. The probable nationality of the "mound builders." *The American Antiquarian and Oriental Journal* 4:9–18.

Broadhead, G. C. 1880a. Prehistoric evidences in Missouri. *Smithsonian Institution, Annual Report* (1879), 350–59.

———. 1880b. Prehistoric remains in Missouri. *Missouri Historical Society Collections* 1(3):3–4.

———. 1881. The mastodon. *Kansas City Review of Science and Industry* 4:519–21.

Bronitsky, G., and R. Hamer. 1986. Experiments in ceramic technology: The effects of various tempering materials on impact and thermal-shock resistance. *American Antiquity* 51:89–101.

Brooks, R. L. 1979. Prehistoric find spots, localities, and archaeological context: A cautionary note from Kentucky. *Tennessee Anthropologist* 4:167–74.

Brose, D. S. 1985. Good enough for government work? A study in grey archaeology. *American Anthropologist* 87:37–77.

Browman, D. L. 1978. The "Knockers": St. Louis archaeologists from 1904–1921. *Missouri Archaeological Society Newsletter* no. 319:1–6.

———. 1981. Isotopic discrimination and correction factors in radiocarbon dating. In *Advances in archaeological method and theory,* vol. 4, ed. M. B. Schiffer, 241–95. New York: Academic Press.

Brown, I. W. 1990. Cyrus Thomas and the mound explorations of the Bureau of Ethnology. In *Edward Palmer's Arkansaw mounds,* ed. M. D. Jeter, 23–27. Fayetteville: University of Arkansas Press.

Brown, J. A. 1983. Summary. In *Archaic hunters and gatherers in the American Midwest,* ed. J. L. Phillips and J. A. Brown, 5–10. New York: Academic Press.

———. 1984. *Prehistoric southern Ozark marginality: A myth exposed.* Missouri Archaeological Society, Special Publication no. 6.

Brugman, R. B. 1980. Postglacial diatom stratigraphy of Kirchner Marsh, Minnesota. *Quaternary Research* 13:133–46.

Bryan, K. 1950. The geology of Ventana Cave. In *The stratigraphy and archaeology of Ventana Cave, Arizona,* ed. E. W. Haury, 75–126. Tucson: University of Arizona Press.

Bryson, R. A. 1966. Airmasses, streamlines, and the boreal forest. *Geographical Bulletin* 8:228–69.

Bryson, R. A., D. A. Baerreis, and W. M. Wendland. 1970. The character of late-glacial and post-glacial climatic changes. In *Pleistocene and recent environments of the central Great Plains,* ed. W. Dort Jr. and J. K. Jones Jr., 53–74. Lawrence: University Press of Kansas.

Bryson, R. A., and W. M. Wendland. 1967. Tentative climatic patterns for some late glacial and post-glacial episodes in central North America. In *Life, land and water,* ed. W. J. Mayer-Oakes, 271–98. Winnipeg: University of Manitoba Press.

Buckingham, J. S. 1842. *Eastern and western states of America.* Vol. 3. London: Fisher.

Buikstra, J. E. 1977. Biocultural dimensions of archaeological study: A regional perspective. In *Biocultural adaptation in prehistoric America,* ed. R. L. Blakely, 67–84. Southern Anthropological Society, Proceedings 11.

———. 1979. Contributions of physical anthropologists to the concept of Hopewell: A historical perspective. In *Hopewell archaeology: The Chillicothe Conference,* ed. D. S. Brose and N. Greber, 220–33. Kent, Ohio: Kent State University Press.

Buikstra, J. E., and C. C. Gordon. 1981. The study and restudy of human skeletal series: The importance of long-term curation. *Annals of the New York Academy of Sciences* 376:449–66.

Buikstra, J. E., L. Koningsberg, and J. Bullington. 1986. Fertility and the development of agriculture in the prehistoric Midwest. *American Antiquity* 51:528–46.

Bushnell, D. I., Jr. 1904a. *The Cahokia and surrounding mound groups.* Harvard University, Peabody Museum of American Archaeology and Ethnology, Papers 3(1).

———. 1904b. Archaeology of the Ozark region of Missouri. *American Anthropologist* 6:294–98.

———. 1907. Primitive salt making in the Mississippi Valley I. *Man* 7:17–21.

———. 1908. Primitive salt making in the Mississippi Valley II. *Man* 8:65–70.

———. 1914. Archaeological investigations in Ste. Genevieve County, Missouri. *United States National Museum, Proceedings* 46:641–68.

————. 1915. Fragmentary textiles from Ozark caves. *Washington Academy of Sciences, Journal* 5:318–23.

Butzer, K. W. 1977. *Geomorphology of the lower Illinois Valley as a spatial-temporal context for the Koster Archaic site.* Illinois State Museum, Reports of Investigations no. 34.

————. 1978. Changing Holocene environments at the Koster site: A geo-archaeological perspective. *American Antiquity* 43:408–13.

Byers, D. S., ed. 1967. *The prehistory of the Tehuacán Valley.* Vol. 1, *Environment and subsistence.* Austin: University of Texas Press.

Byers, D. S., F.-C. Cole, and W. C. McKern. 1943. The first archaeological conference on the Woodland pattern. *American Antiquity* 8:392–400.

Calabrese, F. A., R. E. Pangborn, and R. J. Young. 1969. *Two village sites in southwestern Missouri: A lithic analysis.* Missouri Archaeological Society, Research Series no. 7.

Caldwell, J. R. 1958. *Trend and tradition in the prehistory of the eastern United States.* American Anthropological Association, Memoir no. 88.

————. 1964. Interaction spheres in prehistory. In *Hopewellian studies,* ed. J. R. Caldwell and R. L. Hall, 133–43. Illinois State Museum, Scientific Papers no. 12.

Camilli, E. L. 1988. Interpreting long-term land-use patterns from archaeological landscapes. *American Archeology* 7:57–66.

Canouts, V., assembler 1972. *An archaeological survey of the Santa Rosa Wash Project.* Tucson: Arizona State Museum.

Carr, C., and D. W. G. Sears. 1985. Toward an analysis of the exchange of meteoric iron in the Middle Woodland. *Southeastern Archaeology* 4:79–92.

Casteel, R. W. 1980. National Science Foundation funding of domestic archaeology in the United States: Where the money ain't. *American Antiquity* 45:170–80.

Chang, K. C. 1962. A typology of settlement and community patterns in some circumpolar societies. *Arctic Anthropology* 1:28–41.

Chapman, C. H. 1935. Stone age man of Crawford County. *Missouri Resources Museum Bulletin* 16:1–9.

————. 1941. Horse bones in an Indian mound. *The Missouri Archaeologist* 7(1):2–8.

————. 1946. A preliminary survey of Missouri archaeology (part 1): Historic Indian tribes. *The Missouri Archaeologist* 10:1–56.

————. 1947. A preliminary survey of Missouri archaeology (part 2): Middle Mississippi and Hopewellian cultures. *The Missouri Archaeologist* 10:57–94.

————. 1948a. A preliminary survey of Missouri archaeology (part 3): Woodland cultures and the Ozark bluff dwellers. *The Missouri Archaeologist* 10:95–132.

————. 1948b. A preliminary survey of Missouri archaeology (part 4): Ancient cultures and sequence. *The Missouri Archaeologist* 10:133–64.

————. 1952. Culture sequence in the lower Missouri Valley. In *Archeology of eastern United States,* ed. J. B. Griffin, 139–51. Chicago: University of Chicago Press.

————. 1954. Preliminary salvage archaeology in the Pomme de Terre Reservoir, Missouri. *The Missouri Archaeologist* 16(3–4).

————. 1956. A resume of Table Rock archaeological investigations. *The Missouri Archaeologist* 18(1–2):15–45.

————. 1957. Open house at Jakie Shelter. In *A report of progress, archaeological research by the University of Missouri, 1955–1956,* ed. C. H. Chapman, 18–20. Missouri Archaeological Society, Special Publication no. 1.

————. 1959. The Little Osage and Missouri Indian village sites, ca. 1727–1777 A.D. *The Missouri Archaeologist* 21.

————. 1960a. Excavations at Jakie Shelter, 23BY388. In *Archaeological investigations in* the *Table Rock Reservoir area,* comp. C. H. Chapman, 1116–30. Report submitted to the National Park Service, Lincoln, Neb.

————. 1960b. The Cantwell site II, 23SN137. In *Archaeological investigations in the Table Rock Reservoir area,* comp. C. H. Chapman, 184–91. Report submitted to the National Park Service, Lincoln, Neb.

————. 1960c. *Archaeological investigations in the Table Rock Reservoir area, Missouri,* comp. C. H. Chapman. Report submitted to the National Park Service, Lincoln, Neb.

————. 1961. Preface. *The Missouri Archaeologist* 23:iii–v.

————. 1962. Preface to archaeological salvage in Joanna Reservoir area. In *Archaeological investigations in the Joanna Reservoir area, Missouri,* by C. H. Chapman, D. P. Heldman, and D. R. Henning, iii–vi. Report submitted to the National Park Service, Omaha.

————. 1965. *Preliminary archaeological investigations in the Kaysinger Bluff Reservoir area.* Report submitted to the National Park Service, Lincoln, Neb.

————. 1974. The aboriginal use and occupancy of lands west of the Mississippi River by the Osage Indian tribe, and village locations and hunting territories of the Osage from time immemorial to 1808 A.D. In *Osage Indians,* vol. 4, ed. D. A. Horr, 173–249. New York: Garland Press.

————. 1975. *The archaeology of Missouri, I.* Columbia: University of Missouri Press.

————. 1980. *The archaeology of Missouri, II.* Columbia: University of Missouri Press.

————. 1985a. The amateur archaeological society: A Missouri example. *American Antiquity* 50:241–48.

————, ed. 1985b. *Osage and Missouri Indian life cultural change: 1675–1825.* Report submitted to the National Endowment for the Humanities.

Chapman, C. H., and L. O. Anderson. 1955. The Campbell site: A late Mississippi town site and cemetery in southeast Missouri. *The Missouri Archaeologist* 17.

Chapman, C. H., and R. T. Bray. 1960. Vaughn 1, 23SN203. In *Archaeological investigations in the Table Rock Reservoir area, Missouri,* comp. C. H. Chapman, 268–300. Report submitted to the National Park Service, Lincoln, Neb.

Chapman, C. H., J. Cottier, D. Denman, D. Evans, D. Harvey, M. Reagan, B. Rope, M. Southard, and G. Waselkov. 1977. Investigation and comparison of two fortified Mississippi tradition archaeological sites in southeast Missouri: A preliminary comparison. *The Missouri Archaeologist* 38.

Chapman, C. H., A. Grimshaw, W. Klippel, R. B. McMillan, J. Mori, R. E. Pangborn, W. E. Sudderth, and R. L. McNair. 1965. *Preliminary archaeological investigations in the Kaysinger Bluff Reservoir area,* part 2. Report submitted to the National Park Service, Lincoln, Neb.

Chapman, C. H., and D. R. Henning. 1960. *Salvage archaeology in the Joanna Reservoir, Missouri.* Report submitted to the National Park Service, Lincoln, Neb.

Chapman, C. H., T. J. Maxwell Jr., and E. Kozlovich. 1951. A preliminary archaeological survey of the Table Rock Reservoir area, Stone County, Missouri. *The Missouri Archaeologist* 13(2).

Chapman, C. H., and R. E. Pangborn. 1962. The Broyles site, 23CE123. In *A preliminary investigation of the Stockton Reservoir,* by C. H. Chapman, M. J. Powell, J. R. Bradham, and R. E. Pangborn, 98–140. Report submitted to the National Park Service, Omaha.

————. 1965. The Brounlee Shelter, 23SR103. In *Preliminary archaeological investigations in the Kaysinger Bluff Reservoir area,* comp. C. H. Chapman, 413–48. Report submitted to the National Park Service, Omaha.

Chapman, C. H., M. J. Powell, J. R. Bradham, and R. E. Pangborn. 1962. *A preliminary investigation of the Stockton Reservoir.* Report submitted to the National Park Service, Omaha.

———. 1963. *Archaeological investigations in the Stockton Reservoir: 1962.* Report submitted to the National Park Service, Omaha.

Chapman, E. F. 1953. How to draw artifacts. *The Missouri Archaeologist* 15(1–2):78–83.

Childe, V. G. 1946. Archaeology and anthropology. *Southwestern Journal of Anthropology* 2:243–51.

Chomko, S. A. 1976. *The Phillips Spring site, 23HI216: Harry S. Truman Reservoir, Missouri.* Report submitted to the National Park Service, Denver.

———. 1978. Phillips Spring, 23HI216: A multicomponent site in the western Missouri Ozarks. *Plains Anthropologist* 23:235–55.

———. 1983. *Cultural resources survey, Harry S. Truman Dam and Reservoir Project.* Vol. 7, *Archeological test excavations in the Harry S. Truman Reservoir, Missouri: 1975.* Report submitted to the U.S. Army Corps of Engineers, Kansas City District.

Chomko, S. A., and G. W. Crawford. 1978. Plant husbandry in prehistoric eastern North America: New evidence for its development. *American Antiquity* 43:405–8.

Clark, G. 1970. *Aspects of prehistory.* Berkeley: University of California Press.

Claypole, E. W. 1896. Human relics in the drift of Ohio. *The American Geologist* 18:302.

Cobb, C. R. 1988. Mill Creek chert biface production: Mississippian political economy in Illinois. Ph.D. diss., Department of Anthropology, Southern Illinois University, Carbondale.

———. 1989. An appraisal of the role of Mill Creek chert hoes in Mississippian exchange systems. *Southeastern Archaeology* 8:72–92.

Cole, F.-C., and T. Deuel. 1937. *Rediscovering Illinois: Archaeological explorations in and around Fulton County.* Chicago: University of Chicago Press.

Cole, K. W. 1964. The Popke site (23MN302). In *Archaeological investigations, Joanna Reservoir, Missouri,* by D. R. Henning, A. E. Henning, and K. W. Cole, 1–23. Report submitted to the National Park Service, Omaha.

Colton, H. S. 1953. Potsherds. *Museum of Northern Arizona, Bulletin* 25.

Conant, A. J. 1877. The mounds and their builders, or Traces of prehistoric man in Missouri. In *The Commonwealth of Missouri,* ed. C. R. Barns, 1–122. St. Louis: Barns.

———. 1878. Archaeology of Missouri. *Transactions of the Academy of Science of St. Louis* 3:353–68.

———. 1879a. The mounds and their builders, or Traces of pre-historic man in Missouri. In *Switzler's illustrated history of Missouri, from 1541 to 1877,* 1–122. St. Louis: Barns.

———. 1879b. *Footprints of vanished races in the Mississippi Valley.* St. Louis: no publisher.

Conkey, M. W., and J. M. Gero. 1991. *Engendering archaeology: Women and prehistory.* Oxford: Blackwell.

Cook, D. C. 1976. Pathological state and disease process in Illinois Woodland populations: An epidemiological approach. Ph.D. diss., Department of Anthropology, University of Chicago.

———. 1979. Subsistence base and health in prehistoric Illinois Valley: Evidence from the human skeleton. *Medical Anthropology* 3:109–24.

Cook, D. C., and J. E. Buikstra. 1979. Health and differential survival in prehistoric populations: Prenatal dental defects. *American Journal of Physical Anthropology* 51:649–64.

Corbett, J. M. 1961. River basin salvage in the United States. *Archaeology* 14:236–40.

Cottier, J. W. 1977. An area archaeological construction. *The Missouri Archaeologist* 38:49–69.

Crampton, D. B. 1983. Phase I cultural resources survey and phase II archaeological testing for the Route 79 Old Monroe relocation, Lincoln/St. Charles counties. Report on file, Missouri Highway and Transportation Department, Jefferson City.

Cressman, L. S. 1942. *Archaeological researches in the northern Great Basin.* Carnegie Institution of Washington, Publication no. 538.

———. 1960. Cultural sequences at The Dalles, Oregon: A contribution to Pacific Northwest prehistory. *Transactions of the American Philosophical Society* 50(10).

Cresson, H. T. 1890a. Early man in the Delaware Valley. *Proceedings of the Boston Society of Natural History* 24:141–50.

———. 1890b. Remarks upon a chipped implement, found in modified drift on the East Fork of the White River, Jackson County, Indiana. *Proceedings of the Boston Society of Natural History* 24:150–52.

Croswell, C. 1878. Mound explorations in southeastern Missouri. *Transactions of the Academy of Science of St. Louis* 3:531–38.

Curry, M. 1979. Cataloging procedures and analytic techniques. In *Cannon Reservoir Human Ecology Project: A regional approach to cultural continuity and change,* ed. M. J. O'Brien and R. E. Warren, 203–23. University of Nebraska, Department of Anthropology, Technical Report no. 79–14.

Curry, M., M. J. O'Brien, and M. K. Trimble. 1985. The classification of pointed, hafted bifaces. In Archaeology of the central Salt River valley: An overview of the prehistoric occupation, by M. J. O'Brien. *The Missouri Archaeologist* 46:77–189.

Cutler, H. C., and L. W. Blake. 1973. *Plants from archaeological sites east of the Rockies.* St. Louis: Missouri Botanical Garden.

Dall, W. H. 1877. On succession in the shell-heaps of the Aleutian Islands. *U.S. Department of the Interior, Contributions to North American Ethnology* 1:41–91.

Damon, P. E., C. W. Ferguson, A. Long, and E. I. Wallick. 1974. Dendrochronologic calibration of the radiocarbon time scale. *American Antiquity* 39:350–66.

Dana, J. D. 1875. On Dr. Koch's evidence with regard to contemporaneity of man and the mastodon in Missouri. *American Journal of Science and Arts* 109:335–45.

Dancey, W. S. 1973. Prehistoric land use and settlement patterns in the Priest Rapids area, Washington. Ph.D. diss., Department of Anthropology, University of Washington.

———. 1974. The archeological survey: A reorientation. *Man in the Northeast* 8:98–112.

———. 1976. Riverine period settlement and land use pattern in the Priest Rapids area, central Washington. *Northwest Anthropological Research Notes* 10:147–60.

Daniel, G. 1981. Introduction: The necessity for an historical approach to archaeology. In *Towards a history of archaeology,* ed. G. Daniel, 9–13. London: Thames and Hudson.

Darrah, W. 1951. *Powell of the Colorado.* Princeton: Princeton University Press.

Davis, E. L. 1975. The "exposed archaeology" of China Lake, California. *American Antiquity* 40:39–53.

DeBoer, W. R., and D. W. Lathrap. 1979. The making and breaking of Shipibo-Conibo ceramics. In *Implications of ethnography for archaeology,* ed. C. Kramer, 102–38. New York: Columbia University Press.

Deevey, E. S., and R. F. Flint. 1957. Postglacial Hypsithermal interval. *Science* 125:182–84.

de Hass, W. 1869a. Archaeology of the Mississippi Valley. *American Association for the Advancement of Science, Proceedings* 17:288–302.

———. 1869b. Report on archaeology and ethnology. *American Association for the Advancement of Science, Proceedings* 17:303–4.

———. 1881a. Progress of archaeologic research in the United States. In *Abstract of transactions of the Anthropological Society of Washington*, ed. J. W. Powell, 9. Washington, D.C.: Anthropological Society of Washington.

———. 1881b. The mound-builders: An inquiry into their assumed southern origin. In *Abstract of transactions of the Anthropological Society of Washington*, ed. J. W. Powell, 55. Washington, D.C.: Anthropological Society of Washington.

Dellinger, S. C. 1932. The bluff shelters of Arkansas. In *Conference on southern prehistory*. Washington, D.C.: National Research Council.

———. 1936. Baby cradles of the Ozark bluff dwellers. *American Antiquity* 1:197–214.

Dellinger, S. C., and S. D. Dickinson. 1942. Pottery from the Ozark bluff shelters. *American Antiquity* 7:276–89.

Denny, S. 1964. A re-evaluation of the Boone Focus: A Late Woodland manifestation in central Missouri. Master's thesis, Department of Anthropology, University of Missouri–Columbia.

Deuel, T. 1935. Basic cultures of the Mississippi Valley. *American Anthropologist* 37:429–45.

———. 1937. The application of a classification method to Mississippi Valley archaeology. Appendix I in *Rediscovering Illinois: Archaeological explorations in and around Fulton County*, by F.-C. Cole and T. Deuel, 207–23. Chicago: University of Chicago Press.

Dexter, R. W. 1966. Putnam's problems popularizing anthropology. *American Scientist* 54:315–32.

Dickeson, M. W. 1846. Report at meeting of October 6, 1846. *Proceedings of the Academy of Natural Sciences of Philadelphia*, 106–7.

Dixon, K. A. 1977. Applications of archaeological resources: Broadening the basis of significance. In *Conservation archaeology: A guide for cultural resource management studies*, ed. M. B. Schiffer and G. J. Gumerman, 277–90. New York: Academic Press.

Dixon, R. B. 1913. Some aspects of North American archaeology. *American Anthropologist* 15:549–77.

Donham, T. K. 1982. Chronology of the ceramic period. In *The Cannon Reservoir Human Ecology Project: An archaeological study of cultural adaptations in the southern Prairie Peninsula*, ed. M. J. O'Brien, R. E. Warren, and D. E. Lewarch, 117–30. New York: Academic Press.

Donham, T. K., and M. J. O'Brien. 1985. Ceramics and chronology. In Archaeology of the central Salt River valley: An overview of the prehistoric occupation, by M. J. O'Brien. *The Missouri Archaeologist* 46:191–202.

Dorsey, J. O. 1886. Migrations of Siouan tribes. *The American Naturalist* 20:211–22.

Downer, A. S. 1977. Activity areas, surface collection, and factor analysis at the Phillips Spring site, 23HI216, Missouri. *Plains Anthropologist* 22:299–311.

Dunnell, R. C. 1971. *Systematics in prehistory.* New York: Free Press.

———. 1978a. Archaeological potential of anthropological and scientific models of function. In *Archaeological essays in honor of Irving B. Rouse*, ed. R. Dunnell and E. Hall Jr., 41–73. The Hague: Mouton.

———. 1978b. Style and function: A fundamental dichotomy. *American Antiquity* 43:192–202.

————. 1979. Trends in current Americanist archaeology. *American Journal of Archaeology* 83:437–49.

————. 1980. Evolutionary theory and archaeology. In *Advances in archaeological method and theory*, vol. 3, ed. M. B. Schiffer, 35–99. New York: Academic Press.

————. 1982a. Missouri. In Current Research. *American Antiquity* 47:225–26.

————. 1982b. Science, social science, and common sense: The agonizing dilemma of modern archaeology. *Journal of Anthropological Research* 38:1–25.

————. 1984. The ethics of archaeological significance decisions. In *Ethics and values in archaeology*, ed. E. L. Green, 62–74. New York: Free Press.

————. 1985a. Archaeological survey in the lower Mississippi alluvial valley, 1940–1947: A landmark study in American archaeology. *American Antiquity* 50:297–300.

————. 1985b. The interpretation of low density archaeological records from plowed surfaces. Paper presented at the 50th annual meeting of the Society for American Archaeology, Denver.

————. 1985c. Methodological issues in contemporary Americanist archaeology. In *Proceedings of the 1984 Biennial Meeting of the Philosophy of Science Association*, vol. 2, ed. P. D. Asquith and P. Kitcher, 717–44. East Lansing, Mich.: Philosophy of Science Association.

————. 1986. Methodological issues in Americanist artifact classification. *Advances in archaeological method and theory*, vol. 9, ed. M. B. Schiffer, 149–207.

————. 1988a. Low-density archeological records from plowed surfaces: Some preliminary considerations. *American Archeology* 7:29–38.

————. 1988b. Archaeology and evolutionary theory. Manuscript on file, University of Missouri–Columbia, Museum of Anthropology.

————. 1988c. The concept of progress in cultural evolution. In *Evolutionary progress?*, ed. M. H. Nitecki, 169–94. Chicago: University of Chicago Press.

————. 1989. Aspects of the application of evolutionary thought in archaeology. In *Archaeological thought in America*, ed. C. C. Lamberg-Karlovsky, 35–49. New York: Cambridge University Press.

————. 1990a. Artifact size and lateral displacement under tillage: Comments on the Odell and Cowan experiment. *American Antiquity* 55:592–94.

————. 1990b. The unhappy marriage of the philosophy of science and archaeology. In *Critical traditions in contemporary archaeology*, ed. V. Pinsky and A. Wylie, 5–9. London: Cambridge University Press.

————. 1992a. The notion site. In *Space, time, and archaeological landscapes*, ed. J. Rossignol and L. Wandsnider, 21–41. New York: Plenum Press.

————. 1992b. Archaeology and evolutionary science. In *Quandaries and quests: Visions of archaeology's future*, ed. L. Wandsnider, 209–24. Southern Illinois University at Carbondale, Center for Archaeological Investigations, Occasional Paper no. 20.

————. 1993. Chemical origins of archaeological aerial signatures. In *Looking into the future with an eye to the past, ASPRS Technical Papers*, vol. 2, *Remote sensing*, ed. A. J. Lewis. Bethesda, Md.: American Society for Photogrammetry and Remote Sensing.

————. n.d. *The Langdon site*. Manuscript on file, Museum of Anthropology, University of Missouri–Columbia.

Dunnell, R. C., and W. S. Dancey. 1983. The siteless survey: A regional scale data collection strategy. In *Advances in archaeological method and theory*, vol. 6, ed. M. B. Schiffer, 267–87. New York: Academic Press.

Dunnell, R. C., and J. K. Feathers. 1991. Late Woodland manifestations of the Malden

Plain, southeast Missouri. In *Stability, transformation, and variation: The Late Woodland Southeast,* ed. M. S. Nassaney and C. R. Cobb, 21–45. New York: Plenum Press.

Dunnell, R. C., M. Ikeya, P. T. McCutcheon, and S. Toyoda. 1994. Heat treatment of Mill Creek and Dover cherts on the Malden Plain, southeast Missouri. *Journal of Archaeological Science* 21:70–89.

Dunnell, R. C., and M. K. Jackson. 1992. Technology of late Mississippian polychromes. Paper presented at the 49th annual meeting of the Southeastern Archaeological Conference, Little Rock.

Dunnell, R. C., and J. Simek. 1995. Artifact size and plowzone processes. *Journal of Field Archaeology,* 22:305–19.

Dunnell, R. C., and F. H. Whittaker. 1990. The Late Archaic of the Eastern Lowlands and evidence of trade. *Louisiana Archaeology* 17:13–37.

Edwards, R. L., J. W. Beck, G. S. Burr, D. J. Donahue, J. M. A. Chappell, A. L. Bloom, E. R. M. Druffell, and F. W. Taylor. 1993. A large drop in atmospheric $^{14}C/^{12}C$ and reduced melting in the Younger Dryas, documented with ^{230}Th ages of corals. *Science* 260:962–68.

Eichenberger, J. A. 1937. Notched chipped implements classified. *The Missouri Archaeologist* 3(2).

———. 1939. The Saverton site. *The Missouri Archaeologist* 5(1):6–15.

———. 1944. Investigations of the Marion-Ralls Archaeological Society in northeast Missouri. *The Missouri Archaeologist* no. 19. [Publication of *The Missouri Archaeologist* was interrupted during World War II. Volume 8(2), published in August 1942, was followed by number (not volume) 19 in December 1944.]

Emerson, T. E. 1986. A retrospective look at the earliest Woodland cultures in the American Heartland. In *Early Woodland archeology,* ed. K. B. Farnsworth and T. E. Emerson, 621–33. Center for American Archeology, Kampsville Seminars in Archeology no. 2.

Emerson, T. E., and A. C. Fortier. 1986. Early Woodland cultural variation, subsistence, and settlement in the American Bottom. In *Early Woodland archeology,* ed. K. B. Farnsworth and T. E. Emerson, 475–522. Center for American Archeology, Kampsville Seminars in Archeology no. 2.

Emerson, T. E., G. R. Milner, and D. K. Jackson. 1983. The Florence Street site. *American Bottom archaeology, FAI-270 site reports.* Vol. 2. Urbana: University of Illinois Press.

Evers, E. 1880. The ancient pottery of southeastern Missouri. In *Contributions to the archaeology of Missouri, by the Archaeological Section of the St. Louis Academy of Science,* Part 1: Pottery, 21–30. Salem, Mass.: Bates.

Fagan, B. M. 1977. *Elusive treasure: The story of early archaeologists in the Americas.* New York: Scribners.

Falk, C. R. 1966. Preliminary report on salvage excavations in 1966 in the Kaysinger Bluff Reservoir, southwestern Missouri. *Plains Anthropologist* 12:213–14.

———. 1969. *Archaeological salvage in the Kaysinger Bluff Reservoir, Missouri: 1966.* Report submitted to the National Park Service, Omaha.

Falk, C. R., and K. A. Lippincott. 1974. *Archaeological investigation in the Harry S. Truman Reservoir, Missouri: 1967–1968.* Report submitted to the National Park Service, Omaha.

Farnsworth, K. B., and D. L. Asch. 1986. Early Woodland chronology, artifact styles, and settlement distribution in the lower Illinois Valley region. In *Early Woodland archeology,* ed. K. B. Farnsworth and T. E. Emerson, 326–457. Center for American Archeology, Kampsville Seminars in Archeology no. 2.

Feathers, J. K. 1988. Explaining the transition from sand to shell temper in southeastern Missouri pottery. Manuscript on file, Department of Anthropology, University of Missouri–Columbia.

———. 1989a. Effects of temper on strength of ceramics: Response to Bronitsky and Hamer. *American Antiquity* 54:579–88.

———. 1989b. Ceramic analysis, variation and data base construction: A selectionist perspective. In *Analysis and publication of ceramics: The computer data-base in archaeology,* ed. J. A. Blakely and W. J. Bennett Jr., 71–80. British Archaeological Reports, International Series no. 551.

———. 1990a. An evolutionary interpretation for the predominance of shell tempering in late prehistoric southeastern Missouri ceramics. Paper presented at the 55th annual meeting of the Society for American Archaeology, Las Vegas.

———. 1990b. An evolutionary explanation for prehistoric ceramic change in southeast Missouri. Ph.D. diss., University of Washington. Ann Arbor: University Microfilms.

Feathers, J. K., and W. D. Scott. 1989. Prehistoric ceramic composite from the Mississippi Valley. *Ceramic Bulletin* 68:554–57.

Fenenga, F. 1938. Pottery types from Pulaski County. *The Missouri Archaeologist* 4(2):5–7.

Ferguson, J. A. 1990. Pottery classification, site patterns, and Mississippian interaction at the Common Field site (23STG100), eastern Missouri. Master's thesis, Department of Anthropology, University of Missouri–Columbia.

Ferring, C. R. 1986. Rates of fluvial sedimentation: Implications for archaeological variability. *Geoarchaeology* 1:259–74.

Ficklin, W. H. 1894. Antiquities of Boone County, Missouri. *The Archaeologist* 2:144–46.

Figgins, J. D. 1927. The antiquity of man in America. *Natural History* 27:229–39.

Fischel, H. 1939. Folsom and Yuma culture finds. *American Antiquity* 4:232–64.

Fisk, H. N. 1944. *Geological investigation of the alluvial valley of the lower Mississippi Valley.* Vicksburg, Miss.: U.S. Army Corps of Engineers.

Fitting, J. E. 1978. Client-oriented archaeology: A comment on Kinsey's dilemma. *Pennsylvania Archaeologist* 48:12–15.

———. 1979. The role of market analysis in archaeological planning. *Journal of Field Archaeology* 6:229–35.

Fitzhugh, W. W. 1972. Environmental archeology and cultural systems in Hamilton Inlet, Labrador. *Smithsonian Contributions to Anthropology* no. 16.

———. 1975. A comparative approach to northern maritime adaptations. In *Prehistoric maritime adaptations of the circumpolar zone,* ed. W. W. Fitzhugh, 339–86. The Hague: Mouton.

Flannery, K. V. 1965. The ecology of early food production in Mesopotamia. *Science* 147:1247–55.

———. 1966. The postglacial "readaptation" as viewed from Mesoamerica. *American Antiquity* 31:800–805.

———. 1967. Culture history v. cultural process: A debate in American archaeology. *Scientific American* 217:119–22.

———. 1968. Archaeological systems theory and early Mesoamerica. In *Anthropological archeology in the Americas,* ed. B. J. Meggers, 132–77. Washington, D.C.: Anthropological Society of Washington.

———, ed. 1976. *The early Mesoamerican village.* New York: Academic Press.

Flannery, K. V., M. Winter, S. Lees, J. Neely, J. Schoenwetter, S. Kitchen, and J. C. Wheeler.

1970. *Preliminary archeological investigations in the Valley of Oaxaca, Mexico, 1966–1969.* Manuscript on file, University of Michigan, Museum of Anthropology.

Foley, R. 1981. *Off-site archaeology and human adaptation in eastern Africa.* British Archaeological Reports, International Series no. 97.

Ford, J. A. 1936. *Analysis of Indian village site collections from Louisiana and Mississippi.* Department of Conservation, Louisiana Geological Survey, Anthropological Study no. 2.

———. 1938a. Report of the Conference on Southeastern Pottery Typology. Ann Arbor: University of Michigan, Museum of Anthropology, Ceramic Repository (mimeographed).

———. 1938b. A chronological method applicable to the Southeast. *American Antiquity* 3:260–64.

———. 1954. The type concept revisited. *American Anthropologist* 56:42–57.

———. 1962. A quantitative method for deriving cultural chronology. *Pan American Union, Technical Manual* no. 1.

Ford, J. A., P. Phillips, and W. G. Haag. 1955. *The Jaketown site in west-central Mississippi.* American Museum of Natural History, Anthropological Papers 45(1).

Ford, J. A., and G. R. Willey. 1941. An interpretation of the prehistory of the eastern United States. *American Anthropologist* 43:325–63.

Fortier, A. C. 1985. Selected sites in the Hill Lake locality. *American Bottom archaeology, FAI-270 site reports.* Vol. 13. Urbana: University of Illinois Press.

Fortier, A. C., T. E. Emerson, and F. A. Finney. 1984. Early and Middle Woodland periods. In *American Bottom archaeology: A summary of the FAI-270 Project contribution to the culture history of the Mississippi River valley,* ed. C. J. Bareis and J. W. Porter, 59–103. Urbana: University of Illinois Press.

Foster, J. W. 1864. Ancient relics in Missouri. *Smithsonian Institution, Annual Report* (1863), 383–84.

———. 1873a. On the pottery of the mound builders. *The American Naturalist* 7:94–103.

———. 1873b. *Pre-historic races of the United States of America.* Chicago: Griggs.

Fowke, G. 1894. Archaeologic investigations in James and Potomac valleys. *Bureau of American Ethnology, Bulletin* 23.

———. 1905. The Montezuma mounds, explored by N. D. McEvers, John M. Wulfing, and David I. Bushnell. *Missouri Historical Society Collections* 2(5):1–16.

———. 1910. Antiquities of central and southeastern Missouri. *Bureau of American Ethnology, Bulletin* 37.

———. 1912. Some notes on the aboriginal inhabitants of Missouri. *Missouri Historical Society Collections* 4(1):82–103.

———. 1922. Archaeological investigations. *Bureau of American Ethnology, Bulletin* 76.

———. 1928. Archaeological investigations II. *Bureau of American Ethnology, Annual Report* 44.

Fowler, D. D. 1984. Review of *The Cannon Reservoir Human Ecology Project: An archaeological study of cultural adaptations in the southern Prairie Peninsula,* ed. M. J. O'Brien, R. E. Warren, and D. E. Lewarch. *American Anthropologist* 86:196–98.

Fox, G. L. 1992. A critical evaluation of the interpretive framework of the Mississippi period in southeast Missouri. Ph.D. diss., Department of Anthropology, University of Missouri–Columbia.

Frink, D. S. 1984. Artifact behavior in the plow zone. *Journal of Field Archaeology* 11:357–63.

Fritz, J. M. 1972. Archaeological systems for indirect observation of the past. In

Contemporary archaeology: A guide to theory and contributions, ed. M. P. Leone, 135–57. Carbondale: Southern Illinois Press.

Fritz, J. M., and F. T. Plog. 1970. The nature of archaeological explanation. *American Antiquity* 35:405–12.

Gamio, M. 1913. Arqueología de Atzcapotzalco, D.F., México. *Eighteenth International Congress of Americanists, Proceedings,* 180–87.

Garrison, E., J. A. May, W. Marquardt, and A. W. Sjöberg. 1979. *A final report on the effects of inundation on cultural resources, Table Rock Reservoir, Missouri.* Report submitted to the National Park Service, Santa Fe.

Garrison, E., [J.] A. May, J. Newsom, and A. [W.] Sjöberg. 1977. *Progress report on the effects of inundation on cultural resources: Table Rock Reservoir, Missouri.* Report submitted to the National Park Service, Santa Fe.

Gibbon, G. 1989. *Explanation in archaeology.* Oxford: Blackwell.

Gibbs, G. 1862. Instructions for archaeological investigations in the United States. *Smithsonian Institution, Annual Report* (1861), 292–96.

Gilmore, M. R. 1931. *Vegetal remains of the Ozark bluff dweller culture.* Papers of the Michigan Academy of Science, Arts and Letters 14:83–102.

Goodyear, A. C. 1975. *Hecla II and III: An interpretive study of archeological remains from the Lakeshore Project, Papago Reservoir, south-central Arizona.* Arizona State University, Department of Anthropology, Research Paper no. 9.

———. 1982. The chronological position of the Dalton horizon in the southeastern United States. *American Antiquity* 47:382–95.

Goodyear, A. C., L. M. Raab, and T. C. Klinger. 1978. The status of archaeological research design in cultural resource management. *American Antiquity* 43:159–73.

Gould, R. A. 1980. *Living archaeology.* New York: Cambridge University Press.

———. 1985. The empiricist strikes back. *American Antiquity* 50:639–44.

Gould, R. A., and P. J. Watson. 1982. A dialogue on the meaning and use of analogy in ethnoarchaeological reasoning. *Journal of Anthropological Archaeology* 1:355–81.

Grady, M. A. 1977. Significance evaluation and the Orme River Project. In *Conservation archaeology: A guide for cultural resource management studies,* ed. M. B. Schiffer and G. J. Gumerman, 259–67. New York: Academic Press.

Grady, M. A., and W. D. Lipe. 1976. Conservation archaeology, research, and environmental law. Paper presented at the 41st annual meeting of the Society for American Archaeology, St. Louis.

Graham, R. W., C. V. Haynes, D. L. Johnson, and M. Kay. 1981. Kimmswick: A Clovis-mastodon association in eastern Missouri. *Science* 213:1115–17.

Graham, R. W., and M. Kay. 1988. Taphonomic comparisons of cultural and noncultural faunal deposits at the Kimmswick and Barnhart sites, Jefferson County, Missouri. In Late Pleistocene and early Holocene paleoecology and archeology of the eastern Great Lakes region, ed. R. S. Laub, N. G. Miller, and D. W. Steadman. *Bulletin of the Buffalo Society of Natural Sciences* 33:227–40.

Grayson, D. K. 1983. *The establishment of human antiquity.* New York: Academic Press.

Green, E. L., ed. 1984. *Ethics and values in archaeology.* New York: Free Press.

Green, W. 1984. Review of *The Cannon Reservoir Human Ecology Project: An archaeological study of cultural adaptations in the southern Prairie Peninsula,* ed. M. J. O'Brien, R. E. Warren, and D. E. Lewarch. *The Wisconsin Archeologist* 65:389–97.

Griffin, J. B. 1936. The archaeological remains of the Chiwere Sioux. *American Antiquity* 2:180–81.

———. 1937. Culture identity of the Ozark "top-layer." *American Antiquity* 2:296–97.

————. 1941. Report on pottery from the St. Louis area. *The Missouri Archaeologist* 7(2):1–17.

————. 1943. *The Fort Ancient aspect: Its cultural and chronological position in Mississippi Valley archaeology.* Ann Arbor: University of Michigan Press.

————. 1946. *Cultural change and continuity in eastern United States archaeology.* R. S. Peabody Foundation for Archaeology, Papers 3:37–95; 307–48.

————. 1952a. Prehistoric cultures of the central Mississippi Valley. In *Archeology of eastern United States,* ed. J. B. Griffin, 226–38. Chicago: University of Chicago Press.

————. 1952b. Culture periods in eastern United States archeology. In *Archeology of eastern United States,* ed. J. B. Griffin, 352–64. Chicago: University of Chicago Press.

————. 1952c. Radiocarbon dates for the eastern United States. In *Archeology of eastern United States,* ed. J. B. Griffin, 365–70. Chicago: University of Chicago Press.

————. 1952d. Some Early and Middle Woodland pottery types in Illinois. In *Hopewellian communities in Illinois,* ed. T. Deuel, 93–129. Illinois State Museum, Scientific Papers no. 5.

————, ed. 1952e. *Archeology of eastern United States.* Chicago: University of Chicago Press.

————. 1959. The pursuit of archaeology in the United States. *American Anthropologist* 61:379–88.

————. 1960. Climatic change: A contributory cause of the growth and decline of northern Hopewellian culture. *Wisconsin Archeologist* 4(2):21–33.

————. 1965. Hopewell and the dark black glass. *Michigan Archaeologist* 11:115–55.

————. 1967. Eastern North American archaeology: A summary. *Science* 156:175–91.

————. 1974. Foreword to the new edition of *The Adena people,* by W. S. Webb and C. E. Snow, v–xix. Knoxville: University of Tennessee Press.

————. 1985a. The formation of the Society for American Archaeology. *American Antiquity* 50:261–71.

————. 1985b. An individual's participation in American archaeology, 1928–1985. *Annual Review of Anthropology* 14:1–23.

Griffin, J. B., A. A. Gordus, and S. A. Wright. 1969. Identification of the sources of Hopewellian obsidian in the Middle West. *American Antiquity* 34:1–14.

Griffin, J. B., and A. C. Spaulding. 1952. The central Mississippi River valley archaeological survey, season 1950: A preliminary report. In *Prehistoric pottery of eastern United States,* ed. J. B. Griffin, 1–7. Ann Arbor: University of Michigan, Museum of Anthropology.

Gross, H. 1951. Mastodon, mammoth, and man in North America. *Bulletin of the Texas Archeological and Paleontological Society* 22:101–31.

Guthe, C. E. 1930. The Committee on State Archaeological Surveys of the Division of Anthropology and Psychology, National Research Council. *International Congress of Americanists, Proceedings* 23:52–59.

————. 1934. A method of ceramic description. In *Standards of pottery description,* by B. March, 1–6. University of Michigan, Museum of Anthropology, Occasional Contributions no. 3.

————. 1952. Twenty-five years of archeology in the eastern United States. In *Archeology of eastern United States,* ed. J. B. Griffin, 1–12. Chicago: University of Chicago Press.

————. 1967. Reflections on the founding of the Society for American Archaeology. *American Antiquity* 32:433–40.

Haag, W. G. 1985. Federal aid to archaeology in the Southeast, 1933–1942. *American Antiquity* 50:272–80.

Haggett, P. 1965. *Locational analysis in human geography.* New York: St. Martin's Press.

Hamilton, H. W. 1967. *Tobacco pipes of the Missouri Indians.* Missouri Archaeological Society, Memoir no. 5.

Hamilton, H. W., and J. T. Hamilton. 1972. Clay pipes from Pamplin. *The Missouri Archaeologist* 35(1–2):1–47.

Hamilton, H. W., J. T. Hamilton, and E. F. Chapman. 1974. *Spiro Mound copper.* Missouri Archaeological Society, Memoir no. 11.

Hamilton, T. M. 1982. *Native American bows.* Columbia: Missouri Archaeological Society.

———, comp. 1960. Indian trade guns. *The Missouri Archaeologist* 22 (whole volume).

Hardy, G. L., and F. B. Scheetz. 1883. Mounds in Ralls County, Missouri. *Smithsonian Institution, Annual Report* (1881), 533–36.

Hargrave, M. L. 1981. Woodland ceramic chronometry and occupational intensity at the Carrier Mills Archaeological District, Saline County, Illinois. Master's thesis, Department of Anthropology, University of Southern Illinois at Carbondale.

Hargrave, M. L., and D. P. Braun. 1981. Chronometry of mechanical performance characteristics of Woodland ceramics: Methods, results, applications. Paper presented at the 46th annual meeting of the Society for American Archaeology, San Diego.

Harlan, R. 1843. Description of the bones of a new fossil animal of the order Edentata. *The American Journal of Science and Arts* 44:69–80.

Harn, A. D. 1986. The Marion phase occupation of the Larson site in the central Illinois River valley. In *Early Woodland archeology,* ed. K. B. Farnsworth and T. E. Emerson, 244–79. Center for American Archeology, Kampsville Seminars in Archeology no. 2.

Harrington, J. C. 1935. The task of a state archaeological society. *The Missouri Archaeologist* 1(1):1–3 (unpaginated).

———. 1938. Report on the excavation of mound Bo1:1. *The Missouri Archaeologist* 4(1).

Harrington, M. R. 1924a. The Ozark bluff dwellers. *American Anthropologist* 26:1–21.

———. 1924b. Explorations in the Ozark region. *Indian Notes* 1:3–7.

Harris, M. 1968a. *The rise of anthropological theory: A history of theories of culture.* New York: Crowell.

———. 1968b. Comments. In *New perspectives in archeology,* ed. S. R. Binford and L. R. Binford, 359–61. Chicago: Aldine.

———. 1979. *Cultural materialism: The struggle for a science of culture.* New York: Random House.

Haven, S. F. 1856. Archaeology of the United States. *Smithsonian Contributions to Knowledge* 8(2).

Hay, O. P. 1924. *Pleistocene of the middle region of North America and its vertebrated animals.* Carnegie Institute, Publication no. 322A.

Hayden, B., ed. 1979. *Lithic use-wear analysis.* New York: Academic Press.

Haynes, C. V. 1976. Late Quaternary geology of the lower Pomme de Terre Valley. In *Prehistoric man and his environments: A case study in the Ozark Highland,* ed. W. R. Wood and R. B. McMillan, 47–61. New York: Academic Press.

———. 1985. *Mastodon-bearing springs and late Quaternary geochronology of the lower Pomme de Terre Valley, Missouri.* Geological Society of America, Special Paper no. 204.

Haynes, H. W. 1888. The bow and arrow unknown to Palaeolithic man. *Proceedings of the Boston Society of Natural History* 23:269–74.

———. 1892. Palaeolithic implement recently discovered by Mr. W. C. Mills in the valley of the Tuscarawas, Ohio. *Proceedings of the Boston Society of Natural History* 25:49–51.

———. 1893. Paleolithic man in North America. *The American Antiquarian and Oriental Journal* 15:37–42.

Healan, D. M. 1972. *Surface delineation of functional areas at a Mississippian ceremonial center.* Missouri Archaeological Society, Memoir no. 10.

Heizer, R. F. 1951. A preliminary report on the Leonard Rockshelter site, Pershing County, Nevada. *American Antiquity* 17:89–98.

———. 1966. Salvage and other archaeology. *The Masterkey* 40:54–60.

Heldman, D. P. 1962. Salvage archaeology in the Joanna Reservoir area, Missouri, 1960. In *Archaeological investigations in the Joanna Reservoir area, Missouri,* by C. H. Chapman, D. P. Heldman, and D. R. Henning, 1–86. Report submitted to the National Park Service, Lincoln, Neb.

Hempel, C. G. 1965. *Aspects of scientific explanation, and other essays in the philosophy of science.* New York: Free Press.

Henning, A. E. 1964. Starr mound. In *Archaeological investigations, Joanna Reservoir, Missouri,* by D. R. Henning, A. E. Henning, and K. W. Cole, 71–93. Report submitted to the National Park Service, Omaha.

Henning, A. E., and D. R. Henning. 1964. The Calvert mound. In *Archaeological investigations, Joanna Reservoir, Missouri,* by D. R. Henning, A. E. Henning, and K. W. Cole, 94–106. Report submitted to the National Park Service, Omaha.

Henning, D. R. 1959. The Loftin mound (23SN42). *Missouri Archaeological Society Newsletter* no. 128:9–10.

———. 1960a. The Loftin mound (23SN42). In *Archaeological investigations in the Table Rock Reservoir area,* comp. C. H. Chapman, 366–67. Report submitted to the National Park Service, Lincoln, Neb.

———. 1960b. Additional house excavations: The Loftin component (23SN42). In *Archaeological investigations in the Table Rock Reservoir area,* comp. C. H. Chapman, 829–42. Report submitted to the National Park Service, Lincoln, Neb.

———. 1961. Archaeological research in the proposed Joanna Reservoir, Missouri. *The Missouri Archaeologist* 23:131–77.

———. 1962. The Garrelts site I (23MN221). In *Archaeological investigations in the Joanna Reservoir area, Missouri,* by C. H. Chapman, D. P. Heldman, and D. R. Henning, 212–37. Report submitted to the National Park Service, Omaha.

———. 1964. The Davis site. In *Archaeological investigations, Joanna Reservoir, Missouri,* by D. R. Henning, A. E. Henning, and K. W. Cole, 24–70. Report submitted to the National Park Service, Omaha.

———. 1970. Development and interrelationships of Oneota culture in the lower Missouri River valley. *The Missouri Archaeologist* 32.

———. 1979. History of the Cannon Reservoir Human Ecology Project. In *The Cannon Reservoir Human Ecology Project: Recent advances in the archaeology of northeast Missouri,* ed. M. J. O'Brien and D. E. Lewarch, 3–16. University of Nebraska, Division of Archeological Research, Notebook no. 5.

———. 1987. Chapman. *Iowa Archeological Society Newsletter* 37(2):5–6.

———. 1993. The Oneota tradition. Manuscript on file, University of Missouri, Museum of Anthropology.

Henning, D. R., A. E. Henning, and K. W. Cole. 1964. *Archaeological investigations, Joanna Reservoir, Missouri.* Report submitted to the National Park Service, Omaha.

Henshaw, H. W. 1883. Animal carvings from mounds of the Mississippi Valley. *Bureau of Ethnology, Annual Report* 2:117–66.

Hesse, B., and P. Wapnish. 1985. *Animal bone archaeology: From objectives to analysis.* Washington, D.C.: Taraxacum.

Hester, T. R. 1981. CRM publication: Dealing with reality. *Journal of Field Archaeology* 8:493–96.

Hill, F. C. 1975. Effects of the environment on animal exploitation by Archaic inhabitants of the Koster site. Ph.D. diss., Department of Biology, University of Louisville.

Hinsley, C. M., Jr. 1981. *Savages and scientists: The Smithsonian Institution and the development of American anthropology, 1846–1910.* Washington, D.C.: Smithsonian Institution Press.

———. 1994. *The Smithsonian and the American Indian: Making of a Moral Anthropology in Victorian America.* Washington, D.C.: Smithsonian Institution Press.

Hoard, R. J. 1992. Woodland-period cooking vessels from Missouri. Ph.D. diss., Department of Anthropology, University of Missouri–Columbia.

Hoard, R. J., and M. J. O'Brien. n.d. Limestone as a tempering agent in prehistoric midwestern pottery. Manuscript on file, Museum of Anthropology, University of Missouri–Columbia.

Hoard, R. J., M. J. O'Brien, M. G. Khorasgany, and V. S. Gopalaratnam. 1995. A materials science approach to understanding limestone-tempered pottery from the Midwest. *Journal of Archaeological Science* (in press).

Hodder, I. 1985. Post-processual archaeology. In *Advances in archaeological method and theory,* vol. 8, ed. M. B. Schiffer, 1–26. New York: Academic Press.

Hodge, F. W. 1910. Handbook of American Indians north of Mexico. 2 vols. *Bulletin of American Ethnology* 30 (1907–1910).

Hoebel, E. A. 1946. *The archaeology of Bone Cave, Miller County, Missouri.* American Museum of Natural History, Anthropological Papers 40(2).

Hole, F. 1966. Investigating the origins of Mesopotamian civilization. *Science* 153:605–11.

Hole, F., K. V. Flannery, and J. A. Neeley. 1969. *Prehistory and human ecology of the Deh Luran Plain: An early village sequence from Khuzistan, Iran.* University of Michigan, Museum of Anthropology Memoirs no. 1.

Holland, T. D. 1989. Fertility in the prehistoric Midwest: A critique of unifactorial models. *American Antiquity* 54:389–426.

———. 1991. An archaeological and biological analysis of the Campbell site. Ph.D. diss., Department of Anthropology, University of Missouri–Columbia.

———. 1994. Skeletal analysis. In *Cat monsters and head pots: The archaeology of Missouri's Pemiscot Bayou,* by M. J. O'Brien, 307–47. Columbia: University of Missouri Press.

Holmes, W. H. 1884. Illustrated catalogue of a portion of the collections made by the Bureau of Ethnology during the field season of 1881. *Bureau of Ethnology, Annual Report* 3:427–510.

———. 1886a. Origin and development of form and ornament in ceramic art. *Bureau of Ethnology, Annual Report* 4:437–65.

———. 1886b. Ancient pottery of the Mississippi Valley. *Bureau of Ethnology, Annual Report* 4:361–436.

———. 1892. Modern quarry refuse and the Paleolithic theory. *Science* 20:295–97.

———. 1893a. Distribution of stone implements in the Tidewater Country. *American Anthropologist* 6:1–14.

———. 1893b. Are there traces of man in the Trenton gravels? *Journal of Geology* 1:15–37.

———. 1893c. Gravel man and Paleolithic culture: A preliminary word. *Science* 21:29–30.

———. 1893d. Traces of glacial man in Ohio. *Journal of Geology* 1:147–63.

———. 1893e. A question of evidence. *Science* 21:135–36.

———. 1893f. Man and the glacial period. *The American Antiquarian and Oriental Journal* 15:34–36.

———. 1894. *Natural history of flaked stone implements.* International Congress of Anthropology, Chicago, Memoirs, 120–39.

———. 1897a. Primitive man in the Delaware Valley. *Science* 26:824–29.

———. 1897b. Stone implements of the Potomac-Chesapeake Tidewater Province. *Bureau of American Ethnology, Annual Report* 15:13–152.

———. 1903a. Aboriginal pottery of the eastern United States. *Bureau of American Ethnology, Annual Report* 20:1–201.

———. 1903b. Traces of aboriginal operations in an iron mine near Leslie, Missouri. *American Anthropologist* 5:503–7.

———. 1903c. Flint implements and fossil remains from a sulphur spring at Afton, Indian Territory. *Report of the U.S. National Museum for 1901,* 233–52.

———. 1907. Prefatory note. In Skeletal remains suggesting or attributed to early man in North America, by A. Hrdlička. *Bureau of American Ethnology, Bulletin* 33:3.

———. 1919. Handbook of aboriginal American antiquities. Part 1. *Bureau of American Ethnology, Bulletin* 60.

Hopgood, J. F. 1967. The Burkett site (23MI-20). In *Land leveling salvage archaeological work in southeast Missouri: 1966,* by J. R. Williams, 293–304. Report submitted to the National Park Service, Lincoln, Neb.

———. 1969. Continuity and change in the Baytown pottery tradition of the Cairo Lowland, southeast Missouri. Master's thesis, Department of Anthropology, University of Missouri–Columbia.

Horr, W. H. 1955. A pollen profile study of the Muscotah Marsh. *University of Kansas, Science Bulletin* 37:143–49.

Houck, L. 1908. *A history of Missouri, from the earliest explorations and settlements until the admission of the state into the union.* 3 vols. Chicago: Donnelley.

House, J. H. 1975. Prehistoric lithic resource utilization in the Cache Basin: Crowley's Ridge chert and quartzite and Pitkin chert. In *The Cache River Archeological Project: An experiment in contract archeology,* assembled by M. B. Schiffer and J. H. House, 81–91. Arkansas Archeological Survey, Research Series no. 8.

House, J. H., and M. B. Schiffer. 1975a. Archeological survey in the Cache River basin. In *The Cache River Archeological Project: An experiment in contract archeology,* assembled by M. B. Schiffer and J. H. House, 37–53. Arkansas Archeological Survey, Research Series no. 8.

———. 1975b. Significance of the archeological resources of the Cache River basin. In *The Cache River Archeological Project: An experiment in contract archeology,* assembled by M. B. Schiffer and J. H. House, 163–86. Arkansas Archeological Survey, Research Series no. 8.

Howard, E. B. 1935. Evidence of early man in America. *The Museum Journal* 24:53–171.

Hrdlička, A. 1907. Skeletal remains suggesting or attributed to early man in North America. *Bureau of American Ethnology, Bulletin* 33.

———. 1910. Report on skeletal material from Missouri mounds, collected in 1906–7 by Mr. Gerard Fowke. In Antiquities of central and southeastern Missouri. *Bureau of American Ethnology, Bulletin* 37:103–12.

———. 1912. Early man in South America. *Bureau of American Ethnology, Bulletin* 52.

————. 1918. Recent discoveries attributed to early man in North America. *Bureau of American Ethnology, Bulletin* 66.

Hudson, J. C. 1969. A location theory for rural settlement. *Annals of the Association of American Geographers* 59:365–81.

Hunt, W. J., Jr. 1976a. The Lick Lake site, 23RA302. In *Cannon Reservoir Archaeological Project report* (Appendix 4, part 1), ed. D. R. Henning. University of Nebraska, Department of Anthropology, Technical Report no. 76–06.

————. 1976b. The Foss site, 23RA271. In *Cannon Reservoir Archaeological Project report* (Appendix 4, part 2), ed. D. R. Henning. University of Nebraska, Department of Anthropology, Technical Report no. 76–07.

————. 1977a. The Victor Bridge site (23MN380). In *Cannon Reservoir Archaeological Project reports,* vol. 1, ed. D. R. Henning. University of Nebraska, Department of Anthropology, Technical Report no. 77–03.

————. 1977b. The Muskrat Run site (23RA151). In *Cannon Reservoir Archaeological Project reports,* vol. 2, ed. D. R. Henning. University of Nebraska, Department of Anthropology, Technical Report no. 77–05.

Iroquois Research Institute. 1980. *Prehistoric archaeological reconnaissance in the Harry S. Truman Dam and Reservoir: 50 year flood easement lands, Osage River basin, Missouri.* Report submitted to the U.S. Army Corps of Engineers, Kansas City District.

Ives, D. 1984. Neutron activation analysis characterization of selected prehistoric chert quarrying areas. Ph.D. diss., Department of Anthropology, University of Missouri–Columbia.

————. 1985. Chert sources and identification in archaeology: Can a silk purse be made from a sow's ear? In *Lithic resource procurement: Proceedings from the second conference on prehistoric chert exploitation,* ed. S. C. Vehik, 221–24. Southern Illinois University, Center for Archaeological Investigations, Occasional Paper no. 4.

James, E. 1823. *Account of an expedition from Pittsburgh to the Rocky Mountains performed in the years 1819, 1820 by the order of the Hon. J. C. Calhoun, Secretary of War, under the command of Maj. S. H. Long, of the U.S. Top. Engineers, compiled from the notes of Major Long, Mr. T. Say, and other gentlemen of the party, by Edwin James, botanist and geologist to the expedition.* Philadelphia: Carey and Lea.

Jennings, J. D. 1963. Administration of contract emergency archaeological programs. *American Antiquity* 28:282–85.

————. 1968. *Prehistory of North America.* New York: McGraw-Hill.

————. 1974. *Prehistory of North America.* 2d ed. New York: McGraw-Hill.

————. 1985. River Basin surveys: Origins, operations, and results, 1945–1969. *American Antiquity* 50:281–96.

————. 1986. American archaeology, 1930–1985. In *American archaeology past and future: A celebration of the Society for American Archaeology, 1935–1985,* ed. D. J. Meltzer, D. D. Fowler, and J. A. Sabloff, 53–62. Washington, D.C.: Smithsonian Institution Press.

Jermann, J. V. 1981. Surface collection and analysis of spatial pattern: An archeological example from the lower Columbia River valley. In *Plowzone archeology: Contributions to theory and technique,* ed. M. J. O'Brien and D. E. Lewarch, 71–118. Vanderbilt University, Publications in Anthropology no. 27.

Jeter, M. D. 1986. Review of 1985 reprint of *Report on the mound explorations of the Bureau of Ethnology,* by Cyrus Thomas. *Southeastern Archaeology* 5:148–50.

————, ed. 1990. *Edward Palmer's Arkansaw mounds.* Fayetteville: University of Arkansas Press.

Johnson, D. L., and W. R. Wood. 1980. Prehistoric studies on the Plains. In *Anthropology of the Great Plains,* ed. W. R. Wood and M. Liberty, 35–51. Lincoln: University of Nebraska Press.

Johnson, J. K., and C. A. Morrow, eds. 1987. *The organization of core technology.* Boulder, Colo.: Westview Press.

Judge, W. J. 1973. *Paleoindian occupation of the central Rio Grande Valley in New Mexico.* Albuquerque: University of New Mexico Press.

Kaplan, D. H., R. E. Pangborn, H. T. Ward, and W. R. Wood. 1967. *Archaeological salvage work in the Stockton Reservoir area, southwestern Missouri.* Report submitted to the National Park Service, Lincoln, Neb.

Kay, M. 1981. Obituary: Rolland Edward Pangborn. *Plains Anthropologist* 26:319–22.

————. 1982a. Overview of the mitigation program. In *Holocene adaptations within the lower Pomme de Terre River valley, Missouri,* ed. M. Kay, 1–7. Report submitted to the U.S. Army Corps of Engineers, Kansas City District.

————. 1982b. Stratigraphic studies at Rodgers Shelter. In *Holocene adaptations within the lower Pomme de Terre River valley, Missouri,* ed. M. Kay, 81–106. Report submitted to the U.S. Army Corps of Engineers, Kansas City District.

————. 1982c. Change in depositional environments at Rodgers Shelter. In *Holocene adaptations within the lower Pomme de Terre River valley, Missouri,* ed. M. Kay, 107–36. Report submitted to the U.S. Army Corps of Engineers, Kansas City District.

————. 1982d. Stylistic study of chipped stone points from Rodgers Shelter. In *Holocene adaptations within the lower Pomme de Terre River valley, Missouri,* ed. M. Kay, 379–559. Report submitted to the U.S. Army Corps of Engineers, Kansas City District.

————. 1982e. *Phillips Spring, Missouri: Report of the 1978 investigations.* Report submitted to the U.S. Army Corps of Engineers, Kansas City District.

————, ed. 1982f. *Holocene adaptations within the lower Pomme de Terre River valley, Missouri.* Report submitted to the U.S. Army Corps of Engineers, Kansas City District.

————. 1986. Projectile point use inferred from microwear of Kimmswick Clovis points. Paper presented at the 51st annual meeting of the Society for American Archaeology, New Orleans.

Kay, M., J. Behm, and C. K. Robinson. 1982. Rodgers Shelter techno-functional studies. In *Holocene adaptations within the lower Pomme de Terre River valley, Missouri,* ed. M. Kay, 263–378. Report submitted to the U.S. Army Corps of Engineers, Kansas City District.

Kay, M., F. B. King, and C. K. Robinson. 1980. Cucurbits from Phillips Spring: New evidence and interpretations. *American Antiquity* 45:806–22.

Keeley, L. H. 1974. The methodology of microwear analysis: A comment on Nance. *American Antiquity* 39:126–28.

————. 1980. *Experimental determination of stone tool uses.* Chicago: University of Chicago Press.

Keeley, L. H., and M. H. Newcomer. 1977. Microwear analysis of experimental flint tools: A test case. *Journal of Archaeological Science* 4:29–62.

Keller, C. M. 1965. Preliminary archaeological reconnaissance and testing. In *Preliminary archaeological investigations in the Kaysinger Bluff Reservoir area,* part 2, by C. H.

Chapman, A. Grimshaw, W. Klippel, R. B. McMillan, J. Mori, R. E. Pangborn, W. E. Sudderth, and R. L. McNair, 171–220. Report submitted to the National Park Service, Lincoln, Neb.

Kelly, J. E., S. Ozuk, D. Jackson, D. McElrath, F. Finney, and D. Esarey. 1984. Emergent Mississippian period. In *American Bottom archaeology*, ed. C. J. Bareis and J. W. Porter, 128–57. Urbana: University of Illinois Press.

Keslin, R. O. 1964. Archaeological implications on the role of salt as an element of cultural diffusion. *The Missouri Archaeologist* 26 (whole volume).

Kidder, A. V. 1936. Speculations on New World prehistory. In *Essays in anthropology*, ed. R. Lowie, 143–51. Berkeley: University of California Press.

King, F. B. 1982a. Vegetational reconstruction and plant resource prediction. In *Holocene adaptations within the lower Pomme de Terre River valley, Missouri*, ed. M. Kay, 9–61. Report submitted to the U.S. Army Corps of Engineers, Kansas City District.

———. 1982b. Ethnobotanical remains from Rodgers Shelter. In *Holocene adaptations within the lower Pomme de Terre River valley, Missouri*, ed. M. Kay, 137–54. Report submitted to the U.S. Army Corps of Engineers, Kansas City District.

———. 1982c. Preliminary analysis of botanical remains from Phillips Spring. In *Holocene adaptations within the lower Pomme de Terre River valley, Missouri*, ed. M. Kay, 701–27. Report submitted to the U.S. Army Corps of Engineers, Kansas City District.

———. 1982d. Analysis of archaeobotanical remains. In *The Cannon Reservoir Human Ecology Project: An archaeological study of cultural adaptations in the southern Prairie Peninsula*, ed. M. J. O'Brien, R. E. Warren, and D. E. Lewarch, 197–213. New York: Academic Press.

King, J. E. 1973. Late Pleistocene palynology and biogeography of the western Missouri Ozarks. *Ecological Monographs* 43:539–65.

———. 1975. *A survey of the Pleistocene spring bogs of the lower Pomme de Terre River valley, Benton and Hickory counties, Missouri*. Report submitted to the U.S. Army Corps of Engineers, Kansas City District.

———. 1982. Palynological investigations at Phillips Spring. In *Holocene adaptations within the lower Pomme de Terre River valley, Missouri*, ed. M. Kay, 687–99. Report submitted to the U.S. Army Corps of Engineers, Kansas City District.

King, J. E., and W. H. Allen, Jr. 1977. A Holocene vegetation record from the Mississippi River valley, southeastern Missouri. *Quaternary Research* 8:307–23.

King, J. E., and E. H. Lindsay. 1976. Late Quaternary biotic records from spring deposits in western Missouri. In *Prehistoric man and his environments: A case study in the Ozark Highland*, ed. W. R. Wood and R. B. McMillan, 63–78. New York: Academic Press.

King, T. F. 1971. A conflict of values in American archaeology. *American Antiquity* 36:255–62.

———. 1977. Resolving a conflict of values in American archaeology. In *Conservation archaeology: A guide for cultural resource management studies*, ed. M. B. Schiffer and G. J. Gumerman, 87–95. New York: Academic Press.

———. 1978. Allegories of eligibility: The determination of eligibility process and the capacity for thought among archeologists. In *Cultural resources: Planning and management*, ed. R. S. Dickens Jr. and C. E. Hill, 43–54. Boulder, Colo.: Westview Press.

———. 1983. Professional responsibility in public archaeology. *Annual Reviews in Anthropology* 12:143–64.

Klempter, L. J., and P. F. Johnson. 1986. Technology and the primitive potter: Mississip-pian pottery development seen through the eyes of a ceramic engineer. In *Technology and style*, ed. W. D. Kingery, 251–71. Columbus, Ohio: American Ceramic Society.

Klepinger, L., and D. R. Henning. 1976. The Hatten site: A two-component burial site in northeast Missouri. *The Missouri Archaeologist* 37:92–170.

Klinger, T. C. 1976. The problem of site definition in cultural resource management. *Arkansas Academy of Science, Proceedings* 30:54–56.

Klinger, T. C., and L. M. Raab. 1980. Archeological significance and the national register: A response to Barnes, Briggs, and Neilsen. *American Antiquity* 45:554–57.

Klippel, W. E. 1968. *Archaeological salvage in the Cannon Reservoir area, Missouri: 1967.* Report submitted to the National Park Service, Omaha.

———. 1969a. The Hearnes site: A multicomponent occupation site and cemetery in the Cairo Lowland region of southeast Missouri. *The Missouri Archaeologist* 31.

———. 1969b. *The Booth site: A Late Archaic campsite.* Missouri Archaeological Society, Research Series no. 6.

———. 1970. Prehistory and environmental change along the southern border of the Prairie Peninsula during the Archaic period. Ph.D. diss., Department of Anthro-pology, University of Missouri–Columbia.

———. 1971. *Graham Cave revisited: A reevaluation of its cultural position during the Archaic period.* Missouri Archaeological Society, Memoir no. 9.

———. 1972. An Early Woodland period manifestation in the Prairie Peninsula. *Journal of the Iowa Archaeological Society* 19.

Klippel, W. E., G. Celmer, and J. R. Purdue. 1978. The Holocene naiad record at Rodgers Shelter in the western Ozark Highland of Missouri. *Plains Anthropologist* 23:257–71.

Klippel, W. E., and M. Mandeville. 1972. The Collins site (23MN223): An Early Wood-land/Late Archaic manifestation in the Prairie Peninsula. In *Report of archaeological investigations in the Cannon Reservoir area, northeast Missouri*, by W. E. Klippel, M. Mandeville, and A. Osborn. Report submitted to the National Park Service, Omaha.

Klippel, W. E., M. Mandeville, and A. Osborn. 1972. *Report of archaeological investigations in the Cannon Reservoir area, northeast Missouri.* Report submitted to the National Park Service, Omaha.

Koch, A. C. 1839a. [Anonymously]. The mammoth [mastodon?—eds.]. *The American Journal of Science and Arts* 36:198–200.

———. 1839b. Remains of the mastodon in Missouri. *The American Journal of Science and Arts* 37:191–92.

———. 1840. *A short description of fossil remains, found in the state of Missouri, by the author.* St. Louis: published by the author.

———. 1841a. *Description of the Missourium, or Missouri Leviathan; together with its supposed habits. Indian traditions concerning the location from whence it was exhumed; also, comparisons of the Whale, Crocodile, and Missourium, with the Leviathan, as described in the 41st chapter of the book of Job.* St. Louis: published by the author.

———. 1841b. *Description of the Missourium, or Missouri Leviathan; together with its supposed habits, and Indian traditions concerning the location from whence it was exhumed; also, comparisons of the whale crocodile, and Missourium with the Leviathan, as described in the 41st chapter of the book of Job, and a catalogue of the whole fossil collection.* London: Fisher.

———. 1842a. *Description of the Missourium Theristocaulodon (Koch), or Missouri*

Leviathan, (Leviathan Missouriensis,) together with its supposed habits, and Indian traditions concerning the location from whence it was exhumed; also, comparisons of the whale crocodile, and Missourium with the Leviathan, as described in the 41st chapter of the book of Job, and a catalogue of the whole fossil collection. London: Fisher.

————. 1842b. On the genus Tetracaulodon. *Proceedings of the Geological Society of London* 3:714–16.

————. 1845. *Die Riesenthiere der Urwelt oder das neventdeckte Missourium Theristo-caulodon (Sichelzahn aus Missouri) und die Mastodontoiden im Allgemeinen und Besodern.* Berlin: Duncker.

————. 1857. Mastodon remains, in the state of Missouri, together with evidences of the existence of man contemporaneously with the mastodon. *Transactions of the Academy of Science of St. Louis* 1:61–64.

Kowalewski, S. A. 1990. Merits of full-coverage survey: Examples from the Valley of Oaxaca, Mexico. In *The archaeology of regions: A case for full-coverage survey,* ed. S. K. Fish and S. A. Kowalewski, 33–85. Washington, D.C.: Smithsonian Institution Press.

Kraelin, C. H., and R. M. Adams, eds. 1960. *City invincible: A symposium on urbanization and cultural development in the ancient Near East held at the Oriental Institute of the University of Chicago, December 4–7, 1958.* Chicago: University of Chicago Press.

Krause, R. A. 1977. Review of *Prehistoric man and his environments: A case study in the Ozark Highland,* ed. W. R. Wood and R. B. McMillan. *American Antiquity* 42:291–92.

Krieger, A. D. 1947. Certain projectile points of the early American hunters. *Bulletin of the Texas Archeological and Paleontological Society* 18:7–27.

Kroeber, A. L. 1909a. Classificatory systems of relationship. *Journal of the Royal Anthropological Institute* 39:77–84.

————. 1909b. The archaeology of California. In *Putnam anniversary volume: Anthropological essays presented to Frederic Ward Putnam in honor of his seventieth birthday, April 16, 1909,* ed. F. Boas, 1–42. New York: Stechert.

————. 1915. The eighteen professions. *American Anthropologist* 17:283–89.

————. 1916. *Zuni potsherds.* American Museum of Natural History, Anthropological Papers 18(1):7–37.

————. 1917a. *California kinship systems.* University of California, Publications in American Archaeology and Ethnology 12, 339–96.

————. 1917b. The superorganic. *American Anthropologist* 19:163–213.

————. 1935. History and science in anthropology. *American Anthropologist* 37:539–69.

————. 1939. *Cultural and natural areas of native North America.* University of California Publications in American Archaeology and Ethnology 38:1–242.

————. 1940. Statistical classification. *American Antiquity* 6:29–44.

————. 1952. *The nature of culture.* Chicago: University of Chicago Press.

Kuchler, A. W. 1964. *Potential natural vegetation of the coterminous United States.* American Geographical Society, Special Publication no. 36.

Kuhn, T. 1977. Second thoughts on paradigms. In *The Structure of Scientific Theories,* 2d ed., ed. F. Suppe, 459–517. Urbana: University of Illinois Press.

Lafferty, R. H., III. 1993. Evolution of settlement structure in the New Madrid Floodway. Paper presented at the 58th annual meeting of the Society for American Archaeology, St. Louis.

Lafferty, R. H., III, M. C. Sierzchula, R. F. Cande, M. T. Oates, M. Dugan, D. Porter, M. Guccione, L. Cummings, and K. M. Hess. 1991. *Cairo Lowland archeology: The* second step. Report submitted to the U.S. Army Corps of Engineers, Memphis District.

Laird, R. T., and M. Worcester. 1956. The inhibiting of lime blowing. *Transactions of the British Ceramic Society* 55:545–63.

Lapham, I. A. 1855. The antiquities of Wisconsin. *Smithsonian Contributions to Knowledge* 7(4).

Layhe, R., S. Sessions, C. Miksicek, and S. Plog. 1976. The Black Mesa Archaeological Project: A preliminary report for the 1975 season. Southern Illinois University, University Museum, Archaeological Service Report no. 48.

Leeds, L. L. 1979. Surface sampling and spatial analysis, the study of a major Mississippian ceremonial center at the Rich Woods site in southeast Missouri. Ph.D. diss., Department of Anthropology, University of Washington.

Lehmer, D. J. 1965. Salvage archaeology in the Middle Missouri. Multilithed for limited distribution.

Leidy, J. 1889. Notice of some fossil human bones. *Transactions of the Wagner Free Institute of Science of Philadelphia* 2:9–12.

Leonard, R. D., and G. T. Jones. 1987. Elements of an inclusive evolutionary model for archaeology. *Journal of Anthropological Archaeology* 6:199–219.

Lewarch, D. E. 1979. Controlled surface collection in regional analysis. In *The Cannon Reservoir Human Ecology Project: Recent advances in the archaeology of northeast Missouri*, ed. M. J. O'Brien and D. E. Lewarch, 42–51. University of Nebraska, Division of Archeological Research, Notebook no. 5.

———. 1982. Analysis of lithic artifacts. In *The Cannon Reservoir Human Ecology Project: An archaeological study of cultural adaptations in the southern Prairie Peninsula*, ed. M. J. O'Brien, R. E. Warren, and D. E. Lewarch, 337–68. New York: Academic Press.

Lewarch, D. E., and M. J. O'Brien. 1981a. The expanding role of surface assemblages in archaeological analysis. In *Advances in archaeological method and theory*, vol. 4, ed. M. B. Schiffer, 297–342. New York: Academic Press.

———. 1981b. Effect of short term tillage on aggregate provenience surface pattern. In *Plowzone archeology: Contributions to theory and technique*, ed. M. J. O'Brien and D. E. Lewarch, 7–49. Vanderbilt University, Publications in Anthropology no. 27.

Lewis, T. H. 1886. The "Monumental Tortoise" mounds of De-Coo-Dah. *American Journal of Archaeology & the History of the Fine Arts* 2:65–69.

———. 1892. The "Old Fort" of Saline County, Missouri. *The American Antiquarian and Oriental Journal* 14:159–66.

Lewontin, R. C. 1974. *The genetic basis of evolutionary change.* New York: Columbia University Press.

———. 1983. The organism as the subject and object of evolution. *Scientia* 118:65–82.

Lightfoot, K. G. 1986. Regional surveys in the eastern United States: The strengths and weaknesses of implementing subsurface testing programs. *American Antiquity* 51:484–504.

———. 1989. A defense of shovel-test sampling: A reply to Shott. *American Antiquity* 54:413–16.

Limp, W. F. 1989. *The use of multispectral digital imagery for archeological investigations.* Arkansas Archeological Survey, Research Series no. 34.

———. 1993. Multispectral digital imagery. In *The development of southeastern archaeology*, ed. J. K. Johnson, 184–206. Tuscaloosa: University of Alabama Press.

Linderer, N. M. 1983. *Cultural resources survey, Harry S. Truman Dam and Reservoir*

Project. Vol. 3, *Architectural survey.* Report submitted to the U.S. Army Corps of Engineers, Kansas City District.

Linton, R. 1944. North American cooking pots. *American Antiquity* 9:369–80.

Lipe, W. D. 1974. A conservation model for American archaeology. *The Kiva* 39:214–45.

Lippincott, K. 1972. *Archeological salvage in the Kaysinger Bluff Reservoir, Missouri: 1969.* Report submitted to the National Park Service, Omaha.

Logan, W. D. 1952. *Graham Cave, an Archaic site in Montgomery County, Missouri.* Missouri Archaeological Society, Memoir no. 2.

Longacre, W. A. 1981. CRM publication: A review essay. *Journal of Field Archaeology* 8:487–91.

Lopinot, N. H. 1982. Summary of the botanical analysis. In *The Carrier Mills Archaeological Project: Human adaptation in the Saline Valley, Illinois,* ed. R. W. Jefferies and B. M. Butler, 797–806. Southern Illinois University at Carbondale, Center for Archaeological Investigations, Research Paper no. 33.

Lovis, W. A. 1976. Quarter-sections and forests: An example of probability sampling in the northeastern woodlands. *American Antiquity* 41:364–72.

Lowe, J. L. 1940. Archaeological investigations in Carter County. *The Missouri Archaeologist* 6(2):4–10.

———. 1988. The magnificent summer of '38. *Missouri Archaeological Society Quarterly* 5(2):4–7, 12–15, 18; 5(3):4–7, 14–17.

Lubbock, J. 1863. North American archaeology. *Smithsonian Institution, Annual Report* (1862), 318–36.

Luedtke, B. E., and J. T. Meyers. 1984. Trace element variation in Burlington chert: A case study. In *Prehistoric chert exploitation: Studies from the Midcontinent,* ed. B. M. Butler and E. E. May, 287–98. Southern Illinois University, Center for Archaeological Investigations, Occasional Paper no. 2.

Lyell, C. 1830. *Principles of geology, being an attempt to explain the former changes of the earth's surface by reference to causes now in operation.* Vol. 1. London: Murray.

———. 1863. *The geological evidences of the antiquity of man with remarks on theories of the origin of species by variation.* London: Murray.

Lykins, W. H. R. 1878. Antiquities of Kansas City, Missouri. *Smithsonian Institution, Annual Report* (1877), 251–53.

Lyman, R. L., and M. J. O'Brien. 1987. Plow-zone zooarchaeology: Fragmentation and identifiability. *Journal of Field Archaeology* 14:493–98.

Lynott, M. J. 1982. Mississippian archaeology of the upper Current River, southeast Missouri. *Southeastern Archaeology* 1:8–21.

———. 1986. Two Emergent Mississippian sites in the eastern Ozarks, southeast Missouri. Paper presented at the 51st annual meeting of the Society for American Archaeology, New Orleans.

———. 1987. Thermoluminescence dating of prehistoric ceramics in southeast Missouri: A progress report. *Society for Archaeological Sciences Newsletter* 10(2):2–5.

Lynott, M. J., and J. E. Price. 1989. The Late Woodland to Emergent Mississippian transition in the eastern Ozark region, southeast Missouri. Paper presented at the 51st annual meeting of the Society for American Archaeology, Atlanta.

Lyon, E. A. 1982. New Deal archaeology in the Southeast: WPA, TVA, NPS, 1934–1942. Ph.D. diss., Department of History, Louisiana State University.

Lyons, T. R., assembler. 1981. *Remote sensing: Multispectral analyses of cultural resources.* Washington, D.C.: National Park Service.

Lyons, T. R., and T. E. Avery. 1977. *Remote sensing: A handbook for archeologists and cultural resource managers.* Washington, D.C.: National Park Service.

Lyons, T. R., and F. J. Mathien, eds. 1980. *Cultural resources remote sensing.* Washington, D.C.: National Park Service.

Mack, J. 1942. Archaeological field work at the University of Missouri. *The Missouri Archaeologist* 8(1):19–20.

MacNeish, R. S. 1964. Ancient Mesoamerican civilization. *Science* 143:531–37.

MacNeish, R. S., A. Nelken-Terner, and F. W. Johnson. 1967. *The prehistory of the Tehuacán Valley.* Vol. 2, *Nonceramic artifacts.* Austin: University of Texas Press.

MacNeish, R. S., F. A. Peterson, and K. V. Flannery. 1970. *The prehistory of the Tehuacán Valley.* Vol. 3, *Ceramics.* Austin: University of Texas Press.

MacNeish, R. S., F. Peterson, and J. A. Neely. 1975. *The prehistory of the Tehuacán Valley.* Vol. 5, *Excavations and reconnaissance.* Austin: University of Texas Press.

Madsen, M. E., and R. C. Dunnell. 1989. The role of microartifacts in deducing land use from low density records in plowed surfaces. Paper presented at the 54th annual meeting of the Society for American Archaeology, Atlanta.

Majewski, T. 1987. Social status and economic patterning in the central Salt River valley of northeastern Missouri during the nineteenth and early twentieth centuries. Ph.D. diss., Department of Anthropology, University of Missouri–Columbia.

Majewski, T., and M. J. O'Brien. 1984. *An analysis of historical ceramics from the central Salt River valley of northeast Missouri.* University of Missouri, American Archaeology Division, Publications in Archaeology no. 2.

———. 1987. The use and misuse of nineteenth-century English and American ceramics in archaeological analysis. In *Advances in archaeological method and theory,* vol. 11, ed. M. B. Schiffer, 97–209. Orlando: Academic Press.

Mandeville, M. D. 1973. A consideration of thermal pretreatment of chert. *Plains Anthropologist* 18:177–202.

March, B. 1934. *Standards of pottery description.* University of Michigan, Museum of Anthropology, Occasional Contributions no. 3.

Markman, C. W. 1993. *Miller Cave (23PU2), Fort Leonard Wood, Pulaski County, Missouri: Report of archaeological testing and assessment of damage.* Report submitted to the U.S. Army Corps of Engineers, Kansas City District.

Marquardt, W. H. 1977a. Epilogue to *Regional centers in archaeology: Prospects and problems,* ed. W. H. Marquardt. Missouri Archaeological Society, Research Series no. 14, 38–39.

———, ed. 1977b. *Regional centers in archaeology: Prospects and problems.* Missouri Archaeological Society, Research Series no. 14.

Marshall, R. A. 1954. A descriptive typology of Griffin and Tater Hole Shelter pottery. Manuscript on file, University of Missouri–Columbia, Museum of Anthropology.

———. 1956. The Delaware Bridge cairn, 23CN13. *The Missouri Archaeologist* 18:18–33.

———. 1958. The use of Table Rock Reservoir projectile points in the delineation of cultural complexes and their distribution. Master's thesis, Department of Sociology and Anthropology, University of Missouri.

———. 1960. Use of Table Rock Reservoir projectile points in the delineation of cultural complexes and their distribution. In *Archaeological investigations in the Table Rock Reservoir area,* comp. C. H. Chapman, 5–172. Report submitted to the National Park Service, Lincoln, Neb.

———. 1963a. Lander Shelter 2, 23SN245, Stone County, Missouri. *The Missouri Archaeologist* 25:109–34.

————. 1963b. *A descriptive system for projectile points.* Missouri Archaeological Society, Research Series no. 1.

————. 1963c. Archeology of Jasper County, Missouri: The Ernest J. Palmer collection. *Plains Anthropologist* 8:1–26.

————. 1965. An archaeological investigation of interstate route 55 through New Madrid and Pemiscot counties, Missouri. Missouri State Highway Department, Highway Archaeology Report no. 1.

————. n.d.-a. Highway salvage archaeology at two village sites in Pemiscot and New Madrid counties, Missouri, 1965. Report on file, University of Missouri, Museum of Anthropology.

————. n.d.-b. Archaeological investigations in the Meramec Spring, St. James, Missouri, locality. Report on file, University of Missouri, Museum of Anthropology.

Marshall, R. A., and C. H. Chapman. 1960a. The Rice site, 23SN200, revisited. In *Archaeological investigations in the Table Rock Reservoir area,* comp. C. H. Chapman, 988–1044. Report submitted to the National Park Service, Lincoln, Neb.

————. 1960b. Cultural materials from Jakie Shelter, 23BY388. In *Archaeological investigations in the Table Rock Reservoir area,* comp. C. H. Chapman, 1131–49. Report submitted to the National Park Service, Lincoln, Neb.

Marshall, R. A., and J. F. Hopgood. 1964. A test excavation at Hoecake, 23MI-8, Mississippi County, Missouri. *Missouri Archaeological Society Newsletter* no. 177:3–6.

Mason, H. L. 1878. Mounds in Missouri. *The American Antiquarian and Oriental Journal* 1:14–15.

Mason, O. T. 1880. Summary of correspondence of the Smithsonian Institution previous to January 1, 1880, in answer to Circular no. 316. *Smithsonian Institution, Annual Report* (1879), 428–48.

————. 1896. Influence of environment upon human industries or arts. *Smithsonian Institution, Annual Report* (1895), 639–65.

————. 1907. Environment. In Handbook of American Indians north of Mexico, ed. F. W. Hodge. *Bureau of American Ethnology, Bulletin* 30:427–30.

Mason, R. D. 1982. A regional chronology for the early historical period. In *The Cannon Reservoir Human Ecology Project: An archaeological study of cultural adaptations in the southern Prairie Peninsula,* ed. M. J. O'Brien, R. E. Warren, and D. E. Lewarch, 131–41. New York: Academic Press.

————. 1983. *Euro-American pioneer settlement systems in the Salt River region, northeast Missouri.* University of Missouri, American Archaeology Division, Publications in Archaeology no. 2.

Mason, R. D., R. E. Warren, and M. J. O'Brien. 1982. Historic settlement patterns. In *The Cannon Reservoir Human Ecology Project: An archaeological study of cultural adaptations in the southern Prairie Peninsula,* ed. M. J. O'Brien, R. E. Warren, and D. E. Lewarch, 369–87. New York: Academic Press.

Matthes, F. E. 1951. Rebirth of the glaciers of the Sierra Nevada during late post-Pleistocene time. *Geological Society of America, Bulletin* 52:2030.

Mayr, E. 1982. *The growth of biological thought: Diversity, evolution, and inheritance.* Cambridge, Mass.: Belknap.

————. 1988. *Toward a new philosophy of biology: Observations on an evolutionist.* Cambridge, Mass.: Harvard University Press.

McCutcheon, P., and R. C. Dunnell. 1993. Quantifying lithic raw material variability of Crowley's Ridge gravel, southeast Missouri and northeast Arkansas. Paper presented at the 59th annual meeting of the Society for American Archaeology, St. Louis.

McDermott, J. F. 1948. Dr. Koch's wonderful fossils. *Bulletin of the Missouri Historical Society* 4:233–56.

McGee, A. N. 1897. Anthropology at the American Association for the Advancement of Science. *Science* 6:508–13.

McGee, W J. 1889. Paleolithic man in America: His antiquity and environment. *Popular Science Monthly* 34:20–36.

———. 1893a. Man and the glacial period. *American Anthropologist* 6:85–95.

———. 1893b. A geologic palimpsest. *Literary Northwest* 2:274–76.

———. 1897a. Discussion. *American Association for the Advancement of Science, Proceedings* 46:390.

———. 1897b. Anthropology at Detroit and Toronto. *American Anthropologist* 10:317–45.

———. 1897c. The Siouan Indians: A preliminary sketch. *Bureau of American Ethnology, Annual Report* 15:153–204.

McGimsey, C. R., III. 1976. The past, the present, the future: Public policy as a dynamic interface. In *Anthropology and the public interest: Fieldwork and theory,* ed. P. R. Sanday, 25–28. New York: Academic Press.

———. 1985. "This, too, will pass": Moss-Bennett in perspective. *American Antiquity* 50:326–31.

McGimsey, C. R., III, and H. A. Davis. 1968. Modern land use practices and the archeology of the lower Mississippi alluvial valley. *The Arkansas Archeologist* 9:28–36.

———, eds. 1977. *The management of archaeological resources: The Airlie House report.* Washington, D.C.: Society for American Archaeology.

McKern, W. C. 1935. Editorial. *American Antiquity* 1:81–83.

———. 1939. The midwestern taxonomic method as an aid to archaeological culture study. *American Antiquity* 4:301–13.

McKinn[e]y, J. J. 1954. Hopewell sites in the Big Bend area of central Missouri. *The Missouri Archaeologist* 16:1–54.

McKusick, M. 1970. *The Davenport conspiracy.* Office of the State Archaeologist of Iowa, Report no. 1.

———. 1991. *The Davenport conspiracy revisited.* Ames: Iowa State University Press.

McMillan, R. B. 1963. A survey and evaluation of the archaeology of the central Gasconade River valley in Missouri. Master's thesis, Department of Sociology and Anthropology, University of Missouri.

———. 1965a. The Rodgers Shelter: A preliminary report. In *Preliminary archaeological investigations in the Kaysinger Bluff Reservoir area,* comp. C. H. Chapman, 330–403. Report submitted to the National Park Service, Omaha.

———. 1965b. *Archaeological reconnaissance in the proposed Hackleman Corner Reservoir, Missouri.* Report submitted to the National Park Service, Omaha.

———. 1965c. Gasconade prehistory: A survey and evaluation of the archaeological resources. *The Missouri Archaeologist* 27(3–4).

———. 1966a. *Archaeological investigations in the Stockton Reservoir area, southwestern Missouri: 1962–1964,* part 2. Report submitted to the National Park Service, Omaha.

———. 1966b. *Archaeological investigations at the Rodgers Shelter site, Kaysinger Bluff Reservoir, Missouri: The 1965 field season.* Report submitted to the National Park Service, Omaha.

———. 1968. Fristoe burial mounds from the prairie border region of southwestern Missouri. *Plains Anthropologist* 13:46–62.

————. 1971. Biophysical change and cultural adaptation at Rodgers Shelter, Missouri. Ph.D. diss., Department of Anthropology, University of Colorado.

————. 1976a. Man and mastodon: A review of Koch's 1840 Pomme de Terre expeditions. In *Prehistoric man and his environments: A case study in the Ozark Highland,* ed. W. R. Wood and R. B. McMillan, 81–96. New York: Academic Press.

————. 1976b. Rodgers Shelter: A record of cultural and environmental change. In *Prehistoric man and his environments: A case study in the Ozark Highland,* ed. W. R. Wood and R. B. McMillan, 111–22. New York: Academic Press.

————. 1976c. The dynamics of cultural and environmental change at Rodgers Shelter, Missouri. In *Prehistoric man and his environments: A case study in the Ozark Highland,* ed. W. R. Wood and R. B. McMillan, 211–32. New York: Academic Press.

————. 1992. W. R. Wood's interdisciplinary approach to archaeology. Paper presented at the 50th Plains Conference, Lincoln, Neb.

McMillan, R. B., and W. E. Klippel. 1981. Environmental changes and hunter-gatherer adaptation in the southern Prairie Peninsula. *Journal of Archaeological Science* 8:215–45.

Medford, L. D. 1972. *Site destruction due to agricultural practices in northeast Arkansas.* Arkansas Archeological Survey, Research Series no. 3.

Mehringer, P. J., Jr., J. E. King, and E. H. Lindsay. 1970. A record of Wisconsin-age vegetation and fauna from the Ozarks of western Missouri. In *Pleistocene and recent environments of the central Great Plains,* ed. W. Dort Jr. and J. K. Jones Jr., 173–83. Lawrence: University Press of Kansas.

Mehringer, P. J., Jr., C. E. Schweger, W. R. Wood, and R. B. McMillan. 1968. Late Pleistocene boreal forest in the western Ozark Highlands? *Ecology* 49:567–68.

Meltzer, D. J. 1983. The antiquity of man and the development of American archaeology. *Advances in archaeological method and theory,* vol. 6, ed. M. B. Schiffer, 1–51.

————. 1985. North American archaeology and archaeologists, 1879–1934. *American Antiquity* 50:249–60.

————. 1989. A question of relevance. In *Tracing archaeology's past: The historiography of archaeology,* ed. A. L. Christenson, 5–19. Carbondale: Southern Illinois University Press.

————. 1991. On "paradigms" and "paradigm bias" in controversies over human antiquity in America. In *The first Americans: Search and research,* ed. T. Dillehay and D. J. Meltzer, 13–49. Boca Raton, Fla.: CRC Press.

Meltzer, D. J., and R. C. Dunnell, eds. 1992. *The archaeology of William Henry Holmes.* Washington, D.C.: Smithsonian Institution Press.

Meltzer, D. J., and W. C. Sturtevant. 1983. The Holly Oak shell game: An historic archaeological fraud. In *Lulu linear punctated: Essays in honor of George Irving Quimby,* ed. R. C. Dunnell and D. K. Grayson, 325–52. University of Michigan, Museum of Anthropology, Anthropological Papers no. 72.

Meyers, J. T. 1970. *Chert resources of the lower Illinois Valley.* Illinois State Museum, Reports of Investigations no. 18.

Miller, R. L. 1983. *Cultural resources survey, Harry S. Truman Dam and Reservoir Project.* Vol. 6, *Euro-American settlement of the lower Pomme de Terre River valley.* Report submitted to the U.S. Army Corps of Engineers, Kansas City District.

Million, M. G. 1975. Ceramic technology of the Nodena phase people (ca. A.D. 1400–1700). *Southeastern Archaeological Conference Bulletin* 18:201–8.

————. 1980. The Big Lake phase pottery industry. In *Zebree Archaeological Project: Excavations, data interpretation, and report on the Zebree Homestead site, Mississippi*

County, Arkansas, ed. D. F. Morse and P. A. Morse, 18–1 to 18–42. Fayetteville: Arkansas Archeological Survey.

Milner, G. R., and V. G. Smith. 1986. *New Deal archaeology in Kentucky: Excavations, collections, and research.* University of Kentucky, Program for Cultural Resource Assessment, Occasional Papers in Anthropology no. 5.

Missouri Botanical Garden. 1974. *Environmental assessment: Clarence Cannon Dam and Reservoir.* St. Louis.

Mitchell, R. D. 1972. Agricultural regionalization: Origins and diffusion in the Upper South before 1860. In *International geography,* vol. 2, ed. W. P. Adams and F. M. Helleiner. Toronto: University of Toronto Press.

———. 1978. The formation of early American cultural regions: An interpretation. In *European settlement and development in North America: Essays on geographical change in honour and memory of Andrew Hill Clark,* ed. J. R. Gibson, 66–90. Toronto: University of Toronto Press.

Moffat, C. R., and C. J. Anderson. 1984. *Test excavations at three archaeological sites on Kaskaskia Island, Randolph County, Illinois.* U.S. Army Corps of Engineers, St. Louis District, Cultural Resource Management Report no. 12.

Montagu, M. F. A. 1942. The earliest account of the association of human artifacts with fossil mammals in North America. *Science* 95:380–81.

Montagu, M. F. A., and C. B. Peterson. 1944. The earliest account of the association of human artifacts with fossil mammals in North America. *American Philosophical Society, Proceedings* 87:407–19.

Moore, C. B. 1910. Antiquities of the St. Francis, White and Black rivers, Arkansas. *Journal of the Academy of Natural Sciences of Philadelphia* 14:255–364.

———. 1916. Additional investigation on Mississippi River. *Journal of the Academy of Natural Sciences of Philadelphia* 16:493–508.

Moorehead, W. K. 1892. *Primitive man in Ohio.* New York: Putnam.

———. 1897. Report of field work carried out in the Muskingum, Scioto, and Ohio Valley during the season of 1896. *Ohio Archaeological and Historical Quarterly* 5:165–274.

———. 1914. *The American Indian in the United States: Period 1850–1914: The present condition of the American Indian; his political history and other topics; a plea for justice.* Andover, Mass.: Andover Press.

———. 1922. *A report on the archaeology of Maine: Being a narrative of explorations in that state, 1912–1920, together with work at Lake Champlain 1917.* Andover, Mass.: Phillips Academy.

———. 1927. A report of progress on the exploration of the Cahokia group. In *The Cahokia mounds,* part 1, ed. F. C. Baker, 9–56. University of Illinois, Museum of Natural History, Contribution no. 28.

Moratto, M. J., and R. E. Kelly. 1978. Optimizing strategies for evaluating archaeological significance. *Advances in archaeological method and theory,* vol. 1, ed. M. B. Schiffer, 1–30. New York: Academic Press.

Morgan, D. T. 1985. Ceramic analysis. In *Smiling Dan: Structure and function at a Middle Woodland settlement in the lower Illinois Valley,* ed. B. D. Stafford and M. B. Sant, 183–257. Center for American Archeology, Kampsville Archeological Center, Research Series no. 2.

———. 1992. Ceramics. In *Early Woodland occupations at the Ambrose Flick site in the Sny Bottom of west-central Illinois,* ed. C. R. Stafford, 127–49. Center for American Archeology, Kampsville Archeological Center, Research Series no. 10.

Morgan, D. T., D. L. Asch, and C. R. Stafford. 1986. Marion and Black Sand occupations in the Sny Bottom of the Mississippi Valley. In *Early Woodland archeology,* ed. K. B. Farnsworth and T. E. Emerson, 208–30. Center for American Archeology, Kampsville Seminars in Archeology no. 2.

Morgan, L. H. 1877. *Ancient society.* New York: Holt.

Morris, E. H. 1919. *The Aztec Ruin.* American Museum of Natural History, Anthropological Papers 25(1).

———. 1921. *The house of the great kiva at the Aztec Ruin.* American Museum of Natural History, Anthropological Papers 26(2).

Morrow, C. A. 1984. A biface production model for gravel-based chipped stone industries. *Lithic Technology* 13:20–29.

Morse, D. F., and A. C. Goodyear. 1973. The significance of the Dalton adze in northeast Arkansas. *Plains Anthropologist* 18:316–22.

Morse, D. F., and P. A. Morse, eds. 1980. *Zebree Archeological Project.* Report submitted to the U.S. Army Corps of Engineers, Memphis District.

Morse, D. F., and P. A. Morse. 1983. *Archaeology of the central Mississippi Valley.* New York: Academic Press.

Morse, D. F., and P. [A.] Morse. 1990. Emergent Mississippian in the central Mississippi Valley. In *The Mississippian emergence,* ed. B. D. Smith, 153–73. Washington, D.C.: Smithsonian Institution Press.

Morse, P. A. 1981. *Parkin.* Arkansas Archeological Survey, Research Series no. 13.

Morse, P. [A.] and D. F. Morse. 1990. The Zebree site: An emergent Early Mississippian expression in northeast Arkansas. In *The Mississippian emergence,* ed. B. D. Smith, 51–66. Washington, D.C.: Smithsonian Institution Press.

Morton, S. G. 1839. *Crania Americana; or a comparative view of the skulls of various aboriginal nations of North and South America.* Philadelphia: Dobson.

Moss, J. H. 1951. *Early man in the Eden Valley.* University of Pennsylvania, University Museum, Museum Monographs.

Munson, P. J. 1982. Marion, Black Sand, Morton, and Havana relationship: An Illinois perspective. *Wisconsin Archeologist* 63:1–17.

———. 1986. Black Sand and Havana tradition ceramic assemblages and culture history in the central Illinois River valley. In *Early Woodland archeology,* ed. K. B. Farnsworth and T. E. Emerson, 280–300. Center for American Archeology, Kampsville Seminars in Archeology no. 2.

Nagel, E. 1961. *The structure of science.* New York: Harcourt, Brace, and World.

Nance, J. D. 1971. Functional interpretations from microscopic analysis. *American Antiquity* 36:361–66.

National Research Council. 1929. Report of the Conference on Midwestern Archaeology, held in St. Louis, Missouri, May 18, 1929. *National Research Council, Bulletin* no. 17.

Neff, H. 1992. Ceramics and evolution. In *Advances in archaeological method and theory,* vol. 4, ed. M. B. Schiffer, 141–93. Tucson: University of Arizona Press.

———. 1993. Theory, sampling, and technical studies in archaeological pottery analysis. *American Antiquity* 58:23–44.

Nelson, N. C. 1909. *Shellmounds of the San Francisco Bay region.* University of California, Publications in American Archaeology and Ethnology 7(4).

———. 1910. *The Ellis Landing shellmound.* University of California, Publications in American Archaeology and Ethnology 7(5).

———. 1916. Chronology of the Tano Ruins, New Mexico. *American Anthropologist* 18:159–80.

———. 1921. Recent activities of European archaeologists. *Natural History* 21:537–41.

————. 1928a. Review of *The antiquity of the deposits in Jacob's Cavern*, by V. C. Allison. *American Anthropologist* 30:329–35.

————. 1928b. In re Jacob's Cavern. *American Anthropologist* 30:547–48.

Newton, M. B., Jr. 1978. Review of *Prehistoric man and his environments: A case study in the Ozark Highland*, ed. W. R. Wood and R. B. McMillan. *Journal of Historical Geography* 4:415–17.

Novick, A. L., and C. E. Cantley. 1983. *Cultural resources survey, Harry S. Truman Dam and Reservoir Project.* Vol. 8, *Archeological test excavations*. Report submitted to the U.S. Army Corps of Engineers, Kansas City District.

O'Brien, M. J. 1977. Cannon Reservoir Human Ecology Project research design 1977–1980. University of Nebraska, Department of Anthropology, Technical Report no. 77–01.

————. 1984a. The Cannon project and data publication: A reply to Green. *The Wisconsin Archeologist* 65:398–401.

————. 1984b. *Grassland, forest, and historical settlement: An analysis of dynamics in northeast Missouri.* Lincoln: University of Nebraska Press.

————. 1985a. Archaeology of the central Salt River valley: An overview of the prehistoric occupation. *The Missouri Archaeologist* 46 (whole volume).

————. 1985b. Intensive surface collection and sample excavation of a Middle Woodland Havana community. Paper presented at the 50th annual meeting of the Society for American Archaeology, Denver.

————. 1986. Hopewell in the lower Illinois River valley. *Quarterly Review of Archaeology* 7(2):3–5.

————. 1987. Sedentism, population growth, and resource selection in the Woodland Midwest: A review of coevolutionary developments. *Current Anthropology* 28:177–97.

————. 1988. Comment on "Ecological theory and cultural evolution in the Valley of Oaxaca," by W. T. Sanders and D. L. Nichols. *Current Anthropology* 32:62–63.

————. 1993. Late-period phases and assemblage variation in southeastern Missouri. Paper presented at the 58th annual meeting of the Society for American Archaeology, St. Louis.

————. 1994. *Cat monsters and head pots: The archaeology of Missouri's Pemiscot Bayou.* Columbia: University of Missouri Press.

————. 1996. *Middle and Late Woodland subsistence and ceramic technology in the central Mississippi River valley: Selected studies from the Burkemper site, Lincoln County, Missouri.* Illinois State Museum, Reports of Investigations no. 52 (in press).

O'Brien, M. J., J. L. Beets, R. E. Warren, T. Hotrabhavananda, T. W. Barney, and E. E. Voigt. 1982. Digital enhancement and grey-level slicing of aerial photographs: Techniques for archaeological analysis of intrasite variability. *World Archaeology* 14:173–90.

O'Brien, M. J., J. A. Ferguson, T. D. Holland, and D. E. Lewarch. 1989. On interpretive competition in the absence of appropriate data: Monte Albán revisited. *Current Anthropology* 30:191–200.

O'Brien, M. J., and G. L. Fox. 1994a. Sorting artifacts in space and time. In *Cat monsters and head pots: The archaeology of Missouri's Pemiscot Bayou*, by M. J. O'Brien, 25–60. Columbia: University of Missouri Press.

————. 1994b. Assemblage similarities and differences. In *Cat monsters and head pots: The archaeology of Missouri's Pemiscot Bayou*, by M. J. O'Brien, 61–93. Columbia: University of Missouri Press.

O'Brien, M. J., and D. R. Henning. 1982. Introduction to *The Cannon Reservoir Human*

Ecology Project: An archaeological study of cultural adaptations in the southern Prairie Peninsula, ed. M. J. O'Brien, R. E. Warren, and D. E. Lewarch, 3–11. New York: Academic Press.

O'Brien, M. J., and R. J. Hoard. 1996. Ceramic vessels. In *Middle and Late Woodland subsistence and ceramic technology in the central Mississippi River valley: Selected studies from the Burkemper site, Lincoln County, Missouri*, by M. J. O'Brien. Illinois State Museum, Reports of Investigations no. 52 (in press).

O'Brien, M. J., and T. D. Holland. 1990. Variation, selection, and the archaeological record. In *Advances in archaeological method and theory*, vol. 2, ed. M. B. Schiffer, 31–79. Tucson: University of Arizona Press.

————. 1992. The role of adaptation in archaeological explanation. *American Antiquity* 57:36–59.

————. 1995a. Behavioral archaeology and the extended phenotype. In *Reconstruction theory: A behavioral approach to the archaeological record*, ed. A. E. Nielsen, J. M. Skibo, and W. H. Walker. Salt Lake City: University of Utah Press (in press).

————. 1995b. The nature and premise of a selection-based archaeology. In *Evolutionary archaeology: Methodological issues*, ed. P. A. Teltser, 175–200. Tucson: University of Arizona Press.

O'Brien, M. J., T. D. Holland, R. J. Hoard, and G. L. Fox. 1994. Evolutionary implications of design and performance characteristics of prehistoric pottery. *Journal of Archaeological Method and Theory* 1:259–304.

O'Brien, M. J., and D. E. Lewarch, eds. 1981. *Plowzone archeology: Contributions to theory and technique.* Vanderbilt University, Publications in Anthropology no. 27.

O'Brien, M. J., and D. E. Lewarch. 1984. The built environment. In *Grassland, forest, and historical settlement: An analysis of dynamics in northeast Missouri*, by M. J. O'Brien, 231–65. Lincoln: University of Nebraska Press.

O'Brien, M. J., D. E. Lewarch, J. E. Saunders, and C. B. Fraser. 1980. *An analysis of historic structures in the Cannon Reservoir area, northeast Missouri.* University of Nebraska, Department of Anthropology, Technical Report no. 80–17.

O'Brien, M. J., and R. L. Lyman. 1996. Site structure and sample context. In *Middle and Late Woodland subsistence and ceramic technology in the central Mississippi River valley: Selected studies from the Burkemper site, Lincoln County, Missouri*, by M. J. O'Brien. Illinois State Museum, Reports of Investigations no. 52 (in press).

O'Brien, M. J., R. L. Lyman, and T. D. Holland. 1989. Geoarchaeological evidence for prairie-mound formation in the Mississippi alluvial valley, southeastern Missouri. *Quaternary Research* 31:83–93.

O'Brien, M. J., and T. Majewski. 1989. Wealth and status in the upper South socioeconomic system of northeastern Missouri. *Historical Archaeology* 23(2):60–95.

O'Brien, M. J., R. D. Mason, and J. E. Saunders. 1982. The structure of historic communities. In *The Cannon Reservoir Human Ecology Project: An archaeological study of cultural adaptations in the southern Prairie Peninsula*, ed. M. J. O'Brien, R. E. Warren, and D. E. Lewarch, 301–34. New York: Academic Press.

O'Brien, M. J., and C. K. McDaniel. 1982. Prehistoric community patterns: Surface definition. In *The Cannon Reservoir Human Ecology Project: An archaeological study of cultural adaptations in the southern Prairie Peninsula*, ed. M. J. O'Brien, R. E. Warren, and D. E. Lewarch, 217–53. New York: Academic Press.

O'Brien, M. J., D. M. Pearsall, and R. J. Hoard. 1992. *Report on the completion of curation of archaeological materials from southeastern Missouri.* Report submitted to the National Science Foundation, Washington, D.C.

O'Brien, M. J., and R. E. Warren. 1982a. The approach. In *The Cannon Reservoir Human Ecology Project: An archaeological study of cultural adaptations in the southern Prairie Peninsula,* ed. M. J. O'Brien, R. E. Warren, and D. E. Lewarch, 13–25. New York: Academic Press.

———. 1982b. Chronology of the preceramic period. In *The Cannon Reservoir Human Ecology Project: An archaeological study of cultural adaptations in the southern Prairie Peninsula,* ed. M. J. O'Brien, R. E. Warren, and D. E. Lewarch, 103–16. New York: Academic Press.

———. 1982c. Prehistoric community patterns: Subsurface definition. In *The Cannon Reservoir Human Ecology Project: An archaeological study of cultural adaptations in the southern Prairie Peninsula,* ed. M. J. O'Brien, R. E. Warren, and D. E. Lewarch, 255–89. New York: Academic Press.

———. 1983. An Archaic projectile point sequence from the southern Prairie Peninsula: The Pigeon Roost Creek site. In *Archaic hunters and gatherers in the American Midwest,* ed. J. L. Phillips and J. A. Brown, 71–98. New York: Academic Press.

———. 1985. Stratigraphy and chronology at Pigeon Roost Creek. In Archaeology of the central Salt River valley: An overview of the prehistoric occupation, by M. J. O'Brien. *The Missouri Archaeologist* 46:203–25.

O'Brien, M. J., R. E. Warren, and D. E. Lewarch, eds. 1982. *The Cannon Reservoir Human Ecology Project: An archaeological study of cultural adaptations in the southern Prairie Peninsula.* New York: Academic Press.

Odell, G. H., and F. Cowan. 1987. Estimating tillage effects on artifact distributions. *American Antiquity* 52:456–84.

Odell, G. H., and F. Odell-Vereecken. 1980. Verifying the reliability of lithic use-wear assessments by "blind tests": The low-power approach. *Journal of Field Archaeology* 7:87–120.

Olsen, J. 1987. The practice of archaeology in China today. *Antiquity* 61:282–89.

Osborn, A. J., and C. R. Falk. 1977. Ecological diversity and aboriginal hunter-gatherers in northcentral Nebraska. In *A resource handbook: 1977 archeological field school,* ed. A. J. Osborn and C. R. Falk. University of Nebraska, Department of Anthropology, Technical Report no. 77–10.

Owen, R. 1842. Report on the Missourium now exhibiting at the Egyptian Hall, with an inquiry into the claims of the Tetracaulodon to generic distinction. *Proceedings of the Geological Society of London* 3:689–95.

———. 1843. Letter from Richard Owen . . . on Dr. Harlan's notice of new fossil Mammalia. . . . *American Journal of Science* 44:341–45.

Padgett, T. J. 1978. *Blue Mountain Lake: An archeological survey and an experimental study of inundation impacts.* Arkansas Archeological Survey, Research Report no. 13.

Pangborn, R. E. 1966. The Eureka Mound, 23DA-250, illustrating Caddoan contacts in the Stockton Reservoir area, southwestern Missouri. *Plains Anthropologist* 11:167.

Pangborn, R. E., H. T. Ward, and W. R. Wood. 1971. Flycatcher village: A non-pottery site in the Stockton Reservoir, Missouri. *Plains Anthropologist* 16:60–73.

Parmalee, P. W. 1965. The food economy of Archaic and Woodland peoples at the Tick Creek Cave site, Missouri. *The Missouri Archaeologist* 27(1).

Parmalee, P., R. B. McMillan, and F. B. King. 1976. Changing subsistence patterns at Rodgers Shelter. In *Prehistoric man and his environments: A case study in the Ozark Highland,* ed. W. R. Wood and R. B. McMillan, 141–61. New York: Academic Press.

Parmenter, R. 1966. Glimpses of a friendship, Zelia Nuttall and F. Boas. In *Pioneers of American anthropology; the uses of biography,* ed. J. Helm, 83–147. American Ethnological Society Memoirs no. 43.

Parsons, J. R. 1971. *Prehistoric settlement patterns in the Texcoco region, Mexico.* University of Michigan, Museum of Anthropology Memoirs no. 3.

———. 1972. Archaeological settlement patterns. *Annual Review of Anthropology* 1:127–50.

———. 1976. Settlement and population history of the Basin of Mexico. In *The Valley of Mexico: Studies in pre-Hispanic ecology and society,* ed. E. R. Wolf. Albuquerque: University of New Mexico Press.

———. 1990. Critical reflections on a decade of full-coverage regional survey in the Valley of Mexico. In *The archaeology of regions: A case for full-coverage survey,* ed. S. K. Fish and S. A. Kowalewski, 7–31. Washington, D.C.: Smithsonian Institution Press.

Peabody, C., and W. K. Moorehead. 1904. The exploration of Jacobs Cavern. *Phillips Academy, Department of Archaeology, Bulletin* no. 1.

Peale, T. R. 1862. Ancient mounds at St. Louis, Missouri, in 1819. *Smithsonian Institution, Annual Report* (1861), 386–91.

Peet, S. D. 1887. "Elephant pipes." *The American Antiquarian and Oriental Journal* 9:250–51.

———. 1890. The difference between Indian and mound-builders' relics. *The American Antiquarian and Oriental Journal* 12:251–72.

———. 1893. The archaeologists and the geologists. *The American Antiquarian and Oriental Journal* 15:46–54.

———. 1903. *The mound builders: Their works and relics.* 2d ed. Chicago: American Antiquarian.

Perttula, T. K., and J. E. Price. 1984. The 1882 investigations by Colonel P. W. Norris at the Powers Fort site, 23BU10, southeast Missouri. *Tennessee Anthropologist* 9:1–14.

Petersen, K. L., V. L. Clay, M. H. Matthews, and S. W. Neusius, comps. 1985. *Dolores Archaeological Program, studies in environmental archaeology.* Report submitted to the Bureau of Reclamation, Denver.

Petersen, K. L., and J. D. Orcutt, comps. 1987. *Dolores Archaeological Program, supporting studies: Settlement and environment.* Report submitted to the Bureau of Reclamation, Denver.

Petsche, J. E., comp. 1968. *Bibliography of salvage archeology in the United States.* Smithsonian Institution, Publications in Salvage Archeology, River Basin Surveys no. 10.

Phillips, P. 1970. *Archaeological survey in the lower Yazoo basin, 1949–1955.* Harvard University, Peabody Museum of Archaeology and Ethnology, Papers 60.

Phillips, P., J. A. Ford, and J. B. Griffin. 1951. *Archaeological survey in the lower Mississippi alluvial valley, 1940–1947.* Harvard University, Peabody Museum of American Archaeology and Ethnology, Papers 25.

Phillips, P., and G. R. Willey. 1953. Method and theory in American archaeology: An operational basis for culture-historical integration. *American Anthropologist* 55:615–33.

Pidgeon, W. 1858. *Traditions of De-coo-dah and antiquarian researches.* New York: Thayer.

Plog, S. 1976. Relative efficiencies of sampling techniques for archeological surveys. In *The early Mesoamerican village,* ed. K. V. Flannery, 136–58. New York: Academic Press.

Plog, S., F. Plog, and W. Wait. 1978. Decision making in modern surveys. In *Advances in archaeological method and theory*, vol. 1, ed. M. B. Schiffer, 383–421.

Pool, K. J. 1989. A history of amateur archaeology in the St. Louis area. *The Missouri Archaeologist* 50.

Potter, W. B. 1880. Archaeological remains in southeastern Missouri. In *Contributions to the archaeology of Missouri, by the Archaeological Section of the St. Louis Academy of Science*, Part 1, Pottery, 1–19. Salem, Mass.: Bates.

Powell, J. W. 1881. Report of the director. *Bureau of Ethnology, Annual Report* 1:xi–xxxiii.

————. 1894. Report of the director. *Bureau of Ethnology, Annual Report* 12:xxi–xlviii.

Powell, M. L. 1989. The people of Nodena. In *Nodena*, ed. D. F. Morse, 65–95. Arkansas Archeological Survey, Research Series no. 30.

Price, J. E. 1969. *A middle Mississippian house.* University of Missouri, Museum of Anthropology, Museum Briefs no. 1.

————. 1973. Settlement planning and artifact distribution on the Snodgrass site and their socio-political implications in the Powers phase of southeast Missouri. Ph.D. diss., Department of Anthropology, University of Michigan.

————. 1974. Mississippian settlement systems of the central Mississippi Valley. Paper presented at the Advanced Seminar on Mississippian Development, School of American Research, Santa Fe.

————. 1978. The settlement pattern of the Powers phase. In *Mississippian settlement patterns*, ed. B. D. Smith, 201–31. New York: Academic Press.

————. 1986. Emergent Mississippian occupation in the southeastern Ozarks of Missouri. Paper presented at the 51st annual meeting of the Society for American Archaeology, New Orleans.

Price, J. E., and G. L. Fox. 1990. Recent investigations at Towosahgy State Historic Site. *The Missouri Archaeologist* 51:1–71.

Price, J. E., and J. B. Griffin. 1979. *The Snodgrass site of the Powers phase of southeast Missouri.* University of Michigan, Museum of Anthropology, Anthropological Papers no. 66.

Price, H. M., III. 1988. Bones of contention: Reburial of human remains under RS Mo. 194.400–410. *Missouri Archaeological Society Quarterly* 5(1):4–6, 11, 18.

————. 1991. *Disputing the dead: U.S. law on aboriginal remains and grave goods.* Columbia: University of Missouri Press.

Proudfit, S. V. 1881a. Earthworks on the Missouri River. *The American Antiquarian* 3:139.

————. 1881b. Antiquities of the Missouri bluff. *The American Antiquarian* 3:271–80.

Pulliam, C. B. 1987. Middle and Late Woodland horticultural practices in the western margin of the Mississippi River valley. In *Emergent horticultural economies of the Eastern Woodlands*, ed. W. F. Keegan, 185–99. Southern Illinois University at Carbondale, Center for Archaeological Investigations, Occasional Paper no. 7.

Purdue, J. R. 1980. Clinal variation in some mammals during the Holocene in Missouri. *Quaternary Research* 13:242–58.

————. 1982. The environmental implications of the fauna recovered from Rodgers Shelter. In *Holocene adaptations within the lower Pomme de Terre River valley, Missouri*, ed. M. Kay, 199–261. Report submitted to the U.S. Army Corps of Engineers, Kansas City District.

Purdue, J. R., B. W. Styles, and M. C. Masulis. 1989. Faunal remains and white-tailed deer exploitation from a Late Woodland upland encampment: The Boschert site (23SC609), St. Charles County, Missouri. *Midcontinental Journal of Archaeology* 14:146–63.

Putnam, C. E. 1886. Elephant pipes and inscribed tablets in the Museum of the Academy of Natural Sciences, Davenport. *Proceedings of the Davenport Academy of Natural Sciences* 4:251–348.

Putnam, F. W. 1870. Comment on a letter from T. T. Richards. *The American Naturalist* 4:63.

———. 1875a. [List of items from mounds in New Madrid County, Missouri, and brief description of excavations]. *Harvard University, Peabody Museum, Eighth Annual Report*, 16–46.

———. 1875b. The pottery of the mound builders. *The American Naturalist* 9:321–38, 393–409.

———. 1888. On a collection of Paleolithic implements from America and Europe. *Proceedings of the Boston Society of Natural History* 23:421–24.

———. 1890. Summary remarks. *Proceedings of the Boston Society of Natural History* 24:157–65.

———. 1897. Early man of the Delaware Valley. *Proceedings of the American Association for the Advancement of Science* 46:344–48.

Raab, L. M. 1976a. The structure of prehistoric community organization at Santa Rosa Wash, southern Arizona. Ph.D. diss., Department of Anthropology, Arizona State University.

———. 1982. Cultural resource management in the university: Getting what we deserve. *Journal of Field Archaeology* 9:126–28.

———, comp. 1976b. *Pine Mountain: A study of prehistoric human ecology in the Arkansas Ozarks*. Arkansas Archeological Survey, Research Report no. 7.

Raab, L. M., and T. C. Klinger. 1977. A critical appraisal of significance in contract archaeology. *American Antiquity* 42:629–34.

———. 1978. A reply to Sharrock and Grayson on archaeological significance. *American Antiquity* 44:328–29.

Raab, L. M., T. C. Klinger, M. B. Schiffer, and A. C. Goodyear. 1980. Clients, contracts, and profits: Conflicts in public archaeology. *American Anthropologist* 82:539–51.

Rau, C. 1873. North American stone implements. *Smithsonian Institution, Annual Report* (1872), 395–408.

Ray, J. H. 1985. An overview of chipped stone resources in southern Missouri. In *Lithic resource procurement: Proceedings from the second conference on prehistoric chert exploitation*, ed. S. C. Vehik, 225–50. Southern Illinois University, Center for Archaeological Investigations, Occasional Paper no. 4.

Reagan, M. J., R. M. Rowlett, E. G. Garrison, W. Dort Jr., V. M. Bryant Jr., and C. J. Johannsen. 1978. Flake tools stratified below Paleo-Indian artifacts. *Science* 200:1272–74.

Reaves, R. W., III. 1976. Historic preservation laws and policies: Background and history. In *Symposium on dynamics of cultural resource management*, ed. R. T. Matheny and D. L. Berge, 15–23. U.S. Department of Agriculture, Forest Service, Southwest Region, Archeological Report no. 10.

Redman, C. L. 1973. Multi-stage fieldwork and analytical techniques. *American Antiquity* 31:61–79.

Redman, C. L., and P. J. Watson. 1970. Systematic, intensive surface collection. *American Antiquity* 35:279–91.

Reeder, R. L. 1980. The Sohn site: A lowland Nebo Hill complex campsite. In *Archaic prehistory on the prairie-plains border*, ed. A. E. Johnson, 55–66. University of Kansas, Publications in Anthropology no. 12.

Reher, C., ed. 1977. *Settlement and subsistence along the lower Chaco River: The CGP survey.* Albuquerque: University of New Mexico Press.

Reid, J. J., M. B. Schiffer, and W. L. Rathje. 1975. Behavioral archaeology: Four strategies. *American Anthropologist* 77:864–69.

Reid, K. 1980. The achievement of sedentism in the Kansas City region. In *Archaic prehistory on the prairie-plains border,* ed. A. E. Johnson, 29–42. University of Kansas, Publications in Anthropology no. 12.

———. 1984a. Fire and ice: New evidence for the production and preservation of Late Archaic fiber-tempered pottery in the mid-latitude lowlands. *American Antiquity* 49:55–76.

———. 1984b. *Nebo Hill: Late Archaic prehistory on the southern Prairie Peninsula.* University of Kansas, Publications in Anthropology no. 15.

Renaud, E. B. 1932. Yuma and Folsom artifacts. *Proceedings of the Colorado Museum of Natural History* 11(2):5–18.

Rice, P. M. 1987. *Pottery analysis: A sourcebook.* Chicago: University of Chicago Press.

Richards, T. T. 1870. Relics from the Great Mound. *The American Naturalist* 4:62–63.

Rick, J. W. 1978. *Heat-altered cherts of the lower Illinois Valley: An experimental study in prehistoric technology.* Northwestern University Archeological Program, Prehistoric Records no. 2.

Rindos, D. 1984. *The origins of agriculture: An evolutionary perspective.* New York: Academic Press.

———. 1985. Darwinian selection, symbolic variation, and the evolution of culture. *Current Anthropology* 26:65–88.

———. 1986. The evolution of the capacity for culture: Sociobiology, structuralism, and cultural selection. *Current Anthropology* 27:315–32.

———. 1989. Undirected variation and the Darwinian explanation of cultural change. In *Advances in archaeological method and theory,* vol. 1, ed. M. B. Schiffer, 1–45. Tucson: University of Arizona Press.

Ritchie, W. A. 1961. Highway construction and salvage programs. *Archaeology* 14:241–44.

Roberts, F. H. H., Jr. 1935. A Folsom complex: Preliminary report on investigations at the Lindenmeier site in northern Colorado. *Smithsonian Miscellaneous Collections* 94(4).

———. 1940. Developments in the problem of the North American Paleo-Indian. *Smithsonian Miscellaneous Collections* 100:51–116.

Roberts, R. G. 1965. Tick Creek Cave, an Archaic site in the Gasconade River valley of Missouri. *The Missouri Archaeologist* 27(2).

Robinson, C. K., and M. Kay. 1982. Phillips Spring excavation and archaeology. In *Holocene adaptations within the lower Pomme de Terre River valley, Missouri,* ed. M. Kay, 623–82. Report submitted to the U.S. Army Corps of Engineers, Kansas City District.

Roedl, L. J., and J. H. Howard. 1957. Archaeological investigations at the Renner site. *The Missouri Archaeologist* 19:53–90.

Rogers, L. D., and R. E. Pulcher. 1987. Archaeological investigations. In *St. Louis harbor historic properties reconnaissance, City of St. Louis, Missouri,* by L. D. Rogers, R. E. Pulcher, and R. G. White, 1–48. U.S. Army Corps of Engineers, St. Louis District, Cultural Resource Management Reports no. 31.

Roper, D. C. 1975a. Archaeological survey and settlement pattern models in central Illinois. Ph.D. diss., Department of Anthropology, University of Missouri–Columbia.

————. 1975b. The Truman Reservoir survey: Approach and preliminary results. Paper presented at the 33rd annual Plains Conference, Lincoln, Neb.

————. 1975c. *Cultural resources survey, Harry S. Truman Dam and Reservoir.* Report submitted to the U.S. Army Corps of Engineers, Kansas City District.

————. 1976. Lateral displacement of artifacts due to plowing. *American Antiquity* 41:372–74.

————, ed. 1981. *Prehistoric cultural continuity in the Missouri Ozarks: The Truman Reservoir mitigation project.* Report submitted to the U.S. Army Corps of Engineers, Kansas City District.

————. 1983. *Cultural resources survey, Harry S. Truman Dam and Reservoir Project.* Vol. 4, *The archeological survey.* Report submitted to the U.S. Army Corps of Engineers, Kansas City District.

Roper, D. C., and M. Piontkowski. 1983. Projectile points. In *Cultural resources survey, Harry S. Truman Dam and Reservoir Project,* vol. 5, *Lithic and ceramic studies,* 121–68. Report submitted to the U.S. Army Corps of Engineers, Kansas City District.

Roper, D. C., and W. R. Wood. 1975. *Research design for the cultural resources survey, Harry S. Truman Dam and Reservoir Project: The archaeological survey.* Manuscript on file, Museum of Anthropology, University of Missouri–Columbia.

————. 1976. Research design for the cultural resources survey, Harry S. Truman Dam and Reservoir Project: The archaeological survey. In *Cultural resources survey, Harry S. Truman Dam and Reservoir Project: Lower Pomme de Terre River arm,* by W. R. Wood, D. C. Roper, C. H. Synhorst, and N. Linderer, 41–48. Report submitted to the U.S. Army Corps of Engineers, Kansas City District.

Rouse, I. B. 1939. *Prehistory in Haiti: A study in method.* Yale University Publications in Anthropology no. 21.

————. 1955. On the correlation of phases of culture. *American Anthropologist* 57:713–22.

————. 1964. Archaeological approaches to cultural evolution. In *Explorations in cultural anthropology,* ed. W. H. Goodenough, 455–68. New York: McGraw-Hill.

————. 1972. Settlement patterns in archaeology. In *Man, settlement, and urbanism,* ed. P. J. Ucko, R. Tringham, and G. W. Dimbleby, 95–107. London: Duckworth.

Rowe, J. H. 1953. Technical aids in anthropology: A historical survey. In *Anthropology today,* ed. A. L. Kroeber, 895–940. Chicago: University of Chicago Press.

Ruppert, M. E. 1975. Research orientation, 1975. In *Cannon Reservoir Archaeological Project report, December 1, 1974–May 1, 1975,* ed. D. R. Henning, 1–17. University of Nebraska, Department of Anthropology, Technical Report no. 75–02.

Rust, H. N. 1877. The mound builders in Missouri. *Western Review of Science and Industry* 1:531–35.

Sabloff, J. A. 1989. Analyzing recent trends in American archaeology from a historical perspective. In *Tracing archaeology's past: The historiography of archaeology,* ed. A. L. Christenson, 34–40. Carbondale: Southern Illinois University Press.

Sahlins, M. D. 1958. *Social stratification in Polynesia.* Seattle: University of Washington Press.

————. 1963. Poor man, rich man, big-man, chief: Political types in Melanesia and Polynesia. *Comparative Studies in Society and History* 5:285–303.

————. 1972. *Stone age economics.* Chicago: Aldine.

Sahlins, M. D., and E. R. Service, eds. 1960. *Evolution and culture.* Ann Arbor: University of Michigan Press.

Salmon, M. H. 1975. Confirmation and explanation in archaeology. *American Antiquity* 40:459–64.

———. 1982. *Philosophy and archaeology.* New York: Academic Press.

Salmon, M. H., and W. C. Salmon. 1979. Alternative models of scientific explanation. *American Anthropologist* 81:61–74.

Sanders, W. T. 1956. The central Mexican symbiotic region. In *Prehistoric settlement patterns in the New World,* ed. G. R. Willey. Viking Fund Publications in Anthropology no. 23.

———. 1967. Settlement patterns. In *Handbook of Middle American Indians,* vol. 6, *Social Anthropology,* ed. M. Nash, 53–86. Austin: University of Texas Press.

———. 1970. *The Teotihuacán Valley Project, final report.* Vol. 2. Pennsylvania State University, Occasional Papers in Anthropology no. 3.

Sanders, W. T., J. R. Parsons, and R. S. Santley. 1979. *The Basin of Mexico: Ecological processes in the cultural evolution of a civilization.* New York: Academic Press.

Santley, R. S. 1983. Ancient population at Monte Albán: A reconsideration of methodology and culture history. *Haliksa'i: University of New Mexico, Contributions to Anthropology* 2:64–84.

Sapir, E. 1917. Do we need a superorganic? *American Anthropologist* 19:441–47.

Sassaman, K. 1993. *Early pottery in the Southeast: Tradition and innovation in cooking technology.* Tuscaloosa: University of Alabama Press.

Saucier, R. T. 1964. *Geological investigation of the St. Francis Basin, lower Mississippi Valley.* U.S. Army Engineer Waterways Experiment Station, Technical Report no. 3–659.

———. 1968. A new chronology for braided stream surface formation in the lower Mississippi Valley. *Southeastern Geology* 9:65–76.

———. 1974. *Quaternary geology of the lower Mississippi Valley.* Arkansas Archeological Survey, Research Series no. 6.

———. 1981. Current thinking on riverine processes and geologic history as related to human settlement in the southeast. *Geoscience and Man* 22:7–18.

Saunders, J. J. 1975. Late Pleistocene vertebrates of the western Ozark Highlands, Missouri. Ph.D. diss., Department of Geosciences, University of Arizona, Tucson.

———. 1977a. *Paleontological resources survey, Tebo, South Grand and Osage arms, Harry S. Truman Dam and Reservoir, Osage River Basin, Missouri.* Report submitted to the U.S. Army Corps of Engineers, Kansas City District.

———. 1977b. *Late Pleistocene vertebrates of the western Ozark Highland, Missouri.* Illinois State Museum, Reports of Investigations no. 33.

———. 1983a. *Mitigation of the adverse effects upon the local paleontological resources.* Report submitted to the U.S. Army Corps of Engineers, Kansas City District.

———. 1983b. *Ice age climates: Plants and animals of western Missouri: A 50,000 year record of change.* Report submitted to the U.S. Army Corps of Engineers, Kansas City District.

Sayles, E. B., and E. Antevs. 1941. The Cochise culture. *Medallion Papers* [Gila Pueblo, Globe, Ariz.] no. 29.

Scharf, J. T. 1883. *History of St. Louis City and County, from the earliest periods to the present day: Including biographical sketches of representative men.* Philadelphia: Everts.

Schiffer, M. B. 1972. Archaeological context and systemic context. *American Antiquity* 37:156–65.

———. 1975a. Archeological research and contract archeology. In *The Cache River*

Archeological Project: An experiment in contract archeology, assembled by M. B. Schiffer and J. H. House, 1–7. Arkansas Archeological Survey, Research Series no. 8.

———. 1975b. Archaeology as behavioral science. *American Anthropologist* 77:836–48.

———. 1976. *Behavioral archeology.* New York: Academic Press.

———. 1983. Toward the identification of formation processes. *American Antiquity* 48:675–706.

———. 1987. *Formation processes of the archaeological record.* Albuquerque: University of New Mexico Press.

Schiffer, M. B., and G. J. Gumerman. 1977. Cultural resource management. In *Conservation archaeology: A guide for cultural resource management studies,* ed. M. B. Schiffer and G. J. Gumerman, 1–17. New York: Academic Press.

Schiffer, M. B., and J. H. House. 1977a. Cultural resource management and archaeological research: The Cache project. *Current Anthropology* 18:43–68.

———. 1977b. An approach to assessing scientific significance. In *Conservation archaeology: A guide for cultural resource management studies,* ed. M. B. Schiffer and G. J. Gumerman, 249–57. New York: Academic Press.

———, comps. 1975. *The Cache River archeological project: An experiment in contract archeology.* Arkansas Archeological Survey, Research Series no. 8.

Schiffer, M. B., and J. M. Skibo. 1987. Theory and experiment in the study of technological change. *Current Anthropology* 28:595–622.

Schiffer, M. B., A. P. Sullivan, and T. C. Klinger. 1978. The design of archaeological surveys. *World Archaeology* 10:1–28.

Schoolcraft, H. R. 1854. *Historical and statistical information respecting the history, condition, and prospects of the Indian tribes of the United States,* part 4. Philadelphia: Lippincott, Grambo.

Schroeder, W. A. 1981. *Presettlement Prairie of Missouri.* Missouri Department of Conservation, Natural History Series no. 2.

Schultz, A. H. 1945. *Biographical memoir of Aleš Hrdlička.* Biographical Memoirs of the National Academy of Sciences, 23:305–38.

Schultz, C. B., G. C. Lueninghoener, and W. D. Frankforter. 1951. A graphic resume of the Pleistocene of Nebraska (with notes on the fossil mammalian remains). *Bulletin of the University of Nebraska State Museum, Contribution of the Division of Vertebrate Paleontology* 3.

Schwartz, D. W. 1967. *Conceptions of Kentucky prehistory.* University of Kentucky, Studies in Anthropology no. 6.

Scovill, D. H. 1976. Regional center: Opportunities for federal-institutional partnership in cultural resources management. In *Regional centers in archaeology: Prospects and problems,* ed. W. H. Marquardt, 23–28. Missouri Archaeological Society, Research Series no. 14.

Scovill, D. H., G. J. Gordon, and K. M. Anderson. 1972. *Guidelines for the preparation of statements of environmental impact on archeological resources.* Tucson: National Park Service.

Scully, E. G. 1953. Extinct river channels as a method of dating archaeological sites in southeast Missouri. *The Missouri Archaeologist* 15(1–2):84–91.

Seelen, R. M. 1961. A preliminary report of the Sedalia complex. *Missouri Archaeological Society Newsletter* no. 153.

Seeman, M. F. 1979. *The Hopewell interaction sphere: The evidence for interregional trade and structural complexity.* Indiana Historical Society, Prehistoric Research Series 5(2).

Semenov, S. A. 1964. *Prehistoric technology.* London: Barnes and Noble.

Setzler, F. M., and W. D. Strong. 1936. Archaeology and relief. *American Antiquity* 1:301–9.

Sharrock, F. W., and D. K. Grayson. 1978. Significance in contract archaeology. *American Antiquity* 44:327–28.

Shay, C. T. 1987. Historical settlement in mid-continental North America. *Reviews in Anthropology* 14:132–38.

Shepard, A. O. 1956. *Ceramics for the archaeologist.* Carnegie Institution of Washington, Publication no. 609.

Shippee, J. M. 1948. Nebo Hill, a lithic complex in western Missouri. *American Antiquity* 14:29–32.

———. 1966. The archaeology of Arnold Research Cave, Callaway County, Missouri. *The Missouri Archaeologist* 28:1–107.

Shott, M. J. 1989. Shovel-test sampling in archaeological survey: Comments on Nance and Ball, and Lightfoot. *American Antiquity* 54:396–404.

Silverberg, R. 1968. *Mound builders of ancient America: The archaeology of a myth.* Greenwich, Conn.: New York Graphic Society.

Skibo, J. M., M. B. Schiffer, and K. C. Reid. 1989. Organic-tempered pottery: An experimental study. *American Antiquity* 54:122–46.

Smith, B. D. 1974a. Predator-prey relationships in the eastern Ozarks: A.D. 1300. *Human Ecology* 2:31–44.

———. 1974b. Middle Mississippi exploitation of animal populations: A predictive model. *American Antiquity* 29:274–91.

———. 1975. *Middle Mississippi exploitation of animal populations.* University of Michigan, Museum of Anthropology, Anthropological Papers no. 57.

———. 1976. Determining the selectivity of utilization of animal species by prehistoric human populations. Paper presented at the 41st annual meeting of the Society for American Archaeology, St. Louis.

———. 1977. Archaeological inference and inductive confirmation. *American Anthropologist* 79:598–617.

———. 1978. *Prehistoric patterns of human behavior: A case study in the Mississippi Valley.* New York: Academic Press.

———. 1981. The Division of Mound Exploration of the Bureau of (American) Ethnology and the birth of modern American archeology. *Southeastern Archaeological Conference Bulletin* 24:51–54.

———. 1985. Introduction to *Report on the mound explorations of the Bureau of Ethnology,* by Cyrus Thomas [reprint], 5–19. Washington, D.C.: Smithsonian Institution Press.

———. 1990a. The Division of Mound Exploration of the Bureau of Ethnology and the birth of modern American archeology. In *Edward Palmer's Arkansaw mounds,* ed. M. D. Jeter, 27–37. Fayetteville: University of Arkansas Press.

———, ed. 1990b. *The Mississippian emergence.* Washington, D.C.: Smithsonian Institution Press.

Snyder, J. F. 1877. Deposits of flint implements. *Smithsonian Institution, Annual Report* (1876), 433–41.

Southard, M. D. 1973. Sources of chert present at Towosahgy State Archaeological Site. *Missouri Archaeological Society Newsletter* no. 273:2–7.

Spaulding, A. C. 1985. Fifty years of theory. *American Antiquity* 50:301–8.

Spier, L. 1917. *An outline for a chronology of Zuñi ruins.* American Museum of Natural History, Anthropological Papers 18(3).

Squier, E., and E. H. Davis. 1848. Ancient monuments of the Mississippi Valley. *Smithsonian Contributions to Knowledge* I.

Stadler, E. A., ed. and trans. 1972. *Journey through a part of the United States of North America in the years 1844–1846 by Albert C. Koch.* Carbondale, Ill.: Southern Illinois University Press.

Stark, M. T. 1993. Re-fitting the "cracked and broken façade": The case for empiricism in post-processual ethnoarchaeology. In *Archaeological theory: Who sets the agenda?*, ed. N. Yoffee and A. Sherratt. Cambridge: Cambridge University Press.

Stegner, W. 1954. *Beyond the hundredth meridian: John Wesley Powell and the second opening of the West.* Boston: Houghton Mifflin.

Stein, J. K. 1987. Deposits for archaeologists. In *Advances in archaeological method and theory*, vol. II, ed. M. B. Schiffer, 337–95. Orlando: Academic Press.

Stevenson, C. W. 1878. New mound discoveries. *Kansas City Review of Science and Industry* 2:108–9.

Steward, J. H. 1949. Cultural causality and law; a trial formulation of early civilization. *American Anthropologist* 51:1–27.

———. 1955. *Theory of culture change.* Urbana: University of Illinois Press.

Steward, J. H., and F. M. Setzler. 1938. Function and configuration in archaeology. *American Antiquity* 4:4–10.

Stimmell, C., R. B. Heimann, and R. G. V. Hancock. 1982. Indian pottery from the Mississippi Valley: Coping with bad raw materials. In *Archaeological ceramics*, ed. J. S. Olin and A. D. Franklin. Washington, D.C.: Smithsonian Institution Press.

Stockton, E. D. 1973. Shaw's Creek shelter: Human displacement of artifacts and its significance. *Mankind* 9:112–17.

Stoltman, J. B. 1978. Temporal models in prehistory: An example from eastern North America. *Current Anthropology* 19:703–46.

Strong, W. D. 1935. An introduction to Nebraska archaeology. *Smithsonian Miscellaneous Collections* 93(10).

———. 1936. Anthropological theory and archaeological fact. In *Essays in Anthropology: Presented to A. L. Kroeber in celebration of his sixtieth birthday, June II, 1936*, ed. R. H. Lowie, 359–68. Berkeley: University of California Press.

———. 1940. From history to prehistory in the northern Great Plains. In Essays in historical anthropology of North America. *Smithsonian Miscellaneous Collections* 100:353–94.

Struever, S. 1960. The Kamp mound group and a Hopewell mortuary complex in the lower Illinois Valley. Master's thesis, Department of Anthropology, Northwestern University.

———. 1964. The Hopewell interaction sphere in riverine-western Great Lakes culture history. In *Hopewellian studies*, ed. J. R. Caldwell and R. L. Hall, 85–106. Illinois State Museum, Scientific Papers no. 12.

———. 1968. Flotation techniques for the recovery of small-scale archaeological remains. *American Antiquity* 33:353–62.

———. 1971a. Problems, methods, and organizations: A disposition in the growth of archaeology. In *Anthropological archaeology in the Americas*, ed. B. J. Meggers, 131–51. Washington, D.C.: Anthropological Society of Washington.

———. 1971b. Comments on archaeological data requirements and research strategy. *American Antiquity* 36:9–19.

Struever, S., and G. L. Houart. 1972. An analysis of the Hopewell interaction sphere. In

Social exchange and interaction, ed. E. N. Wilmsen, 47–79. University of Michigan, Museum of Anthropology, Anthropological Papers no. 46.

Struever, S., and K. O. Vickery. 1973. The beginnings of cultivation in the Midwest-riverine area of the United States. *American Anthropologist* 75:1197–220.

Styles, B. W. 1981. *Early Late Woodland subsistence in the lower Illinois Valley.* Northwestern University Archeological Program, Scientific Papers no. 3.

Styles, B. W., and J. R. Purdue. 1986. Middle Woodland faunal exploitation. In *The Woodland period occupations of the Napoleon Hollow site in the lower Illinois Valley,* ed. M. D. Wiant and C. R. McGimsey, 513–26. Center for American Archeology, Kampsville Archeological Center, Research Series no. 6.

Styles, B. W., J. R. Purdue, and M. L. Colburn. 1985. Faunal exploitation at the Smiling Dan site. In *Smiling Dan: Structure and function at a Middle Woodland settlement in the lower Illinois Valley,* ed. B. D. Stafford and M. B. Sant, 402–46. Center for American Archeology, Kampsville Archeological Center, Research Series no. 2.

Sudderth, W. E., and C. H. Chapman. 1965. The Woody Shelter, 23SR146. In *Preliminary archaeological investigations in the Kaysinger Bluff Reservoir area,* comp. C. H. Chapman, 531–41. Report submitted to the National Park Service, Omaha.

Suhm, D. A., and E. B. Jelks. 1962. *Handbook of Texas archeology: Type descriptions.* Texas Archeological Society, Special Publication no. 1.

Suhm, D. A., A. D. Krieger, and E. B. Jelks. 1954. An introductory handbook of Texas archeology. *Bulletin of the Texas Archeological Society* 25.

Swallow, G. C. 1855. *The first and second annual reports of the Geological Survey of Missouri.* Jefferson City: Lusk.

Swanson, E. H., Jr. 1959. Theory and history in American archaeology. *Southwestern Journal of Anthropology* 15:120–24.

Swanton, J. 1939. *Final report of the United States De Soto Expedition Commission* [House Document 71 of the 76th Congress, 1st Session]. Washington, D.C.: U.S. Government Printing Office.

Swartz, B. K., Jr. 1967. A logical sequence of archaeological objectives. *American Antiquity* 32:487–97.

Synhorst, C. H. 1983a. *Cultural resources survey, Harry S. Truman Dam and Reservoir Project.* Vol. 1, *Chronology of Osage River history.* Report submitted to the U.S. Army Corps of Engineers, Kansas City District.

————. 1983b. *Cultural resources survey, Harry S. Truman Dam and Reservoir Project.* Vol. 2, *Historical gazetteer and mitigation recommendations.* Report submitted to the U.S. Army Corps of Engineers, Kansas City District.

Tainter, J. A. 1975. The archaeological study of social change: Woodland systems in west-central Illinois. Ph.D. diss., Department of Anthropology, Northwestern University.

————. 1977. Woodland social change in west central Illinois. *Midcontinental Journal of Archaeology* 2:67–98.

————. 1978. Mortuary practices and the study of prehistoric social systems. In *Advances in archaeological method and theory,* vol. 1, ed. M. B. Schiffer, 105–41. New York: Academic Press.

————. 1981. Reply to "A critique of some recent North American mortuary studies." *American Antiquity* 46:416–20.

————. 1983. Woodland social change in the central Midwest: A review and evaluation of interpretive trends. *North American Archaeologist* 42:141–61.

Talmage, V., and O. Chesler. 1977. *The importance of small, surface, and disturbed sites as sources of significant archaeological data.* Washington, D.C.: National Park Service, Office of Archeology and Historic Preservation.

Taylor, J. L. B. 1921a. Discovery of a prehistoric engraving representing a mastodon. *Science* 54:357–58.

———. 1921b. Did the Indian know the mastodon? *Natural History* 21:591–97.

———. 1947. Again: The mastodon bone. *American Anthropologist* 49:689–95.

Taylor, R. L., J. S. Cable, A. L. Novick, and J. M. O'Hara. 1986. *Archeological survey and reconnaissance within the ten-year floodpool, Harry S. Truman Dam and Reservoir.* Report submitted to the U.S. Army Corps of Engineers, Kansas City District.

Taylor, W. W., Jr. 1948. *A study of archeology.* American Anthropological Association, Memoir no. 69.

———, ed. 1957. *The identification of non-artifactual archaeological materials; report of a conference held in Chicago, March 11–13, 1956, by the Committee on Archaeological Identification, Division of Anthropology and Psychology, National Academy of Sciences, National Research Council.* National Research Council, Publication no. 565.

Teltser, P. A. 1988. The Mississippian archaeological record on the Malden Plain, southeast Missouri: Local variability in evolutionary perspective. Ph.D. diss., Department of Anthropology, University of Washington.

———. 1991. Generalized core technology and tool use: A Mississippian example. *Journal of Field Archaeology* 18:363–75.

———. 1992. Settlement context and structure at County Line, Missouri. *Southeastern Archaeology* 11:14–30.

———. 1993. An analytic strategy for studying assemblage-scale ceramic variation: A case study from southeast Missouri. *American Antiquity* 58:530–43.

Thomas, C. 1884. Who were the mound builders? *The American Antiquarian* 6:90–99.

———. 1887a. Burial mounds of the northern sections of the United States. *Bureau of Ethnology, Annual Report* 5:3–119.

———. 1887b. Work in mound exploration of the Bureau of Ethnology. *Bureau of Ethnology, Bulletin* 4.

———. 1891. Catalogue of prehistoric works east of the Rocky Mountains. *Bureau of Ethnology, Bulletin* 12.

———. 1894. Report on the mound explorations of the Bureau of Ethnology. *Bureau of Ethnology, Annual Report* 12:3–742.

Thomas, D. H. 1969. *Regional sampling in archaeology: A pilot Great Basin research design.* University of California, Archaeological Survey, Annual Report, 1968–1969 11:87–100.

———. 1971. Prehistoric subsistence-settlement patterns of the Reese River valley, central Nevada. Ph.D. diss., University of California, Davis.

———. 1973. An empirical test of Steward's model of Great Basin settlement patterns. *American Antiquity* 38:155–76.

———. 1975. Nonsite sampling in archaeology: Up the creek without a site? In *Sampling in archaeology,* ed. J. W. Mueller, 61–81. Tucson: University of Arizona Press.

Thomsen, C. J. 1848 (orig. 1836). *A guide to northern antiquities.* London.

Thwaites, R. G., ed. 1905. *Early western travels, 1748–1846.* Vol. 14. Cleveland: Clark.

Tolstoy, P., and S. K. Fish. 1975. Surface and subsurface evidence for community size at Coapexco, Mexico. *Journal of Field Archaeology* 2:97–104.

Trader, P. D. 1992. Spatial analysis of lithic artifacts from the Common Field site (23STG100), a Mississippian community in Ste. Genevieve County, Missouri. Master's thesis, Department of Anthropology, University of Missouri–Columbia.

Transeau, E. N. 1935. The Prairie Peninsula. *Ecology* 16:423–37.

Trigger, B. 1967. Settlement archaeology: Its goals and promise. *American Antiquity* 32:149–60.

———. 1968. The determinants of settlement patterns. In *Settlement archaeology,* ed. K. C. Chang, 53–78. Palo Alto, Calif.: National Press.

———. 1978. *Time and traditions.* New York: Columbia University Press.

———. 1989. *A history of archaeological thought.* Cambridge: Cambridge University Press.

Trimble, M. K., and T. B. Meyers. 1990. *Saving the past from the future: Archaeological curation in the St. Louis District.* St. Louis: U.S. Army Corps of Engineers.

Trubowitz, N. L. 1978. The persistence of settlement pattern in a cultivated field. In *Essays in memory of Marian E. White,* ed. W. Engelbrecht and D. Grayson, 41–66. Franklin Pierce College, Department of Anthropology, Occasional Papers in Northeastern Anthropology 5.

———. 1993. The overlooked ancestors: Rediscovering the pioneer archaeology collections at the Missouri Historical Society. Paper presented at the 58th annual meeting of the Society for American Archaeology, St. Louis.

Ubelaker, D. H., and L. G. G. Grant. 1989. Human skeletal remains: Preservation or reburial? *Yearbook of Physical Anthropology* 32:249–87.

Uhle, M. 1907. The Emeryville shellmound. *University of California, Publications in American Archaeology and Ethnology* 7(1).

Vance, E. D. 1989. The role of microartifacts in spatial analysis. Ph.D. diss., Department of Anthropology, University of Washington.

Van Zant, K. 1979. Late glacial and postglacial pollen and plant macrofossils from Lake West Okoboji, northwestern Iowa. *Quaternary Research* 12:358–80.

Vehik, R. 1978. An analysis of cultural variability during the Late Woodland period in the Ozark Highland of southwest Missouri. Ph.D. diss., Department of Anthropology, University of Missouri–Columbia.

Vickery, K. 1970. Evidence supporting the theory of climatic change and the decline of Hopewell. *Wisconsin Archeologist* 51(2):57–76.

Vivian, R. G., K. Anderson, H. Davis, R. Edwards, M. B. Schiffer, and S. South. 1977. Guidelines for the preparation and evaluation of archaeological reports. In *The management of archaeological resources: The Airlie House report,* ed. C. R. McGimsey III and H. A. Davis. Washington, D.C.: Society for American Archaeology.

Voigt, E. E., and M. J. O'Brien. 1981. The use and misuse of soils-related data in mapping and modeling past environments: An example from the central Mississippi River valley. *Contract Abstracts and CRM Archeology* 2(3):22–35.

Voigt, E. E., and D. M. Pearsall, eds. 1986. New World paleoethnobotany: Collected papers in honor of Leonard W. Blake. *The Missouri Archaeologist* 47.

von Morlot, A. 1861. General views on archaeology. *Smithsonian Institution, Annual Report* (1860), 284–343.

Walker, W. M., and R. M. Adams. 1946. Excavations in the Matthews site, New Madrid County, Missouri. *Transactions of the Academy of Science of St. Louis* 31(4):75–120.

Walthall, J. A., and T. E. Emerson. 1991. French colonial archaeology. In *French colonial archaeology: The Illinois Country and the western Great Lakes,* ed. J. A. Walthall, 1–13. Urbana: University of Illinois Press.

Wandsnider, L. A. 1988. Cultural resources "Catch-22" and empirical justification for discovering and documenting low-density archaeological surfaces. In *Tools to manage the past: Research for cultural resource management in the Southwest,* ed. J. A.

Tainter and R. H. Hamre, 90–97. U.S. Department of Agriculture, Forest Service, General Technical Report no. RM-164.

———. 1989. Long-term land use, formation processes, and the structure of the archaeological landscape: A case study from southeastern Wyoming. Ph.D. diss., Department of Anthropology, University of New Mexico.

Wardle, H. N. 1929. Wreck of the archaeological department at the Academy of Natural Sciences of Philadelphia. *Science* 70:119–21.

Warren, R. E. 1976. Site survey and survey design. In *Cannon Reservoir Archaeological Project report* (Appendix 2), ed. D. R. Henning, 1–333. University of Nebraska, Department of Anthropology, Technical Report no. 79–03.

———. 1979. Archaeological site survey. In *Cannon Reservoir Human Ecology Project: A regional approach to cultural continuity and change*, ed. M. J. O'Brien and R. E. Warren, 71–100. University of Nebraska, Department of Anthropology, Technical Report no. 79–14.

———. 1982a. The historical setting. In *The Cannon Reservoir Human Ecology Project: An archaeological study of cultural adaptations in the southern Prairie Peninsula*, ed. M. J. O'Brien, R. E. Warren, and D. E. Lewarch, 29–70. New York: Academic Press.

———. 1982b. Prehistoric settlement patterns. In *The Cannon Reservoir Human Ecology Project: An archaeological study of cultural adaptations in the southern Prairie Peninsula*, ed. M. J. O'Brien, R. E. Warren, and D. E. Lewarch, 337–68. New York: Academic Press.

———. 1984. The physical environment: A context for frontier settlement. In *Grassland, forest, and historical settlement: An analysis of dynamics in northeast Missouri*, by M. J. O'Brien, 95–134. Lincoln: University of Nebraska Press.

Warren, R. E., and T. Miskell. 1981. Intersite variation in a bottomland locality: A case study in the southern Prairie Peninsula. In *Plowzone archeology: Contributions to theory and technique*, ed. M. J. O'Brien and D. E. Lewarch, 119–58. Vanderbilt University, Publications in Archaeology no. 27.

Warren, R. E., and M. J. O'Brien. 1981. Regional sample stratification: The drainage class technique. *Plains Anthropologist* 26:213–27.

———. 1982a. Holocene dynamics. In *The Cannon Reservoir Human Ecology Project: An archaeological study of cultural adaptations in the southern Prairie Peninsula*, ed. M. J. O'Brien, R. E. Warren, and D. E. Lewarch, 71–84. New York: Academic Press.

———. 1982b. Models of adaptation and change. In *The Cannon Reservoir Human Ecology Project: An archaeological study of cultural adaptations in the southern Prairie Peninsula*, ed. M. J. O'Brien, R. E. Warren, and D. E. Lewarch, 85–100. New York: Academic Press.

———. 1984. A model of frontier settlement. In *Grassland, forest, and historical settlement: An analysis of dynamics in northeast Missouri*, by M. J. O'Brien, 22–57. Lincoln: University of Nebraska Press.

Warren, R. E., M. J. O'Brien, and R. D. Mason. 1981. Settlement dynamics in the southern Prairie Peninsula: A regional model of frontier development. In *Current directions in midwestern archaeology: Selected papers from the Mankato Conference*, ed. S. Anfinson, 15–34. Minnesota Archaeological Society, Occasional Papers in Minnesota Anthropology no. 9.

Warren, R. E., M. J. O'Brien, and C. K. McDaniel. 1984. Environmental dimensions of settlement. In *Grassland, forest, and historical settlement: An analysis of dynamics in northeast Missouri*, by M. J. O'Brien, 192–209. Lincoln: University of Nebraska Press.

Watkins, J. C. 1883. Mounds in the southeast part of Pike County, Missouri. *Smithsonian Institution, Annual Report* (1881), 537–38.

Watson, P. J. 1976. In pursuit of prehistoric subsistence: A comparative account of some contemporary flotation techniques. *Midcontinental Journal of Archaeology* 1:77–100.

———. 1983. Foreword to *A study of archeology*, by W. W. Taylor (reprint), ix–xvi. Carbondale: Southern Illinois University Press.

———. 1986. Archaeological interpretation, 1985. In *American archaeology past and future: A celebration of the Society for American Archaeology, 1935–1985*, ed. D. J. Meltzer, D. D. Fowler, and J. A. Sabloff, 439–57. Washington, D.C.: Smithsonian Institution Press.

Watson, P. J., S. A. LeBlanc, and C. Redman. 1971. *Explanation in archeology: An explicitly scientific approach*. New York: Columbia University Press.

———. 1984. *Archeological explanation: The scientific method in archeology*. New York: Columbia University Press.

Watson, V. D. 1950. *The Wulfing plates: Products of prehistoric Americans*. Washington University Studies, Social and Philosophical Sciences no. 8.

Webb, T., III, and R. A. Bryson. 1972. Late- and postglacial climatic change in the northern Midwest, USA: Quantitative estimates derived from fossil pollen spectra by multivariate statistical analysis. *Quaternary Research* 2:70–115.

Webb, W. S., and D. L. DeJarnette. 1942. An archaeological survey of Pickwick Basin in the adjacent portions of Alabama, Mississippi and Tennessee. *Bureau of American Ethnology, Bulletin* 129.

Wedel, W. R. 1938. The direct-historical approach in Pawnee archaeology. *Smithsonian Miscellaneous Collections* 97(7).

———. 1943. Archaeological investigations in Platte and Clay counties, Missouri. *U.S. National Museum Bulletin* no. 183.

———. 1951. The use of earth moving machinery in archaeological excavations. In *Essays on archaeological methods*, ed. J. B. Griffin, 17–28. University of Michigan, Museum of Anthropology, Anthropological Papers no. 8.

———. 1953. Prehistory and the Missouri River Development Program: Summary report on the Missouri River Basin Archaeological Survey in 1949. *Bureau of American Ethnology, Bulletin* 154:66–101.

———. 1959. An introduction to Kansas archaeology. *Bureau of American Ethnology, Bulletin* 174.

———. 1967. Salvage archaeology in the Missouri River basin. *Science* 196:589–97.

Wells, P. V. 1970. Postglacial vegetational history of the Great Plains. *Science* 167:1574–82.

Wendland, W. M. 1978. Holocene man in North America: The ecological setting and climatic background. *Plains Anthropologist* 23:273–87.

Wendland, W. M., and R. A. Bryson. 1974. Dating climatic episodes of the Holocene. *Quaternary Research* 4:9–24.

West, E. P. 1877a. The Missouri mound builders. *Western Review of Science and Industry* 1:15–22.

———. 1877b. Age of prehistoric remains found at Kansas City, and the races of men associated with them. *Western Review of Science and Industry* 1:193–99.

———. 1880. A buried race in Kansas. *Kansas City Review of Science and Industry* 3:530–34.

———. 1882a. Archaeological exploration of the Missouri River. *Kansas City Review of Science and Industry* 5:529–34.

————. 1882b. Human remains in the loess of the Missouri River. *Kansas City Review of Science and Industry* 6:461–64.

————. 1883. The Missouri River mounds, considered from a geological standpoint. *Kansas City Review of Science and Industry* 7:290–93.

Wetmore, A. 1837. *Gazetteer of the state of Missouri.* St. Louis: Keemle.

Whalen, M. 1977. *Settlement patterns of the eastern Hueco Bolson.* University of Texas at El Paso, Centennial Museum, Anthropological Paper no. 4.

Whittaker, F. 1993. Lowland adaptation during the Late Archaic in the central Mississippi River valley. Paper presented at the 58th annual meeting of the Society for American Archaeology, St. Louis.

Whittlesey, C. 1852. Ancient works in Ohio. *Smithsonian Contributions to Knowledge* 3.

————. 1869. On the evidences of the antiquity of man in the United States. *American Association for the Advancement of Science, Proceedings* 17:268–88.

Wiens, J. A. 1976. Population response to patchy environments. *Annual Review of Ecology and Systematics* 7:81–120.

Willey, G. R. 1953. Prehistoric settlement patterns in the Virú Valley, Peru. *Bureau of American Ethnology, Bulletin* 155.

————, ed. 1956. *Prehistoric settlement patterns in the New World.* Viking Fund Publications in Anthropology no. 23.

————. 1966. *An introduction to American archaeology.* Vol. 1, *North and Middle America.* Englewood Cliffs, N.J.: Prentice Hall.

Willey, G. R., and P. Phillips. 1955. Method and theory in American archaeology, II: Historical-developmental interpretations. *American Anthropologist* 57:723–819.

————. 1958. *Method and theory in American archaeology.* Chicago: University of Chicago Press.

Willey, G. R., and J. A. Sabloff. 1974. *A history of American archaeology.* San Francisco: Freeman.

————. 1993. *A history of American archaeology.* 3d ed. New York: Freeman.

Williams, J. R. 1964. A study of fortified Indian villages in southeast Missouri. Master's thesis, Department of Anthropology, University of Missouri–Columbia.

————. 1967. *Land leveling salvage archaeological work in southeast Missouri: 1966.* Report submitted to the National Park Service, Lincoln, Neb.

————. 1968. *Southeast Missouri land leveling salvage archaeology: 1967.* Report submitted to the National Park Service, Lincoln, Neb.

————. 1971. A study of the Baytown phase in the Cairo Lowland of southeast Missouri. Ph.D. diss., Department of Anthropology, University of Missouri–Columbia.

————. 1972. *Land leveling salvage archaeology in Missouri: 1968.* Report submitted to the National Park Service, Lincoln, Neb.

————. 1974. The Baytown phases in the Cairo Lowland of southeast Missouri. *The Missouri Archaeologist* 36 (whole volume).

Williams, S. 1954. An archeological study of the Mississippian culture in southeast Missouri. Ph.D. diss., Yale University.

————. 1980. Armorel: A very late phase in the lower Mississippi Valley. *Southeastern Archaeological Conference Bulletin* 22:105–10.

————. 1983. Some ruminations on the current strategy of research in the Southeast. *Southeastern Archaeological Conference Bulletin* 21:72–81.

————. 1990. The vacant quarter and other late events in the lower valley. In *Towns and temples along the Mississippi,* ed. D. H. Dye and C. A. Cox, 170–80. Tuscaloosa: University of Alabama Press.

Williams, S., and J. M. Goggin. 1956. The long nosed god mask in eastern United States. *The Missouri Archaeologist* 18(3).

Wilmsen, E. N. 1968. Functional analysis of flaked stone artifacts. *American Antiquity* 33:156–61.

Wilson, D. 1863. Physical anthropology. *Smithsonian Institution, Annual Report* (1881), 240–302.

Wilson, T. 1889. The Paleolithic period in the District of Columbia. *American Anthropologist* 2:235–41.

———. 1892. Man and the mylodon: Their possible contemporaneous existence in the Mississippi Valley. *The American Naturalist* 26:629–31.

———. 1895a. On the presence of fluorine as a test for the fossilization of animal bones. *The American Naturalist* 29:301–17, 439–56, 719–25.

———. 1895b. Paleolithic man. *The American Naturalist* 29:599–600.

———. 1899. The Paleolithic period in the District of Columbia. *American Anthropologist* (old series) 2:235–41.

Windmiller, R. 1977. Comment on "Cultural resource management and archaeological research: The Cache project," by M. B. Schiffer and J. H. House. *Current Anthropology* 18:61–62.

Winters, H. D. 1967. *An archaeological survey of the Wabash Valley in Illinois.* Illinois State Museum, Reports of Investigations no. 10.

———. 1969. *The Riverton Culture: A second millennium occupation in the central Wabash Valley.* Illinois State Museum, Reports of Investigations no. 13.

Wislizenus, A. 1860. Was man contemporaneous with the mastodon? *Academy of Science of St. Louis, Transactions* 1:168–71.

Wissler, C. 1917. The new archaeology. *The American Museum Journal* 17:100–101.

———. 1921. Dating our prehistoric ruins. *Natural History* 21:13–26.

———. 1926. *The relation of nature to man in aboriginal America.* New York: Oxford.

———. 1938. *The American Indian.* 3d ed. New York: McMurtrie.

Wood, W. R. 1958. Excavations of a village site in the Table Rock Reservoir. *Missouri Archaeological Society Newsletter* no. 119:3.

———. 1961. The Pomme de Terre Reservoir in western Missouri prehistory. *The Missouri Archaeologist* 23:1–131.

———. 1965a. *Archaeological investigations in the Stockton Reservoir area, southwestern Missouri: 1962–1964,* part 1. Report submitted to the National Park Service, Omaha.

———. 1965b. *Preliminary archaeological investigations in the Kaysinger Bluff Reservoir area,* part 1. Report submitted to the National Park Service, Lincoln, Neb.

———. 1966. The archaeology and paleoecology of the western Ozark Highlands. Proposal submitted to the National Science Foundation, Washington, D.C.

———. 1967. The Fristoe burial complex of southwestern Missouri. *The Missouri Archaeologist* 29:1–128.

———. 1968. Mississippian hunting and butchering patterns: Bone from the Vista Shelter, 23SR20, Missouri. *American Antiquity* 33:170–79.

———. 1970. Review of *New perspectives in archeology,* ed. S. R. Binford and L. R. Binford. *Plains Anthropologist* 15:229–31.

———. 1973. Culture sequence at the Old Fort, Saline County, Missouri. *American Antiquity* 38:101–11.

———. 1976a. Interdisciplinary studies in the Pomme de Terre Valley. In *Prehistoric man and his environments: A case study in the Ozark Highland,* ed. W. R. Wood and R. B. McMillan, 3–11. New York: Academic Press.

————. 1976b. Archaeological investigations at the Pomme de Terre springs. In *Prehistoric man and his environments: A case study in the Ozark Highland,* ed. W. R. Wood and R. B. McMillan, 97–107. New York: Academic Press.

————. 1976c. Vegetational reconstruction and climatic episodes. *American Antiquity* 41:206–7.

————. 1984. Missouri prehistory: A traditionalist's view. *The Quarterly Review of Archaeology* 5(1):1, 9–10.

Wood, W. R., and D. L. Johnson. 1978. A survey of disturbance processes in archaeological site formation. In *Advances in archaeological method and theory,* vol. 1, ed. M. B. Schiffer, 315–81. New York: Academic Press.

Wood, W. R., and R. A. Marshall. 1960. The Loftin component, 23SN42. In *Archaeological investigations in the Table Rock Reservoir area,* comp. C. H. Chapman, 326–65. Report submitted to the National Park Service, Lincoln, Neb.

Wood, W. R., and R. B. McMillan. 1969. Archeology and paleoecology of the western Ozark Highlands: Final report submitted to the National Science Foundation. Report on file, Museum of Anthropology, University of Missouri–Columbia.

————, eds. 1976. *Prehistoric man and his environments: A case study in the Ozark Highland.* New York: Academic Press.

Wood, W. R., R. K. Nickel, and D. E. Griffin. 1982. *Remote sensing in the central and northern Great Plains.* Washington, D.C.: National Park Service.

Wood, W. R., and R. E. Pangborn. 1968. The Eureka and Comstock mounds, southwestern Missouri. *Plains Anthropologist* 13:1–17.

Woodbury, R. B. 1954. Review of *A study of archeology,* by W. W. Taylor. *American Antiquity* 19:292–96.

Worthen, A. H. 1866. Physical features, general principles and surface geology. In *Geological Survey of Illinois,* vol. 1, *Geology,* by A. H. Worthen, J. D. Whitney, L. Lesquereux, and H. Engelmann, 1–39. Springfield: Geological Survey of Illinois.

Wright, G. F. 1888. On the age of the Ohio gravel beds. *Proceedings of the Boston Society of Natural History* 23:427–36.

————. 1890. The age of the Philadelphia red gravels. *Proceedings of the Boston Society of Natural History* 24:152–57.

————. 1892. *Man and the glacial period.* New York: Appleton.

————. 1893. Evidences of glacial man in Ohio. *Popular Science Monthly* 43:29–39.

————. 1895a. *Man and the glacial period.* 2d ed. New York: Appleton.

————. 1895b. New evidence of glacial man in Ohio. *The American Naturalist* 29:951–53.

Wright, H. E., Jr. 1968. History of the Prairie Peninsula. In *The Quaternary of Illinois,* ed. R. E. Bergstrom, 78–88. University of Illinois, College of Agriculture, Special Publication no. 14.

————. 1976. The dynamic nature of Holocene vegetation; a problem in paleoclimatology, biogeography, and stratigraphic nomenclature. *Quaternary Research* 6:581–96.

Yellen, J. E., and M. W. Greene. 1985. Archaeology and the National Science Foundation. *American Antiquity* 50:332–41.

Yellen, J. E., M. W. Greene, and R. T. Louttit. 1980. A response to "National Science Foundation funding of domestic archaeology in the United States: Where the money ain't." *American Antiquity* 45:180–81.

Yelton, J. K. 1991. Protohistoric Oneota pottery of the lower Missouri River valley: A functional perspective. Ph.D. diss., Department of Anthropology, University of Missouri–Columbia.

INDEX

Abbott, Charles, 114

Academy of Natural Sciences of Philadelphia, 85, 454

Academy of Science of St. Louis, 34, 41, 42–43, 61, 63, 129, 205–6, 449. *See also* individual members

Adams, Lee, 241–42

Adams, Robert M., 148, 205–6, 208, 214, 218, 276, 449

Adams, Robert McCormick, 276

Advisory Council on Historic Preservation, 325, 329, 367, 385

Aerial photography, 407–8

Ahler, Stanley A., 296–97, 298, 382, 409, 484

Airlie House Report, 333

Allison, Vernon, 164–65, 168, 170, 171

Alton complex, 263

Ambrose Flick site (Illinois), 417

American Anthropological Association, 92, 139, 142, 183

American Antiquarian and Oriental Journal, 104, 447. *See also* Peet, Stephen D.

American Antiquarian Society, 41

American Archaeology Division, 234, 323–24, 335, 354, 378, 432, 436, 445. *See also* Missouri, University of

American Association for the Advancement of Science, 41, 91, 92, 120, 139, 142, 183

American Bottom (Illinois), 420

American Council of Learned Societies, 234

American Ethnological Society, 41

American Indians against Desecration, 441–42

American Museum of Natural History, 140, 156, 157, 162–63, 164. *See also* Ford, James A.; Nelson, Nels; Wissler, Clark

American Philosophical Society, 85

Anderson, Kimball S., 26

Anderson, Renner S., 26

Anthropological Society of Washington, 92,

139. *See also* American Anthropological Association

Antiquities Act (1906), 184, 191, 433

Archaeological and Historic Preservation Act (1974). *See* Moss-Bennett Act

Archaeological Institute of America, 42, 183. *See also* Knockers

Archaeological Resources Protection Act (1979), 433

Archaeological significance, 325, 330–32, 367–68

Archaeological Survey of Missouri, 8, 193–98, 259–60

Archaeology: as an interest, 1, 3; history of, 4–7. *See also* Interpretation; Explanation

Arkansas Archeological Survey, 339, 342, 354. *See also* Cache River (Arkansas) Archeological Project

Arnold Research Cave (Callaway County), 283, 285, 286, 288

Artifacts: curation of, 432–37; in evolutionary schemes, 68, 71, 73–75

Atwater, Caleb, 33, 34, 36

Baerreis, David A., 280

Bagnell Dam. *See* Lake of the Ozarks

Baird, Spencer, 92, 93

Baker's Mound, 98, 99, 102

Barkley Reservoir (Kentucky), 470

Barnes pottery, 226

Bass, William M., III, 293

Bauer, G. A., 72, 73

Baytown: period, 224–25, 310; pottery, 221, 222, 226; tradition, 181

Bean, Lewis M., 125

Beck, Lewis C., 39, 134

Beckwith, Thomas, 61

Beckwith's Fort (Mississippi County), 61, 99, 100, 147, 310, 311, 313, 314, 370, 408

Beckwith's Ranch (Mississippi County), 98, 99, 108

Beehler, C. W., 447–48

ABOUT THE AUTHOR

Photo by Cliff White

Michael J. O'Brien is Professor of Anthropology at the University of Missouri–Columbia, where he is also Director of the Museum of Anthropology and Associate Dean of the College of Arts and Science. He is the author of several books, most recently *Cat Monsters and Head Pots: The Archaeology of Missouri's Pemiscot Bayou* (University of Missouri Press).